Richard Hughes

A BIOGRAPHY

By the same author:

Lawrence of Arabia and His World
A. E. Housman: The Scholar-Poet
The Brothers Powys
Robert Graves: The Assault Heroic 1895–1926
Robert Graves: The Years with Laura 1926–1940

Richard Hughes

A BIOGRAPHY

Richard Perceval Graves

André Deutsch

First published in Great Britain
in 1994 by
André Deutsch Limited
106 Great Russell Street, London WC1B 3LJ

ISBN 0 233 98843 2

Typeset by Falcon Graphic Art Ltd
Wallington, Surrey
Printed by
WSOY Finland

For my sister
ELIZABETH MARY GOODCHILD

And for my friends
HELEN *and* MICHAEL CALVER
JOHN *and* BARBARA ROBERTS
and
NICHOLAS DOLPHIN

Contents

List of Illustrations

Preface

In the absence of a biography, those under forty-five vaguely remember Richard Hughes (if at all) as the author of *A High Wind in Jamaica*, a story about children and pirates which some of them read at school for examination purposes. Yes, there was a film, wasn't there, with Anthony Quinn as the pirate chief? And didn't Hughes write some other children's stories?

Those (like myself) approaching fifty recall a novelist who was highly revered by the generation above us, but who, by the time we had reached university, appeared to have run out of steam. Living in a remote part of North Wales, and reputedly working on a sequel to his international bestseller *The Fox in the Attic* (which many of us had read and much admired), he was said to be writing at the rate of no more than two or three sentences a week, and failed to hold our attention.

When after twelve years a sequel did eventually appear, it was poorly received; and following Hughes's death in 1976, his reputation faded, and his work slipped into increasing neglect.

Such neglect came to seem shameful; and in the early 1980s I began thinking of a biography which would introduce a new generation of readers to the best of Hughes's work. However, my knowledge of his life was then extremely sketchy. True, Richard Hughes had been a family friend, and I had first met him after one of my uncle Robert's lectures when I was up at St John's College, Oxford in the mid 1960s; but I had arrogantly assumed that everything of interest about the life of this lonely Welsh recluse could be said in a hundred or a hundred and fifty pages. It was as I worked my way with increasing excitement through box after box of Hughes's papers at the Lilly Library in Indiana in the Autumn of 1987 that I first began to realise how very wrong I had been. There was an enthralling story to be told; and it would be my privilege to be the first to tell it in full.

Acknowledgements

My first and greatest debt is to Lucy McEntee, formerly Richard Hughes's secretary, and now his literary executor. Her faith in me was sustained through a difficult period of eleven years which saw every kind of set-back in both my professional and my personal life. She and her late husband Prosper were a continual source of support and sound advice.

I am also greatly indebted to Richard Hughes's daughter Penelope Minney. Not only has her memoir *Richard Hughes: Author, Father* been a valuable source of information; but in the spring of 1992 she passed on to me a number of letters which had previously been withheld from public view, and which threw important light upon some of the more troubled areas of her father's life. Since then she has devoted a great deal of time to answering questions, reading over draft chapters, correcting errors of fact and making constructive critical comments.

I also thank Robert and Sheila Hughes, who invited me to stay with them in Birmingham and introduced me to Sheila's redoubtable mother Rose Basketts (a close friend of Hughes and his inspiration for the Coventry chapters of *The Wooden Shepherdess*). I also thank Owain and Elizabeth Hughes, who entertained me long ago in New York City; Kate Wells (née Hughes) and her husband Professor Colin Wells, who invited me to a family gathering at Parc in North Wales, and who, together with Lleky Papastavrou (née Hughes), taught me much about their family history, and were especially illuminating on the subject of Richard Hughes's wife Frances, a very shadowy character in my earliest draft. I also thank Frances's half-sister Henriette Abel-Smith (formerly Palmer) for her help; and Frances's brother Sir Thomas Bazley and her sister Lady Rachel Bennett for their help and hospitality.

Others who have supplied me with first-hand information include the late Amabel Williams-Ellis (for many years Hughes's confidante), the late Norah Smallwood of Chatto & Windus, Peter Levi, the late Sir Peter Quennell, Jocelyn Herbert, G. Dyfnallt Owen, Jane Rainey,

Rupert and Nicolette Shepherd, Brigid Macnamara, Polly Hope, and Francis and Jenny West.

Like everyone interested in Richard Hughes, I am very much indebted to Richard Poole not only for his pioneering critical work in *Richard Hughes: Novelist*, but also for his valuable editions both of Hughes's Moroccan tales and of his literary writings.

Others who have helped me with advice or information include Sir Keith Thomas, Margaret and Geraint Pritchard, Julie Riley, Peter Duffet-Smith, Paul Bennett Morgan, Tim Hyman, Judith Eagle, Crispin Jackson, Jane Hill, Richard Poole, Mrs A.C. Wheeler and Steven Myslinski of Salve Regina University.

I am also very greatly indebted to all those who welcomed me to the University of Indiana in the fall of 1987. In particular I thank Dr Ernest Bernhard-Kabisch, then Principal of the Collins Living Learning Center, who appointed me Writer-in-Residence and arranged for me to be given a meal-ticket and a room in exchange for being available to his students. It was an invigorating experience. I also express my very great thanks to the Librarian of the Lilly Library, Saundra Taylor, and to her extremely helpful staff. I also thank the then Chair of the English Faculty, Dr Mary Burgan, who gave me an honorary position within the university, arranged for me to give a lecture while I was there, and made me her house guest for two weeks when my period as Writer-in-Residence had expired. She and her husband were most generous and hospitable; as were Professor Roy Battenhouse and his wife, and many others.

I owe much to the late Dr F.W. Dillistone of Oriel College, Oxford, a family friend who entertained me to dinner at high table, and introduced me to the Librarian Dr W.E. Parry. I thank Dr Parry and his staff most warmly for their subsequent helpfulness over a period of many years.

I must also thank Tom Rosenthal of Deutsch for commissioning this biography. At a time when several otherwise enthusiastic publishers had eventually declined the book on the advice of their accountants, he alone was prepared to commit himself to publication. I also thank my editor Anthony Thwaite, who made a number of valuable suggestions which have very much improved the final appearance of the work.

I should add that this book could never have been completed but for the great generosity of the Royal Literary Fund, who bailed me out of debt when the book was two-thirds written, and my financial position had been temporarily rendered desperate by a series of quite unforeseeable domestic misfortunes.

In addition, grateful acknowledgement is made to Lucy McEntee both as Literary Executor of the late Richard Hughes for permission to reproduce extracts from his published and unpublished prose and poetry and in her private capacity for permission to reproduce an extract from one of her own letters; to Sir Nicholas Henderson for extracts from the unpublished correspondence of his mother Faith Henderson; to Lady Quennell for permission to quote from the published and unpublished writings of the late Sir Peter Quennell; to Rachel Bennett for an extract from one of her letters to Frances Hughes; to Sir Thomas Bazley for an extract of one of his letters to Richard Hughes; to Sam Graves for an extract from a letter by Nancy Nicholson; to Pamela Bianco Hartmann for extracts from her unpublished letters to Richard Hughes; to Lord Bullock for permission to quote from one of his letters to Richard Hughes; to Crystal Hale for extracts from letters by her mother Gwen Herbert; to the *Spectator* for permission to reproduce extracts from an article by Dawn MacLeod; to John Murray (Publishers) Ltd for permission to quote from a letter by John Murray; to Martin Secker & Warburg for permission to quote extracts from their publication *Caitlin* by Caitlin Thomas & George Tremlett; to Weidenfeld & Nicolson for permission to quote extracts from their publication *All Stracheys are Cousins* by Amabel Williams-Ellis, and for extracts from unpublished writings by Amabel Williams-Ellis, Clough Williams-Ellis and Susan Williams-Ellis; to the Provost and Fellows of Oriel College, Oxford for permission to quote from the Minute Book of the Arnold Debating Society, the fourth volume of the Minutes of the Plantagenet Society, and from correspondence between Richard Hughes, Gilbert Murray and the then Provost of Oriel L.R. Phelps; to Gerald Duckworth & Co Ltd for an extract from a letter by Henry Duckworth to Frances Hughes; to A.P. Watt Ltd on behalf of the Trustees of the Robert Graves Copyright Trust for letters written by Robert Graves, and for material from *Good-bye to All That* by Robert Graves; to the Community of St Clare, St Mary's Convent, Freeland for permission to reproduce extracts from material by Caroline Glyn; to Richard Poole for extracts from his publication *Richard Hughes: Novelist*; to David Higham Associates, for permission to reproduce a brief extract from an unpublished letter by Caitlin Thomas; and to Faber & Faber Limited for an extract from an unpublished letter by Geoffrey Faber.

In addition, an extract from a letter by Curtis Brown to Richard Hughes is reproduced by permission of Curtis Brown Ltd, London; and extracts from *The Waters and the Wild* by Gwenol Heneker, together with a brief note from Gwenol Heneker to Richard Hughes, are © Gwenol Heneker, reproduced by permission of Curtis Brown Ltd, London; and an extract from a letter by J.L. Garvin (The Observer ©) is published by permission of The Observer ©.

I also owe an enormous debt to the Lilly Library, Indiana University, Bloomington, Indiana for permission (as owners) to publish extracts from the mass of writings held in their Hughes MSS.

In addition, I acknowledge the use of brief extracts from Jeremy Wilson, *The authorised biography of T.E. Lawrence*.

Despite our efforts to do so, it has been impossible to trace copyright owners of writings by Hugh Ferguson, Maurice Ferguson, Joseph Brewer, R.C. Sclater, E.E. Bryant, Frank Fletcher, Louis Wharton, Hugh Lyon, Charles Prentice, William Heinemann, 'Margaret' (who wrote to Richard Hughes on 15 August 1930); and 'Valerie' who wrote an undated letter to Frances Hughes.

Last but not least, I thank Caroline Belgrave who first suggested to me that Richard Hughes would make an interesting subject for my pen.

CHAPTER 1

A Sense of Guilt

A misty morning on a remote estuary in North Wales, sometime in the spring of 1973. Just above the estuary a shadowy outline (looking just at first like a large hermit crab) emerges from the larger outline of an isolated house. This is Richard Hughes, that 'grizzled Tolstoyan sage'[1] as old as the century, carrying a coracle upon his back.

As he comes closer, you can see that he is a tall man with an imposing forehead, clear blue eyes, and a long straggling beard. Swinging the coracle easily into the water, he steps carefully in, and paddles out of sight again into the mist.

To his contemporaries, almost everything about Hughes seems to be equally shrouded in mystery. Strange that this famous novelist, the author of three international bestsellers, chooses to live in such inaccessible surroundings. Unaccountable that he produces so little: no more than two novels and a few dozen book reviews in the past eighteen years.

When interviewed, he will only say enigmatically that what takes the time is not what he puts in, but what he leaves out. And although he is working on what he evidently regards as an important set of novels about the history of his own times, there seems already to be so little chance of completing his work that he has begun talking (more philosophically than gloomily) about his 'race against the undertaker'.[2]

As a cool wind disperses the mist, and Hughes becomes visible once again in the wild setting of his choice, it can be seen that he is paddling out into the sandy estuary of the Traeth, where the rivers Dwyryd and Glaslyn swirl out past Portmadoc to the bar in Tremadoc Bay. Ahead of him is the fairy-tale village of Portmeirion; and at his back, the hills of Merioneth – the Rhinogs, Moel Ysgyfarnogod, and Moel y Gyrafolen – rising as they climb east and north to the Moelwyns, Cnicht, and then the great Snowdon range itself. There could hardly have been a greater contrast with the land of his birth.

It was in Dorincourt, a substantial family house in Underwood Road, Caterham (a small town in Surrey not far south of London), that Richard Arthur Warren Hughes was born at ten o'clock in the evening of 19 April 1900.[3] Everything about the house and its surroundings was redolent of safe, comfortable, middle-class Edwardian prosperity. Richard's father, Arthur Hughes, was a thirty-eight-year-old civil servant who regularly caught the early-morning train to London, where he worked in the Public Record Office; and his mother, twenty-nine-year-old Louisa, was busily occupied with her children, her servants, and her social obligations.

Arthur, born on 18 July 1861, had a solicitor for a father; and his paternal grandfather had been a barrister. Then the male line ran back through a vicar to a captain in the Royal Navy who, after once entertaining King George III at Portsmouth, had been created Sir Richard Hughes of East Bergholt. On becoming a baronet, Sir Richard had very properly commissioned a family tree. He already believed that he numbered among his ancestors Blethyn ap Cynan, Prince of Powis, and Gwaith Vaed Mawr, King of Gwent;[4] and it was now established (at least to Sir Richard's satisfaction) that he was also descended from King Lear and from the legendary Trojan hero Aeneas.[5]

Although by Arthur Hughes's time the baronetcy had gone elsewhere (his barrister grandfather had been a younger brother of the seventh and eighth baronets), Arthur was proud of his descent: especially from another Sir Richard, the second baronet, a distinguished naval officer and Admiral of the Red, who had combined a life of action with one of scholarship, acting as '2nd in Cmd. under Lord Howe in the memorable relief of Gibraltar; ... captur[ing] the "Solitaire" and beat[ing] the French in a sea fight off Barbados in 1782' and also finding time to translate the *Spectator* into French.[6]

Arthur himself had a great love of boating;[7] he was said by one of his contemporaries at Oxford (where he had read History) to be 'strong both in mind and body and brave to endure hardship';[8] and in his twenties he had risen to the rank of sergeant as a part-time 'enrolled volunteer' in the 2nd Middlesex (Artists') Rifles.[9] But his principal interests were academic. At the time of his engagement to Louisa in 1896, he had already written a number of scholarly papers including a 'Treatise on the method of Chronology in the Chancery of the Palatinate of Durham', and was working on a full-length history of English Law.[10]

A sturdy-looking man of medium height, Arthur had a receding hair-line, a bushy moustache, and a kindly smile. He was also deeply in love with Louisa, a small, pretty woman, with sad grey-green eyes set in a sensitive yet keenly intelligent and determined face. In a characteristic letter written during their engagement, he had told her:[11]

> Your last letter, my darling, was sweet as sleep after suffering or dawn after darkening. The thought that my love makes you happy makes my happiness too — and dearest I could not love you so much if I did not also feel that you are just the one to be my best friend and closest companion — The sentences you call trite and commonplace I have kissed many times — and shall kiss many times again . . . Sweet dear one, how I long to feel once more your dear graceful form in my arms, to have your dear soft lips caressing mine . . . Oh! My darling I do love you so, sweetest and best of all the good women that God has ever made.

He continued with details of his current work (he was examining the sixteenth-century papers of the Cecil family), and he added that on Louisa's return from holiday they would 'decide on the title of your novel and on the complexion of the heroine'. For although Arthur himself was as conventional as he sounds, Louisa (to whom he was married in February 1897) would not be content for long with being a mere housewife.

Louisa Grace Warren (born at Epsom on 11 November 1870) had a troubled childhood, largely thanks to the vagaries of her father's career. Edward Ernest Warren was a bluff, good-humoured man. His ancestors included vicars, rectors, and an archdeacon; but Ernest was known as 'a wit' and hoped to succeed as a playwright.[12] However, when Louisa (usually called Lulu) was a young child of three or four,[13] Ernest went bankrupt.[14] His wife Charlotte Pengelly came from a Cornish family which had been settled for some years in Jamaica;[15] and Ernest's solution to the immediate crisis was that she should take their three children out to Jamaica to live with their Pengelly relatives.

There they spent five years while Ernest successfully built up a new career as a journalist: a calling which took him as far afield as Chicago,[16] and made him many close friends on both sides of the Atlantic. Finally, towards the end of 1878, he was ready to welcome his family home to England.

For Lulu and her two younger brothers it should have been an idyllic five years in the sun: before they returned from Jamaica, Ernest had to remind them that it was 'often quite cold in England . . . and I have no bathing hole but have to get into a big tin bath.'[17] Unfortunately the long separation from her father had preyed upon Louisa's mind.

Her fundamental insecurity (allied to a vivid imagination) was such that as a woman of thirty, walking through some dark pine-woods not far from her home, she began to fear that she would never emerge alive; and the church bells of Weybridge, instead of comforting her, seemed to be positively 'demoniacal'.[18] In addition, she had somehow assumed the burden of her father's unfulfilled literary ambitions.

Arthur Hughes, who was not only 'strong, capable and self-reliant',[19] but who also shared her literary ambitions, offered Louisa exactly the kind of constancy and fatherly reassurance[20] that she needed; and at Dorincourt she did her best to be a good wife to him, providing him in rapid succession with Grace Margaret Lilias (born in February 1898); Arthur Warren Collingwood (born in March 1899); and now Richard. So far, Arthur and Louisa had been wonderfully happy; but this happiness was not to last.

Within eight days of Richard's birth, his thirteen-month-old elder brother had died of some childhood complaint; and Louisa in particular felt the loss so keenly that it was two years before she could hope that 'the wound caused by our little darling's death . . . may in time heal over'.[21] And by then Arthur Hughes, whose health had always seemed so robust, had become seriously ill.

Arthur had lost weight and developed an occasional slight feverishness in the early summer of 1901; and Louisa, attributing these symptoms to overwork, persuaded him to join her and the children at the seaside. From there she reported to her mother not only that fifteen-month-old Richard (usually Dick or Dickie) had 'one more tooth through . . . says "Mamma" quite plainly', and was 'getting on splendidly with his walking & crawling', but also that Arthur was 'much better . . . getting quite fat & *so* brown'.[22]

However the feverishness returned, this time accompanied by the spitting of blood. Clearly, it was tuberculosis. Cures were possible, but expensive, as they depended upon combining dry mountain air with rest and careful nursing; and in the autumn of 1901 Arthur went abroad to a German sanatorium for an indefinite period.

In mid October, Louisa sent Arthur a cheerful letter telling him that eighteen-month-old Dickie was[23]

> a most tempestuous little monkey . . . He takes a positive joy in defying one & he is so strong & venturesome. A funny thing is to see him standing by my dressing-table while I do my hair, gravely sticking hairpins into his little locks. He comes into the bathroom with me in the morning, but he has a wicked trick of suddenly

pulling up the plug & letting out the water, which is unpleasant.

Five months later, Arthur was still immured in his distant sanatorium. Not surprisingly, he was feeling lonely and depressed, especially as the tuberculosis had now affected his throat, and his voice had been permanently reduced to a whisper.[24] In the circumstances, Louisa made a determined effort to throw off her own increasing gloom (one of her friends had given her 'a good talking-to' for being so morbid): 'The thought of you and your true courage has often made me ashamed of myself', she wrote to Arthur.[25]

> Cheer up, beloved, our time of trial must pass soon now, & then how great will be our reward. Often . . . I plan & think of all we will do together once more. How I shall take care of you till you are quite well – how Gracie & I & Dick will come to meet you when you are once more going to Town.

As for Arthur's illness: 'it was God's doing', she wrote, 'and He must put it right for us.' Then Louisa turned to family news. Dickie, now almost two years old, was

> becoming more amiable, though his furies are the funniest things imaginable, he gets even too angry to cry. If only he had not such pretty ways we should be better able to punish him, but he gets sweeter & sweeter every day.

He seemed happiest when playing either alone, or with Grace; and when another boy came to play, he kindly collected 'all his toys and laid them at his feet'; but then 'retired under the table from whence he glared at the stranger'.

Grace was so important to Dickie that his earliest memory would be of sitting at the head of a flight of steep stairs and[26]

> playing with a red tin milk-cart. There was a gate at the top of the stairs, since this was the nursery floor; but it was open. There was a room behind me, and in the room on my left my sister was sitting, playing also.
>
> The memory is simply a flash. I did not even during the course of it look round and actually see my sister; but I must have done so shortly before, since I was conscious she was there. The only time I remember her appearance was once when we both naughtily pushed our way through a hole in the garden fence. Another flash. She was ahead of me that time.

Four-year-old Gracie was an affectionate, gentle child who was patient enough to 'sit perfectly still for hours, till the pigeons came and ate crumbs from her hand'.[27]

Later that spring Arthur returned from Germany, apparently well on his way to a complete recovery; and before he returned to work, Louisa took him and their children for a month's holiday down to the Cornish resort of Marazion, recommended to her for its 'three miles of sand, *no* rocks, & absolutely safe bathing'.[28]

This period of hope was followed closely by a further family tragedy. Four-year-old Gracie became seriously ill and died on 12 October 1902. For Dickie, who was then two-and-a-half years old, her loss was both inexplicable and alarming. More than a year later, he had just finished saying his bedtime prayers with his mother, when he turned to her 'with a very shame-faced expression' and confided:[29]

> 'When I say my prayers in the night when I am in bed, I always ask God to make Gracie again & let her come back' . . . Afterwards he added, 'Why doesn't she say to God, "Please, I'd rather go to be with little Dickie again?"' '

It was now that he began to be 'really afraid: more afraid than I have ever been since!' In particular, of being[30]

> *sucked down the waste-pipe of the bath*! Suppose one night my mother carelessly pulled up the plug before I had climbed safely out? . . . it never entered my head I was too big to go through that small hole . . . sucked into that horrible gurgling whirlpool, choked with warm soapy water, dragged down struggling into the mysterious darkness of the waste-pipe, which led down, no one knew whither.

Beside this illogical fear was an equally illogical guilt. When Dick remembered Gracie waiting quietly to feed the pigeons, this happy image was marred by the recollection that he had liked to 'hide in the bushes till the birds were within a foot of her, and then roll out with a loud "boo" to scare them. This I thought very funny; but nobody else did'; and for the rest of his life, Hughes believed that 'those who knew us felt that Death had chosen selfishly in taking my sister rather than me'.[31]

Worse was to follow. Dickie's father, deeply affected by Grace's death, had only been back at the Public Record Office for a few months when his health once again deteriorated: this time to the point where he became a permanent invalid.[32] Sometimes he was well enough to sit up in bed and work on one of his academic papers;[33] but by the latter part of 1903 the Hugheses' income depended largely upon Louisa's earnings from her article and short-story writing. 'If only I can get one or two more cheques in before Christmas it will be all right', she wrote to her mother that December; 'but I am afraid that there will be no story published next week because it is their Xmas too.'[34]

In April 1904, Louisa (now looking as large and robust as

her ailing husband had done in happier days)[35] took Arthur and Dickie down to Boscombe on the Hampshire[36] coast for a seaside holiday. Although Dickie thoroughly enjoyed himself, and dictated a letter to his 'Dear, dearest Gran' telling her that 'I love you very much & send you five hundred kisses & thank you for that nice book';[37] he added, almost as an afterthought, that 'Father is in bed for two days'. And Louisa explained in a covering letter that Arthur had been once again[38]

> spitting up some blood & so went to bed & I got the doctor. He said there was a little fresh place at the top of the left lung which a few days rest would probably put right . . . There has been no rise of temperature & A. keeps very cheerful but it is very disappointing.

Shortly after their return to Dorincourt, Dickie began attending the kindergarten of Eothen, a local girls' school which found room for a few boys in the most junior classes.[39] He had been looking forward to starting school[40] and was quite ready for it; though he later recalled that he[41]

> did not take lessons very seriously my first term, and indeed I generally reached school very late, especially when I walked there alone. I remember that one day I found, to my surprise, that it was half past twelve when I got there and all the children were coming out, instead of nine o'clock, which it should have been. The distance was half a mile. I was not aware that I had dawdled so much, though I remembered stopping to tell a story to a young robin by the road.

What most impressed his teachers was his phenomenal memory: apparently he could recall verses recited by the other children after a single hearing. They also commented on the strength of his imagination, and reported nervously that it would 'have to be restrained a little as he grows older'.[42]

The following summer Dick suffered from a long illness, which kept him away from school for much of the term,[43] and kept Louisa busy looking after two invalids, as well as earning money by her pen. One London editor had strongly encouraged her in this direction, telling her that there was 'plenty of opening nowadays for good article work & with practice you would soon be making two or three hundred a year'.[44] Every penny of her income would soon be needed.

In mid December 1905 Arthur's health deteriorated sharply; and after several days of 'general failure and collapse', he died at about noon on 16 December. He was just forty-four years old.

The following day Louisa wrote to Charles Johnson of the Public Record Office, a close friend of Arthur's who was also one of Dick's godparents:[45]

> Poor Dick, he will never know what a father he had. I have longed so that he should have lived long enough to leave his mark on his boy, and now it has come just when we had almost begun to hope.

A mark had been left; but not the kind of mark for which Louisa had hoped. 'The instant I was told Father also was dead', Hughes later recalled,[46]

> I broke like a dam, water and grief bursting out of me while my soul was feeling the whole bottomless drop into despair. That day instead of tea in the drawing-room with my aunts I had it in the kitchen with cook – a treat I could never have hoped for: yet even then, how salt was the taste of the raspberry jam.
>
> In bed, in the dark, I woke up – and remembered. Surely it must have been a bad dream? That age can still believe things are too *bad* to be true . . . I felt my way to my mother's room – No, it wasn't a dream, she told me – Well, if I couldn't believe her, should she get up and take me to see his body, see that he was really dead? I shrank from that.
>
> Next morning my mouth still tasted salt, and my gummy eyes would hardly open. Breakfast. There was a load of grief on the still house like a heavy fall of snow. And then – I – *forgot*.
>
> It was mid-morning and I wanted to ask Father something . . . so I scampered up to his bedroom, burst open the door. The – the deathroom was darkened with the drawn blinds, heavy with the scent of his favourite narcissus. Under the stiff folds of the sheet lay what – what looked like a not very skilful wax copy of him.
>
> How on earth had I *forgotten*, who loved him so much? At that moment I understood something more frightful than death: I understood *guilt*. *Better* than I understand guilt now. For can any adult sense of guilt, so condoned and qualified with his excuses, at all compare in horror with the searing, excuseless guilt of a guilty child?

The devastating sense of loss and self-doubt which accompanied this 'searing, excuseless guilt' was never satisfactorily resolved. Instead, it ran deep into the bedrock of Hughes's personality, creating a series of minute fissures which, never observable under normal circumstances, had severely weakened his ability to cope with a certain type of emotional pressure.

CHAPTER 2

Dictating to Louisa

Shortly before his father's death, five-and-a-half-year-old Dick Hughes had been dictating to Louisa what she described proudly as his 'first real connected make-up'. When completed, it was to be 'circulated round the family – so much publicity I have promised him', she told her mother, 'failing . . . some money which was his ambition'.[1]

It was not only by circulating his stories that Louisa encouraged Dick's ambition. Frequently she read aloud to him, making clear the importance of the written word: he would learn from her that the very house they lived in had been named Dorincourt after little Lord Fauntleroy's castle in the classic story by Frances Hodgson Burnett; and Louisa also told him numerous tales about her exotic Jamaican childhood. In this literary atmosphere, the composition of stories and poems became one of Dick's chief pleasures; and he would later describe how he was brought up 'as an *only* child, fatherless', and how, with his[2]

> mother mostly busy at her writing (for bread and butter), and the rest of the household a rather grey synod of maiden aunts and great-aunts, I was as happy as a lark. From the earliest age, long before I could read or write, this happiness used to bubble out of me in verse. It was the only way I could get relief from joy, get it under any *kind* of control. When I felt *too* happy, I used to go and hide in the laurel-bushes, and puddle about there with words, like mud-pies, till I had put together some sort of a piece of rhyme. Then I carried it carefully to my mother – trying not to forget it on the way. I said it over to her, and she wrote it down for me in a little notebook. Once that was done, of course, I was free to forget it; and go away and make another rhyme, if one wasn't enough.

By the summer of 1906, one of his stories ('The Adventures of Violet, Jack and I') had been published in the *Eothen School Magazine*.[3]

Dick himself had a friend, a little girl like the Violet in his story, with whom he would play 'in the *neglected* parts [of the garden], away behind the shrubbery, where the soil was too thin to be worth digging, and a rotting summerhouse dribbled on the gangling green weeds'. He avoided the more formal and flowery parts of the garden chiefly because his sense of smell was so acute. 'Motor-cars', he once wrote,[4]

> were rare in my early childhood days, and I can't remember what the early ones *looked* like, at all – but I *can* well remember the *smell*! If one of them *should* come trundling down the lane, even the width of a field away, it set my dear dog Rory sneezing his head off: and it set *me* sneezing *my* head off, too. And yet I *never* disliked the smell of motor-cars quite as much as I disliked the smell of *flowers*. Whew! A crowded herbaceous border in June used to make me very nearly sick out-loud.

Smells that he *did* like were chiefly woodland smells: the 'very delicate and cool' smell of 'the north side of a beech-trunk'; or 'under the hazel bushes'; or 'the smell of a flint newly kicked out of damp earth'; and he recalled that his other senses were just as keen:

> All sound was bell-music. The *sight* of any *friend* was a vision of angels. English summer heat was a blast furnace: a wasp-sting, the martyr's worst pangs.

The intensity of his perception was unusual, even for a child; and already, at the age of six, Dick had 'decided that I should inevitably be a writer';[5] and had dictated to Louisa a poem entitled *Invocation to the Muse*, which runs:[6]

> Oh maiden, fair maiden,
>   Come spin for me,
> Come spin till you're laden,
>   Though hard it may be:
>
> 'Tis an honour and glory
>   To be a King's maid,
> Though (I'll not tell a story),
>   *You won't be well paid.*

'The pessimism of this last line', Hughes later explained, 'was not without reason': Louisa had impressed her father's bankruptcy upon his mind in the most gloomy colours.

Nor, he learned, could poems always work their undeniable magic as and when required. One evening the following summer, having been sent to bed for coming home an hour late for dinner, Dick composed the following lines, and persuaded Louisa to come to his room with her notebook to record them:[7]

So we came to the river's brink
To of those clear waters drink;
And there the fishes, gold and red,
Ever quickly past us sped,

And there the pebbles, red and blue,
Which we saw the green weeds through,
At the bottom shining lay –
It was their *shining* made us stay!

'Surely', he wrote later, 'that explained it all completely, and now I'd be allowed to get up again and dress? But no . . . though Mother smiled at "To of those clear waters drink".'[8]

Louisa was delighted by her seven-year-old's literary gifts; but she also encouraged him to undertake a wide range of other activities, from dancing to riding; from taking photographs (and developing the negatives himself) to spending a day at the Natural History Museum in South Kensington; and from shovelling snow to learning drill. Remembering her own unusual childhood, she even explained how to set tree-snares for birds,[9] as she had done in Jamaica; and she read him extracts from Baden-Powell's *Scouting for Boys*. Louisa also stirred a theatrical element into the brew of Dick's education, taking him to the pantomime, and encouraging him to celebrate April Fool's Day by dressing up as an old woman: in which guise, she recorded with pleasure, he successfully 'took in his Granny'.[10]

Each year saw another seaside holiday: in the summer of 1908 at Selsey in Sussex, where great storms blew up, making it too rough to bathe; and Dick and Louisa watched as a lifeboat set out to rescue all hands from a steamer which had been disabled in high seas off Selsey Bill.[11] Dick was increasingly fascinated by the sea; and holidaying in Essex in the spring of 1909, he found an abandoned duck-punt on the mud-flats. As he wrote later:[12]

I stepped a willow-pole (of all timber!) for mast, in a bit of old iron. A sack ripped open served for a squaresail – two ropes I controlled with my hands, two I trimmed with my bare toes, and I steered (perceptibly) with a board tucked under my arm. No Americas Cup contestant certainly: but the rapture of spanking along at a round knot and a half! Sliding over the mud in a few inches of water, and jeering at the proper yachts stuck fast till the next tide! Vermin that I was, I used to hail them and offer them a tow.

In September 1908 Dick had moved on from Eothen to 'The Dene', a Caterham 'preparatory-school' for boys up to the age of thirteen. Here (at first) his intelligence and enthusiasm for work won him nothing but praise. However the teaching staff at 'The Dene' was largely second-rate,[13] and Dick soon became so bored that within a year he was being classed as an idler. 'He takes so long to change', reported his headmaster in quiet desperation, 'that one day he missed a whole lesson!'[14]

From time to time Dick exhibited flashes of brilliance which showed just how well he could do if he tried: 'He has all the tastes and instincts of a scholar, but is too slow at present',[15] wrote one of his teachers in July 1910; and variations on this comment recurred throughout his prep-school days.[16] It is true that (as he himself admitted) he was 'always a slow worker, and it took me far longer to do my homework in the evenings than most boys'. But the real problem was that Hughes thoroughly disliked the tedious work which was set before him; and years later he wrote angrily about the[17]

> form of child-labour in England which unfortunately does not come under the Factory Acts, although by it children begin to work for their livings from the age of eight or nine. This is the scholarship system . . . a perfect instrument for ruining the intelligence of any child who is suspected of having one.

If ever a teacher *did* succeed in arousing his enthusiasm, then a very different Dick Hughes appeared. To his weekly English essay, one of the few things which he 'heartily enjoyed', he 'generally gave the whole of the week-end, writing sometimes three or four thousand words'; and at home he not only wrote serials for circulation around the family,[18] but also read avidly. During the Christmas holidays of 1910–1911 alone, he devoured more than forty books, plays and long poems, including Dickens's *Nicholas Nickleby*, Bulwer-Lytton's *The Last Days of Pompeii*, Sir Walter Scott's *Guy Mannering*, Mark Twain's *Tom Sawyer*, Kipling's *Rewards and Fairies*, Sheridan's *The Critic*, Coleridge's *Christabel* and Tennyson's *The Princess*.[19]

Like many writers, Dick appears to have felt something of an outsider during his childhood. He put down few if any roots in Caterham[20] (where he and Louisa had now moved from Dorincourt into the smaller and more manageable La Roche); and after the death of his grandfather Arthur Hughes in 1909, his grandmother Penelope encouraged him to take an interest in the Wales of his remote ancestors.[21]

The result was that when (in the summer of 1911) there was a seaside holiday at Barmouth in North Wales, Dick had the curious feeling that he had at last come home. He rapidly fell in love with the remote landscape of Cader Idris, learned by heart (and in

Welsh) the first verse of 'Land of my Fathers'; and on his return to Caterham, feeling 'a homesickness to go back that I never felt for the south country where I was born and bred', he 'determined then and there to live in Wales as soon as I was able'.[22] In the meantime, discovering from the family tree that he was apparently descended both from the goddess Venus 'and from Regan, the ugly daughter of King Lear', he would 'look at his aunts for a long time and wonder whether the Venus or the Regan predominated in each of them'.[23]

Dick's school-work remained 'patchy';[24] though Louisa was determined that he should win a scholarship so that she could afford to send him to a good public school. By the beginning of 1912, she was already thinking seriously about Charterhouse, which had been strongly recommended to her by some family friends: 'especially' wrote one of them, Hugh Ferguson (who had left Charterhouse for Trinity College, Cambridge some eighteen months previously),[25] 'especially as we have just got a new headmaster there, Mr Fletcher, who is going to improve the school, as I think, tremendously'.[26]

When it became clear that it would require intensive coaching for Dick to reach scholarship standard,[27] Hugh Ferguson's brother Maurice, a Cambridge schoolmaster, stepped into the breach. He soon found that Dick had never been properly taught Latin and Greek grammar; but reckoned that he and his brothers[28]

> could guarantee to work Dick up to scholarship standard in a very few months . . . He is undoubtedly clever, and a conscientious worker: moreover, he is a boy of strong affections.
> I showed his article on *The Messenger of Idris* to an older friend of mine, who has had great experience among boys, and his comment was, 'that young man has a great future before him'.

Dick thrived on this encouragement; and although his progress was hampered at this point by an 'almost chronic cough & cold'[29] which lasted right through the winter, he worked much harder during term-time,[30] and assimilated vast quantities of Latin and Greek from the Fergusons during the holidays. The result was that towards the end of May 1913 Hughes spent two days of examinations in the gloomy medieval hall at the old Charterhouse buildings in London (from which the school had long ago removed to Surrey); and that he emerged triumphantly with a scholarship.

Louisa was delighted; but hardly had Dick begun to enjoy his achievement, when she was busily plotting not merely the next stage of his academic career, but the whole course of his future life. On the advice of one of her contacts in the literary world, to whom she had forwarded some of Dick's poems, Louisa told her son that he should now aim to become a civil servant, with literary work as a subsidiary career.[31] His more immediate aims should be to win two further scholarships: an internal one at Charterhouse, and an external one to Oxford.[32]

Wishing to please his mother, Hughes agreed to do his best; but he had learned to his horror that outstanding achievement brings further pressures in its wake; and the episode left him with a deeply ambivalent attitude towards success which lasted for most of his life. He fervently desired it, and often pursued it (especially in his early years) with all the determination of an Arthurian knight searching for the Holy Grail; but invariably, as soon as he had this gleaming chalice within his grasp, it would turn to the dullest lead, increasing rather than diminishing his emotional burden.

CHAPTER 3

Along the Tops of the Hedges

In the autumn of 1913, wearing the regulation dark-grey trousers and black jacket, Dick Hughes set out for Charterhouse. First his train journey took him to the pleasant little country town of Godalming. Trunks had been sent on 'in advance'; and from Godalming station he walked with his hand-luggage out of the town along the winding road which climbs from the river Wey up to the Charterhouse heights.

Following in the footsteps of the Fergusons (two of whom were still at Charterhouse) Hughes had joined 'Daviesites', then one of the smallest and most agreeable of the eleven houses into which the school was divided.

Work was not at first a serious problem. Mr Lake, one of Dick's teachers, referred rather unkindly in a half-term report to his being 'more than half-asleep as a rule';[1] but when, at Lousia's request, the matter was investigated, the words were said to be an observation rather than a criticism. Dick's housemaster, Mr Slater, explained that her son[2]

> appears to me to think more than most boys and gets rather wrapped up in his thoughts so that he appears to be slow in form, but he is regarded as a promising boy. He likes his work and reads good books.

At the end of the 'quarter' (Carthusian for 'term') Slater added that Dick's intellect was 'of an unusual type'; and Frank Fletcher, a slim grey man with a tight-lipped mouth[3] who was also a great reforming headmaster, wrote encouragingly: 'I hope he means to do really well: there is much promise about him.'[4]

Outside the classroom, however, Frank Fletcher's reforms were only just beginning to take effect, and (in Hughes's words) it was 'not . . . a particularly civilised place'.[5] One of his fellow scholars, Charles Graves, commenting some years later on the 'sentimental falling in love with younger boys' and the 'adolescent lust between boys of the same age who used each other coldly as convenient sex instruments', wrote that:[6]

There was a great deal of both at Charterhouse in 1913 and my refusal to take part added to my unpopularity. I forget how many fellows were either swished (birched until they bled) or were expelled that year. No doubt to sublimate the ego of the lusty adolescents, every effort was made to tire them out in a healthy manner before bedtime.

To this end, all boys in the Lower School had to score eighteen 'pricks' each week: with a game of football, for example, counting four pricks, and a game of squash two. 'Any boy who failed to play the requisite number of games', Charles records,

> was beaten with a toasting fork, which was rather worse than being beaten with a cane. One was beaten, really, for almost anything . . . New boys (known as Newbugs) were beaten if they were unable to pass a local knowledge examination after their first fortnight. Charterhouse was full of conventions known as Post-tes which had to be memorized, together with the names of head monitors of other houses, the various football colours, and so on.

Despite all these difficulties, Richard Hughes later wrote that 'unless my memory grossly deceives me, I was very happy there: and more so at the beginning, when I was the smallest cog in the machine, than at the end'.[7]

The Long Quarter (the short spring term) of 1914 was marred by an illness which kept Hughes in sick-bay 'for more than half the quarter'; but he was up and about in time to see the famous inter-house boxing competitions in which Robert Graves, elder brother of his class-mate Charles, and chiefly known outside his own house for the poems which he contributed to the school magazine *The Carthusian*, became 'the hero of the hour'.[8] As Hughes recorded, Graves[9]

> was a completely dark horse, and practically untaught, but he knocked the almost hypnotised school champions one after the other clean over the ropes – like the hero of a school story, except that he drank plenty of cherry brandy between the bouts.

Robert Graves was then just about to be sacked as assistant editor of *The Carthusian*, which he and his fellow editor Nevill Barbour had been filling with revolutionary attacks upon the public-school system.[10] He was also about to leave Charterhouse: as he thought, for Oxford. But before he did so, at the end of the Summer Quarter 1914, Raymond Rodakowski, one of his few close friends, had pointed out Hughes 'as the coming editor of *The Carthusian*'.[11]

So within a few quarters of his arrival, Hughes had already made a mark; and that summer his English teacher, the Revd E.E. Bryant, wrote to Louisa:[12]

It is not difficult to see his interest where the chance comes of trying to make a good piece of literature 'live' to him, or of bringing the outline of some big idea before him . . . I hope [that when he has moved on to his next form] he will come to talk about his reading and interests to me . . . If his mind gets encouragement and the right sort of sympathy, I think it should make something first-rate.

In August 1914 came the shock of war with Germany. Those who had just left Charterhouse, like Robert Graves, went into the army instead of taking up their places at Oxford or Cambridge; and before many months had passed they were most of them out in France, caught up in the mud and slaughter of the trenches. The Charterhouse which they had left behind became both younger and older. Boys slipped away to 'sign up' as soon as they had reached their eighteenth birthdays; while most of the masters of fighting age departed to the Front, leaving behind the sick, the elderly, and those called out of retirement.

For Hughes, the first year of the war was a period of considerable ill-health. In both the Long and Cricket Quarters of 1915 he endured lengthy absences from school; though these did not prevent him from winning one of the six 'senior scholarships' which were awarded that summer;[13] and it was not until the holidays, when Louisa paraded him around Sussex in his OTC uniform, that he began to recover.[14]

Bryant had continued to keep an eye on Hughes; and soon after the start of Oration Quarter 1915, he reported to Louisa that he had talked to Dick about the possibility of confirmation, '& what strain it was likely to put on him; not so much to find if he was in brain & character ready for it, as from what I know of him he is ready in that way'. Dick's view was that he would like to be confirmed, but that he might get more from the preparation for confirmation and from his first Communion by waiting until he was stronger; and Bryant was pleased to find, as he had hoped, that Dick had[15]

a simple and natural thoughtfulness which looks on life as a whole as a growth in the knowledge of God and on Confirmation as a help to assure one of His Presence and Inspiration & help throughout life.

Hughes had now joined the Lower VI, to which in his mid-quarter report he was welcomed as 'The best writer of English who has passed into the form for many years'.[16] Later that quarter, the December issue of *The Carthusian* included a poem by 'Idris' (the

pen-name which Hughes had chosen in honour of his first visit to
Wales). In the poem, Hughes (who in real life had become a keen
soccer player), 'chases the flying ball' at Charterhouse with his
'Brother', before they meet again on the field of battle:[17]

> I met thee once, my Brother,
>   Not so very long ago,
> In a sodden field in Flanders
>   Where we chased the flying foe.
> I met thee, and I knew thee, and even now I'd fain
> Say I love thee still, my brother, love thee still, though
>   thou art slain.

And this is not the end of the story. They will meet once more:

> In the days that are to be,
> When the good God sends to earthwards
> Back to live both thee and me.

Although the poem shows that Hughes had a firm grasp of rhythm
and metre, he had possessed both since he was a small child;
and Hughes would later declare that the verse he had written at
Charterhouse was 'mostly far worse than what I had been writing
ten years before; imitative, sweet, mystic or melodramatic'.[18]

Since the autumn of 1916, Hughes had been working for an
Oxford scholarship; and, as he later recalled, it was not a happy
experience:[19]

> Instead of finding the study of the Classics grow easier, every
> year it seemed to grow harder, and every year I worked more
> slowly. One whole term I slept with an alarm clock under my
> pillow, and worked each day from four in the morning to the
> official hour of Early School. But by the next term, even an alarm
> clock under my pillow failed to wake me; so I took to sitting up
> instead for the whole of one night each week, and working from
> lights-out to the rising bell. The authorities, of course, would not
> have allowed this if they had known it. On the other hand, the
> work was expected of me, and this was the only way I could do it.
>
> The threat of a breakdown, however, and stringent doctor's
> orders, finally brought some relaxation.

After much of the Long Quarter had been marred through illness
brought on by this overwork, a rather slight poem, 'Love and the
Bee' appeared in the June number of *The Carthusian*;[20] and then
for the November number he wrote what Robert Graves, a fellow
contributor, later described as: 'a jolly poem which I remember about
an elf . . . & a little house: full of colour & charming'.[21] It was called
'Fantaisie (1)'[22] and began:

> A little elf lived in a little white house
> On the edge of the dreamy downs;
>   The roof was red, and the grass was green,
>   The cliffs were whiter than ever were seen,
>   And tiny blue flowers clung in between
> In hundreds of prickly crowns.

Contributing to *The Carthusian* led to a friendship with the then editor, G.H. 'Peter' Johnstone (later Lord Derwent), the Saunderite scholar and poet with whom Robert Graves had once fallen romantically in love, and who was now a school monitor and a leading member of the Upper VI.

Literary pursuits were balanced by some determined soccer-playing: that November, for example, Hughes contributed as a wing-forward to the Daviesite victory, after 'a very hard and evenly-contested game', in their house match against Weekites;[23] and at the start of the following quarter, three months before his seventeenth birthday, he was made a house monitor. In this capacity he was soon judged to be doing well, 'in a simple unobtrusive way';[24] and before long he was displaying a talent for practical administration which would soon lead to further official duties being heaped upon him.

Academic progress was once again 'handicapped by perpetual absences'; though he came *prox. acc.* in the Thackeray prize for English Literature that year;[25] and his mathematics teacher discovered, much to his excitement, that Hughes had been making 'some very interesting mathematical speculations outside the ordinary work of the division'.[26] It was at about this time, for example, that he[27]

> conceived the rather eccentric idea of working out laws of perspective for the Fourth Dimension — how four-dimensional objects would look, that is to say, if represented by three-dimensional 'drawings'; and I remember lying awake nearly the whole of one night in a state of ecstasy, while I tried to envisage the proper three-dimensional distortion for a four-dimensional object bounded by eight cubes, sixteen points, and thirty-two lines. Only the writing of poetry has ever given me the same sort of exaltation.

Another consuming passion was astronomy. Hughes had already made 'a perpetual calendar for the Moon, which showed at a glance the dates of the new moons for any year you liked to consider'.[28] Now somebody told him how to make a telescope; and in his spare time (as he recalled some years later)[29]

> and out of my pocket-money I made myself quite a good one. I use it still. The tubes are only made of cardboard; but they

are quite rigid, and have the advantage of being very light. The lenses I bought, of course; they were cheap second-hand ones. I don't think that the whole thing cost me more than fifteen shillings. But it would magnify up to sixty times . . . I could easily read a book sixty yards away, for instance. In fact, this little telescope of mine was as powerful as the one Galileo used when he made the discoveries that revolutionised the whole science of astronomy!

He was able not only to see hundreds more stars than are visible to the naked eye, but to make out the rings of Saturn; to see some of the moons of Jupiter; and to observe sun-spots, of which he took photographs by attaching an old camera that had lost its lens to the end of the telescope, and using gas-light paper on which to record an image.

Nothing could be quite so exciting in the classroom, where for several years Richard Hughes of Daviesites had shared a desk with the equally clever and equally good-natured but much less law-abiding Charles Graves of Gownboys. Close friendships between fellows from different houses were heavily discouraged on moral grounds; but Charles later recalled how they had eventually 'struck up an acquaintance', and how they[30]

> used to have the greatest fun with our sixth-form master, having bets on who could make him use the most unlikely word in a forty-five minute period, without using it ourselves. Hughes, for example, would select hippopotamus and I would choose abracadabra. Sometimes we would pull it off within ten minutes.

In December 1917 they were both made school monitors;[31] and Frank Fletcher was particularly impressed by Hughes, of whom he wrote shortly afterwards that: 'The more influence he can exert, the better both for him and for others. I value his intellectual influence highly.'[32] By the start of Long Quarter 1918 Dick Hughes had not only won an open scholarship to Oriel College, Oxford, matching Charles Graves's to St John's; but he had also been appointed head of the school, head monitor of Daviesites, and editor of *The Carthusian*.

It was while contemplating how best to fill the pages of *The Carthusian* that Richard Hughes had his first really intimate conversation with Charles Graves, whom he knew (outside the classroom) only as Robert's brother. Afterwards he wrote to his mother telling her that:[33]

> I had an interesting talk with Graves yesterday. His father is a minor poet, a friend of Yeats, & also a politician. He is on the Irish Convention. He numbers among his friends Lloyd George,

Kipling, 8 of the poets contributing to *Georgian Poetry* (including Sassoon, Masefield, Nichols etc.) . . . One uncle is on the *Punch* table, another sub-editor of the *Spectator*, another reviewer to *The Times*, another high in the diplomatic service. They are people to cultivate.

Dick added that he was 'going to tea with Mr Mallory, who is on leave'. This was George Mallory, the gifted English teacher who had done much to make Robert Graves's life at Charterhouse bearable; and who agreed to review Graves's *Fairies and Fusiliers*,[34] which the Library Committee had recently purchased at Hughes's suggestion. Hughes also wrote directly to Robert Graves (then instructing cadets at Rhyl in North Wales); and was rewarded with a friendly letter and an anti-militarist poem[35] for the March number of *The Carthusian*.[36]

Later that quarter, both Richard Hughes and Charles Graves were involved in fighting the great Charterhouse Fire (which at one point had threatened the whole main block of school buildings with destruction);[37] and during the Easter holidays Charles (who left Charterhouse at the end of Long Quarter 1918) invited his class-mate up to Erinfa, the Graves's holiday home at Harlech, in Dick's beloved North Wales.[38]

Joining Charles and other members of the Graves family at Paddington, Dick Hughes caught a brief glimpse of Robert and his wife Nancy Nicholson, who were holidaying in London and had promised to see them off, but who only arrived in time to wave as their train pulled out of the station. On the journey north, Hughes was introduced to Charles's mother Amy Graves, upon whom his politeness, modesty and consideration for others made a great impression;[39] to his father Alfred Perceval Graves, that good-humoured Anglo-Irish poet, who had soon promised to supply Dick with a patriotic song for the next *Carthusian*;[40] to his tall, beautiful and unworldly elder sister Clarissa;[41] and to his red-haired younger brother John (another scholar) who had joined Charles at Gownboys in the autumn of 1916.

When they reached their destination, they drove from the station, on the flat, sandy 'Morfa', up the steep twisting road which led into Harlech itself. Hughes was enchanted by this unspoiled hillside village of small granite houses with slate roofs, dominated then as now by the ruined shell of a magnificent medieval castle; and so pleased was he to be back in Wales, which he still thought of as his 'real' home, that from his arrival in Harlech he abandoned 'Dick' as too English. Instead, he asked the Graveses to call him 'Diccon', the Welsh name (possibly taken from one of the central characters in Frances Hodgson Burnett's *The Secret Garden*) by which he would be known for the rest of his life.[42]

From Harlech, they travelled a mile or so along the road leading northwards to Talsarnau, passing through the little row of houses at Llechwedd where Robert owned a small cottage, before reaching the large stone pillars and wrought-iron gates at the foot of the steep Erinfa driveway. Far above them was the house: a substantial building which Amy herself had designed back in the 1890s. It was magnificently situated: from the terrace they could look northwards to the Snowdon range, where mountain after mountain piled up against the horizon; westwards across a corner of the estuary towards Criccieth; or south-westwards towards Harlech castle on its rocky promontory above the sea.

Diccon Hughes spent nearly three weeks with the Graveses at Erinfa: 'he revelled in the Harlech atmosphere', Charles later recalled, 'recreating in his mind the Welsh ancestry which his surname suggested.' Together they roamed over the ancient hills behind Erinfa where it was possible to walk for fifteen or twenty miles without crossing a road or passing close to a farm; and where, as Robert Graves would one day write:[43]

> the passage of the seasons was hardly noticed . . . the wind always seemed to be blowing and the grass always seemed to be withered and the small streams were always cold and clear, running over black stones . . . There were almost no birds except an occasional buzzard and curlews crying in the distance; and wherever we went we felt that the rocky skeleton of the hill was only an inch or two under the turf.

For Diccon Hughes, this was a land which seemed to offer him a geographical base from whose mountain-tops to challenge the stultifying dullness of the dwellers on the plain.

Indeed, Diccon had been roused to such a pitch of excitement that he would soon tell his mother that he was 'not as sane' as his fellow Carthusians, but that his mind ran 'along the tops of the hedges sometimes, instead of sticking to the paths'.[44] It was in this spirit that he began his journey home by setting out after supper ('well-equipped with food and warm clothing', and escorted to the top of the hill above Erinfa by Charles, John and Clarissa) and walking twenty miles across mountainous country to Bala.[45] And in July he published in *The Carthusian* his poem 'High Things', in which, disdaining the 'gentle folk' of the plain, he declared that he wanted to live with the 'wild-eyed mountain men', in a land where:[46]

> The very rock I lean on feels a friend;
> It knows me, whom it knew not at high noon.
> For night is full of some vague Enterprise
> That makes the poet write, the artist draw . . .

Eternal rest! incessant quietude!
Has hell more dreadful punishment than these?
New tasks I ask, new goals — no peaceful home:
By golden-gleaming stars I'd blaze my trail,
And watch great comets singing up the gale
Which blows from Heaven: or for Aeons roam
Among deep black or starry silences,
Where that fine nectar of the soul is brewed
By which men learn to strive, and Godlike, fail.

These stirring sentiments were connected both with his literary ambitions and with his wish to escape from the strangling tentacles of Louisa's love. But they were also influenced (like so much in Hughes's adolescence) by a profound knowledge that adolescence might be all. Beyond the safety of home and school lay the trenches; and then, most probably, the 'starry silences'.

CHAPTER 4

The Shadow of Death

Since the outbreak of war in August 1914, Charterhouse had grown more and more like an armed camp; and in the initial enthusiasm with which they welcomed the prospect of military training, this was what most Carthusians wanted.[1] The Officers' Training Corps, formerly a voluntary body of two hundred fellows, who paraded twice a week without (it was said) much show of enthusiasm,[2] suddenly became compulsory for all. A bugle band came into being to encourage morale; and the number of parades was increased from two to eight, involving at least an hour of drill every day from Monday to Friday, a military lecture on Tuesday evenings, 'marching out' for three-and-a-half hours on Wednesday afternoons, and a 'Field Day' in full uniform every Saturday.[3]

All the service rifles had been commandeered by the War Office at an early stage in the fighting; and so at first the two or three hundred 'recruits', among whom Richard Hughes was numbered, had to drill with staves;[4] but this did nothing to dampen their enthusiasm. At the same time, *The Carthusian* had begun to read more and more like a military gazette, with pages of military appointments, and extensive 'War Lists', principally of those who had died of wounds or had been killed in action.

By the summer of 1916 (when Private R.A.W. Hughes was about to set off for his first summer camp), enthusiasm for the war had hardly diminished. At the annual inspection on 12 July Major-General M.H. Barnardiston declared to the assembled ranks of the OTC that: 'The remark made by me in 1913 that Public school men are the born leaders of people has been amply justified, and by no school more than Charterhouse.'[5] And yet even as he spoke, the battle of the Somme raged in France for the twelfth successive day; and a generation of young men, including many of the Carthusian officers whom he praised, were being pointlessly slaughtered in this major Allied defeat.

For weeks, casualties averaged some 10,000 killed or seriously wounded every day; while the British press carried nothing but good news from the front. In the July number of *The Carthusian,*

Hughes read of the wounding both of Captain R. von R. Graves of the Royal Welch Fusiliers, and of Second-Lieutenant Leslie Ferguson of the Sixtieth Rifles,[6] but these bare facts conveyed little; and when on 1 August Dick and his comrades set off for their camp at Tidworth Pennings,[7] the scale of the disaster was only just becoming known.

Camp itself remained happily remote from the reality of what was happening in France. For one thing, the weather was almost perfect, with a cloudless sky day after day; and, to most Carthusians, the demonstrations seemed more exciting than alarming. 'The night-firing', wrote one participant,[8]

> was really a thrilling performance, especially for the lucky few who formed the firing-party and were privileged to take front seats with fifty rounds of live ammunition. So, too, was the demonstration by the Stokes guns, four batteries of them, which in a final spasm threw at the enemy one hundred and sixty of their shells, or sausages, in one crowded half-minute of glorious noise.

For more sensitive observers it was merely another reminder (as Richard Hughes wrote years later) that they were[9]

> unlikely to live much beyond the age of nineteen; and [we] accepted this as the natural order of things, just as mankind in general accepts the unlikelihood of living much beyond eighty or so . . . So, genera-tion after generation of boys grew big, won their colours, and a few terms later were . . . mere names, read aloud in chapel once. As list succeeded list the time of other littler boys for the slaughter-house was drawing nearer; but they scarcely gave it a thought as they in turn grew into big boys, won their football colours.

And Hughes himself began climbing up through the ranks of the OTC, becoming a Lance-Corporal in Oration Quarter 1916,[10] and a Corporal in the summer of 1917.[11]

But although indifference was then the general rule, it would sometimes happen that 'the death of someone very close – a brother, or a father perhaps – would bring home . . . momentarily that being killed *is* radically different from that mere normal disappearing into the grown-up shadow-world: is being no more even than a shadow on earth'. For Hughes, that 'sudden blinding intimation of mortal-ity'[12] came in June 1917 with the death of Hugh Ferguson, who had risen to be a captain in the South Staffordshire Regiment,[13] and who had been expected to have a great future in literature, had he lived.[14]

The OTC Camp at Tidworth in the summer of 1917 was a slightly more realistic foretaste of life at the Front, with day after day of incessant rain, which turned the campsite into mud, and 'seri-ously hampered the scheme of training'.[15] But when (on returning to Charterhouse for the start of Oration Quarter 1917), Hughes took up his new appointment as editor of *The Carthusian*, he wrote an editorial in which he showed that he was determined not to let the present be clouded by gloomy thoughts of the future: 'Our time is short', he declared. 'Very short indeed is school life: and its end soon looms over us, unavoidable. Very well, let us forget it. There are more important things in life than death.'[16]

Acceptance of things as they were did not blind Hughes to the ills of boarding-school life; but he believed, as he wrote in December 1917, that 'true reform can only come from within'.[17] His headmaster Frank Fletcher, delighted by this attitude, appointed Hughes head of the school the following January;[18] and Hughes took the opportunity to write an impassioned *Carthusian* editorial in defence of the monitorial system, with its teaching of 'the power to command . . . What better training could there be', Hughes asked, 'for an Imperial Nation?'[19]

Some years later, Hughes would feel ashamed of his unregenerate public-school self, and would complain that he had been 'pushed into the position of head boy', and that[20]

> Compared with this position of autocracy, the monarch of an oriental empire is a shadow. One is the absolute despot of six hundred other boys. But I had been very little beaten myself, and took very little pleasure in beating my Juniors when the Law demanded. Moreover, this whole elaborate disciplinary machine, which had looked perfectly right and proper from below, when seen from above (with myself the God-Emperor) I felt to be unmitigatedly ridiculous.

At the time, however, he had believed that only a few small changes would be necessary to make public schools centres of moral excellence;[21] and he had thrown himself into his duties[22] in the most dedicated manner: 'He sets a good moral and intellectual standard', noted his housemaster approvingly in April, 'and maintains it well.'[23]

As his last months at Charterhouse went by, the sense of impending death grew stronger. Early in 1918 he had made a sentimental journey to Dorincourt, the house where he had been born, only to find it 'half its proper size, /And half its magic shorn';[24] and he began to cram as many enjoyable moments as possible into what would probably be his last summer.

In June (having only recently begun to shave every day),[25] Diccon developed a sudden interest in a girl named Molly Taylor. One weekend, after bicycling over to have an early supper with his godfather, Charles Johnson (who lived not far away at Peaslake), Diccon travelled up to London alone, called on Molly, and (with her mother's permission) took her out to the theatre.

When Louisa heard what had happened next, she was furious. Not only had Diccon gone out with Molly *unchaperoned*, but in seeing her home he had somehow contrived to miss his train, and had therefore been invited to spend the night *under her roof!* Disguising her unpleasant possessiveness as a proper regard for good manners, Louisa wrote Dick a very stiff letter, for which, despite a very reasonable protest that 'most of the boys at school I know of have done far more unconventional things than going to a theatre like that, without thinking anything of it', he still had to make profuse apologies:[26]

> Oh Mother how I do wish it hadn't happened . . . I didn't know what the exact rules were. For goodness sake make me a complete list of them that such a thing may never occur again. I would have spent the night on the streets had I thought I ought.
>
> Oh Mother, Mother, I wish I hadn't done it . . . When your letter first came I nearly kicked myself to pieces with rage for having been such a fool. Why can I never think of things when I ought to?

He added that he hoped Molly could still come down with Louisa to an hotel in Godalming the following weekend; and he enclosed a further note to tell his mother that it was very dull of her *always* to want things organised in advance: sometimes people should act as the spirit moved them.

In the meantime, no doubt to redeem himself in Louisa's eyes, Diccon threw himself into noting the works of Dowden, Blake, Carlyle and Taine,[27] before typing a lengthy entry for the Tennant essay prize. 'All Friday I worked at it', Diccon told his mother; 'I typed about 3,500 words without stopping. All night the keys were tapping in my head.'[28]

The prospect of military service grew daily more sharp. In May, Hughes had called at the War Office in an unsuccessful effort to secure a commission with the Royal Engineers;[29] and in June he took a keen interest in the Arthur Webster competition, an annual event in which all eleven house platoons competed for military honours. One afternoon, therefore, Hughes and a group of his fellow officers 'bicycled out to Puttenham Common, the probable scene of the Arthur Webster attack, & examined the ground with military eyes, evolving stunts'; and although it was an overall 'disaster' for Daviesites, who were placed last, Hughes declared that the competition had given him 'quite an opinion' of himself as a strategist, as the winning house had used virtually the same plan as the one which he had outlined.[30]

In other respects, Diccon was feeling more and more wretched. His godfather, his housemaster and his headmaster were all full of praise: Mr Johnson (who had been asked by Louisa to make a special journey to Godalming to lecture Diccon on his vagueness over the theatre visit, and had arrived at the King's Arms to find him 'hobnobbing with the Duke of Connaught') told Lousia that her son had 'gained in self-possession & force . . . It is Dick in a new phase . . . all is well now & we are firmer friends than ever'.[31] Mr Slater added that 'the general tone of the House has never been better than it is at present, thanks to him';[32] and Frank Fletcher declared that Diccon was[33]

> one of the most interesting & promising boys intellectually that I have ever taught . . . and I am the more anxious to be of use to him in any way that I can be . . . I am intensely interested in his mind & individuality & (I may add) I like him personally very much. So does my wife.

Diccon, however, was chiefly conscious that things were coming to an end. For his final editorial in July he had written:[34]

> Have you ever watched a caterpillar turning into a chrysalis? He does not like it a bit. It is the same with leaving school: five years of omnivorous and succulent feeding; five years of waxing fat, and changing a skin or two. Then the time comes: the poor human caterpillar feels very queer, and starts producing all sorts of strings of thoughts in which he gets wound up horribly. For a while he vanishes from all ken, hidden in a stiff khaki case, only able to make jerky movements. Perhaps he will be a butterfly some day. Perhaps a brown moth. Or perhaps he will die of the cold.

And now he sent a gloomy 'last letter' to Louisa. His success in winning the Tennant essay prize went unmentioned; instead he concentrated upon his 'fail[ure] to win the Leech, and the Petilleau', and his feeling that he had 'done extraordinarily badly in the exams . . . Everything', he wrote, 'conspires to make me dismal'.

He had been up until one in the morning doing the Library minutes; his head ached, he still had half-a-dozen other jobs to do, he had no money to tip anyone, and as if that were not enough, his bicycle pump had been stolen. Before he sealed the envelope, he was able to add a PS to the effect that he had won the '1st general Exhibition'. But this triumph, a special award for Carthusians going up to Oriel College, Oxford, appeared to give him little pleasure, as one of his rivals had won both the Classical exhibition and the

Talbot scholarship. 'However', he concluded, 'it provides for me all right – if I ever get to Oxford. Love, from your Doleful Dick.'[35]

Before making his way back to Caterham, Hughes had a bicycling holiday in Hampshire. First he called on some relatives[36] at Romsey, where he made 'a new and highly superior swing, suspended from an iron bar across two trees'; and where he was such a success with two girl-cousins that on saying goodnight to him one evening, they 'each took a firm grip of my neck', and 'not till I had literally torn them off . . . was I allowed to depart'.[37] And one day he part-trained and part-cycled down to the coast to see another girl (a Miss Wilkins) in whom he was taking an interest.

He enjoyed 'rampag[ing] on the beach' and travelling in a wagonette to Studland Bay for a tea of buttered scones; but his return journey was more memorable. Having left his train at Brockenhurst in the heart of the New Forest, Diccon found that his borrowed bicycle lamp did not work, and had to walk most of the way to Romsey through the night. After a while[38]

> the moon got up and shone sadly through [the fog]. The forest was glorious: but it was hard to find my way, & the roads were full of sleeping cattle. However at Lyndhurst Road I picked up an awfully nice Tommy [soldier], Forester born, & thoroughly well-educated, who took me through all sorts of short cuts, warned me of bad pieces of road, & set me on my way again at Totton: a most amiable man. I didn't get in till midnight.

August 1918 was spent at home with Louisa; and then October saw Richard Hughes in a cadet battalion training to be an officer. He was stationed at an army camp in Bedfordshire, from where he conducted a lively correspondence with friends such as Peter Johnstone and Charles Graves. Johnstone was shortly to join the army as a signaller in the 14th London Regiment, and 'wrote hilariously';[39] while Graves had already spent some months with an officer cadet battalion, and was currently at Leamington Spa learning to fire Lewis guns and throw hand-grenades. The Lewis gun presented him with no problems; but he told Diccon that when he threw his 'first live hand grenade . . . Not surprisingly I tried to throw it a record distance, caught my hand on the back of the trench, and had to nip smartly round the traverse to avoid material damage to myself'.[40]

'So I also am a gorblimey soldier', Diccon wrote to Charles, 'drawing 10/- a week with a nice little gorblimey salute.' He added that he was[41] having the time of my life. The O.C. ... is a Captain of the Lancers ... [with] a strong resemblance to Clarissa. He takes us in riding himself 1½ hours per diem for 120 lessons: so we ought to know something about it at the end. Our senior cadet is an ex-Sergt Major & signalling instructor, who has taught in his time most of the Instructors here, but has to go through the course, before he can get a commission. Also there is Peter Dart, who is an old Dear, with the Somali & Egyptian medals & ... ribbon. We all love Peter. He is even more of an old dear in his cups: which is every evening. He and the ex-Sergt M- are priceless wags. The latter talks French, Greek, Hindustani & Kaffir as well as his other accomplishments. Our third old soldier alternately buzzes Shakespeare Robert Bridges & Omar Khayyam from memory at 12 words p. minute.

Some of his fellow trainees were just as interesting to Diccon: there was one 'lad' in his hut who had a scholarship at Brasenose; and another, 'a delightful agnostic', who

has never been to a public school, has never heard of Chaucer, but knows more philosophy & has more brains & less opinion of himself than most fellows I have met. Our mess is A1, & [we have] only 8 hrs parades a day, but a good deal of other work to do. We have just been discussing the 4th Dimension & the Fox Trot.

All this excitement came to an abrupt end after only just three weeks, when it was discovered that Hughes had developed an abscess in his right armpit which was in danger of bursting through into his chest and killing him.[42]

Diccon was rushed to a hospital in Cambridge and operated upon almost immediately. The operation was entirely successful; and within two weeks Hughes was feeling 'pretty fit', and spending his days promenading round Cambridge 'with a hospital armlet & an empty sleeve, looking like an amputated Hero (transferred epithet) & feeling like an ass'.[43]

The abscess may have saved Hughes from something still worse: a deadly strain of influenza was cutting great swathes through the cadet battalions. On Guy Fawkes Day, Diccon received a letter in which Charles Graves announced that he himself had almost died of influenza, and was currently recuperating at Erinfa. He added that he would like to see Diccon, and that Amy sent her love and an invitation to stay.

'My dear Charles, when I saw the postmark of your letter', replied Diccon, 'I wanted to throw up my nose & howl. This damned flat country is stifling me. Oh to be back among the hills! Damn, damn, damn.' Unfortunately it would be impossible for him to spend any of his leave up at Harlech, as his mother needed him at home; but he asked whether Charles had 'any friends here, especially of the juvenile female variety', as he was 'bored to tears' and had 'nothing to do but write silly stories' – which was difficult when he could only use his left hand.[44]

Six days after Hughes had written this letter came Armistice Day. 11 a.m. on 11 November 1918, and the guns fell silent on the Western Front.

For those who had taken part in the fighting, there was a sense of unspeakable relief, mingled with bitterness for the lives that had been lost. But for those who had come close to the fighting without ever taking part, peace came as a shocking anticlimax. Charles Graves, 'completely flabbergasted' by the idea that he might 'go on living', wondered uneasily for the rest of his life whether or not he would have turned out to be a coward.[45] For Hughes also, 'the shock was stupendous. No one' (as he wrote of his autobiographical hero Augustine)[46]

> had warned him he might after all find himself with his life to live out: with sixty years still to spend, perhaps, instead of the bare six months he thought was all he had in his pocket. Peace was a condition unknown to him and scarcely imaginable. The whole real-seeming world in which he had grown to manhood had melted round him.

Before Hughes could leave his Cambridge hospital, there was one last ordeal to be faced. In mid December the next bed to his had been occupied by a seriously ill cadet, Guy Hender, whom Diccon had nursed when the official staff were unavailable.

When at length Hender died, his widow wrote to Louisa to tell her that: 'one night your boy *stood* the whole night by my husband's side, putting cooling things on his poor head. My husband told me the next day about it & the tears came into his eyes with gratitude, & he said "Hughes is splendid, fancy standing there all night looking after me".'[47]

Diccon was allowed home in time for Christmas: a family affair, with the little house in Caterham 'bursting with "sisters & cousins & aunts" '.[48] Diccon spent most of his time reading; and, as he told Charles, he discovered not only 'some delightful Babylonish exorcisms for expelling the Devil' but 'a wandering student's song (mediaeval)',[49] which included the lines:

> Quid iuvat aeternitas nominis, amare
> Nisi terrae filias licet, et potare?

[Roughly: 'What good is the prospect of heaven, if on earth one can't make love and get drunk?']

Now that the shadow of death had been temporarily lifted, Diccon was looking forward with relish to his undergraduate days.

CHAPTER 5

A Jagged Room

Richard Hughes went up to Oriel College to read classics in January 1919, a few days after being formally demobilised from the army at a camp on Wimbledon Common.[1] His Carthusian friends, Peter Johnstone and Charles Graves, arrived in Oxford at the same time, the former to read Modern Languages, the latter to read English. For all three of them (as Hughes later recalled), post-war Oxford was[2]

> a strange place . . . By far the greater number of the student body had been to the front for a long or short time; nearly all the friends I now made had fought. The Government gave education grants to ex-soldiers, which brought many men there of all classes, often already middle-aged, who would not have gone there otherwise. There were several Brigadier-Generals among the undergraduates.

The presence among the undergraduates of so many battle-weary soldiers created an intellectually heady or even hysterical atmosphere, in which it seemed possible that an entirely new and better world might really be created out of the ruins of the old.

Academic work therefore seemed of secondary importance to the debates, society meetings, undergraduate publications and late-night conversations in which the new intellectual framework could be hammered out; and although to begin with Hughes naturally remained very much the product of his conventional public-school upbringing (and he felt 'a sad failure that I should have reached the advanced age of nearly nineteen without having a book or two to my credit, or a year or two's fighting'),[3] he flung himself into this world with enormous relish and delight.

Hardly had Hughes arrived in Oxford before he was addressing the Oriel College 'Arnold Debating Society' about the 'menace to the best interests of the country' posed by the Labour party;[4] and he co-edited with Peter Johnstone an undergraduate magazine which they called *The Topaz of Ethiopia*. The first number of *Topaz* came out in February 1919, and among its poems and short stories there appeared Diccon's 'In the Hills', a hymn of praise to North Wales which begins:[5]

> I have been where there are no men,
>   In a wealth of cool air:
> Yes, beyond that sky line
>   Away up there.
>
> How to speak of those heights?
>   No road – no way –
> Of living things I saw
>   But two all day –
>
> A sheep stared once
>   When I clattered my stick.
> And two great wings from a black lake
>   Rose and fled quick.

This is light and good-humoured; but later it becomes clear that there is a moral to be pointed; and much of Diccon's writing at this time was filled with a sermonising tendency which he would come to regret.

After his first term at Oriel, Hughes spent most of the Easter vacation as Charles Graves's guest in North Wales. On 20 March 1919 the two friends travelled by train to Harlech, where the first night of their holiday was spent with Robert Graves, Nancy Nicholson and their eleven-week-old daughter Jenny at Llys Bach, the Nicholsons' holiday home. Earlier in the year an attack of influenza had prevented Robert from taking up his exhibition at St John's; and he and Nancy were now writing and drawing so busily and happily (their domestic chores undertaken by a nurse and a general servant) that Robert was beginning to regard Oxford as an unnecessary distraction.[6]

After a single lively evening at Llys Bach (a substantial house just above the road to the north of the village) Diccon and Charles moved on to Erinfa. But that single evening was enough: Diccon had been dazzled both by Robert's achievements and by his uncompromising devotion to literature; and he began spending as much time as possible in Robert's company.

A few mornings later, for example (having declined to join Charles in a round of golf), Diccon walked along the road to Llys Bach where he helped Robert and Nancy to dig their vegetable garden; and that afternoon he was rewarded by being shown the draft of a play which Robert was writing for John Masefield, and the manuscript of *Songs of Country Sentiment*,[7] the provisional title of Robert's fifth collection of poems.[8]

Charles was annoyed by Diccon's evident defection; and by Saturday 29 March, when the two of them had set out to walk through heavy snow to Maentwrog, they both (in Diccon's words) became[9]

> tired and cross. A beastly milestone said nine miles to Harlech. One damnably interesting churchyard sheltered us a bit. Then we moved on, at daggers drawn. Almost at once we came to the mouth of the Raven Falls River. I tried to persuade Charles to go back over the hills. So we parted: he went along the coast road and I went over the hills.

Sunday was still worse. Charles's twenty-five-year-old sister Rosaleen had joined them, and she and Charles and Diccon simply argued and argued; until finally Charles 'rushed out into the landscape'.[10]

Fortunately, Monday brought Robert and Nancy over to lunch; and afterwards (as Diccon recorded in a journal) they all enjoyed[11]

> a furious snow-ball fight in the garden, which ended with a massacre of Charles, which he seemed thoroughly to enjoy. I stormed Nancy's position Tank-wise, bending down and buzzing balls between my legs: then Charles enfiladed me, & caught me unawares in the nape of the neck.

Later that day Nancy's brother Kit arrived; and before long a 'Mutual Improvement Society' had been formed.

As Rosaleen explained in a letter to her parents, she was teaching Nancy music, in return for which Nancy was teaching her gardening. Nancy was also teaching Robert 'home duties and gardening'; while Charles was teaching Rosaleen golf (she had crossly refused to learn bridge)[12] and was 'being instructed by her in domestic work'; and Diccon Hughes was 'getting singing lessons and instructing the rest in considerateness'. Rosaleen did not mention that she was also teaching Diccon elementary Welsh,[13] and that she was enjoying long walks with him in the hills behind Erinfa.

On the last day of March, they searched unsuccessfully for the caves which the Graveses had found in the hills when they were children;[14] and on the first of April, Robert was persuaded to join in their search. 'He found where they were', wrote Diccon in his journal,[15]

> but spent some time finding the way in. Then he moved a flat stone: we crawled along a passage, and found ourselves in a jagged room under a big flat rock. It was obviously partly artificial: but they were large rocks to have moved.

Here in this jagged room Diccon suddenly found himself in the presence not only of the man whom he admired as an exemplar of the 'modern' literary life; but also of what he believed to be his own ancestral past. He emerged in such an exalted state of mind that in his journal that evening he set down the words of the Psalmist: 'I will lift up mine eyes unto the hills, from whence cometh my strength';[16] and a few days later, still feeling full of 'superfluous energy', he set out on an adventure.

It was an adventure which began simply enough, with Diccon putting on his shoes for a run; and then exploring over the hills, following tracks with the aid of a map. But then, as he records,[17]

> the tracks it marked all died down in the bog. I went up behind in the hills, & succeeded in striking Llyn Fedw. Then the fog came down. I couldn't see the hills to steer by, & soon arrived in the appalling rough country round Llyn Eiddw Mawr: all bogs and crags and lichen. I had to keep climbing up & down cliffs, & went over my knees in bogs. The fog was so thick that I soon looped back on my tracks & followed a valley down, till I came to a farm.

Here he learned that he had reached Dol Rheiddiog, not far from the sinister Cwm Bychan lake.

At once he set out again, running up the steep pathway known as the 'Roman Steps', in an attempt to find a still more sinister lake, the Llyn-y-Morwynion, where legend has it that Blodeuwedd's maidens drowned themselves, trying to escape from Llew Llaw Gyffes. 'And no wonder', wrote Diccon, because:

> It is nearly surrounded by cliffs. After a hard scramble I found it & then was so sick of scrambling, & it looked so difficult to climb round, that I swam across, waving a map & a £1 note in my hand. It is a gruesome lake: all deep & black, with frozen snow in it, & icicles dripping from the cliffs, & shadowy white things that seemed to clutch at my legs as I climbed out. I got down then on to the marshes beyond the Roman Steps; then ran back over the Steps, bought 15 eggs at a farm (in Welsh) & ran home. I got in about 8, having run 25–30 miles. Had a hot bath, & felt much better for it next day.

Running about on these ancestral hills was all very well; but Diccon knew that Robert owned a small cottage near Llechwedd, between Llys Bach and Erinfa; and he decided that he too wanted a place of his own somewhere in the vicinity.

Diccon had several times walked north-eastward over the hills to Maes-y-neuadd, an old manor-house which was currently being rented by a friend of the Graveses and Nicholsons, the recently widowed 'Edie' Stuart-Wortley.[18] During one of these visits, he had spent almost a whole day distempering some walls for his hostess;[19] and when she heard that Diccon was looking for a property,[20] she offered to sublet him Ysgol Fach, a tumbledown cottage in the Maes-y-neuadd grounds.

He accepted immediately; and noted in his journal that evening that Ysgol Fach had two rooms, dated back to 1750 (like Robert's cottage, it had once been a school), and had[21]

> long been uninhabited. The roof has holes, as has the upper floor; & it was half full of leaves & earth. It is, in fact, just a shell: but the rent is three days work, two pots of honey, & a groat[4d] per annum. Charles and I started on it at once, & got all the earth cleared out before supper.

The following morning Diccon went off to Ysgol Fach 'as early as possible' to continue putting his cottage in order.

The stone floor was scrubbed; and when this scrubbing revealed that there were 'holes you could chuck a pail of water down', cement was purchased and a major repair work was begun. Meanwhile Charles had cut away the bushes which had overgrown the cottage, and had rigged up 'a contrivance for drawing water from the Eisingrug', a little stream which ran past the front door.[22] Next, there was a leaking roof to be fixed. Hughes did what he could from below; and then, because the roof was too frail to bear his own weight, he enlisted the help of a child who positioned roof-slates as he directed.

These renovations could never be wholly successful because, as Diccon soon realised from the water which welled up through his repairs, there was a spring beneath the cottage: it bubbled up beneath the fireplace, wandered lazily across the stone-work, and then ran out through the front door and down to the stream. Undeterred by this, he spent his savings – some four pounds – on 'a really noble kitchen table, two backless oak chairs from somebody's woodshed, and an iron spring mattress one end of which rested at night on the kitchen-table and the other on the windy window-sill.'[23]

When letters arrived from his mother asking plaintively when he would be returning to La Roche, Diccon replied that it was difficult to be precise, as he did 'so want to get the cottage habitable'; but he would definitely be back in Surrey by 16 April.[24] However, the attractions of Ysgol Fach were too great; and two days after he had promised to rejoin Louisa, he moved out of Erinfa, and into what he now thought of as his 'real' home,[25] a place where:[26]

> Green-eyed care
> May prowl and glare
> And poke his snub, bewhiskered nose:
> But Door fits tight
> Against the Night:
> Through criss-cross cracks no evil goes.

And so contented did he feel that he remained in Ysgol Fach for the rest of the holiday; not leaving until it was necessary for him to travel directly back to Oxford for the start of his second term at Oriel.

For his university degree, Hughes had to pass two sets of major public examinations: the first of these, Honours Moderations or 'Mods', normally taken after two years, was chiefly concerned with translation from and into Latin and Greek. Sadly, his aversion to the study of classics was just as strong as it had been at Charterhouse; and although he was fortunate to have as his tutor David Ross, a dedicated philosopher and one of the great Aristotelian scholars of the century,[27] there was some unexplained lack of sympathy between the two men, and Hughes appears to have done as little formal work as possible.

Far more exciting to attend further meetings of the Arnold Debating Society, where he had soon become one of the principal speakers. The chief event of the summer term was a joint debate with the young women of Somerville College;[28] but Hughes made more of a mark at an ordinary meeting where he was said to have 'demolished' G.L. Thorp, one of his opponents, 'piecemeal' – though in such a good-humoured spirit that it did not prevent the two men from becoming firm friends. P.H.B. ('Phoebe' or Hugh) Lyon, the secretary of the Arnold, also became a friend, commanding Diccon's respect both for the Military Cross which he had been awarded during the Great War, and for the Newdigate prize for poetry which he won in the summer of 1919.

Producing several more numbers of *The Topaz of Ethiopia* was a further distraction, though by July 1919 it had 'flared and died':[29] not surprisingly, in Louisa's view. 'As a man of business, my dear boy', she wrote to Diccon, 'you are absolutely hopeless!' She pointed out that she had been taking orders for *Topaz*; but he had delayed so long in sending out copies, that it was now too late for her to be of help. 'Is it possible', she asked, 'for you ever to answer a letter (that needs an answer) at once?' And then she added sadly: 'this term seems dreadfully long. Are you coming home at all?'[30]

Diccon returned home at the start of the summer vacation of 1919, but left almost immediately for London, where he combined voluntary work in a Bermondsey mission for deprived children with searching for a seaman's berth on an ocean-going ship. Both were exhilarating experiences. On his very first day at the mission, he was involved not only with a run 'over Tower Bridge . . . and west through the City'; but also with 'tak[ing] prayers & preach[ing] my maiden sermon – which took exactly 45 seconds'. And as he hunted for a seaman's berth (he began by finding a firm of shipping agents prepared to write him a letter of introduction)[31] he was introduced to the alien world of the London Docks.

To begin with, Hughes was casually charmed: 'who wouldn't live at the Other End of Cathay Street', he wrote, 'or at the Top of Cherry Garden Stairs? Who could lose hope in Prospect Street? What adventures may lurk on the shore of Tiger Bay, what horrid rites take place in Idol Lane?' He was drawn deeper into this world by listening to strange stories: one of the most striking concerned a crew of Lascars sent to Archangel in the month of Ramadan, when no food may be eaten by Muslims between sunset and sunrise: 'But what were the poor devils to do with a Midnight Sun? They swiftly died like flies: & the official report called it "flu".' Hughes also met characters like Captain Kendal, 'a thin man with bright blue eyes', who had been 'torpedoed and mined six times. His recital was singularly like that of St Paul. He offered me a trip to Montreal, and plenty to the Pacific. He made my mouth water. But what could I say? He had no boats that would be back before the 1st of September'.[32]

After tea one day, Hughes walked with a friend through Rotherhithe tunnel into Chinatown, where they found Penny Fields, 'a seething mass of Asiatics: we could hardly move'; and after walking as far as the East India Docks, they ate chop suey at a Chinese restaurant: 'white stringy stuff, soaked in yellow gravy, chopped dog or cat on top'. Other strange sights included[33]

> a party of Niggers in their Sunday clothes: brown holland for the most part, with high white collars, purple shirts, green silk ties adorned with strange devices & lemon spats over brown boots. Add a straw hat on the back of the head with a flaming hat-band, a coal-black face, & a large walking stick . . .

And a little further on, and 'better still . . . a solemn Hindu with a huge (once) white turban, a flowered silk jacket, & (once) white flannel trousers tucked into cloth-top boots'.

Despite the essential innocence of these observations on foreigners (the cultural arrogance was entirely subconscious and later, when understood, would be speedily corrected), Hughes showed that he could turn a sophisticated gaze upon his fellow countrymen. As he climbed into a railway carriage one evening at Blackheath (not long after finding a berth on a ship bound for Holland), he noticed that[34]

> there was a man getting out. A little girl had just been sitting on his knee. Being dislodged, she merely climbed onto the knees

of a soldier, put her arm round his neck, gave her mother a wink & the soldier the glad eye, & proceeded to flirt with an ease and unblushing cunning that told of much practice. She was whispering sweet nothings before her first love was fairly on the platform.

Hughes was amused, and also felt some sympathy for the girl's mother, who 'bewailed . . . the doings there'd be if such practices continued in ten years' time'.

When his work at the Bermondsey mission was completed, Hughes stayed on in London while he waited for his ship to sail; and in the meantime he is said to have spent 'a week in Limehouse, where he ate black pie and earned money as a pavement artist'.[35]

Then towards the end of July 1919, his voyage to Holland was cancelled at the last minute,[36] and Diccon Hughes retreated to North Wales. After cycling the first one hundred and ten miles, his gears broke down; but this was fortunate, for when he caught a train at Birmingham he found himself in the same carriage as the elderly novelist, Frank Penn Smith, a close friend of his mother's whom he had invited to be his first guest at Ysgol Fach.[37]

Frank Penn Smith, who had contributed a short story to the first number of *The Topaz of Ethiopia*,[38] was a lively if rheumatic companion who joined Diccon in a mild flirtation with 'an engaging young female' from the Russian Ballet, who fed her two admirers with chocolates, and 'blushed every time we mentioned Allegorical': 'I don't know', wrote Diccon, 'what she thought it meant.'[39] After supper in Talsarnau, 'in front of a lovely oak dresser & grandfather clock', Hughes and Penn Smith 'padded up the hill' to Ysgol Fach. There (as Diccon explained to Louisa), they had to live[40]

> entirely downstairs until I put the upstairs window in: but it is all very delightful and comfortable. For Sunday dinner we had loin chops & bubble & squeak & tinned fruit. For supper we had soup, made of the cabbage water & the bones. But we can't get cheese: so please send a pound every four days until we cry off.

Diccon had already told his mother that he was going to his cottage chiefly to do as much reading as possible before the start of the new academic year; and her heart must have sunk when she learned that apart from 'pegging away ½ hr per diem' at his Welsh, he had decided to abandon any serious reading 'till the jobs are done!'

These 'jobs' included plastering the walls; sinking a shallow well in the garden (Penn Smith, who had been living in Africa, encouraged Hughes to call it a 'water-hole'); and building steps down to the stream (which became the 'creek'). And when his guest had departed (apparently very much fitter: Hughes claimed that the running water under his bed had cured Penn Smith's rheumatism), there followed a period of great sociability.[41]

Harlech, as usual in those summers, had become 'a hive of Graveses: they have assembled from every corner of the globe', wrote Diccon, '& flooded out Erinfa, & flooded out Llys Bach, & filled three hotels & all the farms within three miles'. Robert and Nancy were there; also Charles, with his new Oxford friend Leonard Morgan; also Rosaleen and John; and many more, including Robert's fey and beautiful half-sister Molly, a water-diviner who was living 'in a little farm right out on the flat'.[42]

Finally it was the end of September, and Hughes closed up 'Rascal Whack' (as Ysgol Fach had been nicknamed during the summer), and then returned to Oriel: all the more happily for knowing that Robert Graves would shortly be joining him at Oxford.

Robert Graves was not so happy about going up to Oxford; but he felt that he had little choice. A number of schemes intended to be money-spinning had come to nothing; Nancy conceived another child; and eventually financial pressures meant that it would be folly not to take up his place at St John's, where at least he could be certain of a government grant. Because of the poor state of his lungs, he was exempted from the normal rule that an undergraduate must reside within three miles of the centre of Oxford; and at length he was lucky enough to secure 'Dingle Cottage', in the garden of John Masefield's house on Boar's Hill.[43]

Diccon was one of the first visitors to 'Dingle Cottage', where he soon met Robert's landlord. John Masefield, though grey-haired, was still a vigorous poet of forty-one, with a deep rich voice; and he and his shrewd, protective wife, Constance, were kind and encouraging. Within a few weeks of meeting Hughes, Masefield had written to tell him that his poems displayed 'a most delicate and original gift, as well as a most charming power of verse';[44] and soon he had also given his blessing to a publishing project which Hughes had dreamed up with his friends Martin Gilkes and Hugh Lyon.

The result was that before the end of 1919, a message had appeared in all the leading public-school magazines, boldly headed 'Public Schools Verse', and declaring: 'It is intended to publish about once a year an anthology of the best serious verse written at Public Schools, the frequency of publication depending on the amount and quality of what is sent us.' The editors then invited contributions, and added that Mr John Masefield would be writing a preface to the first volume; and that arrangements had been made with 'a first class London Publisher' to publish the anthology, 'provided that the material is good enough'.[45]

In the meantime, 11 November 1919 had seen Louisa Hughes's forty-ninth birthday. Diccon had sent her a slim volume of poems by James Elroy Flecker and handwritten copies of some of his own verses, together with a letter in which he told her of his enormous debt as a poet to Robert Graves.

'Beloved boy', Louisa had replied, 'perhaps some day it will be a slim little volume of your own poetry that will be my birthday gift – & one day it will be – The Great Work – poetry or prose – & then I will sing my "Nunc Dimittis" '. In the meantime, she urged him not to attribute too much weight to his connection with Robert Graves:[46]

> When you say that your lightest poems are owing to RG's influence I think you forget the style in which you wrote as a child. From 6 to 10 what you wrote were the direct prerunners of the light verse you write now.

She added that Diccon's godfather, Mr Johnson, thought that Diccon might eventually decide to combine writing with making a secure income as a publisher's assistant.

Diccon wrote back to his mother telling her that he certainly did not want his success to be the occasion of her death, as she had implied; and asking her to explain exactly what Mr Johnson meant. Louisa in her turn declared that:[47]

> It shall not be the Nunc Dimittis, then dear; it shall be the Benedictus. The idea about the 'Assistant Publishing' was Mr Johnson's & he spoke as though he had mentioned it to you. Murray's was the firm he thought he should like for you & he seemed to think a First in Greats would be a great recommendation. Mrs Johnson knows of a little cottage in Hampstead we might get for about £25 per annum (4 rooms) if she had 6 months' notice to secure it – So there you are – all arranged nicely for you for when you have finished at Oxford.

Arranged nicely, indeed: a little cottage in Hampstead with his mother! If this were to be the price of success, Richard Hughes would surely want no part of it.

On the day that Louisa's final letter arrived, Hughes attended another joint debate with a woman's college. The motion, 'That this House regrets the obsolescence of parental control', was carried; though Hughes and others mounted a strong opposition from the floor. Miss [Vera] Brittain told stories of relentless parental tyranny; Miss [Enid] Starkie claimed that parents should hold themselves up as a warning rather than an example; and Mr Hughes reminded the House that Saturn had eaten his own children.[48]

CHAPTER 6

Real Education

The best education has always come from being in the close company of people with stimulating minds. Oxford University, understanding this, had placed the tutorial rather than the seminar or the lecture at the heart of its educational system. Since (sadly) Richard Hughes found his teachers uninspiring, and since at the same time (through his friendship with Robert Graves), he was coming into contact with a remarkable number of distinguished writers and artists, it was naturally enough to them that he turned for what he later described as his 'real education'.[1] 'What I failed to learn from my teachers', Hughes would recall,[2]

> I learnt from my friends; much from the unfaltering kindness of John Masefield, and much also from my friendship with Robert Graves ... That is quite apart from those interminable conversations into the small hours, about any subject under the sun, with whatever young man happens to be handy, which are (in my opinion) the most valuable part of University education.

At first, it was his friendship with Robert Graves that seemed most important. Diccon felt that there was 'more pith in some half-sentence he shot over his shoulder, darting from the scullery with frying-pan in one hand and poem in the other to still some urgent nursery howl, than in any interminable college lecture-room'.

Visits to the Graves household could also be fraught with anxiety. By February 1920, after the collapse of negotiations with a prospective purchaser for his Harlech cottage, Robert was 'in a hopeless financial state'; while Nancy, eight months pregnant, fell into a deep depression. Diccon, after visiting Dingle Cottage one Sunday lunchtime (and incidentally meeting the poet Robert Nichols, whose *Ardours and Endurances* had been so popular during the war), became worried about them both.[3] As a practical gesture, he commissioned Nancy to design a bookplate; though he mistakenly made out his cheque to 'Nancy Graves', which meant that Robert's feminist wife (who insisted on keeping her Nicholson maiden name both for herself and for her daughters) simply tore it up.[4]

By this time Diccon should have been working full-time for Mods, especially since he had learned at Christmas (which had been slightly marred by Louisa's complaints about a bad wrist) that the examinations were to be held not in the summer (as he had quite unaccountably expected), but at the end of February. However, a combination of circumstances meant that he was extremely ill-prepared. He had had little incentive to work for a First in Mods since hearing from his mother where that might lead; he had been spending a great deal of time on Boar's Hill (where the classical scholar Gilbert Murray had been added to the number of his friends); he had been working hard on *Public Schools Verse*, for which material had poured in from every side; he had been trying to earn money by sending some of his short stories to London magazines, so far without success, though one of them was being looked at extremely seriously; and he had also revived (with himself as president and his friend Jim Bennett as secretary) the Plantagenet Society, which had been dormant during the war, and existed to read papers on subjects of literary or general interest.[5]

The result of all this extra-curricular activity was that Diccon secured only a Fourth in Mods. This was an appalling result for a scholar, and he knew that it would probably lead to his being sent down from the university. As if that were not enough, Louisa wrote him one of her most manipulative letters. Reminding him that he already knew of her bad wrist, she revealed that 'the real cause . . . is tubercle', and that she had refrained from telling him so as not to alarm him before Mods. Luckily, she told him, it was unlikely to be fatal. But what were his plans now? 'I wish you had a motor-cycle, or plenty of money', she concluded rather hopelessly. 'Don't stay away longer than you can help but come home & set me up & take care of me.'[6]

In the face of this letter, Diccon's choices were limited; and as soon as the Lent term was over, he removed Louisa to his Welsh cottage, so that he could look after her there full-time.[7] He also wrote apologetically to the Provost, telling him: 'I feel that I certainly owe you a very humble apology for the disgrace I have brought on the College.'[8]

Fortunately for him, both Hugh Lyon (indirectly) and Gilbert Murray (directly) had intervened on his behalf. Hugh Lyon had persuaded his relation P.C. Lyon, the Bursar of Oriel, to put in a word for Hughes, and to remind the Provost of 'Shelley . . . the only poet that Oxford ever turned out, in both senses'.[9] And Gilbert Murray had written to the Provost:[10]

My dear Phelps,

I am extremely sorry for the collapse of your scholar Hughes in Mods. We read over his papers again and again to see if he could be raised, but both his scholarship and his prepared work were very bad indeed. Yet I am sure he is an intelligent fellow, with imagination and ideals, and if he could only concentrate and work seriously, I think he would justify his position as a scholar. It looks to me as if he had been led astray by a sort of cheap literary facility.

And he added: 'I write . . . because I know the man & like him.'

The result was that Diccon's letter of apology crossed with one from the Provost allowing him to stay on at Oriel. Diccon immediately wrote again, to say that he was[11]

very grateful to you for the lenient view you take of things.

I think you are quite just in saying that I enjoy life too much: I have certainly enjoyed the last year more than all the rest put together & I think it has rather overbalanced me. Consequently I have taken Writing far more seriously than at my age, I have any right to (apart from the fact that I have to scrape together every odd guinea that I can.) For the future I shall reduce it to the least possible minimum, & keep it as far from my mind as I possibly can: for if I don't its absorption is a cumulative one: &, as you say, it is far more important for me to learn concentration, & to acquire a certain mental *hardness* that I am conscious of lacking.

He added that he was 'putting every minute I can now into my reading: my only hindrance being my mother's illness'; and he hoped that the Provost would 'find that this catastrophe has knocked what I must candidly call the conceit out of me.' A few days later Diccon wrote a similar letter to his godfather, telling him that he hoped that the Greats reading would 'stick better', and that he was reducing his writing 'to an absolute minimum so as to concentrate better'.[12]

However, this change of heart was short-lived. One of the few distractions of the vacation was a meeting with the child prodigy Pamela Bianco, a painter whose exhibition at the Leicester Gallery in London had been one of the successes of 1919, when she was just thirteen years old. Her father was a great friend of Nancy's father, William Nicholson; and Louisa had already told Diccon (whose circle of friends she tried to make her own) that Pamela was said to be 'very nice & not at all spoilt'.[13]

Diccon's first reaction was not just to dislike Pamela but to forget that he was meant to be reducing his writing to a minimum, and to compose a very pointed short story, 'The Naked Head',[14] in which the rudeness of a child prodigy deserves and eventually secures a 'sound smacking'. And then at the end of April, the *Saturday Westminster Gazette* published a slightly revised version of a 'fable' which Hughes had sent them in February;[15] so when Diccon returned to Oxford for the start of the summer term, he was more in love than ever with the prospect of leading a literary life.

During the summer of 1920, that prospect drew closer.

Within the college, further meetings of the Plantagenet Society began with Robert Graves reading a paper on 'Missing Good Things' (illustrated from the writings of little-known modern poets);[16] and a new literary society was inaugurated, with Hugh Lyon as president, and Diccon Hughes as secretary. This was the 'Brome'. Named after the De Brome who was one of the founders of Oriel, it was to contain ten members who were to meet on a regular basis to hear distinguished speakers, to read their own compositions (at their first meeting Diccon read a descriptive essay and one of his short stories);[17] and to decide upon how best to live.

Louisa realised that his academic studies were once again taking second or third place, and towards the end of May she tried unsuccessfully to recall Diccon to his duty. 'From your somewhat impressionistic letter, dear', she wrote, 'I gather you have been letting yourself go for Eights Week.' She added that she was 'thankful that you should tell me of your foolishnesses[18] when they occur . . . so long as you tell me yourself it takes the sting out'. But she admitted that she was worried about his plans for the Long Vacation. Surely he would come home to get some reading done before setting out once again for North Wales?[19]

Diccon ignored his mother's fears. It was more important to him that on 5 June the *Evening Standard* published his article on 'What's Wrong with the Stage';[20] that later in the month the *Spectator*, although rejecting one of his poems, wrote a friendly letter asking him to continue to send them his work;[21] and that the *Saturday Westminster Gazette* sent him three volumes of poems to review.[22] It was more important to him that he had the friendship of men like Masefield, who on Monday 28 June, soon after the end of the summer term, invited him to a lunch of pasties and carrots and 'gooseberry tart with strawberries to crown the feast'.[23]

Just as they had finished eating, the Masefields' sixteen-year-old daughter Judith arrived. Diccon had become intrigued by her, and had privately named her after the title of Hardy's novel 'Jude the Obscure'. 'And yet', he asked himself,

> is she obscure? What lies behind those shifting delicacies of opinion? There is character in her chin and eyes, & humour in her lips & eyes, & thought & the joy of life in her broad forehead: but is there character & humour & thought in the soul

inside these things; or is the real girl the one that rides horses, & is afraid of them: that paints pictures, and paints them badly: & slips quietly into the background among the painted chairs.

Afterwards, the Masefields took him to Sir Arthur Evans's vast artificial lake on Boar's Hill,[24] where he enjoyed 'the most glorious bathe I have had; & afterwards we walked back, our heads steaming, & a red glint in the deep brown of Judith's curls . . .'[25]

And then the next morning Diccon (who had no intention of spending another vacation with his mother) caught a bus as far as the edge of the city, and set out to walk the remaining one hundred and ninety miles to Ysgol Fach.

A steady tramp through day after day of pouring rain led Hughes up through Oxfordshire and Worcestershire and into the haunted borderlands of south-west Shropshire. By Friday 2 July he had reached Ludlow; and on Saturday, walking through Craven Arms and then taking the road which branches off to Bishop's Castle, he presently[26]

> came to a big yew tree, clipped like a square and with a hole through: so I crept through the hole, and there was a cottage on the other side, but not so big as the yew tree: and there was a woman, though not so big as the cottage, with eight children and six hens & she boiled me an egg of the latter & then bathed a selection of the former in the egg water while I ate my tea in the parlour.

He spent Saturday night in this gamekeeper's cottage;[27] and then on Sunday night he crossed over a stretch of misty and deserted moorland into North Wales, an un-nerving experience which led him to write how:[28]

> The white mists flow like the hair of the drowned
>   Like wolves' in the howl of the wind
> On the moor at night: & the only sound
>   Is the plover's whistle, and the wind.

The only other remarkable incident was on Tuesday, when after being 'half-drowned' in a bog, he found himself sitting down to tea in a cottage 'with the most beautiful woman I have ever seen', who[29]

> simply took my breath away. She had finer, keen features: the fairest of complexions, & the reddest of delicate lips, & great dark brown eyes & black hair. I was desolated to find she was newly married: but somewhat relieved on finding that her name was Mrs Hughes & that she was therefore, as it were one of the family.

Finally on Wednesday evening, after walking over the hills from Dolgellau, he reached Ysgol Fach; and hardly had he arrived when William Nicholson 'turned up & asked me to supper at Maes-y-Neuadd. I was sopping wet, so he rigged me out in a white canvas shirt, white duck trousers – but I will spare you the rest', he wrote to his mother. 'Anyhow it was a very good supper & Pamela [Bianco] was there, spending a few days, as W.N. is painting her.'[30]

This was Diccon's second meeting with Pamela; and a few months appeared to him to have made a great difference. Pamela (he told Louisa) had 'grown & fits quite well' into the Welsh landscape;[31] and before long he was writing of her family that he had 'seldom met people I liked so much, or folk so informal & sensible in their ways. Mrs B. especially is wonderfully nice'.[32]

Pamela's father, Ferdinand Bianco, 'a funny little butterfly of a man',[33] amused Diccon by his odd turn of speech. Once, after sheltering overnight with Diccon in a cowshed, he cried out: 'Oh! Oh! . . . It's the thought of putting on these wet things makes my soul turn a somersault in its case!' Another day he brought Pamela over to Ysgol Fach for coffee and skipjacks;[34] and Diccon (who had already told Pamela about his adventures on the road from Oxford) presented her with 'Gipsy-Night',[35] which would shortly be published by the *Spectator*,[36] and which runs:

When the feet of the rain tread a dance on the roofs,
And the wind slides through the rocks and the trees,
And Dobbin has stabled his hoofs
In the warm bracken-litter, noisy about his knees;
And when there is no moon, and the sodden clouds slip over;
Whenever there is no moon, and the rain drips cold,
And folk with a shilling of money are bedded in houses,
And pools of water glitter on Farmer's mould;
   Then pity Sally's girls, with the rain in their blouses;
   Martha and Johnnie, who have no money:
   The small naked puppies who whimper against the bitches,
   The small sopping children who creep to the ditches.

But when the moon is run like a red fox
Cover to cover behind the skies;
And the breezes crack in the trees on the rocks,
Or stoop to flutter about the eyes
Of one who dreams in the scent of pines
At ease:
   Then would you not go foot it with Sarah's girls
   In and out the trees?
   Or listen across the fire

To old Tinker-Johnnie, and Martha his Rawnee,
In jagged Wales, or in orchard Worcestershire?

Diccon liked to cultivate aristocrats as well as writers and artists; and in July his wealthy Oxford friend Louis Wharton came to stay with him at Ysgol Fach, where he rapidly succumbed to a bout of malaria.[37] This meant that he was unable to join in the revels at the end of the month, when Diccon went sailing with the Biancos off Barmouth, returned with them to Harlech for supper, and then enjoyed 'a moonlight bathe (no moon)', a bonfire on the beach, and a game of sardines among the sand-dunes.[38]

Robert and Nancy were also in Harlech, staying this time at Erinfa, where Robert was licking his wounds after the commercial failure of his *Country Sentiment* collection; and where Nancy was recovering from the birth of her son John David, whose persistent crying (ignored by Nancy as a matter of up-to-date principle) made life exhausting for everyone within ear-shot.[39]

Diccon was enjoying himself too much to write home very often; and he received one furious postcard from Louisa, who wrote: 'I suppose you are too happy & busy to think of this poor wretch ... it may be you intend to repudiate me altogether so I send no more letters.'[40] However, she was pacified for a few weeks, first by the appearance in the *Saturday Westminster Gazette* of Diccon's poetry reviews; and then by the news that he had won an exhibition from the Skinner's Company valued at £50 per annum.[41]

Later in the summer, however, Louisa wrote again: this time dwelling on her domestic difficulties, and begging Diccon to come home; but he replied that although he was sorry for her, he would not be much of a companion, as he had so much work to do. In any case, he declared, it was important for his career that he should stay on to cultivate the Nicholsons and their friends. On one occasion (as he told his mother) he even[42]

> ran into the original Augustus John one day, roaming about the terrace at Maesyneuadd ... A great lion-headed creature with masses of hair & beard & most wicked eyes. I don't think I have ever seen more concentrated villainy in a face. I went straight back & counted the spoons.

Gradually the summer holiday drew to a close; and on 27 August, Hughes enjoyed a farewell expedition with the Biancos. He and Nancy's brother Kit Nicholson, together with Pamela Bianco, Pamela's brother Cecco and her mother Margery, set out one evening to walk to Cwm Mawr, a remote farm in the hills near Cwm Bychan. Reaching it at ten-thirty by the light of a full moon, they built an open fire, and prepared a supper of melons, sardines, mutton cutlets, fried potatoes, baked potatoes, onions, carrots, and bread and cheese. Some time after midnight, they moved into a barn, where they slept in the hay: where by morning, they had all rolled together and where Diccon (as he reported to Louisa), found that he had 'Pamela in the small of my back, breathing stertorously under my coat pocket, M[rs] B[ianco] on my feet, [and] Kit & Cecco on my head'.[43]

By the time Richard Hughes returned to Oxford for the start of the Michaelmas term of 1920, this twenty-year-old undergraduate had acquired a real position in the literary world. Not only had he become an occasional contributor to the *Spectator*; but by sending him more volumes of poems (by Edward Thomas and W.H. Davies and others) the *Saturday Westminster Gazette* had confirmed him in the post of their new poetry critic.[44]

Not all his friends were impressed by this. Louis Wharton, for example, writing from his parents' country estate in Sussex, had already told Diccon that:[45]

> Many people (by the mercy of God, no friends of mine) admire the *S.W.G.* Some, without great dishonour, write for it for gain. For the former a decent man can have nothing but contempt; for the latter, a sort of anger against the necessity that drives a man to such deeds.

'But you have heard all this before', Wharton concluded, 'And I ought to congratulate you on your job . . .'

Literary work occupied more and more of Diccon's time: six issues of the *Saturday Westminster Gazette* that term carried his poetry reviews; he was editing a second volume of *Public Schools Verse* (the first appeared successfully in November 1920); and he was also busily writing short stories and poems, including his ferocious 'The Ballad of Benjamin Crocker' (which John Graves published in *The Carthusian* that autumn.)[46] The ballad begins in a lively manner:

> Benjamin Crocker in sixteen-three,
> (Here's to the Devil in flaming rum!)
> Made his fifth voyage to West Carribee,
> (Drink to the Devil, man, and don't look glum!)
> Fierce was his scowl, and his skin tanned red,
> And a knotted silk kerchief covered his head
> That was scarred with ivory, steel, and lead:
> He wore three knives and a cutlass too
> To slit the gullets of men of thew:
> Or his thumbs could strangle a whole ship's crew;
> (Here's to the Devil and his jolly chum!)

But then it becomes horrific. Benjamin Crocker kills the witch-like 'Old Gal-gar-ul'; whose familiar, 'a black beast hobbling, one leg gone', follows him back to his ship and wreaks a bloody revenge.

Diccon Hughes also became a leading light of a group calling themselves the 'New Elizabethans'. One of their members was the forty-three-year-old writer A.E. Coppard (at that time still unpublished), who already had a following among the undergraduates. Coppard later recalled that their aim was to read Elizabethan plays together, and that they met at the 'Paviours Arms', 'located in that unheavenly slice of Oxford called Paradise'.[47] Diccon himself told Louisa about this 'low pub', where they met secretly every Saturday night (undergraduates were not allowed in pubs) to drink beer and to read plays 'amid the sound of concertina, mouth organ, barrel organ, banjo, & divers kinds of music from the dancers in the next room. There are two flaring gas-jets; & occasionally there is an irruption from the next room, some Syrinx fleeing from a Pan, or Daphne from an Apollo'.[48]

In the meantime, the Brome was going from strength to strength; its members were treated to 'The Ballad of Benjamin Crocker' on 27 October;[49] and a month later one of them wrote this sketch of a meeting in Oriel, with empty coffee cups and empty coffee pots on the table,[50]

> milk jugs and sugar basins. There is good sherry on that table, and a corkscrew. There are wine glasses in the room, and each glass has an owner . . . Louis [Wharton] is sitting on a cushion by the fire: Diccon is sprawling on a large armchair. Tiny is sitting bolt upright in a chair behind Diccon; James Burch is reposing on a sofa: Hugh [Lyon] is lying on the floor.

The room is warm and cheerful; the air is thick with smoke; and Louis is reciting 'his sixteenth and last ballade'. A little later, and it is time for the sherry to be handed round. By this time, Diccon Hughes, who is chain-smoking panatellas,

> has finally attained a satisfactory pose, and he ignores the proffered sherry. His feet are sticking out straight in front of him: his shoulders are arched; his brows are beetled and his eyes half closed. His jaw is thrust forwards and upwards. He has a vague idea that he resembles Lord Tennyson.

Through the Brome there also came a number of important meetings with distinguished guests who included John Masefield, with his 'lovely reading voice',[51] W.B. Yeats, and T.E. Lawrence.

Lawrence (to whom Hughes had written mentioning the name of their mutual friend Robert Graves) generously invited the Brome to come to his rooms in All Souls. There, for a magical evening, he recounted the amazing history of his adventures in Arabia during the Great War. John Buchan, when Governor-General of Canada, would recall that although he was 'not a very tractable person or much of a hero-worshipper', he 'would have followed Lawrence over the edge of the world';[52] and Diccon Hughes felt something similar in the presence of this remarkable man, who had a gift for showing people the best of which they were capable.

Here too was a man who had managed to combine the intellectual, the adventurous and the artistic. Having taken 'a most brilliant First Class'[53] at Jesus, and embarked upon a career as an archaeologist, Lawrence had played a leading role in a theatre of war far removed from the senseless slaughter of the Western Front; and then retired to Oxford in order to transmute his experiences into literature.

Lawrence became an important influence upon Hughes, who had soon acquired a number of typically Lawrentian habits and attitudes. These included a love of mystery; a determination to see the best in men and women of every class; a delight in poking fun at authority; a desire for personal freedom; a strong belief in the central importance of the written word; and a still more powerful conviction that great writing could only be the result of great experience.

Meetings of the Plantagenet Society were dominated for some months by magic and the supernatural (a speaker in June 1920 was said to have 'a remarkable, almost sinister acquaintance with the subject');[54] and at this time Hughes had a positive relish for horror, which was expressed in his prose as well as in his poetry. John Masefield, who read through several weird short stories, commented that:[55]

> Their certainty & condensation of form are most remarkable in so young a writer. All the tales have this sureness of construction, but the best of them have more than this, of strangeness of invention & power, that can leave no doubt of your future rank as a writer.

And he hoped that Hughes would 'go ahead & write lots of tales in this uncanny mood'. Charles Johnson, by contrast, was slightly alarmed by the tenor of his godson's work. He felt that Diccon was showing some symptoms of a dangerously overheated imagination; and he wrote criticising some of his recent work, and warning him about the difficulties of making his living as a writer.[56]

Eight months earlier, in March 1920, Diccon had told his god-father that in his view Truth was like an island: which meant that[57]

> whatever direction you walk *in a straight line* you are bound to fall off sooner or later. Also that positive & negative, right

& wrong, are only differences of direction (like East & West) not differences in nature, so that whichever you pursue straight you will still fall off. Hence circular thought rather than logically straight pursuit of conclusions.

And his mind had been in a whirl of activity ever since. Thinking of himself as an artist, he had come to the general conclusion that the creation of beauty was the most important function of an artist's life; and, far more important, he had lost his religious faith.

For one of the fundamental beliefs which Hughes and his intellectual friends had acquired was that Freud's theories had made Christianity and Christian morals irrelevant. Their generation, they believed,[58]

> really was a new creation, a new kind of human being, *because of Freud*! For theirs was the first generation in the whole cave-to-cathedral history of the human race completely to disbelieve in sin ... the whole 'God' idea had now subsided below the level of belief or disbelief. 'God' and 'Sin' had ceased to be problems because Freudian analysis had explained how such notions arise historically.

In other words, they were 'merely a primitive psychological blemish which, once explained, mankind can outgrow'.

When on 21 November 1920 Charles Johnson's warning letter arrived, Diccon was actually having breakfast with T.E. Lawrence and J.C. Squire, the distinguished author and literary editor of the *New Statesman*.[59] In the circumstances, Diccon drafted a reply which can have given his godfather little comfort: he said that he had 'no earthly intention of working the "spooky" vein out. I very seldom write two things alike running ... It is at any rate no more than a temporary mood. Of course', he added,[60]

> I know too about writing being a bad crutch; but it bites both ways: to do it at all well, which is the most important thing, will need all my energies. Anyhow, my head's in too much of a ferment for it to dry up just yet, I think ... As for leaving off a bit, I can't: if I try, an especially violent outburst follows. I am afraid it has bitten too deep, now: I must live that way or not at all. God save me from marrying.

This was an attitude which could only be sustained at all easily by continuing success. However Diccon's 'Martha', a story about life in the East End of London over which he had 'sweated blood', was judged by Squire to be a complete failure.

Diccon, not believing the verdict, immediately sent it on to the *Cornhill*;[61] and during the final days of the Michaelmas term he continued to concentrate upon his literary life, having numerous meetings with the Masefields, and taking tea with John St Loe Strachey, editor and proprietor of the *Spectator* (whose son John was also up at Oxford).

When term was over, the pace grew still faster. Hughes spent the best part of a week with the Biancos in London, where he met both Walter de la Mare and the actor-manager Nigel Playfair; and when the *Cornhill* also returned *Martha*, complaining that 'The shadow of a human character-struggle passing across the grimly-sordid background . . . flitted across the stage to its hapless extinction [with] . . . no alleviating [catharsis] to qualify the depressing savour with a full tragic note';[62] he telephoned the Hogarth Press, and found himself talking to Virginia Woolf.

'I couldn't help asking him to dinner', she explained to her sister Vanessa Bell;[63] and the result was that before long Diccon found himself sitting down to dine with Virginia and her husband Leonard. 'I was shy', he recalled, 'and found them both very frightening.' And then a few days later he received[64]

> a chilly letter from Leonard not only turning *Martha* down but seeming to imply – to my perhaps over-sensitive mind – that if I sued them I had no leg to stand on as they had given no undertaking to publish it.

Diccon found this distinctly upsetting; and his immediate reaction was to believe that his problems stemmed from the fact that he was doing too much academic work.

On returning to Oxford for the start of the Lent term 1921, Hughes added the name of Edmund Blunden to the list of his new literary friends;[65] and then in mid January he spent ten days living on Boar's Hill with the Masefields, who had enrolled him as Theseus for their production of Gilbert Murray's *Hippolytus*. The play was a success, it had been enjoyable living so close to Robert and Nancy for a few days, and Diccon himself had done particularly well;[66] but suddenly the strain of balancing his academic work with his literary life had become too great.

A week later, Diccon wrote to his godfather announcing that his affairs had been going through a series of crises, and that he had decided to go down from Oxford at the end of the term. 'Greats', he explained,[67]

> have been becoming more and more distasteful to me, till at last it has become almost an obsession: a mental twinge whenever my thoughts reverted to it. So I asked Masefield's advice, & he agreed that it would be best to go down: that the time had come when I could safely go into the fight. He prophesied me five lean years: but not so lean that I might not live through it: for as he pointed

out, it is unusual for a person to have got so well on the way to a reputation at twenty. Nor does he think there is any fear of writing myself out.

So yesterday I went and told the Provost. It took him by surprise: and he very kindly indeed offered to let me read English Literature, that for my own purposes rather than with regard to Schools.

Hughes had 'jumped at' this offer; but David Ross, his tutor, was made 'of sterner stuff', and insisted that if his pupil were to read English Literature, he should do so with the aim of winning high honours, and with the intention of sacrificing everything else to that end. But that, wrote Diccon, was impossible:

The truth is, that a writer's working day is 24 hours, & he must face it. He is always either taking in, ruminating, or giving out. It has bitten too deep for me to be able to put it aside for 18 months . . . You cannot believe the blessed feeling of relief it is to me now that I have burned my boats.

'I have stuck to Greats', he concluded, 'until I found that two hours work at it was enough to knock me out.'

Fortunately, on the afternoon of the day when Hughes posted this letter, he had tea with his friends Golding and Louis Wharton[68] who convinced him (as he wrote to Charles Johnson the following morning) that he had written 'in greater haste than I should'. The truth was that he had been 'struggling on the edge of some sort of breakdown: I am not sure that I am clear of it yet: but at any rate I feel now it would be the saner course to give the English school at least a trial'. After all, the option of going down remained open; and this action did no more than postpone the way of life upon which he had resolved.[69]

To his mother, Diccon wrote that he would 'give the English school a trial, as soon as I am well enough'; and he added the news that the American journal *Poetry* were giving him thirty shillings for his poem 'Dirge'; and that the *Athenaeum* were paying him 'only . . . £1' for 'The Horse-trough', in which he described how the youngest and most innocent-looking in a group of children:[70]

> . . . sits the sunny steps so still
> For hours, trying hard to kill
> One fly at least of those that buzz
> So cannily . . .
>   And then she does.

The immediate crisis was over; but Richard Hughes was determined that in future no demands from any person or any institution or any code of morality should be allowed to threaten his independence both as a human being and as a writer. From now on he would be chiefly governed by the need to preserve his integrity, come what may; and by the need to experience whatever it was necessary for him to experience in the service of his art. They were needs which would inevitably conflict.

CHAPTER 7

A Steerage Passenger[1]

Having hovered on the edge of a breakdown before accepting the change from Classics to English, Hughes allowed himself time to recuperate before plunging into his English studies. Meanwhile, in February 1921, he acquired a motor bike: a second-hand Douglas with choked valves and no lights, bought at auction on £12 of borrowed money.[2] Once it had been put in order, it was much easier for him to visit friends like Robert Graves (who was running into serious difficulties with a recurrence of shell-shock, and the problems of managing the shop which Nancy had opened on Boar's Hill); or A. E. Coppard, who entertained him 'in winter, at any rate, with a basket full of walnuts'.[3]

Both Hughes and Coppard continued to attend the secret meetings of the New Elizabethans (occasionally joined by W.B. Yeats); and eventually there came an evening when (as Coppard relates):[4]

> without a waft of warning, the Proctor entered . . . He was fully gowned, mortar-board on head, and behind him in the doorway stood two substantial bullies. About a dozen of us were sitting in a circle, each with a book of words in his hand. The Proctor began with the first man on his right. Lifting his mortar-board hat, he said: 'Good evening sir. Are you a member of this University?'

Once their names had been taken, Hughes 'dashed off to report this disaster to W.B. Yeats', who obligingly wrote him a letter to be presented to the university court. In it, he

> assured the Proctors of his knowledge of, and his personal association with, our genuine literary enterprise, and so on, with the result that the lads were let off with fines of half-a-crown each, which were imposed only because the inviolable rule about pubs had been violated and could not be forgiven.

Indeed, while the court was still in session, the New Elizabethans were commended, and the hope was expressed that their meetings would continue – but at some other venue.[5]

In the summer term of 1921, Diccon had a far more serious

clash with authority. This stemmed from his submission to the undergraduate magazine *Isis* of 'The Heathen's Song', a poem in which he asked for pagan gods and devils to worship: gods who would encourage him to 'dance the moon down, up the sun/ In wine fuse night and day'; devils 'with hell-fire in their veins' who would allow him to 'stretch Beauty on a stone/ Naked and young and dead':[6]

> For gods and devils give me these
>   And each shall have his due:
> But shall I tumble on my knees
>   At name of bastard Jew?
>
> Or bow, while wrinkled maids devour
>   Like kine with harmless cud
> A God new-made of wheaten flour
>   With sweetened wine for blood?

Hughes ended his poem (which was published under a pseudonym) by telling the 'Shapeless Master of the fold':

> I'd sooner damn my soul, would I,
>   Than sell it for Thy Grace!

Not surprisingly, he was summoned before the Vice-Chancellor, and lectured on the subject of blasphemy. All that saved him from being sent down, was his willingness to make a public apology. This appeared in the next number of *Isis*, and was followed by an attack upon him in the undergraduate newspaper *Cherwell*, which unkindly described 'The Heathen's Song' not only as offensive and legally indefensible, but also as 'artistically without merit or originality'.[7]

Perhaps Diccon would not much have minded being sent down, apart from the upset that it would have caused Louisa. For although he was now doing a certain amount of work for his English degree, he was once again concentrating chiefly upon his literary career. He had been encouraged in this both by J.C. Squire of the *London Mercury*, who had told him: 'We want to print you & if you give us a good enough chance we shall';[8] and by Leonard Woolf, who had now decided that he would 'like to print a small book' containing two of Hughes's short stories. Woolf had added that he would not give a definite date for publication, as it seemed to him that Diccon was 'in the stage of rapid development, and . . . [might] in the meanwhile produce something which you would much prefer to have produced in the more permanent form of a book than these two stories'.[9]

In the Easter vacation of 1921, Diccon had written to tell his godfather that he was in pursuit of a good plain prose style; and that his intention was to work[10]

> from the Subjective to the objective — begin by discovering what is true to oneself in things, & then sift out the universal truth or reality from it. The successful *story* is in a way the highest form of literature: & the hardest: & *must* be simply treated.

He had also found a theme for a more sustained piece of prose writing than any he had yet attempted.

In mid February, when Pamela Bianco and her family had sailed for Philadelphia,[11] it had been suggested that Diccon should join them in America for part of his summer vacation. Since then, he had discovered that he could make the journey very cheaply if he was prepared to travel as a steerage passenger on an emigrant ship: an experience which might also provide him with the material for an interesting set of articles.

Sailing from Tilbury at ten-thirty in the morning of Monday 4 July 1921, Diccon's first impression was that 'This is Babel. Except for German and a little French patois, I do not know what languages I am hearing'. Immediately outside his steerage-class cabin (a cubicle seven feet each way, in which three other men were also to sleep) there was a notice announcing that the fine for seduction was one hundred dollars; the dark corridors were full of 'a sort of mush of Slovak children: you feel their little hands warding you off as you go by'; and in the cabin itself he could feel rather than hear 'a noise and throbbing under me' from the ship's engines, 'as if I was living in a water-mill'. Their first port of call was Cherbourg on the French coast, where they took on more passengers; and then they began their long, slow journey across the Atlantic.

On the second day out of Cherbourg, Hughes was writing his journal from a perch 'in an iron girder up in the bows', and watching 'amorous Letts' some of whom were 'drinking bass and chanting dolefully' while others 'danc[ed] extravagantly on the deck'. 'How I am enjoying it', he commented, but added that if he stopped to think, he became 'struck with a quite unnecessary terror'.

Later, he fell into conversation with Harold, a snobbish young man who wore a particularly loud purple check tweed cap, and who was

> deploring that he had not gone second. 'To be taken out of your class like this', he confided, 'is fuckin' orrful.' He explained that he had climbed through the barrier & sat for half an hour in the 2nd class lounge 'without anyone guessing I didn't belong there'. This

was such a salve to his dignity that he was able to endure another day in our company.

After talking to another fellow passenger, Diccon began to feel a little more sympathetic towards Harold. Apparently they were sailing aboard 'an old boat, only fit, some say, for cargo'; and he was told that

> on a recent trip they took 1200 3rd class passengers, & . . . typhus was the result. We shall be lucky if we don't get an attack this trip: for you can't pack even 400 of the undesirables of the filthiest races of Europe in an old tin for nothing . . . If the decks stink with them, and a fair breeze blowing, what will it be like if we are shut below?

Diccon then found that the bath he had hoped to use was 'lined with a black grease – thick as tar, which I could not wash off my fingers, so I gave it up'; and he was still more appalled by almost a whole day spent in being

> publicly bathed and searched for lice . . . Our heads were supposed to be scrubbed with soft soap and paraffin. Then the stewards who did it told us frightful tales of the horrors of Ellis Island: & how we should be lucky if we got through in a week: & how we should have 3 paraffin baths a day.

On hearing this, Hughes temporarily lost his nerve, and went to ask the purser whether he could be transferred to the second class when they put in at Halifax.

When he was told that a transfer was impossible, Hughes accepted the situation with a good grace, and settled down to learn and to record. As an Englishman, he found himself wondering especially 'what all these dagos feel about the British', and at first he believed that 'at the bottom they hate us: or at any rate fear us'.

Within a few days he had changed his mind, returned to the offending passage, scored through it half-a-dozen times, written 'tommy-rot' in the margin, and added: 'It seems to me that I have overestimated the race feeling. It seems to be almost entirely on the side of the British. The more intelligent dagos . . .' And then he paused, crossed out 'dagos', replaced it with 'square-heads', and continued: 'The more intelligent square-heads deplore it: while the absolute peasants find the whole life on the boat one of such luxury that occasional [insults] are only a harmless, necessary fly in whole pots of Balm of Gilead.'

Everything on board ship was done 'to bells: at 6.30 a bell to wake us: at 7, breakfast: at 12, dinner: at 5, tea: a separate bell for each batch'; and Hughes soon learned not to offend against etiquette,

> by going into dinner without my cap. It should not be removed

till the soup arrives, & then put on again to show the steward when you have finished. The food is unpleasant, but plentiful. The cigarette, too, should be kept behind the ear between meals: but should be more carefully extinguished than mine was.

In the 'ultra-respectable' mornings, people kept themselves to themselves; but in the evenings there was much fraternising.

One evening very early in the voyage, Diccon made his way forward, and found himself playing kiss-in-the-ring with the Czechoslovaks: after which

a young German brought his mandolin on deck, & sat up against a capstan with it, while the young folk danced, and the old ones started hand clapping the time. They did waltzes & one-steps & several curious dances . . . There were two yellow-haired Hungarian flappers, with red cotton handkerchiefs on their heads, & their brother, & Finns, & Danes, & Letts & Dutch:

not to mention a Jugoslav/Canadian girl called Rosa who talked fluent German and English and so acted 'as interpreter and general master of ceremonies'; and they continued with their songs and dances 'till the stewards drove us out'.

The following evening Diccon went forward again. Finding that Rosa was already playing forfeits with some fellow Jugoslavs, he 'tried to pick up a little Hungarian', from a good-looking girl of seventeen with a 'mobile, sensitive face', 'the wickedest innocent eyes', and a 'beautiful neck and shoulders'. Communication was difficult; but after a while Rosa and her friends came over. Then there were 'many smiles' and an 'exchange of names' (the pretty Hungarian girl turned out to be called Bozska); and Hughes talked to Rosa until nine o'clock, the fixed hour when all the women had to go below.

However, Diccon had soon learned that both the nine o'clock rule and the 'no seduction' notice were little more than a farce. A number of the girls were bound for brothels in South America: 'Some of them', Hughes was told,

have been at the 'Sign of the Red Lamp' before: notably one Emma (& Luba probably); others don't know what they are going to: in fact, there is a certain amount of white slave trafficking going on. The girls are told they will be given a job in New York, and so lured over.

And prostitution was already thriving aboard ship, where at night the third-class saloon was regularly used by the crew as 'a sort of makeshift brothel, as there is a way up to it from the [emigrants'] quarters'.

Intrigued by this news, Diccon decided to inspect the third-class saloon for himself (though not at night); and one afternoon he made his way down to what was no more than 'the spare space round the engine-room: hot as hell, nearly dark, and with only dirty benches to sit on', where he found both Rosa and Bozska.

While Bozska flirted with a good-looking Austrian called Hans, Hughes

> talked to Rosa, & through her to Hans' two sisters. When he grew too pressing Bozska ran over to me, to make him jealous; & there was I in a quandary: for everything I would say to her I had to say to Rosa, who translated it into German to Wilma, who translated it into Hungarian to Bozska – & so back again. Presently B[ozska] ran off with H[ans] in pursuit, & I went and ate a great and glorious tea.

To make communication with his new friends easier, Hughes spent most of Saturday 9 July

> in study – that is to say, an hour's Danish, and the rest, German & Hungarian, sitting down in the Square before dinner with Rosa and Wilma & Bozska . . . In German I can now make myself fairly comprehensible: Hungarian is rather a tongue-twister, so that I make slow progress, though Bozska has a Hungarian-English phrase-book, as well as highly expressive eyes.

And in the evening, after talking 'broken German' to Luba, 'a little Polish Jewess Luba', he gave 'highly entertaining English lessons to Bozska, over cocoa and ship's biscuits, in the dining room'.

Diccon had just begun to feel very fond of Bozska (and had learned 'enough Hungarian to make [her] blush') when on Sunday morning he found her weeping bitterly over Janos, a handsome young Yugoslav who had apparently broken her heart. He did his best to comfort her, but was secretly irritated to realise that she had simply been 'playing with the others – and me', and commented in his journal that she was 'far too silly and pretty to be travelling alone from Budapest to Pittsburgh, & the Lord knows how she will keep herself out of trouble in Pittsburgh either'.

However, Bozska gave Diccon a keepsake to thank him for his kindness, and on the morning of Tuesday 12 July he was able to do her one more favour. A group of passengers from the upper decks was being taken round 'steerage' on a tour of inspection, 'specially conducted', as Hughes explains, 'with their handkerchiefs to their noses (for which I can't blame them, as the only thing which prevents you smelling your neighbours is that it is drowned in the general stink of garlic)'.

But Hughes's sympathy for the visitors was rapidly stifled by their nauseating self-importance and condescension. 'Lord', he wrote in his journal that evening, 'how we did hate them. I doubt if I ever hated anyone so: there wasn't a she-bitch among them with as much delicacy of voice or expression as the lousiest of us; they were ugly to a fault, vulgar, & what is worse bored.' And then came his chance for action.

> One fat chap with a patent cigar stayed behind a moment to roll lascivious eyes at Bozska. So [an English friend] and I jabbered [an invented tongue] of our own at each other and presently pulled out knives and pretended to fight which soon sent him flying.

Afterwards Bozska vanished from sight: 'which is as well,' Hughes commented, 'for she's a silly little goose at best'. But his hatred of the upper-deckers lasted and, having observed one of their parties from a vantage-point, he wrote: 'believe me, there wasn't a woman I would have touched with the end of a billiard-cue, much less dance with as I danced with Gina or Luba'.

On Thursday morning 14 July they were moored in Halifax harbour, 'a big dingy expanse of water with natural breakwaters'; where there were 'fond farewells' to Rosa and other friends; and then Diccon and his remaining companions sailed away southward in a dense fog. On Friday, the weather changed to 'sun, a high wind, & a high sea. Both continued to rise, till some of the waves were breaking right up onto the forward deck'. After lunch, they passed through a little fishing fleet, 'bobbing in the water like corks, with hardly a rag of sail to the wind'; and their own ship began pitching so badly that Hughes

> fell to wondering what sort of chance a man overboard would get on a day like this. Some of the waves are 30 feet from crest to trough; and the curlers when the bows dip are six feet deep of green roaring foam with the spring of a tiger.

But by the evening of Saturday 16 July they had reached the safety of New York where they anchored at first in the quarantine ground.

Doctors came aboard, and Hughes and his fellows were all stripped to the waist on the after-deck, examined, formed in line, marched past and re-examined. Then, when the ship had been cleared, they steamed to the docks, past the Statue of Liberty, a terrible mockery as it seemed to Diccon, for he and any steerage passengers who were not yet American citizens remained prisoners on board ship while they waited their turn for the immigration authorities on Ellis Island.

By Sunday evening, the passengers were 'all in the most doleful state, relieved only by repeated and promiscuous copulation'. There were few men or women aboard, wrote Diccon, 'whose chastity has been able to stand the test of this intolerable boredom: the few ex-harlots set the ball rolling, and the others joined in'. It was also

> hot as Hell ... not a breath of air ... I doubt if I have ever been quite so hot in my life. From 9 a.m. to 5 p.m. you can't bear yourself, & in the dining room you don't get much chance of breathing. The afternoon I spent writing, & so passed it fairly quickly, tho' I was sweating onto the page.

The ship's crew had lost interest in them: 'every day we are on board is dead loss to the company, & they let you know it.' Even the evening cocoa was cut out, so that there was nothing to eat or drink from five in the evening until breakfast fourteen hours later.

On Monday, after 'a night like a bread oven', came 'another broiling day ... only things are a shade worse today', recorded Hughes,

> as they are coaling the vessel on one side, unloading it on the other; we are crowded up in a small part of the deck, with the coal dust and steam drifting over us, the mosquitoes biting like mad: not a breath of air, nor room to breathe it ... If I was to call it Hell I would be understating it ... I am just comatose.

Tuesday came; and at last they were on their way to Ellis Island, where the experience was as bad as Hughes had been warned, with the immigrants being treated as though they were subhuman.

After going through customs, they were 'loaded into some sort of a two-storey cattle boat' whose doors were then locked. Later (when they had been abandoned for some time without food, water or information), a tug began towing them over to Ellis Island; and as they set out, the tug man cheerfully shouted to one of his comrades: 'We got a good load of shit this time, friend!' On arrival, they were 'stripped & medically examined again'. Hughes wrote angrily:

> They didn't bother to speak to you, if they want you to go anywhere, they knock you there.
>
> So we went, and were presently shouted and banged into a large central hall, where we sweated malodorously till noon. At noon we were given coffee and a ham sandwich ... & at one o'clock I got examined. I was then labelled, & chucked about here and there: finally put back on the cattle-boat, and ferried to the docks again by two, and locked in a waiting-room.

Finally, at three o'clock, rescue came, in the form of 'a large, fat, silent man' who released Hughes, took him to a railway station, and put him on board a train.

Hughes was 'amazed simply by looking through the windows', and records that he

> must have gaped like a zany: the slap-dash houses, the odd flowers: the curious promiscuous way the train had of running through any and everything, without fences or gates: & most of all, the glass insulation of the telegraph wires.

But at last he reached Port Pleasant; and, 'after a sandy walk, the house'; and the Biancos 'so used to my blowing [in] unexpectedly as not to be in the least surprised'.

His voyage as a steerage passenger on an emigrant ship was safely over. Hughes had more than enough material for a substantial contribution to the *Saturday Westminster Gazette* when he returned to England (rather more comfortably than he had left it) three weeks later. He had also learned to see his own race and class from the outside: a valuable experience for a writer, and one which made him a very different human being from the undergraduate who had walked into the London's Chinatown to observe the amusing habits of 'a seething mass of Asiatics'.

CHAPTER 8

The Sisters' Tragedy

Mid August 1921 found Diccon Hughes back in North Wales, living in his beloved Ysgol Fach. The Harlech summer was as sociable as usual; and this year Diccon made several new friends: principally the Satows, whom he had previously met only briefly through the Graveses.

Mrs Satow was a beautiful, amorous and yet curiously innocent widow who often gave dances in Dolfring, the large house which she rented in the foothills of Snowdon. She had four attractive young daughters, whom she brought up in an utterly unconventional manner. Diccon soon felt very much at home with them all; and especially with Gwenol, the third daughter, who was then thirteen or fourteen, and who later recalled that although he worked 'tirelessly', he was 'always ready to give time to us'; that Diccon, in those days,[1]

> was a young companion with whom one laughed and played, delighting in his quick inventiveness, his unfailing sense of fun. If you planned an excursion to the top of Snowdon or a picnic to the sea, you never dreamed of going without [Diccon]. Some-one had to jump on to the grey horse and canter over the Roman road, to dig him out of his little cottage where he sat painting dragons on the walls or writing a new book.

He would entertain them with ghost-stories, go swimming with them, or (when they were half-asleep on some mountain-top) give them his famous recitation of Vachel Lindsay's *Congo*[2] in which, 'looking ominously like an old witch-doctor himself', he would begin (as Gwenol remembered) 'in a dark velvet voice:[3]

> 'Fat black bucks in a wine-barrel room,
> Barrel-house kings with feet unstable,
> Sagged and reeled and pounded on the table,
> Pounded on the table,
> Beat an empty barrel with the handle of a broom
> Hard as they were able, boom, boom, boom,
> With a silk umbrella and the handle of a broom,
> Boomlay, boomlay, boomlay, BOOM!'

His voice softened to sudden tenderness;

> '*Then* I had religion, *then* I had a vision,
> I could not turn from their revels in derision.
> Then I saw the Congo creeping through the black
> Cutting through the forest with a golden track – '

Swaying in unison to the rhythm of his voice, [we] joined together in the chorus:

> 'Boomlay, boomlay, boomlay, boom,
> Boomlay, boomlay, boomlay, BOOM!'

Until the sound of [our] own voices, rising and falling across the lake, hypnotized [us], at long last into sleep.

Diccon had a real gift for friendship with pre-adolescent girls – possibly he sought them out quite subconsciously not only as a kind of replacement for his dead sister, but also to expiate some of the guilt he had always felt about surviving her. And the summer progressed very happily until there was a threat to Diccon's position in the neighbourhood.

Almost two years earlier, in the autumn of 1919, Diccon's landlady 'Edie' Stuart-Wortley had married William Nicholson.[4] The two of them had no further use for Maes-y-Neuadd; and they had allowed Edie's lease on the estate to expire in the summer of 1920. When Colonel Kirkby, the owner, had arrived to repossess his property, he had not been best pleased to find an undergraduate in possession of one of his cottages, but had told Diccon that he could stay on at Ysgol Fach for a period of less than one year, for a nominal rent of only one penny: however, he must be prepared to vacate the property at any time at his request.[5]

That request came in September 1921; and Hughes felt deeply upset by the imminent loss of his home. Later he would call his landlord 'hard-hearted';[6] and now, describing himself as a 'banished mourner', he wrote some verses entitled 'Cottager is Given the Bird' which end:[7]

> See how the Past rustles
>   Stirring to life again . . .
> Three whole years left I lockt
>   Behind that window-pane.

He also began searching for a new home in the same area; and one afternoon he joined the train from London on its way north to the village of Penrhyndeudraeth, where he was intending to make some enquiries. During the brief journey, he was intrigued by a family group which included a striking young woman with 'three small children [one of them a baby], two dogs, a sort of nursemaid girl ... a pram ... and a typewriter' – 'it was the typewriter', the young woman would later observe, 'that made [Diccon] curious'.[8] Still more intriguing, they were also stopping at Penrhyndeudraeth station, and he was able to carry some of their baggage on to the platform.

Diccon quickly realised that he had given a helping hand to Amabel Williams-Ellis, who was the wife of the architect Clough Williams-Ellis, the sister of Diccon's fellow undergraduate John Strachey and the daughter of John St Loe Strachey, who was editor of the *Spectator* and a highly influential figure in the political world. Amabel had spent her childhood among some of the most eminent characters of Victorian and Edwardian London. Politicians like the young Winston Churchill had come to stay; explorers like Mary Kingsley and Gertrude Bell had told her personally of their adventures in Africa and Arabia; and she had sat on Rudyard Kipling's knee to listen to his *Just So Stories*.

Amabel was also a woman with a formidable intellect. At the age of twenty-seven she had a career in her own right on the literary side of her father's magazine; and Diccon had already corresponded with her over one of his poems. Soon he was writing again, asking Mrs Williams-Ellis if he could come over from Talsarnau to visit her at Plas Brondanw, the tall granite house which she and her husband owned, some two miles to the north of Penrhyndeudraeth. She replied that he was very welcome to visit; and then, in her own words:[9]

> he came to see us ... [on] a terrible [Douglas] motorcycle, which he called Lord Douglas ... and he fell off more or less at our feet, you see, cutting his leg quite badly, so my first consciousness of this young man was binding up a nastily cut leg with gravel in it.

At first Amabel found Diccon 'very shy'; and many years later she would describe him as 'looking ... slightly furtive I always thought ... one of the many young furtive poets that I had'.[10] However this was the start of a friendship which came to mean much to both of them.

With her position on the *Spectator*, and her various contacts in the literary world, Amabel Williams-Ellis was certainly a useful person to cultivate; and she fully realised that Hughes 'started wanting to talk to me because I could help him there; and indeed I could and did, with introductions as well ...'[11] However, they had soon become genuinely fond of each other. Diccon was strongly attracted not only by Amabel's wit and intelligence, but also by the sheer force of her personality; while Amabel not only delighted in intellectual debate, but (the difference between twenty-one and twenty-seven seeming so great) she rapidly established an ascendancy over him which was much to her liking.

When Clough Williams-Ellis joined his wife at Plas Brondanw, he also liked this tall somewhat gangling young man who had evidently joined the ranks of Amabel's admirers; and when he heard that Diccon needed somewhere to live, he suggested Garreg Fawr, a deserted cottage within a few minutes' walk of Plas Brondanw.

The only access to Garreg Fawr was by a footpath which led from a quiet road up over the side of a hill under a canopy of oak and ash. The building was primitive: there was no lavatory; and water had to be fetched from a nearby stream. But it was an attractive building, with grey stone walls, dormer windows and a good slate roof overhead; it commanded magnificent views down a long wooded valley towards the distant sea; and Diccon fell in love with it at once.

Before long, Diccon had contacted the managers of the estate upon which Garreg Fawr stood, and had been given permission to take the property for a few months on a trial basis, with payment of the rent guaranteed by Louisa. So towards the end of September Diccon moved in and spent the following days painting and decorating the cottage, and digging over the garden.[12] He also saw much both of Clough Williams-Ellis, who promised that he would draw up a scheme of improvements to Garreg Fawr if Diccon should decide to stay, and of Amabel, with whom he was frequently locked in spirited debate.

It was for Amabel Williams-Ellis that on 7 October (shortly before returning to Oxford for the start of the Michaelmas term) Diccon wrote a long letter detailing 'some sort of a poetic Athanasian creed'. The letter was never posted, but in it he declared that beauty was 'an absolute end in itself', and that his own intention was[13]

> to follow beauty as my real aim, & to be moral not as an end in itself, but (a) because, all things considered, it is one's natural inclination; (b) because it is the line of least resistance; and (c) because it is impossible to be immoral without hurting other people, which is very rarely justifiable, & then only for the sake of some very great beauty.

Hughes concluded that he had purposely left 'religion, as opposed to morality . . . out of the discussion';[14] perhaps because he had been dealing with the relationship between Christian precepts and 'true' morality in *The Sisters' Tragedy*.[15] This was a one-act play which he had written at a single twelve-hour sitting, during 'an attack of chronic appendicitis which freed me of any necessity to stop for meals'.[16] It contains an unusual vision of childhood (partly the product of Hughes's close observation that summer of the unconventional Satow girls); and retains its power to shock.

The Sisters' Tragedy tells the story of Philippa, aged twenty-eight; Charlotte, aged nineteen; and thirteen-year-old Lowrie, whose 'curious trend of logic' precipitates the final tragedy. The three sisters live together in a country cottage with their twenty-four-year-old brother Owen, a deaf-mute from the age of seven, who presents them with a series of moral dilemmas.

Philippa has long ago decided that she can never marry, but must look after Owen for the rest of her life, though she is reconciled to this, as 'a sacrifice acceptable unto the Lord'; while nineteen-year-old Charlotte is engaged to be married, but as a good Christian feels duty-bound to stay at home to help her sister.

The play opens violently. A rabbit has been badly mauled by their cat, and Philippa urges Charlotte to put the rabbit out of its misery. When she does so, Lowrie is outraged, calling Philippa a brute and Charlotte a murderer; but then she is told by Philippa that 'it's right to put a thing out of its pain, you little idiot, when living is only a burden to it'.

When Lowrie protests that all killing must be wrong, because it directly disobeys one of the Ten Commandments, Philippa reminds her that it was right to kill Germans in the 1914–1918 war: so killing can be 'right, when it's done from high motives'.

Lowrie fully accepts these arguments; and then later that day, overhearing Charlotte telling Philippa that their lives are being spoiled for the sake of someone whose life is no longer worth living, she decides that it would be morally correct (even if wrong when looked at from a narrowly Christian viewpoint) for her to put Owen out of his misery. Her own soul may be damned if she murders Owen; but at least she will have saved Philippa and Charlotte, and sent Owen from his present half-life to be 'a little boy again among the angels'.

The tragedy unfolds with Lowrie first trying to smother Owen and then (having thoroughly frightened him) allowing him to blunder into a pond and be drowned. Philippa and Charlotte weep over the body of their dead brother but they are quite prepared to agree with Charlotte's fiancé John that Owen's death has been for the best, until Lowrie blurts out what she has done.

Everyone is appalled: John rushes out to denounce Lowrie to the police, after making it clear that he could never marry the sister of a murderer. Charlotte, devastated by the ruin of all her hopes, pursues him. Philippa, who no longer has a clear path to heaven, also rushes out. And then Lowrie, unable to cope with the knowledge that by her selfless act she has not only damned herself but has made things worse for the very sisters she was trying to help, goes completely mad.

When writing his long, unposted letter to Amabel Wiliams-Ellis, Hughes had mentioned *The Sisters' Tragedy* (describing the ideas as good, but the writing as unpolished), and told her that he would 'very much value your opinion, as I don't yield an inch to Robert in my admiration of your critical abilities'.[17] On reflection he must have decided that he would rather show his play to a less thoroughgoing critic; and soon after returning to Oxford (where he now had rooms in Longwall Street, and where his slanting sitting-room was full of drawings by Pamela Bianco),[18] he travelled out to Boar's Hill to ask John Masefield for his advice.

Masefield promised to read the play; and then, much to Diccon's surprise, handed him some sheets of headed notepaper for 'The Hill Players' upon which the name of R.A.W. Hughes appeared as publicity manager. 'I was elected to my honourable position without being told', Hughes wrote to his godfather a few days later; 'anyhow it doesn't mean anything, except the pasting up of notices in the college lodge.' He added that Oxford suddenly seemed 'very empty of my friends now: hardly one of them is still left up'; but that he was 'on fairly good terms' with his tutor, having been awarded an alpha minus for his collections, 'which I don't consider bad seeing I spent two months wandering on the face of the earth, & another fortnight in the building and decorating business'.[19]

One friend who could still be visited was Robert Graves, though he was newly transplanted from Boar's Hill (where Nancy's shop had completely failed) to the most peaceful corner of the village of Islip, some five miles north-east of Oxford; and on Saturday 22 October Diccon walked over to see him for tea. Robert and Nancy's debts had been cleared (partly by a gift from T.E. Lawrence) and they were enjoying a fresh start. So although Nancy was pregnant with her third child, there was an unusually carefree atmosphere, and Diccon found Robert 'better in health than I have ever seen him, & a sturdy centre-forward in the village soccer team'. Diccon accepted an invitation to stay on for supper; and afterwards he walked back to Oxford with his fellow guests, one of whom, E.J. O'Brien, was fiction editor of the American *Pictorial Review*.[20]

On Monday O'Brien called on Hughes for tea in Longwall Street, where he asked to see some of his host's work: 'at which pleasing suggestion', Diccon records, 'I promptly allowed him jam with his muffins.' What happened next seemed extraordinary. Hughes showed him *Martha*, his story of the East End, for which he made an immediate offer of £100. Diccon 'gasped a little & said I wouldn't haggle over the price'. Two more stories were similarly offered and accepted, at which Diccon began to think that his visitor 'must be drunk. I certainly felt drunk myself (and later in the evening *was*)'. Before leaving Longwall Street, O'Brien expressed his surprise that Hughes had been allowed to leave New York with those stories unsold; and promised 'to cable me the decision [in mid November] when he gets back to New York'.[21]

Hughes's own excitement cooled a little when he learned that O'Brien was well-known for his sudden enthusiasms; but, as he pointed out to his godfather, 'if it does come off, it will support me in poetry-writing for years: & be damned to reviewing';[22] and for the rest of that term, buoyed up by the prospect of imminent riches, he did very little formal work. Instead he concentrated upon pursuing literary connections and enjoying himself with old and new friends.

On Monday 24 October, for example, Hughes had lunch with Amabel's father (John St Loe Strachey of the *Spectator*), attempted unsuccessfully to call on Robert Graves (who was taking his children for their afternoon walk), and went on to see Walter de la Mare;[23] while two days later he was having tea at the 'George' with Robert's brother John (a classical scholar in his first year at St John's) and their mutual friend Loveday. As John records, his two companions[24]

> insisted on discussing Elemental [and] Elementary Spirits and others – Black Magic and Blood Ritual, but so earnestly that they obviously were sincere! Then we went to the Hypocrites' Club ... and ... had some rum. Then to the 'Royalist' meeting at the Martyrs' Memorial: Diccon asked one of the speakers if he would help him regain his hereditary kingdom of Wales – & promised to produce his pedigree going back 'Through Adam' – The policemen that were there were shaking with suppressed mirth.

Other friends included Bennett and Thorp from Oriel, and the gentle Alan Porter of Queen's who had been a member of the New Elizabethans; while elsewhere in Oxford Hughes had made a friend of Stella Watson;[25] and a girl called Violet caught his eye for the last few weeks of the Michaelmas term.[26]

By then, Diccon's hopes of American riches were fading. 'O'Brien has melted into the blue with my three stories', he wrote to a friend, '& not been heard of since.'[27] To offset this disappointment (which made him roundly curse America) came news that Harold Taylor of the Golden Cockerel Press proposed to publish a selection of Hughes's poems under the title *Gipsy-Night* in the spring of 1922. The frontispiece was to be a lithograph of the author by Pamela Bianco[28] (probably executed during Diccon's visit to New Jersey); and it was hoped that John Masefield could be persuaded to write a preface.[29]

In the meantime Hughes was co-editing with Robert Graves and Alan Porter successive volumes of *Oxford Poetry*, the second of which appeared in November 1921 to a warm review from Walter de la Mare;[30] and the third of which was due out the following spring. Hughes also continued to co-edit volumes of *Public Schools Verse* with Hugh Lyon. Hugh had now become an assistant master at Cheltenham College, and would recall wryly that Diccon was 'much the best critic of all the stuff that came in . . . and much the worst at returning the stuff in time for publication'.[31] From time to time Diccon had to send him a placatory letter, one of which (written early in January 1922 after a brief holiday in Paris)[32] begins:[33]

> My irascible Hugh,
> I was much astonished at your letter. I did not know of the existence of the said packet. I remember you saying you had left me some rejection slips at Longwall, but failed to find them, so guessed that Arabella had used them for washing bills, and put it out of my mind. As for the rest of the STUFF I have it here . . . duly marked at variance with any existing marks.

Diccon concluded with the hope that Hugh would not 'prove obstinate over small points', since from the moment of his return to Oxford on 17 January he would be 'bloody busy' working on 'a mixture of Anglo-Saxon with Modern Tragedy, Fiction, & Reviewing'. This list was incomplete; but perhaps he hardly liked to admit that he had undertaken yet another extra-curricular activity which was bound to push *Public Schools Verse* still further to one side: namely, the production of his first play.

After reading *The Sisters' Tragedy*, John Masefield had sent Hughes 'Congratulations', telling him that it was 'streets ahead of anything you have done', and asking for it to be staged at his home on Boar's Hill.[34] So on 24 January 1922 it was performed for the first time by the Hill Players before a distinguished audience which, as

Hughes later recalled, included Asquith. 'I produced it', he added, 'and played "Owen" myself.'[35]

So successful was the production that Masefield (without a word to his protégé) sent a copy of the script to the thirty-nine-year-old actress Sybil Thorndike,[36] a friend whose actor-manager husband Lewis Casson was then producing a series of short and horrific so-called 'Grand Guignol'[37] plays at the Little Theatre, Adelphi, in London's West End. As Masefield had hoped, Sybil Thorndike liked the play so much that she immediately wrote to Hughes with the news that she wanted to play the part of Philippa;[38] and before long she had persuaded her husband to produce it as part of his eighth Grand Guignol series.

Although Hughes was not altogether pleased to have his play labelled 'Grand Guignol' (and would later instruct producers that it should under no circumstances 'be acted in a Grand Guignol manner'),[39] it was tremendously exciting news that his first play was to be produced on the West End stage, with one of the finest actresses of her day in a leading rôle. The disappointment of finding that Masefield (pleading lack of time) had declined to write a preface to *Gipsy-Night and Other Poems*[40] at once evaporated.

After receiving Sybil Thorndike's letter, Diccon Hughes had written to tell her how honoured he felt by her interest in his play; and he was invited to travel down to London to watch a rehearsal of *The Sisters' Tragedy* one Saturday afternoon in May.[41] Accepting this invitation (as one of Diccon's friends recounts) necessitated a visit to the Proctors.[42]

> 'I want permission [said Diccon] to go to London for the weekend.'
> And they said: 'Why?'
> And he said: 'To see my own play!'
> And they said: 'That's a good one. We normally have dead grandmothers. We've never had somebody of your age going back to see his own play! Certainly you can have leave.'
> And then [a few days later] they saw the papers blazing out about this play . . . [Diccon] chuckled over that, and after[wards] he said: 'They didn't believe me!'

Before the rehearsal began, Hughes already knew that the censor had made a number of small changes, cutting out two 'Christ!'s, for example, and altering Lowrie's blasphemous 'God damn my soul to hell!' to the comparatively anodyne 'God send me to hell'.[43] However, Hughes was quite unprepared for the extensive series of alterations made to the text by Casson; and on returning to Oxford he wrote an eight-page letter of complaint.[44] His Boar's Hill audience had been able to understand what he had written: were Londoners less intelligent?

Casson replied the following day with a firm but good-humoured letter, in which he declared plainly that Hughes seemed to be living in cloud-cuckoo-land. Despite claims that his Boar's Hill audience had been an ordinary one, he was 'quite wrong in attributing such a high degree of intelligence to the general Londoner', who was 'almost incredibly stupid in appreciating subtleties'. All the changes had been effected 'with a view to making the main motives clearer', and all would remain.[45]

Casson's alterations were amply justified when eight days later, on 31 March 1922, the first public performance of *The Sisters' Tragedy* opened to rapturous reviews. Although it had been sharing a bill with a play by Noel Coward (then equally unknown) *The Sisters' Tragedy* was hailed by *The Times* as:

> incomparably the best play of the evening. First, it is indeed tragedy; secondly, it is mental tragedy, not physical horror . . . The play has suspense and – a rare quality at the Grand Guignol – beauty, and it gives distinction to the Eighth Series.

Later, the *Evening News* would call it: 'The most remarkable play of the year . . . [and] one of the most discussed plays that have been seen at the Little Theatre.'

Casson was so delighted by the success of *The Sisters' Tragedy* that on 16 June he wrote to Hughes begging to be shown any future work, and mentioning that the distinguished critic James Agate of the *Saturday Review* had been 'in the other night and was most enthusiastic about your piece'.[46] It also made Hughes some money. He had secured the services of James Pinker & Son, Robert Graves's literary agents; and although he received no advance,[47] a contract was drawn up on 9 June, after which royalties were paid regularly each week.[48]

Sadly, towards the end of June Hughes learned that Casson was soon to bring his Grand Guignol series to an end. 'It looks as if we were shutting down for good', wrote Casson gloomily, explaining that 'the censorship difficulty' was one of the chief causes. He added that even *The Sisters' Tragedy* had been passed by the censor ' "most unwillingly" & only after I had gone on my knees to him . . . So the chances of revival are I am afraid very small'.[49]

As the run of *The Sisters' Tragedy* drew to a close, so did Diccon's time at Oxford. He took his English Finals, and retreated with his mother to North Wales. From there he was called back for his oral examination or 'viva'; and there, in mid July, news reached him that despite having begun his last year at Oxford with an alpha minus for his collections, he had ended it not with the First Class degree that Masefield had been predicting,[50] but with another Fourth.

This was hardly surprising: there had been little chance of Hughes doing himself justice when he had been so heavily occupied with extra-curricular activities. (Book reviewing was not the least of these. In March 1922 Hughes had written to Hugh Lyon: 'I'm having a stiff time with reviewing: 2 books on metaphysics, one on whaling, one on mysticism, one on the Russian revolution and one on pedagogics: all wanted by tomorrow.')[51] However, he was disappointed, and in his letter of apology to the Provost he wrote:[52]

> I am very sorry to have given a second justification to the opinion of me which Mods gave you. But this time I cannot honestly credit it to inattention – though the necessity of adding to my income & laying the slow foundations of a future income & reputation were naturally a severe hindrance; for in spite of them I imagined myself to be doing some pretty steady reading during the last part of my time.
>
> Of course I knew that my knowledge of Wilde's theory of Philology was singularly weak, & that a good many of my critical opinions were heterodox. But I hardly expected to do so badly as this. I suppose it is bad policy, really, to take Schools in a subject in which one is passionately interested, as one is then too liable to pursue the reading as an end in itself, instead of merely as a means to passing an examination.

He concluded by assuring the Provost that his apology was 'absolutely sincere . . . I have not wantonly failed in my duty'.

Another letter went to the Bursar (who had taken Diccon's side two years previously when he had been in danger of being sent down). 'I am very sorry indeed', he wrote, 'so ill to have justified what you have done for me.' But then, after repeating much of what he had written to the Provost, Hughes added that he had hardly expected 'Brett-Smith in my viva to condemn as "unfamiliar" terms which are the clichés of contemporary criticism even in such conservative papers as the *Spectator*'.[53]

In any case, with the publication of *Gipsy-Night and Other Poems* and the success of *The Sisters' Tragedy* Hughes had made so good a start upon his literary career that his Double Fourth was unimportant. He had also attracted growing admiration as a reviewer. 'My dear Hughes', a letter from St Loe Strachey had begun back in February,[54]

> I must write a line in my capacity as journalist as well as friend to tell you with what delight and admiration I read your novel review

of 'Mountain Blood' . . . I do hope that you will be able from time to time to do some work for us. It will be a great pleasure to me, and I am sure also to my readers. The congestion of the *Spectator* is my only difficulty . . . I want you . . . to have a word with my wife, who runs the Fiction Department for me, in regard to some future work.

Further recognition had come from Sir Edward Marsh, who had met Hughes in June, and promised to include several of his poems in the fifth and final volume of *Georgian Poetry* when it was published later that year.

Everything suggested that Hughes would have no difficulty in supporting himself by his pen; especially as he had arranged to reduce his ordinary expenses to a minimum.

For the foreseeable future, he would share a home with his mother, just as she had always intended; and that home would be Garreg Fawr, on its wild hillside in North Wales. Louisa had liked the cottage when she had seen it; Clough Williams-Ellis had designed a number of improvements, including the conversion of a cowshed at the rear into an outside lavatory;[55] and fifty-one-year-old mother and twenty-two-year-old son had taken up residence there in July.

However, before Diccon was ready to settle down to earn his living as a writer, he wanted another taste of excitement. During his voyage to America the previous summer, he had collected a number of middle-European addresses from his fellow passengers in steerage; and before going down from Oxford he had persuaded his friends Jim Bennett, Christopher Thorp, Peter Brown and Stella Watson[56] that they should join him on a journey through the Balkans.

There followed a period of doubt. Was he being fair to Louisa? Robert Graves, when consulted, advised that 'on your Mother's account, you being her only one left ought not to go on this stunt'.

Then Diccon dreamed a strange dream, in which a figure appeared who was partly Robert's wife Nancy and partly one of the Satow girls. At one moment, Diccon knew that he was on a motorbike in danger of running down a child; and then he seemed to be in a graveyard where another child was calling in vain for its mother.

When he wrote to Robert Graves asking for elucidation, Robert replied: 'The composite character Nancy–Joyce [Satow] expresses the conflict of restraint and freedom. The graveyard and the child calling Mother are your relations with Mrs Hughes and myself.' Robert believed that it was now time for Diccon to become more independent, both of Louisa, and of Robert's own influence. He added: 'Your motorbike fright about running into the little boy is transferred to the thought of this journey; qualms, not on your own account, but on your mother's.'[57]

Formally absolving Diccon from 'any loyalty or gratitude you still feel to me', Robert declared that in future he intended to treat Diccon as 'Richard Hughes playwright', and to cut short their old relations which had 'gone a bit miffy'. It was time for 'a clean start', and he advised Diccon to:

> disjoin my influence from your relations with your mother about this journey ... and then if you decide to go still I will be sure that the case is a simple one & Mrs Hughes is quite confident about things.

Robert concluded that despite his 'deep affection for Mrs Hughes' he had been 'wrong in saying anything to you about her in view of this other conflict'.

Doubts eventually allayed, Hughes met three of his comrades at a rendezvous in London on Sunday 6 August. They were due to catch the boat-train for the continent at 8.55 the following morning, but there was no sign of Stella Watson. Diccon began to fear that he would have to wait behind for her, while the others went ahead to Vienna. Then at six in the morning, just when he had almost given up hope, the telephone rang. It was Stella. She had arrived in London, and their adventure was about to begin.[58]

CHAPTER 9

Paddling down the Danube[1]

When Richard Hughes and his four companions reached Vienna, late one August night in 1922, every hotel was crowded out; and they wandered round the city for two hours in search of rooms, driving in vain from one big hotel to another. At length they started trying the smaller hotels; and had worked their way down to 'a filthy little Gasthaus near the Sudbahnhof' when a friendly waiter took pity on them. Escorting them to his flat, he himself slept on the kitchen table, presumably so that Stella could take his place in bed with his wife.

Or was Stella disguised as a boy? (This would be in keeping with the rest of this episode, some of which reads like a Dornford Yates story, with its mettlesome young woman joining a band of Englishmen on a dangerous foray into Europe.) The hunt for five separate rooms seems to have been the last occasion when any concession was made to Stella's sex; and her presence as a member of the party was a closely guarded secret from all but Louisa Hughes (who must have trusted her intimately) and a few other close friends.[2]

The following day then went bed-hunting again, and 'finally came to roost on the fourth-floor of [a] curious back-street international rabbit-warren', where all five shared a single room. The advantage was that it cost only fourpence a night; the disadvantage that from behind one of the paper-thin walls came 'a steady stream of cursing', which

> rose and fell; higher as it grew less furious, and sinking to a hiss of speechless anger. The rain-water dripping from the ceiling was quite green; and even by sleeping on the floor one could not escape vermin. An uncomfortable night.

By morning, the cursing had 'died away to a deep rumble'; but those who had managed to snatch a few hours of sleep were then woken by the knocking at their door of 'a fat rabbi in a night-shirt', who impressed them by his ability to ask the time 'in several different languages at once', and by the 'long and carefully curled ringlets that swung in front of his ears'.

The rest of the week was spent exploring Vienna. Entertainment was cheap, and the people and the buildings were 'notoriously beautiful'; but the back streets seemed 'pitifully empty' of children; while at almost every corner sat 'disabled soldiers in a pitiable condition', besides 'old peasant women without feet being wheeled about in chairs'.

By Thursday 10 August England already seemed so remote that it was odd for Hughes to receive a letter from the Provost of Oriel. It was a most generous letter, in view of his Fourth, and Hughes replied:[3]

> there is little I can say, except to express my sincere gratitude for the point of view you adopt towards the 'débâcle': & assure you I shall always do my best to justify it. I am well aware that I have been unwittingly the thorn in the College side for some time;

but he had never imagined, he said, that it was anyone's fault but his own; and he was glad that the Provost bore him no grudge.

Saturday lunchtime found Diccon sitting in a restaurant at the same table as two Egyptians, who helped him order his meal and asked his plans.

> Was I going to stay in Vienna? No. Where was I going? [Down the Danube] to Budapest? And then? I projected walking about the Balkans on foot and hoped to arrive some day at Salonika. The elder . . . looked serious: 'Ach, that was not good. Albanians – Macedonians – they are not peoples of good conduct.' Here he drew a significant thumb across his throat, and tapped my pocket: 'Ach, no don't go there.'

Excited by this warning, Hughes immediately acquired 'a large and shockingly new dinghy', for which unfortunately only canoe-paddles were available.

Sunday was a day of rest, with 'a dim and odorous Mass in the Cathedral of St Stephen', followed by lunch in the garden at the top of the Leopoldsberg, 'a steep, sandy little mountain covered with trees, with an ancient fortress on top, a church and café'. Then on Monday 14 August[4] Diccon and his companions loaded their luggage into the dinghy, together with provisions of black bread, sausage and chocolate; and at four in the afternoon they began paddling down the canal that leads from the city into the main stream of the Danube.

For several miles the canal ran through 'an industrial quarter, half-deserted, where goats and geese wage war on the banks, and old women sit on steps washing their feet'; and then their boat was 'caught by the enormous force of the main stream' and whirled along at ten knots or more. The river was of magnificent breadth, though full of whirls and rapids, and all along the bank they could see 'little fishermen's shanties, scarcely five feet each way, with a chimney on top, and in front the square basket net and the winch with which they dip it endlessly into the Danube'. At night they reached a little stone-flanked harbour, ate bread and beer in the local Gasthaus, enjoyed a moonlight bathe, and then slept on the rocky shore.

It rained while they were sleeping, and they were bitten by mosquitoes; but early on Tuesday morning they set out once more, and were soon rewarded by the sight of the sun rising ahead of them,

> golden in a host of small clouds, like little green fish-scales: every swirl and eddy of the river was caught with colour and light . . . The country became every minute more glorious: it was hilly, and the river had burst its path through; moreover, the banks were densely wooded.

The current was still fierce, and in little more than an hour they had reached Theben, where a ruined castle stood on a sheer rock thrust up from the left bank of the river; but they were unable to explore it, because they had no entry visas, and a Czech sentry waved them on their way.

The Danube now formed a boundary between hostile nations, which made their journey hazardous. On the right bank was Hungary, which had been reduced by more than two-thirds and forced to pay massive reparations since having fought on the losing side in the Great War. On the left bank was Czechslovakia, which had 'managed by the obscure processes of "self-determination" to obtain dominion over millions of foreigners who detest [her]', so that, as Diccon wrote, 'in all our landings on the left bank, we did not find a single Czech among the native population; it is as purely Magyar as the right'. This seemed so grossly unfair, that Diccon began to think of Hungary as a 'cause' in which he might become personally involved.

Soon after passing Theben, they found an unguarded stretch of the Czech shore: 'deep forest, full of gorgeous flowers and utterly deserted', where they pulled into the bank and bathed. This was the first of their 'surreptitious' incursions into Czech territory. The next was at Pressburg, a small town where they slipped ashore for breakfast. Scarcely were they once more on their way, when a large motor-launch in charge of a Czech officer shouted to them to heave-to.

This encounter, the first of a number of arrests, was soon over. After inspecting their passports, and asking for 'a manifest of the ship's crew with its port of departure and destination', the officer allowed them to continue down-river.

On they drifted, with the countryside on each bank becoming more and more wild. There was no protection from the sun in their little craft, and the heat grew so intense that Diccon presently removed his clothes, and swam behind the dinghy for a few miles.

Much later that day, tired, hot and hungry, they reached a sandy beach on the Hungarian shore. There they could see several little goose-girls,

> with tight long blue frocks, and big handkerchiefs hooded on their heads, [who] were minding their flocks, making shrill noises to them, which the geese answered cheerfully; swishing at them with long boughs. We drove the boat in: I landed: they fled at once, driving their flocks ahead.

Diccon pursued them, but since he knew no Magyar, his efforts to communicate were in vain. However, he could now see a church spire about a mile inland and so, holding a Magyar grammar under his nose, he set off to search for food; while his friends 'took off what little clothing they still had, and lay in the water'.

By the time he returned from Halászt, having discovered an inn and ordered a meal from the innkeeper (who was lying ill in bed), Diccon found to his amusement that 'they had all been arrested, stark as they were, by the frontier guard; but, by the time I arrived, were teaching them to read 'The Shropshire Lad', and things were smoothed over'. The little goose-girls had also returned, and escorted them 'with smiles and excited eyes' all the way to the village. There Diccon and his companions sat by their host's sick-bed,

> and ate bread and red pepper and hard-boiled eggs, and drank several litres of wine; and gradually all the village collected, and with the help of the wine we conversed with them fluently in any tongue under the sun, and went singing to our boat, and singing down the river at a great pace, with the sunset at our backs, and distant lightning flickering, and a stormy sky.

They paddled on until darkness eventually made them seek the river bank; and there they were so badly bitten by mosquitoes that their hands and faces started to swell, and they endured a cold, painful and utterly sleepless night.

At the first hint of dawn, therefore, they set out again, knowing that at least there would be few mosquitoes in midstream; and after several hours they reached the village of Száp. This was surprisingly oriental in appearance: the houses had dazzling white plaster walls, with verandas and long courtyards; the streets were deep in sand, and edged with heavy mulberry-trees; and they watched in astonishment when a man came by driving a bullock-cart, and wearing 'a blue shirt with full sleeves, a black waistcoat, enormous white cotton trousers like a divided skirt, Turkish slippers, and a broad-brimmed black hat'.

Finding an eating-house, they were just settling down to drink 'wonderful coffee, with clotted cream upon it', when they were arrested again. They were allowed to finish their coffee, but were then deported 'with great politeness' by the soldiers, who 'st[ood] at the salute while our disreputable craft put to sea'. Clouds came up, and the wind rose; but when they attempted to land further down-river they were once again arrested; and so they continued to the town of Gönyö,

> a straggled little town, where we were arrested by police, navy, army, and customs officers at the same time, so we left them to fight it out, and went to the village shop, where at least we were able to buy food: *szallámi*, bread, butter, cheese, and fruit; so we sat in the inn and ate a very great deal, while the authorities searched for us about the town.

At length the authorities caught up with them and this time, instead of being formally deported, their passports were stamped, and they were allowed to walk back to sit in their dinghy. They had a choice now, to go on or to stay; but a hearty meal had made them more deadly tired than ever, and for once they 'wrangled, with . . . a very great deal of bitterness, for no one knew his own mind, and one would loll forward and sleep in a sentence's middle'.

Somehow it seemed easier to let the Danube draw them on southward than to continue arguing; and that Wednesday evening they reached Komáran, where they slept in the waiting-room of a steamer company, under blankets and greatcoats lent them by friendly Hungarian soldiers.

On the morning of Thursday 17 August, they put in at an Hungarian village, which Diccon Hughes believed was the most beautiful he had ever seen. Arriving at Nesmély 'in the early heat of the day', he and his friends

> landed on a little beach that was a farmyard, full of mulberry trees and apples and happy goats, sided by big, dazzling, white buildings, with a mill at the back. From there, a little path wound by a stream under thick trees to the village: a broad, sandy street, edged with mulberry trees: an inn that looked like a monastery, with thick walls and rooms twenty feet high;

and there they 'sat in the cool, drinking wine, served by barefoot girls with brown skins'.

Each day the Danube had been running more slowly, so that progress had become more and more dependent upon their own efforts; and it was after weary hours of paddling that on Friday evening the voyagers reached Esztergom, with its ancient fortress on a plateau of rock above the river.

One of their discoveries on Saturday was 'a wonderful little chapel in the ramparts, full of mural painting', which had been the setting for the christening of St Istvan, first king of Hungary; and the next day, Sunday 20 August was 'his festival, the chief fête of the year in Hungary'. Early in the morning they heard troops marching on their way to a mass presided over by

> the Archbishop of Hungary ... [with] very wonderful music ... [and] a congregation of peasants from the town and country round. All the afternoon was given to jollity: fairs, and bicycle races, houp-la with live ducks, football matches that were nearly all speechifying. By the evening, the town band was an octave out of tune; so we gave them five hundred crowns, and they made speeches to us and followed us about the town playing at us.

By this time Diccon had become so attached to the Hungarian cause that he was much moved when, later in the evening, after all the orchestras had ceased, he 'heard a solitary horn', and was told that it was 'an old Hungarian national tune, of the First War of Independence, played by a patriot on the Czech shore'.

For half a day, Diccon toyed with the idea of taking a house in Esztergom, in the old part of the town: now that his rural retreat in Wales had to be shared with Louisa, it would be good to have a place of his own, somewhere she would be unlikely to follow. Realising however that this was probably just a fantasy, he 'thought better of it, and on Monday at noon we put out to stream once more'.

At Szob, where the Danube winds wholly into Hungary, they failed to steer their dinghy into the shore for a customs check, and so came under fire from the frontier guard. Fortunately no one was hurt, and the only consequence was that they were kept under arrest for about an hour and had to sit 'without clothes eating water-melon in the sun till they let us go'.

Below Szob, the Danube flows into mountainous country, where it narrows by half, and its pace therefore doubles. The urgency of the flow seems to have communicated itself to the spirits of the company; and on Monday (after putting in at Visegrad and admiring 'the magnificence of the castle ruins on the mountain above'), they

started off again under the stars, paddled half the night, slept a few hours on the way, and breakfasted in Budapest, where we were once again arrested for the crime of importing a boat, and charged heavily for it by the customs.

'So our boat trip ended', records Hughes, 'and we took to city life once more.'

Diccon and his friends spent just over a week in Budapest, arriving in the early hours of Tuesday 22 August, and leaving late the following Tuesday or Wednesday evening. Rooms were expensive, but they found that for two shillings a day they could eat 'very well indeed, with unlimited cigars and liqueurs'; and although Pest was 'dullish', Buda was 'very lovely, with the Palace and the huge rock of St Gellert overhanging the Danube, and strange old houses and flowered courtyards'. However, Diccon's principal concern was now political adventure.

Making it his business to interview the most influential and knowledgeable people he could find, Hughes 'spent a great deal of time talking politics' to them; and they for their part 'sketched endless revolutions, invasions and insurrections' in those parts of the old Hungary which remained under foreign domination. In particular, he met a group who talked of restoring the Hungarian monarchy; and at first it was exciting to sit with these royalist conspirators in the imperial cellars drinking the finest Hungarian Tokay.[5]

After a while, however, Hughes decided that they had no intention of doing anything more than talk, and became so disenchanted that he wrote scornfully of the Hungarian preference for 'a slow death to a desperate remedy. They dare not take the initiative'. His disillusion was complete when one of his English friends was 'drugged and robbed in a back street'. Budapest, he decided, was 'no place, at the moment, even for the most modest adventurer'. (Later Hughes would write of having 'dabbled mildly in one of the futile monarchist conspiracies then going on'.)[6]

A new political cause rapidly filled the gap. Hughes heard 'hints' that 'things might be expected to happen' in Zagreb, capital of Croatia, once part of the Austro-Hungarian empire, but now unhappily united with Serbia, Slovenia and Montenegro, and effectively dominated by the Serbian authorities in Belgrade. Money was running short; but it seemed that there was a real chance of becoming involved in a Croatian national uprising, and Diccon became determined to travel to Zagreb.

Three of his four companions, including Stella Watson and Jim Bennett, were persuaded to follow him.[7] (By a rather long coincidence, Jim was already carrying a letter of introduction to a Croat politician, given to him shortly before leaving London by a casual acquaintance whom he had met when dining at the Cafe Royal.)[8]

So they sold their boat, 'invested all but our last few thousand crowns in tickets to the frontier' (though Diccon also wired home for £10 to be forwarded to him at the British Consulate in Zagreb); and left Budapest by train at eight o'clock one evening, 'with the prospect of a night journey into the Balkans ahead of us'.

On reaching Zagreb, they spent the last of their money on eating 'well and with great dignity at the railway restaurant', and then (intending to sleep in the fields), they balanced their packs, and set out 'under an enormous moon' to find their way out into the countryside.

Within an hour they were walking along a road which wound up among trees, maize-fields and vineyards; but then, as they passed beyond the last of the houses, they began to hear

> a curious whistling – here, there, in the fields and hedges. It was neither cicada nor owl; though sometimes it imitated one, sometimes the other, but poorly. There was a rustling in the hedges too, and presently a man hiding behind a tree, who hooted softly when we had passed and was answered from the fields. Then, in the far distance, a sudden burst of rifle-shooting, and faint shouting.

Zagreb had been swarming with heavily-armed soldiers and police; and Diccon and his friends suddenly realised that they had been followed. Waiting until they felt that they were unobserved, they crept through the roadside hedge and lay down on the ground, 'aching with weariness'.

Diccon himself was lying on his back, looking up at the moon and the stars, and feeling very much afraid, when he heard 'another burst of shooting, quite close; followed by furious screaming, then more shots, and then men creeping about quietly, looking for us'. The hunt drew closer and closer, with the hunters 'firing at every shadow'.[9] Through the hedge Diccon could see the legs of some of his pursuers as they tiptoed by; and then suddenly

> behind us we heard the click of a safety-catch, and a man snapping something out in a language of which we knew not one word. We had not a firearm between us, and sat up where we were, thrusting our empty hands up into the moonlight. Other men hurried up, cocking and aiming their rifles at us as they ran – their eyes shone with nervousness and their voices were high – for they saw there were several of us, and probably expected us to open fire at any moment from the darkness of the hedge.

They managed to convince the leader of the gunmen (who knew a few words of French) that they were harmless, and were sent back into Zagreb. It was now one o'clock in the morning. The cafés were closing, though the streets were still pretty full; and they found seats in a public garden where they sat and slept bolt upright.

An hour or so later, Hughes woke to find himself alone. In the distance he could see the last of his comrades disappearing round a corner. Running after them, he found that one of their number was being led away by the police. They reached a police barracks, the prisoner was taken inside, and the rest of them were turned back from the gates at bayonet-point.

Later, they too were arrested; but instead of being imprisoned they were escorted to student sleeping-quarters in the university. And in the morning the prisoner escaped from the police barracks through a window and (in Diccon's words) 'having a certain psychic gift, succeeded in finding the way to where we were'.

Within a few hours of being reunited, all four of them were safely in the British Consulate, where Diccon was relieved to find his £10 waiting for him. After their recent difficulties, they might have been tempted to use the money to set out for home. But they remained in Zagreb, where (for Diccon and Jim at least) the really exciting part of their Balkan adventure was just about to begin.

It was on the morning of Sunday 3 September 1922 that Diccon Hughes and Jim Bennett 'shaved ourselves, polished our boots on our blankets', and presented Jim's letter of introduction. The addressee, a 'broad man with a small smile, a quiet manner and a shrewd sort of visionariness', received them amiably, and then drove them to the house of his political master Stjepan Radić.

Wearing carpet-slippers, and without a collar, Radić was a strange figure to western eyes. He was also a fervent Croatian nationalist and peasant leader who at the age of fifty-one had been active in Balkan politics for more than twenty years. Delighted by the break-up of the Austro-Hungarian empire at the end of the Great War, he had at first been happy to see Croatia join a new triple kingdom of Serbs, Croats and Slovenes; but he soon began to want more autonomy than the predominantly Serbian government in Belgrade was prepared to offer; and (after a period of imprisonment in 1919–1920) he now dreamed of establishing a Croatian Peasant Republic.

The arrival of two enthusiastic Englishmen excited Radić considerably, as their conversation led him (quite wrongly) to suppose that they represented a substantial body of European support for his political aims. He therefore treated them to what Hughes later described as[10] a speech in bad French which lasted four hours and which so entranced the detectives sent to watch him that they glued their noses to the window like a child outside a tuck-shop. Then – it was now afternoon – we were given the world's worst cocktails and whisked off in a car to a political meeting in the country, still foodless.

Lack of food was outweighed by the excitement of being part of a 'triumphal progress'. As they bounced along over bumpy roads in their well-sprung Daimler, Radić bowed and smiled to the passing peasants, 'who all cheered him heartily'.

Shooting up the mountain from ravine to ravine, they stopped for wine and a few speeches at one little mountain inn; and then went on to another, very old, with a long low chamber, where they were to hear a concert of children's orchestras, and where 'our party were very kindly set on window-sills, and the rest of the space was filled with peasants in their gorgeous costumes'. Hughes had learned that the Croats were a peasant people with an ancient culture, and 'no nobles: every peasant owns his own land, grows his own vines and corn and fruit and stock'. And now he was moved by the experience of watching 'the children, in their own tiny dresses, boys and girls', being conducted by 'a serious little girl of six', and playing their national tunes, old battle songs, and melancholy songs, 'very lustily . . . on curious native stringed instruments that very weirdly suited the music'.

For the rest of that week Hughes and Bennett spent much of their time with Radić. During the day there would be more drives to more public meetings in more villages; and before long the two Englishmen had begun to promote the Croat cause with their own speeches, made either

> through interpreters, or in the few words of the language we had managed to pick up: and the little peasant girls bought us bouquets of the national flowers, and the local leaders gave touching expression to their belief in the purity of British Foreign Policy.

In the evenings they would usually return to Zagreb, where (joined by their other two companions), they would all be 'very hospitably entertained . . . by our first friend' who introduced them to most of the other nationalist leaders.

For a while it seemed to Hughes that the Croatian peasants were on the verge of a great revolution; and on Tuesday that week he wrote an excited letter to Hugh Lyon, telling him that 'by great luck' he had[11]

> stumbled on a small nation in the Balkans at the psych[ological]

moment, am now living a life exceeding the wildest dreams of Anthony Hope. Within a week I (a) shall be running like a hare over the mountains to the Adriatic: or (b) shall be going on a triumphal progress over much the same ground.

Sadly, there was to be no triumphal progress.

One evening Diccon noticed that 'the papers I had left loose in my bedroom had been disturbed', a sure sign that the secret police were taking a close interest in his activities; and by the night of Saturday 9 September it had been decided that it was too dangerous for him and his comrades to remain anywhere in the triple kingdom.

The adventurers were therefore roused before dawn on Sunday morning, 'picked up by our host's car' (in which they hid under the seats until they were well clear of Zagreb)[12] and 'driven twenty miles towards the frontier before breakfast'. Nationalist groups had been told of their coming; and parties of cheering peasants lined their route. At lunch-time the car dropped Diccon and his friends, and turned back;

> but the peasants entertained us: gave us a very good lunch and wine; and we addressed them through an interpreter. So we were passed on, in peasant carts from village to village in a sort of triumph, drinking and listening to and returning speeches at each until nightfall.

Sunday night was spent close to the frontier with some friendly cottagers; and when they woke in the morning, the girl of the family offered to guide them to the frontier station.

They accepted her offer, and she led the way, carrying a basket of plums on her head. Suddenly they were hailed; and, looking up, found themselves covered by a party of six soldiers. This was another moment of real danger. The girl was driven away; and Hughes and his friends were taken to a guardroom, which not surprisingly (as Hughes records) 'put us in a cold sweat; partly because of . . . [our] performances of the day before'. Their position seemed hopeless (though Bennett had the presence of mind to drop, as though worthless, a potentially incriminating letter from Radić to the Soviet Foreign Minister);[13] and then a large crowd of peasants appeared 'as if from nowhere', and began to make menacing noises.

The handful of soldiers (who so far had done no more to the English party than examine their passports) very soon decided that it would be prudent to move on, 'shouldered their rifles with bayonets fixed and marched us off up the lane'. Bennett had pocketed his letter again, unnoticed; and now Hughes found that one of their captors knew German, and set about trying to prove 'that we were sufficiently lunatic to be harmless'.

Perhaps he was successful. At any rate, after marching for several miles, the soldiers simply 'stopped, saluted, and wished us *bon voyage*'. 'The whole incident', as Hughes concluded, 'was very odd, very obscure indeed; but by now we had given up looking for any rational process in the mysteries of arrest and release.'

Their freedom was all that really mattered; and after walking across the frontier, they celebrated their escape with much wine and *Sljivovica* in a friendly mountain inn, before setting out for the coast.

Soon after they arrived in Trieste on 16 or 17 September, they found that they had enough money for Stella to buy a steamer ticket to Venice and begin making her way home; but until more funds arrived from England, the other three had to stay behind in a doss-house.

Fortunately one of their companions in the doss-house (where Diccon began growing a beard) was a Montenegrin named Zović[14] who took a liking to the young Englishmen. An ex-brigand who had 'descended via the ironmongery trade, the white slave traffic and communism in the American Red Cross, to being a mere opium-smuggler',[15] Zović was an agreeable rogue who secured credit for them while they waited for their money from England, and entertained them with

> excellent stories about ... how he had eloped with the most beautiful girl in Montenegro on her wedding-day ... of how he had held up six policemen in a railway station at revolver-point ... [and] about Miss Perunic, the Leading Lady Bandit, who had thrown more Austrian officers over precipices than all her men put together.

Eventually their money arrived. After saying goodbye to Zović,[16] making 'a visit to Fiume by a bus which burst five tyres', and engaging in 'a little bit of quite neat smuggling' they followed Stella's footsteps back to England.

While they were abroad, Hughes had been writing a series of letters about their adventures to the *Weekly Westminster Gazette*. The first of these, telling of Vienna and the beginning of their voyage down the Danube, had appeared on 9 September 1922 (the eve of their flight from Zagreb); and the letters made good copy, even when Stella's name had been deleted from the company, Zagreb had become 'a certain Balkan city', and Radić a mysterious 'president'. By the time Hughes returned to England, his story had aroused enough interest for him to be interviewed. Sporting his new beard, he joked that it had been grown 'largely because, in Serbia, razors seem to be used chiefly for social purposes'.[17]

It had certainly been an exciting adventure. But although at the time Hughes believed that his involvement with Radić had been significant, and was also pleased that he had managed to accustom himself to 'crude danger'; he later realised that nothing of political importance had been achieved, and that in his own life he had done no more than[18]

> to shift the gamut of my powers of perception, not to extend it. In becoming able to face, for instance, being woken at night by the muzzle of a rifle shoved into my ribs ... what I gained at one end I lost at the other. By the time I got back to London my finer perceptions, both in intellectual and in human relationships, were badly damaged. It was many months before I returned to normal, and before I was able to write anything except a florid and worthless kind of journalism.

As for Radić, Hughes visited him once more in Croatia; and later, when outlawed, Radić would escape to England, where he stayed for a while at Garreg Fawr. Then, tricked into returning home, and[19]

> run to earth in a secret chamber, he was given the choice of being shot or becoming a Cabinet Minister, and chose the latter. But nevertheless, not long afterwards, he was shot all the same; in the stomach, so that he survived in increasing agony for two months.

When at last he died (on 8 August 1928), he was allowed to lie in state; 'and for three days and nights the procession of peasants ... passing his body to take their last look at it, never ceased for a moment'.

CHAPTER 10

A Comedy of Good and Evil

On returning to Garreg Fawr in October 1922, Richard Hughes had to consider how best to earn his living. The *Weekly Westminster Gazette* was still running the series of articles based upon his letters from abroad; he could find plenty of work as a book reviewer; and he continued to write short stories. But none of these seemed likely to bring him the money and reputation he desired: so where did his real future lie?

Probably not as a poet. It was flattering when a Chicago publisher wrote to tell him that he was 'recognised in this country as a poet of distinction';[1] but *Gipsy-Night and Other Poems* had been a critical and commercial disaster, with the only decent review in the *Spectator*, no more than 250 copies sold in England, and only 130 in America.[2]

Perhaps as a playwright? Hughes had already proved his talent for the stage; the complimentary verdicts of Masefield and other critics had been reinforced by W.B. Yeats, who wrote to tell him that although *The Sisters' Tragedy* was unsuitable for the Abbey Theatre in Dublin, it proved his 'real dramatic gift, a gift in character development and plot'.[3] Clearly, the 'rational thing' was 'to write at once plays and more plays, and thrust them into the breach which *The Sisters' Tragedy* had made in the managerial defences'.

Lacking a compelling new theme, Diccon decided to dramatise two of his own short stories: 'Poor Man's Inn' (written at Oxford) and 'The Stranger' (written one night during a thunderstorm under the Biancos' roof in New Jersey);[4] and as soon as he was able, 'and had begun to sleep soundly again and not look for an ambush in every thicket on the Welsh hillside', he 'settled down quietly' to some steady work, finding that he could write 'about two minutes of acting-time each day'.[5]

'Poor Man's Inn' was adapted as a one-act play entitled *The Man Born to be Hanged*, and Hughes had completed it by Christmas 1922. Its principal themes are the violence of thwarted love and the absurdity of passion; but the story itself is a simple one.

Bill, a travelling entertainer who is down on his luck, seeks shelter with several others in a ruined cottage where they find that a tramp is sleeping off a bout of heavy drinking. Bill is engaging and larger-than-life, and we are tempted to condone his failings until one of his companions, a cloaked woman, reveals herself as his victim.

This is Nell, his jilted wife, a fundamentally good woman absurdly but passionately in love with this sentimental rogue. She is so angry with Bill that she shoots at him, but then realises that she cannot live without him; and later a shaft of moonlight picks out her dead body: she has committed suicide.

Bill (who was only playing dead) is shocked by the depths of Nell's feelings for him, but has no wish to risk arrest; so he leaves her corpse next to that of the sleeping tramp, who by a savagely ironic twist has become the man born to be unjustly hanged for her murder.[6]

By the time he had completed *The Man Born to be Hanged*, Hughes had also begun adapting 'The Stranger' which, as *A Comedy of Good and Evil*, would become his first full-length play. It is in part a celebration of the good humour and vitality of Welsh village life; and as he wrote it, Hughes was aware of a number of parallels between the Welsh villagers and the Croat peasants, both of them politically and culturally enslaved by their foreign masters.

A political revolution in Wales might not come (Hughes thought) for a generation.[7] But if Croatian nationalism (as he had seen) was immensely strengthened by the songs and festivals which sprang naturally from a peasant way of life, could not Welsh nationalism be similarly encouraged by the establishment of a living theatrical tradition?

Sometime over Christmas, he discussed the matter with the Satows, to whom he appeared (after his 'mysterious wanderings' in the Balkans) like 'some mythical hero, straight from the heights of Olympus'. Gwenol was particularly pleased to see Diccon, as from time to time he would 'walk over the mountains just to educate' her, pulling 'a much-thumbed copy of Butcher and Lang's translation of the *Odyssey* from his coat pocket . . . [and] rolling the words lingeringly around his tongue, like tasting a sweet food'. Now he had brought back not only a fund of good stories, but also a new trick to amuse her: striking matches with his toes, which he claimed he had learned from a lion-tamer in Budapest.[8]

On New Year's Day 1923, Diccon also called on Alfred Perceval Graves, Robert's seventy-six-year-old father, who had produced several pageants at Harlech Castle, and with whom he discussed his plans over lunch at Erinfa. Several other members of the clan were present (including Rosaleen and John); and the first thing they all noticed was Diccon's beard. Gwenol had detested it; but APG (himself heavily bearded) thought it 'rather improved him', and listened with interest as Diccon recounted his adventures in Croatia and then stayed on until after five to talk about 'the question of plays for Portmadoc and here'.[9]

At the heart of Diccon's thinking was the establishment throughout Wales of local theatre companies from whose ranks would eventually be drawn the company of a Welsh National Theatre; and he told the Graveses (as he had told the Satows) that he had already decided to start the ball rolling in his own area by gathering together a company of amateurs.[10]

Exactly a fortnight after Diccon's conference with the Graveses came the first performance (in the old kitchens at Brondanw, by kind permission of Clough and Amabel) of a double bill consisting of *The Poacher* by J.O. Francis and *The Man Born to be Hanged* by Richard Hughes. In his own play, Diccon gave what APG described as 'a very realistic rendering of his hero'; while the lovely Gwenol Satow (who had easily been persuaded to play opposite him) was 'excellent' as Nell.[11]

The evening was such a success that Diccon felt confident enough to form his amateurs into a proper company, of which he undertook to be actor-manager. 'We had no money', he later recalled, 'except five pounds I put up myself towards the venture: and for rehearsals I used to collect out-lying members of the cast on the carrier of a motor-cycle.' A.O. Roberts, another young playwright, was co-founder of the 'Portmadoc Players'; and the local magnate Lord Howard de Walden agreed to be president.

Diccon was developing a gift for publicity; and he drew up a declaration of intent which on 27 February 1923 appeared in the *Manchester Guardian*. According to this, the aims of the Portmadoc Players were:[12]

(1) To read and produce as artistically as we can plays by the best authors, especially those of young Welshmen, whether writing in Welsh or in English.
(2) To encourage the serious study of the technique of playwriting, acting, and play production, and of all those crafts which help towards artistic stage production.
(3) To support enthusiastically all those who are striving towards the common ideal of a Welsh National Theatre which shall be worthy of the race and country to which we belong.

They were to open at Portmadoc Town Hall on Wednesday 4

April, with three one-act plays: A.O. Roberts's *The Cloud Break*, together with the two plays previously performed at Brondanw.

When Robert and Nancy came up to Erinfa for a short holiday, and went over to spend a night with Diccon and Louisa at Garreg Fawr,[13] they learned that Amabel Williams-Ellis had persuaded Nigel Playfair, the highly regarded London actor-manager, to attend Diccon's opening;[14] Robert's father had promised to cover the event for the *Liverpool Post*; and in due course Robert himself was persuaded to review the evening for the *Manchester Guardian*.[15]

Alfred Perceval Graves, who attended the first night with a party which included Robert, Nancy and Charles, afterwards noted in his diary that:[16]

> *The Man Born to be Hanged* went off better than I hoped fr[om] such an audience; *The Poacher* was well played; & considering that *The Cloud Break* had been so little rehearsed it was well played by Gladys Williams [a young Welsh girl who was one of the 'discoveries' of the evening], Diccon, and [Roberts].

Nigel Playfair had been so impressed that he had told Hughes that arrangements must be set in hand for the Portmadoc Players to bring their productions to the Lyric, Hammersmith (his London theatre); and Diccon's pleasure was flawed only when he saw the *Manchester Guardian* review on Friday morning. It was A.O. Roberts who had persuaded the *Manchester Guardian* to ask Robert to review the plays – and yet in the review (jointly written by Robert and Charles, to whom Robert had turned for help) there was no mention at all of *The Cloud Break*. Diccon sent an angry telegram demanding to know which of the brothers had been responsible.[17]

Robert vigorously protested his innocence, and Charles was allowed to shoulder the blame,[18] but in any case Diccon had no time to follow up the matter. He had already made plans for a continental excursion. By Sunday morning he was already on his way to London; and from there, on Monday 9 April, he and Jim Bennett set out for Paris.[19]

Diccon spent a few days in Paris with Bennett; and then he travelled on alone to Rome where he met the eighteen-year-old poet Peter Quennell, with whom he had arranged to spend a week or ten days in Sicily. Hughes had been acting as a kind of literary godfather to this outstanding young poet, publishing his work in *Public Schools Verse*, and bringing it to the attention of men like John Masefield (who found it unreadable), Edward Marsh (who included some of Quennell's poems in his final volume of *Georgian*

Poetry), and Robert Graves (who was 'enthusiastic').[20]

In Rome, the two men acquired a third travelling-companion, Pilley, 'an amusing young man', and also an extremely brilliant one, with whom they travelled on to Palermo, a 'lovely town . . . set in . . . a semi-circle of . . . golden cliffs'. The very next night found the three of them roped together on the side of a 4000-foot mountain, waiting for the dawn and enjoying what Hughes described as[21]

> the most wonderful view in the world: inland mountain after mountain stretching away towards Aetna; the whole north coast of the island, with the great rock of Cefalu: late at night, Stromboli sending flashes of light up out of the sea.

They also inspected the unfinished Greek Temple at Segesta, and scaled Mount Eryx which in Greek times, as Diccon reported to Louisa,

> was supposed to be the favourite temple of Aphrodite . . . Imagine a mountain nearly 3000 feet high, precipitory on *all* sides, hanging right over the sea, with a large town at the very top . . . practically unchanged since the middle ages.

Diccon was pleased by the effect of Pilley's brilliance upon Peter Quennell. Previously, Diccon had found the young poet a little too full of himself; but now he had become 'quiet, thoughtful and efficient . . . oh so changed', Diccon told Louisa, 'you would hardly know him'.[22]

On the way back to England, Hughes escorted Quennell as far as Rome; where he found a letter waiting for him at the British Consulate. Before leaving England, Hughes had written to J.L. Garvin of the *Observer* asking whether he would be prepared to pay for an article on various Balkan matters; and now Garvin had replied:[23]

> As it happens I am very specially interested in the connected group of Adriatic and Danubian questions on which you are making yourself an authority . . . the best thing would be to send us an article of a thousand words upon the new situation in Yugoslavia.

Hughes immediately set out by land first for Venice (which he reached on 30 April); and then 'trusting in the disguise of my newly-grown beard', he crossed the border into Yugoslavia. Soon he was back in Zagreb, where he spent 'a few nights with my former leader. An intrepid old gas-bag and a genius [Radić] had completely won my devotion'.[24]

After gaining the information needed for his article, Diccon 'did a sort of Phillips-Oppenheim dash across Europe, by steamer aeroplane motor-boat train and car, to get back [to London] and sell it before it was stale'. 'Balkan politics', he told Louisa on his return to London, 'keep worse than eggs.'[25]

Back by the end of May 1923 in the cloyingly domestic surroundings of Garreg Fawr, Hughes resumed work on *A Comedy of Good and Evil*, which he had set in a 'rather poky little Welsh kitchen'.[26] Like *The Sisters' Tragedy*, it is a play full of moral ambivalence. Hughes later wrote that it derived partly from 'a predilection I then had for taking a conventional notion and turning it inside out to see how it looked like that: a predilection which was the mainspring of [much of my work] at the time. On this occasion of course the notion turned inside out was that of Conscience'.[27] Soon after the curtain rises, the Revd John Williams tells himself that it is 'a grand terrible thing to be a humble soldier, fighting the shadowy battles of the Lord: fighting for the forces Good against the forces Evil. Yes. But there are times when it is not easy to tell which is which'.[28]

John Williams and his one-legged wife Minnie are visited by a little girl thought by Minnie to be an angel, until Gladys (as they call her) burns her hand when she touches the Bible, which shows that she is really a devil in disguise. However, just as a saint might have a powerful faith in God, and yet be tempted by evil thoughts, so Gladys has a powerful faith in the Devil ('If I'm not bad,' she cries out, 'I'm nothing!')[29] but is constantly tempted to do good.

But if faith in good and evil are equally strong, and if in any case good and evil cannot exist without each other, then how on earth are we to behave for the best? As usual at this stage of his writing, Hughes delights in moral paradox. John Williams, for example, is condemned to Hell for consorting with a devil, and yet he has only followed the Christian precept of loving his enemy; while Gladys, trying to do her worst, falls so far short of her ideals that she cannot resist conducting him to Heaven.

But although this is essentially a play of ideas, Hughes stirred into the plot a good deal of broadly theatrical humour: as when Gladys (who has risked using good means for a bad end) replaces Minnie's wooden leg. Not only is the new leg made of real flesh and blood, but (much to Minnie's alarm) it behaves independently with a seductiveness and sophistication utterly at odds with the body to which it is attached.

Besides dealing with *A Comedy of Good and Evil*, and his normal burden of book reviewing, Hughes was preparing for the Golden

Cockerel Press[30] an edition of the poems of John Skelton, a largely forgotten poet to whose work he had been introduced by Robert Graves.

Skelton had been born about the year 1460, and in his own day (as Hughes pointed out in his introduction) Skelton's reputation[31]

> was international. Oxford, Cambridge, and Louvain crowned him with laurel: he was tutor to Henry VIII and Orator Regius: Erasmus, Caxton, and other smaller fry praised him immoderately.

After his death in 1526, however, his style of writing had been overtaken by the Elizabethan revolution; and since then he had been largely forgotten. True, there had been a scholarly edition by Dyce in 1843; but, as Hughes commented, 'God help any poet who hopes to be rescued from oblivion by the scholars!'

Hughes's intention was to produce 'a selection from his poems, aimed rather at the lover of poetry than the lover of literary, social, or linguistic history', and declared that his work had been 'undertaken in the hope of winning for [Skelton] his just place (after four centuries of neglect) among the poets who are read'.

Richard Hughes himself particularly admired Skelton's 'descriptions of birds and young girls'. In lines like those on 'Maystres Jane Scroupe', Skelton depicted pre-adolescent girls with all the joy and radiance which Hughes recognised in his own friends of that age. Jane, in Skelton's words,[32]

> is the vyolet
> The daysy delectable
> The columbine commendable
> The jelofer amyable;
> For this most goodly floure
> So Jupiter me succour
> She florysheth new and new
> In beauty and vertew.

Hughes also put in a word for Skelton's single surviving play *Magnyfycence*: 'the idea of drama it serves was not then invented', he tells us; but if it were produced in modern times 'it could not fail to create a sensation'.

While working on his various projects, Diccon was also doing his best to be a good companion to Louisa, attending the Harlech music festival with her in drizzling rain,[33] or joining her for an evening of supper and bridge with the Graveses (where for once he seemed to APG to be 'rather a fish out of water').[34] But he found her too demanding and oppressive; and in the autumn of 1923 he told her that he must go down to London to sell some of his work, and he escaped to lodgings in Adelphi Terrace.

Hughes had taken with him the completed text of *A Comedy of Good and Evil*, a number of short stories and the determination to stay away from Louisa for as long as possible. (She still washed his clothes, though, and they would exchange bundles of clean and dirty clothing through the post.) When in mid October Louisa wrote a plaintive letter asking about his return, Diccon replied very firmly that there was 'no immediate prospect of my coming back'. So far, his earnings were no more than £60; but he was 'meeting all sorts of people I ought to meet, and beginning to make some headway'. In particular, he had showed *A Comedy of Good and Evil* to J.C. Squire, who had liked it so much that he had offered to encourage the Stage Society to give a performance.[35]

By the end of November, he had moved to a tiny and often extremely chilly attic in New Oxford Street, where he busied himself with writing bread-and-butter reviews;[36] and he had also acquired a new agent, Curtis Brown, who had very rapidly succeeded in selling his short story 'Poor Man's Inn' to *Hutchinson's Mystery Magazine* for seven guineas.[37]

Louisa had become increasingly depressed during his long absence,[38] but he returned to Garreg Fawr for a week or two at Christmas; and while he was at home he began exploring the dramatic possibilities of an altogether new medium.

When the British Broadcasting Company was established in 1922 (within a few months of the very first authorised wireless broadcasts) part of its remit was to provide 'theatrical entertainment'; and yet by Christmas 1923 not a single play had been broadcast. Sitting in his chilly attic in Oxford Street, Hughes had become intrigued by the possibilities. A successful play for the wireless would involve a new combination of skills, in particular[39]

> the poetic technique of sensory stimulation, using the devices of indirect suggestion, the tricks and feints by which Keats and the Elizabethans make you sweat or shiver or dazzle at will; all this, together with the action, breathing through the dialogue . . . men talking . . . as if for them . . . the visible world really existed.

And over Christmas at Garreg Fawr he produced the first draft of a 'broadcasting play', and left it behind for his mother to read when he returned to London.

Writing to Louisa in the early hours of New Year's Day 1924

(Diccon was now mixing in high society, had been supping and dancing till 2 a.m. at Lady Townshend's, and had then gone on with 'a few indefatigably to the Ritz, where we danced some more'), he asked his mother to bring the play with her when she came up to London on 5 January.[40]

And then one Friday night (less than a week after Louisa's arrival in London with his play) Diccon Hughes was dining with Sir Nigel Playfair. Sir Nigel had kept the promise he made to Diccon the previous April, and their chief business was to discuss arrangements for a forthcoming performance by the Portmadoc Players at the Lyric Theatre. Over coffee, however (as Diccon later recalled), Sir Nigel[41]

> mentioned that he was engaged to put an hour's semi-theatrical entertainment on the air the next [Tuesday] evening. He was himself reading a passage from Jane Austen, he said; and one of A.A. Milne's *Punch* dialogues would be read in parts by actors. He had not quite decided on a third item.[42]
>
> 'You know, Hughes', he remarked suddenly, 'I believe what is really wanted for broadcasting is something specially written for the job. A pity there's no time now to get it done; we begin rehearsing after lunch tomorrow.'

With a play already in draft form (though it seemed politic not to mention this at the time) the opportunity was too good to miss.[43] Diccon modestly hoped that he could write something suitable in the time, and would like to have a try. 'Sir Nigel's eye', as Diccon continues the story,

> went small; and bland, like the eye of a calculating fish. 'Ten guineas,' he said, 'for all rights.'
>
> 'You mayn't like my play when you read it. Let's leave terms till the morning', I countered.
>
> But I didn't really care about the terms: I was afire with excitement . . . I went home and wrote all night.

And over breakfast the following morning, Hughes was ready to read out his revised and polished work to Playfair. He had called it at first *A Comedy of Danger*; and then simply *Danger*.[44]

Since wireless drama would be a new experience, Hughes had the idea of setting *Danger* in the dark; so an announcer asks the audience to turn out their lights, explaining that the scene is a coal-mine. Then, in the darkness, two voices are heard:

> MARY [sharply]. Hello! What's happened?
> JACK. The lights have gone out!

At first the young lovers assume it is a temporary power failure; and just when they are beginning to become frightened, they are joined by Bax, a crusty old English gentleman, who complains:

> I'd expect anything of a country like Wales! They've got a climate like the flood and a language like the Tower of Babel, and then they go and lure us into the bowels of the earth and turn the lights off!

But then an explosion is heard, followed by the sound of rushing water. In the distance, trapped miners sing until their voices are extinguished.

Realising that they have been caught up in a pit disaster, and are in danger of death, Mary and Bax are by turns frightened, angry and resigned; while Jack, with his occasional wild laughter, betrays the most neurotic and morbid nature of the three. Like Hughes, Jack is a writer who believes strongly in the importance of his work: 'What do you think I've got to live for, besides myself and Mary?' he asks Bax. 'Why, my work! If it wasn't for that, I'd go to death without caring a tuppeny damn! I'd die just for the fun of the thing, to see what it felt like.' And by the time the water has reached their waists, Jack has begun to welcome death: 'Now I am so nearly dead', he declares, 'I wouldn't come back to life for anything. There's such a lot to find out, the other side.'

It is Bax who desperately wants to live. When Jack unkindly remarks that the prospect of death must be easier for an old man, Bax retorts:

> D'you think it is any easier for the old to die than the young? I tell you it's harder, sir, harder! Life is like a trusted friend, he grows more precious as the years go by. What's your life to mine? A shadow, sir! Yours, twenty-odd years of imbecile childhood, lunatic youth; the rest a mere rosy presumption of the future! Mine, sixty solid years of solid, real living; no mere rosy dream! Do you think it is as easy for me to leave my solid substance as you to leave your trumpery shadow?'

However, when rescuers break through the roof of the tunnel, and lower a rope, it is Bax who drowns because he nobly refuses to be hauled up until the other two have reached safety. Jack is left with Bax's encouraging words ringing in his ears: 'Give you something to write about . . . my boy.'

Sir Nigel Playfair liked what he had heard. *Danger*, by Richard Hughes, went into rehearsal a few hours later, and was broadcast on Tuesday 15 January 1924. It was the world's first radio play, and received excellent notices. Not only had the story been dramatic; but the special effects had worked well: hollow mine-entombed voices were produced by speaking into buckets; the Welsh miners' chorus had sung uninterrupted behind doors which were simply opened whenever the sound was wanted; and the press (who listened to the play in darkness from a room inside Broadcasting House) were particularly excited by the deafening explosion. (In rehearsal, the first 'explosion' had shattered the microphone; so in performance, a much smaller 'explosion' was arranged close to the microphone; while at the vital moment the press were treated to a truly terrifying bang from the room next door to the one in which they were sitting.)[45]

Much of the six weeks after the premiere of *Danger* was spent on arranging for the London appearance of the Portmadoc Players. Nigel Playfair and his fellow directors had been willing to offer them the free use of the Lyric for a series of matinees; but because of the financial risk, the players decided to give only one performance. 'Even that', Nigel Playfair told them, 'would probably mount up to a risk of several hundred pounds, with the company to transport and house.' However, as Diccon later wrote, 'they were not to be daunted'. He himself worked hard[46]

> at the unfamiliar task of theatrical organisation ... [and] got together a committee ... [After which,] the Welsh Colony in London was canvassed, and proved most enthusiastic: a Welsh hotel-keeper even put up the company at his hotel entirely free for a week.

The press became intrigued; and when on 26 February, Richard Hughes and his Portmadoc Players gave a matinee performance of three one-act plays (including of course *The Man Born to be Hanged*), the house was

> packed twenty minutes before curtain up. Lloyd George was there, and many other prominent Welshmen. The Prince of Wales sent messages of good will: and the whole thing went off with a swing. The actors thoroughly enjoyed themselves, and seemed absolutely guiltless of stage-fright.

Amabel Williams-Ellis was also in the audience, and wrote to Diccon to 'congratulate you ... It really surpassed my wildest dreams. I thought your acting ... was excellent'.[47]

Three days after the performance of the Portmadoc Players, Hughes gave a celebratory party; but he was too overworked to derive much pleasure from his success. 'Yes', he wrote grimly to Hugh Lyon,[48]

> the matinee is all over, and now I have nothing to do except

finish my edition of Skelton, finish a volume of short stories, write a quarter of a novel, review 43 books, and rehearse a new production. So it looks as if I shall be really able to deal with the [Public Schools Verse] towards the end of the week. I mean this.

The nervous strain of supporting himself as a writer had become terrible. He had hired a secretary who was helping him clear the enormous back log of work[49] (though she was a little taken aback one morning to find him scrubbing the floor while she typed up one of his short stories);[50] but even her help was not enough. His 'grumbling appendix' flared up; and on 24 March he wrote to Heinemann (who had taken over his *Skelton*) that his doctors had advised an immediate operation.[51]

The operation was a success; lying in bed in Guy's Hospital came as a wonderful relief; and on Friday 4 April, after a week and a half in hospital, Diccon sent a postcard to a young woman called Nancy Stallibrass who had recently caught his eye. The attraction seems to have been mutual: for hardly had it been posted when he received a letter from her, saying that she proposed to come and visit him.[52]

Nancy Stallibrass was a highly attractive and highly-strung poet with dark soulful eyes which contrasted decoratively with her ash-blonde hair. Just a few weeks short of her nineteenth birthday, she had been educated at an expensive girls' school, but was open, frank and unspoiled. One admirer described her as the prettiest girl he had yet seen; another recalls that she was small and slender, and 'intensely feminine', with 'a charmingly cat-like head poised upon a graceful neck'.[53]

Nancy's father was an engineer who had made his money laying cables in South America, and then married into society; he now owned a country house in Gloucestershire, as well as the town apartment in South Kensington from where Nancy had written.[54] Through her mother's family, Nancy was related to one of the Oxford heads of college; and she and Diccon are thought to have met at a reception in Oxford.[55]

'Dear Miss Stallibrass', Diccon now replied, 'I'd love you to come and see me: but isn't hospital visiting rather an ordeal? I've never had the courage to visit a friend in hospital myself.' He added that he was 'getting on famously: well ahead of schedule: they take out my stitches tomorrow, so I shall then cease to look and feel like an untidily darned stocking'; and on Tuesday he would be moving to his godfather's house in Hampstead. Could Nancy visit him there?

'Bring your new poems', he urged her. 'I'm not really a bit ill: but I should like you to come!'[56]

She did so; and then one evening after he had returned to his attic in New Oxford Street, he called upon her out of the blue. Afterwards he felt that she had been bored, and wrote apologising: 'I'm afraid it was a great shame to drag you out like that.' But they had arranged to meet on the following Sunday; and she had given him some small trifles as 'hostages' to ensure her arrival.[57]

They were clearly attracted to each other, and for several weeks they continued to meet regularly; but Diccon had no idea how to advance the relationship. He was very good at dealing with women as honorary sisters, and thought nothing of defying convention and sleeping out on a Welsh mountainside next to a girl of fifteen;[58] but like many ex-public-schoolboys in those days he was alarmed by sexual warmth (he later admitted to having been 'scared stiff by the extrovert manners of stage people', with their intimate endearments and their social kissing);[59] and the prospect of an intimate relationship filled him with guilt and self-doubt.

Soon after Diccon's twenty-fourth birthday, he and Nancy were sitting in 'the garden at Battersea', when she asked him[60]

> what was the best way to give their quietus to people who were in love with you? 'What age?' I asked: 'sixteen?' 'No; older', [she] said. My heart sank into my boots. 'Twenty-four?' I said. 'Yes, more about that age', [she] answered.

Diccon immediately assumed that he was the twenty-four-year-old she meant; and felt so utterly wretched that after one more meeting he retreated to Garreg Fawr, from where at the end of April he sent her a letter of chilling formality, which he must have assumed would bring their friendship to an end.[61]

Nancy was not so easily deterred. She replied to Diccon's letter accusing him of making her feel 'like a very respectable nursery governess'; added diplomatically that she had been reading and admiring the work of his protégé Peter Quennell; and also enclosed two poems of her own, asking him not to comment upon them too severely.[62]

Diccon was delighted. Abandoning his customary 'Dear Miss Stallibrass', he addressed her warmly in his letter of 2 May as 'My dear Nancy', apologised for making her feel respectable ('I will not err again'), and promised not to say devastating things about her poems. 'In fact', he declared, 'they seem to me much the best things of yours I have yet seen.' He continued with some detailed criticisms; and in his enthusiasm, he suggested that she should take one of the poems to Squire, and see whether he would have it for the *Mercury*, '& if he won't, then call him all justifiable names & take it to the *Spectator*'.[63]

'It was simply too angelic of you', Nancy replied on 14 May, 'to take so much trouble criticising those wretched poems.' She had done as he suggested[64]

> and sent that poem and two others to J.C. Squire who returned them with the following exasperating remarks 'I like your poems very much and indeed I nearly accepted "The Ghost" but it takes a lot to get past us at present as we are overcrowded. I should be very pleased to see some more later on'.

After what she described as this 'crushing defeat', Nancy had not dared to try the *Spectator*. And now she asked Diccon: 'When are you coming back? How are the stories getting on? You say nothing whatever about yourself – which I most wanted to hear', and she added: 'I've been getting horribly disillusioned about everyone & everything – and can write nothing but morbid poems about dead bodies!'

Nancy's letter demanded some kind of emotional response; but instead of replying to it at once, Diccon brooded over it for a few days, and then took himself off to spend a week among the Welsh islands.

When Diccon returned, he heard that definite arrangements had been made for *A Comedy of Good and Evil* to be performed on 6 July (under the auspices of the Three Hundred Club) at the Royal Court Theatre.[65] Diccon decided to attend the rehearsals;[66] and on Friday 6 June, shortly before going down to London, he finally replied to Nancy's last letter.

Instead of being more open with Nancy, as she had hoped, Diccon had become extremely guarded. He began not with the affectionate 'My dear' but with plain 'Dear Nancy'; though he informed her that he had[67]

> a passion for islands ... & the Welsh ones are some of the best I have seen: mostly uninhabited, except by puffins and seals, with the most wonderful cliffs and caves, and often quite large. One, with fifty inhabitants, has a King – so far as I know the only other monarch in the British isles, besides George: he has a crown and full regalia, and duly declared war on Germany [in 1914] by posting a notice on the chapel door! I met him not long ago, in a pub in Aberdaron: & bought a lobster from him.[68]

He added that Nancy 'ought to see Wales', and not only for its 'oddities', but because 'I think there is going to be a most holy psychological explosion in a generation or so, & it is just as well to see these things beforehand'.

In the meantime (saying nothing about the play rehearsals which would bring him down to London almost immediately and keep him there for weeks), Diccon revealed only that he was 'making an attempt to come to London for the week-end', and he asked her:

> may I descend on you on Sunday? Because I am sure you have written fourteen or fifteen pounds of poetry during the last two months: & unless I apply for them personally it is quite plain I shall never see them!

Should he succeed in his attempt to reach London, he would telephone.

There was of course no problem in reaching London: Diccon travelled down to Hampstead on Saturday. The real attempt was to keep his feelings for Nancy in check; and in this he very happily failed. On Sunday he called on Nancy for tea, and stayed to supper; and on Monday he took her out to supper himself. Impressed by Nancy's intelligence, and deeply touched by her sensitivity (she told him about the 'nightmare feelings' she sometimes had as she lay awake at night), Diccon was falling in love. Explaining that he would now be in London for some time, as rehearsals of his play were due to begin the following morning, he invited her to a performance of *Romeo and Juliet* on the coming Friday.[69]

The cast of *A Comedy of Good and Evil* was a respectable one, with Leslie Banks playing the part of Mr Williams, and Louise Hampton that of Minnie; but what most pleased Diccon was that the central role of Gladys was to be played by Hermione Baddeley, a young actress whose beauty, warmth and deliciously seductive voice had excited him the previous autumn.[70] Diccon took her out to lunch on the second day of rehearsals; and she was one of several young women (including Gwenol Satow) whom Diccon entertained during the next ten days, as if to convince himself that his passions were not becoming fully engaged elsewhere.[71]

However, by the time *A Comedy of Good and Evil* was presented on Sunday 6 July, Diccon could no longer conceal the fact that he was wildly in love with Nancy; and, to his incredulous delight, she returned his feelings. Louisa had come down from Wales to watch the performance; and afterwards, by using her as an occasional chaperone, Diccon and Nancy were able to spend most of the following week together.

During that week, they began talking about getting married. Diccon's only fear was Nancy might not take to being the wife of a Welsh cottager; and so it was agreed that they should become engaged as soon as possible, and then travel up to Garreg Fawr, where Nancy could experience Diccon's way of life at first hand. But before they could become engaged, they must consult Nancy's parents: not only for loving family reasons, but because if they wished to get married before Nancy's twenty-first birthday (almost two years away) they needed her parents' permission. And so (believing that she would be the more sympathetic of the two) they began by taking Nancy's mother into their confidence.

CHAPTER 11

Unofficially Engaged

Mrs Stallibrass was a deeply conventional woman who thoroughly distrusted writers and artists (especially when they were poor), and was horrified by the prospect of her daughter marrying someone so obviously unsuitable as Diccon Hughes. As for the two of them going off to Wales together, with only Diccon's mother as chaperone, it was clearly out of the question. However, she could see that Nancy was head-over-heels in love; and she decided that the safest thing to do was to play for time.

It was fortunate, she told them, that they had come to her first. It would have been madness for them to confront her husband. Their engagement would have to remain unofficial for the time being; but if they agreed to defer their Welsh holiday (at least for a few weeks, until Mr Stallibrass had left the country on a business trip), she would endeavour (in due course) to win him over to their cause.[1]

Mrs Stallibrass appeared to be on their side; and Diccon and Nancy reluctantly agreed to fall in with her demands (though Diccon was extremely annoyed about being unable to take Nancy to Wales at once, and later regretted the fact that he must have appeared to be 'an absolute bear-cub'). So on Monday 14 July Diccon and Louisa (installed in the sidecar of his motor bike) set out alone for North Wales.

It was a terrible journey: the machine 'collapsed utterly' at Coventry, and they had to 'leave it behind and come on by train, travelling all night – 13 hours – five changes'. And on waking up at Garreg Fawr on Tuesday morning, Diccon found (as he wrote to Nancy), that it was[2]

> just as I expected, Wales seems an absolute MONSTER without you: coming back like this and seeing everything & then remembering in my mind's eye I had seen YOU against its background, rubs in your not coming a thousand times worse.

He was determined, he wrote, that they should 'get full measure' for their self-sacrifice; he asked her to let him know 'as soon as you can where you are going and when I can see you'; and he added:

Darling, darling, DARLING, I love you so I feel it will burst out of me suddenly like a thunderclap, & leave my body all cracked up on the grass. But I hope it isn't! And it shan't: all that gigantic shadowy force bottled up inside me, when we're together, dearest, will move the earth, shelve the rocks into the sea. And then at times I feel awful to think that YOU should be wasted on a person like me: who am really worth nothing at all, couldn't shift a pebble, except for the love of you in me . . . I feel even now the dread that you MUST someday open your eyes, and see how misguided you are to tolerate me!

And now it was time for him to stop writing long letters, and begin 'the work that shall make the money that shall pay for the house that Jack shall build . . . Dearest', he concluded, 'write to me fifty times a day, & I'll write to you as often as I can't help!'

Diccon had been working at Garreg Fawr for just over a week, when he heard from Nancy that she and her mother were planning to holiday in the West Country once her father had gone abroad; and she asked whether he would like to join them there for a few days. 'Beloved', he replied, 'Devon would be simply wonderful: and as SOON as possible.' He was now so much in love, that in his eyes Nancy embodied every kind of perfection. 'How *DO* you write sonnets?' he asked her.[3]

And isn't it rather a shame that you should pinch all the beauties, and all the talents, and all the virtues the way you do; & really leave none for the rest of the world at all? It really does convince me that heaven isn't just! You ought to be either stupid, or ugly, or villainous, to make up for having the other two!

In his waking moments, Diccon was alarmed by how happy he felt, fearing divine retribution; and when he was asleep, perplexing images bubbled up into his mind. One nightmare was particularly vivid. He knew that he was on the banks of the Danube; and he could see a canoe floating downriver, empty but for Nancy, who was seated 'very primly' at its 'extreme end. So I seized hold of a handy trapeze', he told her, &

swung myself about half a mile out into mid-stream, ready to land in the canoe. And when I got there, I found I had made a mistake: it was not you at all, but a Serbian policeman, who promptly put us under arrest. So I stamped on the canoe till it sank, and woke up yelling.

Attributing this nightmare (to which he attached no significance) to his having eaten cheese sauce at supper, he went on to ask Nancy for a photograph of herself: 'Because, if I had your face pinned firmly down on a piece of paper, perhaps it wouldn't be quite so given to floating in between me & the book I am trying to review, & then skipping out of the window the moment I whistle for it.'

Hughes's work that summer of 1924 included not only book reviews for the *Spectator*, but also articles for the *New Statesman*, correcting the proofs of his *Skelton* for Heinemann,[4] and dealing with the English and American editions of his collected plays (published by Heinemann as *The Sisters' Tragedy and three other plays*, and by Knopf as *The Rabbit and a Leg*).[5] At the same time, Hughes was searching for a publisher for a book on *The History of the Lyric Theatre* which he had agreed to 'ghost' for Nigel Playfair, but it was an idea about which both Heinemann[6] and the Bodley Head[7] were deeply pessimistic; and he even wrote some material for a prospective music-hall entertainer, who then 'decided not to go on the Halls after all, so that is a whole fortnight's work down the sink. However, I am getting used to that sort of thing,' he told Nancy. 'The *Spectator* seem the only honest people anywhere.'[8] At the beginning of August, feeling somewhat dispirited, Diccon used the Bank Holiday weekend as an excuse to escape from his desk and catch a train to London.

Mrs Stallibrass found that she was surprisingly pleased to see Diccon Hughes again. Although he was a writer, he seemed to work hard; he had been to a good school; and (most important) he had been ready to defer to her wishes over the proposed Welsh holiday, even when he had clearly disagreed with her. She was unwilling to lose Nancy, upon whom (having a moderately unhappy marriage) she had come to depend for emotional support; but perhaps in acquiring Diccon as a son-in-law, the area of her control might actually be extended.[9]

Unfortunately, Diccon now made what he would later describe as 'a fatal mistake'. Had he acted pragmatically, and tried to smooth over any areas of difficulty between himself and his prospective mother-in-law, all might have been well. Instead (since it was 'inconceivable' to him 'that anyone could *really* disagree with things which seemed so crystal-clear') he 'expressed open disagreement, believing it to be the only way of arriving at ultimate agreement'.

In particular, Diccon 'made open confession' of his wish to alter Nancy's 'way of thinking & living'. He explained very forcefully (with Nancy present) how important it was for his future wife to develop into an independent adult capable of making her own moral choices, 'for God forbid', as he would later repeat to Nancy, 'that I should want to substitute *my* control for your mother's'.

Possibly he spoke so strongly because he was fighting on Nancy's behalf the very battle for emotional freedom which he had never successfully fought and won with his own mother. At any rate, this appears to have been the moment when Mrs Stallibrass, realising (as Diccon put it) that she would be losing a daughter rather than gaining a son, made a clear decision against him. From that moment (Diccon came to believe), she set out to prove to herself that in trying to keep Nancy wholly hers she was acting in Nancy's best interests: 'Therefore, I *must* be a bad character: therefore, I *am* a bad character! Q.E.D.'

Diccon did not see this at the time; but although it was still agreed that he should join Nancy and her mother for part of their holiday in the West Country, he realised that something had gone very wrong; and on returning to Garreg Fawr he sent Nancy a penitent letter. 'Beloved', he began on Tuesday 5 August,[10]

> I really feel ashamed to write to you, after being so rude to your mother: she may well hesitate to trust you to so unrestrained a creature! . . . But it was so difficult to get her to speak out without speaking out myself . . . & once I began I overdid it. I don't suppose she will ever really quite forgive me for it: not only the things I said, but the things I led you into saying (which was why I didn't want you to be there).

In an attempt to retrieve the situation, he told Nancy: 'It seems an odd thing, but all the time I was being so abusive I was really getting to love [your mother] more than I had ever before, there was a sort of magnificence in her expression.' But as the days went by, he felt unhappily that he was 'sinking slowly in a bog of burnt porridge'. In an effort to clear his head, he spent most of one night walking up Snowdon; and it was an enormous relief when on Friday morning a letter reached him from Nancy.[11]

She was safely established with her mother at the Foresters' Arms Hotel in Dunster, where he could follow her as soon as he pleased; and she wrote so anxiously and trustingly that his self-confidence was wonderfully restored. He replied that he would travel south as soon as 'Lord Douglas' had recovered from its latest mechanical failure (probably the following Tuesday); and he begged her not to like Dunster 'as much as you are one day going to like Wales!'

He wrote again on Saturday 'to soften the gap between Saturday and Tuesday, adding that when he saw her, he would 'kiss you like mad'; but now that he felt so secure, his journey south seemed less urgent. 'Don't worry yourself ill', he told her. 'It sounds callous to confess it, but I am fit as a fiddle! And writing like mad.'[12] And when on Sunday he wrote that his motor bike might easily not be repaired until the end of the week; but that in the meantime he was enjoying the weather, and had been 'finding all sorts of urgent jobs to do in the garden (at the expense of my reviewing, I am afraid!)'[13] Nancy wrote to complain that he was 'finding absence getting easier'.[14]

This drew from Diccon a cry of anguish. 'My dear, my dear', he began, 'What have I done or not done that you should reproach me?' And he promised to leave 'the very *minute* I have finished the *New Statesman* articles – even if it is at midnight, & I have to hold the broken bits of my machine in my hand!'[15] Two days later, on Thursday morning, he gave up waiting for 'Lord Douglas' to be repaired, and set out for Somerset by train. He arrived at the Foresters' Arms Hotel at about four o'clock. Much to his pleasure, Mrs Stallibrass had not yet returned from her afternoon constitutional; and so he and Nancy were able to sit down to tea alone.

This time, Mrs Stallibrass made it clear from the first that Diccon Hughes was not a welcome guest, and had only been invited on her daughter's absolute insistence. That evening, the young lovers were allowed to walk on to a nearby hill-top to watch for an eclipse of the moon which was due at 9.20;[16] and she made her displeasure felt when they failed to return until 10.40, twenty-five minutes later than had been agreed.

The following afternoon they drove over to Exmoor for a picnic lunch; and that evening Diccon wrote to Louisa with some satisfaction, begging her for another clean shirt and collar, because Nancy was being quite agreeably 'fierce about my clothing habits. When I pleaded that it wasn't so much the suits' fault in that I didn't look after them properly, she said I oughtn't to keep suits long enough for them to *want* looking after!'

Diccon was so happy in Nancy's company that he could not imagine an unsuccessful outcome to their relationship; and (recalling that members of the Brome had pledged, in the event of their marrying, to give their fellows a dinner) he sent Hugh Lyon a cheerful letter telling him that he was in the West Country, 'endeavouring to owe a dinner to the Brome'. He added that he was confronted with[17]

> a Dragonry of incredible efficiency ... which regards me as a Bad Wicked Artist up to No Good, with No Sense of Responsibility and so on, & so forth. All the same I do take a certain illicit pleasure in a fight – & I am certainly getting one!

However, he would be returning to Wales 'on Friday [29 August], Round One being over'.

He was wrong about that. On Thursday evening Mrs Stallibrass summoned Nancy and Diccon to her room, and laid down a new set of conditions, much fiercer than the last. She now believed, she told them, that she had probably been wrong to think of persuading her husband to agree to a wedding.

However, there was some doubt in her mind. She would therefore promise to raise no further objections to their marriage if (and only if) they would agree to a 'contract' by which they should not see or communicate with each other for six months. In the meantime, should Nancy prove to be 'disobedient', should she persist in communicating with Diccon, then her allowance would be cut off. Mrs Stallibrass added that she would be quite willing to call in the law if necessary; and that in any case she intended to take Nancy abroad as soon as possible for an indefinite period.

Diccon was so stunned by this onslaught, that he hardly knew what to say; but he agreed to consider the matter of a contract; and the following morning he set out miserably for North Wales, not arriving home (because of missed connections) till after midnight.

In his absence, Stella Watson and a woman friend of hers (an artist) had come to stay at Garreg Fawr; and after an agreeable Saturday morning spent talking to them, Diccon had only just sat down to write to Nancy, and 'had finished illuminating the address and date, so to speak, when something loomed out of the mist: & enter Robert Graves & his wife'. After lunching together, they spent the afternoon in 'wandering all over the house with kettles and things in our hands, talking all at once & very loud'; and in the evening Robert and Nancy invited Diccon, Stella and her friend to join them for supper at Erinfa.

Lord Douglas had been mended by now, and the sidecar was also serviceable; and so after Robert and his Nancy had 'melted into the mist' again, the others followed. Unfortunately Diccon had left his sidecar open to the elements, and it came on to rain, so that Stella and her friend were soaked to the skin by the time they roared up the steep driveway at Erinfa; but after they had dried out by a blazing fire in the drawing-room (surrounded by a host of Graveses), everyone had supper; and then they took turns telling stories to each other until after ten o'clock in the evening.[18]

Diccon had thoroughly enjoyed such congenial company; and he had also had a long and fruitful conversation with Robert about the psychology of his problems with Mrs Stallibrass.[19] On Sunday morning, when he sat down to write a long letter to the woman he loved, he mentioned Robert's visit (though he discreetly said nothing

about their evening at Erinfa, or about the presence of Stella and her
friend at Garreg Fawr), and he told Nancy that he had been 'thinking
a lot about your mother's Exposition t'other night: & I think I have
come to some fairly clear conclusions'.

It was evidently 'quite hopeless' to try and convert Mrs Stallibrass,
since her method of thought was not rational but emotional; and she
sincerely believed that[20]

> the rational arguments, invented originally as a secondary jus-
> tification, were really the mainspring of her thought: to use
> psychological jargon, she is very prone to False Rationalisation.

Diccon added that she clearly liked Nancy to be absolutely dependent
upon her, wished to control every aspect of her life, and very much
disliked the idea of her growing-up, and 'becoming a really *separate*
identity'.

So what was to be done? Diccon suggested to Nancy that she
should avoid all conflicts with Mrs Stallibrass ('for they can do no
good'); while simultaneously avoiding all control. 'You must make
her see', Diccon advised,

> that you are *not* a child any more: but that ceasing to need her
> authority and protection does not in the least mean ceasing to love
> her. For her to talk about obedience and disobedience with a girl
> of nineteen is simply fantastic: I mean, you can completely *ignore*
> it.

Most of her threats were 'pure bluff'; if she persisted about going
abroad, Nancy should 'simply refuse. She can't make you go'; and
if the situation became completely intolerable, Nancy should

> say that you will leave home & earn your own living altogether
> – which you can always do, remember, *by coming as secretary to
> me*. Provided you come as a secretary, & duly chaperoned by my
> mother, she cannot prevent you.

In the meantime, they would have to meet surreptitiously in London:
it should be easy enough for Nancy to 'invent various pretexts for
going out'.

Diccon concluded his letter by apologising for so many 'dry-
as-dusteries', and writing a paragraph of ecstatic adoration:

> Beloved & beloved & BELOVED ... It is *because* you are so
> wonderful that I feel the fight to make you altogether & wholly
> *you* is so absolutely necessary ... never was it more important than
> to free such a holy & wonderful thing as you! There is not an inch
> of your body, a single twist of your thought, a millimetric fraction
> of you, mind, body, or spirit that isn't so absolutely different and
> distinct from everyone else in the world, so worth all the rest of the

world put together! I love you, darling, with an absolute devoted love: I am all transmuted into love of you, liquid love that you can run through your fingers & over your shoulders, or drink with your lips: & yet which can crouch itself together strong as a lion to fight for you & protect you, & then melt away into a liquid gold again, gentle as water, rather than EVER 'protect' you against your will! Except *you*, there is nothing of me left: I am become the ends of your fingers & the tips of your hair, the lashes of your eye: we are as much one being as a single flame springing from two logs of wood. Darling and beloved Nance, with so much one-ness burning in me it cannot be for long that we shall be in any way separate.

On the morning of Monday 1 September, when Diccon was just about to post this, he received a very distressed letter from Nancy.[21] Almost soon as Diccon had left, she told him, a storm had broken about her head. She had been informed that her allowance was to be cut off immediately, and that if she had any further communication with Diccon, then her father would be informed. It was therefore not safe for Diccon to use her home address, and he should send his letters to the post office in Harrington Road, from where she could collect them unobserved.

Diccon replied by return of post, and for the rest of that week he and Nancy wrote to each other almost every day.[22] His first inclination was to rush down to London '& bear you straight away'; but instead he left the initiative firmly with Nancy, telling her on Monday that it was 'a little difficult to suggest what to do'. Personally, he felt that unless the situation improved rapidly, she should 'run away to here, & make terms with your Mother before your return'. But perhaps she had better wait another week until her father had gone away again on one of his frequent business trips, 'so to avoid a row between him and your Mother – I feel we ought to save her that if we can'. In any event, the important thing was for Nancy to decide for herself. He would simply 'do *whatever* you want me to'.

The following morning, hearing that Mrs Stallibrass had slipped into a more sympathetic gear, and had drawn up a 'treaty' of the kind which had been talked about at Dunster, Diccon rushed this warning into the post, unprefaced by any endearments:

> *DON'T* sign that treaty, whatever you do, I hope to goodness this arrives before you are in any way committed to it. In the first place, what do we gain by it? Nothing: except a hazy promise from your mother 'not to do anything more to prevent our marriage'. That doesn't get us past your father, even if she honestly keeps her bargain: she could safely trust to *him* to refuse his consent, & we would be no better off.

Diccon reminded Nancy that the last time they had agreed to a 'treaty' with her mother, she had failed to keep her side of the bargain. 'But the really important point', he continued,

> is quite apart from this. I have put it to your mother again & again, but she is such an incredibly stupid woman she cannot see it. She cannot see that what I have in mind is not so much the immediate question of marriage – which at worst she can postpone for eighteen months, when you will be of age – but the far more important one of happiness *after* marriage.
>
> To be quite flat – if we were completely separated for six months, & if at the end of it she & your father were willing to have an immediate wedding, I myself would refuse to marry you until you had a real opportunity of trying my way of living. Six months isolation would test nothing whatever except the obstinacy of our emotions . . . How your mother can imagine that we are to come to any *real* conclusions about each other, *really* know any more of each other when 'we are not even to hear about each other' only a person as crass as herself can conceive.

Diccon was now very angry. He declared that entrusting their happiness to Nancy's mother would be 'like trusting the wheel of a car to a man who didn't know the difference between an accelerator and a brake'; that she had 'shown herself utterly unfit to be entrusted with shaping your life'; and that 'by disuse and misuse' her brains had entirely 'atrophied'.

If however Nancy was 'really convinced' that a treaty must be drawn up (and he would far prefer her to run away to him in Wales), then it could only be acceptable on the following terms:

> in the first place [that] your father should be a party to it, with what the diplomatists call 'adequate sanctions' to prevent them wriggling out of their bargain; & in the second, that you should first come down here for a month, to see me in my own setting & have some definite experience to meditate on during that absence: & that during that six months you should be free to mingle with intelligent people (your mother would want to prevent your meeting any of my friends either) in order to get illustration, as it were, of their world.

By the time Nancy received Diccon's letter, Mrs Stallibrass had cunningly consolidated her position by making two fraudulent claims upon Nancy's good nature. The first involved depicting herself as a cruelly treated wife whose daughter was her only remaining solace; and the second centred upon the suggestion that it would be selfish of Nancy to marry a struggling writer, thereby dragging him completely into the mire.

On Wednesday afternoon, therefore, Diccon heard from Nancy that she was worried about her mother's suffering; and that, however much she loved him, it was 'fundamental' that she could never marry him unless she could bring a substantial dowry to the wedding.

'My darling', he replied, 'Don't you see it isn't fundamental at all, but just one of those deadly, specious ideas which possessive parents instil into their children, in order to keep them dependent on them?' He admitted that she might feel more comfortable if she were financially independent of him (just as the lower, possessive side of him would like to feel that he was wholly supporting her). 'But', he continued,

> I recognise the selfishness in that instinct of mine, & sit on it: you have no more reason to refuse to marry me if you hadn't an income, than I have to refuse if you had! As for being a 'drag', it is absurd: you must realise you could never be that, but an incentive: while if you were to refuse to marry me, you would not simply be a 'drag' you would be *destruction utter and bottomless*.

It might be different, he told Nancy, if they were faced with 'a life of perpetual poverty from which the only escape was for me to sacrifice my art and write pot-boilers' but such was not the case. He was involved in two areas of writing, 'fiction & the drama, in both of which it is possible to make quite a tidy sum without in any way "pot-boiling" ... the question of being a "drag" simply doesn't enter into the question'.

As for Mrs Stallibrass: Diccon hoped that Nancy had not been 'hurt by the things I said about your mother yesterday'; he promised that he understood that Mrs Stallibrass had suffered; and he appreciated Nancy's feelings of loyalty to her mother. But having made a mistake in her own life hardly gave her more of a claim to decide her daughter's; and he disliked the way she tried to play Nancy

> like a trout: she storms as much as she dare, but stops just short of angering you enough to break the line: then immediately slackens the tension in order to weaken your resistance before the next try.

This was all true; and Nancy's mother was relentless.

Her next step was to bully Nancy into half-believing that she should agree to submit to the decision of a 'jury' of family friends about her future; and then she reminded her daughter of a romantic attachment she had formed as a seventeen-year-old schoolgirl on holiday in France: despite all Nancy's protestations at the time, was she not glad that her mother had intervened, and put a stop to it?

Mrs Stallibrass added that twenty-four-year-old Diccon was 'a mere boy'; that once he had Nancy in his power, he would love her no longer; and finally she descended to a number of utterly trivial complaints: item, that Diccon had thoughtlessly inconvenienced her by not arranging for the return of a typewriter which he had loaned while staying in Dunster; item, that he had arrived at Dunster with a wardrobe so disgracefully limited that he had hardly ever changed his socks; and so on, and so forth.

When Nancy retailed all this information to Diccon, she added that he must not be too hard on her mother, who was only doing what she thought was right; and she herself had no wish to 'offer . . . up two poor unhappy parents to Venus'.

The minor attacks were easily dealt with by a few strokes of Diccon's pen; and he dismissed 'the French incident' as 'an almost certain accompaniment of growing up, and thought that it was 'downright, & rather black, lying' by Mrs Stallibrass 'to pretend that something of that sort at seventeen is to be compared with real love at nineteen'. However, the idea of a jury alarmed him. 'My own beloved darling', he wrote on Thursday:

> Though all the devils in hell were to come together over afternoon tea, & to tell you your mother was right, don't believe them: would the lamb believe a jury of wolves who came together to decide whether it was justifiable to eat her or not? And if your mother insists on the jury, refuse to be present unless you can have an equal number of *your* friends.

Those friends, said Diccon, should include Amabel Williams-Ellis, who 'has had plenty of experience of life, & knows me pretty thoroughly'; and he suggested that Nancy should ring her up and go to see her at once. He added that it was all very well for Nancy to excuse her mother 'by saying she is doing right according to her convictions: it is the excuse for half the wickedness in the world'.

Nor did he like the suggestion that, after marriage, he would cease to love her. It was this, Diccon believed, that was the only argument 'with any real bearing'. However, he dismissed it as 'bizarre': if his love had been 'only the emotional, temporary sort,' he would not have spent so much time planning for the future. 'Why', he commented,

> we shouldn't be in this mess at all if it wasn't that I was absolutely determined you should get to know all my faults & sharp corners now, not after you were married to me: that I was determined we should not only be wonderful lovers but wonderful friends too.

As for offering up her parents to Venus: there could be 'no obligation for you to destroy your whole life before you have begun it in order to humour people whose life is mostly over'.

This exchange of letters had reduced Diccon to a highly nervous state in which work had become virtually impossible. On Thursday he promised Nancy that he would come down to London 'at a moment's notice, if you wire to me'; but made it clear that he was hoping to avoid a journey at least until after the weekend; and if he did come down, it would be for a secret meeting with Nancy, whom he asked to 'start thinking out alibis', rather than for a confrontation with the Stallibrass parents. And by Saturday he was feeling so ill with worry that he disengaged himself from the contest in London altogether, writing to Nancy:

> it is simply *enraging* to think of the time you are going through . . .
> I try not to think about it . . . because thinking about it doesn't do
> any good . . . This stage of the battle is all yours, I am afraid.

Then he settled down to a period of sustained writing.

There was a pile of books waiting to be reviewed, and three radio plays to be written for the British Broadcasting Corporation; but in order to 'work off my feelings', as he put it, Hughes threw himself full-tilt into a highly personal retelling of a tale which he had heard two years before, in a doss-house in Trieste. That old rascal Zović became 'Lochinvarović',[23] moving with skill and grace and cunning through a dangerous world in which the illusions and pretensions of Mrs Stallibrass and her kind have been stripped away; a world in which quite extraordinary things may be expected to happen (and to be recounted by the author in a dead-pan manner which gives an ironic effect to everything he writes); a world in which received notions of justice and morality are very likely to be turned on their head; a world in which passionate love is both an absurdity and 'a strange and beautiful invention of the Deity'.[24]

At the time, Richard Hughes explained to Nancy Stallibrass that he was writing in 'altogether a different style, a sort of bogus Anatole France, where one gets one's irony chiefly by the mere juxtaposition of unlikely sentences'.[25]

Having written the first ten thousand words of 'Lochinvarović' (I doubt if he will ever get published', Diccon told Nancy. 'He certainly won't do for the Queen!') Diccon heard of new developments in London. Mrs Stallibrass, learning that Nancy had been invited to tea by Amabel, asked whether she too might have a private conversation with Mrs Williams-Ellis. Diccon was sceptical about the outcome of this meeting, supposing that Nancy's mother would be 'Oh, so reasonable and broad-minded, so that Amabel may tell me how I have misjudged her'.[26] In the event, it was Mrs Stallibrass who was highly impressed (not to say overawed) by Amabel, and agreed that (after all) Diccon and her daughter might continue to meet;[27] while Amabel herself wrote so warmly to Diccon about his intended that he reported to Nancy: 'I think she's very nearly in love with you herself.'

By Friday that week, Diccon had completed 'Lochinvarović'; and on Saturday (now that Amabel had smoothed things over with Mrs Stallibrass) he went up to London. There he stayed for the weekend with Joseph Brewer, a genial and sympathetic American Rhodes Scholar with whom he had become friendly in his undergraduate days; and on Sunday afternoon he spent a few hours with Nancy.[28]

It was not as joyful a reunion as they had expected. In a recent letter, Diccon had commented: 'One *talks* in letters: but when we are together we don't talk, which is odd.'[29] It was in letters that Diccon could pour out his heart to Nancy: in her presence he felt terribly nervous. Nor was Nancy able to give him much help: although she was naturally warm-hearted, she had been brought up by her mother to be so prudish in sexual matters that she once pasted together two pages of the Mallarmé poem about a boy being seduced by 'une negresse'.[30] For two such sensitive people, to be so much in love, and yet so inhibited about expressing that love, was an extreme form of torture; and Diccon may well have been relieved that the BBC were now clamouring for their radio plays, so that on the morning of Monday 15 September he had a good reason for hurrying back to Garreg Fawr.[31]

During the next two and a half weeks, Diccon did a great deal of writing. Louisa was entertaining a succession of guests, but she took care to distract him as little as possible. However, he was glad to join her on the Thursday following his return from London, when Amy Graves invited the two of them to spend the evening at Erinfa. Robert Graves and Nancy Nicholson were in residence; and they all enjoyed what Robert's father described as 'a rare good supper after which Robt. excelled himself singing Folk Songs with & without Amy's accompaniments'.[32] At eleven o'clock that night, Louisa astonished her son by suggesting that they should walk home. So, as Diccon wrote to Nancy Stallibrass, 'we started off from there at 11 at night, & came back over the mountains, getting in at five in the morning. It's I who am getting old, not she!'[33]

Diccon was now working on a wireless play about Christopher Columbus; but by the beginning of the following week he had only reached 'the Preliminary Squabble between the Portuguese sailors in mid-Atlantic', and had to tell Nancy that he was 'up to my eyes in things to get through', and that although he was planning to take lodgings in London as soon as possible, there was 'no hope' of his managing to see her for the time being.[34]

By Wednesday 24 September Diccon had completed his three plays, only to find that he need not have troubled to work on them so late into the night. As he told Nancy, the 'wretched' BBC had written asking him 'to postpone for "a month or two" '; so when on 1 October he came up to London, he could not afford to take lodgings, but had to live with his godfather in Hampstead.[35]

However, better things were to come. On his previous visit, Diccon Hughes had met Nigel Playfair with whom he had discussed a synopsis for the *Lyric Theatre* book which he was to 'ghost'. Now Hughes sent out a revised version to several publishers,[36] and a deal was rapidly concluded with Chatto & Windus.

Alongside writing ephemeral reviews and articles (one of which, on 'The Renaissance in Wales', he posted during a brief visit to Garreg Fawr in the last week of October);[37] and alongside chasing Heinemann over their long delay in publishing *The Sisters' Tragedy and three other plays* (which finally appeared towards the end of the year), it was a relief to have a really substantial project under way. Indeed, there was so much work to be done that Diccon re-employed his former secretary Miss Wardale, whom he described to Nancy as 'tappity tapping [on the *Lyric* book] like one o'clock, and me trying in vain to keep up with her!'[38]

Shortly after Diccon's arrival in Hampstead, Nancy had come to tea with him at the Johnsons'; the very next day they had gone out together for a walk;[39] and other walks had followed, whenever Diccon could escape from his desk. At length he and Nancy had a proper discussion about their future with Nancy's parents; and the upshot was an informal engagement, with various conditions attached.

Diccon was to be allowed to correspond with Nancy, and to see her (properly chaperoned) whenever he was in London; but he was to make no objections to Mr and Mrs Stallibrass taking her to Paris for Christmas; and early in 1925 he was to go abroad on a long 'holiday'. This was the very kind of enforced separation which Diccon had wanted to avoid; and he conceded the point only in return for a promise that while he was abroad Nancy should spend a long holiday with Louisa at Garreg Fawr, so that she could see for herself the kind of life which, as Diccon's wife, she would be expected to share.[40]

When Nancy and her parents left for Paris, Diccon went up to North Wales to spend Christmas at Garreg Fawr, taking with him

Peter Quennell, the good-humoured and generous Joseph Brewer, and 'Tommie', an American friend of Joe's who was 'not noticeable except for a good fire-side voice & an enormous repertory of coon-songs'.[41]

Since their Italian holiday together, Diccon Hughes had continued to keep a fatherly eye on Peter Quennell (who had recently completed his fifth term at Balliol College, Oxford), and now enjoyed stocking his mind with strange stories:[42]

> The whole neighbourhood was full of ghosts and spectres, including ... a phantom dog that pattered up and down the mountain paths; and almost every farmhouse that he pointed out had some strange and dismal history – a tale of incest or murder or suicide – concealed behind its white-washed walls.

But although Diccon was fond of Peter Quennell, his more important friendship was with Joseph Brewer. There were considerable differences between the two men, not least the fact that Joseph was a convinced Christian, while Diccon was a determined atheist; but Joseph's Christianity owed little to the dead weight of official doctrine, much to the spirit of unselfish love which shines through the first four books of the New Testament. His intellect, his largeness of spirit, his tolerant good-humour and his reluctance to judge were gradually making him Diccon's most reliable and (after Amabel Williams-Ellis) his closest friend and confidant.

On arriving at Garreg Fawr, one of the first things Diccon discovered from Louisa was that the *Cambrian News* had been 'stiff with virulent attacks on the Portmadoc Players'; and so he wrote to Nancy's Parisian address asking whether she would mind telling the *News* that[43]

> as a DISINTERESTED person, familiar with the stages of London and Paris ... you were not altogether surprised at their local correspondent's disappointment, since the subtlety and quietness of their style of acting would probably be wasted on people not familiar with the best modern acting.

Or did she, asked Diccon, have 'any conscientious scruples about perjury?!' He had no other news, except that he was 'vegetating wonderfully ... all sleep & open air, like a cow'.

A few days after Christmas, Diccon wrote again to thank Nancy for her 'lovely long letters'. He also told her that (thanks to Joe) the land was flowing with port and caviare; that Peter had 'acquired my taste for cold water and spends quite a lot of the time sitting under waterfalls'; and that he himself had been thinking about his immediate future. He would have to return to town to finish the *Lyric* book; and then it looked as though[44] my so-called 'holiday' will have to be New York: it is time I worked up some sort of a connection there, with magazines & so on. James Bennett has fallen on his feet: he is getting sixty pounds a month for one hour's work a day teaching English literature at a girl's school! He has rooms down in Greenwich village, & has offered to put me up, which would be useful.

Diccon did not mention that he had also been writing to Pamela Bianco, whom he had told of his hope to be in America by the end of January 1925.

In the event, Hughes was considerably delayed. For one thing, the *Lyric Theatre* book took far longer than expected (he was badly held up by influenza at one point), and it was not until mid February that he had 'finished all I can do . . . & will have to leave two chapters to Playfair to finish'. For another, there was more trouble with Nancy's parents. They worked upon her so effectively that eventually it seemed to both Nancy and Diccon that their unofficial engagement must lapse, at least for the time being. While the trouble was at its height, Diccon had left several of Louisa's letters unanswered; and she had accused him of not bothering about her now that he had Nancy. At length, apologising to his mother for having 'been a *pig* about writing', Diccon went on:[45]

> there's no need for you to come up and shoot Nancy: we aren't engaged any more. Perhaps why I didn't write was because I hoped to be able to come down to explain by word of mouth . . . But don't worry, dearest: there was nothing that could – or should – be helped: it seemed in the end inevitable. Whether it is final or not only the future can show.

While he was delayed in England, Hughes collected numerous letters of introduction for his American journey;[46] and he and Peter Quennell spent five 'heavenly' days with Robert Graves and his family at Islip (from where Hughes travelled into Oxford and 'at last' took his degree).[47] Hughes also secured commissions for two more wireless plays from the BBC; and he arranged a meeting with Margaret Kennedy, a young novelist whose second book *The Constant Nymph*[48] (first published in October 1924) he liked so much that he wished to dramatise it for the stage.

The Constant Nymph is a minor classic, an unsentimental tragedy full of insight and wit and ironic wisdom. In the background is the figure of Albert Sanger, an eccentric composer of unrecognised genius and bohemian life-style whose death precipitates the tragedy. In the foreground is Lewis Dodd, a brilliant composer in his late twenties who (like Sanger) has rejected bourgeois morality; and who is very close to Sanger's fourteen-year-old daughter Tessa. Shortly after Sanger's death, Lewis (who should have waited for the similarly unconventional Tessa) foolishly marries Florence, who is charming and clever, but cannot help being part and parcel of the middle-class society which he despises; and by the time he has had the good sense to run away with Tessa (now fifteen) it is too late: Tessa has become ill, and she dies in an hotel room in Brussels before their relationship can be consummated.

The novel appealed to Richard Hughes not only because it was a forceful and clear-sighted attack upon the bourgeois 'morality' of people like Mrs Stallibrass, but also because the central relationship, between Lewis Dodd and Tessa, closely paralleled his own experience with Gwenol Satow; and because the difficulties of the relationship between Lewis and Florence threw his own problems with Nancy into sharp relief.

At first Margaret Kennedy expressed considerable reservations, telling Hughes (through Heinemann) that she '*does* object in principle' to Hughes writing a play, but 'in practice might not hate it'.[49] And when (on Wednesday 25 February) they met for lunch,[50] it was agreed that he should take things further. Diccon's cause can only have been helped by the news that the theatrical producer J.B. Fagan was to put on *A Comedy of Good and Evil* at the Playhouse in Oxford for a week beginning on 9 March, and then intended to take it up to the Ambassador Theatre in London's West End.

The day after lunching with Margaret Kennedy, Diccon went to Oxford to read *A Comedy of Good and Evil* to the cast, and then (after returning briefly to Wales to prepare for his journey to America),[51] he went back to Oxford, and stayed once again with Robert Graves while he assisted with the production.[52]

Shortly before the curtain went up at the Playhouse on the evening of 9 March, Hughes was delighted to receive a telegram from John Masefield 'Wishing you the greatest possible success tonight';[53] and he himself was pleased with the 'general excellence' of the production. This he attributed in large part to the stage-manager and assistant producer James Whale, who went on to become a highly-paid Hollywood director.[54] However, there were problems: the very 'Welshness' of the play was a 'severe handicap', as at that time 'few actors could be found who had any knowledge of the Welsh accent, or any understanding and sympathy for the Welsh character';[55] but in any case, before Hughes could witness its transfer to the London stage (a prospect which, in his abnormally sensitive state, filled him with nothing but alarm), he had departed in a state of nervous depression for his second voyage to New York.

CHAPTER 12

Furthest North

On arriving in New York in the third week of March 1925,[1] Richard Hughes moved into a garret in Eighth Street on the outskirts of Greenwich Village, where a corner of his depression was lifted by the singularity of filling in his first questionnaire for a biography in *Who's Who* while 'sitting on a table to escape the vermin'.[2] Although his attic was (in his own words) 'beastly', it was also 'economical', and it had the advantage of being just around the corner from Pamela Bianco's studio in MacDougal Alley, which he rapidly made his headquarters.

What Diccon found most soothing to his nerves was the anonymity of the New York streets. 'I was not so fatuous', he wrote later, 'as to suppose that all London was ringing with my name; on the other hand, there was at least the liability that anyone I met there might have heard of me, to which I was abnormally sensitive at that time, and for which I had a ridiculous and unnatural dislike . . . But in New York I was blessedly unknown.'[3] In mid April, when Diccon heard that (following his departure for America) Nancy had also been in a state of nervous depression, he suggested fancifully that she had[4]

> better come here for a rest cure, too! Or, we might start a Home for Nervous Wrecks, in Broadway (really bad cases might need special treatment in Wall Street). And take in all those who find the Welsh mountains too crowded.

By this time he had been sent a number of press-cuttings from London, and he added that: 'The poor *Comedy* seems to have had a short life and hardly a gay one.'

Perhaps because it had seemed 'wild and incomprehensible when performed by Englishmen for Englishmen',[5] *A Comedy of Good and Evil* had aroused strong feelings: there had been 'violent abuse and quite as violent praise'. Audiences had rapidly dwindled away; until the play could not be saved even by 'a most generous article by George Bernard Shaw',[6] who declared: 'Give me a play at which I have not the faintest notion what anyone will say next or how the play will end; how else can you expect me to keep awake at my age? Now I can say without reserve that Mr Hughes's play held me all the time in this delightful fashion.'[7]

Nor did Shaw's conclusion (which was that 'anyone who cannot enjoy all this must be an idiot'),[8] encourage any New York producer to take *A Comedy of Good and Evil* seriously;[9] and so after three weeks in America, Hughes was chiefly aware of how little he had accomplished.[10] But then, towards the end of April, he was jolted into action when Margaret Kennedy's novel began rapidly climbing the American bestseller lists.

Hughes had intended 'to let [the idea of adapting *The Constant Nymph*] simmer for several months'; but with its enormous popular success, the dramatic rights suddenly became extremely valuable. In mid April, Margaret Kennedy wrote to explain that she had been approached by 'a New York dramatic Manager ... about the dramatisation of *The Constant Nymph*';[11] and Diccon (as he explained much later to Nancy Stallibrass)[12]

> couldn't help seeing it, in a flash, as a possible solution of the financial side of our problems, for a successful play here may make almost any amount of money. Ordinarily, the commercial complications, which were obviously going to tie my hands considerably ... might have tempted me to resign straight away; ... but under the circumstances Fate seemed to be playing straight into my hands by giving me the chance.

One danger was that a sale of the film rights might preclude an independent theatrical production of *The Constant Nymph*; and Hughes urgently cabled Margaret Kennedy, begging her not to sell any such rights before she had received his letter on the subject.

In her reply of 26 April, Miss Kennedy pointed out that large sums of money were involved – perhaps as much as $25,000 – 'and I do not want to risk losing it by any delay or muddle.' However, her agent's New York representative was instructed to keep in close touch with Hughes 'on the ground that you may have an interest in the dramatic rights';[13] and within days an agreement had been reached which fully protected him, subject to Margaret Kennedy's final approval of his completed script.[14]

Armed with this agreement, which (he believed) made the production of his stage version 'fairly secure', Diccon Hughes decided to 'bolt ... from New York',[15] and find a place in the country where he could work in solitude: both on *The Constant Nymph*, and on the two wireless plays he had been commissioned to write before leaving England.

By good fortune, an admirer of Pamela's (an 'Oil King' known as 'the O.K.') was just about to drive the Biancos out to a farm at Bearsville in the Catskills, where they rented a shack for holiday use. Diccon was invited to accompany them; and just a few fields away he found an empty chalet, consisting of 'a large studio with a bedroom in one end'[16] which he had soon 'borrowed'; although, as he told Louisa, 'borrowed is a euphemistic word: the owner doesn't know yet'.[17]

The chalet was in a remote, wooded area by a flowing stream; but there was no solitude at first, because although Ferdinand Bianco and his son Cecco returned to New York after the weekend of 2–3 May, Margery and Pamela and the O.K. lingered on for another week. Diccon took advantage of their stay by borrowing the O.K.'s Chrysler to explore the mountainous countryside round about. Much to his satisfaction, he found that the 'big six-seater' could 'tackle anything'; and its powerful engine was particularly valuable when on Thursday 7 May, after collecting a bottle of wine from a bootlegger, 'a suspicious-looking car' began pursuing him.

Hughes was anxious, not least because under prohibition regulations, any car taken with drink was automatically confiscated; but there was a two-mile straight on his journey home; and as soon as he reached it, he put his foot down on the accelerator, and was soon hurtling along the dusty road at 68 m.p.h. 'That did the blighter', he told Louisa. 'I slipped into the farm & disappeared with the bottle before he got near again.'[18]

That Sunday the O.K. left with Margery and Pamela. At last Diccon had 'the place to myself, except for chipmunks ... & woodchucks'. The result was that by Tuesday he had completed the second of his two radio plays:[19]

> rather amusing, a dream, called 'The War in Spain'. Missing trains, chases, no clothes, & all the usual gadgets of dreams. The other is rather a pig: a semi-expressionistic melodrama ... called 'The Serenade'.

Working on these plays, he had recovered 'something of the speed' with which he had written *The Sisters' Tragedy*; and now, by 'sheer concentration', he intended to complete *The Constant Nymph* 'in a very short time ... Three weeks, I thought, would see me through'.[20]

He said nothing to Nancy of his hopes: partly because of a feeling that if he failed to make a great success of *The Constant Nymph*, 'there would be little harm ... if nothing had been said'; and partly because he remained extremely nervous and uncertain where she was concerned.

Nancy wrote far more often to Diccon than he did to her; and when in mid May she arrived at Garreg Fawr, it must have been galling to find that while two of her own letters remained unanswered,[21] Diccon had chosen to write to his mother; and instead of bothering to enclose even a brief note inside the same envelope, he had only acknowledged Nancy in an aside which read: 'My love to N: I suppose she will have arrived when you get this.'[22]

Although Diccon was now devoting all his energy to his adaptation of *The Constant Nymph*, it would not be hurried. Despite working a punishing fifteen hours a day, by the end of the month he had only completed the first act.[23] 'It never entirely stuck', he explained later, 'but it moved at the same pace as the *Comedy* – a page a day. Each difficulty I passed, I thought the rest would be plain sailing – & of course it wasn't.'[24] In other aspects, his new venture was[25]

> about as different from the *Comedy* as it well could be: all emotions and practically no ideas. The method is absolutely different, too: short, varied scenes. One of them (this sounds like radio influence) is in the pitch dark: I follow it by one of dazzling sunlight, and so on.

It was only when Diccon heard from Nancy that she had contented herself with a single week at Garreg Fawr that at last he wrote; but his letter of 5 June must have been deeply disappointing. He wrote amusingly enough about the bootlegging restaurants in New York; about the poets and artists who crawled over the nearby countryside 'like lice', congregating especially at Woodstock (where they went 'for long walks in the woods with each other's wives to talk about Gauguin'); about the wild strawberries 'nearly as big as garden ones'; and about the porcupines who 'get up trees in the hope you will come underneath: then they drop on you'. But the personal content of his letter was kept to the absolute minimum.[26]

Admittedly, Diccon told Nancy about his bathing-pool, 'made . . . in three days, by building a dam on the Welsh stone wall principle'; and he confessed that he was finding *The Constant Nymph* 'a much tougher proposition' than he had expected. But there was not a word about loving Nancy or missing her; and there is far more honest feeling in a slightly drunken letter which he wrote a few days later to Joe Brewer, telling him 'I am a pig not to have written', acknowledging that he was reduced to 'living on $4 a week' (and was now down to his last $20), asking to borrow money, and adding:[27]

I am tight: home-brewed mead.
I don't like porcupines.
Nor trout which tickle your testicles if you fall asleep in the water
Nor snakes which bite (one chewed a hole in my finger).
I am sorry to be importunate . . . but my need is getting sore.

His need became still greater when Nigel Playfair's personal assistant pointed out that in Diccon's absence Playfair had been forced 'to put in a lot of extra work' on *The Story of the Lyric Theatre*, and demanded £10 by return of post towards the expense of having it typed.[28] And then the owner of his chalet 'arrived, & wanted to have a nervous breakdown in it'. Diccon was told that he could stay if he wanted, in return for literary conversation;[29] but he declined the offer, and 'cleared off for New York'.[30]

Arriving virtually penniless in Manhattan, Hughes sold a poem 'at the critical moment' for $40;[31] he also showed Act One of *The Constant Nymph* to Curtis Brown who was suitably encouraging;[32] and then he received an unexpected offer. After eighteen months' uncertainty, Pamela's O.K. was suddenly 'given his final congé. He wanted to drown his sorrows in a wet country', Diccon later recalled, '& offered to drive me up to Canada. So I took the chance'.[33]

In the third week of June, the O.K. and Diccon began their journey (in Diccon's words) with 'a most wonderful drive, right up through the Adirondack & the White Mountains. Except for one or two trails it is pathless'.[34] And after crossing the Canadian Border, their first night in the country was 'fairly gay. At any rate', Diccon told Joseph Brewer,[35]

we chased a detective ten miles, *made* him fighting drunk, relieved him of gun and badge & tucked him up in bed with a merry widow, assisted by her three daughters just home from the convent (which means Paris had nothing to teach them except caution).

By the end of June, Diccon was established 'as viper in the bosom of a very amiable French peasant family' a few miles from Montreal in the village of Ste Genevieve de Pierreford. There was a local prejudice against Englishmen, since the last one had 'held up the whole village stark naked in mid-winter, & was only deterred from scandalising its name when the wolves ate him'; but Diccon's command of French pleased his hosts; and he enjoyed a 'bedroom, sitting-room, board, washing, gin, & fishing-boat all inclusive for $1.25 a day!'

Diccon observed that the villagers were 'as prolific as rabbits';[36] and that the girls were fully grown at twelve, and married at fifteen. His own landlady already had nine children at the age of thirty-one, and Diccon recounted to Joseph the 'strange vices' of her daughters: thirteen-year-old Helene, who 'eats lemons, peel and all, plentifully dipped in salt'; eighteen-year-old Isabelle, who 'goes into shrieks of laughter reading the telephone directory'; and above all 'Cecile (16 & pretty)', who 'sits comparing the girth of her leg at different (& often extreme) altitudes with a piece of tape'.[37]

Diccon was fascinated by Cecile (who later reappeared in one of his novels),[38] and something about the curiously bohemian atmosphere not only enabled him to start racing ahead with *The Constant Nymph*; but also encouraged him to break his five-week silence, and write a repentant letter to Nancy. 'My dear love', he began very nervously on 8 July,[39]

> I haven't had any news of you since the long time ago you left Wales . . . Is it – that you don't want to hear from me any more? That is why I haven't written again till now . . . I know only too well . . . what I deserve: it seems incredible that you shouldn't be hating me by now, violently . . . Dear – unless you would very much rather not – do, please, write.

By the end of the following week Diccon had completed his play, and had sent it down to New York to be typed. He intended to follow in person within a few days. But then (as Hughes later explained) the O.K. decided that 'he wanted to drive round for a few days before taking me back'; and this 'driving round' developed into 'an attempt to do farthest north by motor-car'[40] . . . [an] 'insane expedition . . . in town clothes and without the least preparation'.[41]

They drove up beyond Quebec. When the roads ran out, Hughes and the O.K. took to bridle-paths. Then they reached a point of no return, and there was 'nothing but to lumber somehow over the Laurentian mountains, by a hundred miles of back trails, to[wards] Chicoutimi'.[42]

By this time (in Diccon's words), they were 'practically carrying the car . . . which is no joke for two people with a semi-closed six cylinder';[43] and there were moments on the long haul when Diccon wanted 'to sit down and weep, every fresh swamp we stuck in'. But the shared hardship drew the two men together: 'I never expected', wrote Diccon, 'to get to like a Strong Silent man as much as I like him';[44] and it was thrilling when 'after a week of it', they 'finally tobaganned down with what was left of the car to the far side [of the mountains]',[45] where their Chrysler became 'the first automobile ever to reach Lake St John overland'.[46]

The north still beckoned. On 21 July, leaving the Chrysler to be repaired in Chicoutimi, they set off[47]

in canoes with a party of Red Indians who were migrating through the bush towards Hudson Bay for the winter's trapping: . . . they poled their canoes up rapids which were practically waterfalls, with a wife and family and luggage in the front, when the slightest failure of skill would mean drowning for everyone concerned.

On the third day, coming to an easier stretch of the river, Diccon and the O.K. asked to take a turn at the poling. 'Standing on the thwart', and propelling their canoe up-river through the icy water in the midst of a wilderness – this was the adventure for which they had craved; and there suddenly seemed no need to go further.

Borrowing one of the Indian canoes, they turned toward the south. They 'shot down in a little over an hour what had taken us three days to work up';[48] and forty-eight hours later (after a voyage by river-steamer, and a journey by road) they were back once again in the teeming streets of New York.[49]

While he was still in the elated mood brought on by his 'furthest north' adventure, Diccon found a cable waiting for him from Nancy. She still loved him, she said, though she had been unable to understand his long silences; and she hoped that he would soon return to England.

'You angel', he replied, 'I can't think why I was such an imbecile as not to have explained [my long silence]: I was pig-headed, & wanted not to till it was all over, having no idea that "till it was all over" would be so long.' Now at last he told her about his hopes for *The Constant Nymph*, and about his difficulties in producing 'a saleable play without sacrificing at all the kind of play I wanted to write . . . I couldn't help counting my chickens to *myself*', he went on,[50]

> – hoping to have soon a nice fat brood to spring on you as a surprise: instead of which, of course, as I ought to have seen, I was simply giving you a hell of a time & steering straight for shipwreck. It was incredibly, *abysmally* stupid of me.

He added that his adaptation still needed the critical approval of his agent, of Margaret Kennedy, of a theatrical manager, and of the paying public: so it was still 'rather early to talk of chickens!' But whatever happened, he would be sailing for home by the *Berengaria* on Wednesday 5 August, and it was 'wonderful' that she had 'any patience left at all . . . Dearest', he concluded, 'I have been a terrible ass, & I love you from the bottom of my heart'.

By the time he boarded the *Berengaria* (accompanied by the O.K., who was now talking of joining the Riffs of Western Morocco in their struggle for independence), Diccon Hughes had received a deeply disappointing letter from Curtis Brown. While recognising that Hughes had 'preserved the atmosphere of the CN quite wonderfully', and 'kept to the spirit of the book with great delicacy', he doubted very much whether Hughes had 'got a powerful dramatic story that stands without the aid of having read the book'. Margaret Kennedy would be cabled for her views; but his own were clearly hostile.[51]

Instead of being plunged into depression, Diccon was so immensely buoyed up by the prospect of seeing Nancy again that he shrugged off the probable ruin of four months' work. All that was important now was to take Nancy in his arms, and sweep her off to North Wales.

CHAPTER 13

Invitations to a Wedding[1]

The *Berengaria* docked in Southampton on Tuesday 11 August 1925,[2] and Hughes immediately travelled up to London, where he called on Nancy at Sussex Mansions. It was a joyful return: he had kept his side of the bargain with the Stallibrass parents; after their long separation, he and Nancy still loved each other; and he had very soon removed her to Garreg Fawr, insisting that she should have a further experience of the way of life which he wanted her to share.[3]

Diccon sometimes took Nancy down to Portmadoc Harbour, where (as Amabel noticed) he liked spending time with the poet and boat-builder Elias Pierce. Pierce had spent many years at sea as a ship's carpenter; and had once very much pleased Diccon with an account of an Atlantic storm ending: 'You know, Mr Hughes, after so much peril a man is apt to give way to his natural impulses! I went below and I wrote an ode.'[4]

Pierce introduced them to his friend Captain Coward, master of the trading schooner *Elizabeth* then moored in Portmadoc harbour. Coward liked them so much (especially Nancy, whom he said had the makings of a finer seaman than Diccon) that he offered them work: Diccon should be the second mate, and Nancy the cook, on his forthcoming voyage to the south seas. The idea was immensely attractive; but as soon as Mrs Stallibrass heard of the possibility, she 'put down her very plump foot'.[5]

Next came the 'collapse' of what Diccon now called 'this C.N. play business'. But the news was half-expected; and far from bearing Margaret Kennedy a grudge, Diccon corresponded with her in the most friendly manner later in the year,[6] and even took her out to lunch.[7]

After all, as Diccon told Nancy, although he would like another more substantial project, he could easily support the two of them on his journalism and his broadcasting (and within the next six months, his prodigious output would include a paper on Skelton, a long piece on 'Aspects of the Cinema', and several more radio plays). Nancy was happy to believe him, especially as she had been very much enjoying her stay at Garreg Fawr.

When Diccon was in a cheerful mood he was a wonderful companion, whose 'way of being able to live almost totally in the present – like an animal' meant that in his presence the world became richer and more magical;[8] and now that Nancy had approved his way of life, there seemed no reason why they should not get married as soon as possible.

On Nancy's return to London, therefore, she insisted that her parents should agree to a formal engagement; and so on Monday 14 September, the Court Circular page of *The Times* carried the following notice:

> The engagement is announced between Richard Warren Hughes, son of Mrs Hughes of Garreg Fawr, North Wales, and the late Mr Arthur Hughes of the Public Record Office, and Nancy Marianne, daughter of Mr and Mrs Edward Stallibrass, 11 Sussex Mansions SW.

Before long, as Nancy wrote to her new fiancé, she was inundated with correspondence. She wished that Diccon would come to London to help her. Could he really be getting any work done at Garreg Fawr, now that Peter Quennell had come to stay before the start of his Michaelmas term?

'You poor dear', replied Diccon, 'I *am* sorry you are being so severely battered.' He himself had been 'saved by the magnificent (but fortunately insufficient) address given – "Garreg Fawr, North Wales" ',[9] adding 'What an imposing country seat that looks! . . . Also, so far as [the] press is concerned, the "Warren" is an admirable disguise'. Although he was missing Nancy 'frightfully', remaining in Wales was his only hope of getting any work done; and Peter was certainly 'not so distracting as you: how modest of you to imagine he could be! I lock myself up in my study and pull the switch in my head marked "radio-plays" – and out comes a letter to you instead!'

In suggesting that Diccon would find Peter Quennell distracting company, Nancy was reading her own emotions into the situation. As Diccon's protégé, Peter had been conducting a kind of approved flirtation with her: she regularly sent him kisses through the post, and he had told her (in front of Diccon) that she had an open invitation to run away with him. But although this had been said lightly enough, it was a flirtation with passionate undertones.

Peter Quennell had greatly profited by his friendship with Diccon Hughes, who continued to look over his work and introduce him to literary figures: notably Edith Sitwell, who had received them 'in all her Gothic elegance, sheathed in a golden robe, and wearing a cap, or toque, of gilded feathers, with many encrusted rings on her long noble hands, and on her breast a large jewelled cross that had once belonged to Cagliostro'.[10] It was a friendship which had prospered not merely for literary reasons, but because the two men had much in common. Both, for example, had a nervous, highly-strung side to their nature (Quennell recalls having been 'the victim of many fears and manias'); both men were rebels against their upbringing; and both had gone up to university with their knowledge of women confined largely to what they had read about them in books.[11]

In this latter sphere, however, Quennell had been rapidly outgrowing Hughes. Failing to succumb to what he later described as the 'strongly homosexual leanings' of the Oxford society of his day, he had gradually felt excluded from the intimate society of his peers, and had taken 'to assuming the rather silly pose of an inveterate malcontent. I decided that Oxford was not for me, and lost no opportunity of abusing the place and neglecting every chance it afforded'. He had also spent many 'happy hours' on his sofa with one or other of his women friends from Oxford or London – though, as he explains, he 'respected [their] innocence'; and more recently he had lost his virginity in a Parisian brothel.[12] Like Diccon Hughes, he had wit, charm, and a powerful belief in himself as a writer; but his growing sexual assurance had already given him a darkly attractive edge over his former mentor.

Besides working on his radio plays, Hughes had begun preparing collected editions of his poems and short stories, in both of which he had interested Chatto & Windus; but he was still looking for another major project to replace his dramatisation of *The Constant Nymph*. At various times he had worked on a number of 'embryo novels',[13] but although he turned these over in his mind, none of them seemed satisfactory for his purpose. (In later life, Hughes liked to assert that he had taken an early decision not even to attempt a novel before he was 'at least twenty-seven', since it was 'inevitable that writing a novel should take longer than most other forms of composition; and if it is to have any cohesion it needs (as well as greater experience) that slowing-down of mental development which only comes with advancing age'.[14] But this must be taken more as preaching than practice.)

Then came a stroke of good fortune. Louisa Hughes had always enjoyed reminiscing about her childhood experiences in Jamaica in the 1870s; and (knowing this) a family friend arrived at Garreg Fawr one day with a fascinating manuscript written in her old age by a Miss Jeannette Calder, who had lived in Jamaica fifty years before Louisa. Jeanette's story concerned the year 1822, when (as a young child) she had been a passenger on an English barque returning from

Jamaica, which was captured by pirates off the western edge of Cuba.

Once Captain Lumsden and his crew had been overpowered, Jeannette and the four or five other children aboard were shut in the deckhouse. The pirates then threatened to kill them unless Lumsden revealed where he had hidden his money; and when he refused to talk, they fired a volley into the deckhouse above the children's heads. This, Hughes noticed, was where[15]

> the story took a strange turn. The pirates were not so bloodthirsty as they pretended. They let the frightened children out, and petted them, and comforted them, and took them on board their schooner and fed them on crystallised fruit.

The whereabouts of the money was soon discovered by the more direct expedient of tying up Captain Lumsden, sprinkling gunpowder under his toes, and showing him a flaring match. Later, after transferring both money and cargo to their own ship, the pirates returned the children, and sailed away. 'There', explained Hughes, 'the "true" story ends.'[16]

However, he became intrigued by the possibility of a dramatic confrontation between a group of children (who appear innocent but are actually quite amoral) and their pirate-captors (who appear wicked but are actually quite principled). 'Suppose, I thought', that the children[17]

> had never been returned to the brig; and, instead, the pirates had somehow been landed with this uncomfortable booty?
>
> The idea took fire in my mind. I looked up the records of the case . . . and determined to make a novel of it.

Soon he was gathering background material, reading 'pamphlets by Quaker abolitionists on the state of the negroes in Demerara, and so on', with the idea of 'gradually getting a sort of hot-pot of miscellaneous information into my head: when I have forgotten it I shall begin to write'.

Richard Hughes now had the substantial project he had wanted; but once Peter Quennell had left for Oxford, the atmosphere in Garreg Fawr became increasingly oppressive. Louisa, finding it hard to accept that her only surviving child was now formally engaged to be married, began to show physical symptoms of distress. 'Mother rather worries me', Diccon told Nancy in late September,

> she gets so easily tired. I think she must have consistently starved herself all the summer & is now feeling the effects. She will write this evening to you. She had meant to write for the post, but I have made her go to lie down.

When Louisa suffered, Diccon suffered too; and his suffering took
the form of occasional black moods during which he wondered
whether it would really be possible for him and Nancy to be
happy together.[18] On one occasion, having failed to communicate
with Nancy for several days, he explained that he had been

> rather knocked in the eye lately with bad headaches, & have
> been trying to work them off by violent and continual exercise:
> one day I walked over the Roman Road to Dolfring, from there
> across the Glaslyn, over the top of Moel-Ddu & down the other
> side to Portmadoc & back across the flat.

And on another day, he had 'helped load about ten tons of fine
brick & cast iron stoves in the *Elizabeth*, & so on: that's why I
haven't written'.

Diccon's happiest hours were now spent in Portmadoc harbour;
and when he was in a particularly cheerful mood (having helped
Captain Coward to bend the topsail, which meant working out on
the highest yard), he told Nancy that he had been thinking:

> What a wonderful time we could have, if I succeeded in learn-
> ing enough to sail a small vessel myself . . . cruising about the
> Mediterranean together! I don't see, later on, why we shouldn't get
> a 35-footer or something like that, that could wiggle in and out of
> all the little fishing ports: turn the fo'c'sle into a nursery, hang the
> washing from the halyards, clamp a typewriter to the foretopmast,
> and take a barrel of ink . . . and only be in to such callers as could
> swim.

It would certainly be 'much simpler than a London flat, simply to
tie up to the Victoria Embankment for the season!' And he asked
her seriously to consider the idea.

Another weekend, he told her that Clough Williams-Ellis had
announced his purchase of *Twinkler*,[19] which Diccon described as
'a little 20-foot sloop, which should be fun for pottering about
the bay in'. Clough encouraged Diccon to think of himself as a
'part-owner' of the sloop; and during the next few months, when
things were difficult at Garreg Fawr, Diccon often found his way
to Plas Brondanw to see Amabel, or down to Portmadoc Harbour
to go 'Twinkling' with Clough.[20]

Early in October, it was Nancy's turn to be silent for almost a
week; and then Diccon was devastated to receive a letter in which
she explained that she hadn't felt able to write, because her parents
had been once again trying to bully her out of her engagement.
'My dear', wrote Diccon, 'why didn't you tell me you were being
excoriated? Of course you haven't felt like letter-writing – I had no
idea till your letter came this morning . . . How long are they going

on with it? They are absolute brutes.' Within twenty-four hours he was down in London, pouring oil on troubled waters; but he was dreadfully torn between fiancée and mother, and it was only a few days before he felt that he must once more return to Wales.

Travelling back through Oxford, Diccon spent a few nights at Islip with Robert Graves, 'terribly cock-a-hoop' at having recently been offered a job as Professor of English at Cairo at £1500 a year. Diccon told Nancy that he had also lunched with Mrs Masefield (who had been 'especially inquisitive about you'); and on his return to Garreg Fawr he had found Louisa 'pretty well'. The only sad piece of news was that Peter Quennell had been rusticated: 'ridiculously conventional of him', Diccon commented, 'just as if he was no better than Shelley!'[21] Despite this insouciant tone, Hughes had already begun to feel a little uneasy about Quennell's effect upon his fiancée: '*Still* no letter from you', he had complained to Nancy during her period of silence. 'I'll begin to think you have accepted Peter's invitation & vamoosed!' And he did not mention that the reason for Quennell's rustication was that he had spent several nights and days far from Oxford in the arms of Nina, an 'expert guide' of uninhibited sexuality, in whose welcoming arms 'the dreams that had first been inspired by *Hero and Leander* assumed a dazzlingly concrete shape'.[22] Rustication involved being sent down for a single term only; but after his experiences with Nina, Quennell felt that he had altogether outgrown Oxford. He decided never to return, and not long afterwards went abroad to stay with Osbert and Sacheverell Sitwell in Amalfi.

November 1925 was unusually fine. 'The country is at its best now', wrote Diccon to Nancy, 'the visitors gone, & the floods out in the valleys. I bathed yesterday under my favourite waterfall: I have never seen it in such spate.'[23] The weather seemed to have had a good effect upon Louisa; until, at the very end of the month, Diccon mentioned that he was contemplating another visit to London to see Nancy.

Within days, Louisa's health had deteriorated so sharply, that Diccon had to tell Nancy that he had no idea how soon his mother would be fit enough to be left alone. 'She seems to have sprained a muscle in her leg', he explained,[24]

> & to have got rheumatism on top of it. Yesterday she couldn't even turn in bed without help: it is a little better today, but she can't get out of bed yet. Hence awful rush: cinema article for *Outlook*, housework & nursing all at once!

But when Nancy wired offering to catch the next train to North

Wales, so that she could nurse the invalid back to good health, there was an even more sudden change for the better.

'I wish to goodness', Diccon replied, 'I could have righteously said yes.' Unfortunately for them, as soon as Nancy's wire had arrived,

> Mother came clambering downstairs & announced her intention of being better! It's a way she has: she is one of those Quick Recoverers . . . oh how PIGLY of Mother to go and get better just then!

However, if she was better, then he would be able to come up to London on Thursday or Friday.

Or would he? On Thursday he had to write again with the disappointing news that[25]

> Mother is considerably better now, & up; but I can't leave her to do heavy things yet. And there is no help to be had. So I shall stay for the week-end: not much *Twinkling*, I am afraid, there is not a breath of breeze.

It was only on the following Monday when (as Louisa knew) he had a business appointment in London, that Diccon was finally allowed to make his way down to the metropolis; and there he stayed for ten or twelve days, until shortly before Christmas.

In his absence, Louisa wrote to Amy Graves, who had congratulated her upon Diccon's engagement. Despite describing Nancy as 'a particularly lovely & charming girl, & very unselfish & considerate for me', Louisa could not bring herself to be more than 'quite pleased' about the engagement; and openly lamented the fact that she would be losing her only child.[26]

When Diccon returned, Louisa must have become still more despondent. He told her that he could not spend Christmas with her, because on Christmas Eve he would be travelling down to Kemble in Gloucestershire. There he would be joining Nancy and her parents for the Christmas weekend at a country house belonging to her extremely wealthy aunts.

After an appalling journey, Diccon arrived at Kemble on Christmas Eve (a Friday) 'bedraggled as a wet sparrow'. But very soon (as he reported to Louisa), he was finding everything 'all very exotic & interesting & exciting – quite as fascinating as the steerage'.[27]

Saturday was a traditional Christmas Day, with an abundance of presents, matins presided over by a parson whose face was 'like a parody of a convivial monk', and a hearty Christmas lunch. Then in the evening they were driven through deep snow to have dinner with

The wedding of Arthur Hughes and Louisa Warren, February 1897.

Louisa tending her tubercular husband, now a permanent invalid, 1903.

4-year-old Richard ('Dickie') at home in Dorincourt, 1904.

19-year-old Richard ('Diccon'), at Oriel College, Oxford, summer 1919.

13-year-old Richard ('Dick'), shortly before winning a scholarship to Charterhouse, May 1913.

Mid-European peasants on an emigrant voyage to Ellis Island, taken by Hughes, July 1921.

Signed photograph of the Croatian nationalist Stjepan Radić, for whom Hughes made speeches in September 1922.

Hughes, actor-manager of the Portmadoc Players, as Bill in a scene from *The Man Born to be Hanged,* February 1924.

Nancy Quennell (née Stallibrass), whom Hughes courted unsuccessfully from April 1924 to February 1926.

Hughes, now best-selling author of *A High Wind in Jamaica*, summer 1930.

Hughes and Frances Bazley after
their marriage at Hatherop Castle,
8 January 1932.

House-party for the wedding with (back l. to r.) Anthony Bazley,
Lance Sieveking, Louisa Hughes, Esmé Howard; (mid) Rachel
Bazley, Mrs Cadogan, (an aunt), Thomas B., Mrs Sieveking;
(front) Henriette C., Mrs Johnson, Christopher C., Mr Johnson.

Stiffkey Hall, Norfolk, where the Hugheses lived from summer 1932 to summer 1934.

With his baby son Robert, born November 1932.

Portrait of Frances Hughes by Augustus John.

Hughes entertaining a group of children at Laugharne, mid-1930s.

Hughes relaxing at the tiller of a boat.

Laugharne Castle, principal home of the Hughes family from 1934 to 1942.

Parc, the ancient stone house in North Wales which Hughes rented from Clough Williams-Ellis from the summer of 1934.

Nancy's uncle, Gordon Macmillan. Diccon found Nancy's relatives 'so wonderfully clear-cut & concrete, like people out of a particularly lurid & consistent novel'; and at the end of the meal, when the ladies had left the table, he decided that Gordon Macmillan was[28]

> straight out of the 18th Century: stupid as a block & generous as a thundercloud: sitting over his port in his beautiful scarlet tail-coat watching the country go to the dogs – he is magnificent.

On Boxing Day the Macmillans paid a return visit, and there were charades. 'Ours was a very grand one', Diccon told Louisa;

> we spent the day rehearsing it: a comic melodrama called *The Vamp the Villain & the Victim of the Murder at the Mouldy Mill* with N[ancy] as the Vamp, me as the Villain, & Anne as the Victim: Mrs S[tallibrass] as the Aged Mother & Mrs P[rince, one of Nancy's aunts] as the Comic Servant: complete with an epilogue in heroic couplets.

Afterwards, there was 'a little dancing, & parlour gymnastics'.

The following day, there was 'nearly a disaster', when Nancy announced over breakfast that she 'wasn't going to church today, as Sunday seemed such an anticlimax after Christmas'. However, she gave way to family pressure; and shortly afterwards Diccon was invited to stay on at Kemble until New Year's Day. (Apparently it had always been intended that Diccon should stay until then; but the aunts had decided to 'leave themselves a loop-hole' in case they could not stand him in the house for any longer than three nights.) 'Darling', Diccon wrote to Louisa, 'I hope you don't mind. It is so lovely being in the same house as Nancy, & not having to spend all my time saying good-bye.'

Three dances had been arranged; but as the days went by, Diccon's pleasure in Nancy's company was offset to some extent by the boorishness of her relatives. He found that he was unable to take Nancy over to Cheltenham to visit Hugh Lyon, because 'the two aunts have only five cars between them', so 'naturally' (as he told Hugh) 'there isn't one to spare'. Diccon added that he was 'being inspected by the county', whom he described as 'the most amazing collection of oppulent bumkins'. He had just been for a walk with 'a young dragon', with whom he had[29]

> discussed the pernicious spread of education. 'After all' [the young dragon] ended, 'my idea is that there's the upper class and the lower classes, & all this school rot is only unsettling. I don't see, myself, why they need even learn to read'?!!!?

On New Year's Day, when Diccon was due to leave, he was finally allowed to borrow a car for the day; and so instead of travelling 'straight back to Wales to my sorrowing mama', he drove Nancy first to Cheltenham to be introduced to Hugh Lyon; and then on to Islip to meet Robert Graves and Nancy Nicholson.[30]

Robert met them at the door of The World's End to warn them that Sam (almost two years old) had had mumps earlier in the month; and that although Sam was now out of quarantine, and three-year-old Catherine and five-year-old David appeared to be clear, six-year-old Jenny was showing some symptoms of the disease, and was confined to her bedroom until they could be certain of her condition. Neither of the visitors had ever had mumps; but the danger seemed so slight that they ignored it, and entered the long, low house: two old stone cottages knocked into one.

It was there, sitting in semi darkness before a blazing fire, that Nancy Stallibrass and Nancy Nicholson met each other; and the contrast was extreme. One of them, in her twenty-first year, was inexperienced, beautiful, and full of romantic dreams about being a writer's wife. The other, only seven years older, was worn out by having given birth to four children in five years, suffered from a thyroid imbalance which had made much of her hair fall out, was thoroughly disillusioned and desperately needed a winter in the sun.

After visiting Islip, Diccon Hughes returned Nancy Stallibrass to Kemble; and then he travelled up to North Wales, and began looking for a home for them to share after their marriage. He was in a highly excited state of mind, and would soon be telling a friend that he had no particular news, *except* that he was engaged to be married; that he and his fiancée had been offered jobs on a schooner bound for the South Seas; that he was a kind of part-owner in a little 20-foot sloop; that he was completely broke; that he had a novel in preparation, and that his collected stories and collected poems would be appearing in the spring.[31]

Diccon and Nancy were soon corresponding about possible wedding-dates. Diccon favoured St David's Day (St David being the patron saint of Wales); but Nancy pointed out that 1 March fell on a Monday in 1926, and that a Saturday would be far more convenient for their guests: so they settled on Saturday 27 February.

When Diccon broke the news of this agreed wedding-date to his mother, it came as a severe shock. 'Result: a fainting attack, miles from home, when we were prospecting the Ffestiniog country.' Nancy's mother reacted equally badly, working herself into a terrible state over 'the money question'. Diccon spent a morning writing her 'a careful financial statement. I hope it will calm her', he told Nancy.

I was afraid she'd have one more fling. If a crisis arises, however, wire & I'll come up. It is absurd to talk of pauperism:
we shall *start* with six or seven hundred a year between us, &
Hope!

He himself remained happy and excited as he went house-hunting,
and as the wedding became 'realler every minute! Hoorooosh!'
   Diccon had hoped at first for Cwm Mawr, that remote farmhouse where he and the Biancos had once cooked supper by
moonlight. Finding it unavailable, he examined numerous
other properties, including Dolwyddelau Castle, which (as he
told Nancy)

> really *is* exciting ... the walls are all ruined but the Keep is
> in perfect repair, a large square tower *with a roof* ... It belongs
> to a small freehold farmer's mother-in-law ... there seems quite
> a chance of letting ... Does this excite you? or make you think
> of DRAUGHTS?'

When Nancy said that it sounded highly impractical, he continued
his search; though he thought it was worth seeing whether they could
acquire the castle 'for next-to-nothing ... & just camp in it when we
felt Romantick'.
   As for the details of the wedding: at first they both favoured
a small formal ceremony, followed by a large informal reception.
Nancy then changed her mind, and suggested a larger but informal
wedding, with no reception to follow; and Diccon had just agreed,
when Mrs Stallibrass decided that (if there had to be a wedding
at all) it should be a very large formal wedding at Holy Trinity
Church, Brompton, followed by a very large formal reception at
the Rembrandt Hotel; and she had invitations printed to that
effect.
   This was irritating to the engaged couple, but relatively unimportant. More worrying was the possibility (which began to prey
on Nancy's mind) that one or both of them might have contracted
mumps during their visit to The World's End. Nancy asked Diccon
to find out whether Catherine (with whom she had played) had since
gone down with the disease; and he replied that he had 'written to
RG/NN to ask very tentatively after Catherine's health. My blessed
angel', he added, 'I was an idiot to take you into the house at all:
we ought to have bolted at once'.
   His letter never reached Robert and Nancy, who had hurried off to
London several days earlier than planned; and by 17 January, when
it was clear that no answer would be forthcoming, Louisa wrote on
Diccon's behalf to Amy Graves asking if she knew whether Robert's
children had mumps or not, explaining that[32]

Diccon took his Nancy down to see them & found that Jenny was suspect. It is rather important for him to know as he is getting married next month & as neither he nor Nancy have had it they will have at least to observe quarantine – if worse things do not befall them.

Amy replied that it had been a false alarm: the children had only had swollen glands, and had been able to set sail for Egypt on 8 January with a clean bill of health. She was sorry that Diccon had been anxious, and she enclosed a cheque for one guinea as a wedding-present.

Diccon was not much impressed by Amy's generosity, and asked Nancy whether her cheque should be 'an exhibit in its own self, or shall I go to the docks, & lay it out in a pair of tarry trousers to *Twinkle* in, & label them "From Mrs Graves"? She tells me to buy something "nice" with it'. However, he was highly relieved by Amy's news about the mumps, and told Nancy that he would now be able to join her in London as soon as he had 'cleared off my arrears of journalistic work'. In the meantime, he asked her to extract written permission for the wedding from both her parents, so that the banns could be read out in church on the last Sunday in January. 'Darling', he concluded, 'I shall work like a nigger & let you know as soon as I can about coming up.'[33]

Everything looked promising; but the very next day there was bad news. Despite the story about swollen glands, which Amy had retailed in good faith, Diccon received a wire from his fiancée stating that she had definitely contracted mumps. Within a few days he was wondering gloomily whether or not he too had the disease. Within a few more, he was having serious doubts about getting married.

It was only a few weeks since Diccon had parted from Nancy in a state of almost ecstatic happiness; but as the wedding-day approached he suddenly became deeply alarmed; and his fears took the form of worrying about that very sensitivity in Nancy which had once touched his heart.

In the early days of their friendship, Diccon had enjoyed reassuring Nancy when she told him of her occasional 'nightmare feelings'; but since then he had several times had to write to Nancy begging her not to worry herself ill; quite recently (when Nancy had complained about his delay in sending her a list of wedding-guests) he had commented: 'I'm afraid the truth is that you've been overdoing yourself rather, isn't it? Still, I'm glad you are being careful now'; and on hearing that she had mumps, he had become so used to thinking of her as slightly neurotic that his immediate reaction was not to be sympathetic, but to suspect that it was probably 'a false alarm: it is really two days early for you to begin'.

By the end of January, it was Diccon who appeared to be the one in a thoroughly nervous condition. 'I really am in a quandary', he told Nancy.

> I don't know whether I've been mumping or not. Don't stare: I mean it. I've had all the symptoms *except* the swelling – Hamlet without the Prince of Denmark, in fact ... The result is I don't know just when it began, I shan't know when it is ended, & when I'm uninfectious enough to travel!

And if Nancy herself remained infectious for some time, he could only visit her if he definitely *had* contracted mumps. Otherwise, he wrote nervously, he 'might catch it & come out on my wedding-day!'

A week later, and Diccon was suffering from an altogether new set of symptoms: 'a steadily *sub*-normal temperature & a pulse practically on strike altogether'. In the circumstances, he asked Nancy to forgive him for 'a very wispy little letter', though he added that despite his illness he had 'succeeded over the weekend in wading through all this year's submissions for Public Schools Verse, which is no mean achievement'.

Nancy was now surprisingly cheerful. 'You must have the courage of a steam-engine', Diccon told her. 'My own always gives out like a burst tyre when I am ill.' A few days later, at the beginning of February, he attempted to write a cheerful letter to Nancy from his sick-bed, and began exuberantly:

> My dearest love,
> SPRING really has come, I do believe – I feel it in my bone (but perhaps that is the tonic I am taking) & see it through the window. Hooray! There'll be a full moon at the end of the month, too. We'll be able to leap over the mountains all night.

But then he added gloomily 'Or do you not feel leapish' before filling up half a page with bad news from America, where Pamela Bianco had suffered a severe nervous breakdown.

The truth was that by this time Diccon was racked with doubt; and as soon as he was well enough, he walked over to Plas Brondanw, and poured out his worries to Amabel Williams-Ellis. Although he still loved Nancy very much, he recognised that they were both highly-strung and both liable to alternating moods of elation and depression. Up to now (he told Amabel), the one who was elated had always been able to comfort the one who was depressed. But suppose the day came when their black moods coincided? It would turn their marriage into a nightmare.

Instead of trying to allay these pre-wedding nerves, Amabel agreed that Diccon and Nancy were temperamentally ill-suited, and advised him to break off the engagement.[34]

Diccon could not quite bring himself to take Amabel's advice. If they were really unsuited at present, then surely he could change? Yes, he must be the one to banish his private devils, and see things through.

But Amabel had fatally weakened Diccon's confidence in himself, and his next letters to Nancy have a good deal of false hilarity attempting to mask fundamental unease. In one of them, he asks her to remind Peter Quennell 'about the Epithalamium he promised us . . . It will be probably very indecent, but he *must* be made to produce it. He must, he must'; and he looks forward to being 'in a fit state to plague the life out of London together'. But then comes a thoroughly depressed warning about the danger of their becoming too attached to possessions. In another, after telling Nancy to be careful not to over-do things and 'invite a relapse', he adds:

> Don't you think instead of the wedding march we ought to have 'A hunting we will go' with its chorus of:
> > For all my fancy
> > Dwells upon Nancy
> > And I'll sing tally-ho!

At last, on Saturday 13 February, Diccon arrived in London, and joined Nancy for a walk. It was their first meeting for more than six weeks, and it was only fourteen days before their wedding. But instead of being a joyful reunion, it was more like a wake.

To Nancy's horror, she found herself walking beside someone so sad and withdrawn that she hardly knew him. Since (for once) Diccon seemed utterly unable to communicate what he was feeling, Nancy tried to help him. 'I *know* you love me', she declared at one point; but even this elicited nothing very positive; and when they parted that afternoon she was sick at heart.

Worse followed. For day after day, while Nancy tried to pretend to her parents that all was well, there was no sign of Diccon. He never called at her house, he never wrote, he never even telephoned.

By the following Thursday (with nine days to go to the wedding), Nancy felt that she could only interpret Diccon's behaviour in one way; and she wrote a letter telling him that he had behaved so abominably that he had finally lost her love. In his reply, Diccon began with a frank apology: 'My dear', he wrote,

> you are perfectly right to be angry with me for behaving the

way I have: looked at simply as *behaviour*, it was abominable. And if I have lost your love, it is all along what I have known I deserved: I have known I wasn't really worth putting even in the same room as you. There is nothing I can complain of: only thank you very humbly for the very patient way you have put up with my behaviour hitherto.

However, her letter had sounded angry, '& when people are angry they're not sure'; so perhaps she could forgive him?

If he had seemed distant on Saturday, he explained, it was partly because he had a headache, and partly because he disliked the pressure of being in crowded places: 'I don't in a way feel really *with* you in crowded places', he told her,

> but I had fought my devils and they were dying in heaps: and I was happy just to sit by you & walk with you. Dearest, you said you *knew* I loved you. And I believed you knew it, too. I didn't think that it was really a doubtable thing, except by myself when I am mad.

As for his silence: it had been due solely to his need to get through

> more work than I felt up to doing, & my only hope of pulling through it was to give every minute of the day to it, & if I had rung you up I should not have been able to stop myself coming to see you & so neglecting things.

He added that she was 'such a wonderful creature' that he felt it

> almost blasphemous to plead with you, or ask you anything. But I do ask your forgiveness, & to see me. I have been *thinking* about it, because I didn't dare do anything else. And then suddenly – it is gone. Is it gone, Nancy? I know I haven't any right to hope you will forgive me: but I shall stay in all the morning, at least hoping to hear from you. Oh, Beloved!

He then asked Nancy to telephone him to arrange a meeting; but instead, on Friday morning, he received a letter which finally ended their relationship. 'Dear', he replied,

> if I needed anything else to convince me what an angel of light you are, it would be that letter. I shouldn't have thought any human being could be so unreproachful.
>
> I have wanted this to come right, more than I have ever wanted anything in my life before: and seen it going wrong. If you weren't so precious to me all might, in a sense, have been well: but we are neither of us of a build to be able to put up with the second-best in marriage: it must, for us, be flawless as a gem. We can't take it lightly, cynically: there is a sort of dangerous sensitiveness in us, that means we *might* reach heaven – but missing it would have no purgatory, only hell.

Just what is it has happened? I love you, you are the most precious creature to me; & yet I feel like you that it is 'impossible' – whatever that may mean! The country of the blind: two people walking together hand in hand: so happy that they do not notice when they drop hands: then find themselves a few feet apart, longing for each other, hearing each other's voices – unable to *touch*. I know, in the intuitive way one knows these things, that it is my fault, that somehow I made a mistake, somewhere – & nature never forgives a mistake. If I knew what the mistake *was*, I might even now put it right. But I don't, though I would give my eyes, each separately, for the key. Oh Nancy, my beloved, *where* are you?

I am writing today to catch the post, though I hardly know what I am saying – for though I felt all night your letter was coming, that made it no less of a shock when it did arrive. Perhaps in a day or two I shall feel a little clearer: at present I am only flooded in a sort of paralysing sorrow that stops me thinking. I can only acquiesce in your decision: it was a miracle of God that you ever loved me, & it was the act of a saint that you have borne with me so patiently, & tried to shield me from the consequences of my own mistake: but sooner or later I *had* to be abandoned to them: & now that I am alone with them, either they will destroy me, or I them. When that is over, I believe and hope that I shall love you more passionately than you me: I hope it, even though by that time I may have lost you for ever, though the realist in you has by then fully discovered the despicable in me, & I simply get the kick in the face I deserve.

Oh Nancy, my darling above heaven and earth, HOW have things come to such a pass? How will it all end?

If there had been a central mistake on his part, as he believed, then Diccon might have found the key in his early dream about Nancy: the one in which she was floating down the Danube, and he swung himself out into her canoe, only to discover to his horror that she had become a Serbian policeman, who put him under arrest. Believing (probably as a result of his difficulties with Louisa) that it was dangerous to love anyone too completely, Hughes had 'stamped on the canoe till it sank'; but then it had only been a dream, and he had been able to wake up. This time, he had destroyed something real.

Instead of replying to Diccon's letter, Nancy Stallibrass wrote very unhappily to Peter Quennell (who was then in Ravenna) about the breakdown of her engagement. Peter sent her a sympathetic reply; and would later marry her himself. Diccon for his part retreated to Garreg Fawr, where a period of acute depression was followed by a complete nervous breakdown.

CHAPTER 14

Recovery

Under the grey, slate roof of Garreg Fawr at the head of its remote and beautiful Welsh valley, Richard Hughes lay in bed in a state of utter misery and almost complete nervous collapse. It was Saturday, 27 February 1926, the day which should have been his wedding-day. His face, normally so mobile, seemed like a wooden mask. There had been no public announcement that he and Nancy Stallibrass were not, after all, to marry; and his misery was heightened during the next few days when telegrams and letters of congratulation reached him from those, like Amy and Alfred Perceval Graves, who assumed that the wedding had gone ahead as planned.[1]

Silence and darkness descend upon the next two months of Hughes's life. The publication by Chatto & Windus of his collected poems (*Confessio Juvenis*) and selected short stories (*A Moment of Time*), which would once have given him such pleasure, now seemed almost an irrelevance. It is only possible to guess at the depths of his suffering but no doubt, like the poet Housman on finally realising that his love for Moses Jackson had no future, Diccon felt that his heart and senses had been drowned: 'Far past the plunge of plummet/ In seas I cannot sound.'

Later, Hughes would be extremely reticent about his breakdown, describing it variously as 'a sudden and severe illness which made all work quite impossible for a long while',[2] and as 'a serious illness – chiefly the deferred result of overwork in my schooldays'.[3] Once, fearing that someone who was close to him might be on the verge of a similar breakdown, he drafted (but never posted) a letter in which he wrote that, in his own case, 'the emotional causes were pretty complicated, and after it happened I could do no [intellectual] work at all for 6 months'.[4]

Before then (towards the end of April), Hughes decided that he was convalescent enough to leave Garreg Fawr and seek relief from his mental suffering through physical hard labour; and he cabled to Captain Coward of the schooner *Elizabeth*, then in the Seychelles, asking whether he could travel out to the South Seas and join their voyage.

The reply was disappointing. 'The mistake you made', Captain Coward wrote bluntly,[5]

> was in not joining us in Portmadoc, a chance like that you may never get again: to leave a small place like Portmadoc for such a long voyage the end of which was on the knees of the Gods . . . We have paid off & sent home our Portmadoc crew & now have a native crew & we're leaving Thursday for the Farquhar Islands, & taking fifty labourers down there who'll load us with guano for Mauritius, from there we'll probably go back to the outer islands.

He explained that Diccon had no hope of finding them in the outer islands without chartering a schooner and sailing around in pursuit, possibly for months. 'Still, don't lose hope', the captain concluded, 'as we may be coming home early next year & start another ship, or we may get into some regular trade.'

In the circumstances, Diccon had to settle for something more modest; and he signed up as deck-hand on 'a little cargo-carrying ketch'[6] filled with slates for Ireland. Built for a crew of six, she set sail with only the captain, the mate and Diccon on board. 'We had a very slow passage out', he wrote to his mother from Belfast on Friday 21 May,[7]

> head winds all the way. Anchored in Abersoch Roads Saturday night: were off Holyhead by breakfast Monday, & off the Isle of Man by Tuesday morning. We were becalmed off the Irish coast all Tuesday night, & fetched into here Wednesday afternoon.

He added that he was very busy cleaning and painting; that the cargo would be 'all out tomorrow', and that they were hoping to load a fresh cargo, and sail for Portmadoc on Tuesday. More important, he felt 'very well, and enjoying it all immensely!'

On returning to Garreg Fawr, however, Diccon found that he was still incapable of any prolonged mental effort; and his doctor's advice that he should do no more than half an hour's work a day was superfluous. When he tried to return to his book about the pirates and the children, he could write for no longer than 'ten minutes at a time', and he was often 'unable to write at all for days together'.[8]

What sustained him was his association with Chatto & Windus. They liked his work so much that (as he recalled years later) they decided to take 'a long shot . . . [and] on the strength only of two little books of plays and short stories, neither of which had sold a thousand copies, [they] guaranteed me a minimum income'.[9] This would be an essential support through the months and years to come; and although at first he could hardly do any writing, he began the practical work of examining in the greatest possible detail the psychology of children: something absolutely necessary if his novel was to ring true.

To this end Hughes began (in his own words) 'borrow[ing] friends' children, generally one at a time to come and stay with me for a week'.[10] The child whom he borrowed most frequently was eleven-year-old Charlotte Williams-Ellis who (according to Amabel), had been going through a difficult phase of[11]

> nightmares and that sort of thing, and they used to go off together, [on] walking tours ... It did her a lot of good and Diccon got a lot of copy out of her. But ... very often there w[as] a whole nest of children.

One of the attractions for the children was that Diccon would encourage them to take part in all kinds of potentially dangerous pursuits ('Sometimes with boats and sometimes with going up on mountains in rather perilous conditions'); but none of them ever came to any harm because, as Amabel recounts, 'he was very large and strong [and] could pick them up and carry them, which swayed on our maternal anxieties'.

Occasionally, even when children were with him, Diccon would plunge into a black mood. Amabel once asked her daughter:[12]

> 'What was Diccon doing?'
> Answer: Lying on his bed.
> 'And what doing?'
> Despising.
> Question: 'Despising what?'
> Just despising.

But for some months (apart from the interlude of his voyage to Ireland), he found it much easier to spend time with children like Charlotte, who could accept him as he was, than in the company of other adults. (Years later, he commented that 'during my illness small children had proved to be almost the only human contacts I could tolerate'.)[13]

Early in June, when J.O. Francis (who had written plays for the Portmadoc Players) sent Hughes a letter, he received a reply making it clear that Diccon had been seriously ill, and that he was still very far from a complete recovery, and was finding it almost impossible to work.[14] A few days later, when Amy Graves asked him and his mother to Erinfa, Louisa replied on his behalf that Diccon was much better – but the Graveses must come to Garreg Fawr if they wished to see him, as he was not yet ready to pay social calls.[15]

Later that month, reckoning that Diccon's recovery would now be faster if he were no longer living under the same roof as his mother,

Clough Williams-Ellis came up with an ingenious solution. He was in the process of developing an Italianate hotel-village at Portmeirion, on the Dwyrwd estuary about four miles from Brondanw,[16] and he asked Diccon to spend the summer of 1926

> living at Portmeirion on board a retired 3-masted schooner, the *Amis Reunis*, which Clough had purchased in Portmadoc and kept tied up alongside the quay of the hotel. He gave Diccon free lodging on board and space to write, in exchange for Diccon having vague responsibility for any marine events that might occur at Portmeirion.[17]

This brought Hughes into regular contact with the manager of the hotel, Jim Wyllie (who was also a landscape painter); and the two men had soon become firm friends.

Wyllie's history was unusual: he had travelled to Morocco 'at the age of eighteen to learn Arabic in order to enter the Diplomatic Service . . . instead had stayed there', for several years, and still returned there each winter while Portmeirion was closed.[18] But despite having learned how to bargain in the markets of Tangier, he found from time to time that the Welsh were more than a match for him. On one occasion the following year Diccon Hughes was very much amused when an enterprising Miss Jones 'sold the lid of a motor-grease can to Wyllie as a (Cromwellian) pewter plate. He is pleased', Diccon told Louisa, 'and so is she: & so am I: so why wrong?'[19]

Living on board the *Amis Reunis* made it still easier for Diccon 'to get to know children without their parents – some even used to spend the night on board with him'.[20] With children, Diccon could do more than gain copy for his book: he could relearn in their presence his own childlike capacity for enjoying the simple pleasures of the passing moment. He could also indulge his continuing interest in pre-pubescent girls, an interest just as innocent (in practical terms) as it had been in the author of *Alice in Wonderland*; and yet with a dark side which worked just as powerfully upon his own creative imagination. In later life, Charlotte would vividly recall 'a game he used to get us to play called Muffled Silence when you move about in the dark and pinched people you met and they mustn't shout. It was terrifying'. She also recalled that as she began to mature physically, Hughes lost interest: she could no longer play the part required.[21]

While Charlotte was still young enough, however, she helped to serve as a model for ten-year-old Emily, the central character of Hughes's as yet untitled novel and in some ways a recreation of his mother. For in the first chapter of this novel (which took the entire summer and much of the autumn to draft) Diccon drew heavily upon Louisa's childhood experiences in Jamaica; as well as adding several eccentric touches from the Welsh landscape around him.

Emily Bas-Thornton is introduced to us as the oldest girl in a family from England who discover that Jamaica in the 1820s is 'a kind of paradise for English children to come to, whatever it might be for their parents: especially at that time, when no-one lived in at all a wild way at home'. Out in Jamaica, Hughes tells us,[22]

> one had to be a little ahead of the times: or decadent, whichever you like to call it. The difference between boys and girls, for instance, had to be left to look after itself. Long hair would have made the evening search for grass-ticks and nits interminable: Emily and Rachel had their hair cut short, and were allowed to do everything the boys did – to climb trees, swim, and trap animals and birds: they even had two pockets in their frocks.

There are cotton-trees and coffee-trees, where Emily and her older brother John set 'tree-springes' for the birds (just as Louisa had done when she was a girl); and the centre of their life is a bathing-pool where Emily, for coolness, sits 'up to her chin in water', while 'hundreds of infant fish were tickling with their inquisitive mouths every inch of her body, a sort of expressionless light kissing'.[23]

On the day after Emily's tenth birthday, she and John are invited to spend a few days with the Fernandez family, who own a ramshackle estate to the eastward, and whose driveway runs round rather than through a massive gateway whose iron gates are permanently closed – exactly like the gateway which led to the Satows' house in the hills behind Harlech. There Emily meets Margaret Fernandez, and is down by the sea with her when there is an earthquake. They come to no harm, but see the extraordinary sight of the water in the bay beginning to ebb away,[24]

> as if someone had pulled up the plug: a foot or so of sand and coral gleamed for a moment new to the air: then back the sea rushed in miniature rollers which splashed right up to the feet of the palms. Mouthfuls of turf were torn away: and on the far side of the bay a small piece of cliff tumbled into the water: sand and twigs showered down, dew fell from the trees like diamonds: birds and beasts, their tongues at last loosed, screamed and bellowed: the ponies, though quite unalarmed, lifted up their heads and yelled.

For Emily, this is the most exciting experience of her life; and she is so 'saturated in earthquake' that two days later, back home, she hardly notices the early stages of a tremendous thunderstorm.

While they shelter indoors, their tabby cat is savaged to death by wild cats; their old negro servant Sam is struck by lightning; and then as the wind becomes still more fierce, the shutters begin to bulge,[25]

> as if tired elephants were leaning against them, and Father was trying to tie the fastening with [his] handkerchief. But to push against this wind was like pushing against rock. The handkerchief, shutters, everything burst: the rain poured in like the sea into a sinking ship, the wind occupied the room, snatching pictures from the wall, sweeping the table bare. Through the gaping frames the lightning-lit scene without was visible. The creepers, which before had looked like cobwebs, now streamed up into the sky like new-combed hair.

Soon the floor begins to ripple; the roof is torn off by the hurricane; and Mr Thornton and his wife and children break through into the stone cellar below, and sleep there dead-drunk on Madeira wine, 'while what was left of the house was blown away over their heads'.[26]

Hughes had completed a draft of this wonderfully dramatic first chapter, and was just sinking back into a state of renewed creative exhaustion in which further progress seemed impossible, when he made a new friend.

It began one day when he was walking through Portmeirion, and saw three children dancing on the lawn. It was an enchanting sight; and he had soon introduced himself to nine-year-old Jocelyn Herbert, her younger sister Lavender, and their still younger brother John. They explained that they and their mother had been in a car crash. They had all been hurt, their mother badly. She was still recovering in London with their elder sister Crystal, but would be joining them soon; and in the meantime they were having a holiday and being looked after by a governess and a nurse.[27]

Soon the Herberts had become part of a whole gang of children whom Diccon entertained (including some Stephens from the Essex mud-flats who were related to Virginia Woolf). Sometimes the *Amis Reunis* would be the focus of their activities, and Jocelyn remembers Diccon hauling them up the mast in a bosun's chair; at other times they would go on walks through the mountains, and bathe in cold sparkling streams.

Jocelyn's mother, Gwen, was a tall, dark-haired artist in her early thirties, who had been married for twelve years to the writer Alan Herbert (a friend of the Williams-Ellises, and well-known as APH of *Punch*); and by the time she arrived at Portmeirion with Crystal, she found that Diccon had completely won over her other children; while she herself was so strongly drawn to him, that for several weeks she visited him almost every day.

Gwen found in Diccon a sympathetic spirit: the accident had left her with mental as well as physical scars, and she later thanked him for having done 'so much to make me better – and, as I told you, your interest in my children was a great need';[28] while Diccon found in Gwen one of the first adults whose company he had been able to tolerate since his breakdown. (Another of Gwen's friends would later recall that she was an appealing woman, whose voice had 'an attractive husky quality', and 'now and then, as she talked, she gave a little chuckle that was almost a croak. That doesn't sound attractive when described – but it was'.)[29]

Diccon and Gwen walked over the hills together, talked as intimately as old friends, and found that they even had a common interest in Jamaica: Gwen would be sailing there with her husband shortly after Christmas.

Gwen Herbert was an extremely understanding woman: when she returned to London she delayed writing to Diccon for several weeks, her natural inclination to get in touch, as she told him, having been[30]

> tempered by consideration of your state of mind. I am mindful of our last walk together; – of that Sunday painting & lying often on the hills; of your fear of my failing you Monday night (wasn't it that?); & of our mutual dismay the Tuesday! You are getting well – you will soon be writing again – you will face the past, & want the future: You may now hate letters – or want to forget me – so I meant to refrain from writing!

But she could not 'easily dismiss' him, and did not see why she should: 'All this pretence' being 'so futile when time races us along & we floundering after must needs snatch at what we like or go without'.

Gwen was also acutely perceptive. In her letter, she hoped that Diccon would 'keep above' the community in which he was living, in which he was perhaps too much adored. 'Only exotic or weakly plants', she told him,

> want that hot-house sort of atmosphere. You are too virile and have a rare quality that will develop with difficulty, but should come through under a rather spartan rule with yourself. All the charming paraphernalia of your day:- your clothes, your cookery – your legends – all so right and delicious for those wandering around you – & natural to you perhaps at present – all this and much else that you must suspect when you are introspective might swamp you yourself ultimately.

She understood, however, that it was 'terribly difficult' for him 'not to be charming! To forgo your best trick'.

Gwen also warned him about the unsatisfactory nature of his relationship with his mother:

> You are fond of your Mother, I know, but even the three times I saw you together I saw & felt the tension between you. One that is hopeless as you are on your guard & defensive the whole time. It's a sort of nervous friction that is doing *NO* good.

She made it clear that this was not intended as a criticism of either of them: she was merely 'stating what I know to be the case!' She added that as soon as possible, he should return to the larger world; and now that she had written all this, he 'must be kind & go & smoke that large pipe filled with my tobacco & remember that under this hard exterior a kindlier nature lurks, & that I liked you enough to see you most days ... a thing I have never done before'.

Spurred on, perhaps, by Gwen's letter, Diccon had soon decided that he would go abroad for the winter and see whether he could 'eke out an economical convalescence'[31] in a warmer climate.[32] On his way to the continent he stayed a night at The World's End, Islip, where he found Nancy Nicholson alone with her children, and heard from her the strange account of how Robert Graves and Laura Riding had gone away to work together in Vienna.[33]

By mid November Diccon was comfortably and cheaply established in the Albergo Tomasin on Capodistria, an Adriatic seaport to the south-west of Trieste.[34] Capodistria had been an island until 1825, when it was connected to the mainland by a causeway and drainage works; and its narrow streets and attractive old houses reflect a Venetian influence. From here, Hughes wrote both to Pamela Bianco and to Gwen Herbert to tell them that at last he felt like working again, and he began drafting his second chapter.[35]

Hughes was soon being distracted from his work: but usually in quite pleasurable ways. One evening not long after his arrival he managed to see Pirandello's *Cosi è (se vi pare)*, 'a wonderful play', with the added excitement that when it was over, Pirandello himself 'appeared to cries of author [though] I couldn't see him well'. He also began 'swapp[ing] language lessons every two days' with the son of a local doctor; and he discovered the delights of sailing the local craft, which were 'tricky ... but handy as greased lightning'.[36]

Sailing won him the friendship of two of the sea-captains of the local coasting schooners; and on Christmas Day they invited him to their remote island home, where they entertained him to[37]

> such a meal as I had never eaten before, a meal that has left my stomach elastic-sided for life. Then, after we had visited every

house on the island and drunk a tumbler of maraschino in each, we repaired to the inn, where two policemen lay on the floor so drunk that they could not sit, much less stand, yet firing off their revolvers in the crowded room with a monotonous regularity of aim.

Apparently every bullet either 'went through the window into the street', fortunately without killing anyone; or 'landed with a loud *ping* in an upturned brass spittoon in the corner'.

By this time Diccon had also become deeply involved with his fellow guests at the Albergo Tomasin, the Fassios, 'an enormous nomadic family from Piedmont who looked most respectable but couldn't pay'. Their impressive array of suitcases were 'empty, except for a kitten and a puppy'; there was a grandmother 'who spoke only Piedmontese and smoked a clay pipe in bed'; a mother in search of her husband, 'a consumptive whose habit it was to run away to some distant State sanatorium without leaving his address'; and four children, of whom the eldest daughter 'gave birth to a baby the night she arrived', and the youngest was 'a wizened and skull-faced little girl of seven who smelt'. Since they couldn't pay, the landlord kept them on, but without feeding them; and eventually Hughes took pity on them, and 'set them up in a cottage on the mainland, and fed them when I could afford to'. For this generosity he was 'gently chided' by the local schoolmaster, who thought that it was a waste of money keeping them alive, when they would be bound to die of starvation as soon as Hughes had left Capodistria. 'But I am sure he was wrong', wrote Hughes.[38]

> They were as ebullient and gay as crickets, with uneducated but wildly dramatic and satirical minds and incapable of self-pity even when fainting with hunger . . . They cast me in the dramatic rôle of their saviour, and when the mood was on them would heap me with gratitude and compliments that became all the more extravagant till we could sustain it no longer and dissolved in laughter, the two smallest rolling on the floor convulsed with laughter while the mother, poker-faced, was quoting them as saying that surely this young Englishman was the Good Lord Himself come down from Heaven in Person to help them . . . This was true wisdom, really, for it was the only way which could make tolerable the relationship of a 'rich' benefactor to his proteges which normally is so intolerable. My 'bounty',

Hughes concluded, 'really was keeping them alive; yet, instead of that making us hate each other, *this* way all we felt for each other was the warmest and most unembarrassed affection'.

While her son was abroad, Louisa (who had nursed him patiently through his long illness) had decided that she too deserved a holiday from Garreg Fawr. Early in December she had travelled up to London; and then in mid February 1927 she set out for Paris, where this resourceful woman not only visited the art galleries and attended at least one lecture at the Sorbonne, but tried to increase her range as a writer by working on ideas for film scripts.[39] Diccon as usual tried her patience to the limits with his shortcomings as a correspondent; but eventually on 8 March (when she had written suggesting that he should visit her in Paris for a few days) she received a long letter in which he apologised for not writing, explaining that[40]

> it began with not knowing whether you were in Paris or London, & then ensued an interregnum of earthquakes, liver, arrival of Bennett, long walks, & complete neglect of my fountain pen, so that my every post consists entirely of reproachful letters from people to know why I haven't written.

Jim Bennett had been tutoring in the south of France, and (as he complained to Diccon in January) his status was such that he had been reduced to having only one afternoon off each week. So when Hughes wrote to him about how cheaply he was living, Bennett had thrown up his job and joined his friend on Capodistria.

By this time (chiefly because of his generosity to the Fassios) Diccon could no longer afford to stay even at the Albergo Tomasin; however, as he had mentioned in a letter to Hugh Lyon, there were plenty of imposing palaces 'let in tenements to cuttle-fish catchers & other marine heroes – or empty'. He could therefore tell Louisa that:[41]

> Having run out of money, I have moved into a palace: where Bennett and I have an enormous first floor room with a bed each & some rather lovely but battered furniture, for 4d each a day, including the services of the countess to make our beds! We snack in the room for breakfast and lunch, but still take supper at the Tomasin.

His novel had 'temporarily collapsed: I don't quite know what has gone wrong', he lamented, 'but it won't write'. In the meantime, he was reading about the history of Istria; and very much enjoying living in the Palazzo Borizi, an 'extraordinarily attractive' fifteenth-century building, 'practically unfurnished, just a few incredibly battered pieces of good stuff ... a few old masters, & ... a long sala, where an aspidistra on a lace mat stands on a wicked-looking mediaeval black chest'. The palace was at its best either 'in the early morning ... with sleepy doves cooing all over the window sills'; or at night, when you stumble up the stone stairs & fling open the doors of the big sala: there is a street lamp outside that sends beams of bogus moonlight right through it, till it looks both ghostly and magnificent.

He concluded that he was uncertain about visiting Louisa in Paris, as 'I don't know when I leave here: it depends on funds, weather and whether I start writing again'.

In the event Diccon remained on Capodistria until the spring, by which time he had drafted another two chapters of his novel, moving the story on to the point at which Emily Bas-Thornton and Margaret Fernandez and their brothers and sisters fall into the hands of the pirates. Then Hughes set out in a leisurely manner for home. The first leg of his journey was by a little open four-seater seaplane which plied from Trieste to Venice: so, as he later recalled,[42]

I got my first sight of Venice from the air ... San Marco and the Campanile wheeling up first under one armpit then under the other till we splashed down at the mouth of the Grand canal. When I landed I found Lord David Cecil [a slightly younger Oxford contemporary] and L.P. Hartley [who was Robert Graves's age] gently promenading the Piazza, and joined them in a cup of coffee. *Their* Italian was impeccably Tuscan, and [at first] I did not dare open my mouth in Italian in front of them.

However, the moment came when 'they got into grave semantic difficulties with a gondolier', who found Hughes's Capodistrian Italian 'far more comprehensible – though naturally it amazed him to find this obvious British tourist talking a dialect even more debased than his own'.

From Venice, Hughes made his way back to North Wales, where he spent much of the summer and autumn working on his novel, writing occasional reviews for the *Spectator*,[43] and relaxing either on board *Twinkler* with Clough and Amabel, or ashore in the company of James Wyllie. Once again he spent some weeks living and writing on board the *Amis Reunis*; and once again Gwen Herbert and her children visited Portmeirion, and fell into the same close relationship with Diccon that they had enjoyed the previous summer. Afterwards, Gwen wrote to Diccon about their parting on the platform of Penrhyndeudraeth railway station. Apparently her daughter Crystal had remarked that[44]

you looked so sad as she said goodbye, & I was just seeing you standing aloof from me, & told the children you were going & they raced towards you & threw their arms around you so simply

& truthfully & feelingly – & I envied them their freedom.

It was 'such a right ending, at that moment', she felt, 'to the passage of our days together – with no ulterior or inner meaning!'

Towards the end of the year, Diccon felt that he was growing stale, and needed another foreign adventure. He had remained in touch with Captain Coward, with whom he still hoped to go voyaging; but the wind was blowing most unfavourably from that quarter. The *Elizabeth* had gone down in a cyclone in the south seas; the Board of Trade had presented Coward with 'a staggering bill' for the repatriation of the *Elizabeth*'s crew to the Seychelles; and there was a question about whether or not the insurance company would make good his losses. If not, thundered the Captain, he intended to[45]

> take action against the French Observatory, it was their fault the Elizabeth was lost . . . What's the good of an observatory if they can't see a cyclone coming . . . they can see snow-storms on the moon & floods on Mars & stars up to the 32nd magnitude, yet they can't see a cyclone 100 miles off.

In Coward's view this was 'gross negligence . . . let 'em direct their telescopes to windward where the trouble is!' In the meantime, he was trying to purchase a new ship, but with no luck so far.

This news reached Diccon early in December, when he was staying with his godfather in Hampstead. A few days later, Jim Wyllie, who was en route for his annual winter holiday in Morocco, called in on him; and, as Wyllie records, Diccon asked:[46]

> 'Where are you going?' I said: 'I'm going to Tangier.' He said: 'I'm coming with you!' I said: 'You can't: I've only got a quarter of an hour to catch the boat.' He said: 'Oh yes I can. You stay there.' And he went upstairs and dropped his suitcase down the well of the house into the hall and [it] burst [open] at my feet.

A few moments later clothes began raining down; Wyllie packed them into the case as they fell; and they left the house together, and caught the boat.

CHAPTER 15

In the Lap of Atlas[1]

It was a raw and sleeting December day in 1927 when Diccon Hughes and Jim Wyllie boarded a Dutch steamer calling in at Tangier en route for Java and points even further east. The start of the voyage was choppy, and made still less agreeable by the fact that the Lascar stewards, who padded about in bare feet, their heads wound in batik handkerchiefs, 'understood no request in any language . . . Pathetic little creatures', Diccon recorded in his travel-diary, 'with voices like windy mice and bodies like monkeys'.[2]

By the time they had reached North Africa, the weather was

> luckily fine enough to anchor in Tangier Bay, where [Diccon] got his first distant glimpse of this westernmost . . . outpost of Islam. Away to the right, on two-hundred-foot cliffs, he could see the crumbling walls and minarets of the Kasbah: below lay the scrambled Arab Medina, and outside the walls of the town to the left stood a few new blatantly European blocks which he tried to ignore. At that moment from one of the minarets a muezzin was calling the Faithful to prayer; and his wailing voice, heard over a mile or so of intervening water, sounded as eerie as wolves in Canadian forests.

After being rowed ashore by sweating oarsmen in a kind of wherry, they

> landed in Babel – or Bedlam – or both, with bare-legged hooded porters and touts and hucksters fighting each other and yelling like mad in Arabic, Spanish, or even a lousy word of two of incomprehensible English to get their custom. But [Jim] sorted everything out. Their luggage was hoisted on skeletal donkeys; and soon they were forcing their way through the fancy-dress crowds which thronged the steep and narrow (and only more-or-less-cobbled) streets.

The next day they drove south to Rabat, where they explored old Moorish dungeons; and then (over a period of days) they carried on further

> down the coast past dreary commercial Casablanca to Mazagan;

and on to Saffi, where beautiful bronze Portuguese cannon with handles moulded like dolphins and knobs like bunches of grapes still lay about on the Keshla ramparts just where – centuries back – the Portuguese gunners had left them. Then they turned inland ... towards Marrakesh; and saw for the first time – floating as if detached above the heat-haze – distant snow-covered peaks: the tempting, forbidden Atlas Mountains.

Both Hughes and Wyllie longed to explore these mountains and to reach 'Taroudant and the then forbidden Sous Country'. It was an area only nominally under French control; and while they were in Marrakesh, they secured an audience in his 'vast and desolate palace' with 'The Glaoui', a native prince who was not only Pasha of Marrakesh, but the Premier Lord of the Atlas. An outright request to travel into the mountains would almost certainly have met with refusal; but Jim Wyllie played a clever game. As he sipped his scented coffee, he

hinted (no more) at their crazy impossible pipe-dream of crossing the mountains from Asni towards Taroudant 'had the French been less insanely jealous of British intruders'. This nettled the Glaoui: the Atlas was his domain, and permission had nothing to do with the French ... Without more ado he [gave] his blessing; then turned to one of his Berber bodyguard, Ali [a 'lean and mild-eyed cut-throat'], and told him in Shleuh (the Berber tongue) to guide [these two Christians], and guard them – and not to come back without them ... Whereupon Ali – knowing full well what this warning meant from the merciless Glaoui ... sat up the whole night sharpening knives.

The three men rode southward on horseback the forty miles to Asni, in the foothills of the Atlas; but horses would be useless on mountain tracks; and since this was a region where 'only the scum-of-the-earth went on foot', Wyllie hired 'three miserable little mules, with whom three little slave-boys were thrown in as a make-weight by the owner'. Then, wearing no disguise 'but an Arab jelaba over our European clothes – to prevent us showing at a distance too obviously as Christians; and with no other weapons amongst us than our guide's curved knife and our own impudence', they set off into the mountains 'in the general direction of Taroudant and the forbidden Sous country'.

'The scenery', as Hughes records, 'was magnificent';

the whole mountain-side crimson rock and earth, the snow-capped peaks faint in the intense brilliance of the sky. The path was a narrow one, generally winding along the face of a cliff with a thousand-foot or so drop to the river beneath, that glittered like a little stream of spilt mercury among the olive-groves. There was

a continual coming and going of traffic; runners jog-trotting with
a load on their shoulders; here and there some rich man's wife on
a mule, attended by her eunuchs and covered in draperies like an
unfinished statue; or camels, with great bales done up in Saharan
carpets on each side. Meeting these last was nervous work. One
had to lie flat on one's mule to avoid being swept off and over
the edge; and the mules, moreover, had no saddles; just a kind
of straw pannier flung loose over their backs, on which it was the
custom to loll sideways, and which a nervous rider continually felt
to be about to slip into the gulf he could see between his legs.

When rivers had to be crossed there weren't any bridges:
they had to be forded, towing the three boys behind through
the ice-cold water gripping the tails of the mules in their teeth. At
night they would come to some mud-built village, where Ali would
summon the Sheikh and the magic of Glaoui's name would secure
them lodging of sorts: a carpet to sleep on, mint tea and rock-like
bread — and possibly hard-boiled eggs.

For three magical days all went well; but late on the afternoon of
the fourth, they reached a spreading valley where Ali seemed uncertain which track to take. On cresting a rise in the ground, they saw
below them what Jim Wyllie later described as 'this really magnificent
castle'; and then all the pigeons flew out of their nesting-places on
the walls; and the gatekeepers, alerted to the fact that visitors were
approaching, began swinging shut a pair of 'enormous doors'.

When they rode up, a wizened face looked out through a wicket-
gate, and Ali asked who owned the castle. On hearing the answer,
he turned pale, and whispered to Jim 'that Allah had brought them
to a country where claiming the Glaoui's friendship merited instant
death'. Bluff now seemed to be their only remaining hope. Jim beat on
the wicket-gate; and when it reopened, the castle seneschal appeared,
a huge coal-black man, dressed in a long striped gown, with 'a large
silver ring in one ear, a bunch of heavy keys and a long curved sword
in a silver sheath at his waist; and his expression was not one of peace
and goodwill towards men'.

Jim then 'pleaded the law of Koranic hospitality', naming himself
and his friends ' "deeaf Allah" — "guests sent him by God" '. The
seneschal disappeared, presumably to report to his master; and while
they were waiting, a crowd of small boys appeared. 'For some time',
as Hughes records,

> they stared at us in silence, making no move, their starveling
> faces concealed in their ragged hoods. But apparently we did
> not look quite so abject as we felt: for presently one of them
> came slowly forward and, bowing, lifted the hem of my cloak
> and kissed it ... rather a heartening thing to happen in the
> circumstances.

When the seneschal returned and asked for their papers, they had none; but Jim Wyllie (as he recalled years later)

> put my hand in my pocket and passed him the first thing I thought was a letter and we came in. We went along a dark alleyway, and ... I looked down from my pony and saw the whites of hundreds of Arabs' eyes looking up at us; and we came round a bend into an open courtyard with orange trees in bloom.

There stood the owner of the castle, holding Wyllie's 'papers', which 'turned out to be scarlet-edged, a royal coat of arms in gilt, and written underneath were the words: "With Fortnum and Mason's compliments" '.

The seneschal led them across the courtyard, where they climbed the outside stair of a corner tower, and were shown into a small upper room which was

> quite bare, spotlessly clean, and rather beautiful. The walls and floor alike were of a highly polished white plaster ... Only the ceiling was ornate, the rafters being carved and painted in rich, geometric colours. The single window had for pane a grille of simple and elegant iron. Moreover, what I saw through it was this: the river with its blackening olive-trees; the sunset; the dark crimson soil of the valley and lower mountain slopes; and above, colossal towering snow-capped peaks, rearing ten thousand feet higher into the daylight that had already left the lower earth.

Diccon Hughes turned back from this view to find that slaves were entering with carpets, mattresses, cushions, and candles in tall brass candlesticks. Others followed with

> glowing earthenware braziers poised on their heads, and incense thrown on the white-hot charcoal filled the room with blue aromatic smoke. The jittery Ali must have been badly in need of warmth, for he squatted on top of one of these braziers tucking it under his skirts as a personal central-heating system, and groaned with pleasure as tiny smoke-wisps of incense came curling out at his neck.

Before long, supper arrived: a magnificent supper which included a lamb roasted whole, and a couscous, 'a cone of white meal sprinkled with powdered sugar and cinnamon, with roast quails inside'. Jim and Diccon, having enjoyed their meal, felt less alarmed about their host's intentions; but Ali, as suspicious as ever, 'post[ed] the boys to sleep in dark corners of the stairs (if trodden on they could be guaranteed to yelp like any watch-dog). Then he laid himself out gingerly across the draughty doorway, his beloved dagger drawn and his cheek pillowed upon it'.

When Diccon woke the following morning,

it was with that vague uneasy feeling one gets sometimes, that there is something one has to remember . . . I lay still, chasing this elusive memory, enjoying the softness of my pillows and the sunlit morning air that streamed through the window . . . And then in a flash I remembered what it was – that I might never have woken up at all.

The danger had been real enough; and this was almost the southernmost limit of their wanderings. The next chieftain whose territory they entered gave them a superb lunch; but then, 'once we had again crossed his threshold into the open air, sent out a message that he would give us till sunset to be out of his reach. As he completely guarded the way to the Sous, there was nothing for it but to return'. It was an uncomfortable journey. Speed was essential: they had learned privately that once they had been given a few hours' start, they might very well be hunted down and killed. However, if the boys suspected that their masters were so much out of favour, they would probably decamp with the mules; so prizes were promised for whichever boy's mule was fastest, and they were cajoled into keeping going all day 'by jokes and mockery laced with bribes'.

Despite their speed, and their attempt to cover their tracks by taking a different route home, they learned from a friendly peasant that news of their retreat had reached the village at which they had hoped to pass the night, and orders had been given that no hospitality was to be shown them, a dictat which effectively placed them outside the law, and at the mercy of any anti-Christian fanatic.

The peasant risked the displeasure of his local lord (against whom he had a private grudge) by sheltering them 'in a windowless mud-walled stable half-full of dung and lit by a single candle'; but even so, they only escaped serious trouble, as Hughes recalls, 'by the skin of our teeth. In the first place, the village priest came and sat with us; and this prevented any sort of general mob attack'. But then, after midnight, they heard 'a staccato drumming outside, and a voice crying "Where are those dogs of Christians? Death to the Infidels!" [Diccon] peeped through a crack in the door: a single Negro with frothing lips was waving an awesome axe in one hand and wildly rat-tatting his drum with the other'.

Once again it was Jim's quick thinking which saved the day: as Hughes recalls, their bloodthirsty enemy 'was soon rendered helpless with laughter by [Jim's] celebrated imitation of a monkey catching fleas'.

Occasionally, Diccon Hughes was still liable to suffer from black moods (described to Pamela Bianco as 'relapses'),[3] during which he 'had to drop everything and just retire to bed with a detective story or something like that;'[4] but he had been invigorated by surviving extreme danger; and on returning to England, he threw himself into his work with more energy than he had shown since before his breakdown almost two years previously.

To begin with, Hughes wrote up his latest adventures for a wireless broadcast. This led to a useful association with Lance Sieveking, a childhood acquaintance of Diccon's who was now a BBC executive in his early thirties, and was also married to Gwen Herbert's younger sister April.[5] In the spring of 1928, Hughes gave a talk on 'The Atlas, a Real Journey into the Middle Ages', which he began imaginatively by using the Mohammedan instead of the Christian calendar, and announcing that[6]

> I found myself standing, one winter evening in the year 1363, at the doors of a great castle, petitioning for that hospitality which then was still – even in 1363 – in some parts considered the due of a benighted traveller.

Subsequently (at Sieveking's request) Hughes wrote elaborating upon suggestions for similar talks: on his Balkan adventures; on his experiences as a steerage passenger; and on his 'insane expedition to the Boiling North by Chrysler'.[7]

More important, Hughes continued with his novel about the children and the pirates until he had drafted a substantial section; and his thoughts kept returning to Morocco, and especially to Tangier, where on first 'thread[ing] a maze of alleys all smelling in turn of donkeys and incense and leather and urine and spices [Diccon had] felt strangely elated, as if this was "home" at last!'

Years later, fictionalising his travels in the Atlas mountains, Hughes considered that 'at twenty-six he ought to have had more sense'; but at the time those travels had heightened his sense that life was a dangerous and uncertain game, with horror and violence lurking only a few paces over the horizon. This may have been partly responsible for a shocking twist in his novel: while the pirate ship is anchored at Santa Lucia, the children (with whom the pirates have accidentally been lumbered) are allowed ashore; and while John is watching a curious nativity play (complete with live cow) from an upper window, he leans out too far, loses his balance, and falls 'clear to the ground, forty feet, right on his head'.[8] He dies instantly, and the other children never talk of him again.

Amabel Williams-Ellis, to whom Diccon read out the draft of what he had so far written, took John's death in her stride. What upset her was an obvious weakness in the book as a whole; and her comments were to be of crucial significance. As she later recalled:[9]

When he read me the first draft of it, there was no sex in it at all. I said: 'But my dear Diccon, this is a nonsense. There are all these girls and all these men and *something*'s got to happen. And so he put in . . . the half-grown girl, who is different to the children.

This was Margaret Fernandez, who now became the eldest of the Fernandez children, a girl of such earthy instincts that at the age of thirteen she can 'sort out people's dirty clothes for the wash by the smell: who they belong to';[10] and who would soon be 'follow[ing] the pirates about the deck like a dog'.[11]

But before he could rewrite and then continue with his novel along the lines which Amabel had suggested, Richard Hughes felt that he must enlarge his own experience of life; and he decided to travel once more to America, where he could renew his friendship with Pamela Bianco, now in her twenty-third year.[12]

In the second week in August,[13] while he was arranging his journey across the Atlantic, Diccon stayed in London with the Herberts. Alan and Gwen had lived since shortly after their wedding in 1914 at 12 Hammersmith Terrace, 'a row of houses built', so Lance Sieveking tells us,[14]

> for the mistresses of George the Second . . . They are high, narrow little houses with an elegance all their own. They have long, narrow gardens going down to the river bank, and beyond the low brick wall each garden has a flight of steps from which the residents can clamber into their little sailing-craft . . . one of the things I remember most vividly about Number 12 is the way the sunlight, reflected off the water, dazzlingly sparkles on the ceilings of those rooms whose windows look out across the river.

Here Diccon got to know Gwen's husband, with his 'mixture of open friendliness and intangible abstraction', a man who had surrounded his inner self with an 'invisible and intangible barrier' which even his children could not penetrate.[15] Here, too, Hughes one evening cemented his friendship with Sieveking, whose wife had just left him for another man.

Knowing nothing of this, but guessing from his own experience that Sieveking was heading for a nervous breakdown, Hughes suggested quite casually that he might like to borrow Garreg Fawr. The cottage was shut up, Sieveking was told, but he[16]

> could get the keys from [Diccon's] friends the Williamses down at Penrhyndeudraeth if I thought of going. The matter wasn't referred to again until next day when I, equally casually, asked Diccon Hughes for a few precise instructions.

Thirty years later, Sieveking would write that: 'The time I spent alone in that cottage brought me peace. After half a lifetime, my intense gratitude for that act of brotherly love and understanding is undiminished.'

Not long after his meeting with Sieveking, Richard Hughes boarded the SS *Baltic*, bound for New York.[17] He had already heard from Pamela Bianco that he would be most welcome at the old farmhouse which her family were renting in Connecticut. Indeed, she wrote that she was longing for him to arrive; and that she wanted him to accompany her in stormy weather on a private trek through the woods lasting the best part of a week. She intended, very oddly, to wear shoes which let in the rain; and at the close of her letter she begged him to remember this curious expedition,[18] in a plaintive and slightly possessive tone which he would come to find increasingly irritating.

CHAPTER 16

Pamela and Jane

Pamela Bianco met Diccon Hughes's boat when it docked at New York in mid August 1928;[1] and soon afterwards accompanied him to Merryall, not far from South Kent in the hills of western Connecticut. The two of them shared this sprawling farmhouse with several other members of the Bianco family; and during the next month Pamela's friendly feelings for Diccon seem to have quickened into sexual desire.

Diccon in return treated Pamela with special consideration, waking her each morning with tea and cinnamon toast;[2] but her adult sexuality was an unwelcome intrusion into their relationship. He shut himself away from her and wrote for much of the day; while for relaxation, he hired a horse from neighbours called Cassidy (Pamela did not ride) and explored the nearby woods, where the leaves were so thick on the trees that 'by the time the light reached the ground it was green, like being under the sea'.[3]

When in September the time came for Pamela and the others to return to New York, Diccon announced that he was going to stay on. By this time he had discovered that he could hire Merryall for a nominal sum out of the season; he had already acquired 'a peach of a Ford' (which he had named Ambrose) so there would be no difficulty about keeping himself supplied with stores; and he had taken the precaution of sending away for some tall boots to keep him warm while he finished his novel.[4]

Pamela had hoped and assumed that Diccon would follow her back to New York within a few weeks; but he remained uncommunicatively and (to her mind) stubbornly where he was; and one Tuesday in mid October she wrote miserably from MacDougal Alley about her thwarted hopes. She now wished (she told him) that she had joined Cecco and Max, who had visited him at Merryall the previous weekend; but looking after her new puppy had prevented her. She was doing a little painting, but much disliked waking up without her tea and cinnamon toast; he himself must be feeling very isolated up at Merryall; and she wondered whether he would soon be driving back to the city?[5]

After a further two weeks without a reply, she complained much more forcefully about his absence;[6] and then she tried to awaken his interest by a singularly unsubtle ploy. Sending him a letter, she enclosed a sealed envelope which she asked him to mail on her behalf. This would give some credence, she told him, to her pretence that she was staying with him in Connecticut – a device by which she hoped to discourage a male admirer whom she had met at a party, and who had been in hot pursuit ever since.[7]

All this was to no avail, as Pamela realised early in November after a meeting with her brother, who had spent a weekend at Merryall without letting her know in advance. Had she known, she said, she would have accompanied him; but now she had learned that her presence would have been superfluous; apparently Diccon's spare time was fully occupied in long moonlit rides with Jane Cassidy.[8]

A few days previously, Diccon had written to his mother not mentioning Jane by name, but describing her as his 'riding-companion', a woman 'whose husband is conveniently in Ohio & who has a big wilderness of a stone house on the top of New Preston Hill where she lives alone with a horse, two dogs, & a cat'. They rode together in the afternoons and evenings, averaging some twenty miles a day in temperatures of around seventy degrees; and Diccon's horse, Rowdy, was 'sure-footed, & not too mettlesome to ride by moonlight through the woods'.[9]

The atmosphere of repressed sexuality and romance which Hughes had found in his recent dealings with Pamela and Jane was exactly the right atmosphere in which to rework his pirate novel along the lines suggested by Amabel Williams-Ellis.

On the children's first night aboard the pirate schooner, Margaret Fernandez, questioned by the others about why she is sobbing, can only explain that she is frightened because she is older than any of them; and they are too young to know . . . Some days later, when Captain Jonsen and the sailors become very drunk one evening, and descend into the hold to see the children, Emily notices to her surprise that Margaret has gone as 'yellow as cheese, and her eyes were large with terror. She was shivering from head to foot as if she had the fever. It was absurd'. Then Emily herself is alarmed, when Jonsen staggers up to her, puts one hand under her chin, and begins stroking her hair with the other. Catching his thumb, she bites it as hard as she can. This breaks the spell; the sailors retreat. But over the next few days there is a major change: Margaret, who[10] at first ... seemed exaggeratedly frightened of all the men ... had suddenly taken to following them about the deck like a dog – not Jonsen, it is true, but Otto especially. Then suddenly she had departed from them altogether and taken up her quarters in the cabin. The curious thing was that now she avoided them all utterly, and spent all her time with the sailors.

Margaret, who has become the sailors' sexual plaything, is now heartily despised both by the sailors who use her, and by the children who believe that she has deserted them; and Hughes himself shows her no particular sympathy. However, by portraying (even if somewhat elliptically) what has happened to Margaret, he has significantly increased the emotional range of his novel; and can portray more truthfully the nature of the strong affection which grows up between Emily and Captain Jonsen, and which (like his own friendships with pre-pubescent girls) remains innocent despite containing a strong sexual undertone. It was this innocence at the heart of his story which led Hughes to the title for which he had been seeking: *The Innocent Voyage.*

Diccon had become aware that Pamela was sexually attracted to him: hence his epistolary silence. Where Jane was concerned, he seems at first not to have noticed; or to have wanted not to notice. However, as the weeks went by he felt under increasingly severe emotional pressure; and towards the end of November he wrote to Joseph Brewer (who had returned to his homeland and was now living at 229 East 48th Street in New York City), telling him that he was[11]

> not sure how much longer I'm going to be able to stay on here. I was ill last weekend, but I had a worse attack this one, and I don't much like risking a third attack alone like this: the second was short, but it was pretty bad. If I feel a third coming on, may I just telegraph and come up? ... It's my own fault, I have been getting up at five to work & then spending the afternoon & sometimes half the night riding.

In the meantime he was expecting Amabel's brother John Strachey for a long weekend, and was hoping that Joe would come too, though he warned him to stay away 'if you think you'll freeze: it really is getting, now, what the natives call "kinda wintry" – i.e. the eggs are solid in their shells, & saucepans freeze unless you wash them at once'. Diccon also asked for a loan of fifty dollars, as he could not quite last out until an expected cheque from Harpers arrived on 15 December; and added that he was 'hung up on the very last pages of my novel: not more than 4,000 words to do'.

While John was still at Merryall (he had become a fervent socialist, and took a positive delight in the somewhat Spartan living conditions), Diccon received a letter from Jane. She was angry with him for not visiting her: 'I think you are a louse with a small l, which is not lady-like of me, is it?' she began her letter. Her husband, Bob, had written[12]

> that he was coming home this weekend and then going to Des Moines, Iowa; and in the same mail another letter that he may not be able to get home this weekend and that Des Moines won't be until January. Which, of course, is why I think you are unmentionable for not coming up.

In Diccon's absence, she had had to put up with 'Camp' who, after meeting her out riding, had 'said he was coming up to call & did that evening drunk as a lord & got drunker so I drove him home in his Dodge in all the skids . . . & him making passes'. Then she had gone over to Waterbury to visit her uncle, whose 'kids . . . are swell. They came to sit on my stomach in bed this morning, & I wished you were there'.

When Jane next saw Diccon, he was still unable to complete *The Innocent Voyage*. One reason for the blockage was his anxiety about the separate publication of the first chapter. One of his New York friends, Henry Leach, calling it 'High Wind in Jamaica', had taken this vivid account of a hurricane for the December number of his literary magazine *The Forum*. Illustrated by some block prints of West Indian scenes, and discreetly reduced by a few pages (so that readers were denied the sexually charged paragraph in which Emily sits in the bathing-pool being tickled by hundreds of infant fish), 'High Wind' made an excellent short story in its own right and was widely praised.[13]

Hughes's anxieties were stilled; and then came a physical shock which suddenly made everything seem straightforward. One Tuesday in mid December he wrote excitedly to Joseph Brewer: 'I FINISHED MY NOVEL YESTERDAY. The jolt of somersaulting off Rowdy proved the required cathartic, & I did the last 3000 words in a burst.'[14] What had happened (as he recalled years later) was that a girl (presumably Jane) had baked him a cake, and he had 'started off for an all-day ride with the cake in my knapsack'. When Rowdy threw him, he had landed[15]

> flat on my back on top of the cake. The cake was absolutely intact. And so was I – more than intact – for I rode back and straightway finished the story. All I required was a good

shaking up. Which would go to prove that all books come from the liver.

With *The Innocent Voyage* completed, Diccon was planning to tour the south with Strachey; but first he enjoyed a Connecticut Christmas. This involved setting out late on Christmas Eve, and riding to the house of a neighbouring farmer of his acquaintance, 'through starlit air held motionless in the grip of thirty degrees of frost'. After supping 'solidly in the roaring furnace that was his kitchen', Diccon was[16]

> lulled to sleep, it is true, by the midnight cooing of children ... but there it all ended. By three in the morning we were up, had breakfasted on cold fried steak, and started forth with a willing hound bitch to a serious day in the woods *shooting foxes*!

Recalling the experience for an article in *Harpers* two years later, he concluded by asking wryly: 'Was that the way for a Christian Englishman to spend the day?'

Soon after Christmas, Diccon Hughes travelled down to New York from where he and John Strachey set out in Ambrose for the south. Strachey, as a budding politician, was determined that it should be a fact-finding tour as well as a holiday. So in Baltimore (which they had reached by 7 January 1929) they talked (among others) to Thomas Brown of the Department of Sociology of Morgan College, Baltimore. He gave them an introduction to Mordecai Johnson of Howard University, Washington, asking him to help[17]

> Messrs Strachey and Hughes, of England, [who] are visiting some of our Negro institutions and seeking to meet educated Negroes who are in a position to give them information on problems that vitally concern the colored citizens of America.

Other introductions, had they used them, would have ensured a warm welcome both in Palm Beach, Florida,[18] and in New Orleans[19] (where one of Diccon's plays had been produced at a little theatre in the French Quarter);[20] but for several weeks there is no record of their whereabouts, and both men vanish from sight.

Diccon reappears one bitter January night ('the wind is howling, the rain and cold incredible') at Bellevue, Virginia. A young woman called Annie Churchill is sheltering with her friends Emily and Charlie Abbot in 'the warm charm of the Bellevue Library', and waiting (as Annie recalled in a letter to Diccon written more than thirty years later)[21] for a young stranger who finally came about midnight.

Charlie went out to really help – and Emily to welcome – she came back swiftly with time for just one sentence – 'We are going to love him – his voice is charming – and the top of his Ford car is tied on with a rope' – and then suddenly – there stood a young Shakespeare – and with my enthusiasm I said so! Without a word you reached into your pocket and gave me a dime – probably your last one – and then began that lovely winter – of another world.

Then on 12 February we find Pamela Bianco in her New York apartment addressing an envelope to Richard Hughes at Bellevue in Virginia, where he was staying with Jane Cassidy, presumably while her husband was away in Des Moines.

Diccon had written to Pamela asking her to join them; and she replied with a letter of enthusiastic agreement. Her only two stipulations were first that she must be made to do six hours work a day; and second (thinking perhaps of the times when Diccon and Jane had gone riding together in Connecticut by moonlight) that he must train her to ride, as she wanted to spend a good deal of time on horseback.[22]

Diccon (as he explained when he wrote to Joseph Brewer, enclosing a set of page proofs of *The Innocent Voyage*) had been enjoying himself 'eating too much and living a regular life. My belly gets rounder and rounder'. He was also 'trying to learn to play the guitar'; and sometimes he went riding, though this was 'very painful: both horse and accoutrements being heirlooms; they were left behind by a Northern officer in the Civil War'.[23]

While he had been travelling with John Strachey, Diccon may well have met some 'educated Negroes', and learned something about those 'problems that vitally concern the colored citizens of America'. But here he was faced with the reality of the south in the 1920s, where most black people, though no longer legally slaves, had little chance of a decent education, and could therefore be seen as 'all crazy . . . The poor silly negroes', Hughes wrote, 'actually believe in voodoo'; and he recounted how one of the black servants, Dolphin,[24]

> threw the ice-pick at Hunter [another servant] & it missed him & stuck in the buttocks of the stallion. They had great fun catching the beast to pull it out. Then this morning a kitten that had fits ran up one leg of Hunter's pants & down the other: & that means Hunter is going to have fits too.

But if the blacks were 'crazy', the whites were crazier still – they were 'all Gentlemen and Ladies. Gee, Joseph', Hughes wrote in astonishment, 'they believe in the Unwritten Law! If you get called a Cad for cheating at croquet, shoot your best friend &

say he was your wife's lover & they'll let you into your clubs again'.

However, he and Jane were very happy together. Diccon seems to have treated Jane (though a fully mature woman) in much the same manner as he had once treated Gwenol Satow: guiding her, making her feel utterly secure in his presence, and inspiring her with the confidence to enlarge her own horizons. In particular, he persuaded Jane that since Bob was away so much, she should look for a job. Later she would come to feel that he had 'put on the screws rather hard. I don't believe you ever realised, though I had told you, how actually I accepted everything you said'.25 Under his influence, they were able to live in the same house together as though the love she felt for him was no more than platonic.

In the circumstances, it was a mistake to introduce Pamela into their delicately balanced household. Her letter of 16 February, thanking Diccon for the money he had sent towards her fare down to Virginia, shows that she was in a considerably disturbed state: on each of the past seven days, she told him, she had wept for several hours; and she added a curious story about how she had recently attracted a circle of admiring male shop assistants by trying on a new shirt in front of them.26

Pamela arrived in Virginia on Tuesday 19 February; and within three days everything at Bellevue was falling apart. On Friday evening Jane 'got very drunk, poor girl' (as Diccon reported to Joseph Brewer in a letter written the following morning)27

> & there was a hell of a scene. Pamela is flaring mad with me: the counts of the indictment falling under two main heads, A) that I am cold and B) that I am a lecher. Such is her sweet reasonableness. My wickedness in being Jane's lover is only exceeded by my cruelty in refusing to be Jane's lover. Need I say that I am depressed?

The chief purpose of his letter was to ask Joseph if he could stay with him 'from about March 7–20th', as Harper & Row had now fixed the American publication date of *The Innocent Voyage* for 13 March, '& want me in town for the week preceding'. But in the increasingly difficult atmosphere at Bellevue, Diccon Hughes added that 'I *may* get thrown out before the seventh'.

What had gone wrong? Years later, when Hughes drew heavily upon the experiences of these days for his account of Augustine Penry-Herbert's American adventures in the opening section of *The Wooden Shepherdess*, he wrote much about the totally different sexual expectations of young Americans and young Englishmen. To the Americans, almost complete sexual licence was considered normal: being a 'good' girl 'merely meant not taking the ultimate step which made you a bad one, finding it simple – with practice, and help from the boy – to get complete satisfaction without'. To the young Englishman, however, 'you didn't kiss any girl until you and she were engaged'; and 'one started off from the premiss that girls are 'cold' and 'pure', which means that Nature has left them without any carnal urgings at all unless and until engendered by love'.[28]

The more that Pamela betrayed her feelings for Diccon, the more he misunderstood, pitied and even despised her. Pamela in her turn began by being furious with Diccon for being more attracted to Jane than to herself; and was then still more furious when (in her American view) this lecherous Englishman, having got Jane interested in him, lacked the common decency to follow through and give her the physical warmth which she desired and deserved. Under Pamela's influence Jane too began to feel that Diccon was treating her badly, and had prolonged crying bouts.

On Wednesday evening there was a great deal of drinking; and the following morning Diccon wrote a long letter to Joseph Brewer telling him that between the two women he was being driven 'nearly crazy'; he also felt that Pamela, now merely a 'star illustrator', was betraying her earlier promise as a great artist, and he concluded that the only sensible remark she had made lately was 'to curse me for not having married her when she was fifteen'.[29]

A few days later Diccon suddenly departed from Bellevue, leaving behind two profoundly distressed young women. Pamela still wished to be Diccon's friend; and his growing dislike upset her so much that within a few months she would be completely re-evaluating the direction which her life was taking. Jane returned to her husband and (in her own words) 'tried' to dislike Diccon for a while; but because she understood that there had been no malice in what Diccon had done (or rather, failed to do), she 'could not' dislike him – or at least, not yet.[30]

On leaving Virginia Diccon had returned to New York where (as he had told Joseph) he had the promise of 'a bed (only) round the corner [from you] in 46th Street'. During the day, he hoped to 'be in-and-outish' at Joseph's house; and there he awaited publication of *The Innocent Voyage*: after which nothing would ever be quite the same again.

CHAPTER 17

The Innocent Voyage and Celebrity

The Innocent Voyage was published on 13 March 1929; and (as Richard Hughes later recalled) it made[1]

> a very slow start. It was taken up by just one or two critics, notably Isabel Peters and Burton Roscoe, who plugged it for all they were worth, week after week. I was in New York myself at the time, and Harpers kept me in constant circulation, at lunches, cocktail parties and so on.

Eventually, 'this worked'. other critics began to write glowing reviews; a great deal of interest was stirred up; 'about the eighth week after publication', the book climbed into the bestseller lists; and Hughes was suddenly a celebrity.

It was not just the quality of the story-telling which attracted readers, though this was outstanding. (The first chapter alone had won so many admirers when it appeared in the December 1928 number of *The Forum*[2] that Chatto & Windus had decided to retain the title – slightly altered to *A High Wind in Jamaica* – for English publication, now scheduled for late September.) But what would make the book such a talking-point on both sides of the Atlantic was its sharp, bleak, decidedly original (and some thought cynical) view of childhood.

In the Christian societies of the west (at least until the mid eighteenth century) children had been prized chiefly as potential adults. The doctrine of original sin meant that children were seen as fundamentally flawed on coming into the world: which had tended to obscure Christ's teaching that 'except ye be converted, and become as little children, ye shall not enter into the kingdom of heaven'.[3]

Then in 1762 Rousseau published his *Émile*, which he began with the striking sentence: 'God makes all things good; man meddles with them and they become evil.'[4] Rousseau's central thesis, that children must be treated not as embryo or miniature adults, but as human beings with specialised and separate needs, was highly beneficial; but his declaration that children were fundamentally good on coming into the world had been (ever since then) the basis not only for all kinds of sentimental nonsense, but also for books about children which were wholly untrue to life.

When Hughes was writing *A High Wind in Jamaica*, for example, one of the best-loved children's classics was R.M. Ballantyne's *The Coral Island*. This rousing adventure story, first published in 1858, carried the message that a group of children cast away on a deserted atoll in the south seas would prove to be naturally good, decent and self-reliant. That was not at all how Hughes saw his children; but instead of replacing the prevalent and somewhat dogmatic belief in the innocence of childhood with an equally dogmatic return to the doctrine of original sin (as Golding would do years later in his *Lord of the Flies*) Hughes accomplished something both far more subtle and far more profound.

Through his fictional group of children, ranging from three to thirteen, Hughes presents a comprehensive view of childhood in which his central thesis is that children cannot be judged in terms of adult values: for childhood, like the past, is another country. In describing Laura, for example, he writes that:[5]

> Being nearly four years old, she was certainly a child; and children are human (if one allows the term 'human' a wide sense): but she had not altogether ceased to be a baby: and babies of course are not human – they are animals, and have a very ancient and ramified culture, as cats have, and fishes, and even snakes: the same in kind as these, but much more complicated and vivid, since babies are, after all, one of the most developed species of the lower vertebrate.
>
> In short, babies have minds which work in terms and categories of their own which cannot be translated into the terms and categories of the human mind.

Hughes adds that a case might be made out for saying that children are not human either, but that, in his view, would be wrong:[6]

> Agreed that their minds are not just more ignorant and stupider than ours, but differ in kind of thinking (are *mad* in fact): but one can, by an effort of will and imagination, think like a child at least in a partial degree – and even if one's success is infinitesimal it invalidates the case: while one can no more think like a baby, in the smallest respect, than one can think like a bee.

As an example of how profoundly a child's mind differs from that of an adult, Hughes observes that children 'have little faculty of distinguishing between disaster and the ordinary course of their lives'.[7] In the immediate aftermath of the hurricane, for example, when the Thorntons are camping out among the literal ruins of their former life, it is the adults who are devastated; while the children accept the change quickly and easily. Indeed, they enjoy what seems to them like 'a sort of everlasting picnic', which leads them 'to begin for the first time to regard their parents as rational human beings, with understandable tastes – such as sitting on the floor to eat one's dinner'. And if Emily was occasionally silent, Hughes tells us,[8]

> and inclined to brood over some inward terror, it was not the hurricane she was thinking of [as her parents believed], but the death of poor Tabby. That, at times, had a horror beyond all bearing. It was her first intimate contact with death – and a death of violence, too.

The death of old Sam (far more horrifying to an adult) had made no such impact. To Emily's childish mind there was 'after all' (as Hughes writes with characteristic irony) 'a vast difference between a negro and a favourite cat'.

When children and adults perceive things so differently, there are bound to be misunderstandings. Mrs Thornton, we learn, would have been very much surprised to find that before the hurricane struck[9]

> she had meant practically nothing to her children. She took a keen interest in psychology (the Art Bablative, Southey calls it). She was full of theories which she had not time to put into effect; but nevertheless she thought she had a deep understanding of their temperaments and was the centre of their passionate devotion.

In reality, Mrs Thornton is 'congenitally incapable of telling one end of a child from the other'. When, for example, the children are first embarked on the *Clorinda*, and the time approaches for Mr and Mrs Thornton to go ashore, there is a difficult period when Emily and John are somehow 'captured' by their parents, and stand talking to them 'uneasily . . . as if to strangers'. For John it is a particular ordeal: 'With a rope to be climbed dangling before his nose', Hughes tells us, 'John simply did not know how this delay was to be supported, and lapsed into complete silence.' Mrs Thornton, noting this, but completely misinterpreting what she sees, will later remark to her husband: 'John is so much the most sensitive: he was absolutely too full to speak.'[10]

While the children remain in this largely unselfconscious stage of their development, they may (like Rachel) have an extremely keen sense of what is right and wrong – but their scale of values is quite different from an adult's. Months after their voyage with the pirates is over, when Emily has been asked to recall 'something nasty' about them, Rachel immediately butts in to remind her of an incident which (at the time) all the children found deeply shocking.

They had been tobogganing happily on the wet, sloping deck of *Clorinda* when Captain Jonsen, exasperated by the antics of these unwelcome guests, cried out:[11]

> 'If you go and wear holes in your drawers, do you think *I* am going to mend them? – Lieber Gott! What do you think I am, eh? What do you think this ship is? What do you think we all are? To mend your drawers for you, eh? To *mend . . . your . . . drawers*!'
> There was a pause, while they all stood thunderstruck.
> But even now he had not finished:
> 'Where do you think you'll get new ones, eh?' he asked, in a voice explosive with rage. Then he added, with an insulting coarseness of tone: 'And I'll not have you going about my ship without them! See?'
> Scarlet to the eyes with outrage they retreated to the bows. They could hardly believe so unspeakable a remark had crossed human lips. They assumed an air of lightness, and talked together in studied loud voices: but their joy was dashed for the day.

Other childish traits which Hughes records include the ability to close one's eyes to anything too disagreeable. When the children realise that they have been captured by pirates, they all 'shared Emily's instinct that it was better to pretend not to know – a sort of magical belief, at bottom'.[12] And when (knowing nothing of his death) they are faced with John's utterly inexplicable disappearance, the other children find it too frightening to be discussed: so that thereafter, 'if you had known the children intimately', Hughes tells us, 'you would never have guessed from *them* that he had ever existed'.[13]

After all this detailed observation of how children actually think and behave, we are still left with the problem of how the child develops into the adult; and Hughes tackles this triumphantly. At the heart of *A High Wind in Jamaica* lies an account of the psychological changes which begin at the critical moment when Emily becomes aware of her own separate identity, and (therefore) of her vulnerability and mortality. It is this awareness which will gradually propel her into adulthood.

The moment occurs when Emily is on board the *Clorinda*, 'walking rather aimlessly aft, thinking vaguely about some bees and a fairy queen'. Suddenly, it flashes into her mind 'that she was *she*'. Stopping dead, she begins to examine herself, though she[14]

> could not see much, except a fore-shortened view of the front of her frock, and her hands when she lifted them for inspection: but it was enough for her to form a rough idea of the little body she suddenly realised to be hers.

She began to laugh, rather mockingly. 'Well!' she thought, in effect: 'Fancy *you*, of all people, going and getting caught like this! – You can't get out of it now, not for a very long time: you'll have to go through with being a child, and growing up, and getting old, before you'll be quit of this mad prank!'

Climbing up to the mast-head so that she can avoid being disturbed in the middle of this new revelation, Emily continues with her self-examination by[15]

> examining the skin of her hands with the utmost care: for it was *hers*. She slipped a shoulder out of the top of her frock; and having peeped in to make sure she really was contiguous under her clothes, she shrugged it up to touch her cheek. The contact of her face and the warm bare hollow of her shoulder gave her a comfortable thrill, as if it were the caress of some kind friend. But whether the feeling came to her through her cheek or her shoulder, which was the caresser and which the caressed, that no analysis could tell her.

Convinced at last 'of this astonishing fact, that she was now Emily Bas-Thornton (why she inserted the 'now' she did not know . . .), she began seriously to reckon its implications'.

Chief among these is her vulnerability. 'As a piece of Nature', Emily had been 'practically invulnerable'. But with her new self-awareness, 'as *Emily*', she suddenly feels that she is 'absolutely naked, tender'.[16] It is not long afterwards, while she is still in this extremely anxious state, that this conventionally 'innocent' child commits a murder for which her conventionally 'wicked' captors will later hang.

The pirates have boarded the *Thelma*, a small Dutch steamer, whose captain is tied up and left on the floor of Jonsen's cabin. Emily is close by, lying on the bed in a feverish state after being accidentally gashed in the leg several days previously. Before long she notices that the stranger, who can just move his head, keeps turning his eyes[17]

> first on a very sharp knife which some idiot had dropped in a corner of the cabin floor, then on Emily. He was asking her to get it for him of course.
> But Emily was terrified of him. There is something much more frightening about a man who is tied up than a man who is not tied up – I suppose it is the fear he may get loose.
> The feeling of not being able to get out of the bunk and escape added to the true nightmare panic.

Then the Dutchman, seeing that Emily will not help him, begins rolling himself across the floor to the knife. Emily screams for help; but most of the pirates are still on the *Thelma*, and there is no one within ear-shot.

At last the Dutchman is within reach of the knife, and his fingers begin to grope, behind his back, for the edge of the blade. At that moment Emily,[18]

> beside herself with terror, suddenly became possessed by the strength of despair. In spite of the agony it caused her leg she flung herself out of the bunk, and just managed to seize the knife before he could manoeuvre his bound hands within reach of it.
>
> In the course of the next five seconds she had slashed and jabbed at him in a dozen places: then, flinging the knife towards the door, somehow managed to struggle back into the bunk.

The Dutchman begins bleeding to death. Margaret arrives, but has no idea what to do, and simply watches. Then comes the first boat-load of sailors returning from the *Thelma*. They find the Dutch captain 'on the floor, stretched in a pool of blood. *"But, Gentlemen, I have a wife and children!"* he suddenly said in Dutch, in a surprised and gentle tone: then died'. Margaret is blamed for the killing and dropped unceremoniously into the sea (from which she is picked up a few moments later by the second boat, bringing back the rest of the crew and the four children from the *Thelma*). But much later, back in England, it is the pirates who are tried for murder.

Emily, to protect herself, has said nothing; and when she finally breaks down in court, her only articulate words: 'He was all lying in his blood . . . he was awful! He . . . died, he said something and then he *died*!' are enough to secure the conviction of Jonsen and his crew.

A few days later Emily starts at her new school at Blackheath; and Hughes shows her making friends with the other pupils. 'Looking at that gentle, happy throng of clean innocent faces and soft graceful limbs', he concludes his story, 'listening to the ceaseless, artless babble of chatter rising, perhaps God could have picked out from among them which was Emily: but I am sure that I could not.'

And yet Emily had murdered the Dutch captain, and Margaret had become the sexual plaything of the crew. The shock (in 1929) of seeing children portrayed as creatures whose ideas, feelings and morals were so different from those of adults that it made no possible sense to think of them as in any way innocent, was neatly encapsulated in a review of *The Innocent Voyage* written by Ford Madox Ford in *The Forum* that summer. 'There used to hang on the walls of country public houses and farm labourers' cottages', he wrote,[19]

> a lithograph that, seen from close quarters, represented two innocent children against the light on a balcony beneath an arched

window. When you receded from it you saw that in truth it showed as a skull, with crossbones complete beneath. Mr Hughes's book is that lithograph come to life in another art.

It revealed Hughes's great 'literary gift and sheer magic of implication', but was also 'the most horrible' work of fiction that Ford Madox Ford had ever read. 'I feel inclined to say, as a final tribute', he concluded his review:

> that if ever a book deserved the attention of the censor it is the *Innocent Voyage* – and that compliment will do Mr Hughes no harm, for the censor is too stupid to attend to the book – he will probably give it to his daughter for a Christmas present.

For two months since the publication of *The Innocent Voyage*, Hughes had done as his American publishers requested, and remained firmly in the public eye while sales climbed to more than four hundred copies a week; but eventually (as he wrote to a friend), 'There just seemed no end to the lionising process. I had used up all my money and wasn't allowed a minute to make more'. So (although he remained in New York), he began 'officially' living in the country. This was achieved by the simple ruse of[20]

> say[ing] many farewells, and walk[ing] through Grand Central Station and out at the other side. If there is anyone I have to see, of course, I 'come up for the day'. Meanwhile Harpers send out press bulletins in all innocence, describing my life in Connecticut: how I rise at six, lave in the brook, go for a gallop on my mustang and then write for the next fourteen hours or so at my new novel.

There was certainly no new novel (though there may have been some short stories); but his increasing celebrity had given Diccon's existing body of work a new lease of life.

During 1928 and the early part of 1929 there had been no more than a trickle of interest in his work: a request from Vancouver for the USA and Canadian vaudeville rights of *Danger*;[21] another from a German publisher wanting translation rights to *A Comedy of Good and Evil*;[22] and a letter from Maurice Browne (writing from the Savoy Theatre in London) enquiring whether Hughes had any full-length plays to offer.[23] But with publication of *The Innocent Voyage*, the trickle becomes a steady stream. *Vanity Fair* sends him $100 for the first American serial rights of his short story 'The Ghost';[24] the editor of the *Yale Review*, Helen McAfee, introduces herself by mentioning that 'my friend Thornton Wilder has told me that you have recently come to this country for a visit', and asks whether he has anything for them;[25] Louis Untermeyer, revising

Modern British Poetry, wants to include 'Vagrancy' and 'Poets, Painters, Puddings', asks whether he has anything more recent ['Memo: send him *Confessio*' writes Hughes], and congratulates him on the success of *The Innocent Voyage*;[26] Viola Gaylord of New York asks whether *Danger* could go into a book of plays for a small High School[27] . . . and so on, and so on.

While he remained in New York City, Hughes (who always had something of the chameleon about him) was amused to discover the extent to which he was adapting to his environment. 'Curiously enough', he told a friend in May 1929, 'I find myself now enjoying the heat as much as I used to loathe it.' The temperature in his rooms had been over eighty degrees; and yet he had deliberately walked along the sunny side of Park Avenue to soak up even more heat. 'After that', he declared, 'I feel as if there is nothing durable at all − no Absolute − ME enjoying HEAT!' He added that 'Pamela complains of my American accent . . . and [J.C.] Squire [of the *London Mercury*] says he couldn't tell me from a mid-Westerner!'[28]

Although Pamela occasionally tracked him down, Hughes saw very little of the Biancos that spring or summer; but by now he had built up substantial circles of friends both in Connecticut and in New York City − where he was a particular intimate of Henry Leach, editor of *The Forum*.

Sometimes the two circles overlapped. For example Hal Smith, a New York publisher who became a close friend, was married to the woman from whom Diccon had rented Ambrose; and August 1929 found Diccon cruising with Hal on the New England coast in the yacht *Cossack*.[29] Fogbound for a while in Nantucket, the two men introduced each other to the rising stars of English and American literature − Diccon lending Hal his copy of Evelyn Waugh's *Decline and Fall* and receiving in return bound copies of William Faulkner's earliest novels *Soldiers' Pay* and *Mosquitoes*, and galley proofs of his first masterpiece, *The Sound and the Fury*, which Hal's firm was publishing. So impressed was Hughes that he contacted Chatto & Windus, who would (in due course) publish both *Soldiers' Pay* and *The Sound and the Fury* in England, with introductions by himself.[30]

Hal's sister-in-law Margaret also became a friend. She worked on the books section of the *New York Herald Tribune*, and wrote to Diccon the following year telling him that she had[31]

> thought of you times innumerable, especially here at [West] Cornwall [in Connecticut] this summer where everything is so wound around with memories of you: at the lake after a wild flight on the raft; at the study where I yearn for a recorder player; at meal-time when I need a city beginning with X or Y; during wild rides in the Ford, and so on quite endlessly.

Diccon Hughes had already showed that he was quite handsome and intriguing enough to break a few female hearts. (Jane Cassidy would later write to him about 'Hortense', telling him: 'You did a good job there. Let me tell you something – if you let a woman feed you breakfast she will fall in love with you as sure as shooting.')[32] Margaret herself was so fond of him that she signed her letter 'lovingly'. However, there was another woman who was fleetingly closer to him than Pamela or Jane or Margaret had ever been.

In the American section of _The Wooden Shepherdess_, Hughes depicts his _alter ego_ Augustine feeling 'ashamed in such strangely conflicting ways'[33] for having hurt the under-age Ree so badly by refusing to sleep with her; and soon afterwards, there is a scene in which Sadie comes to Augustine's bed. She says simply: 'Move, and give a wench some room.' Augustine's priggish moral resistance has been eroded by his guilt over Ree: 'It was Fate, he had no more fight'; and he allows Sadie to begin his sexual education.[34]

This is an echo of what happened to Hughes himself. Full of ambivalent feelings about how he had treated Pamela and Jane, he came across an attractive and slightly eccentric young woman of seventeen or eighteen who was shortly to begin her studies at Smith College in Northampton, Massachusetts. It is certain that they slept together; but all that survives of their meeting is this much-folded letter which Diccon preserved among his papers for the rest of his life:[35]

> Dear Dickens,
>
> I just can't tell you how ashamed I am about Tuesday night, I mean Monday nite – really tho' – I needed it – I was getting too damned confident about the amount and mixture of liquor I could contain – don't kid me about always being the lady – I'll admit I didn't remember a damned thing – but I have a vague recollection of me crawling across the floor on my hands and knees – oh horrors! And I prided myself on my dignity, and poise! Who could be dignified in that position – it speaks too much of my evidently not too distant ancestry!
>
> You asked for my impressions of Smith . . . The rules would amuse you, particularly when applied to a certain young Smith girl _you_ know! Oh well – I have become horribly rah-rah and am exceedingly happy being normal – Believe it or not!
>
> Don't be too fatherly when you write to me, after all, you know, I _have_ slept with you (or maybe you've forgotten).
>
> Ever   Ann

It was only towards the end of September 1929, when *A High Wind in Jamaica* was about to be published in England, that Richard Hughes was able to tear himself away from a country in which he had grown to feel very much at home. When he was being interviewed by some reporters who had followed him on board his ship, the SS *De Grasse*, he lamented that he had failed to master the American language, a task which he said would take an Englishman at least twenty years. Then he went on (in the purest American he could muster):[36]

> Get a load of this – in literature, England has more to learn from America than America has from England. Present day American authors are the goods. I give every new one the twice over. It wouldn't burn me up if one of them kicked in as the biggest noise since Shakespeare.

He had some conscience about having played to the gallery in this enjoyably shameless manner, and wrote to Joseph Brewer begging him to deny any suggestion that he had said anything uncomplimentary about America. 'I said nothing that was not silly', he explained, 'but nothing that was not complimentary.'[37]

Hughes had just finished dealing with the reporters when Henry Leach 'came galloping across the pier', asking him to speak to his cousin Miss Thayer who was also on board. Assuring Leach that he would do so, Hughes escaped to his cabin, leaving orders that the crew were to reveal his whereabouts to no one.

This meant (as he discovered only when the moorings had been cast off, and the SS *De Grasse* had begun its leisurely journey across the Atlantic) that he avoided a potentially embarrassing farewell with Pamela Bianco. A note in her hand was brought to his cabin, from which he learned that she had pursued him aboard, but had been unable to locate his cabin. She hoped that he would enjoy his voyage, and begged for letters.[38]

CHAPTER 18

A High Wind in Jamaica and Fame

It was while the SS *De Grasse* was still at sea that *A High Wind in Jamaica* was published in England, where it was already a *cause célèbre*. The distinguished critic and literary editor Desmond MacCarthy had devoted the complete August 1929 number of his magazine *Life and Letters* to an abbreviated version of *A High Wind in Jamaica*, which he prefaced with the words:[1]

> When *Life and Letters* started we said that we would sometimes give up a whole number to a controversy or to one long contribution. It is time this promise was fulfilled. But before venturing on a course unusual in the conduct of magazines, editors must be certain that they have found a work of unusual merit and originality.

On both those grounds, he felt able to introduce *A High Wind* 'with complete confidence'. He added that 'there was no dead wood in it which could be lopped off; all the excisions were losses'; and therefore, he declared, everyone who read the abbreviated version would wish to buy the complete work when it was published in the autumn.

The *Life and Letters* version not only whetted the appetite for more, but also helped to generate so much advance publicity that when Chatto & Windus published *A High Wind in Jamaica* in late September, it immediately shot to the top of the bestseller list. One of the very first English reviews (described by a family friend as 'a full-blast encomium') appeared in the *Observer*, where Gerald Gould wrote: 'Mr Hughes has the divine gift of imagination. His phrases have often the fatality of poetry and often the unexpectedness of wit.'[2]

In New York Hughes had been merely a celebrity: by the time the SS *De Grasse* docked in Southampton, he was famous. 'Going like hot cakes!' he wrote excitedly to Joseph Brewer. 'Over twelve thousand in a fortnight!'[3] And there were further glowing reviews, several of them from well-known novelists. Arnold Bennett, for example, praised the style, the ingenuity of the narrative, and the characterisation; while Hugh Walpole declared: 'It has genius because it sees something that a million people have seen before, but sees it uniquely.'

Unqualified praise always begins to seem suspect; but fortunately there were enough dissenting voices to stir the public interest. St John Ervine dismissed *A High Wind in Jamaica* as 'an amazing stunt'; the critic of the *English Review* objected to 'some, at least, of the horrible and cruel and disgusting things described'; and Humbert Wolfe complained that the children were no more than 'brilliant robots'. Correspondence columns became filled with letters both for and against Hughes's portrayal of the children, and he aroused the particular anger of the headmistress of a girls' school in Bath, who described *A High Wind in Jamaica* as 'a disgusting travesty' of child life, and found such things as the children's silent acceptance of John's sudden disappearance, and Emily's killing of the Dutch captain, quite 'unthinkable'.[4]

There were also numerous letters from family and friends. Uncle Walter Warren declared that Diccon had 'found out in thirty years what it has taken me nearly sixty to discover';[5] Gilbert Murray confessed to having opened *A High Wind* 'in the state of mind which is normal in a don approaching a best-seller'; but he had then fallen 'instantly under the charm. I do think it an extraordinarily clever and original book, & a remarkable achievement'.[6] Alan Porter wrote wisely: 'Perhaps you de-sentimentalise with too much intellectual ferocity, but I don't think that could be mended; it is so much in the quality of the book, a distortion which clarifies, too.'[7] And Hugh Lyon, knowing Diccon better than most, warned him: 'If you don't watch out, my dear, you will be one of the "Great Writers" of this epoch. Beware!'[8]

Hughes certainly found success as alarming as ever, and was already wondering how on earth he could live up to the enormous enthusiasm which had been generated for his work. This led to numerous requests. Some were agreeable, as when the *Saturday Review* asked for a contribution to their Christmas number. Others were disagreeable, as when the *Evening News* asked for '1000 words for a series "WHAT I EXPECT OF LIFE" by men and women who think straight and are young enough to expect much of it'. Hughes scrawled across this request the single word: 'Unanswered!'[9]

Should he write another play, perhaps? In December he lunched with Maurice Browne,[10] to whom he had written earlier in the year saying that he had no new play for him at present, but that 'I expect I shall be turning back to the theatre pretty soon'.[11] However, no suitable theme suggested itself.

Or a new novel? For several years there had been an idea at

the back of Diccon's mind, for a novel whose central characters were to be[12]

> a family of Italians [clearly based upon the Fassios whom he had befriended in Capodistria], destitute to the point of starvation, completely incapable of work, by no means picturesque, and always merry. The theme of the novel was [to be] the contrast of their insecurity against the security of the background upon which they were set.

For the time being, however, this seemed too large a project; and Hughes contented himself with articles and short stories, which were eagerly snapped up as soon as written by his agents George Bye in New York and Elizabeth Marbury in London.

In between times Hughes picked up the threads of his social life. Within a few weeks of returning to England he had seen his mother, and lunched with Jim Wyllie; and then on 25 October he dined with the Quennells.[13]

It was already more than three and a half years since Nancy Stallibrass had broken off her engagement to Diccon Hughes, and she had now become Mrs Peter Quennell; but it was their first meeting since those terrible days when Nancy had realised that Diccon's heart was no longer in their wedding plans, and Diccon had cried out: 'Oh Nancy, my darling above heaven and earth, HOW have things come to such a pass? How will it all end?' On both sides old resentments came to the surface, no prettier for having been so long repressed.

Nancy, having 'waited for years' to meet Diccon again, and having read and much admired his *A High Wind in Jamaica*, had looked forward enormously to their meeting; but then found herself spoiling the evening by making what she later admitted were 'unkind and *insincere*' comments about his book.[14] Diccon retaliated by reminding her that he was growing richer from day to day – which was also a way of pointing out that Nancy's family had been utterly wrong to worry about his financial prospects.[15]

Peter's easy familiarity with 'Stally' (as he called Nancy) also grated on Diccon's nerves; and in order to pretend that he felt no jealousy, he said enough about his American adventures to make it clear that he was no longer the sexual innocent of Nancy's memory.[16] The result was that the evening ended awkwardly.

So much had remained unspoken, that afterwards Nancy was uncertain whether or not they had quarrelled. As for Diccon, six or seven weeks later he sent Nancy what she described as 'an exquisite little present' for Christmas;[17] but he took good care to avoid any further meetings with her or Peter for many months to come.

Other friendships were less troubled. Diccon travelled to Wales to see Clough and Amabel Williams-Ellis and their children, to Oxford to stay with the Masefields, and to Charterhouse to call on Frank Fletcher; while in London he lunched or dined with the Herberts, Margaret Kennedy and Lance Sieveking.[18]

Sieveking noticed that Diccon's hair had receded, 'leaving a large and impressive dome, above the quiet grey-blue eyes from which the ripple of a private twinkle was rarely absent';[19] and to many of those he visited, Hughes seemed both older and more enigmatic, though (as Sieveking recalled) he could also be an extremely entertaining guest. One evening, for example, recalling his time in Virginia, he surprised his fellow guests by breaking into a negro song over the dinner-table; and then he told them a story with a bizarre ending.

With his 'ragged beard wagging up and down, and the unself-conscious eyes under the bald dome regarding us with the seriousness of a child', Diccon had been describing 'in his gentle, quiet, reasonable voice' the exploits of an enormously wealthy and eccentric family, in which 'the son of the house was a wild youth who had evidently been completely spoiled from birth'. Then he told them how[20]

> one evening at sunset the boy had suddenly driven off to visit the family crypt in the cemetery a few miles away. Here he forced open the glass fronts of several cases in which lay or sat the embalmed remains of his departed relations. He spent a long time rearranging the wrong uncles with the wrong aunts.
>
> 'At last he seemed to get bored with tweaking their noses and un-tidying their hair, and with a quick twist he snapped off his grandmother's head and ran up the steps. He chucked her head into the dicky seat and drove home.'
>
> It was said so quietly, and with such an air almost of apology for mentioning such a common-place little event, that it was a second or two before the shock registered.
>
> And then, as if doubting her own ears, a girl's voice came: '*What* did you say?'

It was easy enough for Diccon to sing for his supper in this manner; but it was disagreeable to feel (in most company) that he was valued chiefly for his fame; and by mid December, the burden was becoming insupportable. On his mantelpiece there were invitations to a number of parties and dances.[21] but none of them seemed very attractive; and one evening, in conversation with the traveller and translator Arthur Waley, Hughes talked of retreating to Morocco for a while. Shortly afterwards, Waley wrote advising Hughes to[22] look up my friend Beryl de Loete who has been living [in Fez] for some time. She knows some Arabic and could, I think, show you a good many things that are not generally seen. She is living now at the Grand Hotel, but is negotiating for a house in the Medina (native town).

On his first visit to Morocco, Hughes had felt 'strangely elated, as if this was "home" at last!' And now the mention of Beryl de Loete's negotiations reminded him that ever since his visit to Budapest he had longed for a small house of his own in some exotic foreign location: why not Tangier? If Waley's friend could buy a house in Fez, it would be still easier for Diccon to buy one in Tangier, which since 1923 had been an international city, 'ruled like a tiny stagnant separate state "on the Sultan's behalf" by a concert of European powers, including the English'.[23] Within a few days, Hughes had set out for North Africa.

CHAPTER 19

Retreat to Morocco

Hughes's reputation had preceded him to Tangier, where he spent Christmas 1929 'in the . . . exotic surroundings of a formal dinner at [the] British Legation';[1] where he made a friend of Walter Harris, a 'nonchalant, witty and resourceful' man, who had been *The Times* correspondent in Tangier since 1887;[2] and where, early in 1930, he bought a house in the Casbah for two donkey-loads of silver. (The vendor is said to have been so excited that he stayed awake for two days and two nights while he bit every coin in turn to make certain it was real.)[3]

The chief attraction of the property was that (unusually for houses in the Casbah) it had a small garden, last remnant of the magnificent gardens of a seventeenth-century British governor. Having passed to the British crown during Charles II's reign (as part of the dowry of Catherine of Braganza), Tangier had been returned to Morocco in 1684; and since then, as Hughes liked to point out, no Christian had ever owned property within the Casbah: he was the first.

Its chief disadvantage (if one ignored its generally run-down condition) was that it was hidden away in a labyrinth of streets; and according to Jim Wyllie, 'The Arabs used to roll with laughter and say [of Diccon]: "He owns a house and he doesn't know how to find it!" '[4]

His base secure, Hughes purchased Arab clothing, and a number of sumptuous brocade-lined tents which 'had once belonged to the famous Kaid Sir Harry [MacLean], the Scotsman who became the Moorish Commander-in-Chief'. Then (having also acquired four Arab servants), he travelled to somewhere still more remote than the depths of the Casbah: the cork-woods of north-west Morocco.

Pitching camp in a glade where 'gladioli and asphodel and marigolds grew in profusion', Hughes lived 'in some comfort', having brought with him 'one large tent for use by night, and another by day, as well as cook-tents and store-tents. I had embroidered cushions and gaudy carpets, and braziers and trays and basins and ewers of polished copper and brass and silver'. By night, he found that 'there was nothing to disturb me but the nightingales ... the grouching of an occasional wild boar ... and the distant high piping howl of young jackals'.[5] Night and day, across the marshes to the westward, 'the surf thundered on twenty miles of deserted sandy beach'; and there, in 'the hot middle of the day', he would 'ride ... in and out of the water: and swim'.

At last Hughes could relax from all the pressures of the past year, secure in the knowledge that Hamed, his principal Arab servant, was capable of supervising his life like 'a kind of Oriental Jeeves'. Hamed, who was 'villainous to look at, very small, very dark, but highly intelligent', pretended 'that he knew no English (which was untrue), but talked French – in the [past] tense only'.[6] He also 'cooked like an angel', and possessed 'a remarkable tenor voice, great ability as a story-teller, and handiness in the use of a knife', the latter skill having been acquired 'only after much practice, as two murderous scars across his own throat witnessed'.[7]

Their camp soon became 'a recognised stopping-place for travellers – what few passed'. Hughes grew accustomed to the sight of 'some complete stranger helping with the work of the camp; and, if his gifts lay that way, he would often come to my own tent after supper in the evening and sing, or play the lute'; or the stranger might tell 'long stories that were own blood-brother to those in the Arabian Nights'[8] and which gave Hughes much useful material for stories of his own.

Occasionally Hughes rode back into Tangier to check on his house and keep an eye on what was happening in the outside world; and while he was in Morocco a number of personal letters reached him both from New York and from London. On reading them, he must have felt relieved that he could ride back to his retreat in the cork-woods, and lie awake listening to nothing more disquieting than the thundering of the surf.

A communication from Jane Cassidy arrived first. Writing from an apartment which she had recently purchased at St Luke's Place in New York, she told him that it was 'the genteel block in a slum'. Bob, her husband, would visit her at weekends; and she was looking for a job – busily, but not under as much pressure as when Diccon had been her mentor. She reproached him for his complete control over her life: 'I don't think I'd [accept everything you said] again, though I could not dislike you when I tried'; and finished damningly: 'I hope you won't come back too soon.'[9]

Earlier in her letter, Jane had mentioned that everybody was 'poverty-poor', that Mr Bianco was 'having a nervous breakdown, mostly on account of his children', and that in the circumstances

'Pamela daren't go home'; and Diccon's next communication was a Christmas letter from Pamela herself. After only a few lines, in which she told him what a dreadful autumn it had been, with her father being so ill, and herself and Cecco both out of work, Pamela wrote that she would not continue with her letter in case it was unwelcome; but no Christmas should go by without her sending him a loving message of goodwill.[10]

Diccon's heart was touched; he had already cabled the Biancos on Christmas Day; and now he sent Pamela a family ring as a late Christmas present. It was exactly the right gesture: Pamela wrote that the gift had filled her with happiness, and allowed her to feel that she was forgiven. She added that she had come to a terrible awareness of the severity of her illness during his last stay in America. Her own behaviour had caused her the most bitter regret; and now she wanted Diccon to blot out the memory of those days, and try to remember her instead just as she was when she was a thirteen-year-old child. In future, she intended to live somewhere far from the world, abandon all social life, and concentrate entirely on her painting: for it was only in her life as an artist that she could see any glimmer of light.[11]

This melancholy letter was followed a month or two later by much more cheerful news. 'Pamela wanted me to tell you', wrote Jane Cassidy, 'that she got the Guggenheim fellowship . . . She thought you might feel more at ease about her if you knew.' The award would enable Pamela to travel to Florence to paint; and in the meantime she wore Diccon's ring on her middle finger, had his portrait on her wall, 'and is sure she has alienated you for ever by the way she acted. I told her', Jane continued,[12]

> that if you're fond of a person you only get fonder when they (he or she) is mentally ill, and gave an example or two, too near home for any pride (you didn't know the half of it, dearie). But let that rest: you quite apart, she's looking for a philosophy or God – and thinks she can find one. What a child.

Then Jane repeated how troubled Pamela had been 'because you thought she was too animal', and accused Diccon of being[13]

> not very bright sometimes. And you should *not* have gone about making dramatic exits. You wouldn't ride Sukey with spurs. And [Pamela] is troubled because you can't talk with her. That's too bad. If you can't relax and forget wisdom and reticence, let down your barriers, play, be silly, confidential, metaphysical, *sentimental* yes – you might as well go whoring and be done with it. Better, because you don't hurt people.

She had tried (she wrote) to explain this to him before. His pride in

himself was all very well up to a point, but sometimes she suspected
that he had

> set up an little ideal image and are moulding yourself to it.
> Sometimes when you say 'I'm not built that way' you mean
> that your idea of yourself isn't, so you won't let yourself be.
> But there's something deeper than introvert, gentleman, artist, or
> even son-of-a-bitch: not good or bad, but real, and the introvert
> *et al* will get much further by building on that instead of trying
> to undermine it. Even the artist, I do believe . . .

Having begun her letter 'Dear Diccon', Jane concluded bitterly:
'Please give my love to Richard Hughes. I'm very fond of him.'

Soon afterwards came a letter from Pamela herself, also giving
news of her Guggenheim fellowship, but adding that in the months
before it came, she had often thought of suicide. Even when she
heard of her success, she had at first regarded it as a kind of
epitaph; and several times when out walking through the city she
had been tempted to step in front of a taxi. However, she was now
feeling more hopeful, and begged him for a letter.[14] Diccon replied
immediately with both cablegram and letter, which elicited a tender
response.[15]

This emotionally charged correspondence with Jane and Pamela
was accompanied by an equally difficult exchange with the
Quennells, who sent Diccon a joint letter at the beginning of
March. (By this time, rumours were circulating in London about
Diccon having bought a house in Tangier. And by midsummer –
since people knew of Diccon's friendship with Robert Graves, about
whom far stranger rumours had been circulating since he decamped
to Majorca with Laura Riding – it was being reported that Diccon
was 'living in Morocco as a native, complete with turban and surrounded by swamps, & that . . . Robert is to join him there'.)[16] Peter
wrote first, with the news that he was heartily sick of literary journalism, and had secured a teaching job in Tokyo for three years. He and
Nancy would be leaving England for Japan in exactly a month's time
on 2 April. 'Stally is looking forward to a Japanese house', he went
on. 'It is a pity that you have been fighting so shy of us for the last
six months, as we probably shan't see you now: *unless* you come to
stay. N. would very much like that . . . Are you still getting richer
every day?'

Then Nancy wrote, saying that she had been 'on the point of
writing to you several times to thank you for the exquisite little
present you sent me at Christmas time. It was so sweet of you and
I was terribly pleased with it'. In the meantime, she would be 'sad
at not seeing you to say goodbye before we go'. He could borrow
any furniture from them while they were away:[17]

And of course you must take care of the lovely green lustres you once gave me . . . Come and stay with us in Japan? After knowing you all these years you *ought* to be our best friend . . . but perhaps you don't like us any longer? . . . Diccon dear – I hope you are happy & well.

Love from Nancy: don't think this provocative!

At length Diccon replied to this letter by inviting the Quennells to visit him in Tangier. His reward was this cross postcard:

Marseilles, 4 April

Beastly old Diccon: Your lovely invitation came far too late to be any use . . . We should have liked to have come had we known in time to accept it. But I think if you had *really* wanted us you would have sent a cable . . . Your new home sounds more than inviting. I hear news of your friendships with various of my discarded friends . . . I hope we shan't disappear (as you put it) but that depends on you; so do come and see us. Nancy.

In the meantime, his nerves restored after some weeks in the cork-woods, Diccon had moved on (with his tents and his servants) to join the annual pig-sticking camp, a social event organised by British army officers from Tangier. Here he renewed his friendship with the young artist Teddy Wolfe, whom he had met on his first visit to Morocco, and who had rented a house in Tangier in order to paint.

Teddy (who had a penchant for decorating his letters with line drawings of beautiful bare-breasted dancing-girls with plumes in their hair) jealously observed Diccon making an impression upon a party of young English women in the camp. They had soon learned that he was the author of *A High Wind in Jamaica*; and then the day came when a wild pig, 'driven by beaters, as was the custom, towards the hunters – turned on a horse which reared, unseating its lady rider'. Hughes, who up to this moment had refused to take part in the pig-sticking, quickly 'grabbed a spear and chased the pig away'.[18]

After this, he was a great favourite with the women; and Teddy Wolfe saw that Diccon himself was particularly attracted to Margaret, a spirited twenty-four-year-old who had come out from England with her two younger sisters on an extended holiday. Teddy also noticed that Margaret's father, a colonel, was not best pleased by this development. At a camp-fire entertainment, after Diccon had demonstrated one of his party-tricks, which was to[19]

open a box of matches with his bare feet and strike a match with his toes. There was a round of applause. But in the darkness Teddy heard the girl's father muttering furiously that he wasn't going to have a monkey as a son-in-law, however famous a writer he might be.

When the pig-sticking camp broke up, Hughes decided upon a second attempt to reach Taroudant and the Sous valley. This time he was accompanied not by Jim Wyllie, but by Monty Corcos,[20] 'a Moorish-Jewish friend'; and by Monty's father's personal assassin.[21]

Passing themselves off as slave-smugglers, they succeeded in reaching Taroudant, where they found that the whole Sous valley was 'a desert in the grip of a famine and a seven-years drought';[22] and where Hughes 'observed a crowd of starving people collapse like a house of cards when a push was administered to the foremost'.[23] There, too, he[24]

> made friends with one of the Ait B'Amram, or Blue Moors, who veil their faces like the Touarreg, and whose leader styles himself Sultan of the Sahara; and there too, I attended a circumcision feast among that strange tribe known as the Fighting Jews; a jovial if rather bullying crowd, who claim to be one of the Ten Lost Tribes.

When the feast was over, they all 'sat on the floor of the mud synagogue beneath the Ark of the Covenant, eating cold chicken and stale bread, and drinking a very potent kind of brandy which these people distil from dates'.

There had been dangerous moments on their journey south. Once, for example, an old snake-charmer said a spell over Hughes 'to make me immune from snakebite', and then held up 'two cobras to kiss my hands and forehead with their flickering, tickly tongues'. And later on, when they had left the Sous valley and reached the seaport of Agadir, Hughes quarrelled with the town poisoner,[25]

> who straightway offered him tea. When Hughes protested at the crudity of his host's methods, the poisoner blushed but proceeded with the ceremony of pouring the tea, which he managed with the dexterity of a conjuror, his sleeves well rolled-up. A macabre game began, one attempting to introduce the poison, the other to detect it.

'In the end', recalled Hughes, 'I managed, by skilful juggling, to acquire my host's cup. We raised our cups, made loud quaffing sounds, but drank no tea!'

On his return to Tangier Diccon immediately contacted Margaret and her sisters; and for a few days these respectable English girls from Reading enjoyed what Margaret described to Diccon as 'the greatest fun and mostly due to you'. The resourceful Hamed had proved quite capable of 'arranging a dinner-party . . . (complete with a string quartet) at ten minutes' notice';[26] and it seemed strange to Margaret when at the end of March she found herself back in England and 'going to bed at nine o'clock, no more eggs and bacon at one in the morning'. She added that her sisters Marie and Jocelyn were 'missing very much all the spoiling they got from you'; but at least the Moorish tunes which they had acquired in his company were 'a succes foue: we play them every evening'.[27]

From the rest of Margaret's letter, Diccon learned that he had not been altogether successful as her mentor. She had not yet (she confessed) begun the prescribed 'brain-work'; and although, after his censorious parting remarks about her powder and lipstick, she had 'quite seriously thought of giving it up for Lent', she had come to the conclusion

> that anything so temporary would be no good so I am not giving it up after all and besides as in three days time I am breaking into the quarter of a century I feel that . . . it will be hopeless to try and look like sixteen!

She then consoled him with the fact that she was putting on 'less [make-up] every day'; hoped that he would visit her when he was back in England; enjoined him not to smoke too much *Kif*; and asked him (if propriety permitted) to give her love to Hamed.

Diccon spent another month in Tangier; and then, leaving Hamed in charge of his house, he returned to London where he resumed the life of a successful literary man.

CHAPTER 20

A Literary Life

By mid June 1930 Diccon Hughes was living at 12 Hammersmith Terrace, where he was reminded of his recent travels by one of the massive tent-poles which had last seen service in a Moroccan cork-wood within sound of the Atlantic rollers.[1] His new flat overlooked the river Thames; and one morning he walked along to the moorings where Nancy Nicholson had been living in a barge with her four children and Geoffrey Phibbs. The barge was 'empty of Graveses', who had recently decamped to Sutton Veny in Wiltshire; but Diccon was given their new address,[2] and subsequently he made it his business to befriend the children whom Robert had deserted.

As Hughes settled down once again to a literary life (mainly writing children's stories, reviews and articles), news of other friends reached him from abroad. Pamela Bianco wrote to announce that she had suddenly 'got married about a week ago to Robert Schlick, an American boy from Oregon, a poet, and I think I am going to be happy'. In a month's time she would be sailing alone to Europe, so that she could 'do some real work at last'; she hoped very much to see Diccon; and she declared that she was[3]

> a little bit worried about the garnet ring you sent me, for since I know it belongs in your family, I feel I have no right to it. You must tell me what to do. It would make me happiest to keep it.

Which of course he allowed her to do.

A less intense letter came from Nancy Quennell, who apologised handsomely for having dealt unkindly with Diccon in the recent past, asked him in a friendly way whether there had been 'any more ravishing or being ravished?' and told him that he had been right about Tokyo being intolerable. 'So sordid', she wrote,[4]

> so provincial, and worst of all so expensive. The question now is how to return. Peter has most inopportunely developed a conscience and feels it would be a dirty trick to leave before a year, since they paid our passages out . . . P. grows more Christian every day; but I, alas, have become a continuation of *Emily*.

A High Wind in Jamaica continued to bring Hughes fame, so that in August 1930 he was invited to a luncheon given by the *Daily Mail* at the Savoy Hotel for the aviator Miss Amy Johnson: Evelyn Waugh, J.B. Priestley, David Garnett and many other well-known names were present; and his old school-friend Charles Graves sat at the next table. *A High Wind* also continued to earn substantial royalties, which enabled Hughes to buy himself a magnificent Bentley touring car and (later in the year) to move from his flat in Hammersmith to a house at 21 Lloyd Square.

In September,[5] he drove up to North Wales in the Bentley, taking with him thirteen-year-old Jocelyn Herbert (who would normally have been at St Paul's but had broken a leg and was recuperating at home), and another girl, who had been depressed and also needed a holiday. When they reached Portmeirion, Diccon took them sailing in *Tern*, and then carried them off to Garreg Fawr, where he cooked them a stew which they ate by candlelight; after which he told them stories and recited poems, until it was time for them to go to sleep on camp-beds covered with exotic furs and burnouses.[6]

Later that month, Diccon set out for another holiday: this time in Holland, where he joined Clough and Amabel Williams-Ellis and their children for some cruising on the Dutch canals and the Zuider Zee in a flat-bottomed sailing barge. Afterwards, they drove on to Austria, where it had been arranged that they should stay with one of Amabel's friends Aemethe, the wife of Count Leo Zeppelin of Schloss Wernberg. This was a large, romantic castle, described by Clough as[7]

> built around a courtyard on a rocky bluff above the rushing river Drau with cone-topped towers, winding stone stairs, a vast empty and echoing 'Prälaten-saal' with frescoed walls, surviving from its religious past, and great wolf-hounds prowling around.

Count Leo himself was 'a lively muscular little man usually in national green hunting-dress, leather shorts, feathered hat and so on – extrovert', and so 'pleasantly eccentric' that while they were there he came back from an auction not with the bull that he needed for his farm, but 'a lion cub he had taken to instead'.

Unfortunately the visit went badly wrong. Susan, Amabel's eldest daughter, had to be carried off to hospital dangerously ill with mastoid; and shortly afterwards Clough followed her, in a delirious state with double pneumonia. Diccon himself was ill with an abscess on one of his teeth; and once it was clear that Susan and Clough were out of danger, he wrote a grimly entertaining letter to one of his friends in which the Schloss Wernberg seemed 'like the scene of several Elizabethan tragedies'.[8]

During the rest of 1930, and the first few months of 1931, Hughes was chiefly engaged upon routine literary matters, not all of them agreeable. There was (for example) a tiresome correspondence with the *Spectator*, whose literary editor had written begging him for an article for their December number on children's books. Hughes wrote 1500 words; but first they refused to offer him more than five guineas; then the acting editor announced that his article had been held over due to pressure on space; and finally it took an angry letter to the editor to secure even the five guineas which had been promised.[9] There was also a disappointing production by Tyrone Guthrie of *The Man Born to be Hanged* at the Grafton Theatre in Tottenham Court Road;[10] and it took months for Diccon and his agents to secure any payment from the theatre management.[11]

On the more positive side, there was news that *Danger* was to be staged by a small travelling theatre in England at half a guinea a performance,[12] and broadcast on Australian radio at a guinea a time;[13] and that *The Sisters' Tragedy* had been a 'sensation' in Edinburgh.[14]

Richard Hughes was learning how to cope with fame by becoming elusive. The poet Robert Nichols (already sinking into obscurity after his brief period of wartime fame) tried once or twice to scrape an acquaintance, but was politely discouraged.[15] Dick de la Mare of Faber and Faber wanted Hughes to contribute to a series of pamphlets, 'The Poets on the Poets' (for which Eliot had written on Dante), and also wanted him to meet his wife. But Diccon seemed impossible to track down, and in October 1930 de la Mare wrote to him disconsolately 'as I went along Tottenham Court Road the other day, I saw you in front of me forging along in a Bentley. I tried to attract your attention but you were gone in a flash'.[16]

Not that Hughes was becoming a recluse: he actively cultivated the company of those like Virginia Woolf whom he admired. In 1925 (four years after dining with Woolf and her husband), he had written a glowing review of her *Mrs Dalloway*, in which he declared that 'Mrs Woolf has, I think, a finer sense of form than any but the oldest living English novelist'; and this, appearing as it did in the American *Saturday Review of Literature*,[17] was influential in securing attention for her work on that side of the Atlantic.[18] Now (in November 1930) he wrote privately to Virginia Woolf in praise of her latest novel *The Waves*. 'I can assure you', she replied,[19]

> It was a very great pleasure to me to get your letter. *The Waves* was a book that gave me a great deal of difficulty − I know it is in many ways wrong now − & I was sometimes afraid that what I was trying to do couldn't possibly get through − I mean it would only seem an ambitious failure. So I am greatly encouraged by what you say; & especially because I so much admired your *High Wind*.

She added that she was 'rather knocked up at the moment and have to keep quiet', but she hoped that he would come to visit her 'in a week or two', and concluded: 'I have it on the tip of my tongue to ask − but perhaps you will think it foolish − if you would give me a copy of *High Wind* in return for a copy of *The Waves*?'

Nor did Hughes ever turn his back on friends in need. He continued to give emotional support to Pamela Bianco, whose life had entered another downward spiral. In the autumn of 1930, thanking Diccon for his recent letters, she explained that she had contracted a serious physical illness, from which (according to her doctors) it could take six years to make a full recovery.[20] The following August, she would write that she had been treated by doctors in Zurich, and was now back in Florence, where she hoped that her husband would be joining her in September. She added that Diccon's latest letter had given her great happiness; and she much regretted not having been able to visit him in Wales as he had suggested.[21]

Other friends in some difficulty were his Oxford friend Alan Porter, and Alan's wife Iris Barry. They were both writers (she was principally a film critic), and they were finding it very hard to make ends meet in London, and thinking of crossing the Atlantic to make a fresh start in New York. It was all very difficult (especially for Iris, who seems to have been almost as fond of Diccon as she was of her husband); but eventually they decided to make the move; and Diccon gave them all the help he could − both in terms of introductions to friends like Joseph Brewer, and financially. When early in 1931 he sent them a present of fifty dollars, Iris thanked him most warmly, telling him that it had enabled her to pay the final instalment on their furniture; they were 'just managing the rent', and she hoped that 'by God's help and the *Herald Tribune* by the beginning of next month we shall be solvent'.[22]

However, letters or requests that seemed unimportant or unjustified simply went unanswered; and Nancy Quennell would complain to Diccon in the summer of 1931 (when she and her husband were about to return to England) that 'Peter has written you *dozens* of letters, persuasive, insulting − and of every SORT. He is heartbroken at the cruel way you have ignored them'.[23]

In one of Peter Quennell's more difficult letters, Diccon had been asked 'about the enclosed cutting'.[24] This was of a poem by Hughes entitled 'Burial of the Spirit of a Young Poet', which had appeared in the *New Statesman* and which began:

> Dead hangs the fruit on that tall tree:
> The lark in my cold hand is dead.
> What meats his funeral stars decree
> By their own light I've spread:
> The bearded fog among the leaves
> Too sad to move, excludes the air:
> No bursting seed this stiff soil heaves
> Nor ever will again, when we have laid him there.

Peter had scrawled across the foot of the cutting: 'Whose funeral?' because (as Nancy later confirmed) he had 'promptly [taken it] to refer to himself'.[25] What made his letter unanswerable was that he was right. Only recently, he had published a volume of poems which Hughes thought very poor; and for the rest of his life he would lament that Quennell, as a poet, had altogether failed to live up to his early promise.

The more agreeable part of Quennell's letter had been written to congratulate Hughes upon a significant landmark in his career: his first major literary prize. It was towards the end of March 1931 that he had received a letter informing him:[26]

> Dear Sir,
>   I am pleased to tell you that at a meeting of the French Femina Vie Heureuse Committee held in Paris under the Presidency of Mme Saint-René Taillandier, your novel *A High Wind in Jamaica* was awarded the Femina Vie Heureuse prize of £40.

The prize (he was told) would be formally presented to him at the Institut Français, Cromwell Gardens, later in the year. This was exciting news which set a seal of approval upon Hughes's new status in the literary world; and his immediate reaction was to seek out some fresh challenge.

Towards the end of March, therefore, Hughes came to an agreement with a flying school which promised him half-price tuition in return for copies of any articles he wrote about his experiences as a pupil;[27] and subsequently 'My First Day in the Air' appeared in the *Daily Express*, describing what it was like to take over the controls of a light aeroplane for the first time.[28]

In other respects, Hughes's life proceeded for some months in what was (for him) a comparatively routine manner. In April he spent two weeks in Morocco, where he continued putting his house in order;[29]

despite having protested to Nancy Quennell that he was broke,[30] he acquired a Gauguin;[31] there was a production of *The Sisters' Tragedy* at the Globe, after which he invited the cast to dinner;[32] and he began some serious work on his novel about an Italian family, but became unhappy with it, and had soon laid it permanently to one side.[33]

His two most satisfactory accomplishments during this period were a wireless broadcast, and the compilation of a volume of children's stories. The broadcast (given on 22 April) was called 'Under the Nose and Under the Skin', and Hughes declared provocatively that although people 'generally suppose that a writer naturally writes best about what is under his nose', he himself found it 'far easier to write about places that I haven't been to than the places to which I have been'. In his view, what writers 'really' wrote about was 'not so much what is under their noses as what is under their skins; and that they can no more help than a hen can help laying an egg'.[34]

The volume of children's stories, *The Spider's Palace*[35] (to be published that autumn in both London and New York), was the fruit of hours of story-telling. It was a favourite device of Diccon's to begin by asking each child present to name an item to be included. Then, unleashing the full force of his powerful imagination (including its darker side), Hughes would concoct some more or less elaborate fantasy. In his stories, little girls can travel down telephone wires, or live permanently inside whales; but they can also be sucked down the waste-pipe of a bath, or shrink down to a size at which they can be chased through underground passages by an army of ants wanting to bite them in half.

In one of the stories, a child radiates darkness; in another, when a gardener calls out 'I'm not afraid of you! You're only a silly old rabbit!', Hughes has told his story so well that it comes as no surprise when the rabbit cries out:[36]

> 'Oh, I am, am I?' . . . in a most wicked voice, and before their very eyes he began to swell and grow, and his teeth grew sharp as a tiger's, and his eyes flashed fire. Then he sprang at the first elephant with a savage growl, and plunged his teeth in its trunk.

The title-story is especially interesting. When Richard Hughes had been at the height of his passion for Nancy Stallibrass, spiders' webs had formed an important part of the secret erotic world which they had begun to develop. Now, in 'The Spider's Palace', he tells of a little girl (afraid of snakes) who is invited by a friendly spider to live in his palace. This turns out to be a palace in the air, which is completely transparent. Only one room is permanently shrouded in curtains and mystery. Once a week the spider goes there and locks himself in for an hour; and when the little girl discovers his secret:[37]

All the clear walls and ceilings of the palace started to go milky: and when she woke up in the morning she couldn't see through them at all. They had all turned into white marble. She got up and went to look for the spider, and, as you might expect, he was now changed back into a man altogether. He didn't say anything, and she didn't either, even when they found the palace had sunk down and was now in the middle of a valley.

Later, she realises that it is 'a very nice palace as palaces go; but, after all, marble palaces on the ground are much commoner than ones up in the sky you can see through'; and we know that something of great importance has been permanently lost.

Diccon regularly corresponded with some of the children who had inspired him to write these stories, children like 'Toby', a schoolgirl whose mother, Faith Henderson, was a friend of Amabel's. Faith had begun to worry that there was something unhealthy in Diccon's relationship with her daughter; and one evening in July 1931 he visited her London home in an attempt to set her mind at rest.

Diccon did most of the talking. After telling Faith that her fears for Toby were absurd, he explained that he liked the company of children as a distraction from the pressures of adult life. He also mentioned that he had a pronounced 'anti-Mother' complex, deriving no doubt from his personal difficulties with Louisa.

Faith spent several days turning their conversation over and over in her mind, and then sent Diccon a closely-written six-page letter of reply. She agreed that she was wrong to be worried about Toby – as Diccon had said, she was probably reading her own feelings into the situation; 'but I also think it is possible', she added, 'that had I not taken a liking to you I might have taken a much more detrimental view of your friendship with Toby'. However, she had no wish to go into all that again. What she did have was an alternative explanation for Diccon's behaviour, which was:[38]

> That your anti-Mother complex may have led you subconsciously to devote yourself to the task of rescuing children from their parents. To this end you have yourself to become first a child so as to realise vividly where & how they have need of rescue, and then a parent to take the place of the parent you are rescuing them from. You are playing a dual rôle. The parent side of you satisfies itself in ... tying up cut toes etc ... the child side is playing & fighting & tumbling about with them & entering into a conspiracy with them against the adult world.

In this way, Faith suggested, he was not so much trying to escape from his problems, as to come to terms with them.

At the same time, she believed that the 'stumbling-block between us, which has been so intangible & yet which I have felt so strongly' was her feeling that Diccon was trying to rescue Toby from her, or even to 'stab me in the back ... because I was her Mother, & because by rescuing her you are helping to rescue yourself'.

She herself (she explained) had been first dominated and then exploited by her own mother, and was just as keen as Diccon to make sure that this pattern did not continue into the next generation. So could they not work together? Her own guiding principle was one of benign neglect – to be available to her children, to try to understand them, but not to dominate them, 'seeing their point of view & interfering hardly at all except to give them a feeling of confidence that they *can* do what they want to do, & get what they want to get, & be loved if they want love as I believe they always do'.

Finally, she begged most movingly for Diccon's help, saying that every step of the road they were in was

> to me more or less a step in the dark, & the road itself gets more unfamiliar ... You are one of the few people I know Diccon whose help I would care to have. You have an innate respect for each human spirit ... You wouldn't tamper with it yourself, or let anyone else tamper with it if you could help it.

Hughes took this letter very seriously indeed; not only did he continue to keep a watchful eye on Toby; but years later, although his individual method of bringing up his own children evolved to some extent by trial and error,[39] the principle of 'benign neglect' lay at its heart.

In the meantime, events of which he was completely unaware were propelling him towards an important meeting: one which would make him both happier and less cynical than he had been ever since Nancy Stallibrass had broken off their engagement some five years previously.

It happened like this: Diccon's godfather, Charles Johnson, had begun taking his wife Violet up to North Wales to be close to Louisa for occasional holidays; and there they had met a youthful baronet, the shy, bespectacled and utterly charming Sir Thomas Bazley of Hatherop Castle in Gloucestershire. Sir Thomas had found the Johnsons such congenial company that early in 1931 he asked his older sister Frances (then in her twenty-sixth year) to accompany him on his next visit to their holiday home. 'So', as Frances later recalled,[40]

> we went to stay up there and they were very very interesting, not

like anybody I'd ever met, and they kept talking about Diccon, very worried as all his friends were because he hadn't written a book . . . since *High Wind*, and they were asking each other why he didn't and how he didn't and whatever. And they said: 'Would you like to meet him?' And I said I would. So in a few months they said: 'He's coming to stay – would you like to come?' And I said I would.

Diccon (who was staying with the Johnsons on his way to lecture on nationalism and literature at the Bangor Eisteddfod) heard from his godfather that Frances was young, good-looking, and a talented artist; and he was intrigued. Learning that she was due to arrive at Penrhyndeudraeth station at six o'clock on a certain evening in August, he decided to intercept her train at Dolgellau and pick her up in his Bentley. Charles Johnson and his wife both protested that Diccon would not recognise her; to which, as Frances later heard, he merely answered quietly:[41]

'I expect I will.' And the wife said: 'Well, I daresay she will be wearing a brown tweed suit.' So he set off in the 113th-ever-made Bentley for Dolgellau station. The train stopped there for a while, and I was reading; and he walked down the train, and I was dressed in red; and he said: 'Are you Frances Bazley?' I said: 'I am.' And he said: 'I'm Richard Hughes. I came to meet you to save you the longer journey.'

This meeting had soon led to a rapid courtship which contrasted very dramatically with Diccon's long-drawn-out, tortuous and unsatisfactory wooing of Nancy Stallibrass.

CHAPTER 21

Frances Bazley

Frances Catherine Ruth Bazley, the product of an unconventional upbringing and a form of home tuition to which she was hopelessly unsuited, had accomplishments rather than an education; but her accomplishments were remarkable, and she had an independent and naturally eccentric turn of mind which Richard Hughes found wholly delightful.[1]

During the past twelve months, Diccon had entertained a succession of young ladies to dinner; but none of them seems to have made any significant impression. Mollie, Esther, Faith, Elizabeth Cameron of Glebe Place: their names appear for a brief moment or two on the pages of his engagement diaries, and are heard of no more.

Frances, however, was different. Offering a friend some 'irrelevant details' about her, Diccon declared: 'The first is that she is a quite exceptional girl, and well worth waiting for to my advanced age [as Hughes described his thirty-second year]; the second that last year she almost became a Master of Foxhounds; the third that she paints.'[2]

Diccon soon learned that Frances had been born into a family which combined new wealth and old aristocratic breeding in almost equal measures. Her grandfather Sebastian Bazley, a mill-owner who was an enlightened employer and an astronomer of some repute had inherited from his wife's family a substantial fortune derived chiefly from cotton; and it was he who in 1867 had purchased Hatherop Castle, an imposing stone-built country house (chiefly early Victorian but with parts dating back to the seventeenth century) at the centre of its own estate in Gloucestershire. Two years later, Sebastian had buttressed the estate with a title, allowing Gladstone (then Prime Minister) to know that his father Thomas Bazley, the wealthy Liberal MP for Manchester, would not refuse a baronetcy. On Sir Thomas's death in 1885, Sebastian inherited both the baronetcy and a further substantial fortune, also largely from cotton.[3]

Sebastian once described his estate as 'a devouring beast';[4] but although it was a tremendous drain on his resources, it brought the family the social status which he desired; and in 1903 he had the satisfaction of seeing his own son (another Sebastian) marry Ruth Howard, a member of the leading house of the English Catholic nobility. They produced a family of five children: Elizabeth, born in 1904; Frances, in 1905; Thomas, in 1907; Rachel, in 1909; and Anthony in 1911.

However, Anthony was only eighteen days old (and Frances five-and-a-half years of age) when on 21 June 1911 their father Sebastian died suddenly and unexpectedly, of fatal complications which had set in after an apparently routine appendicitis. This family tragedy had left Frances with the sad, vulnerable quality which had aroused Diccon's protective instincts. Not only had she lost her father; but the remainder of her childhood had been desperately unhappy.

Within two years, her mother Ruth (still a glamorous young woman) had remarried, swept off her feet by a naval officer, Lieutenant-Commander Francis Cadogan, who had noticed her when he was looking through a telescope on the sands at Torquay.[5] As a stepfather he was 'not very kind to his step-children, though kinder to the girls';[6] but in any case, he had only been married to their mother for about a year when the Great War broke out;[7] and from then on, he was away from home so much that he had little practical effect on their lives, apart from fathering two more children – Henriette and Christopher (who were both extremely fond of him).

The responsibility for the children's happiness thus fell chiefly upon their mother, who neglected it for two reasons in particular: not only was running Hatherop Castle a great responsibility, which (not surprisingly considering that there were at least twenty-five servants) took up much of her time; but also she had been brought up in the Victorian tradition of handing over one's children to professional nannies. Never entirely comfortable with young people, Ruth contented herself with seeing Frances and the others for an hour each afternoon after tea-time.[8]

This system could work perfectly well; but it depended for its success upon the nanny being an effective mother-substitute; and unfortunately Frances and her siblings spent most of their childhood dominated by 'Nanny Taylor, a fierce woman hired to look after the little Cadogan offspring, [in whose] eyes the . . . Bazley children could do nothing good'.[9] Not surprisingly, they disliked and dreaded her. At first her activities were largely confined to the nursery; but once her organisational abilities were realised, her status was raised to that of housekeeper, and she 'ruled the entire household fairly strictly'.[10]

Frances had a particularly difficult time, because Nanny Taylor expected a degree of formal behaviour to which she could never attain; for although Frances is remembered as a very sunny and lovable child, she could usually be relied upon to lose everything, and to appear at the wrong time, in the wrong place, wearing the wrong set of clothes (and perhaps even an odd pair of socks). It was as though there was some minor but essential circuit in her brain which refused to function.

The clever and highly independent Sir Thomas (who inherited the baronetcy at the age of twelve when his grandfather died in 1919) escaped from Nanny Taylor to boarding-school; as, a few years later, did his brother Anthony. Frances and her sisters, on the other hand, remained at home, where they and fifteen or twenty other girls of approximately the same age and social background (the Mitfords among them) were brought together by Ruth Cadogan to become the pupils of a small private school.

Within this school (which met in Hatherop Castle from 1917 to 1929), the only teacher was a resident governess. This was supposed not to matter, because the teaching was done under the direction of PNEU (the Parents' Natural Educational Union) whose system had been designed especially for British mothers in India:[11] so the formal part of Frances' education was not only (with its emphasis upon precise feats of memory) particularly unsuited to her talents; but it was also exactly the same as it might have been had she spent her childhood as an expatriate in some remote and sun-scorched corner of the empire, rather than among the misty hills and valleys of her native Gloucestershire.[12]

It was to that natural world beyond the classroom that Frances fled whenever she could. In that world she developed her private interests and her independent turn of mind. In that world, parental neglect was almost a virtue: she was always inventing secret societies and having adventures; and the tales which she would later tell of her childhood were chiefly[13]

> of wild escapades, such as the time when they made a raft secretly and launched it in the river which flowed past one corner of the Hatherop estate. It wasn't a big raft so to test it they put the youngest of the family, little Christopher Cadogan, on board. They were careful to undress him so that his clothes wouldn't get wet.

Then they pushed him out into the river, and watched as it carried him away. Fortunately, it was not too long before someone caught sight of this little boy, 'blue with cold, drifting by on a raft, recognised him, and raised the alarm'.

Frances had her solitary hours. She had learned to read young, and used to say that she had spent a great deal of her childhood 'sitting in the top of a tree somewhere in the grounds of Hatherop with a book of poetry, just day-dreaming'. A romantic, like Catherine Earnshaw in *Wuthering Heights*, she was attached with passionate intensity to the beauty of the landscape in which she lived. Despite falls (and 'having no balance', as her half-sister recalls, she 'fell off rather a lot'),[14] Frances liked few things better than galloping side-saddle over the fields of the Hatherop estate; and she was also an enthusiastic self-taught artist.

Frances had begun by finding drawing almost as difficult as spelling; and it is not too much to say that the discovery of oil-painting transformed her life.[15] Here at last was a medium in which she could express, with impressionistic dashes of paint, the inmost yearnings of her spirit, yearnings which were heightened during her adolescence by a strongly religious phase. This phase had ended long before she met Diccon; but it left her with passionate feelings about poverty and social injustice which lasted for the rest of her life. And so important did painting become to Frances that when (at the age of twenty-one) she came into a substantial inheritance[16] from her father, she 'took herself to Chelsea Art School, but kept a hunter in Hatherop, ... lived both lives simultaneously',[17] and often exasperated her more formal relatives by arriving at Hatherop with unconventional friends who were quite likely to appear at the breakfast-table without a collar and tie.[18]

A little later, when her great-uncle Lord Howard of Penrith (her mother's favourite uncle, and known to Frances too as 'Uncle Esmé') was British ambassador in Washington, Frances had managed a little travelling. Chaperoned by her brother Sir Thomas (who abandoned Oxford for a term), the twenty-three-year-old Frances had sailed across the Atlantic to the United States of America. After staying for a while with Uncle Esmé in his embassy (where this man of principle saddened many of his guests by allowing Prohibition on to a piece of English soil), brother and sister went on to New York, Boston, and then further north to Toronto and Montreal.[19]

Diccon Hughes admired Frances Bazley's dedication to her art; and in the evenings he would drive her in his Bentley 'to places where she could paint the sun setting from somewhere high in the Snowdon foothills'. But what really impressed him was the fact that she helped run a wolf cub pack in the village. Years later, Diccon would recall that there was no one else among the many writers and artists of his acquaintance 'who gave up time on a regular basis for voluntary work and got a great deal out of the human contact that resulted, *as well as* being an artist. He said she upset his ideas, made him less of a cynic'.[20]

They met again in London in mid October, when Diccon took Frances out to dinner;[21] and another time, a happy afternoon was spent in an antiquarian bookshop poring over old maps.[22] By now, Diccon was so much in love with Frances, and yet so uncertain about what her reply would be if he asked her to marry him, that he was becoming rather confused.

Diccon's emotional situation was further complicated when his mother became ill (just as she had done at various crucial moments of his courtship of Nancy Stallibrass), and needed him to look after her at Garreg Fawr. As soon as she had recovered, he returned to London, and sent her some money which he told her sternly was to be applied 'without any arguments, to having someone in to work *at least* twice a week. Particularly you mustn't clean the bath. Now, please be good and agree: it simply isn't worth getting ill again, is it?'[23]

By now Hughes was planning to spend Christmas in Morocco, perhaps to give himself a breathing-space from both Frances and Louisa; but when in late October he heard (from a travel agency) that Jim Wyllie was hoping to be joined by him on board the SS *Patria* sailing on 6 November from Southampton,[24] he declined this invitation (announcing that he would follow Mr Wyllie to Morocco at a later date),[25] and retreated once again to North Wales. There he battled with storms, and indulged his recently revived passion for reading mathematical works.[26]

This rekindled enthusiasm made it particularly interesting when a letter reached him from Naomi Mitchison (who had recently written a glowing review of *The Spider's Palace*), explaining that she was editing an *Outline of Knowledge* for ten to fourteen-year-olds. This, in her view, represented 'a gorgeous chance of getting at the minds of the intelligent young' and she asked whether Hughes would write 'on dancing and drama? I want it short', she added, 'about 4000 words, so it would take you very little time'.[27]

On returning to London, Hughes wrote to Naomi Mitchison saying that he would far prefer to write about mathematics, physics and astronomy. The obvious difficulty of this course of action (as he pointed out) was that[28]

> it would appear inappropriate to my reputation: on the other hand, I think there is something to be said for it. At the age for which I should be writing, these subjects, and especially Astronomy and Mathematics, were my ruling passion . . . This bent of mine

appeared to atrophy as I grew older, yet this last twelve or six months it has returned with almost full force.

Naomi agreed to him writing on his chosen subjects, provided that he would allow his facts to be checked by the scientist John Pilley of Bristol University; and the result was a remarkable fifty pages in which Diccon Hughes wrote that:[29]

> In taking you to the very large and the very small I am taking you *beyond* common sense. Before starting on that journey your mind will have to turn a complete somersault, and come up ready to think things and believe things that common sense would say are untrue and impossible.
>
> After all, this may not be so difficult for a boy or girl as for a man or woman. When you are young, *all* thinking is something fairly new.

For that reason, he told his audience of children, 'I may very likely expect *you* to tackle new ideas too difficult for the average grown-up'.

Towards the end of November, Diccon dined again with Frances: this time on the night of a full moon.[30] It was a romantic occasion. Diccon had found in his post an early map of Wales. There was no covering note; but, recalling his visit with Frances to the antiquarian bookshop, he assumed that she had sent it to him. In that case, he reasoned, it was clearly a lover's gift: which meant that he could safely propose marriage. He did so, and she accepted. (The map, to which Diccon fortunately made no allusion, had really been sent to him by James Wyllie, a fact which only came to light a year later.)[31]

Now that he was certain of Frances Bazley's love, Hughes decided that he could safely depart for Morocco; and he reached Tangier on 8 December in time for cocktails with Teddy Wolfe.[32] His plan seems to have been that in the New Year of 1932 Frances and various members of her family should join him in Morocco; but if so he was disappointed.

Hardly had he arrived in Tangier before he was handed a telegram (presumably from Frances) which read:

THOMAS CANNOT COME RACHEL MIGHT TRAVEL JANUARY FIRST POSTED LETTER AIRMAIL TODAY

And then on the 22nd Diccon's godfather cabled from North Wales with this enigmatic message about the Johnsons' adopted son Tony Leach:[33]

ANXIOUS TONY CAN YOU RETURN BAZLEY APPROVES
– JOHNSON.

And on the same day a cable arrived from Frances (who was
in London) with the news:

> JOHNSON CABLED ABOUT TONY IF YOU RETURN
> CAN MEET YOU ANYWHERE ANYTIME RETURNING
> HATHEROP TOMORROW AFTERNOON CAREFUL CAB-
> LING TELEGRAMS READ PUBLICLY AT HOME.

Diccon replied that he would return immediately after Christmas.
Could Frances meet him somewhere?

So, the Bazleys-as-mountain would no longer have to travel
out to Morocco to meet Diccon Hughes-as-prophet! Frances was
delighted, and replied on 23 December:

> ANYTHING CONVENIENT SOUTHAMPTON BY TRAIN OR
> CAR IF PREFERRED VERY HAPPY AND CERTAIN SINCE
> MOUNTAIN NOW HATHEROP.

Diccon was back in England by New Year's Eve; Frances met him;
and they decided to waste no more time, but to get married as soon
as possible.

A few days later they drove to Hatherop, and Diccon stepped
for the first time into the massive front hall of Hatherop Castle,
where he was welcomed by the boyish Sir Thomas (six years Diccon's
junior) and his tall, elegant sister Rachel. It was Rachel, with the
help of an ageing Nanny Taylor, who now ran the considerable
household, their mother having decamped some years previously
with her Lieutenant-Commander to Quenington Old Rectory, a
couple of miles away.

However, the Cadogans were waiting for Frances and Diccon
by an open fire at the far end of the long library at the west end
of Hatherop, just beyond the massive flight of stairs. It was now a
Tuesday afternoon; and, as Diccon explained not long afterwards
to Joseph Brewer, Frances, introducing him to her mother for the
first time, immediately[34]

> t[old] that lady that she was expected to produce a wedding for
> us by Thursday. When she said that this was hurrying her rather,
> and she had somebody coming to tea on Thursday anyway, as a
> great concession we gave her until Friday!

Lance Sieveking (who happened to be staying at Hatherop with
his very pretty second wife Nathalie) heard Frances deliver this
ultimatum, and recalls what happened next:[35]

> But how, wailed her mother and stepfather, *how* were all the proper

preparations to be made? How could all the relations and friends be assembled? What about the wedding-dress, the bridesmaids, the licence, the announcements? What about – ? Frances swept them aside. She would be married in the chapel of the castle (which was also the parish church) and the family could make any other arrangements they liked. She didn't say this unkindly; but merely as if it didn't interest her. They must, of course, have their fun, but they must organise it themselves.

'For the rest of the week', Sieveking concludes, 'the castle was in an uproar.'

Louisa Hughes came down from North Wales to join the small house party of close friends and family which was rapidly assembled for the wedding; and a photograph, taken to record their number, shows her looking positively haunted. She stands, peering nervously towards the camera, in sharp contrast to the genial figure of Lord Howard of Penrith, with his white moustache, and a watch-chain stretched across an ample waistcoat; and to that of her friend Mr Johnson, Diccon's kindly godfather, with his thin, wise, bearded face.

Diccon had asked Tony Leach to be his best man; and the two of them spent the eve of the wedding at an old haunt of Diccon's from Oxford days, the Spreadeagle at Thame, still presided over by that brilliant, surly, unpredictable genius John Fothergill. As Diccon describes their stay:[36]

> Fothergill was disturbed and displeased at the care with which I brushed my trousers and had the [Bentley] washed the following morning, so I told him that I was going to a wedding, and even confided, in a morose voice, that it was the wedding of the girl I wanted to marry myself. So Fothergill was brusquely sympathetic, and off we went.

Diccon drove (as Sieveking heard the story), leaving Tony to map-read; and Diccon, normally 'so quietly imperturbable no matter what is going on', must have been on that morning 'in what was for him a very highly strung state'. For they were driving across open country, and already running a little late,[37]

> when Diccon saw that a quarter of a mile ahead the road divided into two.
> 'Which way?' he asked his best man.
> 'Er – ' answered the best man, his finger moving doubtfully about the map.
> They were going at about seventy miles an hour, and in

another moment would have to take either the right or the left road.

'Which WAY?' shouted Diccon, with a harsh edge in his voice that rarely appeared.

'Er – I – er – ' said the best man.

Diccon frowned with silent impatience and drove to neither right nor left, but straight through an open gateway between the two roads, and brought the car to a standstill in the middle of a field. He got out and stood gazing at the view as if they had all the time in the world. At last he turned to his companion and, in a very gentle voice, asked once more: 'Which way?'

The wedding took place at 2.15 on Friday 8 January 1932. Frances, who was dressed in blue velvet, was escorted up the nave by her brother Sir Thomas, and given away by her mother. Apart from the Sievekings (who were horrified to discover when a notice finally appeared in *The Times* that they headed the list of tenantry) almost the only guests were 'relatives and the village'; although the Duke of Hamilton's sister Margaret flew herself down from Scotland in her own private aeroplane.

After the wedding ceremony they returned to the castle for tea – to which the local wolf cubs had been given a special invitation; and when the cake had been cut, the health of the newly married couple was proposed by 'Uncle Esmé' with all the (very considerable) eloquence at his command.[38]

Having 'managed the whole business' (as Diccon told Joseph Brewer) 'with the most commendable speed and lack of publicity', he drove his bride back to the Spreadeagle, where they found Fothergill[39]

> as astonished as anyone could reasonably have wished: [he] called me a bloody fool, kissed me on the cheek, and told Frances not to giggle; and was nicer to us for the next few days than I knew he could be.

After their honeymoon at Thame, Diccon and Frances moved temporarily into his London house in Lloyd Square, and then set sail for Morocco.

It should have been an idyllic start to their married life; and numerous congratulatory letters from John Masefield and others followed them out to Morocco, as news of their wedding gradually percolated through their circle of friends. Iris Barry wrote of New York being a hotbed of rumours about the wedding, with Joseph Brewer acting as a clearing-house for any new scraps of information;

and she added the news that Charles Laughton and Elsa Lanchester were great admirers of his work; and that one Jed Harris, a producer, 'much wants to film "High Wind".;[40]

There was also a letter from Margery Bianco. This very much pleased Diccon, who wrote back to say how remote he had felt from the Biancos for the last few years. Margery immediately sent him a further letter full of regret, explaining that after the difficulties of 1929 (when Diccon had had so much trouble with Pamela and when, Margery now believed, every single person including herself had acted very selfishly) she had gained the impression that Diccon was completely alienated from her. Now, whether that was true or not, she felt it less. She added the news that Pamela and her husband Robert had returned just before Christmas, and that Pamela was expecting a baby in July; but that Robert, though agreeable in some respects, had no sense of responsibility whatever; so while Pamela lived at home, Robert had lodgings elsewhere, which, she concluded, said just about all there was to say.[41]

From Chicago came a particularly charming letter from Ernestine Evans, an editor with J.B. Lippincott, to whom Hughes had once given 'gracious asylum' when she was visiting London. 'Salute your bride for me', she wrote,[42]

> and tell her that I wish her well; that it is sweet and astonishing in this ill-natured world, that so many people this side the Atlantic wish her joy, and believe that she will have it, and have a lively curiosity to meet her.

But despite all these good wishes, the first six weeks of Diccon's married life could hardly have been more difficult. As he explained to Joseph Brewer in a letter from Tangier,[43]

> Frances [has] . . . indulged in gastric flu, appendicitis and peritonitis. That last two she waited for till now, when, as the first and only Englishwoman in the Arab quarter, she was well installed in a house without light or water, & drains built by the Portuguese in 1460. However, I got her to hospital, she has been operated on with great success, & is now sitting up in bed trying to dot me one with a medicine bottle. But it was hell for a bit.

The next set-back was that Frances (as she told her half-brother Christopher Cadogan) developed 'a damaged toe since my appendicitis, so I can't walk on it, nor can we go back to our own house, as we cannot get a car anywhere near it'. She added that she found Morocco 'a queer country', and that Christopher would only be able to stay with them in the Arab Quarter 'if we buy the house next to ours in which to accommodate you. Otherwise you will have to sleep on a bunk on top of the cupboard of our room'.[44]

But although the house was small, the way of life was exotic. Frances later recalled that there were[45]

> cushions all around the side of the room and we sat on the floor, and there was a little tiny round table with short legs, and they brought in a big copper tray which was always cleaned by the old women – the men weren't allowed to clean copper – they brought this in and put it in front of us.

Apart from the bed, 'a sort of platform with mattresses on, and white muslin curtains across it', the table was virtually the only item of furniture in the house; and this appealed to Frances, who commented that 'there wasn't any worry with tables and chairs, and all those stupid kind of things. We had absolutely beautiful copper dishes and copper jugs for carrying water, and every single thing in the house was beautiful'.

Sometimes, 'in the middle of dinner', when their manservant had finished waiting on them, he would 'sit down cross-legged and tell us a story: one of which, "The Red Lantern" must have made [Diccon] about £700, I should think, it was so good. He just wrote it as our servant told it'. Frances was enormously impressed by Hamed, and not just for his story-telling ability. He seemed to her to be 'very much grander than anyone I'd ever come across'. He always looked impressive, in his magenta robes; he still refused to speak English, communicating only in French or Arabic (which Frances began in desperation to learn) and still only used the past tense: so that he had always done everything, and was never going to do anything. Indeed, Frances (who was not allowed to go out without Hamed) found that when they went to market

> he hired a boy to carry things for him, so we walked like that, me first, him next, and then the boy to carry the things. Even the bunches of flowers I wasn't allowed to carry, and he didn't carry either. But if it was a question of sending messages, that was very grand, and he always went. He never paid a little boy a silver coin to go. He always went himself. But he always had his servant in the house, who did all the work.

The only serious drawback in Frances's eyes was the lack of proper sanitation; and as soon as it could be arranged, she and Diccon left their house and stayed with friends, while their typically Moroccan hole in the ground was replaced by a western-style lavatory. This was such a novelty that Hamed 'had people who came in, in procession, from early morning till late at night to look at what they called a Christian cup . . . the first that had ever been seen in the native quarter'.

Even this improvement did not satisfy Frances when she realised that she was carrying a child. They had in any case been thinking of returning to England in April;[46] and (in the words of a close relative): 'Frances reckoned Tangier was no place for an extremely inexperienced young mother . . . She decided things by intuition, and once she had decided, she was unbendable.'[47] So when Frances was four or five weeks pregnant, she and Diccon left Walter Harris in charge of further alterations to their house,[48] and began the long journey back to England.

After a brief family reunion at Hatherop Castle, Diccon and Frances set out for North Wales, where they stayed partly at Garreg Fawr, and partly on the *Amis Reunis*: a hulk since the terrible storm of October 1927 (later known as 'the tidal wave'), during which she had been lifted from her moorings, poked her bowsprit in through the dining-room window of Clough's hotel, and broken her back.[49] Afterwards, the *Amis Reunis* survived for a few years with her hull concreted into place not far from the hotel:[50] which meant that Naomi Mitchison (then holidaying at Portmeirion) was able to write in her introduction to Hughes's piece on 'Physics, Astronomy and Mathematics' in her renamed *An Outline for Boys and Girls and their Parents*: 'When I first met him he was living partly in a cottage a long way from anywhere in the middle of the Welsh hills, and partly on a slightly wrecked ship.'[51]

During those weeks in North Wales, Frances met many of Diccon's friends: including not only Clough and Amabel, but also Frank Penn Smith, who had been living for many years in Gelli, a romantically dilapidated old cottage not far from Penrhyndeudraeth. Diccon had successfully interested a number of editors (notably Desmond MacCarthy of *Life and Letters*) in Penn Smith's articles; and further work on his behalf ended with the publication by Jonathan Cape in 1933 of Penn Smith's novel *The Unexpected*, to which Hughes contributed a preface.

But although Hughes admired Frank Penn Smith's writing, he disliked his right-wing politics; and Frank once wrote to Louisa to tell her that her son had declared him to be 'the greatest Fanatic (politically) he has ever met (And he has met . . . Stella Watson and many others)'. A more serious difference (for Diccon believed that politics was not a writer's business) was the fact that Penn Smith heartily disliked Amabel, describing her as 'a born Jewess of the dangerous sort'. When Louisa told him that the Johnsons were planning another holiday in North Wales, but were against taking Parc (one of the cottages on Clough's estate), 'if Amabel is to be much about', Penn Smith replied sagely:[52]

Mrs J may have cataract and other failings but she has keen insight. Amabel is a malign influence and she is dominant to some natures. It is not that she wishes to do harm, but she is always doing it. The village sees right through her, and won't let the impressionable girls go to her.

He added that Amabel's judgement was 'dangerously bad. She flies excitedly at the last new contradiction to any accepted thing, and rushes round inoculating people with it'.

Amabel and her circle were certainly stimulating company; but after a while Diccon decided that if any work was to be done, he and Frances must find somewhere to live in a part of the country where they had no friends.

By the late summer of 1932, Diccon and Frances had begun renting Stiffkey Old Hall in Norfolk, near Blakeney and about a mile from the east coast. In a letter to a friend, Diccon described their new home as 'what hasn't yet fallen down'[53] of a house built by Francis Bacon's father, Sir Nicholas Bacon[54]

> early in the sixteenth century in a style half-way between the Normandy château and the Rhine Baronial of some earlier age. It was faced with flint. Half of it was in ruins, including the banqueting hall. Originally it had had at least six tall, thin towers, in four of which were five small circular rooms, one above the other. Only four of these towers were still standing.

'It is much too large for us', Diccon conceded, 'but a pleasant excess after so many years of cottage life.' Stiffkey, a little village with no more than five hundred inhabitants, was also (as he pointed out) 'where the Rectors come from'.[55] He referred of course to the eccentric Rev Harold Davidson (known as the 'Prostitutes' Padre' because of his obsessive interest in rescuing 'fallen women'), who had recently hit the national headlines when his bishop successfully prosecuted him for immorality.[56]

There were few distractions in Stiffkey; but although Hughes continued to write 'bread-and-butter' articles and reviews, he still could not find the major project for which he had been searching. In any case, he was spending a great deal of time looking after Frances, now heavily pregnant; and some weeks before her baby was due they moved back to 21 Lloyd Square in London, so that she could come under the care of a first-class Harley Street specialist.[57]

It was in London on 19 November 1932 that Frances gave birth to a son. Diccon's idea of a congratulatory present was a stuffed crocodile from an antique shop; but the nurse, a powerful woman, was so angry about the germs that might have been introduced into her territory that she physically propelled Diccon and his crocodile from the scene.[58] The boy was christened Robert Elistan Glodrydd. Elistan, as Diccon told Joseph Brewer a few months later, was 'after an ancestor who celebrates his millennium this year: but he is always called Mohammed — not after the prophet, but after my Moorish servant'[59] — who had himself been advised of the birth in a splendidly ornate letter beginning: 'To our respected and faithful servant Mohammed el Kejari, may God prolong his life . . .'[60]

Remaining in London throughout December, Hughes toyed with the idea (put to him by Dick de la Mare of Faber & Faber) of a life of the nineteenth-century writer and explorer Richard Burton;[61] but for two months most of his time was devoted to the revival of his ten-year-old dream of a Welsh National Theatre.

Richard Hughes had decided that the Welsh National Theatre movement should be inaugurated by a London performance of *A Comedy of Good and Evil*. If this seems immodest, it must be said in his defence that he was encouraged to choose his own play partly because of his encounter on 3 December 1932 with two of Robert Graves's children: twelve-year-old David and Jenny Nicholson, just a few weeks short of her fourteenth birthday, and training to be a dancer.[62] Diccon had always specified that the principal role in *A Comedy of Good and Evil* should be played by someone[63]

> as young as is technically convenient. Notable for an unearthly innocence of expression. Her English accent is unimpeachable, and she gives every sign of a most careful upbringing, as well as of a naturally nice disposition.

And now, meeting Jenny again after a gap of several years, he realised that she fitted his specifications precisely. He immediately asked her to play the part of Gladys. She agreed. The Arts Theatre was secured for an evening in late January 1933; and round Jenny he gathered a strong cast of 'distinguished members of the Welsh colony of stage artists in London'. (Most notably, Owain Flatfish was played by Richard Goolden, later to become famous for his annual performances as Mole in *Toad of Toad Hall*, A.A. Milne's adaptation of Kenneth Grahame's *The Wind in the Willows*.)[64]

While rehearsals were in progress, Hughes worked immensely hard on securing backers for his new venture. The Earl of Donegal was asked: 'Do you recall the Portmadoc Players? . . . *This* scheme is far more ambitious; and even Lloyd George has sent it a guinea and a kind word.' The object of the movement? 'To establish a permanent company of Welsh professionals to tour the Principality with plays by Welsh authors, and also with plays translated into Welsh.'[65] Within a few weeks, a distinguished committee had been recruited under the chairmanship of Lord Howard de Walden (Hughes himself assumed the role of vice-chairman); and then on Thursday 26 January came the inaugural performance.

Produced by Robert Atkins, and played before a distinguished audience which included both Lloyd George and his daughter Megan, *A Comedy of Good and Evil* received generally good notices; and Jenny Nicholson (according to 'Peterborough' in the *Daily Telegraph*) was 'the success of the evening'.[66] 'She was remarkably good', agreed her aunt Clarissa, who watched the play with several other members of the Graves clan, 'her voice as clear as a bell';[67] and the *Daily Mail* said of her performance: 'The fierce venom and terror which she was able to assume alternately was a piece of amazingly skilled acting for a child of this age.'[68]

Afterwards there was a party at which Hughes explained to a reporter that this had been 'the baptismal ceremony only'. It was hoped to present some plays at the Eisteddfod in April, but it would not be until the autumn that they would start in earnest with a full repertory programme.[69]

Socially, it had been an amusing time for Diccon Hughes. Charles Laughton and Elsa Lanchester came to dinner;[70] he met the distinguished biologist Julian Huxley, who invited him to lunch at the Gargoyle;[71] he saw the de la Mares;[72] and he also met the bestselling novelist Storm Jameson, who had to decline an invitation to Stiffkey because it would have meant leaving her husband to look after himself for a day or two – an impossibility, she declared, as 'he can't make himself a cup of tea without blowing his eyebrows off'.[73]

For Diccon's own work there had been little time; though while he was in London he had managed a wireless broadcast on African music,[74] and an article on 'The National Theatre in Wales' for the *Manchester Guardian*;[75] and there had been more discussions about a biography of Burton.

Then in March 1933 news arrived of the death of Walter Harris. Hughes, as one of the friends of Harris's old age, had heard from his own lips the stories of such dramatic incidents as his abduction by the bandit-chieftain Moulay Ahmed er-Raisuli. So when he was asked to write an official biography, it seemed like a wonderful opportunity, and he began collecting further material.

At about the same time, Diccon received two accounts of a storm which he found 'so extraordinary' that he felt 'very strongly moved to make that storm the basis of a short book'.[76]

*

A hurricane had raged across the Caribbean in November 1932; and it had seized the steamer *Phemius* and sucked it across the sea, so that the ship was battered almost unceasingly for five days and nights. Only the heroism and ingenuity of the ship's officers had prevented a disaster. Captain D.L.C. Evans (who had coped with both the fury of the wind, and the panic of his Chinese crew) sent a detailed report to Laurence Holt (chairman of the line to which the *Phemius* belonged); and Holt was so impressed that he passed it on to John Masefield (now Poet Laureate) 'feeling like Gengi "There are things that must never be forgotten" '. Much to Holt's chagrin Masefield simply returned it with a polite acknowledgement; and Holt then discussed the matter with Clough and Amabel Williams-Ellis, and showed them reports both by the captain and by another member of the ship's company.

As Amabel subsequently wrote to Diccon on 15 March (enclosing both accounts of the hurricane):[77]

> [Holt] told us a lot more of the low-down than is in the printed account, and of course anyone who was using it would need to go and see the captain and the others, but with Holt feeling that it ought to be written about this would not be hard.
>
> You came to my mind directly he began to talk as the *right person* – dearly as I would love to do it myself – but you would do it a damn sight better and well I know it. Also it would be hard for a woman to make the people talk – they would make it all much too proper! Now would you like to have it?

Diccon wrote to Laurence Holt on 27 March, expressing a strong interest in the story, and explaining that he would keep to the incidents of what had happened to the *Phemius*, but would invent his own crew.[78]

Holt replied the following day, saying that Hughes should see Captain Evans, now of the *Myrmidon*, whom he could accompany on a coasting trip.[79] Later that day he wrote again, with the news that Captain Evans would be sailing from Amsterdam on 7 April, calling in at Swansea and then going on to Birkenhead. Would Hughes like to sign on for this voyage?[80]

Diccon sent an immediate telegram of acceptance. On Tuesday 4 April Holt gave him lunch in London at Brown's Hotel, having 'come armed with all instructions and credentials'; and Hughes crossed over to Amsterdam on the night of 5th.[81] Captain Evans found him 'a very agreeable shipmate';[82] and Diccon also had a brief meeting with R.J. Wolfe, who had sailed on the *Phemius* as chief engineer.[83]

*

Soon after returning from his voyage on the *Myrmidon*, Diccon took Frances to Morocco: partly for a holiday, and partly in order to collect material for his life of Walter Harris. (Five-month-old Robert was left behind in the care of the Sievekings, who 'had agreed to come and live at Stiffkey until they came back'.)[84]

Frances enjoyed her second visit to Morocco much more than the first, and it was just as full of exotic incident. Hamed's servant, they discovered, 'had a liking for opium, so all our garden . . . was opium poppies, and he got terribly dozy; but still', as Frances recalled, 'that couldn't be helped. That wasn't our affair. He wasn't our servant, he was our servant's servant'.[85]

Next door, there was an hereditary saint, who to begin with was 'very upset' that infidels should be living so close at hand: one reason why Diccon and Frances took care to observe local customs. For example, breakfast was usually eaten on one of their roof-top balconies, above either the bedroom or the kitchen; but Diccon never went there in the afternoons, because that was when the Moorish women went on to their roofs with their heads unveiled: so only Frances saw the women 'combing out their marvellous black hair, raking it out of ribbons', and 'really looking absolutely wonderful'.

When they returned to Stiffkey in mid June, Lance Sieveking was there to observe how their 'Bentley touring car snorted powerfully along the drive and came to an impressive halt beside the house'. He could see that it was 'piled high with exotic-looking bundles', and that 'Diccon, at the wheel, was wearing an Arab burnous as an overcoat'. Then, greatly to his surprise,[86]

> someone in the dicky seat, in similar headgear, rose up. It was not, however, [Diccon's] friend, T.E. Lawrence, but a very tall, elderly Arab, with a small red watering-can in one hand. He silently clambered out of the car, and gathering his robes about him in a dignified way, walked over to the nearest flower-bed and began to water it.

This was Hamed. All the way from the south coast, Sieveking learned, he had been shouting curses in Arabic at every car that overtook them, and heaping scorn on all those who were overtaken. But now, 'he was at peace. He had refilled his little can from the stream and was watering another flower-bed farther off as if he had quietly lived there all his life'.

Hughes had come back to several letters from Laurence Holt. On 20 April 1933, reporting that the *Phemius*, returning from

Penang, was due at Le Havre on 13 May, and in Liverpool on 17 May, Holt had asked whether Hughes would care to join her at Le Havre;[87] on 8 June he had written again, sending him a list of the crew of the *Phemius*, which was 'here' at Liverpool '& empty'. Hughes could stay with him, and 'I could show you the ship' – including the water-marks which had remained in the holds since the hurricane – '& bring on one or two of the crew'.[88] Then on 14 June he mentioned that the *Phemius* was refitting, and would sail early in August. In the meantime Kavanagh, the first mate, was on holiday in Ireland; but Holt could send Midshipman Timms to see him; and he himself asked for a few days' notice before Hughes made his Liverpool visit.[89]

Diccon wrote at once to say that he was now free to travel; and he was again invited by Holt to stay for a weekend. This gave him a chance to see the *Phemius* for the first time, and also to meet not only Timms, but also the chief steward and the junior engineers.[90] The final stages of this early research were concluded in September, when Kavanagh visited Hughes at Stiffkey Hall, taking with him the log record so as to unravel Diccon's 'meteorological difficulties'.[91]

Sadly, it would take many years for the novel based upon the story of the *Phemius* to be written.

In the short term, besides collecting material both for this new novel[92] and for his Walter Harris biography, Hughes was involved in complex and protracted negotiations with Dick de la Mare of Faber & Faber about his projected life of Burton. These had begun in March, and were still continuing in September, when Hughes rejected de la Mare's latest offer (of £100 on signature, £250 on delivery and £150 on publication against a 20% royalty)[93] in a long letter which began: 'Dear Dick, I'm afraid it won't do. I must stick to my request for half the advance to be payable on signing the contract – or, if you prefer, by Christmas.'[94]

Still more time-consuming was the business of finding (and putting in order) a new home; and indeed (for this and other reasons) it would be several years before Diccon resumed anything like a normal pattern of work.

The Hugheses had begun to integrate themselves into the local community at Stiffkey, where Diccon had become a pillar of the village cricket club;[95] but Stiffkey Old Hall was expensive to lease, and expensive to run. It was also hopelessly impractical for family life: the impossibility of heating the large rooms meant that Frances would later recall eating breakfast in the courtyard on a chilly February morning, it being no colder outside than in.[96] Besides, Diccon wished to return to Wales; and he also wanted to be somewhere within easy reach of the sea, especially as his brother-in-law Thomas

Bazley had given him 'the wherewithal for [a] boat, a part of your belated wedding-present'.[97]

In the summer of 1933 Hughes fell in love with a dilapidated Georgian-looking house in the grounds of a still more dilapidated medieval castle in the remote and somewhat decaying village of Laugharne on the coast of South Wales. The castle (extensively rebuilt during the late sixteenth century by Sir John Perrot, but then ruined during the Civil War in the seventeenth) made a powerful appeal to Diccon's romantic imagination. In September he told Clough Williams-Ellis that he had found 'the perfect place', and asked him to go down to cast a professional eye over its state of repair.[98]

Clough reported that 'Laugharne Castle' (whose name had attached itself to the house) was 'terribly tempting', despite the lack of a damp course, the lack of electricity, and the fact that water had to be pumped from a well; and in October Hughes began negotiations with the owner, Mrs Starke. These lasted until February 1934 (by which time Frances was seven months' pregnant with their second child); and then, after numerous journeys back and forth from Norfolk, Hughes was finally granted a fourteen-year lease. Stringent conditions had been imposed, including that a specific and substantial sum of money must be spent on improvements and repairs; and (with Clough as architect) the builders moved in almost immediately.[99]

CHAPTER 22

Laugharne Castle

When Richard Hughes had first inspected his new home, he had had to cut his way through the brambles which grew almost up to the doors on every side. It was a wild, desolate place, set high on a hill, with the nearby castle ruins looking out over the sea. The whole property occupied a kind of no-man's-land between the two parts of Laugharne. At the foot of the steep hill on which it stood was the area known as Downstreet. There, around an open space called the Grist,[1]

> lived the cockling families, the fisherman, the coal-merchant. They were knit together by the fact that every autumn at the equinox the tides flooded the whole area. People kept barricades in readiness from year to year, and moved their belongings upstairs.

At the head of the steep hill, and behind the castle, was Upstreet, home of 'the more well-to-do – the butcher, Brown's Hotel, the various small-gentry'.

Laugharne as a whole had a well-deserved reputation for eccentricity (not least because it was a self-governing borough with an ancient charter); and Clough Williams-Ellis would later regard this reputation as having been one of its principal lures. Diccon, he believed, had been 'determined to settle down somewhere as odd as possible with as odd a population as possible', and nothing could have been better than 'this little old borough', where 'Everything had gone down, population, income, the harbour silted up, the castle falling down: it was perfect, what you might call ' "Diccon country" '[2]

Another attraction was that whoever lived in the Castle House was accorded an almost feudal respect, 'more play-acted than real, but all concerned enjoyed acting it'.[3] By mid March the vicar of Laugharne, S.B. Williams, was already writing to Hughes as 'Dear Seigneur', in a letter which began:[4]

> I hear you have come & gone – & I have been no use to you! But do, please, let me know of anything where I may be of any service,

at any time – & my home is always open for you, whether I may
be here or not.

I expect you had no difficulty in finding 'spadesmen'; as you
say, a few fine fellows under supervision will soon knock the
garden & grounds into shape.

Nothing, however, went easily; and at the end of March, when the
builders began work on the house, Diccon succumbed to a severe
bout of influenza which left him feeling run-down for weeks.[5]

By then, Hughes had signed a contract with Faber for a biography
of Richard Burton, for which he had been paid £250, part of a staged
advance of £1000.[6] However, in all the confusion at Laugharne, it
had been difficult for him to make any serious progress on Burton,
Harris or his new novel. Diccon had also been called away in February 1934 to attend the Chelsea wedding of his brother-in-law
Anthony Bazley; and two months later he was again in London,
where on 27 April Frances gave birth to a daughter whom they
named Penelope.

For much of the next two years Hughes was further distracted
partly by voluntary work for the Welsh National Theatre, the Council for the Protection of Rural Wales and other institutions; partly by
the lure of the sea; partly by a new venture as a playwright; and partly
by his growing involvement with the township of Laugharne.

The Welsh National Theatre occupied huge tracts of Hughes's
time. As vice-chairman, he considered himself duty-bound not only
to attend all committee meetings (even when much of the time was
spent in pointless and irrelevant discussion);[7] but also to do whatever
else might promote the cause; whether it was acting in January 1934
as adjudicator in the Treorchy Drama Competition,[8] or speaking in
February to the South Wales division of the British Drama League in
Cardiff, to whom he retailed an anecdote about Masefield: apparently the poet had tested his earlier works by reading them on street
corners, and seeing if people stayed to listen.[9]

By the beginning of 1934, the committee of the Welsh National
Theatre had at last established a rudimentary organisation. A full-
time secretary had been found in the enthusiastic Miss Evelyn Bowen;
funds had been raised (Hughes himself had generously directed his
dramatic agents to pay the royalties for all performances of his plays,
professional London productions apart, to the Welsh National Theatre);[10] premises had been leased in Llangollen, where a 'First Annual
School of Dramatic Art' was promised for a week in May;[11] and a
company was being assembled, to be taken on tour by Miss Bowen
that autumn.

Richard Hughes ensured that Laugharne was one of the chosen venues for the new company. He then invited Hilda Vaughan (another committee member) to stay with him in November, her visit to coincide with the Welsh National Theatre performances.

In the meantime Hughes had fallen happily into his patriarchal rôle within the borough, making a local reputation for himself in June 1934 (while work on the Castle House was still in progress) by installing his family (including three-month-old Penelope) in one of the Moorish tents which he had brought back from Morocco. This had been their base during the day; while by night (according to one newspaper report) they had sheltered in a room in the western tower of the Castle.[12]

Nancy Nicholson had taken charge of the interior decoration;[13] and in September, Hughes invited her daughter Jenny (now fifteen years old) to bring her newly formed 'Patchwork Players' to Laugharne Castle. There Jenny was Master of Ceremonies in a programme of dancing and music open to the public and described by the *Western Mail* as 'an attempt to develop an English ballet'.[14]

By the time of Hilda Vaughan's visit, the Castle House was habitable, and even elegant. Both living-room and library, at the front of the house, 'retained their "Georgian" appearance';[15] while at the back were the kitchen, various utility rooms, and a handsome dining-room (converted by Clough from two smaller rooms) with new french windows which gave a view south-east across the estuary.

On the first floor, immediately opposite the staircase, Nurse Graham (assisted by Joyce, a fifteen-year-old nursemaid from the Grist) presided over night and day nurseries and 'exerted a benign influence on the household as a whole'.[16] To the left of the staircase was Frances's studio, where she retired to paint whenever possible; to the right was the main bedroom (in which a large wall-cupboard had been converted into a bathroom), with a small child's room leading off. There was also a spare bedroom on this floor (in which Hilda Vaughan was now comfortably installed); and on the second floor, right at the top of the house, there were two further bedrooms, a lean-to attic, and Diccon's study.

It was a substantial house; and the cost of repairs and alterations (which included installing electricity) had been enormous. The original estimate of £550 (then a good professional salary) had been daunting enough; but at the time of Hilda Vaughan's visit, the builder was about to submit a demand for a staggering £1364 3s. 0d.[17] Much of the cost would be met by a trust fund which held money on Frances's behalf;[18] but Diccon was compelled to arrange a large overdraft[19] (for which his mother provided the security);[20] and when a few months later further extensive repairs were necessary, he told the owners that he had already spent far more on the property than had been agreed;[21] and in recognition of this fact they extended the lease from fourteen to twenty-one years.[22]

Hilda Vaughan and Diccon Hughes were both shocked by the low quality of the Welsh National Theatre productions which she had come to see. The two of them made some enquiries among the members of the company; and on Hilda's return to London on 8 November she wrote to Diccon telling him that she had already posted a letter to Evelyn Bowen, advising her to leave producing to others; and now she planned to 'tell Lord Howard de Walden "in camera" just how deplorably bad you and I thought the productions . . . before we unitedly demand a proper reorganisation of the movement at the next general meeting'.[23]

Diccon replied agreeing that the tour had been a 'fiasco'; though he generously described it as one 'for which we, as a Council, are really to blame more than Miss Bowen, in leaving to her more than any human being could possibly cope with'.[24]

Unfortunately rumours had begun to circulate, and it was already too late for matters to be settled amicably. Evelyn Bowen wrote to Hughes telling him that she was 'very distressed' to hear that he had been complaining behind her back to members of the company, and was planning to usurp her position.[25] He replied that he had no intention of becoming secretary: he had a profession of his own, and his real view was simply that the council was seriously to blame for not giving her enough help. 'Did I ever tell you', he concluded, 'I saw it once solemnly stated in the press I had built a mosque in Merioneth, and called the Faithful to prayer from the minaret every evening?'[26]

Shortly after receiving this letter, Miss Bowen was reported to be 'on the verge of a nervous breakdown';[27] and although she apologised to Hughes for her suspicions, she only did so after having summarily dismissed two of the company whom she now believed to be 'at the root of the matter'.[28] Subsequently (having drawn up a memorandum advocating a separate tour committee) Hughes was present at a main committee meeting held on 2 February 1935 in Lord Howard de Walden's house in Belgrave Square, at which Evelyn Bowen was warned that her dismissals could well lead to actions for slander being taken out against her.[29]

Hughes continued to support Miss Bowen; and in March, having learned that she needed larger premises, and believing that the centre of operations should be moved from Llangollen to Llanelli, he even went house-hunting on her behalf, but to no avail.[30] Early in May he wrote a strong letter to Lord Howard calling for more formal agendas, and 'some rather more elaborate and stricter form of organisation', and mentioning that he had received threats of resignation from more than half the council. A few days later, he followed this up with a plea for the company to concentrate for the time being on a single production once a year, and to employ for that purpose 'a competent producer sponsored by us'.[31]

Lord Howard de Walden accepted this advice in part; and secured the services of Dr Stefan Hock, a producer of international reputation. Under Lord Howard's auspices, Hock mounted two successful productions in the Welsh language: Ibsen's *Pretenders* at the Holyhead Eisteddfod, and *Pobun* at Wrexham.[32]

Dr Hock also appeared at the June committee meeting at which Hughes (chairing the meeting in Lord Howard's absence) secured resolutions agreeing in principle to the production of *Pobun* both at Llanelli and in the Rhonda valley. Responsibility for the latter was to belong to Hughes; and he corresponded valiantly with several amateur companies in South Wales suggesting a combined production under Hock. However he soon ran into severe difficulties (not least because the companies were almost entirely non-Welsh speaking);[33] and this was to be his last major effort on behalf of the Welsh National Theatre Company.

In the autumn, Hughes discovered that Miss Bowen had been suddenly and mysteriously replaced by Captain Fleming, who had been acting for some months as her assistant;[34] and the following spring, reminded that he was due to retire from the council, and asked whether he wished to offer himself for re-election, he politely bowed out. Disheartened by all the intrigue and backbiting, and dissatisfied with the quality of what was being achieved, he promised nevertheless to 'remain a member of the movement and a warm sympathizer'.[35]

Fortunately, Hughes's involvement with the Council for the Protection of Rural Wales (the CPRW) was far less time-consuming. Only a few weeks into his tenancy of Laugharne Castle, he had returned from a brief absence to find a letter from Herbert Vaughan mentioning that he had called with Sir Henry Stuart Jones, Principal of the University College of Wales, to ask him to attend a meeting of the CPRW at Tenby on 10 May. Clough Williams-Ellis was to give an address; and they assured Hughes that 'Your own presence will be greatly appreciated there'. A few days later, Vaughan wrote again, to thank Hughes for agreeing to come – and to speak himself for a few minutes.[36] The following month found Hughes writing to the headquarters of the CPRW in London about oil pollution both in the sea and in tidal estuaries; and from then on he would always put pen to paper and contact the CPRW about any threat to the local environment either in Laugharne or in his chosen area of North Wales.[37]

Other voluntary duties which Hughes undertook included acting as president of the Debating Society of University College, Swansea from 1934–1935, in succession to Harold Nicolson, and giving an address to the society in the Michaelmas term;[38] giving a further address on speech-day at the County School for Girls in Ruabon;[39] and sitting (at the request of the artist Cedric Morris, who had become a friend) on the subcommittee of the Contemporary Welsh Show, whose aim was 'to put on a series of concerts of Welsh music to run concurrently with the show & possibly some Welsh plays and a series of lectures'.[40] Hughes was also prepared to involve himself in public controversies: for example, a letter survives in which E.M. Forster thanks him warmly not only for signing an appeal made by the infant National Council for Civil Liberties (of which Forster was president), but also for thinking of 'additional ways of promoting it'.[41]

Sailing was another distraction; and also an escape from the pressures of creative work. Back in 1931, Hughes had written memorably that:[42]

> There is no excitement that I have experienced which equals the excitement of creative writing; especially of writing poetry. It lifts one into a state of consciousness otherwise unattainable. At the same time, there is nothing so fatiguing, no strain so great. If you have flown, you will be familiar with that sudden strain on the body, that uncanny increase in its weight, which comes at the moment of starting a loop . . . In writing, one's mind suffers the same uncanny increase of stress.

Most writers, said Hughes, suffer from this pressure, 'and some of them seek relief in drink, drugs, society, or writing for the fiction-magazines'. He himself found release in physical action and adventure.

In December 1933, while still negotiating for the lease of Laugharne Castle, Diccon had paid Major Lancelot Evans a £5 deposit on the 25-foot, 6-ton, *Tern*, built as a pilot cutter at Heswall on the river Dee back in April 1919, but more recently used as a fishing boat, and now beached at Deganwy on the north coast of Wales.[43] *Tern* was a formidable vessel: everything about her[44]

was built to stand up to heavy weather – the thickness of

her planks, the short, stocky gaff-rig mast, the lowness of the coach-house roof, the smallness of the cockpit. [*Tern*] was a boat tough enough to sail round the world in.

She was also well suited to Diccon's requirements: 'I chose her', he wrote, 'because I needed a boat to cruise from the Carmarthen estuary; something which would combine shallow draft with sea-worthiness, and take the ground without lying down.'[45] In March 1934, he paid a further £65 on account; the following month there was a final payment of £70; and then at the end of May Hughes sailed her south-west from Deganwy, through the Menai Strait between Anglesey and the mainland, and then all the way round the Lleyn Peninsula, and up to Portmadoc, where she remained for several months in the care of Elias Pierce.[46]

Sailing was not just an antidote to the strain of working at his desk, but a social pleasure; and Hughes had already asked Clough to arrange for his election to the Royal Welsh Yacht Club. (Clough reported after a visit: 'The air of decay about the whole outfit will charm you . . . The club staff sleeps in a shelf off the staircase. It's a wonderful old lady with an auburn wig & a cameo brooch. I think she was a stewardess on the *Great Eastern*.')[47] However, within a few days of purchasing *Tern*, Diccon had also joined the Cruising Association. This involved him in time-consuming administrative work, as he accepted the unpaid post of HLR (Honorary Local Representative) of the Association at Carmarthen, with responsibility for finding boatmen for both Laugharne and Ferryside; and later on, he would survey Carmarthen Bar on their behalf.[48]

His own boat was not brought to Laugharne until August, when, with his family safely established in their tent in the castle grounds, and with an offer from Clough Williams-Ellis of a lift to Portmadoc, Hughes decided to sail *Tern* down to his new home. First he wired to Elias Pierce, asking him 'to get her afloat if possible on the evening tide'. Half-an-hour later, having 'eaten my lunch, bundled my sea clothing into a sack, [and] found my charts, book of words, and instruments, in those obscure places where the furniture-removers had stowed them', he was on his way north.[49]

On reaching Portmadoc early in the morning of Monday 6 August, Diccon found to his disappointment that *Tern* was 'still on the hard. There had not been enough water to lift her stern'. But at seven o'clock that evening her stern lifted, and with the help of a crowbar they levered her off. A carnival was in full swing; and when Hughes had anchored in the channel, he sat in the cabin watching the fireworks 'through the port: rockets rushing into the clear sky, like escaping birds, and then seeming to burst into stars like a lark bursts into song – from sheer gladness'.

At six o'clock on Tuesday morning Diccon's crewman came aboard: Richards, a rigger by trade, and a native of Portmadoc. Hoisting sail, they 'ghosted down the channel, against the fag end of the flood'; and were soon out in Tremadoc bay, enjoying the sight of the Snowdon range mirrored in the sea. 'I know no view in the world more lovely', wrote Hughes. 'People would go to Japan, at vast expense, or penetrate a jungle, in great discomfort, to see something one half as good.'

The rest of that day, they sailed slowly down the coast; until at midnight there was no longer enough breeze to hold *Tern* on course, and it was impossible to crank the engine into life. Wednesday morning was a flat calm, and Hughes grew worried; 'it is notorious', he would write, 'that a flat calm in Cardigan bay generally presages a gale'. So as soon as a breeze sprang up (which was not until noon), he decided to make landfall; and that evening they stood in at Aberporth.

There was good shelter 'from everything south of west'; and after going ashore, Hughes 'picked up an excellent mechanic in a bar', and took him on board *Tern* to examine the engine. After working on it 'for two hours (by which time he had gone over the whole engine at least twice)', the mysterious trouble was discovered: 'A bung had been driven right up the exhaust pipe!'

The following morning it was blowing smartly from the south-west. Hughes and Richards left their anchorage under close-reefed mainsail and storm-jib; but as soon as they were out of shelter, 'the reef-points carried away in one single gust; and the sea was ugly'. Returning to the harbour, they waited for better weather until early on Friday morning, when Richards woke Hughes with the news that the wind was veering round to the north, and they 'had better clear out'.

So they left their anchorage, under the same sail as on Thursday. 'The sea', records Hughes,

> was no better: confused and breaking: we were obviously in for a damp day. Once outside, it was plain the wind had not veered, and that we had almost a dead beat for Fishguard. The tide was contrary, and our jury-reef-points carried away, making it difficult to lie close to the wind. Moreover, it was evident at once we were in for severe dinghy-trouble.

The dinghy, a 'flat-bottomed brute made for the former owner by an out-of-work carpenter', could not be stowed on deck; and began filling with water.

Their situation continued to deteriorate. Off Cardigan island ('which carried a battered wrecked steamer as a *memento mori* on its weather side'), the jib-sheets chafed through, the engine began to overheat, and the dinghy was 'almost entirely swamped'. Hoping to find enough shelter in Cardigan inlet to enable them to bale it out, they stood right in: 'only to find the sea worse inside, not better'.

The dinghy went under; and as they tacked out again, they were forced to cut it loose. Setting a staysail, they began to make progress again; but when they were off the entrance to Newport bay, the mainsheet carried adrift. Putting an old iron hook through the shackle which held it to the horse, they somehow got the sheet-block attached again; and then, wondering what would carry away next, they abandoned the attempt to reach Fishguard, and stood in to Newport bay, exploring for shelter.

Fortunately they discovered a little sheltered cove at the foot of Dinas head, where they anchored at three o'clock in the afternoon in about a fathom of water. They had already been spotted by a kindly doctor who owned a house on the sea-wall:

> and when he got us ashore we found hot baths, ready run, with a bottle of whisky on the ledge . . . hospitality could go no further. He and his admirable family treated us with almost embarrassing kindness for as long as we stayed there; and the contents of our water-logged cabin were soon transferred to their drying-room.

The next two days were spent putting *Tern* in order, and waiting for the weather to improve; and then at about midnight on Sunday Hughes and Richards once again set sail.

In the early hours of Monday, after 'a nasty popple off Dinas head', they put in at Fishguard; but they had rounded St David's head by three in the afternoon; and then, to their delight, they found themselves in 'another world; a most eerie thing. Sudden calm, sudden sunshine; and the rushing water as smooth as oil'.

The rest of their voyage was uneventful: that evening they landed at Dale (close to Milford Haven); on Tuesday they enjoyed 'a smiling day; such weather as mariners sail in off the coasts of Elysium'; and by six o'clock on Tuesday evening they had made their way up the river Tâf, and anchored 'off the castle, our voyage ended'.

By the summer of 1935, Hughes had found a more permanent crewman: young Jack Rowlands, slim and beardless, with his frank, open expression and his large hands. Laugharne born and bred, Jack was the ideal person not only to crew *Tern*, but also to act as a 'general factotum'[50] when anything practical needed doing. In August Diccon decided to spend a short holiday with Frances at

Bideford in Devon; and they began (with Jack as crew) by sailing out into Carmarthen bay, from where they planned to make a short journey across the Bristol Channel to Ilfracombe on the Devon coast.

Unfortunately, when they were well out into Carmarthen bay, a storm blew up; the jib blew to ribbons; half-an-hour later the mainsail began to tear; and they were forced to run before the gale and shelter in Tenby harbour. Frances, unnerved by this (and also determined to return home on the correct day to the children she had left behind), abandoned the two men and made her way to Bideford by train. It was not until several days later that Diccon and Jack finally sailed into Ilfracombe harbour – where *Tern* was laid up for repairs until the following spring.[51]

Hughes enjoyed his rôle as unofficial seigneur of Laugharne, and devoted an increasing amount of time to the community. During his first autumn at the Castle House, he was invited by the Portreeve of Laugharne to attend the annual banquet of the Corporation in Brown's Hotel;[52] afterwards, he decided to pay the fee which was necessary for an outsider to become a burgess of Laugharne;[53] and in 1935 he and Frances gave two parties for the local children.[54]

There was a more serious side to all this. Having showed that he was interested in the borough, and having made himself approachable, Hughes found that he would frequently be consulted: almost always when any weighty public matters were under discussion, and often when some private person wanted a word of advice. Diccon was always prepared to listen, and to give an opinion; and on one occasion, seeing that the family of a local bus-driver could not afford to send their 'exceptionally refined' daughter to school, he went so far as to secure her future by paying (anonymously) half her school fees.[55]

Further distractions from his novel and biographies included negotiations over the film rights to *A High Wind in Jamaica* (which led nowhere, but involved considerable correspondence: at one time there was even talk of Shirley Temple playing the part of Emily);[56] and then Hughes became interested in yet another entirely new venture.

On D.H. Lawrence's death in 1930 at the early age of forty-four, he had left behind the draft of a play entitled *The Daughter-in-Law*. His widow Frieda Lawrence wanted the play produced, and early in 1934 she showed it to Leon Lion of London's 'Playhouse Theatre'.

Lion, realising how much work still needed doing on the play, persuaded Frieda to come to an arrangement with Richard Hughes. He was to do whatever was necessary within a month, in return for an immediate advance against 25% of all fees received.[57]

Hughes had been attracted to the piece principally because it dramatised the difficulties of a man caught between the irreconcilable demands of a mother and a wife; but he had revised only the first two acts and sent them to Lion within the specified month. Lion was reasonably pleased with what had been achieved; though he pointed out that the part of the mother in Act One had been severely reduced, and that Sybil Thorndike (whom he had approached about playing the part) might not be very keen unless she were allowed to 'shine out' in Act Three.[58]

Hughes found this a severe problem; and when he had completed Act Three, it was judged unsatisfactory, and he was summoned to a meeting with Lion at which Lewis Casson was present. Casson was both a respected producer, and Sybil Thorndike's husband; and he demanded a complete redraft of Act Three along certain well-defined lines.[59]

A long period of silence followed. Lion wrote in October, and then again in December to ask when he could expect a redrafted Act Three.[60] It was not until 9 January 1935 that Hughes wrote to say that *The Daughter-in-Law* had now been rechristened *My Son's My Son*; that it had nearly been completed when Christmas intervened; and that it was now being typed.[61]

However, this second draft was no more acceptable to Lion than his first. In an interview with Hughes on 19 February, Lion suggested further changes; and early in March he sent Hughes some notes which he had dictated after their February meeting, and told him: 'my time limit for doing the play is rapidly contracting'.[62]

By now, Hughes was convinced that Lion's demands would weaken the dramatic heart of the play; and on 12 April he wrote to him:[63]

> I have tried poring over the play for hours together, and I have tried putting it in the back of my mind for several weeks; and I am afraid I cannot find any opportunity for making an entirely different third act.

It was possible, he said, that he could improve on the last scene in rehearsal; but for the moment it had gone stale on him. Finally, he restated his belief that:

> If there is inherent tragedy in this theme, it lies in this: *the impossibility, try what you will, of ever making a husband out of one who has been too long a son.* That is to me the only tragedy,

and indeed the only culmination, which I feel myself to grow out of the characters and the situation.

This letter greatly displeased Lion. After 'very much regret[ting]' that 'after all this time' Hughes had reverted to the very point on which they had always disagreed, Lion pointed out that it had taken Hughes a year to do what he had promised to do in a month; that he had accepted payment on conditions that remained unfulfilled; and that his own and Casson's views had been crystal-clear. As the play stood, it would be a box-office disaster. 'In the circumstances', he concluded pompously, 'what do you think is the fair and reasonable thing to do?'[64]

At this point Hughes very sensibly abandoned the play as a lost cause, and passed the matter over to his agent, Spencer Curtis Brown.[65] It had all been a great waste of his time: except that it had enabled him to give some serious thought to his own difficulties with Louisa and Frances.

In moving to Laugharne, rather than returning to somewhere near Penrhyndeudraeth, Hughes had sensibly kept a considerable mileage between Louisa and his own household. This was not to avoid the usual complications which arise between mother-in-law and daughter-in-law, but for his own sake: because Louisa's habit of emotional blackmail was too deep-rooted to be easily weeded out, and at least distance gave him some protection.

Frances herself had been made well aware of the difficulties which existed between Diccon and his mother by Violet Johnson, who had wisely advised her:[66]

> that she [Frances] should contrive for the first few years at least that all dealing with Louisa should be her responsibility, not Diccon's, because whenever he was with his mother he seemed to go into a wooden, dazed state, dangerously like his state in the year of his nervous breakdown.

Diccon still loved his mother and still wanted to be able to holiday in North Wales; and in the summer of 1934 (when he was in the process of selling the lease of 21 Lloyd Square)[67] he persuaded Clough Williams-Ellis to rent him Parc. This ancient stone house (then with no mains services) stands in a remote and unspoiled mountainous setting, but is only about a mile further up the valley of the river Maesgwm from Plas Brondanw, and is also within an easy walk of Garreg Fawr.

Diccon could therefore see his mother when he chose to do so; but his relationship with Louisa remained troubled; and (as he worked on *The Daughter-in-Law*) he had become uneasily aware that he had acquired self-protective habits which meant that it was difficult for him to treat Frances as well as she deserved. When she was upset and in need of reassurance, all was well: Diccon could always be kindly and caring to someone in distress. But when Frances flexed her mental muscles, it was difficult for Diccon to cope.

Tearful moments abounded; and it sometimes seemed as though Frances brought disaster upon herself through a curious and perhaps structural deficiency in her memory. Despite having lived with servants all her life, she had an unfortunate knack of upsetting them. 'I have been battered by them from childhood', she once told Diccon, 'so I think they all *know* at once I have an inferiority complex about them.'

Early in 1934,[68] for example, Frances was planning to leave Robert and his nurse at Hatherop, while she and Diccon enjoyed a brief holiday in Norfolk. She therefore wrote to her former 'Nanny' to tell her what arrangements needed to be made; but her letter was returned with a covering letter from her sister Rachel which began:[69]

> My dear Frances,
> You are a mutt. You have written a long letter to Nanny starting 'Dear Taylor' & she said she wouldn't even read it ... considering how much bother she has when your babies come to stay I think you might be a bit more friendly.

Apparently Frances had committed a serious breach of etiquette. She *should* have begun the letter 'Dear Mrs Taylor', as although their mother had always called her 'Taylor', housekeepers did not really expect to be addressed *tout court* by their surnames.

Frances (who was in London at the time) forwarded Rachel's letter to Diccon, telling him that she had been 'horrified and rather insulted', and had 'cried rather a lot'. Apparently she had then had to listen to the worries of Robert's nurse for one and a half hours, which had yet again reduced her to tears; and she was now 'dreading being telephoned for, the moment we get to Norfolk', to be told that 'nurse is so tiresome all the maids want to leave! ... If God is good', she concluded, 'we shall soon be too poor to afford nurses and servants, or travelling, riding and sailing, so we won't mind being tied to babies'.[70]

When however Frances felt secure enough to take a firm line, she often did so in an extremely exasperating manner. To give just one example: early in 1934, while Diccon was in London for a week, she had taken Robert to Hatherop. Her brother Thomas liked having artistic people around him; and one of her fellow guests was a brilliant German architect called Mendelssohn. Frances found his ideas so fascinating that, although Diccon had just spent months on planning for their move to Laugharne, she wrote telling him bluntly that her conversation with Mendelssohn had made her 'more than ever convinced not to spend more than £800 on Laugharne House and in the future we can still have something of unbelievable perfection'.[71] After an anguished protest from Diccon about the waste of his winter's work, Frances relented a little (though it may have seemed to her that it was Diccon who was being exasperating, spending so much of his time and her money on a house that could never be wholly theirs). The Mendelssohns left Hatherop; and she turned her attention towards 'two silly girls', whose idle chatter she ended (as she told Diccon) 'by denouncing the *Tatler* in bitter words'.[72]

There would be times when Diccon found it very difficult to be close to Frances; and (although he loved her dearly) he would often find good reasons for being away from home. Despite this, the years which they spent together at Laugharne Castle were probably the happiest of their marriage. By January 1936, with Robert three years old, and Penny one and three-quarters, Frances was already two months' pregnant with her third child; and Diccon, although still unable to make progress on any of his more serious work, was delighted (on being elected to the Corporation of Laugharne as a Petty Constable) to have found an official position for himself within the borough. (He had already learned that the Corporation, governed by a charter granted in 1307, consists of a Portreeve, two common Attorneys, one Recorder, four Constables, a Bailiff or Crier, and a Foreman of the Jury.)

The other nine members of the Corporation had been invited to the Castle for a splendid four-course supper whose principal ingredients were to be cockle soup, roast turkey, cold pie and plum pudding,[73] when Diccon received news which had him gathering up his sailing clothes and driving as fast as he could to Swansea. He missed the feast; but the events of the next twenty-four hours began to break up the creative log-jam from which he had suffered for the past two years, and set him once more upon his proper course.

CHAPTER 23

In Hazard

There was a storm in the Bristol Channel; and during the early evening of Sunday 5 January 1936, one of the Holt Line vessels *Ulysses* under Captain D.T. Williams was caught in heavy seas just off Swansea. There was damage to the forecastle head, and the *Ulysses* began shipping water. Just when things were looking serious, there was a lull in the storm; and Captain Williams ordered his men to get the forecastle head squared up.

A working-party went out onto the open deck, and began repairing the damage. Suddenly, without any warning, a heavy sea rose up out of the darkness and swept down upon them. There was no time to run for cover. Three men were killed outright, and four others were seriously injured.

When news of this disaster reached Richard Hughes on Monday afternoon, he also learned that no one had yet managed to reach the ship to take off the dead and injured. Immediately he set out for Swansea, which he reached at seven o'clock in the evening. Three and a half hours later, having secured the use of a pilot cutter (similar to *Tern*), and taken on board a volunteer crew and seven stretchers, he set sail for the *Ulysses*. The waters were still choppy; and although he managed to board the ship in the early hours of Tuesday morning, it was impossible to transfer the injured or the dead.

Hughes therefore sailed his boat a short distance away, and lay down from five-thirty until seven, when the sea was calm enough for him to approach *Ulysses* with a greater chance of success. By seven-thirty the dead and injured had been unloaded, and he cast off. In recording the event (which he never talked about in later life), Hughes noted that the ensigns in the *Ulysses* and on his pilot cutter were at half-mast, 'the pale morning light and grey swell our only farewell'.[1]

Seeing the dead and wounded on board the *Ulysses* had revived and sharpened Hughes's interest in his sea-story about the *Phemius*, upon which he had done no serious work for more than two years. In the interim, Charles Prentice of Chatto & Windus had retired, telling Diccon with commendable patience that he would continue to be well-treated by his successors at Chatto, who were 'as keen on [his works] as I, their only complaint is the same as mine: that there are too few of them'.[2] At the same time, Diccon thought of his other outstanding obligations – especially the life of Walter Harris (for which one of Walter's friends had been hoping to write a preface as far back as November 1934).[3]

Planning to work on both projects, Hughes arranged with Laurence Holt to take a job on board the *Eurymedion*, which would be sailing from Amsterdam towards the end of January, and calling in at Tangier on its way to the Middle East.

Signing on in Amsterdam, Diccon discovered that he had been given 'a vast great cabin with no less than four port holes . . . And me in rank but an "assistant purser" at one shilling a month!'[4] The sea was rough in the channel, and there was fog off Finisterre; but the voyage was a considerable personal success.

The captain, who had been hostile at first, 'thawed a lot' when he found how well Diccon knew his home town, Portmadoc; and by the time they arrived off Tangier on 6 February, Diccon had been invited to go on in the *Eurymedion* to Jeddah. On declining, he was told: 'that another year I was to go right out to Java with him. [The captain] had me on the bridge all the time', Diccon reported to Frances, 'and lent me his sextant, & taught me to find out latitude and longitude by the sun & the stars, which I have always wanted to know, & which was easy to be taught but very hard to learn from a book'.[5]

Jim Wyllie had come on board to meet Diccon; and after discovering that his own house was in need of repairs and 'looking a bit desolate', Diccon stayed with Jim and spent much of the next six weeks in his company. It was an amusing time. For one thing Gwenol Satow turned out to be living in Tangier, 'with a very beautiful and nice young man who is A.D.C. to the Governor of Gibraltar'. For another, Jim Wyllie had gathered 'some fine new disreputable friends', including Francois Pierrefour, a French count with a colourful history who had built the harbour at Casablanca, and whose principal passions were yachting, women and poetry; and a Spanish marquis, 'a fine rogue' who had been 'a great friend of Diaghilev', and now sniffed cocaine and talked 'with an excited brilliance that one can listen to without stopping till morning'.[6] With companions like these, Diccon had to admit to Frances that after being in Tangier for almost a week, he had 'not been very successful in getting any *Harris* information'.

There followed a period of incessant rain – 'day and night with the force of a thunder at its worst'. The Arabs took to sea-boots and oilskin Jellabas; Diccon's shoulder became rheumatic; and at last (more or less confined to quarters) he began drafting the first chapter of *Walter Harris* – which Jim found 'very amusing: but I don't know', added Diccon, 'whether the Harrises will find it so'.[7]

When the weather improved again, Hughes conducted a few more interviews with Harris's friends; but he reverted to doing very little serious work, and his letters to Frances were chiefly about his social life. One evening, for example, their friend Jaime Betridio 'dashed round' to say that he was arranging a Moorish dinner at the big café in the old palace for a party from Paris. Would Diccon and Jim come along as Moors? They agreed, dressing themselves 'as rich Shereefs'; and, as Diccon reported to Frances, they carried it off[8]

> very successfully. I had a lovely time pulling the leg of an elderly Russian lady in all sorts of ways. There were two beautiful young women in the party & two Spaniards who tried to flirt with them but cut no ice at all because the poor young creatures hoped to sleep with us but were so impressed by our dignity that they didn't dare suggest it!

Later, Diccon heard that the Russian lady had 'said afterwards that I was the very finest type of Arab'.

Hughes remained in Morocco for another month; but his heart was not really in the *Walter Harris*; and there was a distressing incident when he had to sack Hamed, whom he discovered trying to cheat Wyllie out of a substantial sum of money.[9] So early in March Diccon turned his back on Tangier and his work, and motored with Jim over the Atlas mountains and into the desert. It was a journey which almost ended in disaster.

As they travelled towards the oases of Tafilet, Diccon found the desert 'more beautiful than can be imagined … an *infinite* variety (which I had not expected) and a sort of colour-box purity of colour'. But then, in recrossing the Atlas, he and Jim were[10]

> caught by a blizzard after dark at a height of over 6,000 feet (twice the height of Snowdon) and very soon stuck in a snowdrift. There was nothing for it but to stay put. The blizzard blew the snow in through the side-screens till the front seats were nearly full; but we built barricades of our suitcases, put on all the clothes we had got and crouched behind the suitcases in the back.

It was a terrifying night, as they huddled in the back of the car listening to the howling of the blizzard, and watching themselves being slowly buried alive. The snow crept up and up. First the bonnet was entirely covered; next one door was completely snowed in.

And then came the dawn. Up to then, one door had been kept clear by the very force of the wind; but now the wind had fallen, and soon that door would also be snowed in. So as soon as it was light enough, the two men

> abandoned the car and everything in it, and began to walk, though the snow was soft and in places up to our waists, following the telephone poles and hoping to get somewhere, though at that height the mountains [are] practically uninhabited except for panthers and wild bear.

In the first two hours, they covered less than three miles. Diccon's beard and moustache were 'solid ice', and the handkerchief which he had tied over his head to protect his ears was 'hard like a helmet'. Their strength was running out, and they had almost abandoned hope, when they reached

> a refuge built by the road engineers, with some berbers in it and a French engineer. It was just a hut with an earth floor, no window and snow drifting through the door, but they had a fire and food, and a telephone.

At length a snow-plough arrived, followed by a lorry on caterpillars, and they were taken down to Azrou: though even that journey of seven miles was hazardous, as the blizzard blew up again, the engine of the lorry froze, and it took the snow-plough two and a half hours to tow them to safety.

Richard Hughes now knew at first hand what it was like to be at the mercy of the elements. So interested did he now become in the psychology of men under extreme pressure, men in hazard of their lives, that on returning to Laugharne he laid aside the draft chapters of *Walter Harris*. Instead, he made preparations for writing *In Hazard*, his novel of a ship caught in a hurricane on the high seas.

While he was working on reviews or articles, Hughes was content to remain in his study at the top of the Castle House; but *In Hazard* required greater concentration than was possible in a noisily child-centred household; and so he decided that he would write it in a little summer-house which had been built into the walls of Laugharne Castle, and which looked out across the mud-flats and the estuary towards the open sea.

There he installed a telescope (for observing either distant shipping or the still more distant stars), a desk, a chair, pen, ink, paper, a handful of reference books, and a pouch of tobacco for his pipe. And there one morning in the summer of 1936 he took up his pen and began to write.

Since the heroine of his story was to be the *Archimedes* (as Hughes had decided to rename the *Phemius*) he wanted his reader to have a vivid impression of the workings of the ship; but nothing could be more off-putting than a mechanical description without human interest, so Hughes began with the chief engineer, and identified him immediately with a broadly comical stroke.[11]

> Amongst the people I have met, one of those who stand out the most vividly in my memory is a certain Mr Ramsay MacDonald. He was a chief engineer: and a distant cousin, he said, of Mr J. Ramsay MacDonald, the statesman. He resembled his 'cousin' very closely indeed, in face and moustaches; and it astonished me at first to see what appeared to be my Prime Minister, in a suit of overalls, crawling out of a piece of dismantled machinery with an air of real authority and knowledge and decision.

Mr MacDonald's ship, the *Archimedes*, is 'a single-screw turbine steamer of a little over 9000 tons'. She belongs to the Sage Line, 'one of the most famous Houses in Bristol'; and we are told how the owners 'loved each vessel as if she was their child', never insured their ships, and therefore built them to the most demanding specifications:

> Look at the funnel-guys of the *Archimedes*, for instance. They were designed to stand a strain of 100 tons! But how could a strain of 100 tons ever come upon funnel-guys? A wind of seventy-five miles an hour would blow every shred of canvas out of a sailing-ship; yet even such a hurricane, the designers reckoned, would only lean against the funnel of *Archimedes* with a total pressure of ten or fifteen tons.

A detailed description follows of Mr MacDonald's territory, which includes the engine-room, the fire-room, and various outlying territories; and which is contrasted with the realm of Mr Buxton, chief officer and first mate who controls the rest of the ship: the hull, the decks, and the cargo-space.

And then the voyage begins.

First, a mixed cargo is loaded, at various ports on the Atlantic seaboard; and at Norfolk, Virginia, we are introduced to Dick Watchett, a very young officer who is 'caught up suddenly one night by a troop of Southern boys and girls', and taken to a party at a fine colonial house. There he meets Sukie, a 'lovely fair girl' of sixteen, 'with wide innocent eyes . . . in the first bud of youth'; and when she has sat in his arms for some time, drinking a good deal of bootleg corn-whisky, she suddenly struggles out of his arms, and springs to her feet.[12]

> Her eyes, wider than ever, did not seem to see anybody, even him. She wrenched at her shoulder-straps and a string or two, and in a moment every stitch of clothing she had was gone off her. For a few seconds she stood there, her body stark naked. Dick had never seen anything like it before. Then she fell unconscious on the floor.

Dick rolls Sukie in the hearthrug and makes her comfortable on a sofa before returning to his ship, where she continues to blaze in his mind's eye; and two nights later *Archimedes* sets out for the West Indian island of San Salvador.

Through Dick Watchett's eyes we see Captain Edwards, 'a small man, rather cherubic, but dark', an unimpressive 'native of Carmarthenshire'; the chief officer Mr Buxton (whom Dick would have preferred to see as captain); and the second officer Mr Rabb, who, 'with his steady and brilliant blue eyes, and his firm jaw' has 'the look rather of a naval officer than a mercantile one' – though his nails are 'always bitten right down to the quick'.

As Hughes worked on his first draft of *In Hazard*, these were the principal characters who were to be tested by the coming storm; but much later, it would be felt by those who knew the story of the *Phemius* that the character of the original second mate Brown (who had broken down during the hurricane) was too easily recognisable in Mr Rabb; and so Hughes invented Mr Foster, a new second officer and a 'solid, North-of-England man' who 'looked a highly efficient seaman'; while Rabb became a supernumerary officer, on his way to join another one of the Sage Line ships at Colon.

When he was not writing, Hughes longed for the feel of a heaving deck under his feet. He was irresistibly drawn to the company of the Laugharne fishermen who regularly plied the sea; and in April 1936, not long after his return from Morocco, Diccon and Frances gave tea to forty fishermen and their wives. Also present was Augustus John, who had been born in Tenby, just a little farther along the coast, and who (having met Diccon sixteen years previously, through the Nicholsons) had gradually become a friend, and had taken to calling in at the Castle House for an occasional weekend.

They sang old sea shanties together, consumed three enormous meat pies (on top of which the pastry had been shaped into ships in full sail), and drank vast quantities of mild and bitter beer. Hughes then proposed the King's health; Augustus John toasted the cockle – explaining that he had been raised on cockles during his boyhood; and Diccon made a short speech in which he deplored the death of the Laugharne Regatta, and proposed (to enthusiastic cheers) that it should be brought back to life; after which there was more singing and dancing until midnight.[13]

The Regatta, with Hughes as its president, was duly revived later that summer; and Hughes himself competed both in the coracle race (for which he ordered a new coracle),[14] and in the principal race of six sailing-boats from Tenby to Laugharne (for which he acquired a small racing yacht, the *Dauntless*). But some weeks before the Regatta, there was a far more dramatic event: the Bristol Channel Pilot Cutter's Race of 1936, for which Hughes had ambitiously entered *Tern*.[15]

First *Tern* had to be recovered from Ilfracombe, where she had been laid up for the winter under the care of Sid Williams, a local boatman. Diccon sailed over to collect her with Jack Rowlands, and was pleased to find a letter waiting for him from Frances, who was six and a half months pregnant, and had been feeling too unwell to join them. Now she wrote that she was feeling better, and that fifteen-year-old Jocelyn Herbert had arrived to keep her company for a few days. 'How lovely', Diccon replied on Friday 22 May. 'All the way over I wished you were with us: sun: lovely smooth sea. And Ilfracombe is very nice in its way.' He added that he and Jack had been 'working like Trojans', and hoped to be ready for sea by Saturday night. His only regret was that the fine weather was breaking: 'Well', he concluded, 'we shall be glad of a west wind, going up to Barry' where the race was to begin.[16]

The fine weather broke in no uncertain manner. Reaching Barry on Tuesday 26 May, Diccon began looking for a pilot to accompany him and Jack in the race; but the outlook was so bleak that no one could be found. Finally, at eleven o'clock on Friday morning, with only three hours to go before the start of the race, Hughes recorded in *Tern*'s log-book that he had signed on Jack Strong, who was no pilot, but had been 'born and bred in channel, [and boasted that he] could sail it blindfold'.[17]

At one-thirty that afternoon, they edged out of the harbour.

By now it was blowing such a gale that two yachts were dismasted before they had even crossed the starting-line.

From then on, the struggle against the elements was so severe that log-book entries are few and unrevealing. For three days and three nights the race continued in the teeth of the gale. Jack Strong's boasts proved to be worthless: he was so terrified by the violence of the storm that after a short while he hid himself away below-decks, and refused to come out for the rest of the race.[18] Diccon and Jack toiled on alone, both so absorbed in their struggle that they felt no need of sleep.

Finally, on Monday morning, after battling her way (at an average speed of only three knots) through one hundred and twenty-five miles of heavy seas, *Tern* sailed back victoriously into Barry, where among the crowd of well-wishers who cheered them into the harbour was Jocelyn Herbert.

Two days later the gale had blown itself out; and Diccon, Jack and Jocelyn set sail for home. After crossing Carmarthen Bar, they could begin to see Laugharne in the distance, and for a while[19]

> they could not make out what had happened: it looked as if a tornado had hit the town. For the news of their success had reached Laugharne ahead of them, and from every window hung a brightly-coloured tablecloth or bedspread to greet them. When they came ashore they found a crowd waiting to welcome them. They were sat on two kitchen chairs and carried shoulder-high through the streets.
>
> 'A Laugharne boy winning the big race!'
> 'A Laugharne boat!' people were shouting.
>
> [Diccon] got a lot of praise but it was Jack Rowlands who was the hero of the hour, because he was a Laugharne boy. Laugharne, for its people, was still the centre of the world.

Although Hughes's chief work was now as a novelist, he still wrote poetry and occasionally had it published. *Time and Tide* for 24 March 1934, for example, included his poem 'I Had a Doe', which contains the striking lines (perhaps a reminiscence of Nancy Stallibrass):

> I had a friend with love like gold
> Whose beauty lighted every place:
> And so I blinded both my eyes,
> Never to see her face.

In November the following year, when asked by the editor of the

Saturday Review for poems, he was able to send him half-a-dozen;[20] in the same month W.B. Yeats wrote with the news that he hoped to include nine of Hughes's poems in his *Oxford Book of Modern Verse*;[21] and Diccon continued to review poetry, and to keep an interested eye on younger, undiscovered poets, just as he had done ever since co-editing *Public Schools Verse*.

This led (in the late summer of 1934) to a nineteen-year-old Welsh poet travelling over from Swansea, where he lived with his parents in the house in which he had been born. Since leaving the *South Wales Daily Post*, where he had been employed as a junior reporter, the young man had spent the past year and a half trying to interest literary editors in his work; but he was still virtually unknown.

His journey came to nothing: Hughes was away. But in October 1934, he tried again. This time, he wrote in advance:[22]

> Dear Mr. Richard Hughes,
>   As I'm going to spend this coming week-end in Llanstephan, I wonder whether I could call and see you some time on Saturday? Only a few days [ago] I was shown an old cutting from a local newspaper in which you said you'd read some of my poems. That does give me some sort of an introduction, doesn't it, however vague? I was in Laugharne in the late summer, but the ferryman, who knows everything, told me you were away, and so I didn't batter at the Castle gates. I do hope I'll be able to see you this time.

And he signed himself: 'Yours sincerely, Dylan Thomas.'

Unfortunately this attempt also ended in failure; and it was not until 14 July 1936 Dylan Thomas wrote to Richard Hughes a second time.

The intervening twenty-one months had seen important developments in Dylan Thomas's life. In November 1934, he had left Swansea and shared lodgings with friends in London; the following month his first book, *18 Poems*, had been published; this had run to a second impression by February 1936; and in April that year he had met and fallen in love with a beautiful and voluptuous twenty-five-year-old Irish girl.

Caitlin Macnamara was the offspring of an eccentric alcoholic Irishman, and an essentially lesbian Frenchwoman. She had been largely brought up by her mother, who had settled in Hampshire, not very far away from Augustus John. By 1936 Caitlin (who had trained as a dancer), was modelling for John. Much to her disgust, at the end of every session he 'pounced' on her 'like a hairy animal'; but she stoically endured these sexual assaults, and even joined him on occasional expeditions to London. It was there, in a public house (having temporarily escaped from Augustus John), that on 12 April 1936 Caitlin first met Dylan Thomas.[23]

The attraction was instant and mutual. 'I was sitting on a stool', Caitlin records,[24]

> and I don't know how Dylan managed to get his head on my lap; I don't know how he did it, or how he was standing, but he seemed to fold up over me, and I immediately felt a great sense of closeness that I had never felt before with anyone. He told me that I was beautiful, that he loved me and that he was going to marry me.

That very night they booked themselves into an hotel; and for the better part of a week they lived together, spending their days in the pubs, and their nights in bed.

Eventually, one evening in the pub, Caitlin became quietly angry. She was very hungry (because Dylan had never offered her any food); and she disliked his being 'the centre of attention as always, telling stories', while she was 'ignored by everyone'. So she simply 'walked off and caught the next train home'. Back in Hampshire, she resumed her work as Augustus John's model; but she could not dismiss Dylan Thomas from her mind; and somehow she let Dylan know when Augustus invited her to join him for a few days at Laugharne Castle for 'a change of air and scene'.[25]

Receiving this news on Tuesday 14 July (the day that Augustus John and Caitlin Macnamara were due to arrive at the Castle House), Dylan Thomas acted at once. 'Dear Richard Hughes', he wrote:[26]

> I'm going to Fishguard by car tomorrow, and passing awfully near Laugharne. I do hope you'll be there because we – that's painter Alfred Janes and me – would very much like to call on you. We shall, shall we, some time in the afternoon? Hope I shan't miss you as I did last time.

And late on Wednesday morning, Dylan was knocking on the door, having been driven over from Swansea by Fred Janes.

The appearance of these two young men 'immediately put Augustus on edge';[27] but Diccon greeted them warmly, and invited them both to stay to lunch, which was just being served up. So Frances had her first sight of Dylan Thomas as he entered the dining-room. She felt that he was 'one of the most vivid and alive young men I'd seen in years – he was quite thin then', she later recalled, 'with very brilliant eyes and curly hair and [he] looked somewhat ethereal'.[28]

After lunch Augustus was due to adjudicate in the painting section of the National Eisteddfod over at Fishguard: so he and Caitlin left in his enormous black six-cylinder Wolseley. They were followed by Fred and Dylan in their much more modest vehicle; but Diccon remained behind, promising to have a special supper prepared for them on their return, with fine wines that he had been saving for just such an occasion.

The journey, as Caitlin remembers it, 'soon turned into a splendid pub crawl, and we must have stopped for pints of beer at nearly every pub between Laugharne and Fishguard'. After a relatively short stay at the Eisteddfod, the pub crawl was resumed. And then after one stop, Dylan climbed into the back seat of Augustus John's car with Caitlin, leaving Fred to make his own way back to Laugharne. In another moment, Dylan and Caitlin were 'kissing and cuddling and fondling'.

This astonished Augustus, who knew nothing about their five days and nights together in April, and later wrote that 'A more instantaneous case of mutual "clicking" can hardly have occurred in history!' It also enraged him. Caitlin had not been brought down to Wales to be seduced on the back seat of his car by someone else! Saying nothing, but driving even faster and more furiously, Augustus turned off towards Carmarthen where they stopped for another prolonged drinking session. When they were ready to set off again, and Caitlin was climbing into the Wolseley, she heard[29]

> shouts and a scuffle going on somewhere behind the car . . . and a few moments later Augustus jumped back into the driving-seat and drove off fast, very fast. As I looked through the window there was Dylan lying on the ground, having obviously come off worse in the fight.

They arrived back at Laugharne to find Richard Hughes 'mourning the burnt remains' of his special dinner; and later that night Augustus restored his wounded pride by coming to Caitlin's room and taking her by force.

What followed (as Diccon remembered it) was 'a little like a French farce'. Dylan Thomas re-appeared the next morning, and stayed with the Hugheses for another four or five days. However, he did not relish the idea of being knocked down again by Augustus John; and so 'whenever Augustus was out, Dylan wandered in; and just before Augustus arrived, Dylan would go out again'.

With the departure of these colourful guests, Frances began making serious preparations for the birth of her third child. Jenny Nicholson,[30] staying with her grandmother Amy Graves at Erinfa, was surprised to get an anxious telephone call from Frances on Sunday 19 July. Frances explained that her baby was due in less than a month; that she wished to go to London as soon as possible; but that she 'must not travel with Diccon by car, or alone by train, & she could think of nobody but Jenny to accompany her'.

Jenny did as she was asked, travelling down to South Wales the very next morning, and then on Tuesday escorting Frances up to London. There she joined Diccon and Frances[31] at the flat which they had taken after disposing of 21 Lloyd Square; and with them she listened anxiously to news of the Spanish Civil War, now only a few days old, but already threatening her father in his Majorcan retreat.

On Thursday 6 August 1936 (the day that Robert Graves and Laura Riding and their party, having been rescued by a British destroyer, landed safely on French soil) Lleky Hughes was born. News of her birth was immediately wired both to Gloucestershire and to North Wales, where it reached Louisa Hughes during her last weeks in Garreg Fawr: following Frank Penn Smith's recent death, she was about to take over the lease of his cottage, Gelli, a little further down the valley towards Penrhyndeudraeth.[32]

Returning to Laugharne, Richard Hughes settled down to an autumn of hard work. There were the usual distractions: for example, one Wednesday in November he went to lunch with the High Sheriff of Carmarthen;[33] and he was involved in successful negotiations over a site down by the harbour for a boat-shed, in which (as soon as it was built) he and Jack Rowlands housed *Tern*, *Dauntless* and a powerful winch to drag them out of the water.

Hughes's friendship with Rowlands now bore unexpected fruit. Jack had met and married a newcomer to the village called Sheila; and (as she later recalled) it was in the autumn of 1936, when she had known Hughes casually for almost a year, that he 'found that I could type . . . at least he discovered that I wouldn't be the sort of person to be frantically tidying up, so he asked me if I'd like to go and help him'.[34] By organising his diary, and dealing with his routine correspondence (while taking care to leave his numerous heaps of foolscap exactly where she found them all over the floor of his study), Sheila Rowlands freed her new employer for a sustained assault upon his novel.

As Richard Hughes took up his pen, sitting in his summer-house on the walls of Laugharne Castle, and looking out across the estuary toward the open sea, he saw in his mind's eye how the *Archimedes* steamed through the West Indies, and passed by Navassa island:[35]

a barren limestone sponge, between Jamaica and Haiti. That was the last land they would see before they reached Colon, the entrance to the Panama Canal (where Mr Rabb was to join his own ship). Ahead of them lay a short passage across the empty Caribbean Sea – a passage of about forty-eight hours.

That night, however, it blew a gale; and by nine the following morning, with the barometer rapidly falling, and the wind blowing harder than ever, Captain Edwardes slowed engines, and 'headed her round north-east and north, with her nose splitting the gale, to ride it out'.[36]

By noon, the wind had increased to force ten, and Dick Watchett observes how:[37]

> The seas, huge lumps of water with a point on top, ran about in all directions in a purposeful way at immense speeds. They were as big as houses, and moved as fast as trains. Sometimes they ran into each other, hard, and threw themselves jointly into the air. At others they banged suddenly against the ship, and burst out into a rapid plumage of spray that for a moment hid everything. The windows of the bridge, high up as they were, were completely obscured by spray; it was only through the little 'clear-vision screen' (a fast-spinning wheel of glass which water cannot stick to) that it was possible to see at all. For if you stepped out on to the ends of the bridge, where there was no glass, the wind blew your eyes shut immediately.

And then, a disaster: the steering fails.

The *Archimedes* is turned broadside on to the wind, and heels over at an angle of thirty-five degrees. The force of the wind sweeping across it creates so much suction that the hatch-covers on the foredeck are ripped off; and then the funnel itself is torn away, taking with it the whistle-pipe, through which steam pours out. Pressure drops; and soon there is a general failure of everything steam-operated, including the fans which supply draught to the furnaces; and when those fans are stopped,[38]

> the fires began to blow back, with explosions that burst open the furnace doors and lit the inky engine-room with flashes of flame like lightning . . . At each blow-back a tongue of fire thirty feet long would shoot out of the open fire-door.

In order to reach the emergency cock for turning off steam to the whistle, it is necessary to shut off the oil to the furnaces; and so by ten o'clock that night, the steam has gone, the fires are out, and the *Archimedes* is totally dead.

Captain Edwardes, once the storm has reached such a height 'that plainly this was no longer an issue between himself and his

Owners, but . . . between himself and his Maker', responds to this series of disasters with 'a gigantic exhilaration, and a consciousness that for the time being all his abilities were heightened'.[39] Mr Rabb, on the other hand, has been so overcome by fear that he has hidden himself away in the carpenter's room; while Dick Watchett has been able to keep himself sane only by focusing upon the image of Sukie's nakedness.

In a slight lull, the hatches are replaced; and captain and crew begin to believe that they are passing through the centre of the storm. One more violent contest with the hurricane, another seventeen hours or so, and they would be out of it. But then (from observing the direction of the wind) comes the stunning realisation that 'the storm was not passing over them: it was sucking the *Archimedes* along with it!'[40]

When Hughes returned from his mornings in the summer-house, it would sometimes be to find Sheila Rowlands almost submerged by correspondence connected with the film rights to *A High Wind in Jamaica*. Back in July 1936, Henrietta Malkiel, one of Diccon's New York friends, had written to ask him: 'Would you like to go to Hollywood for a couple of months at a tremendous salary? I am now a Hollywood agent and piling up cash for my friends.'[41] Hughes cautiously welcomed this way of earning 'his screw', and asked her to take a hand in the current round of negotiations.

The situation, as Diccon explained to Henrietta, was confused, with several people trying to put packages together. The leading contender at present was the producer John Krimsky of the American Music Hall in New York City, who had agreed to pay Hughes $6500 for a six-month option on the world film rights. Krimsky had also signed an option on 'the Abbe children' (explaining that Patience Abbe seemed just right for the part of Emily); he was hoping that Hughes could persuade Charles Laughton to undertake the rôle of Captain Jonsen; and he talked of a production date as early as the beginning of November.[42]

In replying to Diccon's letter, Henrietta wrote a little tartly that 'before you come over here you had better start learning the American language again. In America you don't 'earn your screw' by working in an office, or had you forgotten that?' She added that she had been to see Krimsky, who had agreed that Hughes should travel to Hollywood to work on the screenplay of *High Wind* as soon as a deal had been signed with one of the studios.[43]

Diccon then contacted Charles Laughton, suggesting not only

that he should play Jonsen, but that his wife Elsa Lanchester should play Margaret; and at the beginning of September (at Laughton's invitation) he lunched with them at Denham Studios, where Laughton was being directed by Alexander Korda in the title rôle of *Rembrandt*.[44] Laughton was extremely interested in playing Captain Jonsen, though he was also being considered for the leading part in a proposed film of Robert Graves's *I, Claudius* and he made it clear that he was completely tied to Irving Thalberg, the production manager of Metro-Goldwyn-Mayer, so he could only play Jonsen if Krimsky *either* sold the story to MGM *or* came to some special arrangement with Thalberg.[45]

After cabling this news to Krimsky, Hughes wrote to Charles Laughton, asking about the possibilities of getting a trial job as a screen-writer in Hollywood, and asking him and Elsa to come down to Laugharne later in the month.[46] Soon afterwards there was encouraging news from Krimsky, who cabled:[47]

> NEGOTIATING MGM MY PRODUCTION IF SUCCESS-FUL LAUGHTON'S SERVICES POSSIBLE AWAITING REPLY OPTION EXTENSION IMPORTANT TO CONSUMMATE DEAL FAVOURABLE TO ALL PARTIES KRIMSKY.

Henrietta Malkiel, who was now assisting Krimsky in these negoti-ations, found that the studios were confused about who really represented Hughes, and so on 14 September she cabled:[48]

> CALL OFF OTHER AGENTS LET US HANDLE EXCLUSIVELY STUDIOS REFUSE DEAL WITH MORE THAN ONE AGENT.

And then later that very day came disaster.

Irving Thalberg died at the age of only thirty-seven: after which, as Henrietta Malkiel explained, the situation became[49]

> completely unsettled. Krimsky was negotiating with Thalberg for the release of your picture, and we were discussing with Metro the possibility of bringing you over for it. Thalberg's death interrupted these negotiations and Krimsky feels that no other executive at Metro will have courage enough to undertake this picture.

It was little comfort to hear that Henrietta had raised Diccon's wish to be a screen-writer with 'every story editor at the Coast and in New York', and she was certain that, had *A High Wind in Jamaica* gone through, she could have secured him a contract at once.

Gradually, everything fell apart. Charles Laughton and his wife were suddenly too busy to come down to Laugharne;[50] and three months later, in December 1936, there was disquieting news about Krimsky. According to Henrietta's information, Warner brothers had offered Krimsky $35,000 for the rights to *A High Wind in Jamaica*; but Krimsky had turned it down since they refused to allow him to produce the picture. So it seemed that his chief interest in *High Wind* had been as a vehicle to further his own ambitions.[51]

December 1936 was the month that the uncrowned King Edward VIII abdicated, driven from his throne because the woman he loved and wanted to marry, Wallis Simpson, was a divorcee, and (as such) unacceptable as Queen. Hughes very much disliked the way in which the Prime Minister, Baldwin, had (as he thought) hounded Edward into exile;[52] and on 14 December he secured a resolution of the Laugharne Corporation which empowered him to write the following letter, addressed to HRH Prince Edward at Schloss Enzesfeld near Vienna:[53]

> I am today directed by the Portreeve and Court of the ancient Township of Laugharne to convey to you the deep gratitude we feel as Welshmen for the happiness and many benefits we enjoyed during your long tenure as our Prince.

This devoted message was a product both of Hughes's natural human sympathy and of his passionate allegiance to all things Welsh; but although he could be loyal to a Prince of Wales, he also nurtured a powerful (though rarely disclosed) attachment to the Welsh Nationalist cause.

When on 22 February 1937 Hughes visited the Welsh Radio Station in Swansea and gave a talk on 'Nationhood', he arrived with 'a severe cold in the head, which', as he explained to G. Dyfnallt Owen, the producer, 'he had essayed to neutralize by imbibing whisky'. The broadcast itself was unexceptionable; but afterwards Hughes was in what Dyfnallt Owen (who had known him for several years) described as an unusually 'expansive and self-revelatory mood'.

It was not long since Saunders Lewis, the leading figure in Welsh Nationalism, had been imprisoned with two of his friends for setting fire to an RAF aerodrome on the Lleyn Peninsula; and as Hughes talked to Dyfnallt Owen, their conversation turned naturally in that direction. Up until then, Dyfnallt Owen had believed Richard Hughes to be 'something of an Imperialist'; so he was much surprised when[54]

> Richard declared that the Nationalist party had no alternative but to prosecute their campaign against the condemnation of 'Y

Tri Llanc' (i.e. Saunders Lewis, D.J. Williams and Valentine), and to resort to further incendiary action if the Government continued to ignore their protests. He was disappointed to hear that the students of Swansea University had not agitated more effectively against the expulsion of Saunders, and opined that the authorities were remarkably shortsighted in their policy of allowing political prejudices to determine their attitude towards the 'Fuhrer' (presumably Saunders Lewis). There were moral motives involved in the perpetration of the so-called 'crime', he said, and they should have been valued at their real worth.

When, however, Dyfnallt Owen inquired whether Hughes approved of the Welsh Nationalists' attempts to boycott celebrations for the coronation of George VI, Hughes replied that 'such attempts would be abortive for the simple reason that there were too many vested interests concerned with those festivities'. In which case, one could presumably enjoy them with a clear conscience; and three months later found Hughes in the thick of the Laugharne merry-making.

Frances and the three children were away at the seaside while the plumbing was being renewed; but Diccon had stayed on in the Castle House, where Teddy Wolfe joined him for the coronation festivities on Wednesday 12 May 1937. The two men had spent the whole of Tuesday decorating; and Coronation Day itself, as Diccon reported to Frances,[55]

> was marvellous. Even knowing how well Laugharne likes fiestas, I did not know they would do themselves so proud. Decorations all flutter and loveliness, the best I have seen anywhere, especially Frog Street which sat up all the night before frilling coloured paper and stringing it along the street.

The day began with a procession by the Portreeve, Corporation and burgesses of Laugharne to the castle gate, over which was Teddy's principal creation: 'an enormous crown twelve feet high covered in Xmas tree decorations, and lit with coloured electric lights'.

There the Bailiff called out: 'Open in the King's name, and give passage to His Worship the Portreeve and to his free burgesses!' At that, a salute was fired ('Gwylym firing off the big cannon'); and there was a procession into the castle ruins, where Hughes made a speech which began:[56]

> Worshipful Mr Portreeve, and free Burgesses of Laugharne. More than six hundred years ago, Sir Guy de Brian, by virtue of the powers granted him by his king, gave this town its charter. We are standing now in Sir Guy's castle. It may well be that we are standing on the very spot where that first charter was handed to the first Portreeve Laugharne ever had.

Six hundred years is a long time. But three things still remain: the Laugharne charter, Laugharne Castle: and the loyalty of Laugharne towards its King. Long may they remain, all three.

For the grant of that charter meant not one thing, but two. It gave Laugharne her freedom, as a town, for ever. But also it bound Laugharne, for ever, to the King's service.

At the climax of his speech, he presented the Corporation with 'a new flag ... emblazoned with Sir Guy's arms'; the flag was unfurled; another salute was fired; and the procession moved off again to the church.

Later there were sports in the Green Dragon Field, followed by a tea for the village children; but 'best of all', as Hughes wrote,

> was the evening: torchlit procession with fifty torches and the whole town following: all street lights turned out, but the Town Hall and Castle floodlit. Then bonfire on the Grist, and fireworks.

That summer, shortly after the second Laugharne Regatta (in which *Tern* had held the lead until a rival boat was able to pull up her centre-board and cut over a sand-bank which *Tern* had to go round)[57] there was news of a family tragedy. Frances' younger brother Anthony, a happily married gentleman-farmer, died of appendicitis at the age of twenty-six. Diccon and Frances attended the funeral service in the chapel at Hatherop Castle; and Diccon found himself staying on to nurse the sick (a task at which he excelled), after outside caterers had given severe food-poisoning to a large number of the funeral guests.[58]

Returning to his summer-house overlooking the estuary, Diccon resumed work upon *In Hazard*; and there he watched his characters pitting themselves against the terrible natural forces of the hurricane.

The odds against the crew of the *Archimedes* surviving the storm were rising. As soon as he realised that the storm was sucking his ship along with it, Captain Edwardes knew that 'it was impossible any longer to count on anything at all'. And when dawn came on Thursday morning (after twenty-four hours in the hurricane), 'it grew light; but things did not become visible. Spray – atomized ocean – hid everything. It was a white night, now, instead of a black one: that was all'.[59]

Unsuccessful efforts were made to relight the furnaces by Mr MacDonald, who had been 'propelled into the fight against the storm' with a psychological momentum 'so great that henceforth, if he did get a chance to relax, to rest, he would not be able'.[60]

Then the ship ran into the still centre of the hurricane. The roar of the storm was replaced by 'a blanketing silence', in which the air was[61]

> gaspingly thin, as on a mountain: but not enlivening: on the contrary, it was damp and depressing; and almost unbearably hot, even to engineers. Big drops of sweat, unable in that humid air to evaporate, ran warm and salt across their lips.
> The tormented black sky was one incessant flicker of lightning.
> For the first time since the storm reached its height they could see the ship from one end to the other. For the first time they saw the gaping crater left by the funnel's roots. Smashed derricks, knotted stays. The wheelhouse, like a smashed conservatory. The list, too, of the ship.

Down in the water, the ocean was 'full of sharks ... plainly waiting for something: and waiting with great impatience'; but these sharks were not the only living things:[62]

> The whole ruin of the deck and upper-structures was covered with living things. Living, but not moving. Birds, and even butterflies and big flying grasshoppers ... birds like swallows: massed as if for migration. They were massed like that on every stay and hand-rail. But not for migration. As you gripped a hand-rail to steady yourself they never moved.

The deck was so thick with them, that as the barefoot officers walked 'they kept stepping on live birds ... You would feel the delicate skeleton scrunch under your feet: but you could not help it'; and little humming-birds 'kept settling on the captain's head and shoulders and outstretched arm', and 'would not be shaken off'.

When on Friday morning they passed out of the still centre, and back into the fiercest part of the storm, waves so huge began to batter the _Archimedes_, that, with the hatch-covers swept away, it seemed only a matter of time before the vessel would be utterly swamped.

In his childhood, Diccon's mind had been suffused with Christian imagery in which the wind and the sea were potent metaphors of the spiritual life. Creation itself begins with the Spirit of God moving upon the face of the waters; in the midst of Job's sufferings, 'the Lord answered [him] out of the whirlwind'; and the coming of the Holy Spirit is announced by 'a sound from heaven as of a rushing mighty wind'.[63] So now, while the storm rages around the _Archimedes_, Hughes altogether suspends the forward movement of his narrative, and _In Hazard_ deepens into a celebration of moral values, and an exploration of the nature of religious belief.

At the height of the storm, Mr Buxton experiences a kind of revelation about why he first went to sea: it had been, quite simply, 'because he liked virtue'; for although the *raison d'être* of seagoing is clearly economic,[64]

> the practice of it is judged by standards which are not economic at all, which can only be called moral: and which are peculiar to it. For the working of a ship calls for certain qualities – virtues, if you like – which do not seem to be appropriate today to the relations of employers and employed on shore. The shore-labourer's liability is limited: the seaman's is unlimited. The seaman may be called on to give the utmost that he is able, even to laying down his life.

This moral awakening gives Buxton 'a comfortable sort of contentment', which suffuses 'the thin, hollow shell' between 'the wind and incessant noise battering him from without', and the 'hunger and weariness battering him from within', and enables him to cope with them both.

In the meantime, the ship has only been saved from the huge waves (at least for the time being) by the constant pouring of small amounts of oil from the forward and aft latrines: 'a thin film only a few molecules in thickness' which, once it had spread out, 'bound millions of tons of water'. During the twenty hours that Dick Watchett is engaged upon this task, he finds relief from his fear partly in further fantasies about Sukie, with her 'beautiful cool eyes'; but principally in returning to a modified version of the simple religious faith of his childhood. As soon as Dick can manage to pray unselfishly, he feels 'a most distinct and stabbing promise, of the kind he remembered so well, that he should be saved alive kindly'.[65]

Buxton's revelation and Watchett's new religious faith lie at the heart of *In Hazard*; and Hughes's account of Dick Watchett's spiritual voyage is so highly autobiographical that if the latter part of it is descriptive rather than prophetic, we may begin to imagine what thoughts may have been going through Hughes's mind when he and Wyllie were facing almost certain death from exposure on the High Atlas.

Among the stream of book reviews and articles, which (on returning from the summer-house to his study) Hughes wrote alongside *In Hazard*, was a series for *Time and Tide* on 'The Psychology of War'. In one of these, he suggested that ancient cave drawings bore the same relation to hunting that modern lavatory drawings did to sexual desire: 'each line of the animal', he wrote, 'titillates the hunting lust'; and he told one correspondent on the subject that 'in the act of galloping after a wild boar I have felt a pang of pleasure equivalent to sexual pleasure in its intensity'.[66]

This may be taken as an indirect tribute to the sexual satisfaction which Diccon and Frances had come to share,[67] and which saw them through numerous difficulties in their long married life.

Through the summer of 1937 (with Robert now five years old, Penny three, and Lleky celebrating her first birthday) Frances continued to run the household in her typically disorganised and eccentric fashion: meals were at odd times, for example, and clothes for her children were bought not so much for practicality, as for whether they would combine to form a pleasingly artistic ensemble on the washing-line.[68] She herself often appeared in the town wearing 'her side-saddle "habit" made by a very smart firm called Busrine (the Christian Dior of the riding world) – though she had long since given up riding – & a sort of naval jacket on top'.[69]

Very protective towards Diccon – to whom she usually deferred in everything – Frances worried that he might be overworking; and for a few weeks that summer she persuaded him to take her and the children up to Parc for a holiday – even though this meant that she felt obliged to leave Laugharne Castle House in good enough order for it to be sublet to tenants while they were away. Staying in North Wales also involved Diccon in a difficult confrontation with his mother.

Louisa, knowing of Diccon's progress upon *In Hazard*, had worked herself up into a frenzy of anxiety: 'so fearful', she later explained to Frances, '& afraid to expect too much, for a book at his present age is so much more crucial than one written ten years ago'.[70] She was also jealous of the fact that it was presumably Frances (and not she) with whom Diccon was sharing extracts from the novel as it was being written. Diccon found the emotional pressure so severe that after this visit it would be two years before he returned to Parc; and for some while he could hardly bear to communicate with Louisa.[71]

Resuming work upon his novel, Hughes thickened its texture with psychological speculation about the way in which cultural forces work upon the same 'few prime movers common to us all', to produce such different results. After his recent difficulties with Louisa, Diccon was especially interested in considering 'the curious opposition, and tension (or at least tie), which exists in all men, and indeed in all beasts, between parents and child'. He believed that the form in which this emerged was (broadly speaking) a matter of cultural environment. Among Anglo-Saxons, it flowered[72]

> for the most part in revolt: in an exaggerated contempt of the
> adolescent child for the parent: a contempt far greater than he
> would feel for any other human being of the same calibre as his
> father. Amongst the Chinese, it is precisely this same root which
> flowers in obedience, in worship of the parent.

'In both cases', Hughes concluded, the root was the same: 'a tie
felt to be immensely strong, and potentially very painful: so, *we*
tug against that tie, desperately, trying to snap it, while *they* walk
towards the source of the pull faster than the pull itself, so leaving
the cord quite slack!'

At length, *Archimedes* passed through the storm; and was even
making some steam of her own while she was towed to the nearest
port. Then, as Hughes sat in his summer-house on a cold winter's
day, watching her and her crew in his mind's eye, a surprise awaited
him. The chief engineer, overcome by sleep, 'fell off the rail backwards into the sea. The shock of the water, of course, woke him,
and he swam for quite a time'. After writing those words, Hughes
retreated to the Castle House, made his way up to Frances's studio,
and said in a shocked voice: 'MacDonald's fallen overboard – he's
drowned!'

Then at last, very early in 1938, there came an evening when
Hughes was known to be writing the concluding sentences of his
novel. As Sheila Rowlands describes it, she and Jack were waiting
outside in the cold; they were joined by Frances; and then Diccon
emerged from the summer-house 'with this enormous look of relief
on his face and said "Oh, thank God for that!" ' And then he looked
up and said: 'Look, even the heavens are rejoicing.'[73] Most unusually
so far south, there was a spectacular display of the aurora borealis,
and huge red streamers radiated from the zenith of the sky.

Towards the end of March 1938, Richard Hughes was able
to send Laurence Holt the typescript of *In Hazard*; and then
he and Frances went up to London, where they held a party
to celebrate its completion.[74] It was a lively party, but a little
premature, because this was the moment when a problem arose
about protecting the identity of Brown, the second officer whose
nerve had broken during the real hurricane. 'No-one familiar with
the *Phemius* story', Holt declared,[75]

> could fail to identify . . . the officer who shows up unfavourably
> in your manuscript. What you have written about this character is
> not in substance more severe than warranted by the facts reported

to me by the Master and Chief Mate, upon which I acted in dismissing Brown from the Company's service and in advising him to abandon a sea career, and I should, if necessary, be willing to testify to this effect.

Both he and his associate Mr James Miller thought it might be preferable to reduce the risk of any legal action by introducing a rational second mate, and making Rabb 'a supernumerary officer', and this, as we know, was the suggestion which Hughes adopted.[76]

The tedious process of rewriting sections of what he had hoped was a completed work (a process once compared by the novelist John Cowper Powys to being in one's own grave, eating one's own bones) was enlivened by the presence in Laugharne Castle House of some unexpected visitors.

At the beginning of April 1938, Diccon Hughes had received a letter from Dylan Thomas, saying that he and Caitlin (whom he had married the previous July) would be spending Easter in Wales, and wanted to know whether they could call in for a visit. The point was that they were[77]

> hoping to rent a cottage for the summer, somewhere in Carmarthenshire. Do you know of any likely place cheap enough for us? If you do happen to know of anywhere, or know anyone who might know, we'd be very grateful if you'd tell us, when – as we hope – we can meet you again.

After consulting Frances, Diccon replied with an open-ended invitation: Dylan and Caitlin could come and stay until a cottage could be found for them – and why not look for somewhere in Laugharne?

Dylan accepted gratefully, and before long he and his wife were installed in the Castle House.

It was not an altogether easy arrangement, partly because of an underlying tension between Caitlin and Diccon. Although she recognised Diccon's kindness, she claimed later that he thought her 'the most stupid woman he'd ever met' – or was it just that he took no very obvious notice of her beauty? – and she responded by deciding that 'he was the most pompous man I'd ever met'.[78] She particularly disliked 'the way he kept talking about his children as though he understood child psychology better than anyone had ever done'; and she thought him 'mean at table', only producing a bottle of wine 'if there was someone important dining with them. He would pour them a glass and then one for himself, and not offer a glass to us. It caused great resentment'.[79] Diccon's lack of generosity was most uncharacteristic, and may well have stemmed from Frances having nagged him about deadening his faculties by drinking too much, as she is known to have done at a later date.[80] Frances may also have begged him to keep Dylan Thomas's drinking in check while he was staying with them.

At all events, Dylan was wildly happy to be back in Laugharne; Diccon would later describe how he had 'revelled like an intoxicated whirligig in the profoundly humane eccentricities of that unparalleled little township: they ran in at his five senses and out at his mouth day and night';[81] and any resentment over the wine was soon dealt with. Dylan and Caitlin were sitting one day in the summer-house on the watchtower (where Dylan would be allowed to work as soon as Diccon's *In Hazard* revisions were out of the way), when they saw their host 'going down some steps into the bowels of the castle. We watched', Caitlin recalls,[82]

> and saw him return with a bottle of wine in his hand. Needless to say, as soon as he was gone we went down the steps to see what was there and found he had constructed his own private wine cellar. At first we were very careful, creeping down there when it was dark and taking the odd bottle. Hughes didn't seem to notice so we started taking risks and would come back sometimes with our arms full of bottles, laughing at the cheek of it all because Hughes had laid down some really good stuff.

When Diccon realised what was going on, and mentioned his losses as if in all innocence, they 'made horrified noises of sympathy, with Dylan saying: "Now, who the hell could have done that?" '

After a while, Diccon appeared to be persuaded that some Territorial Army soldiers must have raided his cellar (there was an encampment not far away, and this was the best solution that Dylan could come up with at a moment's notice); but in fact he had already decided not to let the theft of the wine spoil an important friendship; and after this he sometimes amused himself by leaving out wine on his dining-room table, and watching from the shadows as Dylan and Caitlin crept downstairs late at night and made off with it.

Years later, when his friend Lance Sieveking had written a piece suggesting that Diccon and his friends had been too easily won over by Dylan Thomas's charm, Diccon commented:[83]

> It wasn't just occasional 'charm' made us fond of him . . . it was his genius ('charm's' two-a-penny). He may have sponged on us economically, but spiritually it was more the other way round . . . New poems in the making . . . the stories in *Portrait of the Artist as a Young Dog* (I suggested the title, incidentally) read out as they were written . . . it was the kind of companionship I badly needed.

After five or six weeks in the Castle House, Dylan and Caitlin moved out to Eros, a tiny two-bedroomed fisherman's cottage in Gosport Street down on the Grist, where they were visited by the poet Vernon Watkins; and one morning after breakfast (as Watkins describes it), they heard 'two knocks on the door. "That will be Hughes", said Dylan, giving the surname 'an accent of awe'. A moment later, and Watkins was immensely impressed to see, standing in the doorway,[84]

> a figure tall and solemn, with a high, white forehead and black, curly beard, his powerful hands resting on a strong cane. On this he leaned in order not to dwarf still further the low doorway on whose threshold he stood. I was quickly introduced, and he moved with an evenness of step and intonation into the room, rising there almost to the raftered ceiling, and then standing stock-still opposite the window, black-bearded and impressive, like a sea-captain who has taken up a vantage point in a small boat, focusing, with an invisible telescope, on something none of us could see.

At first, Watkins believed that Hughes used this 'completely impassive' mask as a way of 'curb[ing] Dylan's natural eagerness and enthusiasm'; but later, when he himself was a guest at Laugharne Castle, he realised that he had been deceived and that

> it was [Diccon's] own exuberance and awareness that he was resisting and keeping under restraint. His acute observation of the barbaric world of children and of animal joy had manoeuvred him out of wonder, which was only bearable for minutes, into immobility ... In gentle cadences he talked gravely and most entertainingly of the past, the present and the future, until each was becalmed by his understatement and the trance of his voice into a condition that conformed to the timelessness of Laugharne itself.

While writing *In Hazard* (which had been revised to Laurence Holt's entire satisfaction by the end of May 1938,[85] and was then promptly despatched to Chatto), Hughes had been wondering what to do next. His interest in the Richard Burton biography had evaporated long ago, and after a lengthy correspondence Geoffrey Faber had eventually agreed to 'relieve you of the £250 already paid to you. It is an unusual state of affairs when an author has to persuade a publisher to take money back!'[86] *Walter Harris* demanded attention, but there was still considerable research work to be done; and Hughes was pleased to be diverted from this task by a proposition which had been put to him the previous autumn.

It was in November 1937 that the publisher John Murray had spent a weekend at Laugharne Castle, and had discussed the possibility of his revising the autobiography of the lone yachtsman Fred Rebell.[87] It was a story full of excitement: without any previous experience of navigation (he took a book with him, to study the subject en route) Rebell had set out from Australia in a boat with a home-made keel, intending to make his way across the Pacific to North America. It was also the story of a confirmed atheist who had returned to Christianity.

Hughes was intrigued on both counts, and would later write of Rebell's voyage:[88]

> The initial passage across the Tasman Sea would have daunted any whose physical endurance was less than sub-human. The boat leaked, by the keel: he had to keep baling, which allowed him very little sleep, and from constant soaking his toe-nails floated off. That goaded him to dive overboard, in spite of sharks, and mend the leak under water. Then, trusting at first to dead reckoning, he missed New Zealand altogether. That drove him to study the art of navigation by sextant. At length his home-made instruments rusted, his watches became unreliable, the storms became unbearably violent. That drove him again to prayer.
>
> In this way he won back his faith: for his prayers were answered. If he prayed for the storm to lessen, the winds and the waves were tempered to his little craft. If he was lost and prayed for a true position, the hidden sun would reveal itself to his sextant at the critical moment: or, lying under the little canvas hood which served him for a cabin, he would be what St John calls 'in the spirit', and as from an immense height would see where islands and reefs lay a hundred miles off.

Hughes had soon agreed both to edit Rebell's account of his voyaging, and to add a short preface; though he commented: 'what I shall have to do really amounts to a kind of collaboration'.[89]

When Hughes and Murray went to meet Rebell a few weeks later, he was living in spartan conditions on a 'Baltic fishing-boat with a keel of reinforced concrete (home-made again)', which had been driven on to a Suffolk beach during a North Sea gale; and he announced that he intended to set sail for Australia as soon as proper arrangements had been made for the publication of his autobiography.[90] Hughes promised to begin work on it in the spring; but when in April he received a typescript copy from Murray,[91] he was busily revising *In Hazard*; and when that was done, his energies were re-channelled into an unwelcome bout of research work on *Walter Harris*.

What had happened was that Sir Austin Harris had written to Hughes in mid March asking whether he was still working on his brother Walter's life, as the family were disappointed, and someone else was waiting in the wings.[92] Hughes replied that it would be more satisfactory for him to complete the work 'some time this winter'.[93] However, Stephen Gaselee was also becoming impatient, writing from the Foreign Office on 25 March:[94]

> Some slight inconvenience is being caused by the two volumes of Morocco print which you began to examine being now kept at your disposal, but not used by you, for some 3½ years. I wish you could come here and finish reading them so that we could wind up the business.

Four days later, Hughes lunched at Pruniers with Harold Nicolson, who had decided to make Harris the central figure in a volume of reminiscences;[95] and this meeting finally spurred Diccon into action. The result was that on 21 June, he went up to London for six or seven weeks: partly so that he would be on hand to see *In Hazard* through to publication; and partly for research into *Walter Harris*.

Frances was saddened to be left behind in Laugharne. 'Diccon Dear', she wrote to him two days after his departure,[96]

> I wonder how you are getting on in that big city of London and if you have started to and fro to the Foreign Office yet. I am sorry to say I have missed you much too much, and was very dawdley 2 days.

To cheer herself up, she had taken 'the Dylans and her mother' to Saundersfoot and Tenby, and had then invited them all to supper. Dylan had been in good form; and Caitlin had 'talked much better than I have known her', and had mentioned that she was now expecting a baby; but Frances had to confess that despite 'that wine lesson you gave me, I poured them all out glasses of Vin Rose, and when we drank it, it was Liqueur Brandy instead!'

Diccon replied with an advance copy of *In Hazard* (now scheduled for publication on 7 July), and a letter telling her that he was having a miserable time, suffering from terrible aches and pains, which he ascribed to lumbago. Frances was sympathetic, though she believed that it was probably 'just . . . stiffness, you know you are old to begin an office stool life, and probably it don't suit you at all. Here you always ramble and wander during work'.[97] No doubt that was partly true; but no doubt that Diccon was also racked with anxiety about his new novel; especially as Chatto, anticipating a success similar to that of *A High Wind in Jamaica*, had arranged to spend a great deal of money on publicity.[98]

Another advance copy had been sent to Louisa Hughes. Not knowing her son's London address, she immediately sent two long, slightly hysterical letters to Laugharne. 'It has come!' she wrote to Frances, '& I can hardly contain myself with happiness. To see it at last, actually there when for so long it had become almost a myth, you can't think how marvellous it is to me.'[99] And to Diccon she began:[100]

> Oh, my dear – to have it at last & see it before me! I have not read it yet, but you may be sure I shall do so before I sleep tonight, & I had to thank you first . . . I have just peeped into it & I can see (with the two chapters I had already read) that I need not have been afraid – it is *good*.

She promised that she was not counting upon *In Hazard* becoming a bestseller; but in any case nothing mattered now she knew that it was really good, '& it is really you. Thank you & God bless you!'

A few days later came the official publication; and very soon it appeared that Diccon's anxieties had been justified.

In Hazard certainly received excellent reviews from Desmond MacCarthy, who described it as 'a tremendous piece of dramatic, narrative description . . . as thrilling a yarn as any you are likely to pick up . . . magnificent'; from Edwin Muir, who said that it was 'outstanding'; and from Graham Greene, who wrote:

> Here is the old simplicity, surprise, outrageous humour. But the most outrageous quality is not its humour but its daring – to take the same subject as Conrad in *Typhoon* . . . it would be foolhardy if it were not triumphantly justified.

But the critical reception was so mixed, that 'on every significant issue, there were violent disagreements of opinion'. Some critics, for example, disliked the lengthy scientific descriptions, described by one of them as 'lectures about engine-rooms and meteorology, and so on'; while others believed that in those very descriptions, Hughes had 'revived our lost sense of wonder'.[101]

Even Virginia Woolf, to whom Richard Hughes had sent a copy of his new novel, was less than enthusiastic: 'I read *In Hazard* with great interest', she told him,[102]

> & am sure it is full of remarkable things. What I'm not sure is whether they coalesce . . . It seems to me possible that on the one hand there's the storm: on the other the people. And between them there's a gap, in which there's some want of strength.

And, as if to confirm her misgivings, sales figures were disappointing in the extreme.

In public, Hughes was his usual imperturbable professional self;[103] but in private, as it became clear how badly *In Hazard* had flopped, his health took another turn for the worse. His aches and pains became so bad that he could take no exercise; and when he managed to get down to Laugharne for a weekend in July, Frances was shocked to see that he had put on a great deal of weight, and was weaker than she had ever known him.

'It was nice being about with you', Frances wrote on Diccon's return to London, but 'all I really want to know is how your aches and pains are, because I feel so sorry for you on that account, and also if you are at all getting your strength back.'[104] And later on, when a family holiday had been arranged: 'I really miss you again, every day, and am quite lonely for your company. It will be lovely for us to be in Cumberland.'[105]

The latter part of August and the whole of September were spent on the shores of Ullswater in the Lake District. Lyulph's Tower, the former hunting-box of the Howards of Greystoke, had been lent to Frances by her cousin, Lady Mary Howard; and they were joined there by her sister Rachel, and her brother Thomas.

It was an enchanted place. Before them, the lake; and behind them, a fell upon which there still roamed one of the few remaining herds of English red deer.[106] Among his family (as Frances reported to Louisa), Diccon grew 'very very happy . . . He got much thinner and stronger again in Cumberland. Though one day he ran too far over the mountains, and looked very tired for two days after'.

Largely abandoning his work, Diccon found a neglected boat on the lake and (cheerfully ignoring the fact that a few minor repairs would have made it usable) he spent over a month putting it into perfect order. He also gave rowing lessons to Robert (now approaching his seventh birthday); and spent some time with four-year-old Penny, whose eyes were 'bright with liveliness and mischief'; though she felt things acutely, and would sometimes baffle her parents by bursting into tears for no apparent reason, and with no subsequent explanation.[107]

On returning to Laugharne, and receiving anxious messages from John Murray asking about his progress on the Rebell typescript,[108] Hughes wrote a long letter explaining that the work was far greater than he had anticipated, and it was not really worth his while doing it for the sum of £25 and a 2½% royalty as originally agreed. After 'careful thought', Murray improved the terms, giving him a 7% royalty; and with this encouragement, Diccon began his rewriting.

The early results were impressive; and by 9 December John Murray was telling him:[109]

You are a magician – and a modest one! You have hidden your hand very cleverly on these four chapters, for you have retained the naive spirit of the man without it appearing so excessive as to be burlesque.

His confidence considerably restored, Hughes worked hard for the rest of that month and all the next; and by the end of January 1939 the revised text of Rebell's work was in the publisher's hands, lacking only a title[110] and an introduction.

In the meantime, the threat of a new World War had begun to loom very large. Hughes had been convinced for many months that 'war was absolutely inevitable'.[111] The spring of 1938 had seen the German annexation of Austria, but even that had not satisfied Hitler's greed. In September, at Munich, the British Prime Minister Neville Chamberlain had signed an agreement with Hitler by which the Czech Sudetenland was surrendered to Germany; and when in January 1939 Hughes successfully completed some negotiations by which he effectively annexed part of a neighbour's land (in order to give his children a safe and secure passageway down to the harbour),[112] he wrote ironically:[113]

> So our Munich Conference has been successful! We have been given our Sudetenland and our passage to the sea: and while we are to recognise the independence of the Rump, we have acquired control over it on all essential points. All this, too, has been done entirely by Peaceful Negotiation – only the threat of force, not force itself, being necessary. I did not realise before how much I had in common with Herr Hitler.

For his part, Hughes had begun organising air raid precautions in Laugharne, and would later write an authoritative letter on the subject to the *Western Mail*, pointing out that speed was vital; and that a village fire watcher party armed with only a stirrup-pump and three or four buckets might do better than a fire-engine coming from fifty miles away.

Or was that all he had been doing?

The autumn of 1938 had seen the American publication of *In Hazard*; and this had brought in its wake a wonderful letter from Ford Madox Ford, who told Hughes roundly that his book was 'a masterpiece. It is rather as if the book itself were a ship in a hurricane'. He declared that Hughes stood 'quite apart from any other writer known to me'; and added:[114]

> I don't know how the book has done here. I have seen one or two notices that quite miss all the points and resolve themselves into

saying that it is or isn't better than *Typhoon*. It isn't, of course, better than *Typhoon*. *Typhoon* was written by a great writer who was a man. *In Hazard* is written by someone inhuman . . . and consummate in the expression of inhumanities.

Hughes was delighted by this, and replied in due course: 'Your letter gave me more pleasure than any other kindness the book has met with, because you are one of the very few men living today who really *respect* the novel.'[115]

Then, as he pondered over Ford Madox Ford's words (and also perhaps recalled Virginia Woolf's comment about the gap between the people and the storm in his book), Hughes began to think that there had been a great subconscious purpose to his writing of *In Hazard*; and later, he would tell one of his children: 'I was carried along in my writing of it by a kind of prophetic fury, seeing so clearly the abyss Europe was about to be sucked down into by war, and wanting to tell people it would be fearful, but they were going to come through.'[116]

Diccon's health remained fragile; and he arranged to spend the worst of the winter abroad, on a cruise arranged by Sir Henry Lunn's 'Hellenic Traveller's Club'. So in February 1939 (leaving Frances recovering from influenza) he travelled down to Plymouth, where he joined the SS *Letitia*, out of Glasgow, and bound for the Bahamas and the West Indies.[117]

It was to be a working holiday: Hughes had been commissioned by the *Geographical Magazine* to write an article about Jamaica;[118] while on board the *Letitia* he was to deliver a number of lectures;[119] he had another article to write for *Vogue*;[120] and he intended to spend much of the homeward journey working on his Walter Harris biography.[121]

As they steamed southward, Diccon soon realised that he had 'not been so interested in the *people* I travelled with, since that steerage voyage to New York'. Many of them were old: Sir Henry Lunn himself was eighty; as was Lord Olivier, a former governor of Jamaica 'who follows his own stomach about looking like a benevolent old bear'; but there was also the forty-six-year-old popular travel-writer H.V. Morton and his wife, 'whom I think you would like', Diccon told Frances; and 'a pretty young girl of fifteen, who seems to have five clergymen for father, but who spends her time down in the barber-shop, sitting on the knee of the barber. When the shop is closed she either hugs the bell-boys in corners or handles other old clergymen'.[122]

At length they came down to the islands. Their first landing was at Nassau in the Bahamas, where Diccon and some of his fellow passengers

> went in little motor-launches with glass bottoms, so that you could look down and see the coral growing, and the strange fish in it. From there we landed on a long island . . . The sand was all coral sand, white as salt: & the water as brilliant and many-coloured as a peacock's tail, & clear as a stained-glass window – yes, like that, for light seemed to come up out of it.

From the Bahamas they sailed on to Miami, where Diccon drove out to an alligator farm and bought

> two charming little alligators for Robert: but as soon as the captain heard of it he sent and had them thrown into the sea, because his ship was not supposed to carry live-stock! Damn the pig, they were so nice.

Monday 20 February found the SS *Letitia* between Cuba and Jamaica, sailing close to Cape San Antonio, 'just outside the reefs where the pirate-ship in *High Wind* lurked to catch the *Clorinda*. It was a very odd feeling', Hughes told his wife, 'to *see* like that for the first time a place which for years has been so vivid in my memory'.

At five o'clock on Wednesday morning they anchored in Montego Bay, and Diccon was 'up at five, to watch as we came in. First, at dawn, the whole long line of the inland mountains, with the morning stars shining big and bright until the sun was up'. Then, as they entered the bay, there was

> a gold sky in the east, behind the headland, so dazzling as to turn the headland a rich black and the water a green steel. It was odd to come in the bay; I saw it as I had described it – even two large schooners lying there, lying at anchor as the *Clorinda* lay when the children went aboard.

On landing at Montego Bay, Hughes left his new friends, promising to rejoin them on board the *Letitia* on Saturday, when they would be putting into Kingston on the far side of the island.

After being interviewed 'by a fine black journalist', who began: 'I shall not tell you an untruth, Mr Hughes; I have never read your book', the rest of Wednesday was spent in 'looking for cousins; & found some: a pleasant young couple with two children, who were very hospitable', and who put him up for the night after taking him

> to bathe at 'Doctor's Cave' (I believe it is the original of the place where the children bathed during the earthquake, but now it is a swell bathing beach!) & was interviewed by another (rival) journalist, just as black, who followed me about taking snapshots.

The result was that, when Diccon left Montego by train early on Thursday morning, the ticket-collector 'came up to me with a beaming face, waving the *Daily Gleaner*, and assuring me that the pictures of me in it (looking like a rather blotchy version of a Jewish rabbi just about to be hanged) were "very sweet and very lovely" '.

By the time he rejoined his ship, Hughes had more than enough material for his article on Jamaica (which appeared in the *Geographical Magazine* later in the year, once the editors had excised that part of it which dealt with the contraceptive practices of negresses);[123] but he was achieving less than he had hoped; he began to feel that the great heat, far from doing him good, was sapping his energy; and then, not long after his return to England, he became extremely ill.

Jaundice was certainly involved;[124] but as week after week went by without any significant improvement, family and friends began to feel that something more fundamental might be wrong. Louisa Hughes was so alarmed that she became accident-prone, and scalded herself quite seriously with boiling water.[125] Charles Johnson's wife urged Frances to 'tell the doctor his family history, & that his father's illness began about his age'.[126]

By mid May, Diccon was still so unwell that he was 'not allowed to attend to any business'.[127] At length there was an X-ray examination. Much to everyone's relief, his chest and lungs were pronounced clear;[128] and during the course of June his strength gradually returned.

As soon as he was well again, Hughes found himself under considerable pressure. There was an introduction to be written for *Escape to the Sea* (the title of the Rebell memoirs);[129] the Harris family were clamouring for news of progress on *Walter Harris*[130] (of which Hughes had still only drafted the first few chapters); and he no longer had any secretarial help from Sheila Rowlands, who had given birth to her first child earlier in the year and was now wholly occupied with domestic duties.

Nor was it always easy to work in a house which was full of boisterous young children, leading a somewhat anarchic life since the recent departure of one of their nannies. No replacement had been found, and Frances was too disorganised to fill the gap effectively.

'From time to time if our games got noisy', Penny recalls, '[Diccon] would descend like a thunderclap from his study at the top of the house.' Once that summer he came in, picked them up without a word, and[131] stuffed us one after another into the empty top level of the bookshelves that lined one wall of the Nursery, one to each shelf. We knew that if we didn't wriggle we wouldn't fall out, and we felt complimented that he knew we would have the sense to keep still. We wailed a bit, tentatively, and then settled down to talk and wait.

They were left there for about half an hour, 'like chickens stacked in cages in a poultry-market', before being released.

At length, work on *Escape to the Sea* was completed; and a family holiday was arranged at Parc. Frances travelled overland to North Wales with the children; while Diccon set sail on 17 August in *Tern* with some unusual passengers: two Catholic Fathers, who kept him company on the two-day voyage up to Portmeirion.[132]

By now, the international situation was rapidly plummeting out of control. In March, Germany had invaded and occupied Czechoslovakia; in April, Italy had invaded and occupied Albania; Hitler was calling for the return to the Reich of the free city of Danzig; and was clearly bent upon the destruction of Poland, with whom Britain had recently signed an alliance.

War seemed so very likely to Richard Hughes that soon after arriving at Portmadoc, he bought a large quantity of stores from a chandler whom he asked to advise him on what he needed for 'a voyage of a couple of years'. These stores (including such unlikely 'iron rations' as tinned poppadums) were transferred to Parc, and there they were 'hidden in the Priest Hole in one of the bedrooms', as an emergency reserve.[133]

Hardly had they been stowed away, when news came that Nazi Germany had signed a Non-Aggression Pact with the Soviet Union. War was now inevitable. Nine days later, the blitzkrieg on Poland began; and on 3 September 1939 Great Britain and France had declared war on Germany.[134]

For Richard Hughes, the outbreak of war was personally momentous. During the past thirteen years, he had fought his way back from comparative obscurity and a severe nervous breakdown, to become internationally known as the author of *A High Wind in Jamaica*. However, fame had brought its own problems. In particular, the pressure of trying to match the quality of his most successful work was severe; and yet Hughes firmly believed that writing was the central purpose of his existence. He was fortunate to have the support of a wife who shared this belief; and yet her very belief in him meant that she expected a great deal (especially now that they had a young family to support), and so there were times when he found her almost as difficult as he had always found his mother.

In August 1939, an official at the Ministry of Labour had written to Hughes telling him: 'If the worst happens I should hope that some use might be made of your exceptional abilities';[135] and the Second World War would soon provide him not merely with a good regular income for the first time in his life, but with the duty of abandoning all literary work for the duration of the conflict.

Paradoxically, the war also made a commercial success of *In Hazard*, whose sales suddenly picked up, so that 'by the end of the war it had sold more copies than *High Wind*';[136] and it provided Richard Hughes with the theme of the literary work which would come to dominate the remainder of his long life.

CHAPTER 24

Finding a Role

By the autumn of 1939, it was almost two hundred years since there had been any serious fighting on the British mainland. After the defeat of Prince Charles Edward Stuart at Culloden in 1745, wars had been carried on abroad by the men-folk (or some of them), while at home the women and children slept safely in their beds. This time, however, it would be different, and everyone knew it. Articles in the newspapers, newsreels from the Spanish Civil War, and both the book and the film of H.G. Wells's terrifying *The Shape of Things to Come* had prepared people for an aerial bombardment which would devastate towns and cities, cause massive loss of life, and perhaps altogether destroy modern civilisation.

Therefore the decision had been taken that, in the event of war, children were to be evacuated from centres of population most likely to be targeted by enemy bombers, and sent into the country. The area around Penrhyndeudraeth would receive eight hundred children from Birkenhead; and when they arrived, early in September 1939, one hundred and seven of them were taken by bus to Llanfrothen, the nearest village to Parc.[1]

Since Richard Hughes had a car at his disposal, he volunteered to help with the billeting. However, he was given a twenty-one-year-old billeting list dating from the end of the Great War;[2] many family circumstances had changed; and he was eventually left with six girls for whom he had been unable to find a home. Not knowing what else to do, he drove them to Parc, where his family was just sitting down to supper.[3]

Frances, though always 'immensely warm-hearted to children with the odds stacked against them', already had three young children to look after in a house with no drains and no running water, and was far from pleased at being joined by so many refugees.[4] And although six-year-old Robert and five-year-old Penny 'thought the evacuee children agreeable new companions', Lleky, 'suffering from an older brother and sister who always seemed to get more attention', felt that it was 'just too much to be invaded by a whole lot more children.' One day (although she was only three), by 'shouting and waving a long broom', she managed to round up some Welsh Black heifers and send them stampeding towards the evacuees: fortunately no one was hurt.[5]

All was well so long as Diccon could take the children out, and go for walks with them, or bathe with them in the stream, where he 'would hold his breath and count to sixty', while all nine children 'sat ourselves on arms and legs, and crowded onto his back. Then the earthquake would begin. He would roll us into the water brushing us off like gnats. We would shake the wet hair out of our eyes and scramble on again as fast as we could'.[6] But indoors, the atmosphere was different, though it was difficult for the Hughes children to understand why. 'It was sometimes', Penny recalls,[7]

> as if the house had declared war on the lot of us. My father once shouted, 'Anne, you shouldn't be carrying that jug!' Her mouth dropped open in fright, she parted her hands, and the jug landed on the slate floor.
>
> Another aspect of the house we had always loved now became an enemy. The centre of our life had always been the fire. All the cooking was done on it; we heated water on it in an urn; we burnt tins on the back of it before burying them in the bog to rust away to nothing. In the old days my mother just lit it when the evening began, but now, with so much cooking to be done, the fire had to be fed almost all day.

'It ate up time', Penny concludes, 'and even though we fed it on a mixture of wood and coal, not wood alone, we children always seemed to be getting in wood.'

Later, Diccon would apologise to Frances both for having given her so much extra work, and for having been unreasonably upset about breakages to his collection of fragile old china. 'It wasn't you that broke it', he wrote. 'It was me that foolishly took on too many evacuees. Six was a bad number to have: too many for a home and not enough for a school, so that we fell between two stools in our way of treating them.'[8] At the time, he had been angry with her for not being more supportive just when he felt that he was patriotically doing his best.

Hughes may also have felt frustrated in his purely domestic role. He had soon learned, to his great sorrow, that he was too old for active duty in the Royal Navy; but he had not forgotten his letter from the Ministry of Labour, suggesting that important work might be found for him in the event of war; and it had been disappointing when his request for an interview had been denied: no appointments could be made during the current rush of work, they had told him on the day after war broke out; but his name and particulars had been forwarded to the appropriate authorities.[9]

In the meantime, Diccon concentrated on his evacuees; and, replying on 12 September to a letter from an admirer, he wrote that he was himself[10]

> involved in a curiously *High Wind* situation, since I have spent the last week or so in my North Wales cottage as nursemaid general (also hewer of wood and drawer of water) to six evacuated children from Birkenhead. Normally that only occupied my time from 6.30 a.m. to midnight; but if they had toothache in the night or anything of that sort, of course the hours were rather longer.

The pressure of domestic duties was eased only a little by the arrival of the uniformed Nurse Cecil. Although she had another pair of hands, she could not grasp the Hugheses' informal way of dealing with their children, and came in for a good deal of scolding from them both.[11]

The happiest hour of the day (in what was now a troubled household) came in the evenings, when 'there was still a time of peace', and all nine children (as Penny recalls) 'would gather round the fire and my father would tell us stories'. As usual, each child had to choose an object to go into the story, and 'the understanding was that as soon as he had gone right round the circle he had to begin'. She added that when adults were present, 'he was inhibited and the stories were never so good . . . These story-telling sessions were intensely private to us and him'.[12]

Sometimes, indeed, Diccon had a particular therapeutic purpose in mind. For example, an evacuee who was always wetting her bed was told of a wooden doll who ran away from ill-treatment, sailing down-river in a china chamber-pot. When the doll reached the open sea, the waves broke upon the chamber-pot, and it sank – but the doll discovered that she could swim. The positive manner in which she continued to advance through a story which was saturated in dampness somehow did the trick, and the evacuee was cured.

Once the children were in bed, the quarrels between Diccon and Frances resumed and intensified. It was no longer simply a matter of too many evacuees, and too much broken china. Other more fundamental grievances (such as the financial improvidence of which each might plausibly accuse the other) were dragged in, adding fresh fuel to the flames; and by mid October Diccon had begun to fear that his marriage was in serious danger.[13]

In the midst of all this, Frances revealed that she had once again become pregnant, with a child which had been conceived in the happier days of July. She decided that they should all return to Laugharne; and one evening she and Diccon 'sat long over the table discussing plans'. Penny, who was sitting reading not far away, 'overheard scraps of conversation about where the evacuees could transfer to, and my father obstinately saying he would stay on till the last of them was settled'.[14]

Frances continued to press Diccon on the matter, but he was adamant. He had another book in mind, he told her: a new collection of children's stories, consisting of the best that he had been telling to the evacuees. It would be much easier for him to write them at Parc, away from the noise and bustle of Laugharne; and he would rejoin her and the children as soon as he could.[15]

So eventually on 4 or 5 October (with all of the evacuees but Anne and Ailsa settled elsewhere), Frances set off alone to open up Laugharne Castle House; where she was followed a day or two later by Nurse Cecil and the three Hughes children.[16]

Diccon's own situation at Parc was eased for a short while by the presence of another recent addition to the household: a German refugee called Ursula who was looking for work, and had been recommended to the Hugheses by a friend of theirs.[17] A tall young woman, with blue eyes and a ruddy complexion, Ursula seemed rather solemn at first: no wonder, as there was some doubt about whether or not she would be interned for the duration of the war;[18] but she turned out to be a great asset.

On arriving back at Laugharne, which immediately put their recent difficulties into perspective, Frances wrote to Diccon apologising for having been so bad-tempered. She also commented favourably upon the various merits of the woman she had left behind with him. Diccon in his turn assured Frances that their troubles had been largely his own fault: he had been 'a pig most of the time and not even the useful sort that eats scraps and makes nice bacon'. As for Ursula: he agreed that she would be[19]

> excellent. She *is* interested in the psychological side, but very sensibly and not (as so often) through being neurotic herself. It is interesting to watch her technique with Ailsa: even in this short time she has done her an immense deal of good. She is very different both from [Nurse] Graham & [Nurse] Cecil, being intelligent and interested in general things as well as her work.

He added that she was also quick to think she might be doing something 'not well', and that they must both be careful 'not to scold her as we did Cecil: and I don't think there would ever be any need to give her an *order*, she is too intelligent'.

In due course, Ursula followed Frances down to Laugharne, leaving Diccon to look after the two girls on his own. A long silence followed, only broken towards the end of October when Diccon wrote to Frances explaining that it was not 'through lack of love but because that miserable finger decided in spite of all precautions to go septic, so I can't hold a pen in my right hand & writing with the left is very tedious'. Anne and Ailsa were still with him, and he found them[20]

> much better, now they are away from the crowd, Ursula did them a lot of good . . . Ailsa is turning most civilised and merry, Anne is boisterous and whoops, or is helpful in turns (she spent all Sunday morning mending my trousers).

Diccon added that 'almost every day I have wished you were here, in conditions as they are now: everything quiet and peaceful, no rush and hurry, no car and . . . the most lovely weather . . . It seems such a shame that you were up here for all the miseries and are missing this'. The septic finger was his only serious problem, as it was handicapping his work (a few days later it would become so bad that it had to be put in a splint for a week); but he had decided to remedy the situation, by 'wir[ing] to Miss Horton to come and be dictated to'.

Frances was not best pleased by Diccon's continued absence, especially when she herself developed a poisoned thumb. Indeed, for a while they almost seemed to be trying to outdo each other in their misery. On the day that he learned of his wife's mishap, Diccon burnt his left hand, and told Frances he had 'thought I was going to be left completely handless, but I am glad to say it has turned out all right. I put a poultice of tea-leaves on it at once: that generally works wonders'.[21] Frances for her part wrote several reproachful letters, questioning the need for him to stay on at Parc, demanding that he write to her every single day, and asking for more details about their financial position. In one of his (dictated) replies, Diccon told her:[22]

> You ask about economics. Well, the thing is that Mr Barclay has allowed me to increase my overdraft until Christmas on the grounds of my income being dislocated by the war, but on condition only that I pay some substantial sums in by then. Now the only way I can be really sure of that is by getting a book of some sort to the publishers and getting advances on it, for it is impossible to be sure of work for magazines or of getting cheques from them by any particular date.

That, he explained, was why he '*must* get this book of children's stories finished and sent off to the publishers at the very first possible moment'. He added that he had now 'got more than half the stories I need for a book and they are going ahead well'.

This answer appears to have considerably mollified Frances; and by 11 November Diccon was able to write in his own hand: 'My dearest darling, Three lovely letters now from you to answer: how much nicer than being rebuked. I too badly want to see you.' Then (after mentioning that he had 'sent off a big batch of stories to Chatto & Windus, and expect to hear in a few days how long they want the work to be') Diccon finally revealed why he had been so determined to remain at Parc. 'Dearest', he confessed,[23]

> I suppose at the bottom of my wanting to do the work here is that we did quarrel so terribly those last few weeks; the fear of that would be far worse than traffic noises to work under. I am sure it is better for us to have a few weeks of wanting each other & not having each other, to drive all that away. And best then to come together again on holiday. I want you as much or more than you want me − & how good for us that is! I have felt a brute leaving you alone with you ill; but I felt that, and I felt this work *had* to be done & never would be done while we were being beastly to each other, so better to go into retreat. Darling, the same sort of friction so nearly did us in once before, I was terrified at it coming back again.

This letter pleased Frances still further: at last Diccon was being open with her again! She wrote him affectionate long letters; and by 21 November he was able to tell her that although he had still heard nothing definite from Chatto & Windus, his present plans were for Miss Horton to leave 'this coming week-end and that I then set to work to shut up the house'. It would take him about a week, he reckoned; and then perhaps he and Frances might have a brief holiday together?

However, before Diccon had finished closing up Parc, he received an emotional letter from Frances in which she said that she had been unwell on and off for weeks, that she was now very depressed, and that she needed him back at Laugharne. This rattled him, and on 1 December he wrote back defensively:[24]

> As a matter of fact I am a bit depressed myself today, as up to now I have been in brutally good health − apparently quite immune to colds − but today I feel like nothing on earth, as if I had got a touch of jaundice (though not with a temperature and all that nonsense). It is rather beastly with all the packing to do: and tomorrow I *have* to go into Portmadoc to lay up the *Tern*,

though how I shall manage in these storms and deluges I don't know. Of course I am eating nothing.

He also mentioned that the children had 'transferred to Garth Foel today, in spite of the dogs'; that he must stop writing now, since he had been heaving heavy things about all day, and '*must* lay my back out flat'; and before posting his letter the following morning, he added a gloomy footnote: his temperature had climbed to one hundred degrees the previous night, though it was 'down a bit this morning'.

Once again, the prospect of returning to Laugharne had begun to alarm him; and jaundice provided a convenient excuse for remaining at Parc for a little longer. This exasperated Frances, who wrote to him: 'We ate a great goose today. The Dylans came. It is the last of the foods I shall order or lay up or put in store for your returning. We have had so many such.'[25]

Frances and her children were not alone in wanting Diccon to return to Laugharne. The rector, S.B. Williams, had sent him a telegram on 30 September asking him to accept the foremanship of the borough for the coming year. Diccon had replied:[26]

GRATEFUL BUT AFRAID PROBABLE CALL TO OTHER DUTIES MAKES ME UNSUITABLE CANDIDATE WARTIME.

The worthy rector, quite undeterred by this, wrote back to say that he had resolved long ago to nominate Hughes as foreman, and that he had arranged for a capable deputy during Hughes's absence. 'You should have been Portreeve instead of me', he concluded. 'Please accept things as they are.'[27] Hughes did so: though he was unhappy about it, as he was still searching for a more significant wartime rôle.

So far (the evacuation of children apart) the war had made astonishingly little impact. As Winston Churchill would later write, Hitler's 'crashing onslaught upon Poland', and the subsequent declarations of war upon Germany by Britain and France, had been[28]

followed only by a prolonged and oppressive pause . . . The French Armies made no attack upon Germany . . . No air action, except reconnaissance, was taken against Britain . . . France and Britain remained impassive while Poland was in a few weeks destroyed or subjugated by the whole might of the German war machine.

It was only at sea that we were actively engaged, chiefly in trying to keep our supply-lines open. Merchant shipping had to be protected from the twin dangers of the U-boats and of the German pocket battleships, the *Deutschland* and the *Admiral Graf Spee*, which had sailed from Germany in August, before the British blockade was in place.

Diccon was now attempting to secure a position in Naval Intelligence;[29] and while he waited to see if those attempts bore fruit (and also made strenuous efforts in other directions) one small job came his way. A Mr MacBride (from the Ministry of Information in London) wrote offering him five guineas for a twelve-hundred-word article on 'Britain's Mercantile Marine', suitable for distribution to the press both of neutral countries and of the empire.

When Hughes asked for more details, he was told that there was no need to include any overt propaganda – an article by the author of *In Hazard* would speak for itself. He then arranged to stay with Laurence Holt in Liverpool early in the New Year in order to undertake the necessary research.[30]

In the meantime, Hughes had returned to Laugharne.[31] He was still suffering from jaundice, which meant that he missed two court meetings in a row, and was unable to take up his duties as foreman;[32] but before Christmas he was well enough to act in an entertainment which had been organised by Frances in aid of the Red Cross. Dylan and Caitlin Thomas were also heavily involved. Caitlin had become very attached to Frances during Diccon's long absences (and had been living in close proximity to her since the summer of 1938, when the Thomases had moved up to Sea View at the top end of the town); while Dylan Thomas not only liked Richard Hughes, but remained very much in awe of his literary achievements.[33]

After a selection by the band, Caitlin did a tap-dance; three-year-old Lleky sang a solo; when (with some difficulty) Lleky had been persuaded to leave the stage,[34] there were several more solo items before the climax of the evening: a one-act farce about a poor tanner. Dylan Thomas, who produced, also took the part of the tanner; while the woodman and his wife were played by Diccon and Frances (now five months pregnant with her fourth child).[35]

The evening was a great success; and afterwards, as Diccon recalled, he and Frances and Caitlin and Dylan sat up[36]

> into the small hours and talked. 'What the people of Laugharne need is a play about themselves', said Dylan. And so we talked about ideas for a plot. In the play the whole town is told that it is to be certified insane by the Outside World and cordoned off. They ask to plead their case. But when they hear what a *sane* town

ought to be like they withdraw their defence at once – say they'd much prefer to be certified mad.

By this time, Laugharne had

> taken the young bard to its uninhibited heart. His landlord obligingly did his laundry. Creditors secretly left offerings of green vegetables on his doorstep. Even the watching eye of the policeman was moist with appreciation the night Dylan thumped a certain tiresome head on the cobbles – so palpably was Dylan doing it 'for the love of man and in praise of God'.

And now, during this late-night conversation, a train of thought had been set in motion which would eventually lead to Dylan Thomas writing his masterpiece *Under Milk Wood*.

In Laugharne Castle House it was a happy Christmas-time, especially for the children. As an economy measure, Diccon had dragged a whole tree-trunk into the house. To begin with, one end lay right across the hallway, while the other end burned in the library hearth; and in the evenings Diccon would sit his children along the tree-trunk, and tell them stories by firelight.[37] However, the war remained at the forefront of his mind; and before Christmas, like almost everyone else in England, Diccon had been much excited by news of a naval engagement off the River Plate.

The *Graf Spee* had become 'the centre of attention in the South Atlantic'. There (under the inspired command of Captain Langsdorff), her 'practice was to make a brief appearance at some point, claim a victim, and vanish again into the trackless ocean wastes'.[38] She had sunk several ships in the first week of December. Then once again she disappeared from view; but Commodore Harwood, whose naval duties were to protect British shipping off the River Plate and Rio de Janeiro, became convinced that the *Graf Spee* was on her way to the Plate; and when she appeared off the mouth of the river on the morning of 13 December 1939, he was waiting for her with the *Exeter*, the *Ajax* (his own ship), and the *Achilles*.

With her six 11-inch guns, her armour-plating, and her speed of 26 knots, the *Graf Spee* was more than a match for any of the three ships which faced her. However, they engaged her closely; and although Langsdorff did severe damage to the *Exeter*, he was 'plastered from three directions, found the British attack too hot, and soon afterwards turned away under a smoke-screen with the apparent intention of making for the River Plate'.[39]

The British ships gave chase. The *Exeter*, pounded by 11-inch shells, was entirely disabled; the two after-turrets in the *Ajax* were knocked out; and the *Achilles* too was damaged. Harwood decided to break off the fight until after dark, but continued to pursue the *Graf Spee* as she made for neutral Montevideo. There she was granted only 72 hours in port; and on the evening of the 17th, after transferring most of his men to a German merchant ship, Langsdorff took the *Graf Spee* out of the harbour, and scuttled her. Two days later, he shot himself.

The *Altmark*, the *Graf Spee*'s auxiliary ship, remained at large; and it was believed that she still had on board the crews of nine ships sunk by the *Graf Spee*. However, as Churchill records, when news of the Battle of the River Plate reached Britain, it gave[40]

> intense joy to the British nation and enhanced our prestige throughout the world. The spectacle of the three smaller British ships unhesitatingly attacking and putting to flight their far more heavily gunned and armoured antagonist was everywhere admired.

Not least by Richard Hughes. At the end of December, there had seemed to be some possibility of 'a war job in the Persian Gulf';[41] but when this came to nothing Hughes (who had gone to Liverpool to collect material for his article on the Merchant Navy)[42] began to think that perhaps he should continue to serve his country as a writer – and how better, than with a book about the pursuit and destruction of the *Graf Spee*?

Hughes therefore asked a well-placed friend to write on his behalf to Rear-Admiral J.H. Godfrey, the Director of Naval Intelligence.[43] Godfrey decided that it was a matter for the Ministry of Information.[44] And then came the breakthrough: Edward Marsh (who had long ago published Diccon's work in one of his *Georgian Poetry* volumes) put him directly in touch with Leigh Ashton, 'a big noise' at the MoI. Ashton, who said that he had 'no objection' in principle to Hughes's plans, interviewed him on 19 February, and introduced him to the man responsible for information about naval affairs.[45] Within a week, a number of official letters had been issued by the MoI stating that: 'Mr Richard Hughes is writing, under our aegis, a book on the *Graf von Spee*', and asking the recipients to give him 'every assistance in your power'.[46]

The Admiralty also gave Hughes's project their blessing; and by this time the story of the *Graf Spee* had been given a satisfactory concluding twist. Her auxiliary, the *Altmark*, had been discovered in Norwegian territorial waters, and boarded. There followed:[47]

> A sharp hand-to-hand fight ... in which four Germans were killed and five wounded ... The search began for the British prisoners. They were soon found in their hundreds, battened

down, locked in store-rooms, and even in an empty oil-tank. Then came the cry, 'The Navy's here'. The doors were broken in and the captives rushed on deck.

Two hundred and ninety-nine prisoners were released; and many of them were soon available for interview.

For the next two months (as he told an agent who was trying to sell articles for him in New York), Hughes led a busy and exciting life, commuting between London (where he sometimes spent whole days in the Admiralty) and the ports of Plymouth, Bristol and Liverpool. 'I have visited the *Exeter* and the *Ajax*', he explained,[48]

> been allowed to examine the damage: have been taken through the Battle of the River Plate, minute by minute, by the officers who fought it (and believe me, the authors of the newspaper accounts of it used their imaginations pretty freely). I am getting first-hand accounts from the men concerned of every one of the raider's captures, and the real truth about their experiences as prisoners in the *Graf Spee* and *Altmark*.

Where possible, Hughes saw each man more than once, 'so as to get him to talk freely and do away with the "interview" atmosphere'. The more he learned of the story, the better he liked it. 'Moreover, although I am getting all this official help', he went on,

> I am left entirely free as to the manner in which I treat the subject. No one has asked me to write a ponderous 'official history': and no-one has asked me to write an over-dramatised piece of propaganda. I am taking full advantage of this freedom: in matter, to stick dispassionately to the exact truth in every detail, in the hope of producing an account of it all which will stand the test of Peace: and in manner, to write vividly, somewhat in the manner of *In Hazard*, so as to try and make the events as living and immediate as the events in a novel.

By 13 April 1940, Diccon had completed his researches, and was back in Laugharne with his family – just four days before Frances gave birth (at home) to their fourth child: Catharine Phyllida, always known as Kate. The other children, as Penny recalls, had been 'sent to a friend at Fern Hill for the day . . . As soon as she was safely delivered, a flag was hoisted on the flagpole to tell us on the other side of the valley the news'.[49]

Hughes had decided that he must write his account of the *Graf Spee* and the *Altmark* 'at the rate of ten thousand words a week';[50] and he began this punishing schedule on Saturday 27 April. Working long hours (often till after midnight), within twelve days he had completed his first two chapters and embarked upon a third.[51]

The new novel had been provisionally entitled *The Navy is Here* (a popular saying since the publicity given to the release of British prisoners from the *Altmark*); and Hughes began it brilliantly, with a vivid descriptive passage which takes us from the shores of the West Indies to the violet coast of South America, and on to a river in the Amazon delta where the *Ajax* lies at anchor. The date is 30 September 1939; and the scene changes to the deck of a merchant steamer, the *Clement*, bound for the port of Bahia on the South American coast. Seeing a shape coming towards him across the sea, the captain assumes that it is the *Ajax*. Then a plane flies over and circles above the *Clement*; and the captain is holding up a board with the ship's name upon it, when 'To his utter amazement, two bullets struck him in the hand'.[52]

The *Clement* is destined to be one of the first victims of the *Graf Spee*; and as Hughes continues his story, with capture succeeding capture, there are numerous striking passages where his novelist's eye is used to the full, as in this paragraph describing the launching of the *Graf Spee*'s seaplane:

> First the few blinding, sickening moments of acceleration as the giant catapult was fired: then steady flight. Below him the pilot saw the long swell flattened, even from a few hundred feet of height: the deep blues and purples of the sparkling sea spread out smooth, like the sheen on damask, without a visible ripple: a great beautiful saucer of colour, stretching to its clear distant rim – yet tipping and swerving, it seemed, while he was steady! It was often like that the first few seconds in the air – till you got your balance! Hard to believe it was you who tipped and swerved, while the world stayed sober.

However, the narrative is too often weighed down by mountains of factual detail; and Hughes had only reached the ninth page of the fourth chapter, when he became disenchanted by what he was doing. The idea for the book was a good one; but he realised that he could not write it at this speed and have any hope of its being equal in merit to its predecessors.

At the same time, financial pressures were becoming acute. His book of children's stories, *Don't Blame Me!* had been accepted for publication by Chatto & Windus (and would appear towards the end of the year); but their advance was not substantial enough to satisfy his bankers. Back in January, Barclays had agreed to increase his overdraft limit from £400 to £500 for the next six months;[53] but by the end of March they had sent him a letter pointing out that the debit on his joint account with Frances now stood at £576.[54]

Clearly, unless *The Navy is Here* could be successfully completed by the middle of the summer (as Diccon had intended), and then attract a substantial advance, the outlook was bleak.

However these personal worries were insignificant when set against the serious dangers which threatened to overwhelm the entire United Kingdom. The twilight or 'phoney' war had ended early in April with Hitler's invasion and conquest of Norway; and on 10 May, German armies had invaded Holland and Belgium.

This crisis had led to Winston Churchill replacing Neville Chamberlain as Prime Minister; but his first two weeks at the helm of public affairs had seen Holland and Belgium go down to a terrible defeat; the French lines broken decisively at Sedan; and the British Expeditionary Force driven back upon Dunkirk. Fortunately Hitler had not pressed his advantage; and by 2 June a quarter of a million British soldiers had been brought home across the Channel.

Despite this successful evacuation, the British position looked increasingly desperate; and it was at this critical juncture in his country's affairs that Hughes was offered two jobs, either of which would enable him to serve his country (without compromising his reputation as an author), while also staving off financial disaster.

On 5 June, Hughes received a letter from the Ministry of Labour asking whether he would be prepared to be considered for a post in the Public Information Office in Tunis, at £350 per annum;[55] and he was still investigating this prospect in London[56] when two days later (by the same post as a further communication from Barclays about his overdraft),[57] there arrived a letter from his friend Jack James, Lleky's godfather, and one of 4000 Admiralty staff whose departments had been evacuated to Bath not long after the outbreak of war.[58] Subject to the satisfactory completion of three months' probation, Hughes was offered an appointment as a temporary assistant in the Administrative Service, at a salary of £450 per annum.[59]

By the time Hughes had returned to Laugharne on 13 June, Italy had entered the war on the German side; and when the following day Paris fell to the German armies, the defeat of France as a whole seemed imminent and certain, that of Great Britain not immediately imminent, but highly probable. In the circumstances, Hughes would have preferred to be fighting for his country on the high seas. Since that was impossible, a position with the Admiralty was undoubtedly the next best thing.

First Frances had to be persuaded. Knowing of Diccon's nervous breakdown back in 1926, of his poor physical health during 1938 and the early part of 1939 and of the nervous depression which had troubled him as recently as the autumn of 1939, she was intensely worried that the constant pressures and confinement of administrative life would undermine his health. She may also have been saddened by his having to lay *The Navy is Here* to one side. However, Diccon was determined, and she very reluctantly gave way.[60]

On Sunday 16 June Hughes therefore wrote to Jack James telling him that he would be reporting for duty to the Admiralty Offices in Bath on the following Wednesday. At long last he had found a wartime role for himself; and for the next five years he would play the part of a civil servant with enormous thoroughness, energy and distinction, making his own aims and ambitions entirely subservient to the common good.

CHAPTER 25

My Cupboard is Bare

Before setting out for Bath on 19 June 1940, Diccon Hughes had to put his house in order.[1] The first priority was to move Ursula (now acting as the children's governess) to a place of safety: although she was a refugee, she was also a German, and he was afraid that the 'hooligans of the town' might attack her.[2] In the event, a place was found for her in Llanfrothen where, after surmounting some early difficulties, she 'made a little niche for herself' in the local community.[3] The next priority (scarcely less urgent) was to settle Frances and the children somewhere secure. Diccon's first thought had been to send them to Parc;[4] but as the threat of a German invasion loomed larger in his mind, he told Jack James: 'I wish to God I could get Frances and my own children out of the country.'[5]

Once again, Diccon was determined; but this was an issue upon which Frances was not disposed to give way, and they 'fought it out' for some time. She said that she would be 'ashamed' to desert her country; and that it did not seem right to escape simply because they could raise enough money to do so. He replied that the good of the children must come first. Eventually the matter was 'practically settled' in favour of a move;[6] Frances agreed to apply for passports for the children;[7] and on reaching Bath, Diccon began finding out what other arrangements it would be necessary for him to make, and whether any help was available for British refugees when they finally made landfall in New York.

It was all far more complicated than he had expected, and telegrams were soon racing back and forth across the Atlantic. There might be some help from a 'Refugee Committee' – but only if he would allow his children to be separated;[8] temporary visas could be granted for up to twelve months – but only if the American Embassy were to be persuaded that Frances and the children had enough money to support them for that space of time.

Various arrangements were made, including a financial guarantee; but the process dragged on through July and August,[9] and eventually Frances decided that she would remain in the United Kingdom. If things became too difficult in Laugharne, she might take the children up to Cumberland;[10] but she was definitely not prepared to go abroad, and that was that. Possibly she was swayed by a worried letter from Mrs Johnson advising her that the children's good might not be best served by an American education, as Robert, Penny and Lleky were not only 'nicer than any American [children] I have ever seen', but had 'more initiative, intelligence & imagination'.[11]

In the meantime, Richard Hughes had established himself in Bath. He had expected to be employed at first in some purely clerical rôle, 'licking envelopes' or whatever; but he was attached as personal assistant to the head of one of the departments.[12] That head was responsible in his turn to Diccon's friend Jack James who, with the rank of Assistant Secretary, was in charge of the Bath section of the Priority or 'P' Branch. This was an independent secretariat branch within the Admiralty, under the overall control of Harry Markham, the so-called 'Principal Priority Officer', who was based in London. The task of 'P' Branch had originally been 'the rigid administration of production priorities by carefully graded certificates'; but it had gradually become[13]

> the administrative pivot of a very much wider field of work, wherever the Admiralty supply machinery came into contact with the ever more complex central machinery of Government and with the other supply departments.

'P' Branch had also begun to represent the Admiralty on manpower questions; and was involved in the allocation of raw materials, and 'concerned', as Hughes explained at the time,[14]

> with all the broad problems of organising ship-building, armament, and supply: and I am now a sort of chief-of-staff and intelligence officer to the head of [my] branch. One of my special pigeons is extracting the meaning from a large complexity of facts, and trying to express it simply enough to be comprehensible to My Lords. It is rather like that time when I tried to write on Wave-mechanics for twelve-year-olds: only stuff for admirals, of course, has to be put far simpler than that. The head of my branch puts the distinction between an admiral and any other boy whose education stops at fourteen rather nicely. It is the difference, really, between the use of the word 'stop' as a transitive and an intransitive verb. The ordinary boy's education 'stops'. The education of the boy who is sent to Dartmouth *is stopped*. These reports are not easy: for in spite of their limitations Admirals object to being written down to even more than children.

Diccon had only spent two and a half weeks at 'P' Branch (which operated from the premises of the former Fernley Hotel), when there was a considerable diversion from his normal routine. He had been asked to think of somewhere[15]

> for the Admiralty to evacuate to, should London suffer an invasion. He soon realised that all the obvious towns had already been earmarked by other departments. So he suggested wildly that the Admiralty should occupy all the hotels clustered round Lake Windermere, connecting together departments on different sides of the Lake by naval launch.

His suggestion was taken so seriously that shortly before nine o'clock on the evening of Saturday 6 July Jack James put his signature to a letter of authority which read:[16]

> TO ALL WHOM IT MAY CONCERN
> Mr Richard Hughes is engaged upon work for
> the Admiralty and should be granted every facility.

Diccon was then sent for, handed his letter of authority, instructed to carry out an immediate reconnaissance and (as he reported to Frances)[17]

> put in a large car with a little comic clerk in a crumpled suit and a bowler hat, and a hatchet-faced naval chauffeur, and pointed north. We drove continuously . . . all that night, steering (in the absence of signposts) by the stars . . .

Much of Sunday (he told another correspondent) was spent[18]

> tramping over the banks and braes . . . We looked like something out of a nightmare of John Buchan's. The suspicion we excited was continuous, and embarrassing: we were pursued even by police in wireless-cars: and owing to the strictly secret nature of what we were up to I had been instructed not even to show my Admiralty pass until actually lined up to be shot, far less explain my business!

On Sunday night they managed a few hours sleep, 'and started off again' (he continued his letter to Frances) on

> Monday morning at six. I got back here, to the office, at nine in the evening and sat down at once to write my report. It is now being typed by two all-night typists and blear-eyed draughtsmen are copying my plans and maps: when it is ready (which will be about 4.30) I have to present it and be cross-examined on it.

Diccon added that he was 'thriving on it'; and he commented on 'the curious mixture of speed and slowness in the Civil Service'. Routine work could take months; but 'when a hustle is decided on – can they run!' He pointed out that the entire scheme, when completed, would be 'about the size of a volume of the encyclopedia', having been 'produced, so far as I can judge, by 24 men, with relays of typists working day and night, and two draughtsmen, in three days!'

When he had first arrived in Bath, Diccon had been allocated a temporary billet in the Christopher Hotel. There he experienced his first air raid, and had to spend three hours in the cellars, listening to the distant 'faint bumping of explosions'.[19] A few days later, when he had found a more permanent billet in a house on the outskirts of Bath, there were two more air raids; and he spent a night in the coal-cellar. However, Diccon soon stopped taking much notice of air raids, whether he was in his billet, or working late at the office.[20] The German raiders were simply passing overhead on their way to the docks at Bristol; and it was only very occasionally that a stick of bombs was jettisoned over Bath by an enemy aircraft that had missed its target and was running for home.

Soon after moving into his new billet, Diccon had asked Frances to pack up his dinner-jacket and other evening clothes, as 'these blighters dress for dinner!'[21] This was not as tiresome as it sounded. 'Even in war-time', as Lance Sieveking pointed out, Diccon's 'gift for finding himself a perfect nest in a perfect tree had not deserted him'. He had been billeted on the seventy-nine-year-old novelist and man-of-letters Horace Annesley Vachell, a 'noble-looking old gentleman, with bright eyes, and a lively genial expression', who 'dressed with the dandified distinction of a past age', and who 'lived in style in a magnificent and very beautiful house known as *Widcombe Manor*', with an Italian fountain in its forecourt, and both a Greek temple and a Roman bath in its grounds. Not only did Vachell insist upon dressing for dinner each evening, but (according to Sieveking)[22]

> he also said: 'We will do our best to drink everything in my cellar before the damned Huns can get it – not that they ever could – '
> The war raged on, and for many months, every evening when he could get away from the Admiralty Offices ... Diccon, in conventional evening clothes, dined with his aged host, waited on by equally elderly servants, gradually emptying bin after bin of the finest chateau-bottled vintage-year wines which Vachell had laid down at one time or another in his long life.

Diccon told Lance: 'The port, particularly ... was something that had to be tasted to be believed.'

The Vachell household was not only hospitable, but one in

which the importance of the literary life was taken for granted. After watching an air raid one evening (a 'pretty sight', with 'full moon and searchlights and distant gunfire'), Vachell had commented: 'I believe what England needs at the present moment is a really first-class light comedy – it's tragic the Haymarket should be shut at times like these!'; and within twenty-four hours, as Hughes reported to a friend, his elderly host was 'already in the middle of the second act'.[23]

Hughes's own literary work had come to a virtual halt. His official working week was fifty-four hours, and 'in practice I don't think any week I have worked less than seventy, and one week it was ninety-seven'. So for the time being, at least, there was no possibility of continuing with work upon *The Navy is Here*: though Hughes had by no means abandoned the project;[24] and he sent the first three chapters to Mrs Johnson for her opinion.[25] 'From your rather grim sentence', she replied, 'I gather you don't think much of it . . . So far it holds me, but there is a danger of dragging unless another complete contrast is coming at once.' She added that 'the great surprise to me is the psychology. It is as if you had suddenly come to reality and had grown out of some unreal fantasy. Do you understand?'[26]

A number of other literary loose ends remained to be tidied up. In August, there were discussions with his publishers about rival illustrators for *Don't Blame Me!* After canvassing opinion, Hughes chose Eichenberg at the expense of Mervyn Peake, of whom he wrote:[27]

> His disgust with animate nature is intense enough to engender in him a considerable skill, where that skill can be used for its expression – just as lust enables a sailor to draw a woman's breasts to perfection, though he hasn't the faintest idea how to draw her face.

There were also the usual flurries of correspondence about the rights to one or other of his works; and later in the year, Hughes was given a performance pass to the BBC studios in Cardiff, from which a dramatised version of *In Hazard* was broadcast.[28]

Hughes had joined 'P' Branch when it was in the middle of a period of reorganisation; and on 9 September, returning to the office at Bath after a short leave with his family, he found that the new arrangements were at last in place. 'P' Branch had officially become the '*Production and* Priority Branch'; while he himself had been promoted to be 'Head of the General Section of "P" Branch';[29] and had been moved into 'a new room, tiny but luxurious', as he told Frances. He was particularly pleased that it had a carpet, to which (with his new Civil Service awareness of such matters) he understood that he was not yet officially entitled.[30]

To begin with (while his literary persona predominated) Diccon had felt out of his element in the Admiralty: 'I never thought to find myself a civil servant', he wrote to Mrs Johnson in July;[31] and at first he was rather shocked by the way in which Jack James imposed his will: 'roaring like a lion', as he reported to Frances, 'and biting everyone, and people are beginning to touch their foreheads'.[32] However, he had very soon adapted to his new environment, and had thrown himself so wholeheartedly into his new role that the changes in his manner and appearance were dramatic.

Lance Sieveking, who was then working in Bristol for the BBC, was invited over for lunch one day in late September,[33] and noticed that even Diccon's beard had apparently been formalised,[34]

> so that it should be more in keeping with his new dignity. Up to then it had been a distinctly untidy and straggly affair. But by curling the two sides outwards with merciless severity he eventually forced the whole of the lower part of his face to confirm and support the impression created by his black trilby (or Eden) hat, his neat collar and tie, his official brief-case, and his tightly-rolled umbrella.

'For he never does anything by halves', Sieveking added; and 'from having been quite one of the most unconventional characters one could hope to meet', he had become, 'almost overnight, a Higher Civil Servant of the most correct kind'.

September 1940 had seen a sustained attempt by the Luftwaffe to break the power of the Royal Air Force, preparatory to a full-scale invasion of England. By 6 September, in what Churchill christened 'The Battle of Britain', 'the scales had tilted against Fighter Command';[35] and after Hughes had driven back to Bath on Sunday 8 September, he reported to Frances that he and his companion 'had a much interrupted journey . . . owing to the invasion scare. Ferocious Home Guards poking guns at us every four hundred yards'.[36] Then on Sunday 15 September came 'one of the decisive battles of the war'.[37] A massive day-light air attack was successfully repulsed; and two days later Hitler decided to postpone the invasion indefinitely.

The chief danger to Britain now lay in German armed raiders and U-boats cutting off our essential supplies from abroad by sinking merchant shipping in the Atlantic. As Churchill would later write, by the end of 1940 'The Battle of France was lost. The Battle of Britain was won. The Battle of the Atlantic had now to be fought'.[38] It was a battle which could only be won if the Royal Navy had the necessary ships and weapons of war; and it was in working to supply those necessities that Richard Hughes spent much of the next three years.

The labour was unremitting. 'I struggle upwards all day from under a pile of work that goes on growing', Diccon told Frances at the beginning of October 1940. He had only 'had one "day off" since my leave – & then was called back in the middle. However, I am beginning to get the organisation of my section into shape now'.[39]

He had been hoping to return to work on *The Navy is Here* once his section was running smoothly; but the pace of work never let up, and extra duties soon rushed in to fill any spare time.

In March 1941, for example, at the request of the Ministry of Information, Hughes composed what he described as a 'clarion-call to the Croats'. Speaking as the mouthpiece of his old friend, the dead Croat leader Stjepan Radić, he begged them to remain loyal to what had been since 1929 the kingdom of Yugoslavia.[40] However, within that kingdom the Croats had continued to be repressed by the Serbs with such ferocity that Hughes's appeal fell on understandably deaf ears. In April 1941, Hitler invaded and rapidly overwhelmed Yugoslavia; and Croatian Fascists, placed in effective control of a new independent kingdom of Croatia, were soon perpetrating the most bloodthirsty massacres upon their former Serbian masters.

Elsewhere, too, the war went badly for Britain. In particular, the German U-boat fleet was rapidly increasing, and each month was sinking some 300,000 tons of shipping on the high seas.

To make good these losses in the most efficient manner possible, production 'war rooms' had now been set up at the Admiralty offices both in Bath and London. In those rooms, facts and figures for 'shipbuilding and a number of critical stores, for manpower, [and] for the location of Admiralty industries' were 'available at a glance in the form of graphs and maps';[41] and in May 1941, no doubt in an effort to improve the flow of accurate information into these 'war rooms', Hughes travelled the length and breadth of the country, visiting Admiralty area offices in London, Glasgow, Belfast, Newcastle, Sheffield, Manchester, Birmingham, Cambridge, Bristol, Reading, Cardiff and Nottingham.[42]

It was during that month that the Royal Navy scored a signal success in hunting down and sinking a superb modern German battleship, the *Bismarck* (which had earlier sunk the battle cruiser

Hood); but later, during November and December, severe losses in the Mediterranean included the *Ark Royal* and the *Barham*; while the battleships *Queen Elizabeth* and *Valiant* were crippled by Italian frogmen while they lay at anchor in the harbour of Alexandria.

Fortunately by the end of 1941 a major German offensive had become bogged down in the Russian winter; and the United States had entered the war. In the short term, the Admiralty faced increasing problems in the Pacific, where on 10 December both the battleship *Prince of Wales* and the battle cruiser *Repulse* were sunk by Japanese aircraft; and in the medium term, the U-boats would prove still more deadly, sinking as much as 500,000 tons of shipping a month during 1942; but Britain no longer stood alone; so in the long term, at least, there was now a gleam of hope.

To begin with, Frances made a determined effort to remain in close contact with her peripatetic husband: in the late autumn of 1940, for example, taking Penny with her,[43] she spent two nights in a Bath hotel. 'As for your coming here', Diccon had written to his wife beforehand, 'it is too lovely to think of';[44] and some months later she repeated the experiment, this time taking Robert.[45]

Official periods of leave were few and far between. Hughes was at Laugharne over Christmas 1940; but his next leave was not until seven months later in July 1941, followed by further leaves in November 1941 and July 1942. All were so brief that on one occasion, as Penny recalls, she and her brother and sisters 'led a newly-borrowed Shetland pony upstairs to show it to [their father, who was in the bath at the time], because it seemed the only way he would have time to see it'.[46]

Diccon's long absences made Frances dispirited and prone to a string of minor illnesses; and when in mid May 1941 Dylan and Caitlin Thomas returned to Laugharne with their son Llewelyn, she was so pleased to have close friends at her side that she put them up in the Castle House, where they stayed very happily for several months.[47] Soon after their departure, at the beginning of August, Caitlin wrote to Frances 'I hope not to leave Laugharne for ever and advise you not to move';[48] but by that time (as Caitlin knew) Frances was weary of Laugharne.

In particular, she wanted her children to mix in better society. They were sent away to boarding-school as soon as possible, which took care of eight months of the year; but she was determined that her daughters should spend their holidays somewhere where it was unlikely that there would be a repeat of such Laugharne experiences as being offered a farthing by older children to 'pull down your knickers and show us your bum'![49] Frances also wanted to be closer to Bath, so that it would be possible to see more of Diccon; and she began to think seriously about moving back to her Gloucestershire roots.

By the time of another unofficial weekend with Diccon in January 1942, Frances had come to a decision; and she told Diccon that she intended to make a move before the spring. It was a happy weekend, described by Diccon as 'wonderful . . . I wonder when we shall ever [enjoy] one so good'; but Frances and Diccon were now leading separate lives for much of the year, and for long periods they completely lost touch with each other. 'Darling', Diccon wrote to Frances in March 1942:[50]

> Where are you now? I never know well where you are going to be or being, but I suppose if I wrote to Laugharne at least you will find it when the hall is turned out now there are no whitewash buckets for it to fall into.

Apologising for the fact that it had been 'a bad long silent month' from him, he explained that life had been

> rather hellish all round. I am having a weekend with Thomas now, but up till now the only time I have had off has been a hurried visit to the Johnsons on my way back from London.
> Most nights I have been writing till after 12. One day they nearly sent me to America disguised as a statistician but they didn't try very hard so it was fairly easy to scotch the idea, I said I wasn't a statistician & anyhow they had jolly well better send a bachelor.

He added thanks for 'all these lovely seegars. As they had a birthday card though I'll wait till my birthday [his forty-second]'. And then, after wondering whether he would be able to be with his family on that day, he broke out:

> Oh Lord how I hate this life, thinking about things all the time which have merely a practical value. Shall I ever get my mind clean again? Scrub it in sea-water & bleach it in stars and hang it up to dry in front of very warm love (don't let it go out, please: please: put on plenty of coal & poke it.)

A moment later, and he was once again the composed civil servant, ending his letter simply with the words, 'Time, now', and signing himself with his customary monogram, a large D with an H tucked away securely inside it.

Diccon's outburst may have owed something to a letter which he had recently received from Storm Jameson, the novelist and at that time president of the writer's organisation PEN (which Hughes himself would join in 1946). She had written to tell him that she was editing a volume of modern writing which would be published in the USA, and sold for the benefit of the American Red Cross. Would he help? She reminded him that 'you once gave me caviar for tea', and mentioned that she had already secured agreement from Edmund Blunden, T.S. Eliot, E.M. Forster, Robert Graves and others.[51] After sitting on the letter for more than a month, Hughes finally replied that in present circumstances, he could do nothing. 'My cupboard', he lamented, 'is absolutely bare.'[52]

Within less than a month, however, Diccon had written a letter which Frances found so 'remarkable' that she had it copied for Louisa 'and parts of it for others. Do show it to whom you like', she told her mother-in-law. 'Diccon writes so rarely for the public nowadays, but this seems to me something really good.'[53] It was his account of the blitz of Bath.

In the early part of 1942, the *Luftwaffe* had been concentrating its resources upon the Russian front, and attacks on British cities had become infrequent. It was now that Sir Arthur Harris of Bomber Command began his attempt to pound the Germans into surrender. His first target (on 28 March 1942) was the port of Lubeck, almost half of which was utterly devastated. Next came a heavy raid on Rostock; and then 'the first "thousand-bomber"' raid on Cologne, when 13,000 houses were destroyed and 469 people killed. The result was that Hitler 'ordered reprisals: a series of attacks on undefended English historic towns'.[54]

The first target of these raids was Exeter (attacked on 23 and 24 April); and then came Bath.

On the night of Saturday 25 April, Diccon was 'on fire-watching duty on the roof of the Empire Hotel, the highest building in Bath', which meant that he had[55]

> a perfect view of the whole thing. I can't help it; it is a most beautiful and magnificent sight. Up high like that you know nothing of humanity, except a shout or so: this city laid out under you in moonlight, and suddenly huge fires full of majesty and compounded of strange colours mounting round you. The twinkle of A.A. fire high up.

The first wave of aircraft carried incendiary bombs, designed to set Bath alight, and make it an easy target for the second wave, which arrived a few hours later with high-explosive bombs. 'They were dive-bombing', Diccon continued his account,

> swooping down almost as low as I was, and then as they rose

again firing from their rear-guns, downwards like a stream of golden rain. Flares hung on parachutes in a great ring round the city to guide them in. They were dropping very heavy stuff mostly, and showers of sparks and flying pieces would go into the air higher than the Abbey Tower. The sounds too: there's beauty in them. The terrific Cr-r-rump of heavy bombs. The Whoosh of the diving planes followed by the whistle of the bombs, then the tatta-tattat of the machine-guns.

There was no direct hit on the Empire; though once (Diccon reported) 'a big one landed on the opposite bank of the river with blast enough to tip me on my back'; and sometimes 'the whole building twisted and wriggled'; but he decided that 'up on the roof . . . was the safest place. There were machine-gun bullets of course, but they used tracer so you could see them coming and shelter behind a chimney-stack'.

When on Sunday the German bombers returned, Hughes was with the Vachells; and he 'spent the night in the garden in case incendiaries fell on the roof, so I could see'. But this time, he had a very different story to tell. 'Seeing Bath burn from the *outside*', he declared, was[56]

> horrible, not beautiful at all. An enormous smoke turned a bloody brown with flames stretching from the station right up through that lovely city to the top of the hill above the Circus. A filthy thing to see. A dog-fight lasting about three seconds & a small black thing dive into the hills – I don't know if it was our plane or [a] raider. Poor brute. Most of the night I spent in a nook in the garden wall to be out of the way of flying stuff, but once I walked . . . to get a clear view of the city.
>
> It seemed to be burning from top to bottom – I felt sure no fire brigade could get it under control. But they did. This morning there is hardly a fire still smoking. But the Assembly Rooms are gone. The Regina Hotel is gone and most of the Railway station. And houses here and there, everywhere (whole patches of the town in some parts) – the amazing thing, I can't get over it, is that the whole city isn't burnt. It is curious how many churches have gone (though not the Abbey).
>
> You don't think of Bath as a city of spires – till you see them with their different lovely shapes standing out black against the glowing smoke, the only masonry you can see in it: there seem to be scores and scores of them.

Monday was 'the most lovely of spring days'; but Diccon's nerves had been badly affected. He described to Frances:

> The sky full of aeroplanes circling round . . . I find I don't like their sound. I don't really like bangs, even banging doors.

Or anything that whines. It was alright that way the first night, because I was responsible for the building I suppose and had 3 other men & four girls to look after.

But on Sunday night (because he was not in the middle of the worst of it), 'the whole thing [had seemed] more a human matter and beastlier'.

Some 417 men, women and children had died in the raids; and everyone feared that Monday night would see a still more massive attack. By the evening, as Diccon reported,

> there was an extraordinary tension in the air. I went home to dinner and as I came back to go on duty met an endless procession of people clutching coats and rugs, off to sleep in the fields and woods. A rumour had got about, which they all firmly believed, that loud-speaker vans were being sent round by the police, telling everyone to be out of the city by dark as it would be laid flat this time.

However, there was no raid that night; and on Tuesday morning 'all the people had a queer look on their faces. I couldn't make out what it meant at first: then I realised for the first time since they were children, probably, they were acutely aware that they were alive'.

A couple of weeks before the blitz of Bath, Diccon had made one of his infrequent visits to Laugharne (the first since the previous November), and had been distressed to find Frances in bed with tonsillitis so acute that (as he told his mother)[57]

> her throat was actually bleeding. The little Nursemaid and equally youthful housemaid were both away with 'flu, and Frances had nobody but Miss Roblin to look after the house, herself and all 4 children. Miss Roblin is a dear but she is over 70, vague and getting more vague and likely as not to bring up breakfast at 3 o'clock in the afternoon. Moreover, the electric pumps have been out of order for the last 4 months, so . . . every drop [of water] has to be carried into the house in a bucket.

Before he returned to Bath, Diccon had managed 'to fix up a certain amount of daily help'; though it was distressing to have to leave Frances still unwell (though 'getting better') and Robert in bed 'with a temperature of 101 . . . but I expect', he wrote to Louisa, 'it was only a feverish cold'.[58]

Frances had now planned her move to Gloucestershire, where her Bazley relatives would be at hand in emergencies of this kind; though she already knew that the move would make it very little easier to see her husband, at least for the time being. For it had already been confirmed that Diccon was to be called away from Bath to take up new responsibilities in London;[59] and no sooner had she effected her move (to Barrow Elm, Quenington, where she would be sharing a house with a Russian family),[60] than he was gone.

CHAPTER 26

A Sweet Flavour

By the second week in June 1942, Richard Hughes was securely established in rooms at 77 Elizabeth Street in Chelsea, where his landlady 'had spent her working life as a governess, and ruled her household of civil servants as she had ruled in her nursery schoolrooms for so many years'.[1] One of his fellow lodgers was the remarkable Harry Markham, who at the age of forty-five was Principal Secretary to the Admiralty; and the two men quickly became friends.

Markham had been 'the first appointee and architect of the "P" organisation';[2] and Hughes had served under him briefly on first joining the Admiralty back in June 1940. Later, Diccon would vividly recall:[3]

> the first time I saw him — two meetings had clashed, but he was contriving to attend both, and somehow managed to be in his chair whenever he was really needed. I was struck then by his extraordinary rapidity of thought, and by that bodily vivacity which made his movements always a pleasure to watch.

They had met only on official business, before Markham was promoted to the rank of Principal Secretary to the Admiralty, which more or less confined him to London.

There Markham faced a task rendered 'peculiarly difficult' by having to use so many 'temporaries', men who were 'not only untrained but often congenitally unsuited' to their work. However, as Hughes recalled, 'he helped us patiently . . . supported us loyally . . . [and] in general, he contrived to make us feel that he trusted us and depended on us equally with his professional colleagues'.[4]

Hughes thought Markham so exceptional, both morally and intellectually, that he was inspired to a new 'conception of what the Civil Servant at his best might be'; and he also very much enjoyed Markham's company when they began walking to work together in the mornings: about a mile and a half from Elizabeth Street, threading their way north-westward to the south-eastern side of Buckingham Palace, and then striding across St James's

Park towards the Admiralty. 'Off-duty', Hughes later commented,

> many Civil Servants seem to let their minds go into a tortoise-
> sleep, as if they had to husband all their wits for the office: but off
> duty Harry's broad intelligence seemed even wider awake, it had
> an edge which he was constantly sharpening. My morning walks
> across St James's Park with him were an extraordinary solace to
> one who was in exile from any normal way of living.

Hughes added that Markham's 'quick wit . . . and his lightness
of heart could on occasion (I am thinking particularly of the dark
middle years of the war) make him the very best of midnight company'.

Under Markham's influence, the transition from author to civil
servant became more complete, and he almost ceased to regret that
there was no time for him to write. On meeting Robert Graves's son
Sam in Trafalgar Square one day in June, Diccon learned that 'Robert
says he has written 4 bad books this year. Surely', he commented in
a letter to Frances, 'Surely it's better to do like me & write none, for
the nonce'.[5]

In the same letter, Diccon explained that his new head of department (who had been off sick for a while) was still absent,

> so my illicit grandeur is prolonged. Perhaps I shan't enjoy being
> demoted again when he does return! Authority has a sweet flavour
> even to someone so unauthoritative as me. Probably best to have it
> like this in one brief dose, over before there is time for the flavour
> to go rotten – as it soon would, with me.

No reservations of this kind were apparent in public where (as Lance
Sieveking was later told) Hughes now became 'such a stickler for the
Correct Way of Doing Things that he struck terror into many of his
colleagues who had spent all their lives in the Service'.[6]

Jocelyn Herbert, who met Diccon by chance at a London railway
station, was so struck by the change that she could hardly recognise
Hughes as the man whom she had last seen leading a writer's life
at Laugharne.[7] Even Diccon's own eight-year-old daughter Penny
felt quite uncertain (when she visited him at his rooms in Elizabeth
Street) about 'whether he was in fact [her father]. He wore a smooth
pin-stripe suit and a bowler hat, and his umbrella and his moustaches
were neatly rolled. He did not even smell of the familiar pipe-smoke'.
So she decided that she would 'privately' keep 'an open mind . . . see
how things turned out'; and meanwhile, she would 'tread warily'.[8]
When however he came to see her at Deudraeth Castle, her school
in North Wales, she recognised him at once.

Deudraeth Castle stands on a peninsula above Portmeirion, looking out over the sandy estuary of the Traeth Bach, and had many advantages beside its superb setting. The children's former governess Ursula was on the staff; Diccon's friend Teddy Wolfe was the art master; it was only a bus-ride away from 'Granny Hughes', with whom Penny (and later Lleky) could spend their half-terms; and above all, it was run on libertarian lines of which both Diccon and Frances thoroughly approved.

They also liked the headmaster; and Diccon in particular got on with him so well that once (as Penny learned) the two men sat up talking until 'It was too late for my father to go back to wherever it was he was staying', and the headmaster 'brought down mattress and blankets, and made a bed on the floor by the fire in what had formerly been the drawing-room'. However, Diccon overslept; and when he finally woke up and opened his eyes,[9]

> he found himself at the focal point of a maths lesson. He was within three feet of the blackboard. Whenever the shy young master needed to check the work of the boys on the far side of the room, he had to step over my father and his mattress.

In the circumstances, Diccon very sensibly 'decided that the only thing to do was to pretend to be asleep until it was over'.

Since Admiralty business had begun regularly taking Hughes up to London, he had run into a number of old friends: some of them in the most unlikely places. Back in March 1942, stepping into a lift at the Admiralty GHQ, he had been astonished to find himself with Susan Williams-Ellis who was on the staff 'drawing maps and things'.[10] 'Dear Diccon', Susan wrote shortly afterwards, 'How absurd meeting you like that, & how very nice!' She asked him to ring her on his next visit, and added: 'Toby Henderson is in London too at the Ministry of Information. She asks me to send you her love and wants to see you next time you appear.'[11]

Diccon also met Peter Quennell, who was then editing the *Cornhill Magazine*; and a few days later he received a letter from Peter's ex-wife, the former Nancy Stallibrass.

She was now Nancy Fielden, having married a wealthy Yorkshire industrialist by whom she had one child. Home was Grimston Park, a country house where in pre-war days she had efficiently managed a large staff of servants — now reduced, very exasperatingly in her view, by conscription.[12] Almost as formidable an Englishwoman as her mother had once been (though with a very much warmer heart), Nancy had no intention of allowing anyone as ill-bred as Herr Hitler to put a stop to her regular visits to London with his air raids and threats of invasion; and she told Diccon that she would be in London at the Mayfair Hotel 'next Saturday . . . *do* come and have a drink'.[13]

Early in December 1942, when Hughes had been stationed in London for less than six months, there was another administrative reorganisation within 'P' Branch, which led to his returning to Bath with a significant promotion. From now on, the Principal Priority Officer (still the head of 'P' Branch) was to be stationed in London, where he could be in daily contact with the Controller who was the fountain-head of production authority. Hughes had been posted back to Bath 'for purposes of local control . . . as [the PPO's] vicar, with the problems of adapting the techniques of statistics to the needs – and speeds – of administrative purposes particularly in mind'.[14]

By this time there was good news from North Africa where General Montgomery, commanding the British Eighth Army in Egypt, had just inflicted the first major defeat upon the Axis forces at El Alamein, and was driving General Rommel's Afrika Korps back towards Tunisia. In Russia, too, a successful counter-offensive had been launched against the German forces. Two German armies had already been encircled at Stalingrad, and would soon be forced into a humiliating surrender.

From the Admiralty's point of view, however, the situation still looked extremely serious. Far away in the Pacific, the Americans had won important victories against the Japanese at Guadalcanal and Tassafaronga; but in the Atlantic, the North Sea and the Mediterranean there had been no effective counter to the submarine menace. Huge tonnages of shipping were being lost, while the German operational strength had risen from 91 to 212 U-boats during the course of the year.

Making the most efficient use of the shipyards therefore remained of critical importance; and (on first returning to Bath), Hughes's principal task was to find a method of assessing 'the overall load imposed on any given shipyard by its particular mixed programme of warship construction in various stages of completion'. He achieved this by instituting 'a close actuarial study' of the man-hours expended[15]

> on different classes of warship at different yards, and the number of men employed together on a ship at any given stage in its progress. By numerical comparison with the calculated resources of the yard, overloading could be assessed and the extent to which completion-promises were likely to be kept or broken could be fairly confidently forecast.

In this way, a 'somewhat crude', but useful 'unit of production' was evolved, which made the necessary numerical assessment possible.

Armed with this assessment, Hughes would occasionally repair to London; where he had to argue the case at the very highest level[16] for the Admiralty being allocated scarce resources. Once, well-prepared, but a little alarmed by the prospect of presenting his findings to no less a man than the Prime Minister, Hughes listened carefully while his opponent went first. He need not have worried. Churchill waited until the other man appeared to have finished, and then asked if there was anything to add. 'I don't need to hear any more, in that case. I award it to the other side', he concluded, and closed the meeting without Diccon having said a word.[17]

With his new responsibilities, Hughes continued to work long hours, with little time for family life. 'I've no news', Diccon wrote to Frances in February 1943. Most of his energy was being directed into[18]

> trying to make this extraordinary team pull together. They range in age from 61 to 13, in sex from male to female, in interests from beer and hunting to mathematics and the Social Revolution, in beauty from hideous to mildly pleasing: they work like niggers and they fight like cats and there are now 114 of them, & probably I shall wake up one morning and find we have been abolished.

He managed a weekend with Frances later that month at Barrow Elm (after which she found that she was pregnant for the fifth time); but when in March he heard that his mother had suffered a minor stroke, it was impossible for him to leave his desk. However, reasonably good news of Louisa's condition reached him from Ursula, who reported on 10 March that Mrs Hughes was[19]

> in her usual courageous and cheerful spirit and seems to talk without effort, also the paralysis seems only hindering but not painful. She was pleased about my visit and leads a careful and sensible life, that is breakfast in bed, lets N. light the fire, no gardening and early to bed ... She is rather sensitive about the disfigurement which is really not at all bad and I had a hard time to talk her out of it. It is only sad to see her dear, familiar face in that state.

When in June it was the children's summer half-term, Louisa was still not well enough to have any of them to stay with her;

and Diccon gave himself a few days' leave and joined his family at Parc. There he roamed with his children 'about that valley that meant so much to him'; and he took them 'to the deep pool below the waterfall and started to teach us to swim ... Long after we were all too cold to stay in any longer he was still swimming to and fro under the waterfall, enjoying the battering of the water'.[20]

Despite the sadness for Diccon of seeing his mother so much less active, it was a far happier visit to Parc than his previous one in the early days of the war. On returning to Bath, and receiving a warm letter from Frances, Diccon replied that he was now 'too fit to sit in an office all day', and added: 'Darling, I miss you quite as much as you do me.'

Gradually it became clear that the events of November 1942 had seen the tide of war turn in the Allied favour. The U-boats remained to be dealt with. By March 1943 their numbers had reached 240, and in that month alone they sank more than 625,000 tons of shipping. However, this proved to be the zenith of their success. The following month, for example, Captain Peter Gretton, Commander of the B7 Escort group, consisting of six ships which he had trained with the use of radar 'to become expert U-boat hunters' fought[21]

> an epic battle around the outward-bound convoy ONS5. The conflict raged over nine days and nights and thousands of square miles of ocean; by May 6, 40 U-boats had been in contact and 12 merchant ships sunk.
>
> Shortage of fuel forced Gretton's own destroyer, *Duncan*, to leave prematurely ... But his remaining escorts, with a support group reinforcement, sank six of the attacking U-boats; [and] two more U-boats were lost in collisions.

This was one of a number of critical convoy battles which were fought and won by the Royal Navy in the spring of 1943. During May, the U-boats sank fewer than 265,000 tons of shipping; and having lost in that month alone a total of 43 U-boats, Admiral Doenitz withdrew the remainder of his fleet from the North Atlantic until the autumn. It was a major strategic victory; and during the whole of the remainder of the war, there would only be three months when the U-boats sank more than 100,000 tons of shipping.[22]

Elsewhere, the fall of Tunis on 7 May led to the rapid collapse of the remaining Axis forces in North Africa; on 10 July the Allies invaded Sicily, which they had conquered by 16 August; and 3

September saw the beginning of the invasion of Italy. The pressure on 'P' Branch was now intense. The invasion of Sicily had been held up for a month because of a shortage of transport ships and specialised landing-craft; and still more would soon be required for the next major assault upon the European mainland: at the 'Trident' conference in Washington in mid May 1943 it had been decided by Roosevelt and Churchill that the following May they would land 29 divisions upon the coast of France.

The strains which this placed upon the Admiralty as a whole were immense. Not only would 'more men [be] needed to man the landing-craft than the entire pre-war personnel of the Royal Navy', but many of those landing-craft still had to be built, not to mention the special support-craft from which covering fire could be given while the landing was in progress; and other specialised equipment including two complete pre-fabricated harbours, known as 'Mulberries'.[23]

In November 1943 (the month when on the 21st Frances Hughes gave birth to Owain, her fifth child and second son),[24] there was a further reorganisation within the Admiralty. A new head of 'P' Branch was appointed, with headquarters in Bath, but without the title or duties of Principal Priority Officer; and Hughes returned to London, where he once again set up home in Elizabeth Street, and where he became the new PPO. In this capacity he was[25]

> in close touch with the Controller (the fountain-head of pro-duction policy) but, being of equal status with the head of [P] branch, he had no longer formal authority over the branch to which he must inevitably look for nourishment and for carrying out the Controller's wishes. Indeed, he had no longer any staff at all under his direct control, except his official deputy – and even that control he shared with the head of the branch.

This new arrangement was unsatisfactory, and Hughes would later describe it as 'a sort of one man job where most things had to be done by myself if they were to be done at all'.[26] However, it did mean that for many months he had 'a finger in almost all economic and industrial and some strategic questions directly or indirectly affecting the British Navy'. Being in charge of priorities in the British shipyards, meant[27]

> constant juggling with the needs of the forthcoming invasion of Europe, of the Japanese war, of the anti-U-boat campaign, and of the constant load of merchant ship repairs so that, in the face of a steadily diminishing labour force, nothing should come too seriously adrift.

Although his duties kept him occupied for an average of ninety hours a week during the first five months of 1944, Hughes found it enthralling to be at the heart of preparations for the invasion of France, now code-named 'Operation Overlord'. This was an unprecedented undertaking, involving the largest invasion fleet in history, including 1200 fighting ships, 10,000 planes, more than 4000 landing-craft, more than 800 transport ships, together with hundreds of amphibious tanks; and involving the landing on 'D-Day' of 156,000 men on the beaches of Normandy.

Since Hughes was far too busy for private correspondence, almost no record survives of this period of his life, though one fragmentary glimpse later became part of his family folklore. It is the cold, grey dawn of 6 June 1944. The previous morning, the invasion had been postponed for twenty-four hours, because of the worst channel weather for twenty-five years. But now at last we are in the early hours of 'D-Day'; and after a week of sleepless nights, Richard Hughes sits on the wing of an aircraft, waiting for news that the invasion has begun.[28]

German resistance was fierce when Allied troops began landing on the Normandy beaches; but by nightfall 'sizeable beachheads had been established on all five landing areas, and the final campaign to defeat Germany was under way'.[29]

'Now this stupendous thing is at last launched', Hughes wrote to his wife a few days later on 11 June, 'I think there is a chance of getting home for a long week-end.'[30]

Hughes's major work was over; but the war in Europe still had another eleven months to run, that in the far East fourteen. In August 1944 he was moved back to Bath, as acting head of 'P' Branch. Here he cut an impressive figure, 'imposing as a rock-cut temple Buddha' (in the words of one of his personal assistants, Dawn Macleod) as he 'sat alone in the Principal's Office, censing himself with snuff'.[31]

The volume of work remained considerable; and Macleod recalls that when the clerks and typists had gone home, he would send for her, to begin 'prolonged consideration of reports which I had drafted to enlighten the Board of Admiralty about the progress (or lack of it) of shipbuilding and other naval armament supplies'. She was chiefly struck by:

> What endless pains he took! Often I wondered if those brassily efficient Sea Lords in Whitehall ever guessed how much electricity was burned, far into the Bath night, while the distinguished author sat meditating with pen poised above my script. I felt like a novice monk under instruction by the Dalai Lama. The sonority of his

voice took me back to the awesome noise heard in childhood . . .
[of] a huge Tibetan trumpet.

'What about a semi-colon here?' he would intone. 'You prefer
the comma. Very well. Would not this long sentence sound better
if bisected?' Macleod writes that in this manner Hughes taught her
a great deal, 'yet with . . . exquisite consideration'.

It was during 1944 that the thirty-eight-year-old John Betjeman
joined 'P' Branch. After serving with great success as the UK Press
Attaché in Dublin from 1941–1943, Betjeman had spent a less
happy time in the Ministry of Information in London before being
posted to Bath, and no one seemed to be quite certain why he had
been transferred. So much did he loathe being confined to an office
that, as Dawn Macleod relates, 'he drooped and wilted day by day,
appearing to be on the brink of suicide or at best an early Victorian
decline'. Hughes, who was aware of his fellow poet's misery,[32] soon
devised a 'plan for lessening the gloom'. This, as Macleod tells us,
consisted of

> lunch-hour strolls around Bath's crescents and squares, whose
> architectural merits were instantly reflected by the poet's counte-
> nance. His sagging cheeks puffed out, pink and soft. His wet-spaniel
> eyes developed glamorous sparkle. Without delay he launched us on
> a sea of inspired commentary, so that we soon lost our bearings and
> all track of time. On one occasion the punctilious Hughes disgraced
> himself by forgetting an appointment with a V.I.P.
>
> We must have made an odd assortment of characters . . .
> Richard Hughes, in harmony with his erect posture and stately,
> un-modern pace, was invariably well barbered and tailored, while
> roly-poly John Betjeman looked as if he slept in his clothes . . .
> [and I], slightly awed and wholly enthralled.

On April 30 1945 Hitler committed suicide in the ruins of the
Chancellery in Berlin; and on 4 May the German forces formally surrendered at Montgomery's headquarters on Luneburg Heath. Four
months later, after atomic bombs had been dropped on Hiroshima
and Nagasaki, General MacArthur accepted the surrender of the
Japanese.

The Second World War was over; and in mid October 1945
Richard Hughes left the Admiralty and began living with his wife
and family at Barrow Elm in Gloucestershire.

The break was very sudden.

'I have spent the last five years in the Admiralty with my seat
on a stool and my nose to the grindstone for up to ninety hours
a week', Hughes told a correspondent. He was not at all certain

what his next step would be, but he expected to be at Barrow Elm, on and off, for most of the winter.[33]

At the end of October, when his appointment as Temporary Principal officially came to an end, he received a formal letter from the Admiralty 'in appreciation of the valuable services which you have rendered to the Department'.[34] So impressed had they been by his administrative abilities (Diccon had after all proved to be his father's son) that he had been called to London and offered the governorship of South Georgia and the Falkland Islands. No doubt this plumed-hat appointment would have been only the first step in a distinguished career set amid declining imperial splendour, with a knighthood and perhaps even a seat in the House of Lords at the end of the day.

However, Hughes had declined (just as he had declined the more prosaic offer of a job in the peacetime Civil Service).[35] First and foremost, he believed, he was a writer. He had been ready and willing to serve his country in an emergency; but now felt that he should return to his proper work. Before leaving London, he visited the room which he had kept on in Elizabeth Street, and 'took off what he regarded as his uniform'. Lance Sieveking found it there[36]

> several years later, abandoned, and for all I know it is there still: a rather worn black trilby hat, a black tie with a faint grey stripe, a black jacket, and a tightly rolled umbrella by Briggs, on the correct gold band of which was engraved 'Richard Hughes, Laugharne Castle, Carmarthenshire'.

Sieveking comments that Hughes had now 'shed the civil servant for ever'; but although he had symbolically cast off the trappings of office, his loyalty to the service remained, and in due course would involve him in a labour of love which occupied (and in Frances's eyes wasted) a good deal of his time over a period of several years.

Hughes was awarded the OBE in the January 1946 New Year's Honours; and when his medal arrived through the post, his daughter Penny noticed that although she and the other children were 'pleased and proud', Diccon 'seemed sad'. He explained it to them as 'a childish sadness ... because he hadn't been summoned to Buckingham Palace to have it presented'; but she later believed that there was also a 'sadness for the work he had left behind him'.[37]

There was a more important residue of his wartime experiences. Hughes's personal life had been substantially disrupted for five years while he was caught up in great historical events; and his renewed religious faith led him to believe that all this must have been for a deeper purpose than the obvious one of making his own personal contribution to the war effort. If his principal function on earth was to be a writer, then these experiences must have been given to him so that he could write about them.

There no longer seemed any point in returning to the story of the *Graf Spee* and the *Altmark*: there were already published accounts of the Battle of the River Plate; and the immediate post-war years would see a continuing flood of novels, memoirs and histories of the war. Instead, Hughes had begun to think on a much grander scale.

Before leaving the Admiralty, he had told the Johnsons that 'he was storing up a lot of material in his head';[38] and he had conceived the idea of a long historical novel of his own times, in which the private lives of a number of fictional individuals would intertwine with the history of the rise and fall of Nazi Germany. At its heart, he knew, there would be a study of the human predicament, and especially of the perennial conflict between good and evil; but for the time being there was only a vague shape forming somewhere at the back of his mind, and it would be almost ten years before he was ready to begin the writing. In the meantime, he had a private life to rebuild, and a family to support.

CHAPTER 27

Trying to Adjust

'I am clear of the Admiralty now', Richard Hughes had explained to Iris Barry in November 1945, 'and starting to write again, but the wheels are still uncommonly rusty, the gears shriek, and I should like to take the whole engine down and get it checked.'[1] After five years of relative freedom from financial worries, Hughes had once again opted to live by his pen; and he decided that the way to begin (as he told Amabel Williams-Ellis) was to put himself 'through a course of a few months' book-reviewing'. Even that was a terrible struggle. 'The first review', he declared, 'was ground out word by word with sweat and blood, and another was so bad that the Lit. Sup. very sensibly wouldn't print it.'[2] He felt that 'every time his pen started to travel over the paper what he wrote sounded like the report for a Select Committee'; and 'many a time', as his children passed his study door, they heard 'weary groans' from within.[3]

When Diccon emerged from his study, he had to confront a wife and family whom he had hardly seen for the past five years; and to begin with he found family life so claustrophobic that he thought seriously about escaping abroad for a holiday with one of his former colleagues in the Admiralty.[4] However, Frances was determined that her husband should once again take his full share of family responsibilities; and shortly before the Christmas holidays began, she went away for a week, leaving Diccon in sole charge of two-year-old Owain, 'the most cheerful and unruffled creature'; and five-year-old Kate, 'very sweet when she likes'. Dearly though he loved these two children, Diccon not unnaturally found them 'as helpful as little djinns out of bottles'[5] while he was trying to work; and Penny recalls that when she and the others returned home, her father 'tended to be remote and rather distracted' when they were all together.[6]

After a while, Diccon decided that the best way of re-adjusting to family life was by spending time with members of the family on an individual basis; and so, one by one, he took each of his three older children on long walks during which he gradually built up a much closer relationship with them.

Lleky, at nine, was said by family friends to have her father's 'enquiring mind at the same age';[7] eleven-year-old Penny was 'in a state of unending bubbling happiness'[8] — later she recalled how much she enjoyed Diccon treating her 'as an adult friend, not retiring behind his age so as not to give himself away, as so many parents do';[9] while thirteen-year-old Robert (now head boy of his preparatory-school) had acquired several of his father's enthusiasms, and especially his love of the sea.[10]

But although Frances understood the 'absolute necessity of sea' for both Diccon and Robert, and although their present living quarters were extremely cramped (as they were still sharing Barrow Elm for much of the time with another family), she was adamant that there should be no return to Laugharne. Quite apart from her worries about the effect upon her children of living cheek-by-jowl with the Laugharne townsfolk, she had somehow got it into her head that it was an enormously unhealthy place in which to live.[11]

To begin with, Diccon resisted. But there was no doubt that Frances had often been unwell in the Castle House; there was no doubt that Robert had suffered very badly from bronchial troubles during his last two years at Laugharne; and even in Gloucestershire (where the family had been much more healthy, on the whole), Lleky was liable to occasional bouts of asthma.[12]

So eventually Diccon had to give way, and agree that a subtenant should be found for the Castle House, which was to be let furnished while they looked for a home elsewhere; but the emotional cost of the conflict with Frances had been high. As he continued struggling not only with reviews but with a 'satire, couched in the form of a bird-watcher's diary', he was suddenly overcome by a wave of nervous exhaustion, which he generously attributed not to the difficulties of adjusting to family life, but to 'five years accumulated fatigue'.

Sitting down weakly in an armchair as the exhaustion swept over him, Diccon found that it took him 'about an hour to summon up sufficient energy to light my pipe';[13] and for days on end he could do 'nothing but sit and stare at the fire or, as a major expedition, go out to see whether one of our four hens had laid an egg'.[14]

The worst of this exhaustion was over by Christmas; though Diccon was still not at all well, and later commented to Amabel Williams-Ellis that Frances's success in 'spread[ing] the revels — stockings and Church only on Christmas Day, with Christmas dinner on Thursday and the tree on Friday' had certainly 'lightened the impact — but by the same token spread it'.[15] It was not until mid January 1946 that he was fit enough for serious work; and then he began preparing for a lecture tour (his subject was 'The Crying Need for Poets'), which he had promised to undertake in

South Wales at the beginning of February on behalf of the Workers' Education Association.[16]

After so many years of working long hours under extreme external pressure, it was hard to be self-disciplined when that pressure was removed. Towards the end of January, Hughes worked out a daily timetable for himself. It worked well; but only for the first day (Tuesday 29 January), when he recorded in his diary that he had made 'Some progress on lecture notes and short story'. On Wednesday morning he 'Failed to begin work till 11.0', and made 'next to no progress'. And after a party that evening, the following day he simply recorded: 'Hangover: walked all day with Penny.' So on Friday 1 February he had to set off for Swansea with his lecture notes still incomplete.[17]

Fortunately, being away from home, and appearing before a friendly public as the well-known author of *A High Wind in Jamaica* and *In Hazard*, revitalised Diccon. After nine days of travelling and seven lectures, he sent Frances a short but cheerful letter, telling her that he would like to have written at greater length,[18]

> but there hasn't been time, what with having hot arguments with T.V. officials about inspiration & grocers about psychoanalysis & octogenarians about tap-dancing and ministers about painting late into the night, & then generally an extra impromptu engagement of some sort the next morning before moving on to the next place.

He added that he would go to Bath for a few days to see old friends, and collect what he had left behind with the Vachells, before returning to Barrow Elm.

By this time the Castle House at Laugharne had been successfully sublet for twelve months (in the face of considerable opposition from Mrs Starke, the owner, who at one point had asked for the lease to be surrendered);[19] and early in March Diccon and Frances moved with Kate and Owain to Lyulph's Tower, where they had once spent such a happy Indian summer, and which was now loaned to them until the end of May. It was there that Diccon received an important letter from Harry Markham, who had become one of Owain's godfathers. 'My dear Diccon', it began:[20]

> You may remember a discussion which we had one morning on the way up to the Admiralty on the subject of a preliminary naval history . . . if the Board should ask you to consider undertaking this work, would your reaction be favourable? From what you said on that occasion I should assume so.

Diccon replied that his 'interest in the subject' had 'certainly not grown any less'; but he hesitated to commit himself before knowing (among other things) 'what fraction of my remaining mortal span goes into the project?'[21] There the matter rested for the time being; but in due course it would return to haunt him.

The hunt for a permanent home continued. Although the Castle House was now out of the question, Diccon tried for several months to find a house up in the hills behind Laugharne, somewhere which would satisfy Frances by being healthy and remote from ordinary Welsh society – 'the more isolated the better' was how Diccon described their requirements – and yet would be within half an hour's drive of his boat-shed on the Grist.[22] A house in South Wales would also keep him a safe distance from his mother for most of the year.

Louisa, who now spent the winters in a London flat, still lived in Gelli for the rest of the year. In the summer of 1945, suffering from 'spasmodic asthma', she had been so ill that, as Charles Johnson had reported, 'the walk to the gate & back is as much as she can do – and sometimes more'.[23] No one expected her to be able to return to Gelli the following spring; but she was an indomitable old lady, and by mid April 1946 she was once more in residence, and writing her son a very characteristic letter to mark his forty-fifth birthday. 'My dearest', she began,[24]

> I hope this will reach you in time ... Alas! I have no gift to send you, nothing to mark the event it celebrates – my love you always have ... Did you see the letter Penny wrote to me? It has given me a good idea of your amusements among the lakes and fells, but I suppose there is work also.
> ... There has been a lot to do to get even approximately straight, & I am feeling rather tired – I have asked the doctor to come and see me next Sunday & try to see if he can do anything to rid me of this pain in my back which comes on when doing any work ... I have also started ... some night cough & am staying indoors, but I think it is getting better ... Everyone asks if you are coming to Parc ... Anyhow very much love always & all possible wishes for your happiness now and to come
> Mother
> P.S. Don't think I am ill – only it takes a bit of getting used to work again after so long a holiday – I am quite all right and taking precautions.

This combination of possessive love and moral blackmail was all too familiar; yet the summer at least must be spent somewhere near Portmadoc, where *Tern* had been laid up during the war. She had been housed 'in one of the empty slate sheds on the wharf'; and although by this time 'Her planks had shrunk so that you could see daylight through her seams', and 'her paint was flaking to powder ... basically she was still sound'; and Diccon was longing to get her back into the water.[25]

When Frances absolutely refused to return to Parc (which would have been the obvious solution), Diccon began making enquiries elsewhere; and at length Clough Williams-Ellis offered to rent him Môr Edrin, a large white house on the other side of the estuary from Portmeirion.

Môr Edrin had no electricity or mains drainage, but was in other respects a perfectly ordinary house. Penny, who saw it for the first time at the start of her summer half-term, recalls finding that:[26]

> Downstairs there were tiled floors, upstairs bare polished linoleum, and the sunlight bounced back from their clean surfaces – a plain and scrubbed and shipshape house. It was sparsely furnished with iron school bedsteads, and chairs and tables ... on loan from Clough.

Its setting, however, was far from ordinary: indeed, it was 'almost an island'. The road which had led to it along the shore when it was built (just before the First World War) had been partially swept away by a tidal wave in the twenties, and now ended at a farm some distance away along the estuary. So the only land access fit for vehicles was by a grass track which led uphill towards another farm, and was practically impassable in wet weather.

Diccon seemed happy at being back in Wales; and very soon, he was busy in Portmadoc harbour, 'getting *Tern* ready for the sea'. The engine was past repair, and *Tern*'s bottom needed re-caulking, 'but I am glad to say' (he told the yachtsman Uffa Fox, with whom he occasionally corresponded on such matters) 'that, apart from a few deck planks, I haven't found any soft wood in her in spite of her long neglect'.[27] Jack Rowlands came up from Laugharne to lend a hand; and at the beginning of the summer holidays Robert and Penny were 'allowed ... to come to Portmadoc in turns', to live on board while they 'help[ed] with the repairing and repainting'[28] before she was sailed across the estuary to Môr Edrin.

Life that summer seemed to Penny to be 'full of celebrations and gaiety', with numerous parties at Portmeirion; and with her parents 'renewing friendships from pre-war days, and making new ones'. Old friends included Amy Graves, who was much excited to meet Diccon Hughes 'on holiday ... with his wife & five children

& a big black beard';[29] and new ones the novelist Arthur Koestler, then living with his wife Cynthia some fifteen miles away at Blaenau Ffestiniog. He invited Diccon and Frances to celebrate his 'coming of middle-age' (as he described his fortieth birthday) on 7 September, telling them that[30]

> Jim Wyllie is coming too and will give you a lift here and back, unless you both prefer to spend the night here, or get so tight that you are compelled to do so, which I sincerely hope will be the case.

A week or two later, the Koestlers came to dinner at Môr Edrin, leaving their car at the place where the road ended further up the estuary; and, as Penny recalls, Arthur Koestler and her father argued passionately[31]

> about the writer and political involvement. Diccon felt there was no reason to suppose that the novelist would be more politically acute than the next man, but there was no doubt that he had far more than average ability to persuade people to believe things – and to mislead them. To use this ability for political ends was irresponsible. Koestler on the other hand argued that this was just an excuse for being hopelessly lightweight and right-wing as far as politics were concerned. For him the whole purpose of writing a novel was to persuade.

Neither of them would give way; and Robert and Penny 'sat enjoying the dispute till unluckily we were noticed and sent to bed'. The next morning, they learned from Diccon that he had set out at about one in the morning to escort his guests along the foreshore back to their car, and

> the tide had come in. They argued heatedly as they walked, with Diccon [presumably followed by Cynthia] weaving uphill into the rocks and shale, and Koestler downhill, till he was up to his waist in the sea, without ever stopping talking.

A few days later, Koestler sent Hughes a spare copy of his great political novel *Darkness at Noon*, with a good-humoured covering letter telling his host: 'We both enormously enjoyed our dinner despite your implicit attempt to drown me on the way back.'[32]

In mid October 1946, *Tern* was sailed to Portmadoc for further repairs, and Diccon and Frances once again set up a temporary home in Lyulph's Tower, where they remained for the rest of the autumn and winter. However, they had enjoyed their stay at Môr Edrin so much that they began considering the prospect of living permanently in that large white house above the estuary, where they seemed free to choose as much isolation or good company as they wished.

It would mean giving up Diccon's idea of living somewhere within easy reach of Laugharne: but better to be at the water's edge than somewhere miles inland. It would mean being closer to Louisa: but only for part of the year. It would mean spending a good deal of money on modernisation: but if that made Frances happy, it would be money well spent, and in any case her trust fund could meet the bill. Above all, the beautiful location would be a continual source of pleasure and inspiration to them both.

Once Clough Williams-Ellis had agreed in principle to their buying Môr Edrin, Diccon and Frances called in a London surveyor who reported that the property was 'well constituted and in reasonably good condition'.[33] This encouraged them to proceed with the purchase; after which they instructed the London architects Maxwell Fry and Jane Drew to examine Môr Edrin and suggest how it might best be modernised.

It was fortunate that this gave them something to which they could both look forward; because their months in Cumberland were far from successful.

Hughes had arrived at Lyulph's Tower full of optimism. Early in November 1946, writing a third-person resumé of his career, he described his current position as: 'settling down to work (after a year spent in "getting the grime of administration out of my soul") on a new novel which will take him, he expects, from five to ten years to write'.[34] This was to be the long historical novel of his own times, culminating with the defeat of Nazi Germany. But as the weeks went by, all his efforts at beginning this novel proved to be utterly fruitless, and his optimistic attitude was difficult to sustain.

To make things worse, there was dismal news from New York. After years of silence, Pamela Bianco wrote to announce that her mother Margery had died after a stroke back in 1944; that her father Francesco had died more recently of bronchial pneumonia (not long after what sounded suspiciously like a suicide attempt on the New York subway); while she herself, after spending the war in a leather factory, was now illustrating children's books, but leading an increasingly reclusive life, with her fourteen-year-old son Lorenzo as her only constant companion.[35]

Still more depressing news came from London, where Harry Markham had died at the age of only forty-nine. Forgetting his recent unflattering words about 'the grime of administration', Hughes immediately wrote to Markham's brother, telling him that it was[36] a tragic thing for the Admiralty and his country, to have lost his services at the height of his usefulness. He was unquestionably a war casualty. I told him once that spending himself at the rate he was doing he would never live out his normal term in office: he answered almost fiercely that he didn't care, provided he saw out the war.

For himself, it was 'a severe loss'; and he felt 'very sorry that ... Owain, whose godfather he was, will never know him, for I cannot think of anyone better fitted for that relationship, which is generally taken so lightly nowadays'.

At home, financial worries re-appeared. As in pre-war days, Diccon found himself writing to Barclays Bank with the declared object of arranging things so that Frances should be encouraged to limit her expenditure – £80 a month was the figure which he now had in mind;[37] and without his salary from the Admiralty, his own income was once again extremely modest. True, 1946 had seen fees for book reviews, for his hostile report on a biography of John Skelton for T.S. Eliot (Hughes suggested that it needed pruning of much speculation),[38] for a wireless broadcast by the BBC of *A Comedy of Good and Evil*,[39] and for a 25 cent reprint in New York of *The Innocent Voyage*;[40] but these were hardly enough to support a wife and five children, especially when it had been decided to educate those children privately. Robert was now at Eton, and Penny at Westonbirt: though fortunately they had both won awards which considerably lessened the cost.

January 1947 saw a cheerful visit from Amabel Williams-Ellis; but not long after her departure (as Diccon told her) the household at Lyulph's Tower underwent a series of illnesses 'almost à la Werzberg'. It began with four cases of influenza, and one of mild rheumatic fever; then a temporary nurse, called in to take charge while Frances was away, 'had a stroke a few days after arrival and we have her upstairs tucked up in bed for the next few weeks at least'.[41]

Hughes remained unable to make any progress with his new novel; and his consequent sense of frustration spilled over both into his family life, where it made him 'tired and irritable',[42] and into his public life: giving his address as the United University Club and writing as 'Richard Hughes, O.B.E. (Author of *A High Wind in Jamaica*)', he sent the editor of the *Daily Telegraph* a fierce attack upon the 'derisory nature' of tax relief for children 'to those in the middle income ranges'. In his view, relief was being given where it was least needed, 'to those whose children are getting their education at State expense'. He argued that under the system then obtaining, only a handful of middle-class parents could[43]

> afford to give their children paid educations out of income if they have families of more than two or three. The practical effect of this is that at the top of the professional and managerial classes – where you would expect to find stock best worth breeding and children best worth educating expensively – present taxation keeps families below a net reproduction rate of unity (which requires three or four children) and these very strains must die out in a generation or two.

'It is a system of crazy selective breeding', he concluded, 'by which brains are being bred out of the race.' (Three years later, Hughes would argue for a substantially increased family allowance, and for a reform of the taxation system which recognised that 'There is no absolute figure for the cost of children: it is proportionate to the parents' earnings'.)[44]

Another matter of public interest in which Hughes became involved in the spring of 1947 (while he and his family were still at Lyulph's Tower) was the campaign of the National Council for Civil Liberties against MI5. It was a campaign with which Diccon strongly disagreed, and he wrote to the Secretary of the NCCL protesting:[45]

> The Communist Party today is avowedly rather in the position occupied by the Catholic Church in England in Elizabethan times: Communists have (or *may* have) what one can only call a religious loyalty, over-riding their loyalty to the State and to their Service.

He therefore believed that security screening by MI5 was absolutely necessary.

Despite Hughes's symbolic gesture in leaving his bowler hat and umbrella behind in London, the Public Servant in him evidently remained strong (perhaps too strong at that time for the Writer to regain control) and he retained a profound loyalty to the service and its traditions.

CHAPTER 28

Môr Edrin

In the spring of 1947, Diccon and Frances moved into Môr Edrin, which would be their joint family home for another twenty-nine years. There was still no electricity, and the bulk of their funiture would remain down at Laugharne for another year and a half; but by mid May an Aga cooker and an automatic boiler had been installed, and Diccon wrote to Maxwell Fry that 'the cook carols all day'.[1]

Diccon himself had been planning to enter the Bristol Channel Pilots' Race a second time,[2] when he was unexpectedly asked by Storm Jameson of International PEN to attend their annual congress, which was to be held in Zurich at the beginning of June. Clough and Amabel had also been invited; and so (leaving Frances behind to look after Kate and Owain), the four of them travelled together to Switzerland,[3] where they stayed at the Hotel Bellerive on the shores of Lake Zurich. Diccon, much impressed by the mountains, sent Frances a postcard telling her: 'I wish I hadn't left it so late in life to come to Switzerland for the first time.'[4]

Diccon returned to find that *Tern* was repaired; and that in his absence Frances had arranged for the *Sir John Perrot* to be sent over from Portmadoc.[5] Both boats were much used during the summer, whose highlight was a visit from Diccon's old friend Joseph Brewer.[6] However, the atmosphere was not quite so festive as it had been the previous year. Diccon was still unable to write a single satisfactory page of the novel which he repeatedly told enquirers was 'brewing';[7] and Penny recalls: 'Those of us whose rooms were above the back door acquired a whole new vocabulary of swear-words from listening as he chopped kindling-wood barefoot before getting dressed in the mornings.'[8]

Penny had come home for her summer holidays 'to find gaping holes where there had once been solid walls on the ground floor, and two Resident Architects'. Maxwell Fry and Jane Drew, who had arrived to supervise the alterations, had run up against a shortage of cement; so work had come to a halt, and they stayed on as guests for several weeks. Warm-hearted and enthusiastic people, they soon became family friends; but 'I had no idea at that time', Penny wrote years later, 'that as well as installing one new lavatory in a house in North Wales they were building a university in Ibadan, a hospital in Persia, and a summer capital in India'.[9]

Another feature of the summer was the increased extent to which Hughes called upon his children for practical help. Three years later (in his article 'Make Parenthood Possible!'), Hughes would point out that it was taken for granted[10]

> that children should be an economic burden on their parents, as if that were a law of nature: whereas in fact it is characteristic of less than the last 100 years. In a simple agricultural community, children start contributing in work towards the cost of their keep as soon as they can walk, and a very few years later they more than pay their own way.

He wrote admiringly of 'the little girl herding her father's geese on the common', or 'the village carpenter's small son sorting old nails for his father': 'happy and healthy', both of them, and 'learning a means of livelihood'; and he had certainly decided that there was nothing to prevent his own children from making a similar contribution, at least during their school holidays. So, as Penny recalls, they would be 'sent out to dig cockles. But it takes a lot of cockles to feed hungry teenagers', so there was 'hunger, and a lot of tedious slow work', though 'in general we were happy'.[11]

The children also 'spent many hours scavenging along the Bar'. Their finds ranged from a tangle of rope (which their father 'spent hours and hours disentangling and coiling', and which was still in use thirty years later) to a dead seal whose blubber (they had high hopes that it would 'provide the family with fat to cook with, and oil to burn in the lamps, for the whole of the coming winter') they only succeeded in melting down into a foul-smelling oil. In later summers, Diccon regularly set out nets in the estuary, in which they caught[12]

> as many as twenty pounds of fish a day, when the weather was right. Some of them, Diccon carried across the sands to Portmeirion and traded for bottles of wine, some we stored in an outside sink with a dripping tap, and sand and mud, to keep them alive till we were ready to eat them.

But the fishing-nets meant more work: one of the children

> had to be out by five in the morning daily in summer, to bring in the fish before the gulls devoured them. And the whole family had to turn out to pick seaweed off the nets, an infinitely tedious job once the first romance had worn off.

Moreover there were times when Diccon's patience wore thin; and

Penny (after Diccon had roared 'You blasted fool!' at five-year-old Owain, who had begun some unauthorised painting of the boats) secretly named him 'Roaring Forties'.

It might have seemed that Diccon's life had 'become completely overrun and its patterns destroyed . . . by the demands of supporting a large family'; but, as Penny observes, 'it was not so much that his attempts at self-sufficiency kept him from writing, as that he snatched at any distraction available, because for complex reasons he could not write'.[13]

One major project, providing Môr Edrin with its own electricity supply, was begun in the early autumn of 1947, while Frances was away in London. She returned to discover 'electric light to turn on in the kitchen, pantry and larder. It is too wonderful,' she told Louisa.[14] Diccon had created a 12-volt circuit, served by a half horse-power Tiny Tim petrol generator and a Lucas Freelite windmill set together.[15] The arrangement was that the windmill (a propeller at the top of a 40-foot mast) generated power either for immediate use or for storing in three car batteries; and if the wind failed and the batteries ran down (which took about four days), then the Tiny Tim served as a reliable back-up.[16]

Frances was less pleased with the amount of time which Diccon had spent during her absence on stocking up with logs. He had done this by buying an outboard motor, attaching it to the *Sir John Perrot*, and sailing it over to Portmadoc, where he filled it with logs until[17]

> the gunwale was nearly under water and only an inch of free board all round and so came home again. It took the farm boys in a cart five journeys to get it from the shore to the woodshed . . . Diccon is very happy because . . . it only took half a gallon of petrol.

'Altogether', she concluded, 'I daresay it cost 24 hours of man labour.'

Probably Diccon's most time-consuming feat was to dig out 'a channel for the boats a hundred yards long' (which he did single-handed); and then to build beside it a causeway made of 'slabs of salt turf, laid on top of waste tins and bottles. There were several hundred of them neatly laid in rows, each carefully weighted'.[18] Anything rather than confront those blank pages in his study.

The strain of Diccon's novelistic impotence was immense. It involved continual financial worries of a kind with which Frances found it hard to cope, probably because she knew that there were times when she could not help making matters worse. Her 'feeling for visual beauty' was admirable in that it inspired her (for example) to 'arrange branches and flowers together in a jug in a vigorous way, so that the rooms were a blaze of colour'; but it also meant that (even when money was short) she would only buy the very best; and in the closing months of 1947, Frances was almost obsessed with what she described as 'the beautification of our home'.[19]

Since in practice the family was now almost wholly dependent upon her private income, Frances limited herself to repainting some of the walls, and buying a few new rugs or cushions; but even this was more than they could afford; and reality caught up with her in January 1948, when she received a letter from Barclays Bank pointing out that during the last eighteen months she had overspent her drawing account by £750.[20] The pressure suddenly became greater than she could bear, and a doctor had to be summoned.

Later in the year, Frances would explain to a friend: 'Like many others, I got tired after the war, and moving the children 4 times, and finally getting settled in here.' At the time, realising that she was on the verge of a serious nervous collapse, her doctor sent her away for three months, telling her that for the first four weeks she must do absolutely nothing.[21] Even so, before she left Môr Edrin, Frances could not resist writing to Nancy Nicholson and asking her to buy for 'the three [eldest] children' some extremely expensive 'Welsh rugs with fringes ... with yellows and greens' which she remembered having seen 'in Blandford Street or Dorset Street, near Gloucester Place'.[22]

Fortunately, while Frances was away, there was news of a timely windfall from a family trust[23] whose capital had reverted to Frances and her surviving brothers and sisters on the death of the beneficiary. On 6 March, writing to Barclays, Diccon explained that his wife's health had broken down; but that she would shortly be receiving a 'legacy of about one fifth of £12,000'.[24] The promise of this money kept Barclays happy until the autumn, when Frances received a cheque for £2363 10s. 0d., which immediately reduced their total overdraft from the colossal heights it had then reached, to a comparatively modest £80.[25]

In the meantime, Frances's illness had given Diccon a considerable jolt. Outwardly (once he had dealt with the task of feeding their increasingly large menagerie of chickens, ducks, dogs, cats and pony) he busied himself much as usual with interesting but non-essential tasks, such as ordering himself a new coracle,[26] or applying to the Admiralty for a warrant enabling him to fly (from *Tern*) the Blue Ensign and the marks of the Yacht Club.[27] Inwardly, however, he

The Hughes children in April 1938: 5-year-old Robert, 4-year-old Penny, 20-month-old Lleky.

Hughes photographing Frances with Kate, born April 1940.

Penny, Robert and Lleky in wartime.

Hughes (with Owain, born November 1943) standing in the hall of Môr Edrin with the architects Maxwell Fry and Jane Drew.

Hughes and Frances at Swedish conference, 1952.

At Môr Edrin, before a portrait by Augustus John.

Photographed by
Harold Strauss.

The lighter side.

In the dining-room, Môr Edrin.

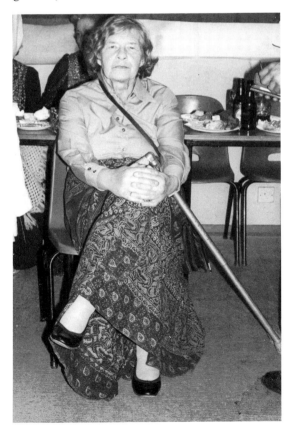

Frances Hughes at an exhibition
of her paintings.

Diccon Hughes as a patriarch: (back l. to r.) Rachel, Richard Minney, Zanni Papastavrou, Lleky Papastavrou, Tom Minney; (mid) Robin Minney, Robert Vassili Papastavrou, Diccon, Frances, Penny Minney; (front) Sheila, Claire, Jim Minney, Kitty Papastavrou, Hugo Minney.

By the estuary, 1975.

On the mud-flats below Môr Edrin with a rowing-boat.

A late portrait.

seems to have done much serious thinking both about Frances and about his work.

So far as Frances was concerned, he realised that the least he could do was to draw her into the more agreeable aspects of his career. Perhaps it had not been altogether kind of him to dash off to Switzerland the previous year for the XIXth congress of International PEN – in effect a holiday with some of his friends – leaving her behind so soon after they had moved house. At all events, he decided that they should both attend the XXth congress; and on 31 May, some weeks after Frances had returned to Mor Edrin, the two of them sailed on the MS *Batory* for Copenhagen.[28]

There they were wined, dined and fêted, and made some interesting new acquaintances (including Evelyn Waugh and his wife, with whom they dined once or twice);[29] and when the conference was over, they spent a few peaceful days in Jutland before sailing for home. But the best thing for Diccon about the holiday (as he told his mother) was that Frances had 'thoroughly enjoyed herself & seems quite recovered'.[30]

However, he realised that the legacy was only a reprieve from financial worries of a kind which might precipitate another crisis; and since his novel would not write, he began racking his brains for alternative sources of income.

Earlier in 1948, Hughes had been reminded that he had some skill as a playwright, when his *A Comedy of Good and Evil* was revived at the Arts Theatre, with the Welsh actor Hugh Griffith playing the part of Mr Williams. Although it was a box-office failure it attracted excellent reviews (one critic wrote that it seemed 'destined to be one of those plays which retains for ever its power to attract and to amuse');[31] and the BBC liked it well enough to televise it on two successive nights in March, which introduced Hughes's work to a new audience, and also earned him the useful sum of £40 per performance.[32]

Not long afterwards, Hughes signed an agreement with the Druid Press of Carmarthen, who were to publish an edition of 1000 copies of *The Sisters' Tragedy*;[33] and in May news came that the New York producer John Gassner (who had already signed an agreement to produce *A Comedy of Good and Evil*) wished to add songs and fresh dialogue, and transform the *Comedy* into a musical he would call *Minnie and Mr Williams*.[34] Hughes was intrigued by the possibilities; he and Gassner began corresponding as soon as the PEN conference was over; and by 21 July he could tell Gassner that he was busy 'revising the whole play in the light of your suggestions'.[35]

The ease with which Hughes was able to revise his play (and the new version of Act One, completed by 3 August, was received by Gassner with great enthusiasm)[36] compared favourably with the torment of trying to begin his new novel. More important, the work he was doing for Gassner gave him a recent track-record in writing dialogue for dramatic scenes.

The result was that by mid August, in a bold career move, Hughes had managed to secure some highly paid work from Sir Michael Balcon, executive producer of Ealing Films. From 1 September 1948, to 1 March 1949 (as Balcon confirmed in writing), Hughes undertook 'to collaborate with us in the preparation of a film treatment and to write the dialogue for our proposed film at present entitled A Nightingale is Singing'.[37]

However, before he could begin work on this project, Hughes was briefly caught up in the world of international politics and intrigue.

The defeat of Hitler in 1945 had been rapidly followed by the partition not merely of Germany but of the whole of Europe into two mutually hostile and mutually fearful power blocs. Churchill expressed it most vividly when he talked of 'an iron curtain' having descended across the continent.[38] On one side lay the liberal democracies of the west, victorious but so impoverished that they were only rescued from bankruptcy and starvation by a massive injection of American funds. On the other lay the totalitarian empire of the USSR, with Communism as its faith, world domination as its avowed aim, and a massive bureaucracy backed up by army and secret police as its practical method of government.

Hughes had already shown in his dealing with the National Council for Civil Liberties that he was well aware of the communist threat; and when in mid July he was asked to attend a so-called 'Cultural Congress for Peace' in the Polish town of Wroclaw,[39] his first instinct was to write to a political contact employed by the Prime Minister at 10 Downing Street.[40]

While he waited for a reply, Hughes received another invitation which he accepted at once: the Sunday Times asked him to review G.M. Gilbert's Nuremberg Diary, a detailed account of the 1945–1946 trials of former Nazi leaders by an International Military Tribunal. It made heady reading for Hughes, as it threw light upon some of the very questions about Nazi Germany which he proposed to tackle in his new novel.

Walking along the sands below Môr Edrin with fifteen-year-old

Robert and fourteen-year-old Penny (both of whom were 'very politically conscious') he talked excitedly about *Nuremberg Diary*;[41] and in his review he wrote how astonishing it was (to people who considered the Nazi leaders to be quite inhuman):[42]

> to learn that for many of them the trial was a period of intense spiritual crisis . . .
> One cannot sum up so complex a picture in a few words. But to understand the effect of the trial on at least some of the prisoners one must realize the part which idealism played in the genesis of the Nazi party — among the leaders as well as among the rank and file.

Hughes's letter about the Wroclaw conference was passed on to the Foreign Office, who were certain that it was intended as 'a marked propaganda stunt', and pointed out that the pro-Rector of Warsaw University had already 'refused to have anything to do with it'. However, they added that on balance they would be pleased if a few level-headed men went to the congress, to offset the influence of British 'fellow-travellers'.[43]

Armed with this advice, Hughes accepted the invitation; though before he left England he reported to the Foreign Office, where he was thoroughly briefed about the political situation in Poland.[44] 'The main thing', as he reported to Frances on the eve of his departure for Poland, 'is to avoid being manoeuvred into a resolution which can be interpreted as anti-Western Powers, which they think will be attempted'. Diccon added that 'only a rather scruffy lot of writers' were going,[45]

> but some good scientists: Jack Haldane, of course. And Julian Huxley & Sir John Boyd Orr. Also Edward Crankshaw the Russian expert whom I want to meet. I saw Jack James yesterday and am dining with Peter Quennell tonight (after a cocktail party at the Polish Embassy).

At seven-thirty the following morning, Tuesday 24 August 1948, he set out in an RAF aeroplane bound for Poland.

Frances heard nothing more of her husband until she received a letter which he had written the following Tuesday from Warsaw. 'My dear;', he began,[46]

> There's a chance to send this home reasonably quickly by tomorrow's courier plane, so I am taking it. I doubt whether I have ever had a more interesting time in my life than these last few days.
> The conference itself was a frame-up: there was no genuine attempt at discussion at all, it was simply a series of anti-American (& to a lesser extent anti-British) tirades, & its object was to secure

at least the pretended support of non-Communist intellectuals for an 'anti Imperialist' resolution. There was a British delegation of 45, which must have included the greater part of the British Communist party: the rest of us were in a very small minority: Sir John Boyd-Orr, Julian Huxley, Edward Crankshaw, Kingsley Martin (ed. of *New Statesman*), a historian called [A.J.P.] Taylor, Olaf Stapledon & myself. The first two fought to the point of exhaustion on the drafting Committee to get the resolution framed in tolerable terms, while the rest of us fought, not altogether unsuccessfully, to make our objections known to the body of the Congress & outside.

'Taken all in all', Diccon commented, 'it was hardly a cheering experience as a world-citizen'; but he had made a friend of Edward Crankshaw, who later wrote to tell him: 'I don't remember anyone I liked so much on so short an acquaintance';[47] and who was a co-signatory to the following dissenting letter published on 4 September in the *New Statesman and Nation*:

Sir – We, the undersigned members of the British group at the Wroclaw Congress, regret that we are unable to accept the resolution there passed as the whole truth. We deplore its oversimplification. The first duty of intellectuals is to be intelligent, and the duty of the Congress should have been to examine impartially the germs of a future war rather than to recapitulate the causes of the war which is finished. Two ways of life and of thought are in conflict throughout the world and it should be the task of intellectuals to resolve that conflict by peaceful means. We feel that the implication of the resolution that one side alone is to blame to be a waste of a great opportunity. We believe that though we were in a minority at the Congress, we represent the majority of men and women throughout the world.

A.J.P. Taylor	Edward Crankshaw	Wroclaw August 28
Felix Topolski	Richard Hughes	1948
A.G. Weidenfeld	Dennis Saurat	
Olaf Stapledon		

And furthermore, as Diccon pointed out to Frances in a letter from Warsaw (to which he had travelled when the conference was over),[48]

for my novel, nothing could have gone better! Opportunities to see beneath the surface, to study character & all that were *far* more than I expected . . . one thing may amuse you. When I had made my position quite clear, Haldane refused publicly to sit at the same breakfast table with me – but one of the Russians did not, and we discussed Dostoevsky for half an hour!

In another incident, 'at a party thrown by the Prime Minister –

a court function in the old style', Hughes was entertained to find
that the fiercest of the Russian speakers 'shook hands with me'; and
that the Polish communist who had staged the conference 'teased me
lightheartedly'; while one of the British communists 'was so abusive
that I had to walk away to avoid a scene!'

Warsaw was just as instructive, though not at all amusing.
Hughes (as he wrote in an article for the *Spectator*) had left
Wroclaw:[49]

> as bewildered as Dr Huxley and Dr Taylor at the complete
> irrationality of Eastern European disputants as soon as the word
> 'Fascism' had justly or unjustly been injected into the discussion ...
> It is a subject on which they are not quite sane.

But then he had seen the ruins of Warsaw. And after hearing
what had happened there, he had become

> a little less bewildered ... Janus-like, Nazism has two faces,
> one turned west, the other east. We only saw the western face.
> We liked that face little enough, heaven knows; but its eastern
> face was unimaginably worse. Auschwitz with its slaughterhouse
> was for the Slav a place in Poland; not, as for us, a place in a
> newspaper report. The Ghetto was in their midst.
>
> Figures of millions of civilians killed cannot themselves move
> the imagination, since human suffering is not susceptible of multi-
> plication by arithmetic. But let me recount one instance out of the
> millions. At the time when all Jews were confined in the Warsaw
> Ghetto, children would sometimes slip out for an hour or two.
> An SS man found one such child crying in a Gentile street. At
> first she denied being Jewish; he cross-questioned her and at last
> she admitted it. He called a Polish policeman, told him to lift the
> man-hole cover off a sewer, and threw the child in alive to drown
> in filth.

'How', asked Hughes, 'could someone who had seen that happen
ever again be quite sane when the sound of the word 'Fascism'
stirred his memories?'

Another RAF aeroplane flew Hughes back to England on 4
September;[50] and when (after a few days in London) he returned
to North Wales, he was still[51]

> excited and on edge. He said he still felt, just as when he used
> to argue with Koestler, that the writer ought not to interfere in
> politics. But the War obsessed him. A letter mentions going to see
> friends specifically to talk about 'the book'.

This might have been exactly the right moment, when Hughes
was fired with passionate feelings about the war, to begin writing
his new novel. He seems to have felt so himself, because in October

he told one correspondent that although his book on the *Graf Spee* had never been written, he fully expected 'to use this material in a novel covering a rather wider canvas that *I am now working on.*'[52]

However, Hughes was already under contract to Ealing Films; and (with a family to support and school fees to pay) it was not a contract he could afford to break; though he had already persuaded Balcon to let him delay work on *A Run for Your Money* (as *A Nightingale is Singing* had been renamed) until he had finished revising *A Comedy of Good and Evil* for John Gassner.

By 7 September 1948 Hughes had sent Gassner his revised version of Acts Two and Three of the *Comedy* for his proposed *Minnie and Mr Williams*; and later that month Gassner replied that he and his associates had 'inserted as much of the new material as seemed to us to strengthen our script'. He added that he thought two of the new speeches 'among the most beautiful things I have read in a long time'.[53]

Gassner's continuing enthusiasm filled Hughes with hopes for a great commercial success: until the Boston try-out, which Gassner admitted 'was in many respects disappointing'. The audiences found it wordy and confusing until Gassner, with 'the benefit . . . of some of the more redoubtable minds at Harvard University whose friendship I enjoy', had made substantial alterations, and added a narrator. The final evenings at Boston were then received 'quite warmly'; and the production moved on to New York City.[54]

However by this time Gassner himself was becoming despond-ent; not surprisingly, when he had lost $16,000 in Boston, and when (taking production costs into account) he now needed to take $11,000 a week on Broadway just to break even. A note of caution had already been sounded by Hughes's theatrical agent who thought *Minnie and Mr Williams* very far removed from the current popular taste. 'My first guess', she wrote, 'is that it will be a failure and will close after a few days. My second guess is that it will have a long run and may win the Drama Critics' Award.'[55]

It was her first guess that proved to be correct. The play received appalling reviews, and was taken off after a couple of nights. Gassner wrote very handsomely: 'I can only say that I am prouder to have failed with this play than I should have been if I had scored a tre-mendous success with most of the trash that Broadway witnesses year after year'; but it was a great disappointment for Hughes, who told his agent Margery Vosper in December that the failure had 'knocked my finances haywire', and asked whether Ealing could advance him £100.[56]

Sir Michael Balcon had offered some work on *A Run for Your Money* to Diccon Hughes chiefly because of his Welsh connections, as it involved two Welshmen, who travel up to London for a Rugby International. Diccon would be collaborating with the established screen-writer/director Charles Frend; and he invited Frend to join him and Frances at Laugharne Castle House at the end of September, so that they could work on the first draft of their script in that quintessentially Welsh setting.[57]

Diccon and Frances had another reason for returning to Laugharne. Their tenant had left the Castle House in April, and they were keen to dispose of the remainder of the lease, and move their furniture and other possessions (including most of Diccon's papers) up to Môr Edrin. They were also worried that if Laugharne were left empty for too long, Mrs Starke might somehow break the lease, and deprive them of whatever value they could still extract from their interest in the property. Louisa Hughes had helped them out by living in the Castle House for a good part of the summer; and on 16 September Frances told Mrs Starke that she and Diccon were returning to live at Laugharne until everything was settled.[58]

Hardly had they moved back into the Castle House when a letter reached them from Dylan Thomas. He had become a national figure since the tremendous acclaim which greeted the publication of his *Deaths and Entrances* in 1946; he worked regularly for the BBC; and he had also signed a lucrative contract with Gainsborough Films, but (as Caitlin later wrote) 'as a man, his life was a mess'.[59] Since the end of the war, he and Caitlin had been very dependent upon the patronage of A.J.P. Taylor's wife Margaret, who first put them up in her summer-house, and later found them a house at South Leigh in Oxfordshire.

But although Margaret very much admired Dylan as a poet, her kindness was far from disinterested. On one occasion she wrote to tell him that sleeping with him would be like sleeping with a God; and there was a long period when she visited him daily in the caravan which he used as an outdoor study. This inevitably put severe pressure upon his troubled relationship with Caitlin. Once she was so angry that she pushed the caravan over while Dylan was still inside it.

When they made up, as they always did in the end, Dylan would tell Caitlin that 'it would all be better if only we could get back to Laugharne'; and as soon as he heard that Diccon Hughes wished to dispose of the lease of the Castle House, Dylan was filled with what Caitlin calls a '*hiraeth*' or 'deep longing' to live there,[60] and persuaded Margaret Taylor to make an offer on his behalf.

Explaining this in his letter to Diccon, Dylan added: 'We would, Caitlin and me, above everything else in the world love to be, if only for 7 years, in the Castle which we have always thought the best house in the best place.'[61] Within a few days, a further letter had arrived, this time from Margaret Taylor, who declared that, in Dylan's eyes, possession of the Castle House had become a symbol of personal salvation.[62]

Diccon was working hard with Charles Frend on 'the Laugharne draft' of *A Run for Your Money*; so Frances replied. She told both Margaret and Dylan quite plainly that the Castle House would do Dylan no good at all: it was an old building whose maintenance endlessly soaked up money; and there were problems, in her view, in dealing with Mrs Starke.[63]

Dylan Thomas was undeterred; and soon afterwards Margaret Taylor herself turned up at the Castle House with a letter from Dylan to Frances in which he explained:[64]

> Unfortunately I can't get away myself: I'm trying to write a musical comedy film, and am weeks behind hand. Margaret Taylor has come to Laugharne to see if she can find out, for me, exactly how the Starke-Hughes-Castle case is going, and what chance there is of my getting the house for some years, and, if I did manage to, exactly what financial commitments I would be held to. Do, please, help her if you can.

In the event, Margaret Taylor found the legal position so complicated that she abandoned her negotiations with Mrs Starke; but her journey to Laugharne was fruitful all the same, because it led to her acquisition of the Boat House, that 'white-painted house on stilts at the water's edge' for which Dylan and Caitlin 'had longed for years'; and when they moved there, in May 1949, it was the start of a much happier and more productive period of Dylan's life.[65]

By then, Diccon and Frances had virtually disposed of the lease of the Castle House,[66] and had left Laugharne for ever. 'It ought to be a melancholy business', Diccon had written to Penny,[67]

> coming back to Laugharne 'for the last time': but somehow it is not . . . The mistake was to imagine it was right, or even possible, to live out one's life in a fairy-tale, which is what Laugharne is. To live one's life in a poem – which is what North Wales is, at least to me – is different.

However, as Penny writes, 'It is clear from the later part of his letter than the enchanted atmosphere of the place still gripped him'. Most afternoons, he told her, he went wild-fowling on the sea-marshes with Johnnie Watts; and he described vividly how 'the most exciting time' to be out on the marshes was at dusk, when the 'flighting' begins. First come the green plover, swooping in over the sea wall only a few feet above your head. Then as the darkness increases come the widgeon and the duck: the widgeon in hundreds, whispering to each other, the duck in ones and twos, silent. They fly higher than the green plover, and because it is darker you can hear them before you see them: a sound like a wind coming, louder and closer, and then a band of birds black against the sky.

Diccon's real feelings of affection for Laugharne were such that he could not bear to part with it completely, and he would retain ownership of his boat-shed for another fourteen years or more.[68]

Diccon Hughes and Charles Frend completed their first draft outline of *A Run for Your Money* with considerable speed. Then on 11 November 1948, while Balcon's criticisms of a second draft were still fresh in Hughes's mind, he wrote Frend a letter saying both that those criticisms were justified, and that he knew why their collaboration had so far been less successful than they had hoped. 'We have been pulling in opposite directions', he explained,[69]

> towards different kinds of film. Your natural tendency is towards character comedy: you want to make the film natural, probable, interesting, even informative (for I detect a streak of the old documentary Adam in you!) Mine is rather towards farcical comedy. I wanted to make it funny, exciting, and happy. In short your approach to the audience is intellectual, mine emotional.

And he suggested that they should 'consider returning to the scrapped Laugharne draft, at least in its essentials'.

A month later, a revised outline had been approved, and Hughes had sent off a substantial batch of dialogue to Ealing, who seemed (as he reported to his agent) to be 'very pleased with it'. But there was much more to be done: and very disagreeable Hughes found some of it.

Summoned to London to attend detailed script conferences, he was amazed that 'everyone seemed to have a say in the script, even the stage-carpenter'. A month later, pouring out his feelings in a letter to Penny, Diccon told her that he had spent a 'very bitter' time in London, 'trying to save some semblance of shape or meaning' for the film; but it was 'like building sand-castles against the tide. All that is left of my work now', he complained,[70]

> is a few scattered scenes, seldom now appearing in the part of the film for which they were written; occasional speeches, often now put into other mouths than they were intended for, incidents

which might have had meaning as part of a balanced whole but now are in different context.

At times he had 'even tried lingering' (when everyone else moved off to the nearby Red Lion Pub at the end of the day), 'and inserting in the script things which he wanted, in various disguised hands'; but it was a dispiriting business, and he looked forward to the day when films were 'written by writers, not by public meetings'.

By mid March 1949 a final shooting script had somehow emerged. Hughes went down to South Wales for five days (he had been asked to adjudicate at a drama festival in Treorchy),[71] leaving Frend behind at Ealing Studios to direct a sterling cast which starred Alec Guinness, and included Hugh Griffith, Meredith Edwards, Moira Lister, Donald Houston and Joyce Grenfell. When *A Run for Your Money* opened in November, Hughes was nervous about going to see the film, telling a friend that although he was 'billed as part-author', so much had been altered that 'I simply might not recognise the result'.[72] However, it was a success (with one paper, the *News Chronicle*, describing it as 'the best film that has come out of Wales');[73] and Hughes had chalked up an important first screen credit.

Financially, the strain upon Diccon was less than it had been immediately after the war (though Frances continued to run up large overdrafts from time to time); but emotionally he was once again under increasing pressure from his mother. She had begun to dangle the prospect of her imminent death before his eyes, and in February 1949 she wrote to explain that she would be leaving everything to him; that her body must be cremated (her ashes were to be scattered in the Llanfrothen churchyard); and that she wished to thank both him and Frances in advance[74]

> for all the happiness you have given me, & the love & care you have always shown me – Rest assured that this latter part of my life has been most happy & that it is your goodness & your love for one another & the dear children which has made it so.

Although superficially charming, this letter filled Diccon with guilt about his dealings with both mother and wife; and that summer he seemed to his three elder children to be utterly distant and withdrawn.

This had the effect of making Frances seem 'remote also' – though she was probably no more disorganised than usual about shopping and meal-times and other distracting pursuits – and Robert, Penny and Lleky 'grew to feel so unwanted at home that', as Penny recalls, 'half way through the holidays the three of us plotted together and ran away'.[75] They were back within fifteen or sixteen hours, having fallen out with each other. Diccon and Frances very sensibly asked them no questions (though the episode must have raised many in their own minds), but fed them, put them to bed, and allowed them a long lie-in the following morning.

That Christmas, some of Frances's cousins lent her a corner of Naworth Castle in Cumberland; but it was a holiday which ended badly. On New Year's Day 1950, Frances 'fell down a flight of stone stairs and broke her coccyx';[76] and then the following afternoon, news arrived from London that Louisa Hughes was dead.[77]

The children, who had been very fond of their grandmother, were devastated. Letters of condolence arrived from some of Diccon's oldest friends like Stella Watson and Gwenol Satow;[78] there were also tributes from Louisa's friends: 'She was the first person', wrote one of them, 'who made me feel it was not a misfortune to grow old, she had the enthusiasm & interest of a young person with the charm & trust & tolerance that is sometimes achieved by people as they grow older'.[79] Frances too found herself the subject of much praise: 'You certainly must have some idea', wrote another correspondent, 'of the depth of happiness & confidence your devotion & wisdom brought to Louisa ever since your marriage . . . It seemed to fill her whole being with tenderness, like a fountain, and to be a rock under her feet as well.'[80]

After breaking her tail bones, Frances had been ordered to lie in bed for a week, and then to avoid sitting down for three months; so she could not accompany Diccon when he went down to London for the cremation. A few weeks later,[81] when all his children but Owain (suffering from whooping-cough)[82] had been despatched to their various schools (an operation which Diccon told Joseph Brewer 'makes *Overlord* seem like a simple route march'),[83] he left Frances and Owain to recuperate at Naworth and returned alone to Mor Edrin.[84] There he began work on an idea for a satirical film to be called *The Herring Farm*;[85] spent a week in bed with flu; and turned his mind to 'five broadcasts and a lecture all to be done during March'.[86]

But what of Hughes's serious work, now that he could subsidise it with his second career as a screen-writer? The Walter Harris biography had been finally set aside: in September 1949, Hughes had returned the family papers 'with deep regret. I still hope', he declared, 'that one day I shall be able to get back to this work, complete my search of the archives, and make a proper job of the book'. But with five children to educate, there was 'no immediate prospect of this', as he simply could not afford to undertake any work for which the return would be so poor.[87]

The way was now clear for Hughes to devote any spare time to his proposed novel; but within a very few months he had embroiled himself in a time-consuming undertaking which was bound to be still less financially rewarding than a biography of Walter Harris. Two days after his mother's cremation, Diccon had met Jack James at the Admiralty, and had been taken by him to see the new Secretary, Sir John Lang, about the project which had been so dear to Harry Markham's heart: the Admiralty section of a history of the *Administration of War Production*.[88]

When Markham was still alive, Hughes had been reluctant to commit himself to this enterprise. Now, however, Markham was dead; in addition, his mother was dead, and it might be years before he could cope with the emotional stress of writing that long novel of his own times, which had already given him such trouble.

So when at this critical juncture Hughes was again asked whether he would work on Admiralty business, feelings of loyalty both to the service and to the memory of his dead friend were reinforced by a strong desire to avoid another wrestle with the opening paragraphs of his novel. In addition, Louisa had left him a small inheritance: how better to spend it than in an act of loyalty to the service which had provided him with a home for five years? Not only would he do the work; but he would do it without payment, for its own sake, (though he might put in for expenses when it was finished), and his novel would have to wait.

CHAPTER 29

Limbering Up

The origin of Richard Hughes's idea for *The Herring Farm*, which he began writing on 5 February 1950,[1] lay in a government scheme for effectively turning a substantial part of Snowdonia into a vast hydroelectric generating station. Much of the land involved had already been designated a national park, and bodies such as the Ramblers' Association and the Council for the Protection of Rural Wales (with which Hughes had been associated since the thirties) were horrified. At its Annual General Meeting in 1950, the CPRW pointed out: 'Some of the vast constructional schemes must deprive much of the selected countryside of the qualities for which it has been marked out as worthy of preservation'; and stated its intention of petitioning against any private bill which the British Electricity Authority might think of laying before Parliament.[2] Hughes himself (in his eldest daughter's words) 'saw the scheme as an attack on the whole Welsh way of life, and counter-attacked furiously in the English Press. We went with him to protest-meetings, and read drafts of articles, and letters to the papers'.[3]

The scheme gave Hughes the idea for a scathing satire upon socialist bureaucracy. His hero would be a decent senior civil servant, Sir Peregrine Madden, who spends his holidays in 'Llanmadoc' – an invented town, a hybrid of Portmadoc (whose position it occupies upon the map) and Llaugharne (whose eccentricities it shares). Encouraged by his secretary Miss Lattery, Sir Peregrine becomes infuriated by the way in which the natural beauty of Snowdonia is gradually being destroyed by the selfish requirements of half a dozen English ministries.

Very early in Hughes's film-script, Sir Peregrine and Miss Lattery are examining a file about yet another damaging new development, on an area one half of which is forestry land. However, as Miss Lattery remarks:

> MISS LATTERY. I suppose they'll think nothing of bulldozing a million ten-year-old trees?

SIR PEREGRINE [a trifle gruffly]. Out-of-date. The Coal Board did that last month, for open-cast.

There is a brief pause while he reads with concentration, drumming nervously with his finger.

SIR PEREGRINE. Not a squeak out of Ag. and Fish, about *anything*?

MISS LATTERY [shrugging, and in sarcastic tone]. Yes indeed! A most urgent phone message – – top secret: Are planned movements of herring shoals *our* pigeon, or *theirs*?

SIR PEREGRINE (snorts, then murmurs as he continues to read). Clupea harangus. A most irresponsible fish. [He scribbles a note in the margin, then continues] Ours, I suppose [with a quick glance up] But Master Herring swimmeth where he listeth . . . quite out of place in a planner's world. [turning to the empty map pocket at the back of the file] But the rest of the site – – what else of the works of God or man do we destroy tonight?

MISS LATTERY [with curled lip and looking at her finger-nails – clearly she is quoting some person well known to them both]. I believe there's 'some tatty old cathedral or other'.

At this point, Sir Peregrine 'springs to his feet, and slams the file on his desk'. That 'urgent phone message' from the Ministry of Agriculture and Fisheries has given him an idea. Soon, he has effectively prevented any more damaging developments in Snowdonia, by[4]

> forging a requisition for the whole region on behalf of the Ministry of Land and Water. This, cunningly backdated, takes precedence over all others. The ostensible purpose of the requisition is to create, by damming and flooding a series of valleys, an inland sea for the farming of herring: but it is, of course, to be no more than an impracticable paper scheme.

The comedy arises from the fact that: 'Sir Peregrine's Minister, the megalomaniacal Dearborn, takes it into his head to realize the scheme, and so erect a lasting liquid memorial to his name'; and Sir Peregrine and the Llanmadoc villagers manage to persuade him that the scheme is actually going ahead. Finally, Dearborn realises the truth, and resigns. By now, so much publicity has been given to the scheme that the government of the day is embarrassed. Once again, Sir Peregrine has a scheme; and one of the final scenes runs:[5]

G.78 EXT. MOUNTAINSIDE DAY
SIR PEREGRINE is back in his Whitehall clothes, standing on a mountainside addressing an official Press party. MISS LATTERY is by his side. Conspicuous in the party are those journalists who

failed to reach the Snowdon Sea. In the valley below lies Llanmadoc.

SIR PEREGRINE. . . . Look around you, gentlemen. Who would
believe, to look at those smiling, prosperous farms, that a mere
few months ago this land was under the sea? That crabs haunted
spots now grazed by sheep, and herrings swam where now the
rooks fly?

The JOURNALISTS gaze in awe at the peaceful valley.

MISS LATTERY. Who indeed?

SIR PEREGRINE reacts, and at that moment a photographer's flash-
light goes off –

The picture freezes to a close-up of Sir Peregrine; the camera tracks
back to reveal that his still photograph is in a newspaper; and we
learn that he has been made a baron in the Birthday Honours for his
arduous work in reclaiming for farming the land under the Snowdon
sea.

Hughes had done no more than draft an outline of *The Herring Farm*, when documents relating to the proposed history of
the *Administration of War Production* began reaching him from
London.[6] The rest of the volume was to be written by J.D. Scott of
the Cabinet office, who was also to be the supervising editor; and in
May, Scott wrote saying that he would be 'very glad to know your
plans for tackling the Admiralty Section'.[7]

There was no reply; but this did not mean that Diccon was
not considering the problem. At the end of the month, he wrote
to Jack James mentioning that he and Frances would be passing
through London in July (en route for a short holiday with Jenny
Nicholson at Portofino),[8] and he would very much like to meet
Jack and discuss the history.[9] Before then, Hughes had also received
a letter from Sir John Lang, explaining that Scott was[10]

stymied over those fields of research which he should undertake
either to cover those parts of the work which lie outside your
knowledge or to assist you where you may desire corroboration
of your recollections or notes.

Lang added that it was hoped to produce the history within six
months, and that in the circumstances a plan would be most helpful.

Prompted by Sir John's rebuke, Hughes did some serious work
soon after his return from Italy; and by 10 August Scott was writing to tell Diccon that he had studied his synopsis, and found it
'admirably comprehensive and clear'.[11] For some months, however,
Scott's letter was answered only by a further long period of silence.

*

August at Môr Edrin was always too busy for Diccon to attempt any literary work. Friends visited; and it was holiday time for the children: seventeen-year-old Robert, just about to start his last year at Eton, and making a separate base for himself (as his father had done before him) in a deserted cottage (Robert had found his at the edge of the disused Ffestiniog railway); sixteen-year-old Penny, trying to discover her own separate identity, angrily realising as she stood by the grave in which Louisa's ashes were being buried that neither she nor Granny Hughes were 'actually Welsh', driven to haunting the attic prowling through photographs and press-cuttings in her efforts to understand her reticent father, and dreaming of going abroad to Greece; fourteen-year-old Lleky, fiercely independent, out of the house at six-thirty each morning and spending most of the day working on a neighbouring farm; ten-year-old Kate, on the surface a sweet, biddable child, who bowed to Frances's changing moods, but who secretly hated the uncertainty and disorder of life at Môr Edrin, and loved staying with her cousins in houses where breakfast was at a regular time, and there was plenty of food on the table; and seven-year-old Owain, a surprisingly adult child, who appeared to observe the doings of his elders with an interest tempered by philosophical detachment.[12]

If that was indeed so, then Owain had learned something from his father, who would write of parental duties:[13]

> One is only responsible for the child from the outside. The world of childhood and of school is the child's own world, where the child does all the living, and the parent just peeps in through the window (if he can) to see if things seem to be alright. Otherwise all he can do is prowl round in the shrubbery outside, chasing away robbers and encouraging the baker to call, and occasionally trying to talk through the window – though even then his voice only gets through strangely distorted.

Hughes made a point of dictating to his children as little as possible, especially in the matter of religion; although he had begun going to church again at Laugharne, and was now a regular worshipper.

From Môr Edrin, it was 'only ten minutes walk through the bracken from our house', to the parish church of Llanfihangel-y-Traethau, a small ancient stone building with no electricity. It dated from the time in the twelfth century when Owain Gwynedd was prince of an independent Powys; and Penny noticed that it 'exercised a strong pull' on her father, who remarked that it had 'none of the "spiritual bailiff for the gentry" atmosphere' which often characterised churches in rural England.[14]

*

Not long after the end of the summer holidays, there was a wireless broadcast of *A Comedy of Good and Evil*. This was attacked in some quarters (notably the *Western Mail*) for caricaturing the Welsh way of speaking; so when Hughes received an admiring letter, he replied: 'praise like yours . . . sounds in my ears like gold'. He accepted that habits had changed, but added: 'I don't think it was a bit exaggerated when the play was written – every idiom and mannerism in it was collected rather than invented.'[15]

Hughes, who should have been forging ahead with his share in *Administration of War Production*, or possibly with *The Herring Farm*, was now working on something else for the BBC: a dramatisation of *A High Wind in Jamaica*. Progress was slow, and for a while he found most pleasure in a light-hearted correspondence with Amabel Williams-Ellis, about her idea for a satirical novel in which Hughes was to appear as Hurricane ap Owain.

'Dear Amabel', Diccon began one letter, 'A suggestion for the name of your female anthropologist: Miss Psyche Savage. (Other possibilities are Barbara Smyth – say that over carefully – Exogama Tribe, and Fertility Wright.)'; and he ended: 'P.S. In Miss Penelope Webb, Hurricane ap Owain has at last found a secretary entirely suited to his Muse. He reports highly satisfactory progress on the novel he has in hand: in the course of the last three weeks he has successfully torn up two whole pages.'[16]

A few days later, Diccon sent Amabel a more detailed contribution, so long that it must have consumed his entire working day. At one point, setting his characters at a dinner-table, Hughes has them canvassing the probable attitude of a local politician to a hydroelectric scheme, when one of them breaks off 'into a eulogy of the extraordinary improvement in the morals of public life which had taken place in little more than a century'.

> 'It is hard to believe', he concludes,[17] 'that "politician" was ever in this country a word of reproach, or that the word "minister" was ever coupled in the mind of the general [public] with self-interest and favouritism.'
>
> 'Indeed', said Lord Pythagoras, 'the statesman we have been talking of is a case in point: for he has taught himself so closely to identify his own with his country's interests that, to him at least, they are indistinguishable . . . and even now that he has held office and power, he is so wholly taintless of the vice of favouritism, that where his career is at stake he will sacrifice a friend as readily as he will his noblest enemy.'

Another piece of work which Hughes agreed to undertake that

autumn was a special broadcast in London on 13 November 1950 to mark the centenary of the birth of Robert Louis Stevenson. In it, Hughes praised Stevenson's technical skill, saying that his 'words are glass. You can see the action through them almost as if there were no words between'.[18]

After the broadcast, Hughes stayed on in London for 'a whirlwind campaign' with J.D. Scott on their *Administration of War Production*.[19] This ended with them descending upon the Admiralty offices at Bath, from where, in the midst of a thick fog, Hughes returned directly to North Wales.

They had agreed that Scott should research in the Admiralty archives, while Hughes produced rough draft material based both upon preliminary interviews, and upon his personal recollections. After Christmas Scott would amend this draft material in the light of his researches, and would then return it to Hughes, who would rapidly prepare a more polished draft of some forty to fifty thousand words.[20]

In practice, Hughes was too busy working on other projects to keep to this schedule. His dramatisation in serial form of *A High Wind in Jamaica* reached Lance Sieveking at the BBC by the end of January 1951 but was declared to be in need of substantial rewriting;[21] and Hughes was also putting the finishing touches to his synopsis of *The Herring Farm*.

When Scott wrote to Hughes on 21 January, complaining that he was 'working in the dark' until some of the draft material arrived,[22] he was sent what Hughes described as 'a first instalment of cock-shy'.[23] But that was all Scott received for a very long time from this 'most maddening colleague', who wrote so slowly that 'months passed, lengthened out into years, and his contribution . . . crept along . . . and halted, and crept again'.

Very occasionally, Hughes would put in an appearance. He was always so courteous and charming that he disarmed criticism; and in any case the two men had much in common: Scott was himself a novelist, and would later become literary editor of the *Spectator*. However, Scott began to feel that the clothes Hughes wore on these visits (those of 'a Whitehall Civil Servant') were a disguise: what he *should* have worn was a pirate's outfit, or that of an Arab with a hawk upon his wrist.

Once he arrived at Scott's office at five in the evening, and talked to him for three hours before they both adjourned for a drink to the nearby United University Club. It was then that Scott first noticed that although Hughes seemed quite indifferent to physical discomfort (it was winter, and he had driven down in an unheated Jeep, so that on arrival his 'great seaman's hands' were 'navy blue' with cold), he was also 'a finnicky gourmet'. Ordering a Manhattan cocktail, Hughes was insistent that[24]

> it must be exactly right ... When ready, the Manhattan looks suitably splendid ... Richard Hughes has drunk it ... he's not absolutely certain if the orange juice was not perhaps after all a shade too sweet?

At the beginning of April 1951, Ealing made Hughes a firm offer of £1000 for his synopsis and future work on *The Herring Farm*. Ealing's plan, as Margery Vosper reported, was that T.E.B. ('Tibby') Clarke should write the screenplay and should then submit it Diccon for his alterations.[25] However, Margery's evident satisfaction with the proposed deal was not shared by Diccon, whose difficulties over the script of *A Run for Your Money* had prompted him to look at film contracts with a very suspicious eye.

First Hughes questioned whether a flat payment was in his best interests (Margery Vosper said that she could try for 5% of the producer's gross, but advised him to stick to his £1000 just in case);[26] and then he decided that before signing anything, he would go down to London to talk to Charles Frend (who was to direct the picture) about exactly how much real control he would be allowed.[27]

Arriving in London in mid April, Hughes established a sympathetic relationship with Frend by taking him to dinner at Pratts (a small and extremely select London club famous for the excellence of its wine-cellar and the wit of its raconteurs);[28] and he also visited Ealing Studios, where he made a striking impression upon Monja Danischewsky ('Danny'), who was to produce *The Herring Farm*.

It happened like this: Danny, on taking him to the Red Lion Pub so that he could introduce him to some other colleagues, asked him what he would like to drink. 'A Worcester Sauce', Diccon replied. 'Do you mean a tomato juice', Danny asked,[29]

> 'or a Bloody Mary?' He looked at me with surprise, and said 'No thanks, just a Worcester Sauce'. Mr Lambeth the licensee, equally puzzled, poured out a glass ... of this highly undrinkable sauce. Silence fell in the bar and we all watched fascinated as Diccon drained the glass.

'From that moment', as Danny records, Hughes 'was number one'.

There followed a period of intensely hard work on the script of *The Herring Farm*, with constant correspondence between Hughes, Frend and Danischewsky; and when the contract was signed at the end of May,[30] it included (at Hughes's insistence) a most unusual clause which gave him the right to prevent his original story-line and ideas from being submerged and distorted.[31]

When in mid June Hughes received his first payment from Ealing (£450 once Miss Vosper had deducted her commission),[32] the flow of his writing mysteriously abated; and so Danny, Tibby Clarke and Charles Frend decided that all three of them would go up to North Wales, where they booked into an hotel not far from where Diccon lived, and drove over daily to Môr Edrin to discuss the script with him. The discussions went well; but, as Danny recalls,[33]

> when it came to putting something down on paper, we found it difficult to get Diccon to write. I suggested to my two colleagues that we would be wise to leave him alone for a few days to get used to the idea of collaborative writing. The weather was glorious, there was a billiards table in the hotel, and a well-stocked bar. T.B. Clarke concurred, Charles Frend was a little dubious: he thought if we didn't stay with Diccon, nothing would get done at all.
>
> When eventually we called on him he was happily working in the garden, his great domed forehead protected from the sun by a wide panama hat. 'There we are', said Charles triumphantly, 'What did I tell you! He is weeding, not writing!'

After this, they kept a close watch upon Diccon, who later told a correspondent that life during the latter part of June, with producer director and script collaborator all in his neighbourhood, had been one long 'exhausting script conference'.[34]

The result was that by mid July a first draft had been completed and submitted to Sir Michael Balcon. As Danny reported to Diccon soon afterwards, 'Mick' Balcon was dubious about one of the premises of the plot: that the failure of a senior civil servant to carry out so large an enterprise as the creation of an inland sea could be kept secret for so long;[35] and then came a very mixed report from Sandy Mackendrick. On the one hand, he praised 'the central part of the story', saying that it was 'fuller of witty and brilliant ideas than any previous comedy from this studio, and one superb climax follows another'. On the other, he disliked Sir Peregrine, commenting acidly that his ideas seemed entirely negative, and that he was the sort of man who appeared to believe that Wales should be preserved as a picturesque backward moribund country, a romantic retreat for authors who were tired of the Savile Club.[36]

Hughes, who was determined not to let his idea be abandoned, took these criticisms on the chin, wrote a letter to Danny apologising for his 'bad' behaviour at script conferences, and was soon busy rewriting the start of the screenplay in an effort to deal with one of Mackendrick's principal criticisms, by making Sir Peregrine more business-like. September saw another new beginning, a title-change (to *Head in the Clouds*),[37] and the withdrawal as director of Charles Frend, who wrote to explain that he was needed elsewhere: Ealing had just bought film-rights to *The Cruel Sea*, a bestselling novel by Nicholas Monsarrat about wartime service on an Atlantic corvette, and they wanted him to make it as soon as possible.[38]

Hughes persevered. By the middle of October 1951, having completed a second draft of *Head in the Clouds*, he took it down to London and handed it over to Danischewsky,[39] before burying himself in the Admiralty for two months' hard work on *Administration*. (This had been the subject of further worried letters from J.D. Scott, who had asked him back in June 'what are the prospects of seeing you in London?', and told him in September that 'The Cabinet Office are now pressing for definite news of progress on our volume'.)[40] While Hughes wrestled with this complex task, it was agreed that the script of *Head in the Clouds* was now satisfactory; he received his final £450;[41] and there was talk of Alistair Sim playing the part of Sir Peregrine.

However, the month in which Diccon completed the script was also the month in which a general election returned the Conservatives to power under Winston Churchill. An anti-socialist satire suddenly began to look out of date; which may have been one reason why in mid January 1952 production of *Head in the Clouds* was indefinitely postponed.[42]

This came as a shock; but it was very far from being the end of the story: on 14 February, Diccon wrote to Danny telling him that Balcon's decision to postpone was 'a blessing in disguise', as the script was still not as good 'as it might be – and shall';[43] and the following day, Danny replied that in any case there appeared to have been a change of heart at Ealing:[44]

> The unaccountable Mick Balcon challenged me the other day by asking what the hell I was doing about *Head in the Clouds*? I said 'Surely you mean *Love Lottery*?' 'Nothing of the sort', says he, 'I mean *Head in the Clouds*. You know we have got a very large investment in it and I want that film made. What are you doing about the script?' 'Nothing', says I. 'Why the hell not', says he. 'Because', says I, 'you, sir, told me not to!' 'So I did', says he. Nevertheless, he has left an unpleasant impression with me that you, Charles and I walked disgustedly out of the picture over his dead body.

His main news was that *Head in the Clouds* now featured once again in the Ealing production schedule as a 'probable alternative' for 18 October; though it seemed more likely that it would be made the following spring.

In March 1952, not long after receiving this unsatisfactory and inconclusive letter, Diccon escaped with Frances to Sweden, where he had agreed to give a series of lectures for the British Council. On different occasions, he talked to university students, Anglo-Swedish societies, and adult education groups. He and Frances were everywhere well-received (the British Ambassador himself entertained them to dinner one evening); weekends were free;[45] and Diccon was soon writing cheerful round-robin letters to his children: including Robert, now in his first year at Oxford; and Penny, who had recently failed to win a place at Somerville, and was lodging in London where she was being coached for a second attempt.

From their father, they learned of the pleasures of meandering by train along the west coast of Sweden, and of arriving in Halmstead, with its 'simple, graceful' castle, and its 'wide quays with 18th century colour-washed dignified houses behind them'. There Frances sat in the sun sketching, while Diccon walked to the harbour mouth and watched in fascinated wonder as nineteenth-century English schooners loaded timber.[46]

After Diccon and Frances returned from Sweden, he divided his time between his chapters for *Administration of War Production*, and looking round for fresh film work. There was also a visit during the Easter holidays from a middle-aged and much more serene Pamela Bianco. She had been stopping-over in London for ten days, when she was persuaded to come up to Môr Edrin for a weekend which introduced her to Diccon's wife and family, and finally laid to rest a few ghosts from the long-distant past.[47]

Film work proved elusive. At one moment, there seemed a chance of working on a film to be set in Tangier with Carol Reed (director of classic pictures like *The Third Man*); at another, there was talk of Hughes adapting Henry James's *The Turn of the Screw* for John Boulting;[48] but all the real work he could find was a rewrite (for £250) of *Head in the Clouds*, which at this stage mysteriously reverted to its original name of *The Herring Farm*.[49]

The original cause of Hughes's anti-socialist satire had now vanished. Early in April 1952, the Second Reading of the North Wales Hydro-Electric Power Bill was passed by the House of Commons by two hundred votes to forty;[50] but then on 20 May it was reported in *The Times* that the British Electricity Authority had decided to 'abandon the promotion of those provisions which relate to the Ffestiniog scheme',[51] and that was effectively the end of the matter. However, at the end of May Danischewsky suggested to Hughes that he could recast his story, making it into a personal conflict between Dearborn and Sir Peregrine, more of a comedy about the abuse of government power, and less of a satire upon government in general.[52] Hughes (who was desperately in need of income) immediately replied that Danny had 'hit the nail on the head', and suggested that they should meet soon in London, where he would shortly be arriving in order (he told Danny) to complete his share of *Administration of War Production*.[53]

Diccon's writing his chapters of *Administration* had become a bone of considerable contention between him and Frances; and while he was in London he sent her a letter which began with a kind of apology:[54]

> I know both you and Amabel think I oughtn't to have done it because it's not my kind of work, and *you* think I hadn't the right to undertake it without pay, and you are right in that, I now agree – I never thought it would take so long and impoverish me so.

But it had still been a job worth doing, as he had 'managed to understand the Admiralty more clearly than it understands itself, and to make clear certain principles, some of them centuries old, which cause trouble when they are forgotten'. It was not his business to be a reformer; but at least he could 'make things *clear* – to show other people just what it is they have to decide between – the choice is then entirely up to them'.

Diccon remained guilty about the extent to which his work on *Administration* had affected his ability to provide for his family; and as soon as drafts of five out of the six Admiralty chapters were ready (and completion of the final chapter was only held up, he declared, as two unregistered memoranda for which he had been hunting had finally come to light), he wrote to the Secretary to the Admiralty saying:[55]

> You will recall that the understanding between the Admiralty and myself was that I did not ask for a fee for this work but that the Admiralty would cover my expenses. I had not intended to ask for any repayment till the job was wound up; but like many people I am now being pressed in accordance with Treasury policy to pay off my overdraft – within the next two weeks, now – and in any case much of the expenditure was incurred a long time ago.

Attaching a summary of this expenditure, he added that it came to more than he had originally expected, partly because of the length of time involved, but chiefly because he had hoped to do most of the work at home, and in practice the bulk of it had had to be done in London. 'As a matter of fact', he concluded, 'it has proved far more expensive to me than could legitimately be charged in any claim.'

Although this memorandum stating that the work was almost complete was dated 29 July 1952, Hughes was still working on the final chapter of *Administration of War Production* in October (running it alongside work on the third draft of *The Herring Farm*); and it was not until April 1953 that a draft of *Administration* had been reproduced by the Cabinet office for wider circulation.[56] Comments continued to come in until August that year; in January 1954 Scott was still asking what the prospects were of getting the job finished;[57] in March there was a more formal letter from the Admiralty;[58] and finally in July 1954 the work was completed.[59]

The intervening two years from the summer of 1952 to the summer of 1954 had seen no very dramatic changes in Diccon's family life; though he was delighted when in December 1952 Penny won an award to Somerville College, Oxford for the following autumn. In the interim she spent several months in Greece as an au pair, having English conversations with the wife of a rich Greek.

Shortly before she left, Diccon spent two days with her in London, 'taking me to visit every friend or acquaintance who had contacts in Greece'. These included Patrick Leigh Fermor. 'More subversive than kind', in Penny's words, he gave her 'a list of names to mention if I wished an explosion in the household to which I was going, which was intricately bound up with the Greek Royal Family.'

Penny was not altogether happy at first in the monied but somewhat dreary atmosphere of her host family; but when she complained to her father about the stultifying effect of riches, he replied wisely:[60]

> Don't blame money entirely: a dull Croesus might not be a whit brighter if he was a peasant. It is only that money shows up his inadequacy, like an enormous Astrakhan overcoat on a weak little man whose knees give . . . Eschew all praise and blame, all appraisal, all wishing they were different, and study your lady for what she is — a member of an utterly strange tribe, with utterly different taboos and rituals . . . Remember, it is the poor we have always with us, not the rich.

Paradoxically, now that she was no longer a child, Diccon seemed much more keen upon playing an active rôle in her life; and when two months later she wrote to tell him that she had been signed on as crew by a Greek friend for a voyage in his Eight Metre from

Alexandria to the Piraeus, Diccon forbade her to go. Upon Penny's complaining 'that he had never made a practice of dictating to me in the past,' he wrote again, explaining that (as he saw it)[61]

> growing up is just this: it is coming out of the childhood world into the world where your parents themselves are living, and have been living for quite a long time.
>
> For the first time, you're walking along together ... *for the first time* they can be useful to your inner living.

That autumn Penny arrived in Oxford, where Robert was now at the start of his final year, and had decided that he would become a priest. For a son of Diccon's to be going into the church came as a shock to many of Diccon's old friends, who remembered him in the days when he was a thoroughgoing atheist. But for Joseph Brewer, at least, the shock was welcome. Joseph (who had seemed such a confirmed bachelor) had married four years previously,[62] and was over in England staying with his wife's relatives when he received an invitation to attend Robert's coming-of-age party, which was to be held on 5 December 1953 in Teddy Wolfe's studio in London. 'Alas', he wrote,[63]

> neither of us can manage Dec 5th. Some people are coming to stay here that day whom we can't put off. Blast. I would so like to have met your son Robert. It is so good to hear of his being a priest. As you know, I'm very churchy and good priests, such as he will be, are hard to find.

On returning to the States, Joseph sent Diccon a magnificent late Christmas present of raw beef, which reached North Wales in the middle of February. It found Diccon and Frances not in Môr Edrin (which, with all three younger children at boarding-school, they had begun closing up in term-time), but in Clogwyn Melyn, which Diccon described as[64]

> that little house on the bluff almost next door (if anywhere could be said to be 'next-door' on a piece of uninhabited coast-line): we have [acquired it,] done it up and modernised it, with the idea of letting it furnished to other families during the holidays when we need to be in Môr Edrin ourselves.

Since the beef was far too much for Diccon and Frances to consume, they sent 10 pounds of it by train to Oxford, where Robert and Penny (as Diccon told Joseph) 'gave a vast skating-party and [after roasting it on a spit][65] devoured it round a bonfire on the ice'.

Diccon's working life during these two years was spent largely upon film-scripts, though he also continued to write reviews, give lectures, and do occasional work for the BBC:[66] most notably a revision of his six-part dramatisation of *A High Wind in Jamaica*. After listening to Lance Sieveking's criticisms, he had made it 'virtually a new work, framed almost entirely in dialogue',[67] and it was finally broadcast in the summer of 1953.[68] That was also the year in which a third draft of *The Herring Farm* was completed; but sadly the film was never made.

The reasons for this are now obscure, though Monja Danischewsky later believed that it might have been 'too fanciful for the studio, whose comedy films tended to be based on a documentary approach'.[69] However, no doubt was cast upon Hughes's ability as a screen-writer; and towards the end of 1953 there were serious discussions about his adapting D.H. Lawrence's *Lady Chatterley's Lover* for the screen. 'Clearly', wrote Diccon,[70]

> it is an ideal subject for a producer of imagination: there is no dialogue (only dissertations), no characters (only types) and no story (only asterisks), so you have a perfectly free hand . . . no, but seriously I see that there are ideas behind it, plenty of them, which could become film.

This also came to nothing, as the censor made it clear in advance that any film version would automatically carry an X-certificate, which would have lost Ealing a good deal of business at the cinema.[71] Next, Hughes was given the chance of working for Ealing on a film called *The Divided Heart*: which marked a watershed in his emotional as well as in his professional life.

It was late in 1953 that Ealing Studios asked Richard Hughes (for a fee of £100) to write an independent report on *The Divided Heart*. At that stage, it was no more than a draft screenplay written by Jack Whittingham; but a production team had already been lined up, consisting of Michael Truman, Charles Crichton (who was to direct) and Whittingham himself. When Hughes's report arrived, it pleased them so much that on Wednesday 6 January 1954 he received a message asking him to come down to the studios to help them produce a revised script by the end of the month.[72]

He agreed at once: partly because he needed the money, but also because the story-line of *The Divided Heart* strongly appealed to him. Set in Europe immediately after the Second World War, it is about a boy believed to have been orphaned, who has become very much attached to the foster-parents who have brought him up. When his real mother turns up and wants him back, he is torn between returning to her, and staying with his foster-mother. Hence the 'divided heart' of the title.

The first script-conference was to be on the very next day; and so, pausing only to send a telegram to Margery Vosper in which he insisted that his contract should be

DEFINITELY TIME NOT PIECEWORK BASIS EQUIVALENT TO SALARY NOT LESS THAN £100 PER WEEK PLUS MINI-MUM EXPENSES,

Diccon set out for London. There he spent both Thursday and Friday in conference, and found that the production team seemed[73]

> genuinely grateful for my report and are accepting its spirit more or less in toto. Moreover they seemed pleased with most of the specific suggestions I put forward in conference. Moreover the bar of the Red Lion opposite is a fair thermometer of favour, and I found there that Balcon seems to have been showing parts of the report that were of general application to others of his producers not concerned with this particular film. Long may it last!

The plan (he explained to Miss Vosper) was that he should suggest revisions and write tentative draft scenes; but he would not displace Whittingham, whose task it would be to put his revisions into effect.

However, at the end of January it was generally agreed that the current draft 'did not in fact provide a wholly satisfactory basis for a shooting-script, and I set to work practically single-handed on a new draft'.[74] This involved him working almost continuously until 15 March; but although there was then 'an unhappy wrangle' about his payment,[75] and although Hughes told Margery Vosper that his final script was 'nothing to write home about', he added that 'it made Mick Balcon cry . . . and it *was* used as the basis for the shooting script'.[76]

Hughes claimed to have 'thoroughly enjoyed' working on *The Divided Heart*; but his involvement with the film had gone deeper than mere enjoyment. With its theme of conflicting loyalties, something which had been at the core of his own emotional life for as long as he could remember, it had been a highly personal film for him to write. Most importantly, it had enabled him at long last to clear the emotional log-jam which had been blocking his creative energies ever since the day some five years ago when he had received that dreadful letter from his mother warning of her impending death.

In the summer, while Hughes waited for *The Divided Heart* to be released, he learned (much to his annoyance) that Jack Whittingham was to be credited as sole author. 'The *fact* is', he told a correspondent, 'that this is a screen-play by Hughes, based on a draft screen-play by Whittingham: but it seems they are under some sort of contractual obligation not to say so.'[77] However, it led to more work later in the year on a film (never to be made) entitled *A Street in Soho*; and when *The Divided Heart* was released in December, the reviews were good, even if audiences in the West End of London were a little disappointing.[78]

Before then, Hughes had received a further boost both to his salary and to his reputation, when in July 1954 he was elected Gresham Professor of Rhetoric in the University of London. His only duties were to deliver 'three sets of lectures a year, each set on [four or] five successive week-nights'[79] (his first set, given early in November,[80] was on 'The Cuckoo's Nest or The Necessity of Rhetoric'); and he told Frances that he had accepted the post (which carried a small annual salary of some £150) in order to 'clear his ideas for starting the long novel'.[81]

By the end of 1954, Hughes had dealt with the galley proofs of *Administration of War Production*,[82] enjoyed the critical success of *The Divided Heart*, and delivered his first Gresham lectures. He had already explained to a correspondent that his intention during 1954 had been[83]

> to make as much money . . . as I possibly could – not only to get out of the red, but to try to build up sufficient reserves to be able to lay off for long enough to start on a new novel.

And now, his 'act of piety to his Alma Mater the Admiralty'[84] completed, his re-awakened capacity for coping with highly personal emotional themes proved by his work on *The Divided Heart*, and his mind sharpened by the preparation of his Gresham lectures, Richard Hughes the novelist felt that at long last he was ready to embark upon what he intended should be the major enterprise of his literary career.

CHAPTER 30

The Fox in the Attic

Sitting on the evening of 15 January 1955 in an hotel garden in the delightfully unspoiled town of Marbella in southern Spain, Richard Hughes had a pen in his hand, and a blank sheet of paper on the table in front of him. He had arrived here the previous day with Frances,[1] having decided that he needed to go abroad to begin writing that long novel of his own times with which a part of his mind had been preoccupied ever since the war. After all this time, he had a title, *The Human Predicament*, and some ideas; but no plan, no list of characters. 'For me', he would explain,[2]

> writing can never be, like a piece of carpentry, done from a blue-print: it has to grow — like a tree.
> You may say that such writing is bound to be formless: but is it? After all, a tree grows from the roots: but would you call a tree 'formless'? The form of every leaf and twig is already laid down in the seed . . . the forester plants it in a picked spot, and tends it and prunes it.

As Hughes sat there in the garden with pen and paper, he could hear 'foreign voices all round me; and four feet away a party of children hung on the railings and stared straight into my face'. And then, as he looked along the road, he saw a man walking towards him carrying a lamb across his shoulders.[3]

This image, looming up out of the dusk, and carrying with it biblical echoes of sacrifice and redemption, was the flash of inspiration for which Hughes had long been waiting. Suddenly, the scene in front of him faded away, and what he saw in his mind's eye[4]

> was a West Wales sea-marsh, a windless damp afternoon . . .
> I saw two figures approaching — I had not the least idea who they were, but as they loomed nearer out of the mist I suddenly saw with a shock what . . . *what* one of them had on his shoulder.

Diccon's pen began to move across the page. 'There was a soft, feathery feeling in the air', he wrote;[5]

for it was a warm, wet, windless afternoon and the rain was so fine it could scarcely fall – clinging, rather, like a mantle of water to everything it touched. The rushes in the choked ditches of the sea-marsh were bowed down with it. The small black cattle glistened and steamed, their horns were jewelled with it: they looked stumpy as they stood there nearly knee-deep in a soft patch. The sea-marsh stretched for miles, and a greyness merging into sea and sky had altogether rubbed out the line of sand-dunes which bound it that way: inland, another and darker blurred greyness was all one could see of the solid hills. In a brief tangle of brambles by a solitary gate the smell of a fox hung, unable to rise or dissipate.

The gate clicked sharply and shed its cascade as two men passed through. They were heavily loaded in oilskins: the elder of them carried two shotguns, negligently, and had a brace of golden plover tied to the bit of old rope he wore round his waist. The younger carried over his shoulder the body of a dead child, its thin, limp, muddy legs dangling against his chest, its cheek pressed against his back. At their heels walked a black dog: disciplined, saturated and eager . . . Only these three beings moving, with their burden, in an empty motionless world.

And it was out of this strange vision, as Hughes later explained, 'that the whole story grew, spreading and ramifying out of those two lonely figures and the burden one of them carried'.[6] Even the incidental detail about the smell of a fox was the origin of an idea so powerful that the whole of the first volume of *The Human Predicament* would eventually be named *The Fox in the Attic*.

Hughes had often said that a writer could write best not about what was under his nose, but about what was under his skin; and there is an autobiographical element which gives much emotional force to the opening chapters of *The Fox in the Attic*. The sea-marsh is immediately reminiscent of the sea-marshes not far from Laugharne Castle where Hughes used to go duck-shooting; while Augustine Penry-Herbert (the man who is first glimpsed in the year 1923 with the body of a dead child over his shoulder) lives in his own country house (Newton Llantony) just eight miles from the town of Flemton, a self-governing township clearly modelled upon Laugharne.

When he filled in Augustine's background, Hughes gave him his own experiences as a public schoolboy growing up under the shadow of the Great War, realising that soon he would be marching to join the dead, and being 'on the last lap of all – at a training camp for young officers – when the guns stopped'.[7] He also gave him a father who had died when Augustine was only five years old; and in his very first draft (from which the relevant paragraphs were soon excised) he even supplied Augustine with his own most upsetting childhood experience: that terrible guilt over having *forgotten* his father's death when he woke up the next morning.[8]

It was Teddy Wolfe who had recommended Marbella to the Hugheses. As a town it was substantial, but very sleepy, with only 'a man in the Bar who had had a street named after his exploits in the Civil War (but it was a *very* short street), a beach below the town, and a 4000 foot mountain behind it'. Teddy had described it as 'a suitably deserted spot for boredom to generate hard work'; but he had recommended it so often that some of the first residents whom Diccon and Frances met, John and Polly Hope, were also friends of his. When asked what they were doing, this young couple claimed to be on their way to Istanbul. In the meantime, Marbella suited them as a quiet place in which to paint.[9]

This immediately gave them something in common with Frances, who confessed that she too was a painter; but Diccon was a little more reticent; and when they privately asked him his profession (not daring to question Frances, who 'talked as if everyone in the world had heard of [him]') he would only admit to being a Professor of Rhetoric. After only three days, however, Diccon had decided that he liked these painters, in particular Polly, a lively woman a little younger than his daughter Penny; and he suggested (much to the Hopes' amazement) that all four of them should climb the mountain.[10]

They agreed; and the result was a revelation. 'Indoors', as they later recalled, Diccon had seemed

> professorial and ponderous, but on the mountain, forging ahead with Polly, he woke up. He seemed able to talk quite a lot of Spanish. He shouted at people they met on the way, scaled walls as if they hardly existed.

They had started in the morning, and it took all day to climb from the concrete bungalows round Marbella, past the shepherds' hovels on the mountainside, and up to the summit. By the time Diccon and Polly and scaled the mountain, they were firm friends; and Frances and John also reached the top, though they walked more slowly, and it took them much longer.

This new friendship of Diccon's presented no threat either to John or to Frances; and did Diccon a great deal of good. Within his own family, as Penny recalls, he had become 'the slightly forbidding "elder statesman" '; and Polly, on meeting Penny the following summer, told her categorically:[11]

> Your Dad suffers dreadfully from all this "famous author"

treatment he gets. He needs to be told he's a hack, not told he's a genius – told he's not getting any lunch till he's done his 500 words a day ... He's a devil, Diccon. If I was driving him he'd keep saying, 'Can't you take the corner faster than that – at *your* age?' He gets treated much too respectfully by everyone.

This was not the whole story: Hughes had come to use his 'eminent writer' persona as a useful barrier between himself and any potentially hurtful intimacy – not least with Frances herself, whose near-idolatry of Diccon-as-author sometimes annoyed her Bazley relatives, but had made it a great deal easier for her husband to carve out that wholly private and independent area within his marriage which he so much needed.

But what a relief for Diccon to come across a young woman with insight and high spirits, a lively and intelligent companion who could cut straight through all the barriers within which he had virtually imprisoned himself, and do so without any danger to either of them! It provided him with the easy intimacy he had once enjoyed with pre-pubescent girls – but this time he was dealing with an adult woman; and just as Diccon's earlier friendships with girls like Charlotte Williams-Ellis and Toby Henderson had given him the insights which he needed for *A High Wind in Jamaica*, so this new friendship (and others like it) would be of enormous value as he worked on successive volumes of *The Human Predicament*.

During the next month and a half, the Hugheses and the Hopes saw a great deal of each other, often dining together, and sometimes sharing expeditions to Gibraltar, Algeciras, or San Roque;[12] and once Diccon had revealed himself as primarily author rather than lecturer (though he was almost certainly working on his next Gresham lectures as well as on *The Fox in the Attic*), Polly and John stopped calling him 'the Professor', and were 'enrolled as listeners'.[13] Reading aloud is the surest way for a writer to detect weaknesses in what he has just written; and when Diccon made the experiment of reading Polly, John and Frances the draft of his first chapter, he found it so valuable that, from then on, reading draft chapters aloud as soon as he had written them became his standard practice.

When Richard Hughes had last visited his house in the Casbah in Tangier, he had left it in the hands of an Arab caretaker, Hausi, who was to be paid one hundred francs a month from an account in a local bank. However, that had been almost twenty-two years ago, back in the spring of 1933. Since then family commitments and a World War had intervened; the account had dried up; and in 1952 Diccon had heard from Jim Wyllie[14] not only that the house was getting in a bad state of disrepair, but that the caretaker was allowing native huts to be built in the garden, and indeed that there was a risk that the caretaker himself would acquire squatters rights and I would lose the property altogether.

Since then he had attempted to remedy the situation, but had found it difficult to achieve anything at long distance. So early in February 1955, Diccon and Frances left Marbella for a while, and crossed over to Tangier. There they visited Diccon's house (visibly in need of urgent repairs) and consulted a local lawyer.

On learning that Diccon had bought his property under Moorish law, and had received only Moorish title deeds, the lawyer explained that it was essential 'to get the property inscribed on the European Central Land Registry and . . . [to] pay up arrears of salary to my caretaker: otherwise' (as Hughes told his bank manager later in the year, when seeking permission to export the necessary sterling) 'I should certainly lose the property and until I did so it could neither be reoccupied or sold'.[15]

There had been one pleasant aspect of the visit to Tangier. That hereditary saint who had once disdained their company, now paid them the tribute of going to see them off on their boat back to Spain: something which, as Frances recognised, 'was considered very very distinguished in the quarter'.[16]

The Hugheses flew back to England on 1 March 1955, and stayed in London for ten days so that Diccon could deliver his next set of Gresham lectures, on 'Poetry and Rhetoric'. Afterwards, making their way back to North Wales, they called in on Penny (now halfway through her second year at Oxford) and Diccon presented her with 'a sizeable manuscript', which she 'read . . . avidly'.

From that time onwards Penny became another of Diccon's principal 'adult advisers' while he wrote *The Fox in the Attic*; and since she was often at home when her three younger siblings were away at school, and since in any case Diccon was so deeply involved in his new novel that he continued writing 'despite the comings and goings of his offspring', she had her first real chance to observe her father at work.

'A typical day for Diccon would begin', as Penny recalls, 'about 5 a.m., for he woke with the light. In the Admiralty he had become an insomniac, and he never threw it off again.' On her first morning at home that Easter vacation, she was[17]

startled out of deep sleep by a very loud bang. Finding myself already out of bed, I went to see what it was. Diccon was standing at the open bedroom window lowering a smoking shotgun: apparently he had been taking aim at a duck bobbing on the tide outside.

'Of course I didn't hit it', he said philosophically. That the noise hit the sleeping household apparently did not occur to him. I asked if it was part of the morning routine. He replied this was an exception: more usually he did the exercises he had done since his twenties, and then sat by the window watching the tide and quietly saying Morning Prayer, following lectionary readings.

This glimpse of Richard Hughes watching the ebb and flow of the tides while reciting from the Prayer Book provides an image that is both significant and haunting. Significant, because it shows that his faith had become so important that he hardly liked to start his morning's work without the spiritual comfort of prayers like the Third Collect (for Grace to live well), in which God is asked to

grant that this day we fall into no sin, neither run into any kind of danger; but that all our doings may be ordered by thy governance, to do always that is righteous in thy sight.

Haunting, because here is a mortal man who, knowing that the tides will continue to ebb and flow long after he is dead, has in a childlike manner placed himself so entirely in God's hands that he can accept everything, and need fear for nothing.

The strength of his faith was noticed at once by the new rector of Llanfihangel-y-Traethau; and Diccon (who in any case rarely missed a service) found himself drawn much more deeply into the life of the church. 'Very often', wrote the rector in an article for the *Church Times* a few years later,[18]

it is he who rings the church bell for the 8 a.m. Service of Holy Communion. In the midst of all his work and engagements he finds time to assist me in the work of the parish, and with his sound judgment and gentleness he is a great asset at the Parochial Church Council . . . [and] on the death of our People's Warden . . . he took over that post.

But although Diccon agreed to read the lessons (which he did in Welsh as well as in English), he was never an official lay reader. 'Indeed', the rector declared in that same article,

I am quite sure that apart from the calls on his time he has no wish to be one: his vocation he feels is in no sense sacerdotal. Indeed he once said to me that he felt a positive vocation *not* to put on a surplice and preach!

'By that', the rector explained, 'he meant no disrespect to the cloth but rather that he feels his vocation as a writer is intrinsically a lay one, and intrinsically different.'

His morning prayers over, Diccon would settle himself down in his study, and then 'work steadily without a break of any kind till three or four in the afternoon'. Often, when he was searching for a word or a phrase, he would 'pace up and down restlessly', but, as Penny records, quiet was his primary requirement:[19]

> When the geese grazing on the salt-flats below the house suddenly took it into their heads to honk at once he was bothered by it. And when for some reason the retriever had to be shut in his study while he worked, even though she simply slept in front of the fire, he said it made work almost impossible, because her rhythmical breathing interfered with the rhythm of the sentences in his head.

When he finally emerged from his study, he would eat; and from then until six o'clock in the evening (when he returned to his study) he combined some useful outdoor activity with his 'planning time'.

Normally, Penny tells us, he 'guarded his solitude' for this planning time. But when she was at home (having made certain that she was up to date with his current draft), she would

> keep him company as he mended the nets or weeded the garden, or would go for a long walk across the sands with him, and he would talk about the political and economic situation he was writing about, [and] about the kind of language people were carrying in their minds at that particular time.

It seemed to Penny that while her father talked, 'his characters were emerging from the mist of their futures – the sheer talking seemed to free his imagination'; and all that she needed to do was 'to listen quietly'.

That summer of 1955, Diccon briefly enrolled another 'listener': Jessamine Weeks, honorary secretary to the Council for Children's Films on which he had recently been serving. 'I wonder very much how the book is going', she wrote to him some months later. 'I remember so well how you read a very small piece to me and talked about it afterwards as the darkness gathered in Môr Edrin. I found it wonderfully exciting with a kind of portentous undertone.'[20] In fact Diccon had been so immersed in *The Fox in the Attic* that when Frances decided to let Môr Edrin (on the grounds that most of the family would be abroad that summer) he had refused to move; so, as Penny records, 'she had to let the house with Diccon still in it, listed as a landlord's fixture'.[21]

'It is a formidable undertaking, as I envisage it', Hughes would write a few months later, ' – a sort of *War and Peace* of the late war.'[22] Formidable indeed: from the semi-autobiographical figure of Augustine, and that of the dead child whom he carried upon his shoulders, Hughes spent the summer and autumn gradually working his way outwards into a panoramic recreation of the whole world of his own youth and early manhood.

The body of the dead child necessitates an inquest; and when old Dr Brinley the coroner is informed, he is sitting down to the annual Flemton (Laugharne) banquet, which enables Hughes to sketch in the life of that eccentric South Wales township. Augustine, feeling that he must get away from Newton Llantony for a few days before the inquest is held, travels up to London. There he stays in the town house of his sister Mary, married to the Liberal politician Gilbert Wadamy; and besides outlining the political life of the period, Hughes gives us a glimpse of the aristocratic world of the Wadamys' near neighbour, Lady Sylvia Davenant.

When Mary wishes to return to her Dorset home, the Elizabethan Mellton Chase, Augustine drives down there in his Bentley with his devoted five-year-old niece Polly, and we are introduced to the country-house life of the twenties; to the visiting Jeremy Dibden, one of Augustine's Oxford friends whose father is a parson of relatively slender means, and who might therefore have to join the Civil Service; and to the hierarchical world of the servants, presided over by Wantage the butler and Mrs Winter the house-keeper.

All these worlds are drawn from Hughes's own experience and observation, and are meticulously realised: one can feel safe in the hands of an author who *knows* (as he did from his experience of Hatherop) how irritating Mrs Winter is likely to find Polly's nanny, Mrs Halloran, since 'constitutionally Nursery was a self-governing province where even a Housekeeper's writ did not run'.

But Hughes was no mere social historian. What principally interested him at this stage (apart from building up a cast of characters who would be useful to him later on) was examining the psychology both of the mass and of the individual. What, he asked, were the formative experiences which might lead nations into war, and individuals to set themselves down on the wrong side in the great contest between good and evil? For that contest was to be at the heart of his novel, just as he understood it to be at the heart of the human condition.

Examining the state of mind which led whole nations to rush into the First World War so joyfully, Hughes asks whether they might have been suffering from a compulsive 'war dream' . . . a 'projection of some deep emotional upheaval'? Suppose that 'modern man' had been 'trying to ignore what seems to be one of the abiding terms of the human predicament'. Suppose that sanity depends upon a clear balance within the personality, a balance dependent upon knowing right from wrong, mine from yours, whom one should trust and whom one should fear; and suppose that 'in the name of emergent Reason', that balance had been destroyed, and

> the very we-they line itself within us had been deliberately so blurred and denied that the huge countervailing charges it once carried were themselves dissipated or suppressed? The Normal penumbra of the self would then become a no-man's-land: the whole self-conscious being is rendered unstable – it has lost its 'footing': the perceiver is left without emotional adhesion any-where to the perceived, like a sea-anemone which has let go its rock.

Into this emotional void, the war patriotism of 1914 had poured 'like Noah's Flood'; and the dangers of such a void (suggests Hughes) remained unrecognised even when the war was over.

To take just two individuals: Polly and Augustine. Polly is being brought up in the 1920s in what is considered to be an entirely modern way: to be unashamed of her body, to talk freely about 'sex and excreta and so on'; but 'shielded from . . . such words as "God" and "Jesus" '. Augustine wholly approves (and blames her nightmares on her old-fashioned Nurse Halloran). He and his sister had been brought up with those words 'God' and 'Jesus' 'knotted in their very navel-strings'; but he had come to believe that he and his generation[23]

> really was a new creation, a new kind of human being, *because of Freud!* For theirs was the first generation in the whole cave-to-cathedral history of the human race completely to disbelieve in sin . . . 'God' and 'Sin' had ceased to be problems because Freudian analysis had explained how such notions arise historically: i.e., that they are merely a primitive psychological blemish which, once explained, mankind can outgrow.

Hating what he thinks of as 'the relics of feudalism', Augustine is also anarchic in his thinking, and declares to Jeremy Dibden: 'There IS NO [social] web! there's no thread, even, joining man to man – nothing!'[24]

When however Augustine Penry-Herbert returns to Flemton for the inquest, he learns that the dead child whom he had carried upon his shoulder was Rachel, the daughter of Mrs Winter's younger sister Nellie. This raises a number of questions in Mrs Winter's mind (for example, about why the brilliant Rachel should have died rather than, say, the much less gifted Polly), which Hughes chooses not to answer for the time being. As for Augustine: because he has failed in his social responsibilities in Flemton, and because there are some awkward questions at the inquest, the jury return an open verdict, the windscreen of Augustine's Bentley is smashed, and he decides to go abroad for a while – to visit some cousins in Germany.

Diccon and Frances and their children spent Christmas 1955 in Gloucestershire with their Bazley relatives[25] – though not in Hatherop Castle, which in post-war circumstances had become impossible for Thomas to maintain, and had been sold for use as a school. And then, on 25 January 1956, with the family dispersed, Diccon and Frances set out (like Augustine) to visit cousins in Germany.

For if Diccon was to write about the Germany of the 1920s, and the rise of Nazism, he could no longer rely upon his own knowledge, and he wanted to talk to people who had lived through the events he planned to describe. After flying to Munich, he and Frances caught a train to Augsburg (travelling 'in a carriage with an old peasant-woman with live hens hidden under her skirts')[26] and there they were met by Frances's relative Baroness Pia von Aretin Gunzbourg, who drove them out to her home, Schloss Neuburg, not far from Krumbach in the heart of Schwaben.[27]

Many of the incidental details of their arrival at Schloss Neuburg made a vivid impression upon Diccon: including the 'newly-painted life-size baroque crucifix a few yards from the castle gateway', the 'dung-heap right alongside Schloss Neuburg's imposing entrance', and (in particular) 'a pet fox who lived in the drawing-room',[28] a curious sight which became inextricably linked in his mind with the scent of the fox about which he had already written in his opening chapter.

For much of the next six weeks, Frances painted in the woods, while Diccon immersed himself in German family life, reading through 'piles of family papers that had lain in the attics at Schloss Neuburg since the twenties'; and having long conversations with Pia's mother, eighty-four-year-old Marie-Lise, who had 'vivid memories' of that period, and who 'passed her days in winter in the main room, either sitting beside the huge porcelain stove, or ten feet from it at the dining-table'.

There were also expeditions to Augsburg (where Diccon and Frances attended a family wedding in the cathedral)[29] and to Munich, where in the most bitter midwinter weather (just a few days previously the temperature had fallen to thirty degrees below zero)[30] Frances watched as[31]

> Diccon and Pia st[ood] together in the Odeonsplatz while Diccon, completely oblivious of the cold, cross-questioned Pia on every detail of Hitler's march down the Konigstrasse, that fateful night of the Munich _Putsch_ in 1923.

Finally, before returning to London on 19 February,[32] the Hugheses spent three nights at 'the larger and grander Schloss Heidenburg two miles away',[33] where they were taken out on a light one-horse sleigh through 'the whiteness and the blackness of [an] endless snow-burdened forest.'[34]

Two weeks after returning to England, Diccon gave another set of Gresham lectures: this time on _The Tale of Genji_ by the Lady Murasaki, a tenth-century Japanese novel of some half a million words, which he is said to have 'rated alongside _War and Peace_ and _The Red and the Black_ as an influence on his fictional practice'.[35] A number of his friends were present at the first lecture: including Lance Sieveking, who, from the moment that he arrived, fifteen minutes early, to find himself the sole person 'in a large hall with seating for about six hundred', thoroughly relished the surreal quality of the experience. As he later recalled:[36]

> Between a quarter past five and half past a trickle of oddly assorted people strolled into the hall and distributed themselves as far apart from each other as they could . . . We sat and waited. One lady began to knit. An elderly man emptied his pockets on to the seat next to him and began gravely sorting out the contents. At twenty-six past five Diccon and Frances arrived.

After piling a large number of books on to a table on the dais, Diccon begged the audience, who numbered no more than thirty, to come and sit at the front ('Most of them did', records Sieveking, 'except two rather shy men at the very back, who only dared to come half-way down the hall'); and then Diccon asked

> those who had read _The Tale of Genji_ to put up their hands. I crouched down to hide my shame, half expecting the entire audience to hold up its hands. To my surprise and relief only three hands went up. One belonged to Amabel Williams-Ellis . . .
> 'As I thought', observed the lecturer, and then thinking this might have sounded unkind, he smiled at us in a fatherly way.

He then explained that 'he proposed to examine . . . what, precisely, happens when a reader and a book meet', and declared that 'meaning' was 'whatever transpires from the transaction'. Sieveking was just beginning to be interested, when Hughes

> gently changed gear, and murmured that as so very few of us had read *Genji*, which he had chosen as a good example of what he had to say, perhaps the best thing to do would be to tell us, in the first place, something of the story and its origins. This he proceeded to do.
>
> But as *Genji* is more than half a million words long, we had scarcely begun to hear what it was about when he looked at the clock and saw that he had been talking for an hour and a half.
>
> 'And there, I'm afraid, we must leave it', he said with a gentle note of regret.

Afterwards, in a nearby public house, Sieveking asked Hughes whether 'he thought he would reach the main theme of his lectures before the fourth lecture was finished'. In reply, Diccon looked at him quizzically, and contented himself with saying gently: 'I hope so.'

By this time, although Diccon had told Frances that the Gresham lectures were helping him to clarify some of his ideas about the novel, he had become disenchanted by the small audiences.[37] So towards the end of March he wrote resigning the professorship, on the reasonable grounds that he had promised his publishers that he would finish his new novel 'in three years, and it is abundantly clear I can't keep my promise if I give so much time and thought to something quite different'.[38]

Progress with *The Human Predicament* was certainly slow. Hughes intended that this should be his masterpiece, and he wrote and rewrote, determined that every sentence should be as perfect as possible. 'My first drafts are ghastly,' he wrote to Lance Sieveking at about this time, in an effort to explain why at the age of 56 he had produced so few books; 'but I work and work on them until they seem effortless . . . Perfectionism and laziness aren't really synonyms, you know'.[39]

In March 1956, on the back of one of the typed announcements of his Gresham lectures for that month, Hughes was still busily redrafting a few paragraphs from the beginning of his seventh page, with its description of the billiard-room at Newton Llantony as (in this version) 'A man's room, this, which no woman (except housemaids) ever used to enter . . .' And the German chapters of his novel[40]

demanded ceaseless reading and research. Parcels of books arrived every few days from the London Library and from Blackwells, and all the spare floor round his desk became a sea of books laid spine uppermost for easy access. The most useful material was always the first-hand accounts – collections of letters, documents, published diaries.

'He read and read, and', as Penny observed, 'seemed as helpless as the Sorcerer's Apprentice to stem the rising tide of books.'

There was a brief escape from the creative tension engendered by all this hard work in the summer of 1956, when Diccon joined Penny and her friend Sally Hinchcliffe on part of their second voyage in their ex-lifeboat _Crab_, of which he was part-owner. On Sunday 1 July the three of them flew out to Malta,[41] where they had to wait for a few days 'for the boat's planks to swell again after nearly a year on dry land'; and where Penny found that her father had 'an insatiable appetite for new experience, and twice our energy'. He encouraged them to explore the island with him; and, as he reported in a letter to Frances, he particularly admired the stone-age temples: especially one underground, which may have reminded him of the Celtic burial chambers he had explored long ago with Robert Graves. He was also interested by the ancient carvings: 'mostly of a very fat old woman (Graves's "White Goddess" I suppose?)' though 'nowadays', he commented, 'it's the Virgin Mary, not the White Goddess'; and he and the others attended a fiesta at which 'people showered the Holy Family with home-made confetti including silver and gold paper strips from the windows'.[42]

At last _Crab_ was seaworthy, there was the 'forecast of a strong following wind', and at ten o'clock on the morning of Monday 9 July they set sail for Sicily.

The atmosphere on board was uneasy: Diccon's physical weight was such that if he made a sudden movement, the two girls were liable to be catapulted overboard; and although Sally was officially skipper, the weight of Diccon's experience was equally difficult to cope with. As they entered the straits between the south-east of Sicily and island of Passero, the wind freshened sharply, and

> a row flared between [Diccon] and the skipper over shortening sail – Diccon wanting to see how fast she would go, Sally cautious, fearing the mast might snap. The row flared briefly and died away again. But rows between generations leave nine-tenths unsaid, hanging over the company like a storm-cloud.

That night they 'beat up the coast towards Syracuse under storm sails', and at dusk they sailed into a cove, pulled the boat out of the water, and 'slept beside her on the sand – Diccon's only comfortable night, for his shoulders were too broad to sleep well on the narrow thwarts'. On Wednesday they reached Syracuse; and on Saturday Diccon flew back to London,[43] leaving the others to collect two more crew members, and continue on their way to Corfu.

Diccon would have preferred to stay in the Mediterranean; but on Tuesday 14 July 1956 he was due to travel up to Bangor, where he and Frances were to dine that evening with the Vice-Chancellor of the University of Wales; and where on Wednesday morning there was a degree ceremony at which (observed by three of his children – Robert, Kate and Owain – and by a number of his friends including Clough and Amabel) he was awarded an Honorary D. Litt. for services to literature. He may not have been best pleased by the moderate praise of Professor J.F. Danby who, in presenting him for the degree, suggested that his particular blend of 'vividness and . . . clear realism and . . . rich fantasy' had been swamped by the changes of the 1930s; and that one of his chief claims to fame was that, like T.F. Powys, he might have been an influence upon Dylan Thomas. However, any kind of public recognition is encouraging to a penurious writer; and since Diccon had decided that everything must be sacrificed to his novel, he was once again running into financial difficulties.

After expenses of £1072, his profit for the year ended 5 April 1955 had been only £422;[44] and in March 1956, replying to a letter from Lang congratulating him upon the publication of *Administration of War Production*,[45] Hughes had asked whether the Admiralty would 'consider the question of an *ex post facto* award related to an estimate of the finished article now in their hands?'[46] In May, while reminding Hughes that he had offered to do the work as a labour of love, Lang had generously offered him an *ex gratia* payment of 700 guineas; but by that time Diccon was becoming desperate; and he kept up an unsatisfactory correspondence with Lang until September the following year, when he accepted the original offer.[47]

He felt able to do so, largely because of an unexpected windfall. In September 1956, the film rights to *A High Wind in Jamaica* were acquired by Twentieth Century Fox. Hughes no longer owned the complete rights; but his share of the proceeds came to a substantial £900. Diccon immediately began trying to sell Fox the dialogue from the radio version he had originally written for the BBC; and towards the end of January 1957 he and Frances once again left for Spain, 'the only country left', declared Hughes, 'in which it seems possible to live cheaply'.[48]

The Hugheses had found 'a Pension at San Roque which costs about 5/- a day';[49] and although (as Frances warned sixteen-year-old Kate, who joined them with a school-friend in late February) it was 'TINY . . . very primitive' and 'entirely SPANISH', it was 'a wonderful place for work, writing, painting'.[50] Diccon himself commented to Joseph Brewer on the 'almost ideal working conditions. For two months . . . I was able to put in an 8-hour day absolutely without disturbance and get a sizable chunk added to my MS'.[51]

However, Hughes's determination to achieve total historical accuracy combined with his lack of any clear notion about what his invented characters would be doing in five or ten pages' time, meant that his overall progress continued to be painfully slow. Ian Parsons, his publisher at Chatto, recalls how Hughes once said 'that he'd done 50,000 words of *The Fox in the Attic*'. Six months later, when Hughes was next in London, Parsons said to him:[52]

> 'Well, now, you must be getting in sight of the end.'
> And he looked at me with blank astonishment and said: 'What do you mean?'
> And I said: 'You'd done 50,000 words back in January, and now it's June.'
> 'Well, oh yes, now I'm afraid the situation's not . . .'
> 'How much have you done, Dick?'
> 'Well, I should think I'm satisfied with about ten thousand, you see . . .' And this went on year in, year out.

It was at San Roque that Hughes had begun drafting the story of Augustine's arrival in Bavaria in November 1923, and his meeting with his German relatives: including Baron Walther von Kessen, wealthy owner of Schloss Lorienburg, and Walther's beautiful half-blind daughter Mitzi, with whom Augustine is soon madly in love.

As he introduced his German cast of characters, Hughes also needed to sketch in the German history of the previous five years. In general terms, this was not too difficult. 'In England', he wrote, 'the ending of the war had come like waking from a bad dream: in defeated Germany, as the signal for deeper levels of nightmare.'[53] Walther's half-brother Otto von Kessen, a retired colonel who has lost a leg during the war, recalls the return of the defeated armies from the Western Front, and cannot understand 'Why . . . God chose . . . to do this thing to His German Army', which is, in Otto's eyes, 'the very salt of His else-unsavoury earth'.[54]

When runaway inflation is added to their other ills, the reasons for their suffering seem more and more inexplicable to the German people. And, as Hughes explains:[55]

inexplicable suffering turns to hatred. But hatred cannot remain objectless: such hatred precipitates its own THEY, its own some-one-to-be-hated. In a hell devoid of real ministering devils the damned invent them rather than accept that their only tormentors are themselves and soon these suffering people saw everywhere such 'devils', consciously tormenting them: Jews, Communists, Capitalists, Catholics, Cabbalists – even their own elected government, the 'November Criminals'. Millions of horsepower of hatred had been generated, more hatred than the real situation could consume: inevitably it conjured its own enemy out of thin air.

On the heels of that hatred came also the inevitable reacting love. All those egos violently dislodged from their old penumbral settings were now groping desperately in the face of that dark enveloping phatasmal THEY to establish a new footing, new tenable penumbral frontiers of the Self: inevitably they secreted millions of horsepower of love that the actual situation also couldn't consume, and therefore precipitating its own fictive WE – its myths of Soil and Race, its Heroes, its kaleidoscope of Brotherhoods each grappling its own members with hoops of steel.

Its Freikorps, its communist cells: its Kampfbund, with all its component organisms: its Nazi movement.

So much for the broad picture: but Augustine arrives at Schloss Lorienburg on the eve of Hitler's abortive Munich putsch; and much of Hughes's time was now consumed by historical research whose detailed nature may be judged by an extract from a letter written to Joseph Brewer in January 1958. 'The thing is', he told his friend (conveniently working as a librarian in New York City),[56]

that I have come up against a snag or two in the historical research for the background of my novel; and I wondered if you could help me. Item (1) entails access to American newspaper files for November 1923 . . .

(1) *The 1923 Hitler Putsch in Munich*
There seems a remarkable paucity of eyewitness accounts. And yet, according to Putzi Hanfstaengl ('Hitler: The Missing Years' page 95 etc.), there was a whole batch of foreign correspondents present in the Burgerbraukeller, including H.R. Knickerbocker, Larry Rue of the Chicago Tribune, and an unnamed woman journalist (could that be Dorothy Thompson?) *Surely* their reports must have been published, however unimportant Nazis seemed in those days! But the Chatham House Press Library has nothing, and apparently the Wiener Library in London can't help either . . .

The march on the Feldherrnhalle the next day seems to be even worse covered! Putzi was not in it himself, and indeed the only account I have come across that was not a second-hand one

I found in Streicher's evidence at the Nuremberg Trial – but it is not very illuminating.

As the years passed and Hughes wrote and rewrote his pages (some fifty to sixty drafts of most chapters), his family grew up and began (as he told Joseph Brewer in that same letter of January 1958) to be 'scattered to the four winds'. Fourteen-year-old Owain was at Shrewsbury School; eighteen-year-old Kate at school in North Oxford; twenty-one-year-old Llecky seemed uncertain about her future, and was 'marking time with a temporary job in a school'; twenty-four-year-old Penny had gone down from Oxford with a Second in Greats ('It was pretty clear she wouldn't get a First as soon as she started giving so much time to small-boat-navigation in the Mediterranean'), was temporarily working as a vegetable cook in the kitchens of a large hotel in Leeds, and was thinking seriously about entering a Franciscan religious order; while twenty-five-year-old Robert had been ordained in Coventry the previous September, and was now said by his father to be 'deliriously happy'.

Diccon could understand Robert's happiness; but Penny's intention of joining a religious order disconcerted him, and in order to try to understand his daughter he 'began reading the mystics – the anonymous _Cloud of Unknowing_, and St Teresa of Ávila and St John of the Cross'.[57]

In the summer of 1958, Diccon arranged to spend a month on board _Crab_, before going on to join Frances in Bavaria for a further period of research.[58] So Tuesday 3 June found him setting sail from Athens with Sally and two other women friends of hers (Penny had been studying archaeology on Crete, and was to join them at Chalcis), and 'lollop[ing] along the coast for only a few miles, anchoring in a bay for the night so as to get everything stowed and shipshape'. The following day, as Diccon told Frances,[59]

> we sailed about 34 miles, in a blazing sun, rounding the point of Sunium (the southernmost point of Attica) where a huge white marble temple to Poseidon still stands on the brink of the cliff, glittering against the blue sky like salt & visible at least twenty or thirty miles.

By Saturday they had voyaged as far as Chalcis where they met Penny. She had arrived with a car-load of friends, including (as she recalls),[60]

> a very beautiful Scottish girl [Catherine Duncan] who had once worked for Diccon as a secretary.

'What are *you* doing here Diccon, when you should be writing your book?' she asked. 'Gaol-breaking as usual?'

Diccon looked at her straight in the eye.

'I'm on my way from North Wales to Bavaria, where I shall do some research', he answered with dignity. 'It's quicker via Athens and Istanbul.'

In the morning, Diccon and Penny woke early and walked up through the town to attend a Greek orthodox service, remembered by Penny as 'a heady experience', in a small crowded church where it was 'dark, but for the flickering of innumerable candles constantly being lit and placed before the ikons, where their glow was reflected by the embossed silver ornamentation'. Afterwards, as father and daughter walked back to the boat, Diccon talked about the present state of his novel.[61]

The first section, which he had named 'Polly and Rachel' (ninety-nine pages in the printed volume) was 'more or less in its final form', though he wanted to alter the sequence of events in one chapter to make it read more dramatically.[62] The second section, to be called 'The White Crow', so far consisted of only six chapters (roughly another twenty-five pages) whose order was not yet decided. And then (slightly to Penny's amusement), he talked about 'his unruly characters . . . not at all as if he were their sole creator', but 'as if he himself were a harassed civil servant trying to marshall [them] into some kind of respectable existence'.[63]

Later that day, they set sail once again — and (as Diccon reported to Frances), they 'passed Aulis, the bay where [Agamemnon] sacrificed his daughter in order to get a fair wind . . . but as we have an outboard engine Penny's life was spared!'[64]

The next few days were full of delightful experiences: such as landing at a little fishing harbour, 'quiet as the grave when we got there but at 2 a.m. they started loading and unloading coasting caiques and fishing boats by the light of torches & continued till after dawn'. Diccon told Frances that he was having 'a really wonderful time . . . My only sadness is it must be at least another week before I get news of you, I do hope you're all right'.[65] Penny recalls how her father's[66]

love of solitude made him a useful person on the boat. When we were passage-making at night he would ask for a double spell of time at the helm, and would be quite content to stay for six hours on end, watching the stars of the Plough circling the polestar, as the night passed.

And she noticed how intensely he was enjoying the holiday, despite the obvious discomforts of life in a 17-foot open boat.

After putting in at Trikeri,[67] they sailed to Skiathos, a fertile 'island of enchantment'; and on to Skopelos with its '34 tiny churches all completely different'; but then on Saturday 14 June they ran into difficulties. A strong current swept them in towards an unknown island; and because the weather looked so threatening, they decided to seek shelter in 'a deep, forked bay' on its western end.[68]

They had arrived on Pelagos, an island which was inhabited only by 'two monks . . . two peasants farming for the monks, and occasionally a charcoal-burner';[69] and there they were stormbound for several days, alongside several fishing boats 'with decking and powerful diesel engines' which had also been forced to run for cover. Penny recalls that food ran short, as _Crab_ carried no reserves of food apart from emergency supplies of biscuit; and when there was no more drinking water, the fishermen 'dug a hole a few feet from the sea's edge and we drank water from there, and gradually got hungrier and hungrier'.[70]

The fishermen also lit fires of myrtle (so full of resin that it burns even when wet), showed them 'how to brew an aromatic tea from a herb which grows there', and allowed them to sleep under the deck of their boats at night, even though 'that meant they had to sleep out in the rain themselves'. In return, Diccon told them 'a very long folk-story from Morocco', which Sally translated, sentence by sentence, into modern Greek.[71]

After four nights on the island, the weather improved enough for the captain of a Greek caique to tow _Crab_ out to sea; where the winds remained so strong and adverse, that he took them all the way to 'the strange volcanic island' of Lemnos. Diccon thanked him for this by making him a present of his pre-war German binoculars;[72] and _Crab_ continued under her own sail to Canakkale in the Dardanelles.

There Diccon discovered that the 'daily plane' in which he had intended to fly from Canakkale to Istanbul was 'a myth, in fact there wasn't even a steamer going for the next five days!'[73] so he was forced to remain in _Crab_; where (as he later wrote) 'the most fantastic part of the journey was only beginning'.[74]

Shortly before dark on the evening of Wednesday 25 June, after three days of sailing towards Istanbul, they reached Kalolimnos, only thirty miles from the Golden Horn, 'just as a north-easter began to get up'. The island had no harbours, but they sheltered behind it for the night, 'in a shallow stony bay, where there was a garden shaded by planes and fig trees; but no houses'.

When they woke the following morning, they found to their amazement that _Crab_ was 'surrounded by a deputation (in their

underpants) waist-deep in the seas . . . proffering bouquets of car-
nations . . . The first thing that seemed really odd about them', as
Diccon observed,

> was that one of them seized our bottle of methylated [spirit] and
> drained it at a draught . . . Then an imperious figure appeared
> on the shore and shouted at them and they scattered. He could
> talk some English, and explained that he was their schoolmaster,
> that the island was a penal colony of 'Six hundred criminals-
> guilty. All mens here and no womans for twenty-two years, all
> criminals-guilty. Too dangerous you remain. Killings with the
> knife; girl-stealings . . . *Very* dangerous but all good men, have
> no fear . . .'

So (as Diccon explained to Frances), 'we and the "good" men
sat in a ring in the shady garden and discussed the situation'.

Penny watched in admiration as her father somehow managed
to communicate with the murderers 'in a monosyllabic broken
English'. All his imaginative powers, she felt,

> were brought into play for that conversation. His interest in them
> as people was self-evident – he leant forward, eyes alight, hand and
> gesture brilliantly conveying what he understood. Since he thought
> of himself as a man with a life-sentence as a writer, perhaps it
> was fellow-feeling for other 'lifers'. Basically their crime was an
> excessive zest for life – and if he had a crime that was his also.

Finally, since it was too stormy for *Crab* to put to sea, the schoolmaster sent for the island's caique, and they were towed to an
artificial harbour. There the governor told them that they must
leave on a steamer which would be calling at the island that very
evening. So *Crab* was hoisted out of the water, and ignominiously
'lashed outside the rail of the upper deck' for the last thirty miles
of her journey to Istanbul.

After spending most of July 1958 in Bavaria, Diccon and Frances
returned to Môr Edrin to find an interesting letter from Margery
Vosper, who reported that Norman Spencer of Horizon Pictures
had been asking whether Diccon had ever done any film work.
She had 'told him at some length about *The Divided Heart*';[75] and
the result was that Hughes was soon studying an Ealing film-script
based upon William Golding's *Lord of the Flies*, that novel about
children reverting to savagery which had been published to considerable acclaim four years previously.[76]

Diccon's first thought was that 'the only thing to do with this
Ealing script is to forget it'. Among other defects, he believed that:[77]

It misses practically everything the book has to offer – except the occasional physical beastlinesses! It casually introduces little girls without an inkling of the profound changes this must have made in the course of events. (Golding left them out on purpose, & if they are to be put in they must be put in very much *on purpose*.)

But although Spencer also disliked the current script, he profoundly disagreed with Golding's fundamental hypothesis, summarised by Diccon in the words:[78]

'There are intrinsically savage traits in the societies little boys evolve for themselves, when they are partially isolated from adult control and feminine influences in prep-schools. So imagine that control and influence removed entirely . . . The savage traits would become completely dominant and their society would revert to total, open savagery.'

Spencer's opposing hypothesis (as Diccon saw it) was

more like this: 'True, there are savage traits innate in the little human animal – female as well as male: but there are civilised, ethical traits just as deep-rooted. Remove adult control, and powerful restraints against his innate savagery would emerge *from within the child himself!*'

Hughes had a number of major reservations about altering Golding's story: for example, that his hypothesis was more startling; that it was simpler; and that: 'Golding has admittedly done a good job: are we so sure we can do a better one? – To put it bluntly: are we so confident our brains are all that brighter than Golding's?' Spencer had no such reservations, and commissioned Hughes to write an entirely new film-script, which would clearly have only a tangential relationship to Golding's original story.

Working 'at top speed', Diccon had completed a rough draft by 29 October.[79] Most ingeniously, the children had become members of[80]

a cast of children being assembled in New Orleans for the production of a film; and that gave me a further notion, that the film they are cast for should be *Lord of the Flies* itself!

This, however, was virtually the end of the matter. After a handful of apologetic letters from Spencer saying only 'that he had *still* not been able to get an opportunity of discussing it with Sam Spiegel', there was silence.[81] It would be four years before a film of *Lord of the Flies* appeared, written and directed by Peter Brook (who appears to have been somewhere in the background of this earlier enterprise),[82] and entirely faithful to Golding's original conception.

Having posted the draft film-script, Hughes had plunged back into his novel. In November 1958 Penny wrote to him about the problems which the von Kessens were facing;[83] in December he ordered twelve additional source-books (including O. Dietrich's *The Hitler I Knew* and A. Kubizek's *Young Hitler: The Story of our Friendship*); in February 1959 (after dining in London with Polly and John Hope) he and Frances travelled out to the south of Spain for another two months of writing and painting; and by August (with Môr Edrin finally connected to a mains electricity supply)[84] Hughes had at last reached the pages in which Hitler is first mentioned.

It is while Augustine is staying at Schloss Lorienburg that Hitler launches his unsuccessful putsch; and the following day, as rumours about what has happened begin to filter out of Munich, Augustine, Mitzi and Franz (Mitzi's twenty-year-old elder brother) are driven in a one-horse open sleigh to a household where they are treated to an eyewitness account of the events in the Burgerbraukeller.

Dr Rheinhold Steuckel, brother of their host, explains that he was present when, on the very stroke of eight-thirty, Hitler fired two shots into the ceiling to attract the attention of all the notables who were present, and[85]

> 'the door burst open, and in tumbled young Hermann Goering with a machine-gun squad! Steel helmets seemed to appear instantly out of nowhere: at every door, every window, all over the hall itself. And then Pandemonium broke loose! Shrieks and shouts, crashing furniture and smashing beer-jugs . . . punctuated by that short sharp ululation peculiar to women in expensive furs.
>
> 'Hitler jumped off his table and began pushing to the front, revolver still in hand. Two of Goering's strong-arm boys half-lifted him onto the platform, and Kahr was shoved aside. So there he stood, facing us . . . You know those piercing, psychotic, popping eyes of his? You know that long, comparatively legless body? . . . But oh the adoring gaze those brawny pin-head gladiators of his kept turning on him from under their skull-caps, those ant-soldiers of his (and there seemed to be legions of them, let me tell you, last night)!'

Dr Rheinhold has finished his story, and 'a rather squat actor-type' is explaining how Hitler makes an impression at dinner-parties (arriving late, saying nothing until he has somehow silenced the rest of the room, and then launching into an impassioned speech for half an hour or an hour before dashing out again into the night) when 'Suddenly Mitzi, forgotten in a corner, gave a startled, poignant cry'. Her remaining eyesight has failed, and she is now stone-blind.

In September 1959, Hughes wrote to an agent who had asked about his new novel, saying that he always hated 'talking about work in progress – I feel there's a hoodoo on it; and (as you guessed) I can't provide any "detailed outline of plot-development" because I can't work to one'; but his letter showed that he was already becoming a little alarmed by 'the intended *scale* of the whole work'. He explained that there were[86]

> plenty of precedents – beginning with Homer himself – for an attempt like this to describe the "human predicament" through a marriage, in epic form, of the two kinds of story-telling, the fictional narrative, where no-one knows what will happen next and the History everybody knows.

'In short', he concluded, 'success and failure depend on the one thing only: on whether I was born with adequate gifts. For I certainly intend to stint neither effort nor time.'

Just before Christmas 1959 there was a family wedding. Penny had become engaged during the summer to Robin Minney (co-owner of *Crab*), having decided (in her own words) that her vocation lay 'in trying to love one person, and to be loved by one, not in trying to love the whole world'; and they were married by candlelight 'in the little ancient church of Llanfihangel'.[87] Christmas itself was spent in London, where everyone but Llecky (who was abroad, teaching English to wealthy Greeks in Athens) squeezed into the 'charming little house in Lambeth' where Penny and Robin were living, and where Penny was expecting their first child in the spring.[88] Robert came down from Coventry (where Diccon had once opened a church bazaar on his behalf);[89] nineteen-year-old Kate (unofficially engaged to the classicist Colin Wells) was also present; as was sixteen-year-old Owain, on holiday from Shrewsbury School.

Passing on some of this family news to Joseph Brewer in January 1960, Diccon commented that he and Frances now spent a lot of time alone at Môr Edrin. This suited both of them: especially Frances, who had more time to paint, and had recently staged her first one-man exhibition. 'But alas!' Diccon lamented,

> that my novel is taking so long. I've now (in four years) written

about as much as *High Wind*: but that's only a flea-bite in a work on this scale. In drafts of course I have written ten times as much: it's the boiling down which takes the time.

'Thank goodness though I've nearly finished with Germany', he concluded, 'and then shortly the scene moves to America (of which my memories are pretty vivid).'

In March 1960, Diccon and Frances were once again in Bavaria.[90] Hughes had already had the good fortune to discover a vivid contemporary account of the Munich putsch by one Major Goetz; and now he and Frances not only met but also stayed with another major participant in his story: Helene Hanfstaengl. In the early 1920s, she and her German-American husband, Dr Ernst Hanfstaengl, had befriended Hitler and enjoyed musical weekends with him; and it was to their little house in the Bavarian village of Uffing that Hitler had fled after the failure of his 1923 putsch. He had found Helene there alone except for her maids and two-year-old son; and stayed with her in hiding for forty-eight hours.

It was during his description of this period (written on his return to England, and based heavily not only upon long conversations with Helene, but also upon her unpublished narrative account),[91] that Hughes made his first attempt to enter Hitler's mind.

By this time, he had already written of the effect upon Mitzi of her blindness. Far from completely destroying her belief in the love of God (as Augustine wrongly assumes it must), 'the very enormity of the shock' (as Hughes told a correspondent)[92]

> topples her head over heels into the experience of 'conversion', so that presently we are watching her first difficult steps on the long road – the lifelong road – of the devoted Christian mystic. Ironically enough, her family have already decided for convenience sake to send her to a convent – doing the right thing, though for quite the wrong reasons.

And now, when Hughes writes of Hitler's demented state of mind during his forty-eight hours at Uffing, he contrasts it with Mitzi's.

Hitler imagines that he is in Berlin, and that he is 'scourging the little flash jew-girls till they screamed'. He sees the dark corners of his room[93]

> filling with soft naked legs: those young Viennese harlots sitting half-naked in the lighted windows all along the Spittelberggasse (between the dark windows where 'it' was already being done). For once upon a time the young Hitler used to go there, to the

Spittelberggasse: to . . . just to look at them. To harden his will.

He knows that his own 'holy flame of sex' must be

> kept burning without fuel . . . After all, how could that monistic
> 'I' of Hitler's ever without forfeit succumb to the entire act of sex,
> the whole essence of which is recognition of one 'Other'? Without
> damage I mean to his fixed conviction that he was the universe's
> unique sentient centre . . . Because . . . the universe contained no
> other persons than him, only things . . .
>
> Hitler's then was that rare diseased state of the personality,
> an ego virtually without penumbra: rare and diseased, that is,
> when abnormally such an ego survives in an otherwise mature
> adult intelligence clinically sane (for in the new-born doubtless it
> is a beginning normal enough and even surviving into the young
> child). Hitler's _adult_ 'I' had developed thus – into a larger but still
> undifferentiated structure, as a malignant growth does.
>
> In Mitzi – as could perhaps happen to you and me – with
> the shock of her crisis the central 'I' had become dislodged: it
> had dwindled to a cloudlet no bigger than a man's hand beneath
> the whole zenith of God. But in this suffering man always and
> unalterably his 'I' must blacken the whole vault from pole to
> pole.

For the rest of _The Human Predicament_, the spiritual struggle
will be between those who favour Mitzi, and those who favour
Hitler. Hughes's reading of the mystics had long ago convinced
him that mystics were 'intensely practical people . . . often with
a bias towards the poor which got them into trouble politically',
and that Mitzi was therefore 'the one person who would be able
to stand up to Hitler'.[94] Before the end of Book Three it will be
Mitzi who finds the body of the political assassin Wolff, swinging
at the end of a rope in the attics of Lorienburg. This was the fox
in the attic – a being of unfettered evil who at one time planned to
murder both Augustine and Mitzi, and whose violent end prefigures
that of Hitler himself.

Augustine, understanding nothing of Mitzi's spiritual life, returns
to Lorienburg after a brief holiday in Munich, intending to ask her
to marry him. Instead, he learns to his horror and despair that she
is about to leave for a Carmelite convent. The colour goes out of
his world, and all solidity. His surroundings seem wraith-like. He
imagines Mitzi 'lying white in the unending darkness of her night'
with a vampire's 'toothmarks on her throat'. He cannot begin to
understand how she can want to be a nun. He cannot begin to
understand why her parents 'allow it, instead of sending for a psy-
chiatrist'. Eventually, 'flinging his things into [a] Gladstone bag', he
flees from Lorienburg:

Where was he going to next? Anywhere anywhere anywhere! Over the frontier to whatever other country was nearest! But then, as he turned again to the wardrobe his bag called after him 'You don't know when you're lucky!'

Augustine turned round in surprise; but he was wrong, it was only a bag.

Richard Hughes had intended to continue at once with Book Four, in which Augustine would go out to America and begin his sexual education. However, there was now quite enough material to fill a first volume, and Chatto urged him not to wait. There were also financial reasons for pressing ahead with publication. Several paintings (including a magnificent Dufy) had already had to be 'sacrificed upon the altar of Volume One';[95] Diccon's gross earnings for 1960 were nil – fortunately Frances had investment income that year of just over £800 – [96] and they badly needed *The Fox in the Attic* to be a commercial success.

By mid October 1960 the manuscript was in the hands of his publishers; and the following month Hughes told the Baroness Pia von Aretin: 'I'm relieved to find them quite enthusiastic about it'[97] – more enthusiastic than the three German publishers who turned it down, in one of whose letters (as Diccon wrote to Pia six months later) 'every line smokes with his anger that an outsider should have the presumption to meddle with such a theme at all'.[98]

It was difficult to begin any fresh work while awaiting publication of *The Fox in the Attic*, now scheduled for the autumn of 1961. During the intervening months, the most important event in family life was the wedding in December 1960 of their son Robert to Sheila, a warm-hearted woman who had been Akela to the cub pack attached to Robert's church.[99]

Diccon and Frances had first met Sheila and her parents (Rose and Joe Basketts) a year or two previously, having been given a meal in their council house after Diccon had opened that church bazaar. Despite Frances's bohemian attitudes, she still had a baronet for a brother, and she found it hard to cope with the fact that her eldest son was marrying into the working class. Diccon was also uncertain at first; and when on one occasion Rose sensed this, she deliberately provoked an argument by saying that she was not at all certain that Robert was good enough for her daughter.[100]

Soon after the wedding, Robert moved with his new wife down to London, where on Sunday 19 March 1961 Diccon and Frances (just back from a ten-day holiday in Paris) heard him preach a sermon at his new church in Woolwich.[101] And that summer, hearing that Rose's mother had just died, Diccon and Frances invited Rose to stay with them for a week at Môr Edrin.[102]

Rose Basketts had won Diccon's respect by her forthright manner; and now he discovered to his delight that they shared a keen interest in gardening. So they took to meandering around the garden together while he showed her his flowers; and then further afield along the shore; and although to begin with Diccon had seemed to Rose to be very shy, they had soon fallen, naturally and easily, into a close friendship.[103]

Rose told him about her childhood in the slums of Coventry back in the twenties: how she had been the leader of the kids in her courtyard; how after having a bath in the wash-tub in her room upstairs, she had been standing on top of the family chest of drawers practising being one of those naked statues which stand in public parks, when someone had called her, and she had jumped off the chest of drawers and crashed straight through the rotten floor-boards into the kitchen below; and how she had once sunk up to the knees in a bottomless bog in a field just outside Coventry, and had had to be rescued by her father. She also told him about the war, when her husband had been a fire-fighter through the midst of the Coventry blitz.

Diccon listened with interest; and in return he asked whether she had ever thought about growing old? 'No, I never think about it', she replied. 'Why, do you?' 'No, not now', came the answer. 'But on my sixtieth birthday I walked down on the beach and I looked at my hands and I thought: "I've got an old man's hands." '[104]

For much of the year, Diccon and Frances now led a very secluded life at Môr Edrin; but occasionally some invitation called them away from study and studio. In the summer of 1960, for example, Diccon had agreed to serve on the selection committee for the Hawthornden Prize;[105] he had also attended an informal buffet supper in Cardiff given by Henry Brooke, the Minister for Welsh Affairs;[106] and a few weeks later he and Frances had been invited to a garden party given by the minister and attended by the Queen and the Duke of Edinburgh.[107]

The summer of 1961 saw the Hugheses promoted to a garden party at Buckingham Palace;[108] soon after which, Diccon developed 'a mysterious fever' and was 'carted off to hospital'. Apparently this was not food-poisoning, as was thought at first, but blood-poisoning following a tooth extraction; and Diccon became 'quite light-headed, and convinced they meant to take my temperature with a cider flagon'.[109]

While Hughes was recovering from the blood-poisoning, welcome news arrived of a serious move by Twentieth Century Fox to film *A High Wind in Jamaica*. Diccon's old colleague 'Tibby' Clarke (with whom he had last collaborated on *The Herring Farm*) was to write the script. There was talk of Hughes himself acting as technical adviser;[110] and of thirteen-year-old actress Hayley Mills playing the part of Emily: to which Hughes objected, saying that this would make Emily a neo-Lolita. Perhaps Miss Mills could play Margaret instead?[111]

As publication day approached in the autumn of 1961, Frances was concussed in an accident, and had a miserable time for several weeks; while Diccon, after so much seclusion for so many years, was suddenly at the centre of things once again: courted by the press (the *Sunday Telegraph* offered him £25 for an exclusive advance interview)[112] and whisked all the way down to Cardiff to be interviewed on television.[113]

There followed a publication party in London, and a massive critical success of a kind with which Hughes had been unfamiliar since the publication of *A High Wind in Jamaica* thirty-two years previously. Kenneth Allsop described *The Fox in the Attic* as:

> An extraordinary creation – extraordinary for its originality of viewpoint, its mixture of the sinister and the frolicsome. Its audacity in mixing fictional and historical characters... Mr Hughes's reconstruction of this nightmare period, his evocation of fermenting evil, is disturbingly real.

Another critic, Goronwy Rees, declared: 'There are few living writers of whom one would say that they had genius; but somehow it seems the most natural thing in the world to say about Richard Hughes.' And the *Times Literary Supplement* magisterially pronounced his novel 'magnificent, authoritative, compassionate, ironic, funny and tragic ... vivid both in the evocation of character and in the unfolding of the action'.

Private letters were equally complimentary. The historian Alan Bullock, who was about to begin revising his *Hitler: A Study in Tyranny* (then the classic work on the subject), had some initial reservations about Hughes's detailed account of the Munich putsch, but asked him for a copy of the Goetz narrative, since he 'had very little to go on in my account of Hitler's Bavarian days'; and he also told Hughes that he had 'particularly enjoyed your picture of the state of mind of the Germans at that time. I found it entirely convincing'.[114] David Garnett was also full of praise, telling him that 'the German part is wonderful and the Germans themselves [were] so almost unbearably like Germans that it was positively all I could do to go on reading'.[115]

Perhaps the most welcome letter came from America, where Diccon's old friend Jane Cassidy had seen _The Fox in the Attic_ advertised in _Encounter_, and decided to break a thirty-one-year silence. She was now, she explained, Mrs Jane Cassidy Holran, 'a real large lady', divorced from her second husband, but with two daughters and three granddaughters, and living 'with too little house-keeping instinct' in Manhattan, where she was editing in-house publications for the United Presbyterian Church. In her letter (which she ended by saying: 'Hasn't it been a wonderful time to be alive?') she also reminded Diccon vividly of her old stone house at New Preston.[116]

Diccon was deeply touched. 'Jane, Jane', he wrote, 'after all these years of silence . . .' He told her that the fall and winter that he had spent around New Preston[117]

> has always been one of my highlights, typing away at _The Innocent Voyage_ till my fingers froze, and riding those comic animals of ours along the overgrown buggy roads. Do you remember the morning I finished the book at last, and climbed on my beast back-to-front in pyjamas and rode it up into your kitchen? Thank heavens you _hadn't_ a housekeeping instinct or you'd have reached for your gun.

She had also returned him, in his memory, to that part of the world in which he intended to set the beginning of the next volume of _The Human Predicament_.

CHAPTER 31

The Wooden Shepherdess

The remains of the temple of Athena Lindia still dominate the acropolis of Lindos on the eastern coast of the island of Rhodes. Standing upon the acropolis (if you had been there one morning in the spring of 1962) you would have looked down upon a scene of ruin and decay. What had once been an important town of some twenty thousand people had shrunk to a village of some eight or nine hundred. But it was the modern buildings which had fared worst from earthquakes; and although a few of the ancient 'knight's houses' were also in a state of collapse (and some of them were empty, or used as donkey stables), most of them were inhabited.

Polly and John Hope, the artists whom Diccon and Frances Hughes had first met in Malaga, had knocked two of these houses together to make a home for themselves and their baby son Augustine (Diccon's godchild), and the Hugheses were staying with them. Frances would have been out in the countryside painting (she caught the 6.45 bus each morning, and set off laden with paints and easel, only returning at night); while Diccon was working on his new volume in a separate house which he had specially rented for that purpose. Its principal room, which looked out over the bay, had a painted ceiling and a patterned pebble floor like a black and white carpet; and he described it as 'about the finest writing-room I have ever found anywhere'.[1]

It was now mid April; and Diccon and Frances had been in Lindos since the third week in March. They had intended to arrive earlier, but had been held up by the news that Frances's mother had suffered a severe stroke. Rushing to her bedside not many days before her death, they had found her blind and unable to speak; but she could still understand what was said to her; and she had taken first Frances's hand, and then Diccon's, written the word 'both' in the air, and then lifted her hand in blessing.[2]

They had been glad to leave England: with *The Fox in the Attic* still riding high in the bestseller lists, interruptions had been frequent. In January (with American publication scheduled for the following month) there had been a day when (as Hughes tells the story):[3]

Time Magazine chased me half across England by fast car – caught me in Wiltshire, lurking in the house of my brother-in-law – held me for grilling – carried me off to H.Q. for photographs – and then, when I was just ready to break down and confess to the murder only to end it all – inexplicably they fed me Lobster Victoria and released me without taking my fingerprints! But I'm still being shadowed.

A few days later he had been asked by his American publisher, Cass Canfield of Harpers, to autograph a thousand sheets for insertion in a special American book-club edition;[4] more letters of congratulation had kept pouring in; and while all this was going on, Hughes had been busily writing pages of commentary on Tibby Clarke's second draft screenplay of *A High Wind in Jamaica*. He had also prepared two sheets of nautical diagrams, telling his agent that he had been 'treating my "technical advisership" as if it already existed: Tibby doesn't know the first thing about sailing vessels, and the script fair bristles with nautical solecisms'.[5]

American publication of *The Fox in the Attic* had been another outstanding success. 'Phenomenal', reported Pamela Bianco on 26 February, 'phenomenal – marvellous reviews everywhere, and of course it is now in the best-seller list.'[6] Even Gloria Vanderbilt felt moved to write a personal letter of appreciation[7] – and there was another great surprise for Diccon, when 'Annie C', from his Bellevue, Virginia circle of January 1929, sent him a poignant letter reminding him of that 'marvellous interlude we loved always', telling him how she and Charlie Abbot and Smiley had always longed for his success – and that sadly, 'now that it is here, [and] your pictures are splashed all over our Virginia and New York papers, only I can rejoice with you – for Smiley died in 1952 – and Charlie a year earlier'.[8]

Now at last, in Lindos, it should have been possible to make good progress with *The Human Predicament*, in the company of the same Polly who had so much encouraged him at its outset. However, the success of *The Fox in the Attic* (for which he had now been offered an Arts Council Literary Award)[9] had the usual effect of any great success upon Diccon: it made it more difficult than ever for him to work; and although he accepted both the award and an invitation to become a Fellow of the Royal Society of Literature, these honours weighed heavily upon him.[10]

Struggling with the first few sentences of his new volume, Hughes thanked one correspondent for an encouraging letter, telling him that it had arrived opportunely, just as he was 'bogged down in a sticky patch in *Fox*'s successor and was reaching the conclusion that nothing I ever wrote could ever have the slightest merit or possibly interest anyone'.[11] However, the 'sticky patch' continued. His principal consolation lay in the extraordinarily long church services all of which (as he reported to Robert with some satisfaction) lasted between two-and-a-half and three hours.[12]

Perhaps he was also comforted by a letter from Laurie Lee, who told him: 'You teach us that the best things are never done in a hurry';[13] and by recalling that his godfather Charles Johnson, who had recently died at the age of ninety-two, had been working with a clear mind up to the age of ninety-one;[14] but the fact remains that Hughes returned to England in June 1962 with virtually nothing to show for nearly three months' work.

Soon after this return, there was a near-tragedy. Robert was riding his motorcycle to church one Sunday morning, with Frances in his sidecar, when the steering jammed. They crashed full-speed into a wall, and were lucky not to have been killed. Amazingly, Frances had no physical injuries worse than a broken wrist and bruises, but the shock to her system had been enormous; while Robert broke a leg and nearly lost a foot, which was practically severed at the ankle.[15]

Diccon, who visited Robert every day in hospital for several weeks, was sustained through this family crisis by the strength of his faith. The previous September, the Bishop of Bangor had devoted 'fully half his sermon' to a discussion of *The Fox in the Attic*, describing it as the fruit of a lay vocation, and declaring that Hughes was 'spelling out the Gospel just as truly as you and I do when we preach';[16] and Diccon was now preparing (at the bishop's request) a paper on *Liturgical Language Today* to be delivered in the autumn to a joint clergy school for the dioceses of St Asaph and Bangor.[17]

Hughes's theme was that the liturgy needed bringing up to date, to make it more accessible; but it needed to be written far more carefully than the New English Bible, whose severe drawbacks included[18]

> its inadequate rhythm and euphony ... Again and again when preparing one's reading before going to church one is struck by how much more clearly the new translation brings out the sense of the passage, and so one decides to use it: then one stands up at the lectern and wishes one hadn't – simply because the language has not been sufficiently composed for reading aloud.

A new liturgical language must also consist of sentences whose 'plain and simple appearance possess that compact multitudinousness of meaning which is the peculiar genius of the English tongue'. So it was not just divines who were needed with their theological meanings, but poets, 'capable of crowding these meanings by the handful into every single pregnant word'.

This strikes a personal note: for although Hughes no longer composed many formal poems, he was writing *The Human Predicament* with a poet's feeling for words. Ideally, he would have liked each of his chapters to be refined until it shone with a multiplicity of meaning like the ancient liturgy: which made his task incomparably more difficult, and gradually made it very doubtful that he would ever live to complete his work. However, his religious faith gave him a kind of fatalism in this respect. Since he felt that he was doing what he ought to be doing, any other questions could safely be left in God's hands.

Fortunately for his readers, Hughes's faith increased rather than diminished the range of his human understanding. The rector of Llanfihangel-y-Traethau records that Hughes regarded many of the distinctions between Christian sects as 'almost meaningless, religiously, in these ecumenical days', and that[19]

> some who with their mouths call themselves atheists yet behave like true Christians are in fact better Christians than he is. In this connection he likens Faith and Works to the heads and tails of a penny: some coins fall one way up, some the other – but the *underside* is there just the same – the upperside witnesses to it if the coin is a true one ... and even the coin itself may be mistaken about what is on the face which lies underneath, he thinks!

The rector added that Hughes's own family of five children was 'almost an ecumenical movement in itself', with one daughter a Roman Catholic, another married to an Orthodox Greek, and three Anglicans ranging all the way from High to Low.

Hughes continued to wrestle with the opening pages of volume two of his novel; but he could make no progress. Nor was there anything to be done on the screenplay of *A High Wind in Jamaica*. Jerry Wald, the prospective director, died after a short illness; and the result (as Tibby Clarke told Hughes in a telephone call towards the end of August) was that everything was thrown into the melting-pot once again.[20]

At least Robert was making a gradual recovery. And the summer was enlivened by the renewal of Diccon's connection with the Betjeman family, when John's daughter Candida came to be his secretary: she was said by her father to be '*thrilled* at the prospect of working for you';[21] though when it came to the point, she stayed with him for less than a year. Another distraction was a writers' conference at the Edinburgh Festival, where Hughes was able to repeat his belief[22] that a writer's duty was to frame questions, not to answer them; and where he stated (as he often did those days) that any generation that preferred non-fiction to fiction must be essentially frivolous, since it was only through fiction (of which he considered biography to be a near-relative) that it became possible to see the world through the eyes of a stranger.[23]

In the autumn of 1962, there was more news about *A High Wind in Jamaica*: but not good news. Darryl Zanuck had returned to Twentieth Century Fox (from which he had resigned six years earlier) and had sent for Tibby to talk to him about *High Wind*. This sounded promising; but in fact, as Tibby told Diccon, Zanuck simply handed over 'the notes he has dictated for the film he intends to make ... a tragically far cry from your book which I have so loved and admired'.[24] There seemed nothing to be done about it, and Hughes tried to dismiss the whole matter from his mind.

In a further attempt at his second volume (there were now 'endless new versions of page one, chapter one')[25] Diccon was planning a return to Rhodes in October. This was delayed when Robert went into hospital to begin 'a five-weeks' sojourn ... for plastic surgery where he is to have some of the missing parts of his foot replaced'. However, all went well. By 29 November Diccon and Frances were boarding a plane at Athens airport for the 8.55 flight to Rhodes; and at the beginning of January 1963, Diccon could write to Cass Canfield:[26]

> For the first time in my life I saw the New Year in while swimming. Out in the bay under the stars, with the bells of Lindos overhead suddenly pealing out Midnight; and a huge shooting star right after, which lit up the whole coast like lightning. I don't at all want to go home!

The best news was that his new volume was properly under way; and by the first week in February, when he and Frances had to return unwillingly home ('our hosts are leaving for Paris', Diccon explained in a letter to Pamela Bianco, 'and one can't very conveniently stay on longer than one's hosts!'), he had written more than thirty pages.[27]

On reaching Môr Edrin, Diccon and Frances were immediately struck down by a strain of influenza so severe that they were ill for six weeks; but they recovered just in time to fly out to Italy on 21 March[28] for the launching of the Italian edition of *The Fox in the Attic*. As Diccon later told Joseph Brewer, his publishers 'did our visit in style'.[29]

Soon after his plane touched down in Milan that Thursday morning, Diccon faced a three-hour press conference. Later there was a dinner; and then he was 'lectured on and publicly interviewed by three leading critics on the stage of a small theatre'. On Saturday the publicity circus moved on to Rome, where Diccon was guest of honour at 'a very large cocktail party', and was 'interviewed at length for television'. On Tuesday there was another lecture, this time in Florence; and, as Diccon told another correspondent, 'The whole affair had very wide coverage in the Press'.[30]

On Friday 29 March[31] they returned to London; and at the end of the following week, when _La Volpe Nella Soffitta_ had been out for just a fortnight, they heard that it had already sold 20,000 copies, and was at the top of the Italian bestseller lists. (By the summer, Diccon could report that it had 'outstripped even the sales in my native England and I believe a fifth printing is now contemplated'.)[32]

At the beginning of April Hughes spent two or three nights in London, where he had coffee at Chatto with his editor Norah Smallwood,[33] and was able to tell her both about his successful Italian journey, and about his progress with volume two. In May there was a similarly brief outing to Cambridge, where he was invited to dinner by the Master and Fellows of Peterhouse;[34] and on Saturday 8 June there was 'a vast party at Portmeirion (estimated at nearly 1,000 including gatecrashers) with fireworks, bands and Welsh choirs', to celebrate Clough Williams-Ellis's eightieth birthday. As Diccon informed Joseph Brewer:[35]

> Bertie Russell wrote him a letter beginning, 'My Dear Young Friend' and going on 'logic forbids me to wish you Many Happy Returns of your 80th Birthday'. Clough seems in excellent form and so does Amabel. The party ended at about half past two with people dancing informally all over the gardens.

And he had been amused to see 'a spectacular little two-year-old still wakeful as a cricket and doing a pas seule all round the parapet of a flood-lit fountain'.

These were the only serious distractions from Diccon's work; but by mid June volume two was actually shorter than it had been when he left Lindos at the beginning of February; and he told Joseph Brewer that it was 'progressing (backwards) pretty satisfactorily at the moment; i.e. in the last weeks I've sweated nearly a thousand words out of the first seven chapters' – only the first thirty-one pages of the printed text.[36]

The prime difficulty faced by Hughes in writing these opening chapters was that[37] although it is intended as a direct continuation of the FOX volume I can't possibly expect the reader to have that volume fresh in his mind – even if he has ever read it. This means that I have to work in a great deal of necessary information about earlier happenings without ostensibly repeating myself.

Another difficulty was that some of his friends had privately complained to Diccon about the comparative 'wetness' in *The Fox in the Attic* of Augustine Penry-Herbert, who seemed to be constantly misunderstanding everything that was going on around him – especially in Germany. Against this criticism could be set a letter from Edward Garnett, who recalled experiencing exactly the same difficulties as Augustine when visiting Germany just before the First World War;[38] and Augustine's lack of comprehension was also a clever device for creating a vivid picture in the reader's mind of a completely alien culture.[39] It was a device which was used again (to great effect) when describing Augustine's American adventures; but in getting him across the Atlantic, Hughes also made him a much stronger human being.

Augustine, the lovesick English milord, is 'slugged for his bulging wallet' on the quays of St Malo 'and flung down any old hatchway alongside the quay – down one just about to be closed as it happened, the ship being ready to sail'. Prohibition is in full swing, and the ship is a rum-runner bound for the coast of North America: her captain, having no other use for Augustine, sets about 'turning him into a rum-running Able Seaman'. Augustine eventually lands 'one pitch-black night on a lonely Long Island beach from a sinking launch with a gunwale-high load of the stuff under gunfire', knocks a coastguard for six in order to escape capture,[40] and then makes his way inland to hide out in the Connecticut woods.

Occasionally there are contrasting glimpses of his sister Mary's life back at Mellton Chase in Dorset; but for the most part Augustine is at the centre of the stage in these early chapters. In his shack in the woods (where his thoughts keep returning to Mitzi in her convent), he is befriended by Ree, a young American, somewhere between girl and woman, who tries to make him feel the coloured-wool turtle on her shirt's breast-pocket. For this was to be the part of his long novel in which Hughes intended not only to introduce some American characters for later use, but also to explore adolescent sexuality; and perhaps to come to terms with his own experiences in America back in the 1920s.

In August 1963, at a ceremony in London, the American ambassador presented Richard Hughes with honorary membership of the American Academy of Arts and Letters and the National Institute of Arts and Letters. Such membership is limited to the fifty most distinguished non-American writers, painters and musicians in the world: the list then included such names as Braque, Britten, Chagall, Cocteau, T.S. Eliot and Henry Moore.[41]

The ambassador praised Hughes for having 'restored to the novel that dignity of intellectual responsibility, political awareness, and moral concern, while creating living characters whose feelings and actions are portrayed with subtle reference to all the psychological dimensions that unite the child with the man, the primitive with the sophisticated, the repressed past with the irrepressible future'.[42] It was a well-deserved tribute; but also another burden to be borne.

In his brief acceptance speech, Hughes declared that neither money nor critical acclaim represented any kind of real success for a writer: for he was a man under compulsion, like a bird laying an egg: and the kind of bird was a cuckoo, because the egg had to be dressed up so that it would be accepted into another brain, and allowed to hatch there.[43]

In October, there was more bad news about the proposed film of _A High Wind in Jamaica_. Tibby Clarke wrote to Diccon telling him that he had seen Nunnally Johnson's adaptation, and that in his view it was 'a horrible massacre of your wonderful story', a vulgarised parody which missed nearly all the points of importance.[44] At Tibby's suggestion, Diccon wrote to Twentieth Century Fox asking to read the script.[45] The reply came that Nunnally Johnson had done a wonderful job – but that as a matter of courtesy the final draft would certainly be submitted for Hughes's inspection.[46]

Such courtesy was considered fitting towards a writer who had become both famous and, for a time at least, comparatively wealthy. When in late November Richard Hughes received his first full-year's accounts for the sales of _The Fox in the Attic_, he found that he had earned the staggeringly large total of £19,055 4s. 10d.[47]

Fame and fortune had finally placed Hughes on an equal footing with Robert Graves, with whom he had been conducting a very occasional correspondence for eight or nine years. Robert had given Diccon and Frances an open invitation to visit him in Majorca back in the fifties;[48] and soon after being elected Professor of Poetry at Oxford in 1961, he had written to tell Diccon that he himself had no more money worries, having discovered how to 'make occasional sallies to [the] U.S. to shake the Dollar Tree'.[49]

Suddenly it seemed like the right moment to take up Robert's invitation. It would mean avoiding Lindos for once; but a little rest is sometimes needed from our closest friends; and Diccon wrote to Robert asking if it would be convenient for him and Frances to come out to Majorca early in the New Year.

While he waited for a reply, Diccon's mind began turning on what would be the next major challenge in *The Human Predicament*: an effective description of Mitzi's life in her Carmelite convent. He had already made contact (through Penny) with a young woman who had once spent six months as a postulant;[50] and in November, he wrote to the Reverend Mother of a Carmelite convent in Dolgellau. He had prefaced his explanation to her with the words: 'I am a Christian, though not a Catholic'; and she agreed to be interviewed by him one afternoon towards the end of the month.[51] (So grateful was Hughes for her kindly instruction, that a few weeks later he arranged for a Christmas hamper to be sent to the convent.)[52]

Robert Graves's reply, when it came, was favourable;[53] so on 13 January 1964 the Hugheses flew to Palma. After driving north-westward across a flat plain, and then steeply up to the mountain village of Valldemosa, they took the coast road leading northward. This winds far above the sea through olive groves and clumps of pine, and occasional orchards of lemons and oranges, and brings one at length to a broad semicircular valley. On the west, this runs all the way down to the sea; and on the east, it settles itself against a tall mountain range. Some distance below the head of the valley, at the point where the road sweeps through a cluster of houses, a long ridge of ground extends itself for a quarter of a mile or so towards the sea, climbing up to the village church.[54]

The centra of Deya is situated in this dramatic setting between the coast road and the church; and just below the church is the Posada, where Diccon and Frances were to stay. A cool, elegant, ancient house, it is built on to the church; and Diccon explained in a slightly awkward reply to a letter from Polly (who had been hoping that he and Frances were on their way to Lindos) that 'if your ears are keen you can hear mass without getting out of bed for it – but I doubt if that counts . . . and for once Frances doesn't mind that it's haunted'.[55]

Diccon went on to tell Polly diplomatically about some of the drawbacks of Deya – such as the sea being very far away and the weather being poor; but he admitted that he was impressed by the mountain scenery; and with its terraces and its 'dramatic mule-tracks, mostly about 1500 feet up, leading from one village to another and now almost wholly deserted', it was 'wonderful country for walking . . . Most afternoons I walk with Robert for 2–3 hours; and Sundays go further afield'.

The one serious disappointment was that work had 'gone terribly slowly – for no very obvious reason'; and when Diccon and Frances flew to London on 22 March (leaving a bottle of wine as a present for Alan Sillitoe, their successor at the Posada)[56] Diccon had little to show for his ten weeks' labour.

Diccon returned home to cope with the consequences of another disappointment. When Candida Betjeman had left him a year ago, he had been lucky enough to find in Sheila Sharp a highly efficient replacement[57] who had at last laid down the foundations of a proper filing system for the mountains of paper which he had accumulated over the years; and now she too had written giving in her notice.[58] She had good domestic grounds for doing so, and had acted quite properly in the manner of her departure;[59] but Diccon was very upset: not simply because he had lost such a first-class secretary, but because, as he told her crossly, 'the whole point of the arrangement was that it should be long-term'.[60]

However, despite Sheila's departure, and despite a number of distractions (including a dinner in June at his old Oxford college Oriel, a diocesan conference at the end of the same month in Dolgellau, and another garden party at Buckingham Palace in July),[61] the spring and summer were an extraordinarily productive time. Perhaps his long conversations with Robert Graves (then in the throes of a deeply troubled relationship with a young Mexican-American woman) had somehow cleared his own mind; because very soon Diccon was moving ahead with his new book at a very regular three hundred words a day; and he had found in _The Wooden Shepherdess_ a title both for the first section, and for the whole of volume two.

'The Wooden Shepherdess', standing at a crossroads in the Connecticut woods, is a wooden church, 'tiny and old, [which] looked nearly disused and stood half buried in trees';[62] and Hughes has made it the presiding spirit of Augustine's Connecticut Eden. For although a good deal of these early chapters concerns Augustine's sexual education, there is something far more important than Augustine's first 'cold porridge' experience with Sadie.[63]

Not long before Sadie tells him to 'Move over, and give a poor wench some room', Augustine has rejected Ree, his first friend. And although he has done so on supposedly moral grounds (because she is legally under-age), he has caused her enormous distress; and he soon realises that[64]

> the pain in that small terrible face as he'd seen it last was something that never could be undone – a weight that he couldn't crawl out from under. For he was the one who had clumsily done it to someone he loved, and who loved him . . . Thus it was no good asking how else could a person with decent instincts behave: somehow he'd somewhere got out of step . . . and this load on his heart, this leaden lump at the very core of his being seemed mighty close to what people like Mitzi must mean by 'sin'!
>
> But there couldn't be '*sin*' if there wasn't a God to offend – which there wasn't, of course . . . And so, was it Freud whom Augustine in fact had offended against? Or the God Who Didn't Exist? Or would some wholly impartial observer, perhaps, have deemed him in Dutch with both?

So when he leaves Connecticut and crossed over the Canadian border on to the security of British soil, Augustine takes with him both the memory of a wooden shepherdess and some disturbing questions to which (at present) he can find no answer.

Earlier in 1964 there was encouraging news about the screenplay of *A High Wind in Jamaica*. At the beginning of May Tibby Clarke wrote to tell Diccon that he had lunched with Sandy Mackendrick, whom Zanuck had asked to direct the picture following Jerry Wald's death. Apparently Sandy had been as shocked as Tibby by the Nunnally Johnson script, and had 'managed to get [it] scrapped'.[65]

The young writer Ronald Harwood was now working on the script under Sandy's guidance (and with the benefit of the notes which Diccon had originally made for Tibby), and was 'trying to get it back to the book as nearly as possible within the framework of what Zanuck will stand for'. In this he had the full support of Anthony Quinn, who was to play Captain Jonsen, and who 'loved the book and hated the Nunnally Johnson script as much as the rest of us'.

Shooting was due to begin in June; and it seemed inevitable to Tibby that there would be 'ructions' when Zanuck found out about the new script;

> but by then there won't be much time for them to go back to Zanuck's ghastly ideas, and with the director and the star both on the side of the book you wrote, we may perhaps hope that the

result will be a great deal better than looked likely when we last corresponded.

Hughes was overjoyed: 'This is wonderful news', he told Tibby, 'like a last-minute reprieve.'[66]

Later in the year, with the shooting of the film almost completed, he went down to Pinewood Studios, where he was relieved to find that[67]

> John _does_ break his neck (and the other children's reaction is much as I portrayed it), Emily _does_ murder the prisoner and _does_ bring the pirates to the gallows. Alexander Mackendrick is a good director, and [Douglas] Slocombe a good camera man. In short, if it isn't spoilt in the cutting-room it looks like being a pretty good – and controversial – picture.

In a letter to Cass Canfield of Harpers, he added that it was to be a 'big-budget' picture, in De Luxe colour and Cinemascope, and that Twentieth Century Fox seemed to be 'planning a fairly ambitious publicity campaign'; so why not a new edition of the book, to keep his name in the public eye?[68]

The following spring, Hughes would attend a private screening of _A High Wind in Jamaica_ in London. It had been competently made, and there are some excellent set pieces (especially the hurricane with which the film opens); but it misses too much of Hughes's psychological detail to stand comparison with the original. It therefore provoked none of the controversy which Hughes had expected; and although it boosted sales of his novel, his payment as technical adviser was to be a percentage of the net takings; and (once the accountants had been to work) there were none.[69]

By the autumn of 1964, three years after the enormous success of _The Fox in the Attic_, Hughes told his own accountant that he was 'having to budget pretty carefully if my money is to last out till the new volume is ready'.[70] Having heard that Robert Graves had been given $30,000 just for the drafts and work-sheets of his poems of the last ten years,[71] he began to think of selling his papers to an American university; and in November he began 'the Augean task of going through the mass of MSS in the attic'.[72]

Fortunately by this time Hughes had a very able assistant. He and Frances had acquired a select circle of local friends and acquaintances (including the sculptor Jonah Jones and the poet Michael Burn); and in the early autumn, a woman whom he had met socially offered to do some typing for him. This was Lucy McEntee (wife of Prosper); and Hughes soon found her so efficient and so loyal, that what began as a casual arrangement developed into a full-time secretarial appointment which lasted for the rest of his life.

In December 1964 Hughes began working on three chapters about Mitzi's first few days at her convent; and when he had drafted them, he sent them to be looked over by the nuns at Dolgellau. In February 1965, the chapters went on to Father Peter Levi, a thirty-four-year-old Jesuit priest who taught in St Beuno's College at St Asaph, and had become a family friend;[73] and in due course they were also inspected by another priest and another nun.[74] Numerous revisions followed; but Hughes remained deeply unsatisfied with what he had written. It therefore came as a great relief when on Sunday 1 July 1965 he was able to abandon his draft chapters for a while, and set out with Frances for a PEN congress in Yugoslavia.[75]

This was the first full PEN congress in an Eastern European country since before the Second World War; and it was to be held in the extreme north-west of Yugoslavia, where the town of Bled lies beside a glacial lake at the foot of the Julian Alps. Along one part of the lake-shore, cliffs rise up some 460 feet; and above those cliffs stands Bled Castle, where there was an eve-of-congress party on Monday evening. Almost at once, Diccon found himself being lionised by the Slovene intelligentsia; no doubt because of the hostile manner in which he had depicted the Nazis in *The Fox in the Attic*. (Although he had eventually found a German publisher, the Germans had hated the novel so much that when 'it was proposed for the Prix Formentor ... the German delegation threatened to walk out if it wasn't withdrawn'.)[76]

The lionising continued a day or two later, at a second party given at an old palace. Photographers were milling round him, flash-bulbs were exploding; and then, not far away, a seventeen-year-old English girl with a drink in her hand suddenly started to feel very unwell, and realised that she was covered in spots. 'Oh!' she cried out. 'I feel ill! I've got chicken-pox, I'm sure!'

On hearing this, Diccon escaped from the lionising, and he and Frances rushed over to help. They soon had her lying down in the back of a car, covered with blankets; and then (abandoning the party) they drove her back to her hotel. There they found that her name was Caroline Glyn; and once Frances had got her to bed, Diccon told her stories to cheer her up. For the next few days (while Caroline waited for her father to travel down from Paris to join her) she felt utterly secure, a kind of honorary granddaughter to this elderly couple who visited her frequently, gave her a copy of

The Fox in the Attic (she said that every paragraph made her think twice), and seemed to believe that she was far more valuable to them than any conference.[77]

This was the start of another friendship which would become important to Richard Hughes as he struggled with _The Human Predicament_. Not only was Caroline Glyn an intelligent young woman who had already published one novel, and was passionate about her chosen career; but she was also a devout Christian, who more and more came to understand and sympathise with Hughes's aims, and later became his confidante in religious matters.

On returning to Mor Edrin, Hughes immediately sent Caroline a copy of _In Hazard_. This followed her from Bled to Paris, where, as she told her benefactor, she was 'more or less walled-up waiting to be uninfectious enough to go to Athens'. She added that her father had been so excited by _The Fox_ that[78]

> he insisted on cancelling our flight and stopping for days in Munich on the way home. There we dashed up and down the Theatinerstrasse [_sic_] and the Odeonsplatz while he shouted (rather unfortunately perhaps) 'This is where Hitler's car was waiting! This is where Natascha fell off her bicycle! This is where Goering crawled for shelter! This is where Lothar went!'

'Fortunately perhaps', Caroline concluded her letter, 'the _Archimedes_ is rather harder to follow.'

The rest of 1965 was spent in steady work on volume two, enlivened only by a visit in November to Oxford. There Diccon attended Robert Graves's final lecture as Professor of Poetry, and heard him talk to a packed house about the influence upon all true poets of the White Goddess, as revealed through a Muse. Afterwards, at an informal gathering in St John's, Diccon recognised a face which he had not seen for more than forty years. Extending his right arm and loudly calling out 'Johnny!' he strode across the room to shake hands warmly with Robert's youngest brother; and to meet John's eldest son Richard, who was then reading History at the family college.

In March 1966, Caroline Glyn was invited to Môr Edrin for a few days. She found it an astonishing experience. Diccon and Frances (or Mr and Mrs Hughes, as she always called them) seemed wonderfully happy together, but their life-style was (to her) hilariously eccentric.

Other visitors during these years would have agreed with her.

One of them recalls beautiful curtains held up not by rings but by broom-handles, and a supper-party at which the central decoration was a jellyfish on a china plate.[79] Another, Monja Danischewsky's daughter Sophie, was quite frightened one night when

> she crept out of her room to go to the bathroom and found [Diccon and Frances] both lying on the floor with their heads by the bathroom door (so it was impossible to get in or out) wearing mandarin robes of the utmost splendour, and as she approached they . . . made a gesture, pushing away . . . so, petrified, she ran off . . . [Later] she discovered that on Thursday evenings they used to listen to a certain programme which was broadcast from the Continent and . . . they could only hear it properly on their set when it was wired up to the bathroom pipes.[80]

Caroline missed this particular experience; but later recalled that she had never in her life been[81]

> so cold and hungry . . . But, of course, I was impressed at the great frugality of [their] life, to put it mildly – the almost spartan simplicity of it. We ate very little and very seldom. They didn't have much heating. They didn't have much in the way of comforts . . . [and] did everything themselves.

And they engaged in some fairly unusual activities. Much time was spent in rebuilding the sea-wall, heaving around reels of barbed wire and pieces of stone. They also took her on expeditions, driving across open fields, or scrambling up rocky gullies in their search for waterfalls for Frances to paint; and all the time Diccon was pouring out a diverting mixture of philosophy, history, legend, myth, reflection and personal anecdote. One incident she recalled in particular: he parked his car by a stone circle, and told her that he found it a rather frightening place, believing (unconventionally for a Christian) that the stones still retained and indeed radiated some kind of malevolent power.[82]

Once again, Diccon gave her the impression that, despite all the other calls upon his time, he had 'nothing else in the world to do but look after me'. (In fact he and Frances had not long returned from a week in Paris; and in a day or two Diccon was due to speak at Sussex University.)[83] In the evenings, Diccon read poetry to Caroline in his study; and once, when they were talking about writing, he let fall a remark which made it quite clear that he had read her novel; and he began encouraging her to begin the next. 'I was delighted by it all, [and] I think', she said ten years later, 'I've never been so happy as I was those two days.'

For the rest of 1966 (with occasional interruptions such as a Diocesan conference in June),[84] Hughes kept working away on that first largely American section of his second volume. Numerous chapter drafts were sent to be inspected by Penny (who was now living with her husband and their three children out in Kenya). 'Many thanks for the drubbing', he told her after she had criticised one section rather fiercely. 'I will rewrite the *Medea* chapter entirely.'[85]

Occasionally work came to a complete standstill for a few days while Lucy McEntee checked on some historical detail. In August, for example, Hughes was rewriting a section in which Augustine, driving along in possession of bootleg whisky, is chased by the police. Deciding that he knew too little about American cars of the 1920s, he dictated a letter to the curator of the Montagu Motor Museum in Beaulieu;[86] and this was followed up by his secretary with a letter to a private enthusiast, and numerous telephone calls. On a later occasion, Hughes had written about a picnic which was meant to have taken place on the day of the General Strike in 1926, when he looked at Lucy McEntee and said: 'Supposing it rained that day'; and she had to secure complete weather reports for Coventry on 8, 9 and 10 May 1926.[87]

However, by the end of November Hughes could tell Joseph Brewer: 'At last I have succeeded in completing a draft of the whole of the American section (i.e. about one-third) of my second volume.' He added that it was 'hard enough anyhow for an Englishman to write American dialogue without setting American teeth on edge', but that[88]

> when it comes to writing *period* American (e.g., which year was it in fact that Cat's Pyjamas became the Bee's Knees?) the task seems hopeless. In consequence I've avoided direct speech as much as I can; but I haven't been able to avoid it altogether, and I'm sure that wherever I have attempted it every single instance will call for your blue pencil.

By now, Hughes had also drafted a good deal of 'The Meistersingers', the middle part of his new volume.

'The Meistersingers' would involve several principal strands: first, the Mitzi chapters, giving a detailed account of Mitzi's entry into the convent, showing how the strength of her convictions overcomes the reluctance of the Carmelites to accept a blind postulant; and how, soon afterwards, Mitzi realises that she cannot always live in the close presence of God, but must be 'resigned to facing the darkness ahead with the confidence born of no longer expecting to see *any* dazzling light'.[89]

Second, the story of how Hitler recovers from the failure of the Munich putsch. That 'eminent jurist' Dr Rheinhold Steuckel, watching how Hitler impresses everyone present at his trial with his 'fire and force',[90] believes that[91]

> the run of Wagner's *Rienzi* is over. We'll see no more of the martyred 'People's Tribune'. His next production is much more likely *The Meistersingers* – of course with appropriate changes of casting: the gifted amateur learning the rules of the silly professionals' game and beating them at it hands down.

And before long, released from his fortress-confinement in Landsberg, Hitler is outwitting one after another of his rivals with consummate political skill.

Third, the contrasting story of English political life (and some of the 'Meistersingers' of the House of Commons, including Augustine's brother-in-law Gilbert Wadamy) leading up to the General Strike of 1926.

Fourth, the story of how Augustine himself returns to Mellton Chase, where there is a tragedy: his sister Mary, thrown from her horse at a Boxing Day meet, breaks her neck. This accident allows an interesting contrast between the way in which Mitzi's faith helps her to cope with her blindness, while Mary's atheist-humanist faith gives her no comfort whatever; and it also advances the plot, since for various reasons it throws Augustine together with Jeremy Dibden's sister Joan. It was also one of those twists in the plot which, like John's fall from the window in *High Wind*, took the author himself completely by surprise. Lucy McEntee, walking into his study one morning, found Hughes[92]

> sitting quite still at the typewriter saying [in astonishment]: 'Do you know, Mary's just fallen off her horse and broken her neck. What am I going to do about this?'
> I said: 'What are you going to do – is she dead?'
> He said: 'No, no. She's broken her neck. I think you can break your neck and still live. I think we'd better get some medical research on this . . .'

Fifth, the story (inspired by Rose Basketts' experiences) of life in the Coventry slums. But although Hughes had begun thinking about this as far back as September 1964,[93] it all remained to be written. And in any case, he and Frances had decided to fly out to East Africa for the winter.

The journey out was a nightmare. On Wednesday 14 December 1966 the Hugheses flew to Basel,[94] where the next day they discovered that the aeroplane which was due to take them from Basel to

Nairobi had not yet arrived from Lourenço Marques. And when it did arrive, 'it taxied once round the airport with us and then gave up the ghost'. All that night they were kept waiting in the airport; and when at five on Friday morning they did get airborne, they set out not for Nairobi, but for Frankfurt,[95]

> to pick up more passengers. We couldn't land at Frankfurt however because of fog, so went on to Stuttgart and spent most of the day there, waiting for the Frankfurt passengers to come over by bus. When they did arrive, it was now time for our crew to sign off: so that evening found us back at Basel again to get a new crew.

After dinner at Basel, a further delay was announced; 'whereupon', as Diccon told Caroline Glyn (now living on a houseboat a few miles north of Cambridge, and working on her next novel),[96]

> everyone went mad in their own national ways. The Germans — being democratic — stood on chairs and made impassioned speeches, with an eloquent shake in their voices at all the proper places. The Frenchwomen seized the pilot by his lapels and shook him, screaming 'Merde!' in his face. The British stood around smiling ingratiatingly at everyone and looking embarrassed. One eighty-year-old Australian strode up and down with blood-shot eyes, shaking from top to toe and announcing that *he* was going on that darned plane even if nobody else did . . . Whereon the Company prudently sent us all away to hotels for the night.

At last, on Saturday morning, they set off for Nairobi; from where on Monday Frances sent a telegram to Lucy McEntee announcing:[97]

> ARRIVED SAFELY EARLY SUNDAY ALREADY SEEN PELICANS GIRAFFES ZEBRAS FLAMINGOES BABOONS AND GRANDCHILDREN FRANCES.

They had found Penny (heavily pregnant with her fourth child) living with her family in what Diccon described in a letter to Teddy Wolfe as[98]

> the garden Suburb to end all Garden Suburbs [Penny's house has 5 acres of garden] with patches of the most appalling African slums — fifty to a hut, and room to lie full length on the floor costing 15/- a month.

However, the climate was 'marvellous, and the vegetation, and the beasts'.

On Christmas Day (after Penny and Robin had introduced them to friends who worked in down-town Nairobi), Diccon and Frances were taken to a Communion service in St John's, a tin church in one of the slums. Although the service was in English, theirs were

almost the only white faces ... and it was packed to the walls –
no possible room to kneel – and there were over twelve hundred
communicants. When it was over we had almost to fight our way
out against an even larger crowd surging in for the Swahili service.

Another day, they picnicked in the Ngong Hills, where they admired
the 'melancholy-looking' Masai, 'carrying spears wherever they go
to keep the lions from their cattle'.[99]

In order to pay for this exotic holiday, Hughes had arranged
with Robin Duke of the British Council (a visitor to Môr Edrin
the previous summer)[100] to take part in three 'book weeks' in the
New Year; but first there was a fancy-dress party for the Classical
Association of East Africa (of which Robin Minney was co-founder),
at which[101]

> Diccon came, bare to the waist and girded in paper seaweed,
> as Neptune. He had been asked whether he would provide a
> 'Cultural Event'; in response he read a poem which began:
> 'Work is the curse of the drinking classes ...'

And then Diccon and Frances went away to spend a few days at
an hotel in the foothills of Mt Kilimanjaro, where Frances painted
a fine waterfall, and was adopted by the local children.[102]

From there they went on to Tanzania as guests of the British
Council, arriving at Dar-es-Salaam on Thursday 26 January 1967.
A busy week followed, with not only speeches, discussions, interviews and a broadcast of Hughes's radio play *Danger*; but also a
great many social engagements, 'ranging from ... a large dinner
party to meet University people to a wholly informal Sunday spent
snorkelling with the Joneses [the local British Council representative
and his wife] on a coral reef – after which', recounts Diccon, 'I peeled
like an onion'.[103]

They returned to Nairobi to find that Penny was in hospital, having
recently given birth to her fourth son (and Frances and Diccon's tenth
grandchild). Twelve days later, on Friday 17 February, the Kenyan
book week was officially opened by the Minister of Education;[104]
but (for the Hugheses) the event was overshadowed by an accident
which had happened earlier in the day. As he complained to Lucy
McEntee: 'The rotten steps outside our front door have taken their
toll at last: after weeks of care, Frances fell on them yesterday, broke
one ankle and sprained the other. She is in hospital.'[105]

Fortunately there had been a first-rate surgeon on duty when
Frances arrived at the hospital. She was out by Tuesday 'with her
leg in plaster and learning to use crutches'; and that very evening
she insisted on joining Diccon at the National Theatre.[106]

There followed another fortnight with no formal engagements

(Diccon used the time to write in 'with a grateful pen' the American dialogue corrections suggested by Joseph Brewer, whose letter on the subject had just caught up with him);[107] and then on Friday 10 March the final book week began: this time at Kampala in Uganda.

For Diccon, this was the most anxious part of his African adventure: partly because Frances insisted on coming with him, despite the fact that she was in considerable pain, and getting very little sleep at night (Diccon was afraid that she might 'overtire herself thereby before the long flight home');[108] and partly because Uganda's President Dr Milton Obote (who officially opened the book week) was in a politically vulnerable position: 'I hope Kampala doesn't stage another coup d'état for the week we are there', Diccon wrote to Joseph Brewer, adding that it seemed 'only too likely on present form'.[109]

In the event all went well; and Frances had a much better time than she could have expected, because the local British Council representative 'most considerately had us to stay in their own house (which has no stairs) instead of an hotel'.[110] The highlights of the week in Kampala included several screenings of *A High Wind in Jamaica* (the first of which was personally introduced by Richard Hughes);[111] and Diccon also enjoyed making the acquaintance of a fellow lecturer, the author Edward Blishen.[112]

At the end of the week, Diccon took Frances for three days to the Hotel Entebbe on Lake Victoria to make sure that she was a little more rested before the flight home; and on 21 March they flew from Entebbe to Paris, where twenty-two-year-old Owain was living, and where he had met Elizabeth, the Frenchwoman whom he would later marry. Frances stayed on with her youngest son for a while, and Diccon flew back to England alone.[113]

Hughes returned home to warm congratulations from Sir Paul Sinker, Director-General of the British Concil,[114] and to renewed work on *The Wooden Shepherdess*: chiefly fresh research. In particular, Hughes wrote to the Librarian of the Foreign Office, asking whether (in his desire to know 'all I can of the atmosphere of the Hitler-Ludendorff Trial at Munich in the Spring of 1924'), he might be allowed to read any relevant despatches from the then British ambassador in Berlin.[115]

It was a time-consuming and sometimes tedious quest for the truth; and when he was in London for part of June and July, Hughes amused himself by reading out draft passages from his new volume for half an hour at a bistro near Buckingham Palace. When interviewed by the *Daily Express* on his reading, he is reported to have said that it was: 'Just an experiment. They were jolly intelligent listeners. I may rewrite one or two bits.'[116]

August found Hughes back in North Wales, where he was heavily involved (as he had been for some summers past) as president of the North Wales Association of Sheep Dog Trials Societies.[117] This was only one of a number of local duties which he had acquired over the years (the earliest had been back in 1947, when he had become honorary local representative for the Cruising Association at Portmadoc);[118] and occasionally Frances became annoyed by the amount of time Diccon spent on these peripheral activities.

In the middle of Diccon's work for the sheepdog trials, a circular letter arrived from Graham Greene, who was calling for mass resignations from the American Academy of Arts and Letters, in protest against American involvement in Vietnam.[119] This received short shrift from Hughes, who began his reply:[120]

> A conspicuous resignation is one of the clumsiest instruments known even to political man: whereas a writer of your parts commands one of the subtlest, most accurate and most powerful. Isn't this a bit as if a skilled surgeon instead of operating on his patient were to down tools and box his ears?

He added that 'its paramount clumsiness is surely that this is a weapon allowing no choice of target'. There might be some point in resigning from the Pentagon, if they were members; but to use the Academy as a kind of Pentagon-substitute 'merely on the grounds that it too is an American institution, seems rather like unloading one's bombs on peaceful villages because one has no hope of reaching the proper military target. A village moreover likely to contain as many friends as enemies'.

Then in September 1967 (having acquired a taste for foreign excursions), Diccon and Frances set off for a holiday and a writer's conference in Hungary.

Despite Frances's continuing obsession with waterfalls, which seemed to Diccon to be 'a plumb crazy speciality for someone with two broken knees and a tendency to arthritis', they very much enjoyed the first fortnight of their holiday. This included a visit to the Matra mountains, 'to see a special stud of grey carriage horses which they export for coronations', and to enjoy 'a drive up a most lovely valley in an open carriage-and-four, complete with footman in tattered livery'.

The remainder of their holiday was ruined by an unfortunate accident. On their way back to Budapest, they were being 'driven fast over Hungarian potholes' in a Russian limousine, and Diccon was 'sitting corkscrew', on what he called 'one of those beastly tip-up seats with no room's for one's knee's, when he seriously damaged his spine.[121]

One disc slipped out, leaving the sciatic nerve to be pinched between the vertebrae; several more vertebrae were twisted, and the nerves controlling his left knee were also twisted and damaged. 'Result,' (as Diccon explained to Jim Wyllie), 'the first three weeks of October in hospital in Budapest' – where the Hungarians looked after him extremely well, even giving him the services of Madam Holapy, the official translator to the Hungarian government, and a highly intelligent woman who had lived through the 1956 uprising. There followed four weeks in the King Edward VII hospital in London; months of exercises (Lucy McEntee recalls him 'rolling about on the hearth-rug in his study each morning while telling me what to write'):[122] and at the end of March 1968 he was '*still* on two sticks out-of-doors', though he believed that he would 'soon be as right as rain', and intended 'spending my seventieth birthday on the top of Kilimanjaro'.[123]

Recently Hughes had again been in London, where, as he told Jim Wyllie, he had moved in a strange mixture of circles. At one party he had 'met Arthur Bryant's wife in a dark corner . . . hiding from the Queen (A.B. *wasn't* hiding) so [I] hid with her'. And he had also seen Teddy Wolfe, who had taken him 'to a vast Psychedelic Party in Carlton House Terrace. London isn't merely "swinging" now, it's swinging from the chandeliers'.[124]

Diccon had already had some contact both with the more purely aristocratic circles of the first party, and with the demi-monde of the more fashionable kind of hippiedom. There were strong links between the two: Frances's half-sister Henriette, a lady-in-waiting to the Queen, was also the mother of the dashing young baronet Sir Mark Palmer, a proponent of the alternative culture who at one stage had taken to the road in a horse and cart to spread the word. Diccon and Frances had become very intrigued by his late-sixties circle, which seemed to contain everyone from pop-stars and models to artists and aristocrats, and which included several of Lord Harlech's children, one of whom, Jane Rainey, was a frequent summer visitor to Môr Edrin.

Lord and Lady Harlech (who had a large estate in the neighbourhood) had themselves been friends of the Hugheses for years:

which involved Diccon and Frances that spring of 1968 in an unusual episode.

Lucy McEntee arrived at Môr Edrin one morning, to find Frances calling out to her from her bed. 'I can't think what to do', Frances lamented. 'Henriette always says "Tell your cook everything, and *no-one else*".' Lucy sat and waited.[125]

> Then she asked me to go down to the Dining Room and fetch up a roll of yellow silk from a cupboard there. When I did, she seized it in both hands and ripped it straight down into two pieces, and told me to hang them in the lavatory.

Eventually it transpired that

> Princess Margaret and her two children were coming to stay with the Harlechs (there were rumours that Viscount Linley might be kidnapped), and no-one was to know anything, and they were all coming here to ride on the shore each day & to have fruit & coffee and use the lavatory. I said that accounted for the £8000 worth of horses grazing in the next field. 'Oh yes – Mr and Mrs Tilley have brought them over from the Vale of Clwyd.'

Lucy then went to Diccon's study to begin work. 'Frances is getting a little worked up', he said, but nothing more.

The following day, Lucy found herself picking raspberries with Madame Holapy, who had been invited down from London for 'a quiet weekend' during her annual visit to England; and then

> the riding party arrived, a little late. They had been preceded up the lane by Mr Quaeck of Portmadoc whose delivery van had broken down, so they all got out and pushed. Frances had thought her lavatory needed a new cork floor, and this was it.

The second day they rode, the tide was further out, and they were held up on the field, 'where they met both Cefn Gwyn bulls. Mr Tilley dug Diccon in the ribs and said: "You'll not get a K for this, Diccon!" And Diccon just roared with laughter.'

That evening, he and Frances dined with the Harlechs; and the following day, Diccon told Lucy 'that he had put his foot into things very badly'. Apparently Frances had been

> all right, she just talked Art with Lord Grafton, but I got Princess Margaret. Her first remark was: 'I haven't read *The Fox in the Attic*, tell me what it's about.' Well, Lucy, I *ask* you. But I did far worse. You know the way one searches for conversation with visitors, in our uncertain misty weather? I said casually 'Have you seen Snowdon' and she said 'Do you mean the man or the mountain?' Oh God!

In the summer of 1968, Diccon was once again revising his 'Mitzi' chapters. Progress was painfully slow; and very occasionally he was overcome by dark moods during which he would remain closeted in his study with a bottle of whisky for company. The strain communicated itself to Frances, who spoiled at least one family visit by provoking quite unnecessary quarrels with one of her daughters. So it came as a welcome distraction for both of them when they received a letter from Caroline Glyn, who had dropped out of sight for so long that, as she herself said,[126]

> you must be wondering if I set off round the world on my houseboat and failed to come back! In fact, it has been a kind of dream voyage – I've been making up my mind to follow in Mitzi's footsteps, and at last here I am [in Oxford] as a novice in an Anglican community of Poor Clares. I've been here nearly a year, in fact.

Reading between the lines, it was clear that she was asking for support: her own parents had been unable to accept her decision, and a friend had written: 'Enclosed there, you will soon forget what real people are like.'

Diccon and Frances responded with long letters. Diccon told her: 'It is all poppycock, of course, about "forgetting what real people are like", in a convent: if nuns aren't ten times more real than most people outside, then . . . they've surely mistaken their vocation.'[127] And as soon as they could obtain permission, they visited Caroline in her convent.[128]

By that time, Caroline had written a further letter in which she told Diccon and Frances that her inclination for the religious life was of a piece with the instinct which from the age of six had propelled her into writing;[129] and it was possibly on this visit (Caroline would later recall the words but not the precise occasion) that Diccon said to her: 'I see increasingly as I get older . . . the great question-mark written on everything by the great questioner.' In the course of subsequent correspondence he made it clear that he regarded his own fiction as 'incarnational', and that he saw himself 'as carrying on a certain work of God'.[130]

It was a work in which Caroline Glyn now had a significant part to play: for early in 1969 Diccon sent her the latest revision of his 'Mitzi' chapters; and she had some searching criticisms to make. In that version, as she later recalled,[131]

> Mitzi went through the complete gamut of Carmelite experience in one night . . . the ascent of Mount Carmel, the dark night of the soul and . . . ravishing in the world of love, all in one night. And it

was terrifying – absolutely terrifying. No human being could have lived through such a night . . . especially not a seventeen-year-old girl entering the convent for the first day . . . I didn't believe it, I had to tell him so.

Diccon took her advice, spun out the first part of Mitzi's experiences over the Christmas season; and saved the most important part for the very last page of his novel. Caroline would be 'almost sorry' when she saw his new version; because the original had been 'the most devastating piece of prose I think I've read'; and yet the new arrangement was more realistic, and provided Hughes with a superb climax for his entire second volume.

But first, Hughes set *The Wooden Shepherdess* to one side, while he prepared to give an important address. On 7 March 1969, he had received a telegram from William Maxwell, President of the American Academy of Arts and Letters, telling him that it was the academy's 'earnest hope' that he would[132]

> JOIN THEM AT LUNCHEON ON MAY 21 OF THIS YEAR AND ADDRESS THEM IMMEDIATELY AFTERWARDS AT THEIR CEREMONIAL.

This was an invitation to travel to New York City (at the academy's expense) to deliver the 48th address on the Evangeline Wilbur Blashfield Foundation.

Hughes had accepted with alacrity, cabling the simple message, 'HONOURED – DELIGHTED'.[133] This would be his first visit to America since 1929, and a wonderful chance to visit old friends; and it would also enable him to pass on his views about the significance of fiction to a highly influential audience.

After arranging that he and Frances should stay with Cass Canfield, Diccon began preparing his speech at once; and although he had been asked to limit it to twenty minutes, composing it took him much of the next two months.[134] He also sent excited letters to Joseph Brewer, Pamela Bianco, Jane Cassidy and others whom he hoped he might be able to meet;[135] and later on he told Robert Graves: 'this time it's *my* turn to give the Blashfield Address . . . but I'm afraid I haven't found any subject so interesting as your *Baraka* (which they have sent me)'.[136]

On Monday 19 May Diccon and Frances flew to New York; the following evening Cass Canfield gave a small dinner-party for them; and Wednesday was the day of the speech. Cocktails at twelve noon were followed by lunch in the National Institute on 632 West 156th Street, and then the ceremonials began.[137] New members were inducted; awards and honours were given to a number of writers, artists and composers; and then Richard Hughes was called upon to speak.

Hughes had entitled his address 'Fiction as Truth', and he declared roundly that the failure to read fiction[138]

> is no ordinary cloud-cuckoo-land escapism: it marks something much more dire, a solipsist retreat into the fortress of his own 'I am', like that of an autistic child. It is a refusal to face the unpalatable fact about his fellow-men which Fiction might compel him to apprehend, the fact that other people are not 'things' but 'persons'.

In real life, even in married love, 'we can't become *self*-conscious with the other partner's own "I-ness": we are still each in solitary confinement, only tapping out loving messages on the dividing wall'; but in novels we are able not just to peer into other people, but to jump inside them and look out.

Hughes added that he knew of only one place to look for anything comparable with fiction, 'and that is in the field of religious experience', where the roles were reversed in the sense that the human being become aware of God is like 'the man-in-the-novel become aware of the Novelist!' The Christian mystic, looking inwards, finds himself looking out upon landscapes of infinite width, for:

> Naked to God no apron can hide him: each word of his mouth, each thought of his mind, each lifting of a finger – God knows its meaning even if he doesn't. God is an Eye and the Eye is inside him, God is an Ear and the Ear is inside and the Eye never blinks nor the Ear mishears. No man can look wide-eyed into the depths of his own soul; needing to hood the eyes he turns inward as from a dazzling by light though this is in fact a dazzling by darkness, by something too dark to bear looking at: yet as an eagle can stare at the brightness of the sun so God stares at even that blackness unblinking.

However, mystics are few; and 'for most of us', Hughes declares, 'Fiction in one form or another offers our only way of experiencing the identity of others': an identity which is 'the necessary ground of Ethics'.

After adding that this is a field in which science is obviously incompetent, Hughes concludes with a warning about the dangers of turning our backs upon Fiction and lapsing into solipsism:

> We know that for the absolute solipsist the asylum doors gape, perhaps the doors of hell. It is also certain that a mankind in which such solipsists gained the upper hand would be a mankind headed for destruction. We neglect the Novel at our peril.

This forceful defence of the novel was warmly received.

The next morning Hughes appeared live on NBC's *Today*; and at a press lunch[139] he enthused over New York City, describing it as 'the one city I have visited that hasn't changed at all in forty years ... *This* building has gone up, and *that* building has come down. The city itself is exactly the same'.[140] However, before leaving for Canada (where he and Frances were to visit Kate and Colin),[141] Diccon did have one sinister experience.

Sitting in the back seat of a taxi, he complained to the driver that his feet were getting wet. The driver said that this was impossible; but the dampness grew worse, so he asked to be set down; and the taxi left him on the sidewalk and drove off. It was only then that Diccon discovered that his shoes were sticky with blood.[142]

On returning to England, Frances held an exhibition of her water-fall paintings in London; and then Kate came over from Canada and (as Diccon told a correspondent): 'while she was here with her two boys almost all of our other nine grandchildren came to visit us in batches. This is a wonderful place for children and they bubbled with happiness (so did we)'.[143] There were also more sheep dog trials, yet another garden party at Buckingham Palace[144] and (much more exciting than either of these) the investiture of Charles Duke of Cornwall as Prince of Wales. The ceremony took place on 1 July 1969 within the walls of Caernavon Castle; and later that day, Diccon and Frances attended the Investiture Ball.

In the autumn, when life had quietened down again, Diccon decided that it was time to make a research trip to Coventry (home of his fictional slum child Norah); and he stayed there for two weeks with Rose and Joe Basketts. Diccon had continued to be very fond of Rose, who remembers it as 'a marvellous fortnight'. There could have been problems: she had to take in a one-year-old granddaughter who had accidentally suffered a hairline fracture of the skull; but Diccon merely said, 'We'll manage to look after her between us', and helped by pushing the pram. Together, they made their way around parts of the city where remnants of the old days had survived the blitz; and at home (when the child was asleep) Rose went over her memories of Coventry in the twenties in great detail.

Once again, they also exchanged confidences. When she was asked what she defined as *home*, Rose answered: 'Home to me is my children, and my husband, and my garden and having things like shells about the house.' In return Diccon, talking about the genesis of *The Fox in the Attic*, mentioned that as a very young boy, when staying away from home, he had seen the mounted head of a fox, and had been terribly afraid that it was coming through his bedroom wall.[145]

Just before Christmas, Diccon and Frances went over to Paris to see Owain and Elizabeth, who were 'just off to Japan via Moscow, then on to America perhaps for several years'. While they were in Paris, they met Caroline Glyn's father (they could not see her mother, who was lying seriously ill in hospital); and when they returned to Wales they found that Caroline had sent Diccon a long, cheerful letter. Not only was her mother more reconciled to Caroline having become a nun; but she herself had begun another novel, the writing of which was giving her 'intense happiness'.[146]

At the end of January 1970,[147] Diccon and Frances set out once again for Rhodes, where Diccon was hoping for 'a concentrated spell of work since I'm determined to finish this volume before 1970 is out'.[148] For the first few weeks, as Frances reported to Lucy McEntee, Diccon was 'well and working well';[149] while he himself wrote optimistically to Caroline Glyn, offering to read a draft of her new novel, and telling her that _The Wooden Shepherdess_ was 'in its final stages'.[150]

Then in the third week of February, Diccon 'overstretched his typing physique'. Each day, as his osteopath had recommended, he had been going on two fifteen-minute walks (usually up to the acropolis and the temple of Athena Lindia); but he had felt too well to bother about 'the lying flat also needed'. The result was that he became very stiff at the top of his spine, and between his shoulders; and then began suffering from neuritis in his right arm. For twenty-four hours the pain was so bad that he had to take to his bed; and for the rest of their time on Lindos, Diccon was unable to type.[151]

By April he had made a good recovery, and was once again working well; and by September Frances was certain that _The Wooden Shepherdess_ was almost ready for the publishers.[152]

During the intervening months there had been the usual distractions such as sheep dog trials and drama festivals;[153] in April it had been Diccon's seventieth birthday; and later on they had seen something of Mick Jagger and his companion Marianne Faithfull, who had met the Hugheses some time ago through Jane Rainey.[154]

Invitations to the seventieth birthday party, held at Môr Edrin, specified long skirts for the ladies and fancy waistcoats for the men. There was 'quite good food and _very_ good drink'; and the highlight of the evening was a 'long and funny speech from Clough Williams-Ellis (aged eighty-seven) starting off: "Well, my dear young chap . . ." '[155]

The visit by Mick Jagger and Marianne Faithfull is remembered by Jenny West (Jocelyn Herbert's married daughter). Jenny had become a regular summer visitor, and recalls an evening at Parc (which was sometimes used as a base camp for a day's walking in the hills) with Mick Jagger smoking a joint while Marianne Faithfull cooked sausages over an open fire. After which, Marianne sat down on a sofa next to Frances Hughes, and began talking to her and to Diccon about time being an illusion:[156] an idea to which Diccon may have felt extremely receptive, as the number of years between the publication of *The Fox in the Attic* and *The Wooden Shepherdess* grew to an embarrassing total.

However, Diccon had been working hard for much of the year on 'Stille Nacht'. This was the third and final section of *The Wooden Shepherdess*, in which he deals partly with Augustine Penry-Herbert, partly with Mitzi; but principally with the events leading up to the so-called 'Night of the Long Knives' on 29 June 1934.

Augustine, fearing that Joan Dibden (with whom he is not in love) is expecting a proposal of marriage, flees with a friend to Morocco. There his adventures are virtually identical to those which Hughes himself had experienced back in 1928, when he and Jim Wyllie had set out on their first unsuccessful attempt to reach Taroudant and the Sous valley. By the time Augustine returns to Dorset, Joan has given him up, and married his American friend Anthony Fairfax; and there we leave Augustine. For the time being, the important strands of the novel lie elsewhere.

Hitler's rise to power in Germany seems inexorable. With his ranting, his uncanny ability to second-guess his opponents, his aberrant sexuality and his love of sticky cream cakes, he is also wholly real. (Olivia Manning would later declare that Hughes's Hitler was 'more convincing than Tolstoy's Napoleon').[157]

In Hitler's private life, his affair with his niece Geli is explained in terms of 'Incest (or quasi-incest at least)' seeming to be:[158]

> perhaps the obvious theoretical answer in cases of psychological blockage which stem from an overweening solipsism, like Hitler's. This sexy young niece was blood of his blood, so could perhaps in his solipsist mind be envisaged as merely a female organ budding on 'him' – as forming with him a single hermaphrodite 'Hitler', a two-sexed entity able to couple within itself like the garden snail.

In practice, Geli is repelled by having 'to do curious [sexual] things for her uncle', who restricts her freedom, while 'behaving towards her in public like any romantical juvenile moonstruck lover'. At last she can stand it no longer, and commits suicide, shooting herself with his pistol.

In his public life, Hitler becomes Chancellor of Germany in 1933; and the Reichstag fire (apparently the work of a communist) enables him to override all guarantees of freedom, and intensify a campaign of violence for his own political ends. However, he knows that he cannot take his revolution too far without alienating the army, and endangering his succession to the Presidency. In this he is opposed by Ernst Rohm, head of the powerful SA and a believer in the 'continuing revolution'.

It is at this moment, while Hitler is undecided about whether or not to move against Rohm, that Augustine's friend Jeremy Dibden (a civil servant in the Admiralty) uses his leave to visit Germany to view the state of that country for himself.

There follows a chilling description of an Augsburg which in June 1934 is 'a blazing sunset of red with its Nazi flags';[159] of 'loving-kindness at every wayside stop' which 'couldn't be normal . . . Suppose it some day went into reverse';[160] of 'something irrepressibly joyous'[161] which nevertheless makes us think of irrepressible evil.

And then comes a night of sheer, unadulterated horror.

Hitler has decided to act. His firing-squads raise their submachine-guns, and unsuspecting SA men are mowed down in droves;[162] Ernst Rohm is arrested, and left with a loaded revolver on the table. 'A German officer knows what to do' says the gaoler, before locking him in;[163] Gregor Strasser, one of Rohm's associates, is lunching with his wife and family when the Gestapo take him away to prison. He is shot to death in his prison cell, and when he bleeds like a pig, the blood is left there as 'a useful exhibit for showing the world what "GESTAPO" henceforth meant'.[164] Other old scores are settled; and even Otto von Kessen is caught up in the 'night of the long knives', and beaten to death with his own wooden leg.[165]

Evil appears to be in the ascendant; but then, just when everything seems hopeless, we find ourselves with Mitzi in her Carmelite cell. She grows aware of 'an overwhelming advent of God; and a God this time so stark she could barely endure his company'.[166]

In this, the final scene of *The Wooden Shepherdess*, Hughes uses part of a crucial extract from his Blashfield address, as he concludes:

> No man can see his own soul clearly and live: he must hood his eyes which look inwards as if against a dazzling by light when the light is too much – though this is a dazzling by darkness, his soul is too dark to bear looking at. Yet God can look: as the eagle can stare at the brightness of the sun, so God stared at even the blackness within without blinking; and under the burning eye of

that burning relentless Love [Mitzi] was molten metal that heaved
in a crucible under its scum – this girl Augustine had thought must
prove so easy to teach his simple, unshakable, childlike faith that
God doesn't exist.

To reach this powerful ending to *The Wooden Shepherdess* took
Hughes until the spring of 1972, some eighteen months after it had
seemed to his wife that the book was almost finished.

Those eighteen months had seen a few diversions: another PEN
conference, this time in Dublin, where for a few days in September
1971 Hughes enjoyed a busy round of speeches and receptions,
and had 'wine and cheese with Sean O'Faolain', the Irish writer
who, like himself, was as old as the century;[167] and five months
later Diccon and Frances had spent a few weeks in Morocco and
southern Spain.[168]

But revisions to *The Wooden Shepherdess* had seemed unending.
Whenever it was Lent, for example, Diccon would be drawn back
to the Mitzi chapters; and he also did further detailed research into
such questions as whether or not Goebbels had demanded Hitler's
expulsion from the party on a particular date in November 1925.
Nor did he find an ending which satisfied him until April 1972:
up to that time, his new volume ended with the death of Rohm
– and (as Lucy McEntee noticed) he 'was very unhappy about
it'.

Both his agent David Higham and his publisher Ian Parsons
of Chatto were now so used to 'saying (still politely, more in
sorrow than in anger), "You said it's nearly finished – you said it
is finished virtually – where is it?" '[169] that to receive the final fair
copy (typed in May 1972) came as an unexpected relief. Publication
was scheduled for the following spring: and Hughes was urged to
begin work at once upon its successor.

Instead, Diccon enjoyed an extended holiday from the 'compulsion to write', which usually held him to his desk 'till too tired
to go on'.[170] Although enjoyed may be too strong a word. It was
more like being out on parole for a certain time, knowing that he
was honour-bound to return to prison to complete his life-sentence,
and that in his case life meant exactly that.

Several members of the Graves family (including the present
author) visited Hughes briefly at Môr Edrin in the late summer of
1972. As always, Diccon could be a lively raconteur when he chose;
and in his study he launched into a vivid account of his Moroccan
adventures. But in other respects he appeared to be nervous, withdraw, remote; and when he mentioned the work which remained

to be done on *The Human Predicament*, a look of intense suffering crossed his face.

When *The Wooden Shepherdess* was published in the spring of 1973, Diccon and Frances held a party in Teddy Wolfe's studio on the river, in the East End.[171] Diccon was determined to enjoy the occasion, and (as Penny recalls) he[172]

> wore a tie given him by Owain, a Present from New York. It was made of rubber simulating plasticine. In realistic 3D the tie depicted a yellow beach, a blue sea, a pile of clothes, and a shark's fin – a tie in monumentally bad taste. He felt it was time to have some fun again.

However, the critical reaction to *The Wooden Shepherdess* was extremely mixed from the first, and he found it difficult to take. (Edward Blishen, who saw a good deal of Hughes at this time, felt that he was 'rather like a boy . . . who's desperately anxious to look at ease and pleased; and yet . . . I had a strong feeling that he was hurt'.)[173] There were some who continued to compare Hughes with the great Russian novelists; but others who censured those very attributes (such as the mixture of fact and fiction) which had been so highly praised in *The Fox in the Attic*.[174]

There were two particular reasons why critical appreciation was bound to be severely muted.

One of these was technical. Although Hughes had deliberately inserted numerous passages into *The Wooden Shepherdess* to help the reader who had never read *The Fox in the Attic*, his new novel was not really constructed to stand alone. (He evidently appreciated this: hence the 'qualified dissatisfaction', which he privately expressed to one critic, with this 'transitional piece' which he now believed he had written 'too quickly'.)[175] The opening section of *Shepherdess*, for example, comes as a delightful pastoral contrast to the horrors with which *Fox* ended: Mitzi's going blind, Augustine's despair, Wolff's madness and suicide. But in isolation it seems not only weak, but also largely irrelevant. And although the volume ends powerfully, there is something unsatisfying about having altogether lost sight of Augustine Penry-Herbert, nominal hero of *The Human Predicament*, for the final eighty-two pages. (In the overall work Augustine was, of course, just about to re-appear.)

The other was to do with the profound change in society which had occurred between the publication of *Fox* and that of *Shepherdess*. In 1961 the social and moral fabric of the immediate post-war western world was still largely in place. British self-confidence had been severely dented by Suez; but there was still substantial respect for traditional authority, and substantial loyalty to the established church.

Then in the mid to late sixties came that intoxicating brew of intellectual, moral and social upheaval; and by 1973 the old order was largely in ruins. By 1973, few things could be more embarrassing to fashionable critical opinion than a work about the human predicament whose fundamental basis was profoundly Christian, and which preached individual responsibility. Realising this, Hughes would later exclaim 'This is me!' when his friend Michael Burn showed him some lines entitled 'A Disappointment', about a writer who could spend a whole year producing only two lines and who also

> . . . possessed that gift, almost amounting to genius,
> Of knowing when the wind of favour would veer,
> And of getting his sails up just in the nick of time
> To see it veer back again.

Caroline Glyn could write warmly from her convent praising *The Wooden Shepherdess*, and agreeing that 'there is nothing more terrible than God's forgiveness – a crucible indeed'.[176] But a critic who was more in tune with the times, would deplore the fact that Hughes appeared to have been chiefly 'interested in setting [his characters] in their moral perspective'.[177]

By the summer of 1973 Penny (who used to take her family to Môr Edrin every summer) had noticed that her father's 'love of solitude' had become 'almost obsessive'; just once, at dusk, she managed to extract Diccon from his study to come sailing. It was a night, as she recalls,[178]

> when there was a spring tide running and the wind was freshening. He was well into his seventies at the time, and by day protested that he was too old and stiff to come sailing. We did not reach home again until nearly midnight, after a long battle in the darkness against head winds and hidden sandbanks, Diccon as gay as a cricket all the while.

Penny was aware that 'such moments of sociability' had become 'rare'; but later that year Diccon struck up an altogether new friendship.

It happened like this. One Saturday evening that autumn (as part of a special weekend course arranged by the Welsh Academy at Coleg Harlech, a residential college for adults), Hughes spoke about the future of the novel. In the chair was Richard Poole, a thirty-year-old poet and lecturer who worked at the Coleg, and who the next morning (with Diccon present) gave a talk on 'Richard Hughes the novelist'. Diccon showed much interest in what was said about him (later commenting that Poole had found many things in his books that he had not consciously put there),[179] and asked for a typescript of the talk.

A few weeks later, Richard Poole sent Hughes 'a copy of an essay – including that material', and also asked him to expand upon his statement that only in novels can one become convinced that 'all men are "persons" '.[180] This was the start of an occasional dialogue which lasted for the rest of Hughes's life. The two men exchanged letters and had long conversations together, usually at Môr Edrin, but once at the flat which Richard Poole and his wife Sandra rented in Harlech; and Diccon explained to Penny that the friendship meant much to him because, *as a poet*, Richard Poole understood better than most what he was trying to achieve.[181]

The last half of 1973, and the early months of 1974, were clouded by ill-health. In July 1973, when Diccon had attended a celebration dance to commemorate the bicentenary of the Hughes of East Bergholt baronetcy,[182] Frances was too stricken by arthritis to join him. In the autumn (not long after Diccon had spoken at Coleg Harlech) she went to London for a major operation on her hip, after which she spent six weeks convalescing in Gloucestershire.[183]

Unfortunately the operation had not been a great success; and when Frances returned to Mor Edrin at the beginning of December, she was still in considerable pain, and could only rest lying face down.

By January 1974 the pain had eased, and Frances could sit in a chair again (though she still had to use crutches to walk);[184] and Diccon felt able to leave her for a short while, and pay a call on Caroline Glyn in her Oxford convent. No long afterwards, however, complications set in. Diccon wrote to Caroline saying that Frances had had to return to hospital, could only write letters face down, and had become so depressed that she had even lost interest in painting.[185]

After a difficult period, Frances recovered her spirits. By the summer, she was once again painting; while her husband: fortified by the encouragement which he had received from Richard Poole, Caroline Glyn and others, was ready at least to begin work upon the third volume of *The Human Predicament*.

CHAPTER 32

Unfinished Business

Stepping into his book-lined study on the morning of 12 July 1974, Richard Hughes sat down at his desk, and was soon observing Augustine Penry-Herbert and his niece Polly at Newton Llantony. They are alone, for although Augustine is now married to an Englishwoman named Noll, his wife is away. In her absence, they celebrate Polly's twenty-first birthday 'with tennis and tea – a large birthday-cake, sandwiches, toast, raspberries and cream'.

Hughes wrestled with this beginning until by 4 September (having typed a hundred and three pages in the process), he had produced a three-page chapter with which he was technically satisfied. However, he had long ago realised that it was a false start, and as soon as he had completed it, the chapter was laid permanently to one side.

The following day Diccon and Frances went down to London, where Diccon had been booked into the King Edward VII hospital for a tooth operation. Afterwards they stayed with Robert and Sheila in Birmingham (where they now lived); and went on to Coventry, for research purposes.

Diccon had decided that Augustine, instead of being married to someone of his own class, should be allowed to fall in love with Norah, the girl from the Coventry slums whose early experiences mirrored those of Robert's mother-in-law (and Diccon's friend) Rose Basketts. Up to this moment, Augustine had been a somewhat shadowy figure: principally because Hughes had given him many of his own experiences, while altogether omitting those which were emotionally the most crucial. It is notable that Augustine's father (like Diccon's) has died when he was a child; but his mother hardly appears at all in either *Fox* or *Shepherdess*; and although Augustine has difficulties in his relationships with women, these are never related back to any central experience which would make enough sense of them to win the reader's sympathy. Now, at long last, Diccon would let Augustine have his head. So when he returned to his desk on 13 October 1974, he made an altogether fresh start.

This time, we find ourselves in a bedroom in Coventry's Slaughter-house Yard in the winter of 1934, some six months after the 'night of the long knives'. Here (in contrast to the very different darkness of Mitzi's cell, with which the previous chapter ended), it is:[1]

> Pitch-darkness warm and smelling of jam-packed sleeping bodies: the only glimmer a small square of window, with a dim blob wavering vaguely outside it and clumsily bumping against the glass. The two 'boys' (now in their twenties) stir uneasily at this familiar sound of the knocker-up's long unwieldy wand but lapse back again into slumber, having no jobs to get up for. Only one candle-end bursts into light, the flimsy curtains screening one bed blossom into an outsize Chinese lantern – and that is their sister's, Norah's.

Norah is about to lose her job at the mill and move down to Dorset, where she will teach tapestry-work to Augustine's crippled sister Mary; and it will be Augustine who meets her at the King's Head Hotel and drives her down to Mellton Chase.

While writing these first two chapters, Hughes made further visits to Coventry. He also went down to London for a Society of Authors dinner (he had been on their council for a number of years); and worked on a wireless broadcast about his old friend A.E. Coppard, who had died back in 1957.[2] The broadcast was to be given on Thursday 5 December, and so two days earlier, Diccon and Frances set out to catch the London train at Llandudno junction. It was a disastrous drive.

Diccon was unused to the car (a recent purchase) and, probably taking a corner too fast, he somehow managed to turn it right over. 'Rescuers', says Richard Poole,[3]

> found the travellers hanging from their seat-belts, and hastened to cut them down. But the seat-belts had saved them: somewhat shocked, they seemed otherwise unhurt and, after spending the night at Conway, carried on to London the following morning.

The broadcast went ahead as planned; but Diccon's secretary Lucy McEntee believes that the shock to Diccon's system was far greater than appeared at first sight, and had severe consequences.

During the first nine months of 1975, a further ten chapters of volume three were written and revised.

Norah becomes a central character: earthy, loving, direct, un-complicated, she seems destined to show Augustine the unselfish side of human love, and to be a partner who (when he has outgrown his fear of the class division which separates them) will be steadfast and true through whatever difficulties lie ahead. By contrast, Gilbert Wadamy (Augustine's brother-in-law), who has a small ministerial post in the National Government, is so besotted by Joan Fairfax (who has returned from the southern United States of America after her husband's death) that adultery is clearly on the cards.

Joan's brother Jeremy, still working for the Admiralty, and increasingly alarmed by the threat from Nazi Germany, points out to Gilbert that the Germans are fast rearming. 'We suspect', he says,[4]

> that they're secretly laying down battle-cruisers of 26,000 tons, far above the Treaty limits. U-boats they aren't allowed at all; but we know that the frames and the parts are already in storage at Kiel, all they need is assembling. They've tripled their naval personnel.

And when Gilbert pours scorn on this, and claims that 'our foremost line of defence is a modern Air Force', Jeremy points out that

> the Germans are building faster than us: their Air Force already's two-thirds the size of our own and will equal our own in a matter of months. In a year from now they'll have fifty-per-cent more machines than ourselves and almost catch up with the French.

At the same time, Krupp, the armaments king, is taking on thousands of extra hands; while I.G. Farben, who make synthetic petrol from coal, have 'stepped up their targets, they aim at a quarter-million tons of oil each year and they'll soon be producing synthetic rubber as well. So blockading's no good this time'.

In the meantime Augustine's nice Polly (who has some things in common with Unity Mitford) has made a God out of Hitler, whom she encounters in his mountain retreat at Berchtesgaden.

There follows a remarkable chapter in which Herr Paganuzzi, one of Hitler's special envoys, asks himself whether he may dare suppose that the Führer[5]

> has no thoughts of his own, just a systematic empathy incarnating a caricature of his hearers whoever they are? Is his mind a mere cinema-screen, portraying a shifting and shadowy caricature of the whole German Race which we Germans ourselves project on it? ... Why not, for isn't this just where the clever man always comes to grief, in assuming that Genius *has* to exemplify deep and original

thought? Who was it said 'Les grands peintres sont toujours un peu bête'? His greatness too is apparent not in his mind but the hugeness of what he effects.

Then Paganuzzi's eye is caught 'by the setting new moon with the old moon, glowing with earthshine, couched in its arms'; and he concludes: 'That huge insensate gravitational pull he exerts and which we choose to personalize as "the Fûhrer's Will": like the moon up there, the hugeness of Hitler's mass is proved by the mighty tides it raises on Earth – among men.'

Back at Mellton Chase, Polly also looks at the moon, and imagines for a while that she can 'read in that very light the answer to all those "ultimate" questions she'd tried to read in so many places, and latest of all in the face of Hitler'.[6] And yet she still needs to find that 'worn three-legged old tedddy bear which she counted on still to keep away bogies'. Polly falls asleep with it 'tightly clutched to her breast'; and in the morning, 'the bear was still there; but alas, no longer the key to the Universe. Somehow that seemed to have taken wing in the night'.

On 2 October 1975, shortly after completing a revision of these first twelve chapters, Diccon and Frances flew to Ottawa to stay with Kate and Colin, enjoy 'the Fall colours', and escape from some of the publicity which had stemmed from Diccon's seventy-fifth birthday earlier in the year. April had seen a literary lunch at Foyle's in his honour; in May, the Archbishop of Wales had come to dinner; and while Diccon and Frances were away in Canada, the BBC screened 'Born in 1900', a tribute to Richard Hughes, which they had filmed at Môr Edrin back in the spring.[7]

From Ottawa, Diccon and Frances went on to New York, to spend 'an Indian summer' with Owain and Elizabeth;[8] and for a few days they left behind the bustle of New York, and travelled with their son and daughter-in-law to what Frances described as 'the infinite peace and quiet of Long Island'. There they all stayed in a sculptor's house, which was 'plain and beautiful, his studio an eighteenth-century barn at the bottom of the orchard. No neglected or overworked garden, just ancient apple trees'. Then came a magical morning, when Diccon[9]

> went a walk with Owain and after lunch we went to the shore near Sag Harbour: it's very like Harlech sands and several dunes, only whiter sand and no-one there at all.
>
> Diccon estimated it was near where Augustine landed from the gun-runner's boat and looked about to see if there was sufficient cover to hide and there was. Next we followed as near as we could

the track to the pub which he went to and everything was right and in its place and possible.

'So you can think', Frances would one day write for her children, 'how happy that made Diccon.'

Not long afterwards, on 29 November, Hughes began writing 'the first tentative paragraph of chapter thirteen'. Tragically, it was to be almost his last hour of work upon *The Human Predicament*.

A number of characters were now in place for the titanic wartime scenes which would have concluded his sequence of novels; and it is easy enough to guess where some of the others would have found themselves. Augustine, after marrying Norah, would probably have been allowed by Hughes to do what he had wanted to do on the outbreak of World War Two, and join the seagoing navy. No doubt he would have seen action against the *Graf Spee* in the Battle of the River Plate; he might have been present when the British prisoners were rescued from the *Altmark*; perhaps he would later have been present offshore at the D-Day landings.

Jeremy was already at the Admiralty, where (Hughes had once predicted) 'the war-time coalition Government' would land him 'with Gilbert as his Minister, to their mutual annoyance. This will give us a summary vantage-point at the centre, to balance individual experiences in the field'.[10]

Two of the younger members of the Lorienburg family were to 'grow up single-minded young Nazis', who would fight on the fascist side in the Spanish Civil War,[11] and were then 'destined for the march on Dunkirk and the Afrika Korps'; but 'ironically', the only one of that family 'destined to cut any figure in the world later on' would be[12]

> the discarded Mitzi! For as the years pass ... she develops alongside the devotional powers of a St Teresa of Ávila – and without ever becoming an intellectual – much of her prototype Teresa's practical capacities in handling the affairs of her convent and Order. Thus in the latter days the 'Blind Abbess' becomes a symbolic and pretty important figure in the anti-Nazi world, occupying among the Romans rather the position the pastor Niemoller occupied among the Lutherans. Her passive resistance to the regime is rock-like, and she only survives concentration-camps because in the last resort Hitler dare not crown her a martyr; but she exasperates sympathizers (including ultimately the American forces) by a refusal equally rock-like ever to lift a finger against it *actively*.

None of these scenes would be written. Overcome in New York by a sudden debilitating illness, Diccon visited a doctor who (after some inconclusive X-rays) was uncertain what he was suffering from and 'told him that there was little advantage to be gained by a hasty return home'. So he and Frances flew back to London on 5 December, as planned; although by this time Diccon was feeling so weak that he had to come off the plane in a wheelchair.[13]

Five days later, on 10 December 1975, Diccon had rallied enough to be able to attend a Foyle's literary lunch in honour of the former Prime Minister, Edward Heath; and he and Frances joined Penny and Robin and their family in Durham (where they now lived) for Christmas. Diccon 'took part in charades, as he had done at so many other Christmases'; but he seems to have realised that he was a dying man. 'When he said goodbye', Penny sadly recalls, 'he promised to come again soon. But the long hug he gave me as he said goodbye belied it: somewhere inside him he realised that time was running out, and that everything he did he was doing for the last time.'[14]

Early in 1976, Robert also realised that his father was not expecting to live long. The two men were watching a television programme 'which presented a fundamentalist view of heaven and hell'. Apparently Diccon 'made no comment, but Robert afterwards saw that he was crying'.[15] Some sadness, perhaps, for his unfinished work. (Until recently, according to Frances, Diccon had remained 'quite extraordinarily confident: he thought he would live to 92 like Bertrand Russell'.)[16] But also perhaps a welling-up of emotion as he realised (because he believed in a life after death) that he would be reunited with Grace, the adored sister who had died when he was a child; with the father whom he had hardly known; with the mother whom (in spite of all their difficulties together) he had dearly loved.

On 23 January, Diccon was well enough to write a long letter to Richard Poole about the difference between conscious and unconscious symbolism: the former striking a single note of meaning, the latter tending 'to be multiple – to convey a whole polyphony of meanings'.[17] And on 3 February, he went to Oxford for a Candlemas dinner at Oriel, where this one-time Double Fourth was now an Honorary Fellow. Sitting at high table, Hughes wrote a teasing but affectionate verse obituary for the Phelps whom he remembered as Provost of Oriel; and he reminisced happily about the Oxford of John Masefield and Robert Graves, of A.E. Coppard and T.E. Lawrence and W.B. Yeats.

Ten days later, Diccon gave a talk to the sixth form at Harlech Ysgol Ardudwy; but his last public appearance (appropriately enough) was one Sunday later that month when he read the lesson at Llanfihangel-y-Traethau church. At the end of the service, after the rest of the congregation had left, the rector found him lying on his pew looking 'ghastly ill'.

Refusing any help, Diccon waited for a few minutes, rose groggily to his feet, and walked home alone. But very shortly afterwards he had to be taken to hospital in Bangor (some forty miles away from his home), where it was confirmed that he was suffering from acute leukaemia.

The specialist placed Diccon in a two-bedded isolation ward (the other bed was empty at first), and decided upon a sustained course of chemotherapy, combined with a blood transfusion every ten days. Then, seeing that his patient was an intelligent man who would want to know the truth, he told him plainly that there was only a fifty-fifty chance of the treatment being successful.[18]

Frances (who found herself a room in a bed-and-breakfast establishment near the hospital) was not strong enough to cope alone, and contacted her eldest son. Robert, pausing only to telephone Penny and ask her to join him at Môr Edrin, drove immediately to Bangor.

There he found that Diccon's primary concern was for Frances: he asked Robert to make sure that she was thinking about her own future, and mentioned that her brother Thomas had once offered to build her a house on the family estate.[19] Then Robert talked to the specialist, who repeated what he had told Diccon, and added: 'Let him enjoy life and see as much of you all as he can in the time he has left.' So for the next few weeks Robert and his brothers and sisters (Kate flew all the way home from Canada, and Owain from New York) 'took it in turns to go to [Bangor] and spend days with him in hospital, and at weekends bring him home'.[20]

When Penny first visited her father in his isolation ward, she was shocked to discover him 'too weak to raise himself in bed to see who had entered'; but then relieved to find that despite being utterly dependent Diccon was still unquestionably himself, with 'the same mischievous light in his eye'. He talked very little, but (as Penny records) he would sometimes rouse himself to joke with them; and she 'had the feeling he greatly appreciated our being with him. The extremities of his illness seemed to make him warmer, more affectionate, instead of making him self-centred'.[21]

In order to keep Diccon company without encouraging him to waste his strength on conversation, his family read aloud to him for several hours a day. 'Robert and Frances had already read the whole of the *Odyssey* aloud to him when I came', Penny recalls,[22]

and were halfway through *Anna Karenina*. Diccon would follow
the story avidly. I remember him shifting eagerly in bed as he
recognised the moment when Levin's brother Nicolai is about
to enter; many a time he would whisper to himself the names
of people about to enter the story.

After a while, the other bed in Diccon's ward was occupied by a
patient who 'neither stirred nor spoke' for the first two days, and
could then only manage a whisper; but having someone else in the
room appeared to Penny to be giving Diccon 'new courage'; and he
had soon[23]

> developed a kind of ju-jitsu movement with his elbow to lever
> himself into a more upright position so that he could look across
> to him. When we asked Diccon how he did it his eyes twinkled
> mischievously and he would not tell us.

And later, when the specialist came in to tell him that he could go
home for a few days, Diccon said: 'Good. The first stop will be the
pub.'

Frances was anxious about coping with Diccon at home; but
Owain rapidly made a ground-floor bedroom out of Frances's
studio; and from there (as Penny recalls) Diccon[24]

> found that through the windows he had a view that commanded
> several miles of estuary, and he could watch the tide as it came
> and went. He sent Robert and me to find saws and trim off some
> lower branches that were blocking his line of vision.
>
> There was an air of gaiety now about Diccon, like a schoolboy
> approaching the summer holidays. He had become warm and
> responsive and appreciative in a way I had never known him to
> be.
>
> 'He's always talked of writing as a life-sentence', Robert said
> to me. 'Perhaps he knows he's getting near the end of his term.'

On Monday 12 April, Luch McEntee told an enquirer that Diccon
was 'responding well to the treatment . . . and has been able to come
home for short periods. Today he is in hospital again, but we expect
him here tonight and he will be here over Easter';[25] and indeed, the
following Monday, Diccon celebrated his seventy-sixth birthday at
home with many of his family around him. He even managed to
dictate two concluding paragraphs to complete an introduction to
a collection of his children's stories which Chatto were about to
publish.[26]

It was an introduction that had been abandoned when Hughes
became ill; and Robert and Penny had (in her own words) 'strung
together as best we could some concluding generalisations. "That's
hopeless! That's not what I want to say at all", he said emphatically

when we read it to him'. And then, hoisting himself on his elbow, he dictated to Robert a brief account of how the stories written for the Birkenhead refugee children had served as a kind of therapy for 'These six alien mites, dumped so suddenly and randomly among total strangers on a lonely Welsh hillside'.[27]

Nine days later, early on the evening of Wednesday 28 April, Diccon died 'very peacefully and suddenly'[28] in his bed. So passed out of this world and (by God's grace) into the next, an outstanding novelist of the human condition.

The funeral service at Llanfihangel-y-Traethau was 'deeply felt', with 'most wonderful Welsh singing', and 'half the congregation unable to get in'. Afterwards, a party developed at Môr Edrin.[29] Some weeks later, there was a further service of thanksgiving for the life of Richard Hughes at the royal parish church of St Martin-in-the-Fields. The lesson was read by his agent David Higham; there was an address by his friend Father Peter Levi SJ; and the blessing was given by the Archbishop of Wales.[30]

The image of the 'Welsh Tolstoy', paddling off into the mist in a coracle, had been very largely a disguise for the benefit of the London newspaper which was running a feature on him. The gale of earthly life had blown through Diccon so much more fiercely than most of those who met him in his latter years could possibly have imagined. It had seen him suffer as a child both from the inexplicable and alarming loss of his sister; and from the horror of 'searing, excuseless guilt', when his father died. It had also seen him with happiness which 'used to bubble out of me in verse'.

It had seen him running over the Welsh hills, and swimming that sinister lake, the Llyn-y-Morwynion, where Blodeuwedd's maidens drowned themselves, trying to escape from Llew Llaw Gyffes. It had seen him as an Oxford undergraduate with the New Elizabethans in their 'low pub' in Paradise. It had seen him sailing over to Ellis Island travelling steerage on an emigrant ship. It had seen him being shot at while he rowed down the Danube. It had seen him making speeches for the Croat leader Radić before being bundled unceremoniously out of Zagreb in the boot of a car. It had seen him canoeing up a Canadian river with Indians bound for Hudson Bay. It had seen him travelling by mule-back through the Atlas mountains, and staying overnight in an Arab stronghold from which it seemed possible that he would never emerge alive.

It had seen him hopelessly in love with Nancy Stallibrass. It had seen him suffering from the severe nervous breakdown which followed. It had seen him battling his way to victory in the Bristol Channel Pilot Cutter's Race. It had seen him as head monitor of Charterhouse, as seigneur of Laugharne and as patriarch of the extensive family of children and grandchildren which followed his marriage to Frances Bazley. It had seen him as atheist, and as Christian apologist. It had also seen him, during the Second World War, playing an important part as a civil servant within 'P' Branch at the Admiralty in paving the way for the crucial Normandy landings.

Above all, it had blown through him with a fierce literary ambition. It had seen him with a play on the London stage while he was still an undergraduate. It had seen him write the world's first play for wireless broadcasting. It had seen him produce, in *A High Wind in Jamaica*, not a children's novel, but the classic twentieth-century novel of childhood. It had seen him proclaim, in the Blashfield address, his central belief in the pre-eminent importance of fiction within any civilised society. And finally, it had seen him write his masterpiece *The Human Predicament* which, though unfinished, is the work for which (after *A High Wind*) he is most likely to be remembered.

By the end of this astonishingly rich life, he had come to a great joy and serenity, born of his Christian faith. Richard Hughes's books live on, though shamefully neglected. His mortal remains lie buried in the churchyard of Llanfihangel-y-Traethau, in the heart of the Wales which he had loved so dearly since childhood that she may safely and gratefully claim him as one of her most distinguished adopted sons.

Notes

Unpublished Sources

AUTHOR The private collection of letters and documents relating to Richard Hughes built up by the present author.

BERG The collection of Graves family MSS which contains both diaries and letters with material relating to Richard Hughes, a family friend.

IND The vast collection of Hughes MSS acquired by the Lilly Library, Indiana University, at Bloomington, Indiana. The basis of this collection (which contains letters, diaries, photographs – almost everything, indeed, from Hughes's earliest school reports to the chapters which he was working on when he died) is the massive personal archive built up during his life-time by Richard Hughes himself.

MCENTEE The private papers belonging to Lucy McEntee, Hughes's secretary for many years and now his literary executor.

MINNEY MSS The private collection of family papers belonging to Penelope Minney (née Hughes).

ORIEL The collection of MSS etc. held by the Library of Oriel College, Oxford.

SCRIPT An important item in MCENTEE above: the typescript of a wireless documentary on the life of Richard Hughes entitled 'A Life Sentence'.

Published Sources

ADMIN J.D. Scott and Richard Hughes, *Administration of War Production* (Her Majesty's Stationery Office and Longmans, Green & Co 1955)

AUTOB Richard Hughes, 'An Autobiographical Introduction' to *An Omnibus* (Harper and Brothers 1931)

FICTION AS TRUTH ed. Richard Poole, *Fiction as Truth: Selected Writings by Richard Hughes* (Poetry of Wales Press 1983)

FOX Richard Hughes, *The Fox in the Attic* (Chatto & Windus 1961)

HIGH WIND Richard Hughes, *A High Wind in Jamaica* (Panther 1976)

IN HAZARD Richard Hughes, *In Hazard* (Penguin Books 1950)

MINNEY Penelope Hughes, *Richard Hughes: Author, Father* (Alan Sutton 1984)

POOLE Richard Poole, *Richard Hughes: Novelist* (Poetry of Wales Press, 1987).

SHEPHERDESS Richard Hughes, *The Wooden Shepherdess* (Chatto & Windus 1973)

SIEVEKING Lance Sieveking, *The Eye of the Beholder* (Hulton Press 1957)

Chapter 1: A Sense of Guilt

1. POOLE p.9; description by Lady Amabel Williams-Ellis.
2. E.g. Richard Poole in SCRIPT p.68.
3. IND Time given by a birth chart drawn up by a friend of Louisa.
4. *Burke's Peerage* for 1876 refers to an emblazoned pedigree drawn up in 1622 by Jacob Chaloner of London.
5. IND 'Descent of Hughes of East Bergholt'.
6. *Debrett*, quoted in POOLE p.16.
7. IND Arthur Hughes to Louisa Warren 16 Aug. 1896.
8. IND C.G. Crump (who met AH at Oxford and went with him to the PRO) to LH 18 Dec. 1905.
9. IND His 'Discharge Certificate' shows that Sergt. A. Hughes served from 27 Jan. 1887 to 4 Dec. 1890.
10. IND AH to LW 16 Aug. 1896.
11. IND AH to LH n.d. [but Aug. 1896].
12. AUTOB p.ix.
13. RH in the *New Yorker* for 28 June 1969 p.31 writes: 'Jamaica . . . My mother had spent four or five years there as a child'; from IND Ernest E. Warren to his children, 1 Sept. 1878, and Charlotte Warren to Louisa, 6 Aug. 1879, we know that Charlotte and her children were still in Jamaica in Sept. 1878, but back in England by Aug. 1879.
14. AUTOB p.ix.
15. This is speculative; but it would help to account both for Charlotte's sojourn in Jamaica some years after her wedding to Ernest Warren; and for the fact that on RH's visit to Jamaica in 1939 (MINNEY p.27) he 'set about looking for cousins; and found some'.
16. IND has some letters of October 1884 from Ernest Warren, then staying with Charles H. McConnell of the National Printing Company, Chicago, who had '9 horses & 6 carriages & is always complaining he has "nothing to drive" '.

17. IND Ernest E. Warren from Putney to his three children, 1 Sept. 1878.
18. IND LH to AH 15 October n.d. [?1901].
19. IND Percy Shepherd-Smith of Caterham to Mrs Hughes 19 Dec. 1905.
20. AH often refers to LH in letters as 'little one' or 'my little one'.
21. IND LH to AH 10 March n.d. [1902].
22. IND LH to Charlotte Warren, enc. a dictated and signed letter from Gracie Hughes n.d. [summer 1901].
23. IND LH to AH 15 Oct. [1901].
24. IND Typescript of RH *Childhood Days (5)* broadcast on 9 July 1950.
25. IND LH to AH 10 March [1902].
26. AUTOB p.vii.
27. AUTOB p.viii.
28. IND Anthony Story of London 22 June 1902 to Mrs Hughes.
29. IND LH to her mother Charlotte Warren 6 Dec. 1903.
30. *Childhood Days* op. cit.
31. AUTOB p.viii.
32. *Childhood Days* op. cit.
33. IND Photographs show AH, thin but alert, sitting up in bed and busily writing while LH looks on lovingly.
34. IND LH to 'Dearest Mother' 6 Dec. 1903.
35. IND Photograph of LH standing by AH's bedside.
36. Boscombe is now in Dorset, but was then in Hampshire.
37. IND RH (dict.) to his grandmother, 22 (misdated 2) April 1904.
38. IND LH to her mother 22 Apr. 1904.
39. IND *Eothen School Magazine 1904*.
40. IND RH (dict.) from Boscombe 26 Apr. 1904 to his godfather Mr Charles Johnson of St Albans.
41. AUTOB p.viii.
42. IND Eothen report summer 1904 on Dickie Hughes.
43. IND Eothen report summer 1905 states RH has 'only been to school for four weeks and two days, so that his progress is not marked'.
44. IND Max Pemberton of Hampstead to Mrs Hughes 4 Dec. 1904.
45. IND LH to Charles Johnson 17 Dec. 1905. 'Dear Mr Johnson', she wrote, 'You have shown so much real affection & kindness to Arthur that I feel you must be one of the first to know that it is all over.'
46. *Childhood Days* op. cit.

Chapter 2: Dictating to Louisa

1. IND LH to her mother n.d.
2. *Childhood Days* op. cit.
3. IND *Eothen School Magazine 1906* pp.43–4, Dick Hughes, 'The Adventures of Violet, Jack and I'.
4. *Childhood Days* op. cit.
5. IND Typescript 30 Sept. 1948.
6. AUTOB p.ix.
7. Lines from AUTOB p.x; their composition from *Childhood Days* op. cit.
8. Ibid. POOLE p.18 wrongly describes the poem as having been written 'in witty anticipation of a late homecoming'.
9. POOLE p.19.
10. IND LH *1908 Diary* 7,8,11,13 Jan.; 1,5,19,27 Apr.; 5 May.
11. IND LH *1908 Diary* 24 Aug. to 14 Sept. for the Selsey holiday. The lifeboat went out on 1 Sept.
12. POOLE p.19.
13. IND Maurice G. Ferguson (a schoolmaster) of Cambridge to LH 10 Nov. 1912 concludes Dick's teaching at school 'left much to be desired'.
14. IND The Dene report for Nov. 1909.
15. Ibid. for July 1910.
16. IND The Dene reports: e.g. Easter 1912, when his work was 'patchy – some quite good, some very indifferent'; or July 1912, he 'does not work hard enough with a subject he does not care about'.
17. AUTOB p.xi.
18. IND has e.g. 'The first large instalment of Dick Hughes' grand new Xmas serial *The Cash Box*'.
19. IND 'Books read by Dick Xmas 1910–11'.
20. Penelope Minney in SCRIPT p.2: RH was 'I think very lonely as a child'.
21. IND Penelope Hughes from South Norwich to RH Dec. n.d. a p.c. of Snowdon hoping 'some day when you are a man you will go & see this mountain . . . & get to the top – Your grandfather went up 7 times'.
22. AUTOB. p.xvii.

23. Penelope Minney in SCRIPT p.2.
24. IND The Dene school report Easter 1912.
25. Hugh Ferguson was at Charterhouse 1905–1910.
26. IND Hugh M. Ferguson from Trinity College, Cambridge to LH 18 Jan. 1912.
27. IND The Dene school report July 1912.
28. IND Maurice G. Ferguson of Cambridge to LH 10 Nov. 1912.
29. IND The Dene Report Apr. 1913: the illness had lasted 'since last October'.
30. IND The Dene at Christmas 1912 RH has excellent reports, and the comment: 'He has worked much harder since half term'.
31. IND to Mrs E. Bicknell from her brother of London 8 Aug. 1913; forwarded to LH by Mrs E.B. of Caterham.
32. AUTOB p.xi.

Chapter 3: Along the Tops of the Hedges

1. IND Charterhouse report mid quarter Nov. 1913: boys in form 27, Hughes R.A.W. (D.) placed fifth.
2. IND R.C. Slater to LH 14 Nov. 1913.
3. Charles Graves, *The Bad Old Days* (Faber & Faber 1951) p.26.
4. IND Charterhouse report Dec. 1913.
5. AUTOB p.xii.
6. Charles Graves, *The Bad Old Days* pp.27–8.
7. AUTOB p.xiii.
8. As Charles Graves described him in a letter home: see RPG, *Robert Graves: The Assault Heroic 1895–1926* (Weidenfeld & Nicolson 1986) p.103.
9. POOLE p.20.
10. RPG, *Robert Graves: The Assault Heroic* pp.100–1.
11. IND Robert Graves to RH n.d. [Feb. 1918].
12. IND E.G. Bryant to LH 12 July 1914.
13. *The Carthusian* vol.XI no.388 Oct. 1915 p.519. Charles Graves was another senior scholar.
14. IND LH ('Lulu') to her mother at La Roche 4 Aug. 1915.
15. IND E.E. Bryant to LH 28 Sept. 1915.
16. IND Charterhouse report mid quarter Nov. 1915.
17. RH (as 'IDRIS'), untitled poem in *The Carthusian*, vol.XI no.390 Dec. 1915 p.551.
18. AUTOB p.xiii.
19. AUTOB pp.xi–xii.
20. RH (as 'IDRIS'), 'Love and the Bee' in *The Carthusian* vol.XI no.393 p.608.
21. IND Robert Graves to RH n.d. [Feb. 1917].
22. RH (as 'IDRIS'), 'Fantaisie (1)' in *The Carthusian* vol.XII no.395 p.15.
23. *The Carthusian* vol.XII no.396 Dec. 1916 pp.50–1.
24. IND Charterhouse report Apr. 1917.
25. *The Carthusian* vol.XII no.397 Apr. 1917 p.69.
26. As n.24 above.
27. IND RH to Naomi Mitchison 11 Nov. 1931 (draft).
28. AUTOB p.xv.
29. RH, 'Physics, Astronomy and Mathematics' in ed. Naomi Mitchison *An Outline for Boys and Girls and their Parents* (Gollancz 1932) pp.329–31.
30. Charles Graves, *The Bad Old Days* p.39.
31. *The Carthusian* vol.XII, no.401 Dec. 1917 p.156.
32. IND Charterhouse report Dec. 1917.
33. IND RH to LH 2 Feb. 1918.
34. *The Carthusian* vol.XII no.402 Mar. 1918 p.181.
35. IND Robert Graves to RH n.d. [Feb. 1918].
36. *The Carthusian* vol.XII no.402 Mar. 1918 p.178.
37. *The Carthusian* vol.XII no.402 March 1918 pp.179–80 carries a good account of the fire, probably written by Hughes, then a member of the school fire brigade. For Charles's part in the operations see *The Bad Old Days* op. cit. p.37.
38. Charles Graves, *The Bad Old Days* p.39.
39. IND Amy Graves to LH 6 May 1918.
40. APG, 'Recruiting Song' in *The Carthusian* vol.XII, no.403 July 1918 p.208.
41. RPG, *Robert Graves: The Assault Heroic* p.79.
42. Charles Graves, *The Bad Old Days* p.39.
43. Robert Graves, *Good-bye to All That* (Jonathan Cape 1929) p.57.
44. IND RH to LH 2 June 1918.
45. BERG Alfred Perceval Graves, *Diary* 24 April 1918.
46. RH (as 'Idris'), 'High Things' in *The Carthusian* vol.XII no.403 pp.216–17.

Chapter 4: The Shadow of Death

1. E.g. the editorial of *The Carthusian* (vol.XI no.379 p.353) in Oct. 1914, bemoaning the fact that 'While history is being made on the Continent and at home . . . we are returning to study the Fall of Troy and the Pelopennesian war'. However, 'If we cannot join Lord Kitchener's army . . . Major Smart is giving the necessary training preparatory to commanding troops'.
2. *The Carthusian* vol.XI no.388 Oct. 1915 p.526.
3. *The Carthusian* vol.XI no.380 Nov. 1914 p.385.
4. *The Carthusian* vol.XI no.381 Dec. 1914 p.407.
5. *The Carthusian* vol.XI no.394 July 1916 pp. 645–6.
6. Ibid. p.626.
7. As n.5 above.
8. *The Carthusian* vol.XII no.395 Nov. 1916 pp.28–9.
9. *FOX* pp.109–10.
10. Promotions for OQ 1916 in *The Carthusian* vol.XII no.396 Dec. 1916 pp.51–2.
11. *The Carthusian* vol.XII no.398, June 1917 p.103.
12. *FOX* p.110.
13. As n.11 above, p.86.
14. IND Gertrude Ferguson to LH 24 June 1917. She has had a nice letter from Dick about Hugh's death; she encloses the copy of a letter from Capt. J.S. Phillips of the 9th South Staffordshire Regt. of 18 June 1917 which has: 'I do not think there is any doubt but that he would have made a great name for himself in literature had he lived.'
15. *The Carthusian* vol.XII no.400 October 1917 p.146.
16. Ibid. p.129.
17. *The Carthusian* vol.XII no.401 p.149.
18. IND Charterhouse report Dec. 1917.
19. *The Carthusian* vol.XII no.402 Mar. 1918 p.165.
20. AUTOB p.xiii.
21. E.g. his editorial in *The Carthusian* vol.XII no.402 Mar. 1918 pp.165–6: 'Public Schools have such a possibility of good: they so narrowly misses [*sic*] what they ought to attain, and it would require so small a change in the relation of master and boy for them to attain it.'
22. IND RH to LH 11 May 1918. These included 'Head Monitor, Head of School, Editor of *Carthusian*, Superintendent of Fire Brigade [a recent promotion], Head Librarian, Tennis Committee, Digging Committee: & president or secretary, I forget which, of any society which may form itself.' On this occasion RH was also school monitor of the week, and was reading the lessons.
23. IND Charterhouse report Apr. 1918.
24. RH, 'Praecox Senectus' in *The Carthusian* vol.XII no.402 Mar. 1918 p.191.
25. IND RH to LH 2 June 1918.
26. IND RH to LH 1 June n.d. [1918 – wrong attribution of 1917].
27. IND RH to LH 11 May 1918.
28. IND RH to LH 2 June 1918.
29. IND RH to LH 19 May 1918.
30. As n.28 above.
31. IND Charles Johnson to LH 6 July[?] 1918. The dating is doubtful. Either this was 6 June, soon after the theatre visit; or Mr Johnson left his lecture until some time later, perhaps not having been informed until then by Louisa.
32. IND Mr Slater to LH 24 July 1918.
33. IND Frank Fletcher to LH 21 May 1918.
34. RH, editorial in *The Carthusian* vol.XII no.403 July 1918 p.197.
35. IND RH to LH 21 July 1918.
36. Uncle George and Aunt Annie.
37. IND RH to LH from Romsey 26 July 1918.
38. IND RH to LH 28 July 1918.
39. IND RH from Class S60 Cadet's Mess Haynes Park, Bedford n.d. [approx. 23 Oct. 1918] to Charles Graves.
40. Charles Graves, *The Bad Old Days* (Faber & Faber 1951) pp.46–7.
41. IND RH to Charles Graves n.d. [approx. 23 Oct. 1918].
42. IND RH to Charles Graves 27 Dec. 1918.
43. IND RH from Ward 12 1st Eastern General Hospital, Cambridge to Charles Graves, 5 Nov. n.d. [1918].
44. Ibid.
45. Charles Graves, *The Bad Old Days* p.48.
46. *FOX* p.111.
47. IND Mrs Clare Hender of Lancashire to LH 26 March 1919.

48.   Hughes is loosely quoting from W.S. Gilbert's *H.M.S. Pinafore*:
        And so do his sisters, and his cousins and his aunts!
                His sisters and his cousins
                Whom he reckons up by dozens,
                        And his aunts!

49.   IND RH to Charles Graves 27 Dec. 1918.

Chapter 5: A Jagged Room

1.   BERG APG *Diaries* 9 Jan. 1919.
2.   AUTOB pp.xviii–xix.
3.   AUTOB p.xix.
4.   Oriel Minute Book of the Arnold Debating Society 1914–1923 (Case D C IV 4) for 3 Feb. 1919. RH spoke third in favour of the motion 'That the advance to power of the Labour Party is a menace to the best interests of the country'. It was carried 18–12.
5.   RH, 'In the Hills' in ed. RH and P. Johnstone, *The Topaz of Ethiopia vol.1 no.1 Feb. 1919 p.6.*
6.   *Robert Graves: The Assault Heroic* op. cit. pp. 211–13.
7.   Published in 1920 as *Country Sentiment* by Martin Secker in London, and Alfred A. Knopf in New York.
8.   IND RH, *Journal* [on 9 sheets, from 26 Mar. to 5 Apr.] 26 Mar. [1919].
9.   IND RH, *Journal* 29 Mar. [1919].
10.   IND RH, *Journal* 30 Mar. [1919].
11.   IND RH, *Journal* 31 Mar. [1919]. For Charles Graves's version see RPG, *Robert Graves: The Assault Heroic 1895–1926* (Weidenfeld & Nicolson 1986) p.212.
12.   IND RH, *Journal* 30 Mar. [1919].
13.   IND RH, *Journal* Friday [4 Apr. 1919] has 'Rosaleen giving me another Welsh lesson'; and entries from 29 March on show RH speaking Welsh to inhabitants of remote farmsteads in the hills behind Erinfa.
14.   IND RH, *Journal* Mionday [31 March 1919].
15.   IND RH, *Journal* Tuesday [1 April 1919].
16.   IND RH, *Journal* 29 Mar. 1919 has 'The hills had brought back my strength'.
17.   IND RH, *Journal* Thursday 3 April 1919.
18.   IND RH, *Journal* entries for 27 and 28 Mar. and 2 Apr. 1919.
19.   IND RH, *Journal* 2 Apr. 1919. Edie had probably mentioned the distempering the previous day, when she had come to supper at Erinfa (with Robert and Nancy); and there had been folk-songs afterwards.
20.   When writing on *Robert Graves*, evidence suggested that Amy had found this cottage for Diccon. But she was in Wimbledon at the time, so unless Charles had asked for help, and she had written to Edie, she can have had no hand in it.
21.   IND RH, *Journal* Friday 4 Apr. 1919.
22.   IND RH, *Journal* 5 Apr. 1919.
23.   POOLE p.22.
24.   IND RH to LH *Sunday* n.d. [Apr. 1919].
25.   RPG, *Robert Graves: The Assault Heroic* p.212.
26.   POOLE p.22.
27.   Assessment of J. David Ross (later Sir David Ross and Provost of Oriel) comes from RH's son-in-law Professor Colin Wells in conversation with the present author in the autumn of 1992.
28.   The motion, won by 54 votes to 38, was that 'In the opinion of this House the influence of the Press is a menace to modern democracy'. Hughes, speaking from the floor, made 'a passing reference to Kilkenny cats', and 'deplored the bad influence of the serial story'.
29.   AUTOB p.xix.
30.   IND LH to RH 1 June 1919.
31.   IND RH, *Journal* Wednesday 9 July 1919.
32.   IND RH, *Journal* 11 July 1919.
33.   IND RH, *Journal* 13 July 1919.
34.   IND RH, *Journal* 12 July 1919.
35.   AUTHOR Newspaper cutting on the performance of RH's *The Sisters' Tragedy* in May 1922.
36.   IND (a) William Gruar[?] of Hampstead to Captain Wills, 14 July 1919; (b) an employee of the General Steam Navigation Company of Irongate & St Katharine's Steam Wharf on behalf of Captain Wills.
37.   IND RH to LH 31 July [1919] p.c.
38.   *The Topaz of Ethiopia* vol.1 no.1 Feb. 1919.
39.   IND RH to LH Friday [?1 Aug. 1919].
40.   IND RH to LH n.d. [?4 Aug. 1919].
41.   IND RH from 'Rascal Whack' to LH 19 Sept. [1919].

42. Ibid.
43. RPG, *Robert Graves: The Assault Heroic* pp.216–20.
44. IND John Masefield to RH n.d. (typewritten copy).
45. E.g. *The Carthusian* vol.XII no.411 Dec. 1919.
46. IND LH to RH 11 Nov. 1919.
47. Ibid. 16 Nov. 1919.
48. Oriel Minute Book of the Arnold Debating Society (Case D C IV 4) 17 Nov. 1919.

Chapter 6: Real Education

1. RH, *An Autobiographical Sketch* written for his American publishers Harper, as a basis for their publicity for his novel *The Fox in the Attic* (1961).
2. AUTOB pp.14–15.
3. IND LH to RH 26 Feb. 1920.
4. IND Nancy Nicholson to RH 25 Feb. 1920. Nancy added that she would do RH a bookplate later on, and would take a new cheque then, but in her depression it only 'worries me to know a thing is paid for beforehand & will probably turn out bad'.
5. *Oriel Record* vol.III Sept. 1920 no.6 p.172; and ORIEL The fourth volume of the Minutes of the Plantagenet Society (Case D C IV 8) shows that the first meeting of the revived society took place in RH's rooms on 3 Mar. 1920.
6. IND LH to RH 11 Mar. 1920.
7. IND RH to LH 12 July 1920 has RH's report of Rosaleen saying that 'it didn't seem like Ysgol at all without you. The cottage was in very good form too: you had packed everything away beautifully'.
8. ORIEL MSS RH to the Provost of Oriel 3 Apr. [1920].
9. Hugh Lyon in SCRIPT p.8. Lyon (an old man when interviewed) misrecalls that he intervened after Hughes's *second* fourth.
10. ORIEL MSS: Gilbert Murray to L.R. Phelps 1 Apr. 1920.
11. ORIEL MSS RH to the Provost of Oriel 5 Apr. 1920.
12. IND RH to Mr [Charles] Johnson 6 Apr. 1920.
13. IND LH to RH 11 Nov. 1919.
14. RH, in *The Carthusian* vol.XIII no.416 Oct. 1920 pp.25–6.
15. IND RH to Mr Johnson 6 Apr. 1920; and IND ed. *Westminster Gazette* to RH 5 Mar. 1920: he had lost RH's story, but just wanted a few words altered to make the end more definite.
16. *Oriel Record* vol.III Sept. 1920 no.6 p.172; and ORIEL The fourth volume of the Minutes of the Plantagenet Society (Case D C IV 8) 19 May 1920.
17. *Oriel Record* vol.III Sept. 1920 no.6 p.172.
18. ORIEL Minute Book of the Arnold Debating Society (Case D C IV 4). On 15 June 1920, RH (speaking against the introduction of Prohibition) 'dwelt on the beautiful multiplicity of barmaids, drinks, money and police-cells produced by intoxication'.
19. IND LH to RH 25 May 1920.
20. *Evening Standard* 5 June 1920 [POOLE p.242].
21. IND Ed. *Spectator* to RH 25 June 1920, rejecting 'The Dirge'.
22. POOLE p.244.
23. IND *notebook* 28 June 1920.
24. IND RH to LH p.c. 29 June 1920: the Masefields took him bathing in Sir Arthur Evans's artificial lake on Boar's Hill. 'It covers about an acre', Diccon told his mother, 'has a sandy bottom, & is dotted with islands covered with rhododendrhons & silver birches.'
25. IND *notebook* 28 June 1920.
26. IND *Notebook* 3 July 1920.
27. IND RH to LH p.c. pmk 5 July 1920.
28. IND RH to LH pmk 6 July 1920.
29. IND *Notebook* 6 July 1920.
30. IND RH to LH 12 July 1920.
31. Ibid.
32. IND RH to LH 27 Aug. 1920.
33. IND RH to LH 7 Aug. 1920.
34. IND RH to LH 14 July 1920.
35. RH, *Confessio Juvenis* [Collected Poems] (Chatto & Windus 1926) p.34. RH annotates this poem: 'To Pamela Bianco 1919'; but 1920 seems a more likely date.
36. IND Poetry Ed. *Spectator* to RH 4 Aug. 1920 accepts 'Gipsy-Night'.
37. IND RH to LH 30 July 1920.
38. IND RH to LH 4 Aug. 1920.
39. RPG, *Robert Graves: The Assault Heroic 1895–1926* (Weidenfeld & Nicolson 1986) pp. 229–30.
40. IND LH to RH p.c. 17 July 1920.

41.   IND Skinner's Hall London to RH 3 Aug. 1920.
42.   IND RH to LH 27 Aug. 1920.
43.   IND RH to LH 28 Aug. 1920.
44.   POOLE p.245.
45.   IND Louis Wharton from Sussex to RH 5 Sept. 1920.
46.   RH in _The Carthusian_ vol.XIII no.417 Dec. 1920.
47.   A.E. Coppard, _It's Me, O Lord!_ (Methuen 1957) p.188.
48.   IND RH to LH 7 Nov. n.d.
49.   ORIEL The first volume of the Minutes of the Plantagenet Society (Case D C IV 8) 27 Oct. 1920.
50.   IND John [? a former member of the Brome] to P.H.[ugh].B.Lyon 23 Nov. 1920, enclosing a script to be read out at the Brome, humorously depicting a 'typical' meeting.
51.   Hugh Lyon in SCRIPT p.6.
52.   Quoted in Jeremy Wilson, _Lawrence of Arabia: The authorised biography of T.E. Lawrence_ (Heinemann 1989) p.939.
53.   L.C. Jane quoted in ibid. p.67.
54.   ORIEL The fourth volume of the Minutes of the Plantagenet Society (Case D C IV 8) 9 June 1920 – a paper by Mr Donaldson.
55.   IND 7 Nov. n.d. RH to LH, copies part letter from John Masefield.
56.   IND Charles Johnson to RH n.d.
57.   IND RH to Mr Johnson 30 Mar. 1920.
58.   FOX p.73.
59.   IND _1920 Engagements_ for Sunday 21 Nov.
60.   IND RH to Charles Johnson p.c. 23 Nov. 1920.
61.   Ibid. 30 Dec. 1920.
62.   Ibid.
63.   Virginia Woolf to Vanessa Bell 7 Jan. 1921; quoted in IND Nigel Nicolson to RH 5 Aug. 1975.
64.   IND RH to Nigel Nicolson 18 Aug. 1975.
65.   INDIANA Diaries 1920 and 1921 engagements include:

November	Friday 19	tea Masefields
	Sunday 21	T.E. Lawrence/J.C. Squire breakfast; lunch Masefields; tea Haldanes
	Saturday 27	PAMELA
	Monday 30	Judith [Masefield] & Mrs Masefield tea
December	Wednesday 1	tea Strachey
	Saturday 4	lunch Bianco
	Sunday 5	Stella tea
	Friday 17 –	Tuesday 21 Biancos
	Saturday 18	lunch F.B[ianco]/Squire, tea de la Mare
	Tuesday 21	tea Playfair
	Sunday 26	_lunch, tea, supper_ Stella
January	Sunday 2	tea de la Mare, supper de la Mares
	Tuesday 4	Nicholsons tea
	Thursday 6 –	Saturday 8 Biancos
	Thursday 6	Pamela, [Peter] Quennell _lunch_
	Friday 7	Blunden _lunch_
	Sunday 9 –	Sunday 16 Masefields
	Sunday 16	_supper_ Robert
	Monday 17	lunch Masefields
	Tuesday 18	PLAY
	Wednesday 19	TEA Masefield
	Sunday 23	lunch Masefields

66.   BERG APG _Diaries_ 10–18 Jan. 1921.
67.   IND RH to Charles Johnson 25 Jan. 1921.
68.   IND 1921 engagements Sunday 25 Jan.
69.   IND RH to Charles Johnson 26 Jan. 1921.
70.   RH, _Confessio Juvenis_ p.23.

Chapter 7: A Steerage Passenger

1.   Much of the material in this chapter comes from IND RH, _Original Draft A SECOND ITINERARY July 4–July 19 1921._ A revised version of this 43-page diary was published in the _Saturday Westminster Gazette Sept.–Oct. 1921._
2.   IND RH to LH pmk 11 Feb. 1921.
3.   A.E. Coppard, _It's Me, O Lord!_ (Methuen 1957) p.240.
4.   Ibid. p.188.
5.   Ibid. p.189. The New Elizabethans briefly 'found a haven' in an attic above 'a varsity club

called The Hypocrites newly established in St Ebbs', of which Diccon was also a member; but they were driven from it by an infestation of fleas; and the club ceased.

6. POOLE pp.27–8. The poem appeared on May 25 1921 under the pseudonym 'Elge'.
7. Ibid. p.28.
8. IND J.C. Squire to RH 10 Feb. 1921.
9. IND Leonard Woolf to RH 4 Feb. 1921.
10. IND RH to Charles Johnson 18 Apr. n.d.
11. IND *1921 Engagements* 18 Feb. 1921 'PAMELA & FRANCESCO SAIL SS Haverford for Philadelphia'.

Chapter 8: *The Sisters' Tragedy*

1. Gwenol Heneker, *The Waters and the Wild* (Macdonald 1972) p.39.
2. Lindsay had recited his *Congo Night* at a meeting in Oxford arranged by Robert Graves the previous autumn: probably RH had been there. In any case, it was a 'party-piece' of his for the rest of his life.
3. Heneker, *The Waters and the Wild* p.54.
4. 'Edie' Stuart-Wortley and William Nicholson had been married in October 1919.
5. IND Captain Wynn Kirkby to RH 16 Oct. 1920.
6. AUTOB p.xviii. POOLE p.30 suggests, perhaps a little unfairly, that Kirkby was 'scandalized at finding a scruffy student occupying a half-ruined cottage in his grounds' and 'lost no time in giving the young man his marching orders'.
7. RH, *Gipsy-Night and Other Poems* (Golden Cockerel Press 1922) pp.57–8.
8. Amabel Williams-Ellis in SCRIPT p.9. See also AW-E, *All Stracheys are Cousins* (Weidenfeld and Nicolson 1983). Where the two accounts differ, the earlier and less artistic but probably more accurate version has been preferred.
9. *SCRIPT* p.10.
10. Ibid.
11. Ibid.
12. IND 31 July 1922 from the Estates Office, Pwllheli North Wales to RH shows that RH had taken over the garden (for which it was proposed to charge him extra rent) on the previous 29 Sept.
13. IND RH to AW-E 7 Oct. 1921.
14. RH had however commented that the religious man 'has no more right to complain that the artist is an ungodly creature & a sorry nuisance to society than the artist has to complain that the good man sings bad hymns in chapels covered with yellow cement, doesn't get Cezanne to design his postage stamps, and won't read his poems'.
15. RH, *The Sisters' Tragedy and three other plays* (Heinemann 1924).
16. IND RH, an autobiog. article dated Aug. 1969.
17. IND RH to Mrs Williams Ellis 7 Oct. 1921.
18. BERG John T.R. Graves *Diary* 1921.
19. IND RH to Mr Johnson n.d. but from internal evidence combined with that of *Diaries* Michaelmas 1921, written between 23 and 27 Oct. 1921.
20. Ibid.
21. Ibid.
22. RH added that the woman editor of the reviews section of the *Saturday Westminster Gazette* was in any case 'fed up to the back teeth' with him. She was someone, he wrote, who liked to 'discover' people, run them for a while, and then throw them out.
23. IND RH *Diaries* Michaelmas 1921 engagements.
24. BERG John T.R. Graves *Diary* 1921.
25. Stella Watson has remained an elusive figure. Not a member of the university, she may have been an art student; she had some connections in the Harlech area; and she gradually became a close friend both of RH and of Robert Graves's sister Clarissa.
26. IND *Diaries* Michaelmas 1921.
27. IND RH to P.H.B. Lyon, 7 Jan. 1922.
28. IND Harold Taylor of the *Golden Cockerel press* to RH n.d.
29. Ibid. 1 Feb. 1922, stating that if RH could secure both Pamela Bianco's signature and John Masefield's preface, there would be no worry about an American edition.
30. IND Walter de la Mare to RH 14 Nov. 1921.
31. Hugh Lyon in SCRIPT p.8.
32. IND *Diaries* Michaelmas 1922 28 Dec. has: 'Sail for France'; and by the time that he was writing 'A Diary in Eastern Europe – 1' for the *Weekly Westminster Gazette* (published 9 Sept. 1922) RH is comparing Vienna with a Paris which he has evidently visited.
33. IND RH to Hugh Lyon 7 Jan. 1922.
34. IND John Masefield to RH n.d.
35. POOLE p.29 suggests RH took the part of John.

36. IND RH, article Aug. 1969.
37. In the nineteenth century, the Theatre du Grand Guignol in Paris was the principal venue for cabarets featuring short plays full of violence and horror.
38. IND Deduced from RH to 'Dear Miss Thorndike' 7 Feb. 1922.
39. RH, *The Sisters' Tragedy and three other plays* p.2.
40. IND Masefield wrote RH two letters on 22 Feb. 1922. In the first, he declined to write a preface, since he had 'a long-standing engagement to write two prefaces for friends and both these may be wanted in this early spring, & though I'd like to bear a hand for you I feel that I must not undertake anything more in the preface way till these are done'. With the second, he enclosed a note from Miss Thorndike about *The Sisters' Tragedy*, which he hoped would be 'a sort of fore-runner of even nicer notes from the management'.
41. IND Mary Groves from The Little Theatre, John Street, Adelphi, Strand to RH 17 May 1922.
42. James Wyllie in SCRIPT p.9. JW was confused, and told the story as though it related to RH's radio play *Danger* which was not written or broadcast until 1924, long after RH had gone down from Oxford.
43. IND Mary Groves to RH 17 May 1922.
44. IND Copy of RH to Lewis Casson 22 May 1922.
45. IND Lewis Casson to RH 23 May 1922.
46. Ibid. 16 June 1922.
47. IND Eric Pinker of James P. Pinker & Son to RH 29 May 1922, explaining that he is asking the Little Theatre for some advance cash.
48. Ibid. 9 June.
49. IND Lewis Casson to RH 19 June 1922. He added that the play might go on tour; but that in all other respects he should consider that it had been released.
50. IND John Masefield to RH Apr. 1922.
51. IND RH to Hugh Lyon 2 Mar. 1922.
52. ORIEL RH to the Provost of Oriel 20 July 1922.
53. IND RH to PCL the Bursar of Oriel 21 July [1922; though annotated 1923].
54. IND J. St Loe Strachey to RH 11 Feb. 1922.
55. IND Estates Office, PWllheli North Wales to RH 31 July 1922; and RH to the Estates Office 31 Oct. 1922.
56. IND RH, 'A Diary in Eastern Europe – 1' in the *Weekly Westminster Gazette* 9 Sept. 1922 has a handwritten note declaring that the 'five young people' who took part in this adventure were: 'R.H. (the author), C.B.L. Thorp, J.D. Bennett, Stella Watson, [and] Peter Brown[?].'
57. Robert Graves to DH 18 July 1922; from a photocopy kindly lent me by Mrs Lucy McEntee.
58. IND RH to LH 6 Aug. [1922].

Chapter 9: Paddling down the Danube

1. Except where otherwise stated, the information in this chapter is drawn from D. [RH], 'A Diary in Eastern Europe' parts I–VII as they appeared in the *Weekly Westminster Gazette* in 1922 on 9, 16, 23, and 30 Sept.; 7 and 21 Oct.; and 4 Nov.
2. IND RH to LH p.c. Friday 22 [Sept.] 1922.
3. ORIEL RH to the Provost of Oriel 10 Aug. [1922].
4. Dating RH's travels in Eastern Europe is a problem. From IND RH to LH 6 Aug. [1922] the date of leaving England was Monday 7 Aug. From ibid. Friday 22 [Sept.] 1922 we have a postcard posted in Fiume.
   However, dates given at the heading of entries in the *Weekly Westminster Gazette* (see note 1 above) are not uniformly reliable. Thus the 7 Oct. *WWG* is headed 'September 23rd'; but after some days of narrative, an entry in 21 Oct. *WWG* is headed 'September 14th'. And the entry in 23 Sept. *WWG* headed 'BUDAPEST, September 4th' has led POOLE p.34 to believe that RH reached Budapest on that date: an impossibility for reasons which include the fact that his subsequent adventures up to Fiume could not possibly have been fitted into the days available. The only safe method appears to be to work from the known dates, and to believe in the narrative when it refers to clear sequences of days.
   One checkable event referred to within the text in 23 Sept. *WWG* is the 'festival' of St Istvan, first king of Hungary; but this is potentially misleading. His feast day is 2 Sept.; but it is on 20 Aug. that Hungarians celebrate the translation of his relics to Buda. Had the celebrations referred to by RH taken place as late as 2 Sept., then once again there would be no room for his subsequent adventures. A crucial factor is the week spent with Radić, which can only have been from 3 to 10 Sept.
5. IND RH to Hugh Lyon 5 Sept. 1922.
6. AUTOB p.xxvi.
7. One of the party turned back at this point, as from now on RH writes in the *WWG* of only three companions; there is also a newspaper cutting of an interview given on his return to England, in which he states: 'One gave up after three weeks at Budapest'.

8. RH to Lance Sieveking, quoted in SCRIPT.
9. IND RH to Hugh Lyon 5 Sept. 1922.
10. IND RH to Lance Sieveking 7 May 1928.
11. As n.9 above.
12. IND RH to Lance Sieveking 7 May 1928.l
13. AUTOB pp. xxvi–xxvii has the story about dropping the papers; and POOLE p.35 mentions the letter from Radić.
14. The name is annotated in IND's copy of the WWG 4 Nov. 1922.
15. IND RH to Lance Sieveking 7 May 1928.
16. IND RH received a brief letter from Zović in Nov. 1922: he had cracked his head and was lying seriously ill in hospital in Rouen intending (if he recovered) to make his way first to Liverpool and then to the New World. 'I never heard from him again', runs a laconic annotation by RH, 'so presume he succumbed.'
17. AUTHOR press cutting n.d.
18. AUTOB p.xxvii.
19. AUTOB p.xxviii.

Chapter 10: *A Comedy of Good and Evil*

1. IND Will Ransom, Maker of Books, Chicago to RH 29 Dec. 1922.
2. IND H. Taylor to RH 26 July 1922.
3. IND W.B. Yeats to RH n.d. 1922.
4. AUTOB p.xxii.
5. AUTOB p.xxvii.
6. POOLE p.98 calls this 'a very early example of the Theatre of the Absurd'.
7. See RH's thoughts expressed later in IND RH to NS 6 June [1924].
8. AUTHOR A two-page MSs headed *Richard Hughes* by John Tiarks Ranke Graves (1903–1980). Gwenol Satow later became Mrs David Heneker; and in 1972 she published an autobiographical novel called *The Waters and the Wild* in which Diccon appears as 'Emlyn'. See AUTHOR Mrs David Heneker to John Graves p.c. n.d. [1978]. The quotations come from Gwenol Heneker, *The Waters and the Wild* (Macdonald 1972) pp.39 and 111.
9. BERG APG *Diaries* 1923 1 Jan.
10. AUTOB p.xxviii.
11. BERG APG *Diaries* 1923 15 Jan.
12. Quoted in POOLE p.37.
13. BERG APG *Diaries* 1923, 28 and 29 March.
14. IND AW-E to RH: 'I slipped in a word about you to Nigel Playfair ... If you like to send me copies of your plays I will see what I can do as your ambassador [or she will try to arrange a lunch] ... and you could come along.'
15. BERG APG *Diaries* 1923 4, 6 Apr.
16. Ibid. 4 Apr. 1923.
17. Ibid. 6 Apr. 1923.
18. RPG, *Robert Graves: The Assault Heroic 1895–1926* (Weidenfeld & Nicolson 1986) p.284.
19. IND RH to LH 9 Apr. 1923.
20. IND RH to NS 2 May [1924].
21. IND RH off the west coast of Sicily to LH 19 Apr. [1923].
22. IND RH, Palermo, to LH 21 Apr. [1923] and ibid. from Rome, 27 Apr. [1923].
23. IND J.L. Garvin to RH at the British Consulate in Naples 11 Apr. 1923.
24. AUTOB pp.xxvii–xxviii.
25. IND RH from 10 Well Road, Hampstead to LH 13 [May 1923].
26. RH, *A Comedy of Good and Evil* in *The Sisters' Tragedy and three other plays* (Heinemann 1924) p.56.
27. IND. *Lico* RH to John Mole 5 May 1966.
28. RH, *A Comedy of Good and Evil* pp.57–8.
29. Ibid. p.139.
30. IND Golden Cockerel Press to RH 27 June 1923.
31. RH (ed.) in his intro. *Poems* by John Skelton (Heinemann 1924). The present author studied copy no. 759 of 780 copies at the Bodleian, Oxford (27976 e.142).
32. John Skelton, 'From the Commendations of Maystres Jane Scroupe' in RH (ed.) *Poems* by John Skelton op. cit. p.87.
33. BERG APG Diaries 21 Ap. 1923.
34. Ibid. 12 July 1923.
35. IND RH to LH 22 Oct. 1923.
36. IND RH to LH p.c. pmk 21 Nov. 1923.
37. IND *Lico* RH to LH 28 Nov. 1923.

38. Ibid. 30 Nov.
39. IND RH, *Will Radio Develop a Literature of Its Own?*
40. IND RH to LH 1 Jan. 1924.
41. IND RH, *Will Radio Develop a Literature of Its Own?*
42. RH's memory was faulty. The final programme consisted of: *The Blacksmith's Serenade* by Vachell Lindsay; the proposal scene from Jane Austen's *Pride and Prejudice*; RH's play, advertised as *A Comedy of Danger*; and A.P. Herbert's '*Ladies' Night, or the Annual Dinner of the National Society for Eating Less Meat*'.
43. This version of events is a little speculative. But RH was a fine raconteur, who learned at an early stage that financial success as a writer is often concerned as much with being a good self-publicist as with being a good writer. His own accounts of his supper with Playfair etc. vary considerably. No doubt he did work all night on *Danger*; but since by his own admission it had taken him a day to produce each two minutes of acting time for *A Comedy of Good and Evil*, it seems highly unlikely (though not impossible) that he could have produced so polished a fifteen-minute play from scratch overnight. And since we know that he had a draft play to hand, the speculation that he used that as the basis for his night's work seems a reasonable one.
44. RH, *Danger* in *The Sisters' Tragedy and three other plays* pp.141–59.
45. AUTHOR Lucy McEntee to the present author 27 May 1993.
46. Nigel Playfair [ghosted by RH], *The Story of the Lyric Theatre Hammersmith* (Chatto & Windus 1925) pp.154–5.
47. IND AW-E to RH 1 Mar. 1924.
48. IND RH to Hugh Lyon 4 Mar. 1924.
49. See IND RH to NS n.d.
50. AUTHOR Lucy McEntee in an undated note to the present author about RH and his secretaries.
51. IND William Heinemann to RH 25 Mar. 1924.
52. IND RH from Luke's Ward, Guy's Hospital to NS of 11 Sussex Mansions, South Kensington, London SW7 pmk 4 Apr. 1924 [a Friday, though RH misdates his letter 'Saturday'].
53. Peter Quennell, *The Marble Foot: An autobiography 1905–1938* (Collins 1976) p.150.
54. Ibid. pp.150–1 supplemented by Peter Quennell in conv. with the present author 24 Nov. 1989.
55. AUTHOR Lucy McEntee to the present author 27 May 1993: 'I seem to remember P.H. Lyon saying Nancy was related to the head of another college and Diccon met her at a reception.'
56. As above n.52.
57. IND RH to NS n.d.
58. Gwenol Heneker, *The Waters and the Wild* (Macdonald 1972) pp.52–4.
59. POOLE p.40.
60. IND RH to NS n.d.
61. BERG Amy G. writes to her son John on Apr. 26 1924 that 'Diccon Hughes is safely back at Garreg Fawr after his operation'.
62. IND RH to NS 2 May [1924].
63. Ibid.
64. IND NS to RH Wed. 14 [May 1924].
65. RH, *The Sisters' Tragedy and three other plays* op. cit. p.52.
66. IND *Diaries* 1924 show the rehearsals were due to begin on Tuesday 10 June 1924.
67. IND RH to NS Friday 6 June [1924].
68. RH added that he had been as far as 'the "City" of St David's, with a vast twelfth-century cathedral, a palace, acres of deans and canons and people, a post-office in a village street. No railway for miles'.
69. IND *Diaries* 1924.
70. IND *Lico* RH to LH 22 Oct. 1923. RH had seen HB on stage in *The Likes of Her* as Florrie Small, 'a fifteen-year-old Iago, finally psycho-analyzed by being compelled to smash an entire roomful of crockery . . . how I should have liked [her] . . . as Lowrie!'
71. IND *Diaries* 1924.

Chapter 11: Unofficially Engaged

1. RH mentions this in IND RH to NS Tuesday n.d. but from internal evidence after RH's trip in mid August to Dunster; and with Nancy aged approx. nineteen and a half.
2. IND RH to NS Tuesday n.d. Garreg Fawr. This refers to RH returning from London by motor bike with his mother: but the machine broke down at Coventry so they continued by train. Now we know from IND RH to 'My dear Hugh' n.d. but dated to mid Aug. 1924 (see n.17 below) that 'a month ago' (i.e. mid July) RH had been travelling back to Wales with LH in his sidecar, and 'had to take the direct route'. Tuesdays in mid July are the 8th, the 15th and the 22nd. The 22nd is most unlikely, as it is within ten days of a further visit by RH to London; and in this letter he has clearly arrived in Wales for a long bout of hard work. The 8th is also unlikely, as RH talks of having only been prevented from leaving on Sunday by an accident to his motor bike; and he could not sensibly have left on

Sunday 6th, the day when his *A Comedy of Good and Evil* was being performed. Which leaves the 15th.

3. IND RH to NS Thursday [?24 July 1924].
4. IND Heinemann to RH 11 and 15 Aug. 1924. RH's deep alarm about the *Skelton* drew this response from Heinemann on 11 Aug.: 'You need have no fear that the book will look anything like a school-book, and, if I may say so, you are a little precipitate in your judgment of the present proofs. On the right paper and, as you say, with the right margins, it will be a presentable book.'
5. IND Heinemann to RH 15, 20, 21, 26 Aug. 1924; at first they hoped to buy sheets from Knopf, to publish 750 copies at 25s., and to pay a royalty of 10% on the first 2000 copies, 15% thereafter. Then the sales manager said *Skelton* must be priced at 15s.; and RH had to accept £100 in lieu of royalties, in the hope that it might be followed by a cheap edition, with a 15% royalty.
6. IND Heinemann to RH 20, 26 Aug. 1924.
7. IND RH to the Bodley Head, telling them that he must close the other offer received, as Lane was not ready to accept the terms asked by Mr Playfair in his letter of 27 Sept.
8. IND RH to NS Sunday [?10 Aug. 1924].
9. This apparently speculative paragraph is firmly based upon IND RH to NS 31 Aug. [1924].
10. IND RH to NS 5 Aug. [1924].
11. RH to NS Thursday n.d. [?7 Aug. 1924].
12. IND RH to NS Saturday [?29 Aug. 1924].
13. As n.8 above.
14. IND quoted in RH to NS Tuesday [?12 Aug. 1924].
15. Ibid.
16. Fellow biographers may relish the fact that only the mention of this eclipse in a letter in the middle of a lengthy undated (except for days of the week) sequence of letters made it possible to establish any kind of certain chronology at this point. The precise dating of the eclipse of the moon to 9.20 (or 8.24 in British summer time) in the evening of Thursday 14 Aug. 1924 was very kindly done for the present author by Peter Duffet-Smith (through Julie Riley) in Sept. 1991.
17. IND RH to Hugh Lyon, n.d. but from Dunster.
18. BERG APG *Diaries* 30 Aug. 1924. APG adds that 'Diccon and co' only left 'after long delays owing to the state of the sidecar in which Diccon brought the two girls'. See also RPG, *Robert Graves: The Assault Heroic 1895–1926* (Weidenfeld & Nicolson 1986) pp.300–1.
19. There is no direct evidence for this; but it is very strongly suggested to me by the tone and contents of IND RH to NS 31 August [1924]. 'False Rationalisation', for example, is pure RG of that date in a didactic mood.
20. IND RH to NS 31 Aug. [1924].
21. IND RH to NS Monday n.d. [1 Sept. 1924] has details of this letter.
22. IND RH to NS, in this clear sequence of letters: Monday n.d. [1 Sept. 1924]; Tuesday n.d. [2 Sept. 1924]; Wednesday n.d. [3 Sept. 1924]; Thursday [4 Sept. 1924]; and Saturday n.d. [6 Sept. 1924].
23. IND RH to NS Saturday n.d. [from internal evidence, esp. on progress with 'Lochinvarović', probably 6 Sept. 1924].
24. RH, *A Moment of Time* (Chatto & Windus 1926) p.116.
25. As n.23 above.
26. IND RH to NS [Tuesday] 9 Sept. [1924].
27. This is mildly speculative, but appears to be borne out by subsequent events.
28. IND RH to NS Friday [12 Sept. 1924].
29. IND RH to NS [Tuesday] 9 Sept. [1924].
30. Peter Quennell in conv. with the present author 24 Nov. 1989.
31. IND RH to NS Friday [12 Sept. 1924].
32. BERG APG *Diaries* 18 Sept. 1924.
33. IND RH to NS n.d. *but* it mentions a walk back from Erinfa which occurred on 18/19 Sept. (see BERG APG *Diaries* 18 Sept. 1924); there has been an intervening Saturday since then; and the letter is clearly written before the letter dated Wednesday [24 Sept. 1924] (see note 35 below); so it must have been written on 21, 22 or 23 Sept. 1924. I would guess the 21st.
34. Ibid.
35. IND RH to NS Wednesday [from internal evidence, 24 Sept. 1924].
36. IND RH to Captain H. Carr-Gomm of Messrs John Lane at the Bodley Head, Vigo Street, London W1, sends a synopsis for a book on the Lyric Theatre, promising that he could finish it by the end of Nov.
37. IND RH to Ronald Tree 23 Oct. 1924.
38. IND RH to C.S. Evans of Heinemann 28 Oct. 1924.
39. IND RH to LH p.c. [Tuesday] 7 Oct. 1924.

40. No documentary evidence exists from 28 October 1924 to just a few days before Christmas that year. Most of the details in this paragraph were deduced by working backwards from IND n.d. [just before Christmas 1924] and 30 Dec. n.d. [1924]. We know from IND 5 June [1925] that NS did holiday with LH while RH was away; and it seems likely (but it is not certain) that this was a condition upon which he insisted.
41. IND RH to NS 30 Dec. [1924].
42. Peter Quennell, *The Marble Foot: An autobiography 1905–1938* (Collins 1976) pp.108–9.
43. IND RH to NS n.d. [shortly before Christmas 1924].
44. As n.41 above.
45. IND RH to LH 18 Feb. 1925.
46. IND has numerous letters between 26 Feb. and 12 Mar. 1925 from e.g. Joseph Brewer, who had contacts with the Boston Press; from Charles Johnson, who introduced this 'up-and-coming dramatist' to Professor Wallace Notestein of Cornell, others in the academic world who might provide him with some lecturing; and from Sybil Thorndike, who introduced him to characters from the New York theatrical world.
47. As n.44 above.
48. Margaret Kennedy, *The Constant Nymph* (Heinemann October 1924.)
49. IND Heinemann to RH 10 Feb. 1925.
50. As n.44 above: 'Margaret Kennedy is coming to lunch on next Wednesday.'
51. IND RH to LH p.c. Tuesday pmk 24 Feb. 1925.
52. AUTOB p.xxix.
53. IND John Masefield to RH telegram, 9 Mar. 1925.
54. As n.51 above.
55. *FICTION AS TRUTH* p.89.

Chapter 12: Furthest North

1.   IND RH to NS 18 Apr. 1925 'I have been here three weeks now'.
2.   AUTOB pp.xxx–xxxi.
3.   AUTOB p.xxx.
4.   IND RH to NS 18 Apr. [1925].
5.   *FICTION AS TRUTH* p.89.
6.   AUTOB p.xxx.
7.   Calcutta *New Empire* 9 May 1925.
8.   AUTOB p.xxx.
9.   e.g. IND RH to LH 8 May [1925] 'Nothing has moved with regard to the *Comedy*'.
10. IND RH to Joe [Joseph Brewer] 'Early in June [1925]' mentions that 'None of *Tommie*'s machinations came off, except the Dartmouth lecture, which I much enjoyed. They didn't'.
11. IND Margaret Kennedy to RH 16 Apr. 1925.
12. IND RH to NS 26 July [1925].
13. IND Margaret Kennedy to RH 26 Apr. 1925. In an earlier letter of 24 Apr. (which must have crossed with RH's cable) MK had said that she was 'quite decided in my wish not to sell the rights to anyone until you have had your go at it'.
14. IND RH to LH 8 May [1925]; and IND MK to RH 2 June 1935: 'I'm glad you've discussed all the dramatic and film rights position . . . I am longing to see the play.'
15. IND RH to LH 8 May [1925].
16. IND RH to NS 26 July [1925].
17. As n.15 above.
18. Ibid.
19. IND RH to LH 12 May [1925].
20. As n.16 above.
21. IND RH to NS 5 June [1925].
22. As n.19 above.
23. IND RH to LH p.c. 25 May [1925]. (He was working from seven in the morning until eleven at night, with only an hour off from 4 to 5 for food and exercise.)
24. IND RH to NS July 26 [1925].
25. IND RH to NS 5 June [1925].
26. Ibid.
27. IND RH to Joseph Brewer 'Early in June [1925]'.
28. IND N. Woolridge from Lyric Theatre, Hammersmith to RH 5 June 1925.
29. IND RH Ste Genevieve, Île de Montreal to NS 8 July [1925].
30. IND RH (in Montreal) to LH 29 June [1925].
31. IND RH Ste Genevieve, Île de Montreal, to Joseph Brewer [late June or early July 1925].
32. As n.30 above, reporting that Curtis Brown 'liked it – or at any rate respected it'.
33. IND RH to NS 26 July [1925].
34. As n.30 above.

35.   IND RH to Joseph Brewer n.d. [early July 1925].
36.   As n.30 above.
37.   As n.35 above.
38.   See *SHEPHERDESS* p.112.
39.   As n.29 above.
40.   As n.33 above.
41.   IND RH to Lance Sieveking 7 May 1928. RH and the O.K. set out on 15 July as is shown in IND RH to Joseph Brewer 15 July 1925. RH had been amusing himself starting a collection of local folk songs.
42.   As n.33 above.
43.   As n.41 above.
44.   As n.33 above.
45.   As n.41 above.
46.   Ibid.
47.   Ibid.
48.   As n.33 above.
49.   Ibid.
50.   Ibid.
51.   IND Curtis Brown to RH 31 July 1925.

Chapter 13: Invitations to a Wedding

1.   The order of events in this chapter is at times conjectural, as the source material consists almost entirely of IND undated letters to NS from RH. All dated letters and other material is acknowledged.
2.   *The Times* Monday 10 Aug.; the *Berengaria* (a Cunard ship) set out again for New York on 15 Aug.
3.   Conjectural; but from a later corres. we know that NS visited Garreg Fawr soon after RH's return from America; and we have his detailed reasons for wanting her to be there.
4.   Amabel Williams-Ellis, *All Stracheys are Cousins* (Weidenfeld & Nicolson 1983) p.89.
5.   IND RH to Hugh Lyon n.d. [but probably the first week of Jan. 1926] has news of this offer of work.
6.   IND Margaret Davies (née Kennedy) to RH, thanking him for a copy of a poem (probably his *Ecstatic Ode*).
7.   Ibid. n.d. Margaret Davies declares: 'I shall be delighted to lunch with you on Saturday – but I'm afraid my husband won't be able to come too as he has to go down to the country.'
8.   MINNEY p.11.
9.   RH's close friends could reach him; and IND has a letter from Gwenol Satow (26 Sept. 1925) in which she teasingly asks: 'Dear Diccon, *shall* you become a city gentleman, with elastic-sided boots?'
10.   Peter Quennell, *The Marble Foot: An autobiography 1905–1938* (Collins 1976) pp.108–9.
11.   Ibid. pp.105–6.
12.   Ibid. pp.123 and 136–7.
13.   IND Jim Bennett (from Manitoba) writes to RH on 7 Aug. 1925 asking which of these 'embryo novels is favourite in the betting at the moment'.
14.   AUTOB p.xxxi.
15.   RH, 'The Gentle Pirate' in the *Listener* 16 June 1938, p.1268; quoted in POOLE p.41.
16.   RH, 'The Children and the Pirates' in the *Radio Times* 14 Aug. 1953.
17.   AUTOB pp.xxxi–xxxxii.
18.   Amabel Williams-Ellis in conv. with the present author April 1983.
19.   Williams-Ellis, *All Stracheys are Cousins* pp.86–7.
20.   IND RH to Hugh Lyon n.d. but probably during the first few days of 1926.
21.   RPG, *Robert Graves: The Assault Heroic 1895–1926* (Weidenfeld & Nicolson 1986) shows that the offer was ultimately less than £1500; which (among other reasons) places the most likely date of RH's visit to Islip as around 18–22 Oct. 1925.
22.   Quennell, *The Marble Foot* pp.138–40.
23.   This is an extract from one of the very few letters which can be plausibly (though not certainly) ascribed to Nov. 1925.
24.   This letter is only dated 'Monday'; but by placing this letter within a short sequence of letters, and taking into account internal evidence (e.g. comments about almost certainly having missed that month's going-to-press of *The Outlook*, in which RH's article finally appeared on 2 Jan. 1926), the most likely date of composition can be established as Monday 30 Nov.
25.   As with so many sequences of RH/NS correspondence, the dating is problematic; though this letter could well have been written on 3 Dec. when (as *The Times* for 4 Dec. records) 'winds became mainly light and indefinite'.
26.   AUTHOR LH to Amy Graves 15 Dec. 1925.
27.   IND RH (from Kemble, Gloucestershire) to LH Sunday [27 Dec. 1925].

28. Ibid.
29. IND RH to Hugh Lyon 31 Dec. [1925].
30. This is speculative; we only know for certain (a) that RH intended to take NS to see Hugh Lyon on that day (he was not in Cheltenham, but somewhere else in the neighbourhood) – but it is possible that the visit never took place; (b) that at some time between mid Dec. 1925 and 2 Jan. 1926 RH took NS to Islip. RPG, *Robert Graves: The Assault Heroic* assumes that the visit probably took place just before Christmas; but on the new evidence (esp. the date when NS went down with mumps, which has an incubation of 17–21 days) 1 Jan. 1926 now seems the only possible date.
31. IND RH to Hugh n.d.
32. AUTHOR LH to Amy Graves [Sunday] 17 Jan. 1926.
33. IND RH to NS Wednesday [20 Jan. 1926]. For once, this letter can be accurately dated. We know from BERG APG *Diaries* 19 Jan. 1926 of the date when Amy received LH's (dated) letter; and Amy always answered important letters by return.
34. Amabel Williams-Ellis in conv. with the present author Apr. 1983.

Chapter 14: Recovery

1. BERG APG *Diaries* 26 and 27 Feb. 1926.
2. AUTOB p.xxxii.
3. IND RH, a two-and-a-half page autobiog. TS marked [enc. 1948, Sept. 30].
4. IND May 1963 Draft of RH to [name withheld].
5. IND Captain Clive Coward to RH 27 Apr. 1926.
6. AUTOB pp.xxxii–xxxiii.
7. IND RH to LH p.c. Friday night [21 May 1926] pmk 22 May 1926, a Saturday.
8. AUTOB p.xxxii.
9. IND RH to Dick de la Mare 1 Sept. 1933.
10. RH in SCRIPT p.14.
11. Amabel Williams-Ellis in SCRIPT p.15.
12. Ibid.
13. IND. RH to Mr Meana 18 Oct. 1962.
14. IND J.O. Francis to RH 4 June 1926.
15. BERG APG *Diaries* 8 June 1926.
16. Amabel Williams-Ellis, *All Stracheys are Cousins* (Weidenfeld & Nicolson 1983) pp.92–3.
17. Penny Minney (née Hughes) in a letter to the present author 9 Aug. 1992.
18. MINNEY p.74.
19. IND RH to LH (then in France) 25 June 1927.
20. Penny Minney (née Hughes) in a letter to the present author 9 Aug. 1992.
21. POOLE p.43.
22. *HIGH WIND* p.8.
23. Ibid. p.11.
24. Ibid. p.18.
25. Ibid. pp.25–6.
26. Ibid. p.27.
27. Jocelyn Herbert in conv. with the present author 19 Oct. 1992.
28. MINNEY Gwen Herbert to RH n.d.
29. SIEVEKING p.290.
30. MINNEY Gwen Herbert to RH n.d.
31. IND RH, a two-and-a-half page autobiog. TS marked [enc. 1948, Sept. 30].
32. By this time, RH had produced virtually nothing for his publishers Chatto & Windus since they had begun paying him a small regular income; and it is notable, as Hughes later remarked in a letter to Dick de la Mare (IND 1 Sept. 1933), that they *continued* to guarantee him this income 'even through my long illness, when they *must* have privately thought they would never see their money again'.
33. BERG Amy Graves to John T.R. Graves 4 Dec. 1926. Robert and Laura had left Nancy on 21 Sept. For a full account of their movements see RPG, *Robert Graves: The Years with Laura 1926–1940* (Weidenfeld & Nicolson 1990) pp.38–41.
34. IND RH p.c. to Mrs Johnson 18 Nov. 1926; IND RH to Mr Meana 18 Oct. 1962 explains that RH had 'travelled by train to Trieste... In the train I made friends with a father and daughter, and they suggested Capodistria. Since I then knew not a word of Italian, the father ... took me there next day himself ... and bargained with the landlord ... for my board and lodging (it worked out at about eightpence a day, which even I could afford)'.
35. IND Pamela Bianco to RH 5 Dec. 1926; and MINNEY Gwen Herbert to RH 9 Dec. 1926.
36. IND RH p.c. to Mrs Johnson 22 and 23 Nov. 1926.
37. IND RH, 'Strange Christmases' (a magazine article) makes him 'the guest of the skipper of a

local coasting schooner'; but IND RH to P.H.B. Lyon n.d. [1927] has: 'I spent Christmas on a remote Dalmatian island as guest of two sea-captains.'

38. IND RH to Mr Meana 18 Oct. 1962.
39. IND *Diaries* LH 1927.
40. IND RH to LH 6 Mar. 1927 [LH's diary shows she received it on 8 March].
41. IND RH to LH 6 Mar. 1927.
42. IND RH to Mr Meana 18 Oct. 1962.
43. E.g. IND the *Spectator* to RH 2 Aug. 1927, thanking him for his 'delightful' review of 'New York is not America' for which he will receive a guinea on publication.
44. Minney MSS Gwen Herbert to RH 1 Sept. [?1927].
45. IND C. Coward of London E15 to RH 9 Dec. 1927.
46. James Wyllie in SCRIPT p.17. Having listened to the BBC recording, I have made some corrections – e.g. 'into a hole' becomes 'into the hall'. Wyllie appears to have muddled his memories of the 1927 journey to Morocco with accounts of a second journey which RH made there alone in 1929.

Chapter 15: In the Lap of Atlas

1. The principal sources for this chapter are:
   (1) RH, *In the Lap of Atlas* (Chatto & Windus 1979; with an intro. by Richard Poole. RP's dating of the Atlas 'jaunt' to Jan. 1927 (see p.9) is wrong. RH was then living on Capodistria. On the same page, RP claims that RH attributed the trip to the Christmas of 1926 in (3) below, when in fact he attributed it to Christmas 1927.
   (2) POOLE pp.47–8.
   (3) RH, 'Strange Christmases' (Harper's Bazaar, 1930).
   (4) *SHEPHERDESS* pp.271–99.
   (5) AUTOB pp.xxxiii–xxxvii.
   (6) James Wyllie in SCRIPT pp.18–21.
   All of these give slightly different versions of what happened to RH and Wyllie during their Moroccan jaunt. The inclusion of (4) above may seem strange; but RH gave his own Moroccan experiences (no doubt slightly embellished) lock stock and barrel to Augustine Penry-Herbert in *The Wooden Shepherdess*; and since his other more strictly autobiog. accounts were also embellished to some extent, pages from *Shepherdess* (used with discretion) are an equally legitimate source for what is (inevitably) a chapter more of imaginative reconstruction (though nothing has been invented) than of scrupulous scholarship. However, much reliance has been placed on (3) above, as the earliest available account.
2. This travel-diary is mentioned in POOLE pp.47–8.
3. IND Pamela Bianco to RH 7 July 1928.
4. IND May 1963 *Draft* of a letter from RH to [name withheld].
5. SIEVEKING pp.163 and 296–7.
6. These words are taken from RH's 'Strange Christmases'; but he begins *In the Lap of Atlas* in similar vein ('I remember standing, one mid-winter evening in the year 1346, at the gate of a grim old castle') and from the title of his talk it may be presumed that he began it in a manner similar to one of these openings.
7. IND RH to Lance Sieveking 7 May 1928.
8. *HIGH WIND* p.69.
9. Amabel Williams-Ellis in SCRIPT pp.15–16.
10. *HIGH WIND* p.19.
11. Ibid. p.91.
12. IND Pamela Bianco to RH 7 July 1928.
13. A shipboard companion gave RH a letter of introduction to be found at IND Able Barne to Mr Fatty McDermott of New Orleans 12 Aug. 1928.
14. SIEVEKING pp. 289–90.
15. SIEVEKING pp.291 and 286.
16. SIEVEKING pp.166–7.
17. IND 12 Aug. 1928 White Star Line on board SS *Baltic* Able Barne to Mr Fatty McDermott of New Orleans.
18. IND Pamela Bianco to RH 7 July 1928.

Chapter 16: Pamela and Jane

1. IND PB to RH 7 July 1928 shows that PB was determined to meet his boat; but whether she actually did so is uncertain.
2. IND PB to RH 27 Sept. 1928.
3. *SHEPHERDESS* p.7.
4. IND PB to RH 27 Sept. 1928; and RH to LH 3 Nov. 1928.

5. IND PB to RH 16 Oct. 1928.
6. IND PB to RH 5 Nov. 1928.
7. IND PB to RH Monday n.d.
8. IND PB to RH n.d.
9. IND RH to LH 3 Nov. 1928.
10. *HIGH WIND* p.91.
11. IND RH to Joseph Brewer Tuesday [27] pmk 28 Nov. 1928.
12. IND Jane Cassidy to RH n.d. [Dec 1928].
13. RH, 'High Wind in Jamaica' (with block prints of West Indian scenes by Lowell L. Balcom) in ed. Henry Leach *The Forum* vol.LXXXX no.6, Dec. 1928 pp.831–44 and 949–52.
14. IND RH to Joseph Brewer Tuesday [most probably 11 or 18 Dec. 1928].
15. Interview with Louise Morgan quoted in POOLE p.49.
16. 'Strange Christmases' in *Harper's Bazaar* Dec. 1930.
17. IND Thomas Brown of the Department of Sociology of Morgan College, Baltimore, to Morcedai Johnson of Howard University, Washington, 7 Jan. 1929.
18. IND Letter from CG of 1035 Fifth Avenue to Martin Sweeney of Palm Beach, 3 Jan. 1929.
19. IND Able Barne to Mr Fatty McDermott 12 Aug. 1928.
20. IND Hamilton Owens of the Baltimore *Evening Sun* to Marshall Ballard of the *New Orleans Item* 7 Jan. 1929.
21. IND Annie Churchill to RH n.d. [1962].
22. IND PB to RH Tuesday pmk 12 Feb. 1929.
23. IND RH from Bellevue to Joseph Brewer Friday n.d.
24. Ibid.
25. IND Jane Cassidy to RH n.d. [but from internal evidence, sometime between Thanksgiving and Christmas 1929].
26. IND PB to RH 16 Feb. [1929].
27. IND RH to Joseph Brewer 22 Feb. [1929].
28. *SHEPHERDESS* pp.74, 60 and 74 again.
29. IND RH to Joseph Brewer Thursday [27 Feb. 1929].
30. IND Jane Cassidy to RH pmk 28 March 1930.

Chapter 17: *The Innocent Voyage* and Celebrity

1. IND RH to Armitage Watkins 13 Oct. 1948.
2. RH, 'High Wind in Jamaica' in ed. Henry Leach *The Forum* vol.LXXXX no.6, Dec. 1928.
3. The Bible: Matthew 18:3.
4. Jean Jacques Rousseau (tr. by Barbara Foxley for 'Everyman's Library'), *Émile* (J.M. Dent & Sons 1966) p.5.
5. *HIGH WIND* p.99.
6. Ibid. p.100.
7. Ibid. p.29.
8. Ibid. p.29.
9. Ibid. p.30.
10. Ibid. pp.35–7.
11. Ibid. p.76.
12. Ibid. p.87.
13. Ibid. p.71.
14. Ibid. p.85.
15. Ibid. p.86.
16. Ibid. p.116.
17. Ibid. p.108.
18. Ibid. pp.109–10.
19. Ford Madox Ford in *The Forum* New York, June 1929 p.xii.
20. IND RH to Charles 27 May 1929.
21. IND Mrs Elizabeth Marbury (who represents dramatists) to RH informing him of a cable from Vancouver.
22. IND The London Office of *Blau-Rot* to RH 28 Dec. 1928.
23. IND Maurice Browne to RH 19 Feb. 1929.
24. IND *Vanity Fair* to RH 14 Aug. 1929.
25. IND Helen McAfee to RH 3 Sept. 1929.
26. IND Louis Untermeyer to RH 3 Sept. 1929. Ibid. 6 Oct. 1929 shows that he selected *Reply to Good Advice, Unicorn Mad, Time,* and *Invocation to the Muse.*
27. IND Viola Gaylord to RH 24 Sept. 1929.
28. IND RH to Charles 27 May 1929.
29. IND *Vanity Fair* to RH Yacht Cossack, Nantucket, Mass. 14 Aug. 1929.
30. *Times Literary Supplement* 22 October 1964 – the year when *Mosquitoes* was first published

in England.
31. IND Margaret to RH 15 Aug. 1930.
32. IND. Jane Cassidy to RH pmk 28 Mar. 1930.
33. *SHEPHERDESS* p.108.
34. Ibid. p.113.
35. IND Smith University; 7 Paradise Road Northampton Mass.; sign. almost illegible [?Ann] to RH n.d. A detailed comparison of the handwriting reveals that this was *not* the Annie Churchill whom he had met at Bellevue, and who wrote to him in 1962; 'Ann' and 'Annie C.' were two different people.
36. POOLE p.50.
37. IND RH to Joseph Brewer n.d. on board the SS *De Grasse.*
38. IND Pamela Bianco to RH n.d. on board the SS *De Grasse.*

Chapter 18: *A High Wind in Jamaica* and Fame

1. Desmond MacCarthy in *Life and Letters* vol.III no.15 Aug. 1929 (kindly lent to me by Sir Keith Thomas, President of Corpus Christi College, Oxford).
2. BERG APG to John Graves 1 Oct. 1929. The article appeared on 29 Sept. 1929.
3. IND RH to Joseph Brewer; a PPPS written *'Years later'* to a letter written on board the SS *De Grasse,* but long unposted.
4. POOLE pp.50–1.
5. IND Walter Warren (decorator/contractor) to RH 14 Nov. 1929.
6. IND Gilbert Murray to RH 22 Jan. [1930].
7. IND Alan Porter to RH 7 Nov. 1929.
8. IND Hugh [Lyon] on board the Cunard RMS *Quitania* to RH.
9. IND Letters to RH of 1 Nov. and 18 Oct. 1929.
10. IND *Calendars* 3 Dec. 1929.
11. IND RH to Maurice Browne 9 Oct. 1929.
12. RH, *Time and Tide* 6 July 1940, quoted in POOLE p.53.
13. IND *Calendars* 25 Oct. 1929 'PCQ & N, Dine'.
14. IND Nancy Quennell to RH 12 July [1930].
15. This is deduced (perhaps unfairly) from a slightly barbed remark in Peter Quennell's letter to RH (IND 2 Mar. [1930]).
16. IND Nancy Quennell to RH 12 July 1930 asks: 'Has there been any more ravishing or being ravished?'
17. IND Peter and Nancy Quennell to RH 2 Mar. 1930.
18. IND *Calendars* 1929, 29 Oct. Lance Sieveking; 8 Nov. Margaret Kennedy; 10 Nov. Herberts; 4 Dec. Charterhouse, James Darling; 7–8 Dec. Masefields.
19. SIEVEKING pp.165–6.
20. Ibid.
21. IND *Calendars* 1929, 1930: 23 Dec. two dances; 2 Jan. Party Spreadeagle Thame.
22. IND Arthur Waley to RH 16 Dec. [1929].
23. *SHEPHERDESS*, pp.271 and 267.

Chapter 19: Retreat to Morocco

1. IND RH, 'Strange Christmases' in *Harper's Bazaar* Dec. 1930.
2. Richard Poole in his intro. to RH, *In the Lap of Atlas* (Chatto & Windus 1979) p.16.
3. Ibid. p.12. See also MINNEY p.74.
4. James Wyllie in SCRIPT p.18.
5. RH, 'The Fool and Fifteen Thieves' from *In the Lap of Atlas* p.35.
6. FH's recollections as told to Richard Poole and recounted in his intro. To RH, *In the Lap of Atlas* p.11. Poole has 'future' tense; but this is contradicted by MINNEY tape-recording of FH talking about her life in Morocco, recorded (in Penelope Minney's words) as 'the result of very skilled interviewing by the freelance BBC interviewer Peter France ... about 1976' (PM to author 9 Aug. 1992).
7. RH, 'The Fool and Fifteen Thieves' from *In the Lap of Atlas* p.35.
8. Ibid. p.36.
9. IND Jane [Cassidy] to RH n.d., but 'in the middle of festivities again'.
10. IND Pamela Bianco to RH n.d.
11. IND Pamela Bianco to RH [Dec.] 1929.
12. IND Jane [Cassidy] from to RH n.d. [pre-7 Apr. 1930 when Pamela herself writes on the same subject].
13. IND Jane Cassidy to RH 28 Mar. 1930.
14. IND Pamela Bianco to RH 7 Apr. 1930.
15. IND Pamela Bianco to RH 27 May 1930.

16. BERG Amy Graves to J.T.R. Graves 4 July 1930.
17. IND Peter Quennell and Nancy Quennell to RH 2 Mar. 1930.
18. POOLE p.52.
19. MINNEY p.74.
20. Robert Hughes in a letter to the present author of 23 Jan. 1993.
21. POOLE p.52.
22. AUTOB p.xxxvii.
23. Poole, intro. to RH, *In the Lap of Atlas* p.8.
24. AUTOB p.xxxvii.
25. POOLE pp.52–3 and Poole, intro. to RH, *In the Lap of Atlas* pp.9–10.
26. As n.7 above.
27. IND Margaret to RH 28 Mar. 1930.

Chapter 20: A Literary Life

1. IND Rotterdam Lloyd to RH 20 June 1930 mentions the landing of the tent-pole; and IND 24 June 1930 has the address.
2. BERG Amy Graves to John T.R. Graves 1 Aug. 1930.
3. IND Pamela Schlick to RH 30 June 1930. She was sailing 'in about a month'.
4. IND Nancy Quennell to RH 12 July 1930.
5. The date is problematic; but on 31 July 1930 RH accidentally met Amy Graves in London, and told her that 'he had not seen Robert but will visit us in September' (BERG Amy Graves to John Graves 1 Aug. 1930). As for the year of Jocelyn Herbert's visit: she recalls that her father's *The Water Gipsies* (1930) had just been published.
6. Jocelyn Herbert in conv. with the present author 19 Oct. 1992.
7. Amabel Williams-Ellis, *All Stracheys Are Cousins* (Weidenfeld & Nicolson 1983) pp.122–3.
8. IND Iris Barry to RH 11 Oct. n.d. begins: 'My endearing Diccon, Your letter was inimitable . . .'
9. IND Celia Simpson of the *Spectator* to RH 22 Oct., 29 Oct., 14 Nov.; acting sub-editor, 25 Nov.; Evelyn Wrench, 8 Dec. 1930.
10. IND Judith Wogan of the Grafton Theatre in Tottenham Court Road to RH 7 Oct. 1930.
11. IND Walter Peacock of *Miss Elizabeth Mercury* to RH 26 Jan. and 6 Feb. 1932.
12. IND Walter Peacock to RH 20 Jan. 1931 about the Noah's Ark Theatre.
13. IND Walter Peacock to RH 6 Feb. 1931.
14. IND Roland J.B. Munro (who played John) to RH 11 Mar. 1931.
15. IND Robert Nichols to RH 6 Aug. and 10 Sept. 1930.
16. IND Dick de la Mare to RH 31 Oct. 1930.
17. *FICTION AS TRUTH* p.131 (Originally in *Saturday Review of Literature* 16 May 1925).
18. Penny Minney to the present author 3 July 1992.
19. IND Virginia Woolf to RH 29 Nov. 1930.
20. IND Pamela to RH autumn 1930.
21. IND Pamela to RH 29 Aug. 1931.
22. IND Iris Barry to RH n.d. 1931.
23. IND Nancy Quennell to RH 12 June 1931.
24. IND Peter Quennell to RH 21 April 1931.
25. IND Nancy Quennell to RH 12 June 1931.
26. IND Winifred Stephens Whale (Hon. Sec.) Femina Vie Heureuse and Northcliffe Prizes Committee to RH 24 Mar. 1931.
27. IND N.I. Smith Sec. Natnl. Flying Servcs. Ltd. to RH 1 Apr. 1931.
28. IND RH, 'My First Day in the Air' in the *Daily Express* 20 Apr. 1931.
29. IND *Calendars* show RH in Morocco 3–19 Apr. 1931; and IND Joy from Tangier to RH 20 June 1931 writes that she has received some 'estimates only yesterday', and is 'sending them on to you now. I saw your article in the Graphic it was most amusing – it seems that you quite enjoyed the revolution in Tetuan'.
30. IND Nancy Quennell to RH 12 June 1931.
31. IND has a letter from the Leicester Galleries 9 July 1931 to this effect.
32. IND *Calendars* the performance was on 20 Apr.; he had the cast to dinner on the 22nd.
33. POOLE p.53.
34. RH 'Under the Nose and Under the Skin', broadcast on 22 Apr. 1931, and printed in the *Listener* June 10 1931 p.979.
35. RH, *The Spider's Palace and other stories* (illus. George Charlton) (Chatto & Windus 1931).
36. Ibid. p.32.
37. Ibid. p.87.
38. MINNEY MSS Faith Henderson to RH 12 July 1931.
39. Penelope Minney in a letter to the present author 9 Aug. 1992.
40. FH in SCRIPT p.23.
41. Ibid. pp.23–4.

Chapter 21: Frances Bazley

1. The present author in conv. (by telephone) with (a) Lucy McEntee 19 Apr. 1992 and (b) Penelope Minney 5 May 1992, about FH's remarkable artistic powers, and being self-taught and never going away to school.
2. IND RH to Joseph Brewer 16 Jan. 1932.
3. For this and other information about the Bazley family background I am much indebted to Colin M. Wells (the T. Frank Murchison Distinguished Professor of Classical Studies at Trinity University, San Antonio, Texas; and also husband of RH's daughter Kate) for sending me a copy of his paper dated 10 Feb. 1991 and entitled *The Benefits of the Industrial Revolution in England: A Little Family History, with Perhaps a Moral.*

   Lleky Papastavrou (née Hughes) writes of Sebastian (15 Apr. 1993); 'Frances's grandfather himself was a very remarkable person. He was a Manchester cotton magnate who was so careful of his workers, their living conditions & children's education that he was visited by both Disraeli and the Prince Regent. He wrote mathematical treatises and was an astronomer (Greenwich Mean Time was not precise enough for him: he used to have his own time, worked out from the stars). He was very public-spirited and became an MP for Manchester . . . [Before he died, he wrote to his son telling him] not to try to mix with the centuries-old aristocracy on equal terms but to be quite open about being nouveau riche.'
4. In a letter of 1872 which forms the basis of the article by Professor Colin M. Wells referred to in n.3 above.
5. Rachel Bennett (née Bazley) in conv. with the present author 25 Sept. 1992.
6. Sir Thomas Bazley in conversation with the present author 26 Sept. 1992.
7. Penelope Minney (née Hughes) to the present author 11 May 1992.
8. As n.6 above. Lleky Papastavrou points out in a letter to the present author of 12 Apr. 1993 that 'One of the reasons my grandmother "neglected" her children was because of all the good works she did in the neighbourhood: e.g., with friends, they started a Co-op in Coln-St-Aldwyns, built and stocked a library in the village . . . built . . . a village laundry to provide employment for the women'.
9. As n.7 above.
10. As n.6 above.
11. From their headquarters in Ambleside, PNEU sent out carefully structured educational materials, mainly in the form of lectures which it required no special expertise to deliver, and whose main points (after a single reading) had to be recalled and written down by the pupils.
12. As n.5 above. Lleky Papastavrou points out in a letter to the present author of 12 Apr. 1993 that although her mother 'didn't give her children much of her own company, she carefully provided other children of the "right age" for her own to play with. By all accounts Hatherop was always a very full and lively house, despite the horrible Nanny Taylor'.
13. As n.7 above.
14. AUTHOR An undated note kindly written for the present author in Sept. 1992 by Henriette Abel-Smith, formerly Palmer (and mother of the present Sir Mark Palmer), née Bazley.
15. As n.5 above.
16. On coming of age at twenty-one each child received an income of some £2000 a year, from capital which was strictly controlled by a trust. (Rachel Bennett née Bazley in conv. with the present author 25 Sept. 1992.)
17. As n.7 above.
18. As n.5 above.
19. As n.6 above.
20. As n.7 above.
21. IND *Calendars* 14 Oct. 1931 '8.0 Frances'.
22. James Wyllie in SCRIPT p.24.
23. IND RH to LH pmk 12 Oct. 1931.
24. IND Bell's Travel Service to RH 28 Oct. 1931.
25. Ibid. 3 Nov. 1931.
26. IND RH to Naomi Mitchison 11 Nov. 1931.
27. IND Naomi Mitchison to RH 5 [Nov. 1931].
28. As n.26 above.
29. RH, 'Physics, Astronomy and Mathematics' in ed. Naomi Mitchison *An Outline for Boys and Girls and their Parents* (Gollancz 1932) pp.307–57.
30. IND *Calendars* 25 Nov. 'Full moon 7.10 Dine F.' (This entry is not conclusive; the previous week he had dined with one Faith.)
31. James Wyllie in SCRIPT p.24.
32. IND *Calendars* 8 Dec. 1931 has: 'Arrive Morocco cocktails Teddy.'
33. IND In the interim, on the 19th, there had been another telegram (from the Lake District) saying simply: 'APPROVED ARRIVE MOROCCO BEFORE JANUARY.'

34. IND RH to Joseph Brewer 16 Jan. 1932.
35. SIEVEKING p.168.
36. As n.34 above.
37. SIEVEKING pp.168–9.
38. *The Gloucestershire Echo* for 9 Jan. 1932; IND RH to Joseph Brewer 29 Feb. 1932; SIEVEKING p.168; and IND A note by Lucy McEntee after a discussion with RH on 2 Nov. 1972.
39. As n.34 above.
40. IND Iris Barry to RH n.d.
41. IND Margery Bianco to RH 11 March 1932.
42. IND Ernestine Evans to RH n.d. [1932].
43. IND RH to Joseph Brewer 29 Feb. 1932.
44. IND FH to Christopher Cadogan 11 Mar. 1932.
45. MINNEY MSS Tape-recording of FH on her life in Morocco, interview by Peter France in about 1976 when he was a tenant of Sir Thomas Bazley and a neighbour of Frances. Lleky Papastavrou comments that 'Frances liked things simple and uncluttered aesthetically; she was not acquisitive'.
46. As n.44 above.
47. Penelope Minney to the present author 11 May 1992.
48. IND Walter Harris to RH 31 Apr. 1932.
49. Particulars of the storm come from McENTEE Copy of letter from the Manageress, Portmeirion, 29 Oct. 1927 to Clough Williams-Ellis. Other details from Penny Minney to the present author 9 Aug. 1992.
50. IND Frank Penn Smith to LH n.d., but annotated: 'Written when the Dicks were living at Garreg Fawr in the summer of 1932.' See also Penelope Minney to the present author 9 Aug. 1992.
51. Naomi Mitchison in *An Outline for Boys and Girls and their Parents* p.305.
52. IND Frank Penn Smith to 'Lulu' (LH), n.d. but annotated 'written when the Dicks were at Garreg Fawr in the Summer 1932.'
53. IND RH to Joseph Brewer 8 Feb. 1933.
54. SIEVEKING p.170.
55. As n.53 above.
56. H. Montgomery Hyde, *Walter Monckton* (Sinclair-Stevenson 1991) pp.27–30.
57. Robert's birth was registered at Clerkenwell.
58. Lucy McEntee in conv. with the present author 19 Apr. 1992.
59. As n.53 above.
60. IND RH to his servant Mohammed 5 Dec. 1932 in Arabic; the School of Oriental Studies at the University of London supplied an original translation which is now at IND, and from which the extract is taken.
61. IND Richard de la Mare to RH 24 Nov. 1932.
62. IND *Diaries* 3 Dec. 1932 (the previous day RH had attended a Book Society lunch at the Park Lane Hotel).
63. RH, note on characters in *A Comedy of Good and Evil* in *The Sisters' Tragedy and three other plays* (Heinemann 1924) p.54.
64. Harold Conway in the *Daily Mail* 27 Jan. 1933. Minnie Williams was played by Christine Silver, the Revd John Williams by Jack Twyman, Scraggy Evans the Post by Llewellyn Rees, Mari Jones by Mary Morgan, Mrs Jones Bakehouse by Gwladys Evan Morris, Timothy YsGairnolwen by Richard Littledale, Mr Gas Jones by Fewlass Llewellyn, and Mrs Resurrection Jones by Hannah Jones.
65. IND RH to Donegal 19 Jan. 1933.
66. 'Peterborough' in the *Daily Telegraph* [?28] Jan. 1933.
67. BERG Clarissa Graves to Amy Graves 28 Jan. 1933.
68. Harold Conway in the *Daily Mail* 27 Jan. 1933.
69. 'Peterborough' in the *Daily Telegraph* [?28] Jan. 1933. The party was given by Mrs Christopher Blunt.
70. As n.53 above.
71. IND Julian Huxley to RH 8 Feb. 1933. 'I was hoping I might see something more of you after our meeting last week', he wrote, inviting him for 15 Feb. – if he was back in town on that date.
72. IND De La Mare to RH 25 Jan. 1933: 'It was so nice to see you again after all this long time, and we hope you will come and see us often.'
73. IND Margaret Storm Jameson to RH 23 Feb. 1933. She asked whether they might go down for a weekend the next term, instead.
74. IND London editor of the *Gramphone* Christopher Stone to RH 1 Feb. 1933.
75. This appeared at some stage before 27 Jan. 1933.
76. IND RH to Laurence Holt 27 Mar. 1933.
77. IND Amabel Williams-Ellis to RH 15 Mar. 1933.

78. IND RH to Laurence Holt 27 Mar. 1933.
79. IND Laurence Holt to RH 28 Mar. 1933 first letter.
80. Ibid. second letter.
81. Ibid. 31 Mar. 1933.
82. Ibid. 20 Apr. 1933.
83. MINNEY MSS Dai Evans to RH 20 Apr. 1933. RH returned to Stiffkey to find IND Laurence Holt to RH 5 Apr. 1933 with Wolfe's address.
84. SIEVEKING p.170.
85. MINNEY MSS tape-recording of FH talking on her life in Morocco.
86. SIEVEKING p.173.
87. IND Laurence Holt to RH 20 Apr. 1933.
88. Ibid. 8 June 1933.
89. Ibid. 14 June 1933.
90. Ibid. 29 June 1933 (in response to RH's letter of 27 June 1933).
91. Ibid. 1 Sept. 1933.
92. IND Joseph Losey to RH 27 June 1933. JL, then a twenty-four-year-old director of stage productions, heard that RH had started work on a new novel; and wrote asking about the possibility of a play for Broadway if it could be dramatised. As his 'credentials' he gave the names of 'The Charles Laughtons, Iris Barry and Ernestine Evans.'
93. IND Richard de la Mare to RH 23 Mar., 26 and 31 Aug. 1933.
94. IND RH to Richard de la Mare 1 Sept. 1933.
95. IND David Garnett to RH 16 June 1933 declining an invitation to play for the Stiffkey Cricket Club on 1 July; and adding: 'How goes your hurricane?'
96. POOLE p.55.
97. IND Sir Thomas Bazley to RH p.c. 9 Feb. 1933.
98. IND *Real Estate* folder.
99. Ibid. On some journeys to Laugharne, RH stayed with his Aunt Margaret in Cardiff (IND M to RH 14 Feb. 1934).

Chapter 22: Laugharne Castle

1. MINNEY p.14.
2. Clough Williams-Ellis in SCRIPT p.28.
3. MINNEY p.16.
4. IND S.B. Williams to RH 17 Mar. 1934.
5. IND R. Cunninghame Graham to RH 28 Mar. 1934. RH's doctor, Hugh Wyllie of 82 Portland Place, prescribed pills and a special diet on 8 Apr. 1934.
6. IND de la Mare to RH 26 and 30 Jan. 1934. The final agreement was sent to RH by C. Stewart of Faber & Faber on 15 Mar.
7. See IND RH to Lord Howard de Walden 2 May 1935.
8. IND It ran from 15–20 Jan. 1934. Plays included *Precious Bane* and *The Taming of the Shrew*. The winner was the Rhondda Players for *A Hundred Years Old* by S. and J. Alvarez Quintero, trans. by H. and H. Granville-Barker.
9. Cardiff *Western Mail* 19 Feb. 1934.
10. MINNEY MSS R. Golding Bright to RH Nov. 16 1933.
11. IND 18–25 May 1934.
12. *Herald of Wales and Swansea Evening Post* 10 Jan. 1935.
13. IND has several letters from Nancy, and a statement of 25 June 1934 of her expenses from 2–5 June at £50 3s. 4d.
14. *Western Mail* 17 Sept. 1934.
15. Paul Bennett Morgan, 'Richard Hughes and "Living in Wales" ' in the *Anglo-Welsh Review* pp.91–103.
16. Penelope Minney in a letter to the present author 9 Aug. 1992.
17. IND Clough Williams-Ellis to RH 16 Nov. 1934.
18. IND Clough Williams-Ellis to RH 22 Feb. 1935: CW-E advises that the trustees may think too much has already been spent on a leasehold property. On RH & FH & their money, Lleky Papastavrou (née Hughes) writes (12 Apr. 1993): 'My memory is of Frances writing out cheques for food, for the coalman & for school fees too. School fees often came out of her capital – they certainly would not have had enough without. Mor Edrin was also bought with her Trust Fund capital, so was Clogwyn Melyn and the fields'.
19. IND On 8 Sept. 1933 RH was given an overdraft limit of £250 for six months; by 3 Sept. 1934 Barclays Bank pointed out that his overdraft was now £523 19s. 2d. and asked him to regularise the situation; and on 14 Sept. they advised him that if over £800 was required they must have a further security; at present they could go to £700 for six months.
20. IND RH to Hubert J. Fripp n.d. showing that Dorincourt, RH's childhood home, remained in the family and had been used by RH as security for his overdraft. Aunt Mary was now offering

£800 for the property, and RH wondered whether to use the cash to pay off his mortgage and overdraft, and then pay his Aunt Mary interest on the £800.

21. IND RH to Mrs Starke and (separately) to her brother Professor David.
22. IND has a draft dated 5 Nov. 1935 of the new lease.
23. IND Hilda Vaughan to RH 8 Nov. 1934.
24. IND RH to Hilda Vaughan 11 Nov. 1934.
25. IND Evelyn Bowen to RH 21 Nov. 1934.
26. IND [Copy] RH to Evelyn Bowen 24 Nov. 1934.
27. IND Hilda Vaughan to RH 28 Nov. 1934.
28. IND Evelyn Bowen to RH 6 Dec. 1934.
29. IND (a) Notice of a meeting for 12 Jan. 1935 in a letter to RH of 2 Jan. 1935, annotated in RH's hand: 'Postponed to Feb 2'. (b) Evelyn Bowen to Messrs. Wiley & Powles 6 Feb. 1935 on what happened in the meeting.
30. IND RH to Evelyn Bowen 9 and 22 Mar. 1935.
31. IND RH to Lord Howard de Walden 2 and 10 May 1935.
32. IND RH to the 'Amateur Players' 5 July 1935.
33. IND See RH to the 'Amateur Players' 5 July 1935; T.J. Lewis of the Barry Players, Glamorgan, to RH 10 July 1935, announcing that they would only work under Hock 'in English'; P.H. Burton of Port Talbot, saying that his company was almost entirely non-Welsh speaking, but that they would like to take up the offer; R.S.T. Fleming of the *Welsh National Theatre Company* at Plas Newydd, Llangollen, to RH 20 July 1935 about the production of the Llanelli cast being 'pretty well assured', and wondering whether Hock could cope with a second cast made up of individuals from six separate companies; and E. Lewis of the Rhondda Valley, to RH 23 July 1935, announcing that his society 'The Garrick' was wholly committed for the next season.
34. IND RH to Captain R.S.T. Fleming 3 Oct. 1935.
35. IND RH to Lord Howard de Walden July 1936.
36. IND Herbert Vaughan to RH 15 and 18 Apr. 1934.
37. IND See for example: CPRW to RH 24 May 1934 about oil pollution in sea and tidal estuaries, thanking him for his letter of the 19th instant; and RH to CPRW 13 Jan. 1936 enquiring about the cutting down of some trees at Laugharne.
38. IND Committee of the Debating Society of University College, Swansea to RH 28 May 1934.
39. IND, showing that RH gave the address on 20 July 1934 at the County School for Girls, Ruabon (where Lord Howard de Walden was chairman of the governing body.)
40. IND Cedric Morris to RH 1 Apr. 1935. IND 18 Dec. 1934 shows that Morris lived near Colchester; and he asked to motor over to visit the Hugheses for a day when staying with friends at Manorbier Castle.
41. IND E.M. Forster to RH 8 Dec. 1935 – about the 'Boriswood Appeal', 'As regards the *Times*', wrote Forster, 'I'm afraid (and Kidd [the freelance journalist who had created the Council] agrees) that they would never publish any letter coming from the Council for Civil Liberties [widely suspected of being a Communist 'Front' organisation]; still less would they publish anything from us which involved, however remotely, the taint of sex!'
42. AUTOB pp.xxiv–xxv.
43. IND. Further work on her had been done by Crossfield at Hoylake in 1920.
44. MINNEY p.21. Just for the record, *Tern* was originally named *My Girl*.
45. RH in *The Cruising Association Bulletin* 1934 p.161.
46. IND Payments were on 6 Dec. 1933; and on 3 Mar. and 7 Apr. 1934; the voyage from Deganwy to Tremadoc took place on 29–30 May 1934. Lancelot Evans to RH 7 Apr. 1934 promises to place the gear on board, including the fishing net; adding that a coat of paint would improve her, as she has been aground through the winter.
47. IND Clough Williams-Ellis to RH 25 Oct. 1933.
48. IND The surveying work was undertaken in 1935.
49. For this and subsequent paras. see RH, 'Tern' in the *Cruising Association Bulletin* (1934) pp.161–2.
50. Sheila Rowlands in SCRIPT p.29.
51. IND The log of *Tern*. See also IND Sid Williams of Ilfracombe to RH 3 Oct. 1935, worrying about *Tern*, as 'The legs we made the day you left broke the first time she grounded. The fault being they were cut too short and when she grounded they went in under the boat and broke so she has been listing down ever since ... I should take her away from here ... could you send her legs here ... best thing ... get her back home'. See also IND 31 Oct. 1935, asking for cash for tobacco for chaps who have helped him; it was a good job RH sent on the legs, or 'I do think the boat would have been smashed up by now'.
52. IND has the invitation for Monday 29 Oct. 1934 at 7 p.m.
53. MINNEY MSS Sheila Rowlands interviewed on tape in 1976.
54. See the Cardiff *Western Mail* for 24 Apr. and IND 25 Feb. 1936 'Jane' in South Africa to RH, having 'read in *The Welshman*' about it all.
55. IND M. Jones to RH. The headmaster wrote: 'I hope to send you a photograph of [Marjorie Davies] in school uniform, later on.'

56. IND has considerable corres. on the subject. E.g. Baroness Budberg for the French Gaumont Film Company to RH Sept. 1935; RH to Walter Peacock 3 Oct., and 8 and 27 Nov. 1935; and WP to RH 7, 11, 12 and 26 Nov., and 3 Dec. 1935.
57. IND Agreement signed 13 Apr. 1934.
58. IND Leon Lion to RH 25 May 1934.
59. Ibid. 3 Oct. 1934.
60. Ibid. 3 Oct. and 4 Dec. 1934.
61. IND RH to Leon Lion 9 Jan. 1935.
62. IND Leon Lion to RH 4 Mar. 1935 (on 22 Jan. 1935 he had written to say that he had not yet received Act Three).
63. IND RH to Leon Lion 12 Apr. 1935.
64. IND Leon Lion to RH 29 Apr. 1935.
65. IND RH to Leon Lion 10 May 1935.
66. Penelope Minney to the present author 9 Aug. 1992.
67. IND Cable to RH 30 July 1934 telling him that 21 Lloyd Square had been let to Mr Rupert Hart-Davis of Jonathan Cape, an acquaintance who was willing to purchase the fittings from RH for £30.
68. The date is conjectural; the incident is not.
69. Rachel Bazley to FH n.d. [?early 1934].
70. IND FH to RH n.d.
71. Ibid.
72. Ibid.
73. IND 6 Jan. 1936, a menu showing details of a supper given to the Corporation of Laugharne at L. Castle on 6 Jan. 1936, as follows:

Cockle Soup
Clear Soup

–

Roasted Turkey   Cockatryce
Potatoes   Sprouts
Cold Pie

–

Plum Pudding
Mince Pie

Chapter 23: *In Hazard*

1. IND *Boats and sailing.*
2. IND Charles Prentice to RH 13 Nov. 1934.
3. IND Cunningham Graham to RH 16 Nov. 1934.
4. MINNEY MSS RH to FH Amsterdam Friday n.d.
5. MINNEY MSS RH to FH from Tangier, 7 Feb. 1936.
6. MINNEY MSS RH to FH 13 Feb. 1936 (with some extracts from the previous letter).
7. MINNEY MSS RH to FH 19 Feb. 1933.
8. MINNEY MSS RH to FH 22 Feb. 1936.
9. MINNEY MSS RH to FH various Feb./Mar. 1926.
10. MINNEY MSS RH from an hotel in Azrou to FH 12 Mar. 1936.
11. *IN HAZARD* p.7.
12. Ibid. p.15.
13. Cardiff *Western Mail* 27 Apr. 1936.
14. IND RH to Mr Elias 10 Mar. 1948: 'About twelve years ago you made me a coracle. Could you make me a new one?'
15. IND The log of *Tern* (confirmed by Sheila Rowlands in SCRIPT p.32) makes the date clear. MINNEY and POOLE state incorrectly that Hughes took part in this race in 1937.
16. IND RH to FH 22 May 1936.
17. IND Log-book of *Tern* 30 May 1936.
18. Penelope Minney in a telephone conversation with the present author 29 Sept. 1992.
19. MINNEY p.22.
20. IND Henry S. Canby of the *Saturday Review* NYC to RH 1 Nov. 1935; RH replied on 17 Nov. The poems were: 'My Head'; 'Cry, my Heart'; 'Burial'; 'Urania'; 'Demon Chained'; and 'Demon Loosed'.
21. IND W.B. Yeats to RH 13 Nov. 1935: 'Chatto & Windus ask me two pounds a poem, and I had proposed to take nine poems. T.S. Eliot and some of the older poets have asked two pounds a page and I calculate that your nine poems will put as seven pages. I have a fixed sum to pay authors with, and if Chatto & Windus ask so much, I must reduce my selection from you to four or five poems.'
22. IND Dylan Thomas to RH n.d. The date of this failed visit can only have been Oct. 1934

or Apr. 1935. DT asks to call on RH on Saturday (6th). He also mentions having been in Laugharne 'in the late summer'. We know from other sources that DT successfully called on RH in Laugharne on 15 July 1936; so this letter must have been written before then (and certainly not in Sept. 1936 as it has been provisionally dated in the IND archives); if in 1936, there is a Saturday 6th in June, but he would not then refer back to having called 'in the late summer'; if in 1935, then the only Saturday 6th occurs in April, and he would have been more likely to say 'in the late summer last year'; if in 1934, then there is a suitable Saturday 6 Oct. which seems most likely. (The only other one in 1934 is in Jan. – before RH was properly in residence.)

23. Caitlin Thomas with George Tremlett, *Caitlin: Life with Dylan Thomas* (Secker and Warburg 1986) pp.1–27.
24. Ibid. p.1. Caitlin records that Augustus John was there on that occasion; but this may be (fifty years after the event) a pardonable lapse of memory, as John himself in 1960 states clearly that the first time he saw Caitlin and Dylan together was at Laugharne: see Augustus John in ed. E.W. Tedlock, *Dylan Thomas: the Legend and the Poet* (Heinemann 1960) pp.25–8. On the other hand, Augustus John May have been lying so as to place himself (as the story unfolded) in a less ridiculous light.
25. Augustus John in ed. Tedlock, *Dylan Thomas* p.25. IND has a preliminary letter (AJ to RH 3 July 1936) in which AJ writes: 'I shall be coming to S.Wales between the 11th & 18th July & would like to look in on you if you are there.'
26. IND DT to RH 14 July 1936. Thomas with Tremlett, *Caitlin* p.7 and p.198 has her arriving 'on the Friday night' and seeing Dylan 'late on the Saturday morning' on 15 July. However, 15 July 1936 (the accurate date) was a Wednesday.
27. Thomas with Tremlett, *Caitlin* p.7.
28. IND *Tapes* spring 1964 at Talsarnau of RH and FH by Colm Edwards with Constantine Fitzgibbon.
29. Thomas with Tremlett, *Caitlin* p.9.
30. Jenny had brought another company of her Patchwork Players to Laugharne the previous summer. See BERG Amy Graves to J.T.R. Graves 18 June 1935; and IND Jenny Nicholson to RH 24 July 1935, with plans for the Patchwork Players. She asks if she may borrow 'a few things that we used when we stayed with you . . . your bell tent . . . a grey top hat . . . your striped sailor trousers sou'wester (yellow) and sailor jersey . . . we will try and have an entirely new programme for Laugharne!! . . . We have got two pianists now *much* better than a gramophone I think . . . Our average age is now 14!!'
31. BERG Amy Graves to John T.R. Graves 20 July 1936.
32. IND Ernest Colin-Smith (who is winding up FPS's estate) on 20 Aug. 1936 encloses a tenancy agreement showing that a Mrs Davis owns the lease, which is fixed at £12 a year. IND 18 Sept. 1936 enclosing an agreement between Mrs Davis, LH and RH in which it is mutually agreed that 'the object in view is to maintain the atmosphere which the late Mr Penn Smith created during his occupation of the cottage and to keep it and the furniture therein in the same way as he left it'.

    The story of FPS's decline is in IND FPS to LH late June 1934, which shows that by then he had moved into a house not far from Portmadoc for which he had paid £140 (presumably feeling too ill to remain in remote Gelli), and IND FPS to RH 24 Oct. 1935 in which he mentions suffering from such low blood pressure that he has fits of unconsciousness.
33. IND High Sheriff of Carmarthen inviting RH to lunch on 11 Nov. 1936.
34. Sheila Rowlands in SCRIPT p.29.
35. *IN HAZARD* p.21.
36. Ibid. p.28.
37. Ibid. p.31.
38. Ibid. p.49.
39. Ibid. p.56.
40. Ibid. p.66.
41. IND Henrietta Malkiel to RH July 1936.
42. IND John Krimsky to RH 31 July 1936.
43. IND Henrietta Malkiel to RH 6 Aug. 1936.
44. IND Charles Laughton to RH. The word 'lunched' should strictly speaking be qualified by 'probably', as we are not certain whether the invitation was accepted, thought that seems most likely.
45. IND RH to John Krimsky 4 Sept. 1936; RH had also cabled Krimsky immediately before writing this letter.
46. IND RH to Charles Laughton 4 Sept. 1936.
47. IND Krimsky to RH (cable) 6 Sept. 1936.
48. IND Henrietta Malkiel to RH (cable) 14 Sept. 1936.
49. IND Henrietta Malkiel to RH 25 Sept. 1936.
50. IND Charles Laughton to RH 1 Nov. 1936.
51. IND Henrietta Malkiel to RH 1 Dec. 1936.
52. RH in *Time and Tide* 19 Dec. 1936 opposes Baldwin, while also opposing Rebecca West,

author of an article calling Baldwin incompetent. On the contrary, says RH, he has strengthened his position immeasurably.

53. IND (draft) RH to HRH Prince Edward. IND has a letter of 6 Jan. 1937 headed 'Buckingham Palace' and containing the formal thanks of Prince Edward, who had by then been created Duke of Windsor.
54. Extract dated 22 Feb. 1937 from the diary of G. Dyfnallt Owen.
55. MINNEY pp.15–16.
56. IND.
57. IND A note by RH on the programme of the Laugharne Regatta Cup Race 1937.
58. Rachel Bennett née Bazley in conv. with the present author 25 Sept. 1992.
59. *IN HAZARD* pp.66–7.
60. Ibid. p.70.
61. Ibid. p.73.
62. Ibid. pp.74–5.
63. The Bible: Genesis 1:2; Job 38:1; Acts 2:2.
64. *IN HAZARD* pp.111–13.
65. Ibid. pp.88–98.
66. IND RH to Karin Stephen 10 Nov. 1937.
67. As Rachel Bennett née Bazley made it clear to the present author in conv. (Sept. 1992) when she said 'that side of things was never a problem' between her sister and brother-in-law.
68. Lleky Papastavrou in conv. with the present author 24 Sept. 1992.
69. AUTHOR An undated note kindly written for the present author in Sept. 1992 by Henriette Abel-Smith, formerly Palmer, née Bazley.
70. IND LH to FH 4 July [1938].
71. This is slightly speculative. It is well-known in the family that there was a time after Diccon's marriage to Frances when there was a serious breakdown in communications between them, and considering the way in which Louisa was raising the emotional temperature over whether or not *In Hazard* would be a success, this seems a likely moment.
72. *IN HAZARD* p.117.
73. Sheila Rowlands in SCRIPT p.31.
74. The party was held on 31 Mar. 1938.
75. IND Laurence Holt to RH 2 Apr. 1938.
76. IND James Miller to RH 3 Apr. 1938.
77. IND Dylan Thomas to RH n.d. [late Mar. or early Apr. 1938].
78. Caitlin Thomas née Macnamara in SCRIPT p.33.
79. Thomas with Tremlett, *Caitlin* pp.54–5.
80. Penelope Minney in a letter to the present author 11 Nov. 1992.
81. IND RH reviewing Dylan Thomas's *Under Milk Wood*; and see Thomas with Tremlett, *Caitlin passim* for Dylan's feelings about Laugharne.
82. Thomas with Tremlett, *Caitlin* p.54.
83. SIEVEKING footnote p.179.
84. Vernon Watkins, a foreword to RH, *A High Wind in Jamaica* (Signet Classics, New York 1961) pp.vi–vii.
85. IND Laurence Holt to RH 27 May 1938.
86. IND Geoffrey Faber of Faber & Faber 23 Nov. 1937. The saga is told in e.g. IND GF to RH 11 Mar. 1937 asking for a reply to his of 19 Oct. 1936 on the subject of Burton; and IND 19 Mar. 1937 hoping RH will keep the money and write the book. IND RH, a memo of 3 Feb. 1938 shows RH returning the £250, and promising to announce 'when he resumes the writing of the said work'. IND also has a note of indebtedness from RH to FH: in Feb. 1938 she lent him £500, of which £250 went to Faber & Faber returning their advance on Burton.
87. IND John Murray to RH 17 Nov. 1937.
88. IND RH cutting.
89. IND RH to John Murray 27 Nov. 1937.
90. Speculative: IND John Murray to RH 17 Nov. 1937 shows a plan for them to meet Rebell, but whether they actually did so is unknown.
91. IND John Murray to RH 11 Apr. 1938.
92. IND Sir Austin Harris to RH 17 Mar. 1938.
93. IND RH to Sir Austin Harris 23 Mar. 1938.
94. IND Stephen Gaselee to RH 25 Mar. 1938.
95. IND Harold Nicolson to RH 24 and 29 Mar. 1938.
96. IND FH to RH 23 June [1938].
97. IND FH to RH n.d.
98. Penelope Minney in a letter to the present author 11 Nov. 1992.
99. IND LH to FH 4 July [1938].
100. IND LH to RH 4 July [1938].
101. POOLE p.61.

102. IND Virginia Woolf to RH 8 Aug. 1938.
103. IND As in RH's scripted interview broadcast from Alexandra Palace on 14 July, when he regaled listeners with such details as: 'I do a great deal of my writing from the top of the watchtower overlooking the harbour. Once when I was up there writing some of my new book the wind blew all the panes out of the windows.'
104. IND FH to RH Tuesday n.d. [?July 1938].
105. IND FH to RH n.d. [?Aug. 1938].
106. *South Wales Echo and Evening Express* 12 Sept. 1938.
107. IND Frances to 'Dearest Mother' 3 Oct. n.d. [1938].
108. IND John Murray to RH 20 Oct. 1938, and (telegram) 27 Oct. 1938.
109. IND John Murray to RH 9 and 14 Nov., and 9 Dec. 1938.
110. Ibid. 10 Jan. 1939.
111. Penelope Minney to the present author 11 Nov. 1992, referring to RH's *Time and Tide* articles on the subject.
112. IND RH to Mrs Murray-Carrington 10 Jan. 1939.
113. IND RH to Henry Duckworth of Messrs Withers & Co 17 Jan. 1939.
114. IND Ford Madox Ford to RH 20 Nov. 1938.
115. IND RH to Ford Madox Ford 11 Feb. 1939.
116. As n.111 above.
117. IND RH to FH 6 Feb. 1939 (from Plymouth), RH to Ford Madox Ford 11 Feb. 1939 on board the SS *Letitia*.
118. IND *Geographical Magazine* to RH 30 Mar. 1939.
119. IND Toby Henderson to RH 8 Dec. 1938.
120. IND corres. *re* an article for *Vogue* of 30 Mar., 21 May, 1 and 13 June.
121. IND RH ('At sea, between Cuba and Jamaica') to FH 21 Feb. 1939; an unpublished part of a letter in MINNEY pp.24–6.
122. IND RH to FH 21 Feb. 1939 and MINNEY p.24.
123. IND *Geographical Magazine* to RH 25 July 1939.
124. Penelope Minney in a telephone conv. with the present author 18 Oct. 1992.
125. IND Mrs C. Johnson ['Pumpkie'] to FH 28 Apr. 1939 and 15 Aug. 1940.
126. IND Mrs C. Johnson to FH 16 May 1939.
127. IND Henry Duckworth to FH 17 May 1939.
128. IND Mrs C. Johnson ['Pumpkie'] to FH 26 May 1939.
129. IND RH to Jock 10 July 1939 encloses the galleys and chapter summaries: intro. to follow soon. John Murray to RH 14 July 1939: the intro. 'seems to me to be admirable'. RH to Jock 27 July 1939 encloses proof of intro.; and the same day RH receives a cheque for £40, and an agreement giving him 2½% on the first 5000 copies sold, then 5%; 2½% on the American edition; and 10% on other rights.
130. IND Arthur Harris to RH 20 July 1939.
131. MINNEY p.17. See also Penelope Minney to the present author 16 Sept. n.d. [1992]: 'Till 1939 we had a lovely professional child-nurse who looked after us. When she left there was probably chaos, so I would put the incident of shelving us all in summer 1939. Perhaps it gave him the idea later for the children's story *Gertrude's Child*?'
132. IND *Tern* 'Aug. 17 1939 Laugharne to Portmadoc: Owner plus two Catholic Fathers; arrived 19th; 11.45 anchored off Portmeirion.'
133. Robert Hughes to the present author 23 Jan. 1993.
134. John Terraine, *The Mighty Continent* (Hutchinson 1974) pp.221–7.
135. IND Ministry of Labour to RH 25 Aug. 1939.
136. Penelope Minney to the present author 11 Nov. 1992.

Chapter 24: Finding a Role

1. MINNEY p.4.
2. Robert Hughes in SCRIPT pp.35–6.
3. MINNEY p.4.
4. MINNEY p.31. Lleky Papastavrou adds that 'Robert had been a tremendous worry from the start, because of severe eczema and asthma'.
5. MINNEY p.4; modified by Lleky Papastavrou and Penelope Minney to the present author 12 and 20 Apr. 1993.
6. MINNEY p.3.
7. Ibid. p.6.
8. MINNEY p.31. Lleky Papastavrou adds: 'This beautiful antique china had all been collected by Diccon: it was not Frances's.'
9. IND Ministry of Labour to RH 4 Sept. 1939.
10. IND RH to Ernestine Evans of Finland 12 Sept. 1939.
11. MINNEY MSS An unpublished part of the RH to FH n.d. in MINNEY p.31. For Nurse Cecil

being uniformed, Robert Hughes in a telephone conv. with the present author 23 Oct. 1992.

12. MINNEY pp.6–7.
13. MINNEY MSS RH to FH 11 Nov. [1939].
14. MINNEY p.13.
15. MINNEY MSS RH to FH 11 Nov. [1939] in which RH explains his *real* reasons for not having wished to accompany FH back to Laugharne.
16. The dating is highly speculative. On receiving a letter from FH telling him that she had arrived at Laugharne, RH wrote back to her on a Saturday: possibly 7 Oct., as has been guessed. It might just as well be the 14th; but not the 21st, as in a letter dated the 25th [Oct.] Diccon apologises for not having written for ages (MINNEY MSS).
17. MINNEY MSS RH to FH 'Parc Saturday' n.d.
18. Robert Hughes in a telephone conv. with the present author 23 Oct. 1992.
19. MINNEY MSS RH to FH 'Parc Saturday' n.d.; but the sentence about being a pig appears in MINNEY p.31.
20. MINNEY p.31; and (for hitherto unpublished sections) see MINNEY MSS RH to FH 25 Oct. [1939].
21. MINNEY MSS RH to FH 8 Nov. 1939.
22. MINNEY MSS RH to FH 8 Nov. 1939. (IND 4 Oct. Barclays of Carmarthen agree to RH's request for a £400 overdraft to the end of the year.)
23. MINNEY MSS RH to FH 11 Nov. 1939.
24. MINNEY MSS RH to FH 1 Dec. [1939].
25. MINNEY p.32.
26. IND RH to Canon Williams.
27. IND Canon Williams to RH 2 Oct. 1939.
28. Winston S. Churchill, *The Second World War: Volume One – The Gathering Storm* (Cassell 1948) p.330.
29. IND a friend of RH to Rear-Admiral J.H. Godfrey CB, Director of Naval Intelligence, 10 Jan. 1940.
30. IND 1939: L.M. MacBride to RH 2 Dec.; RH to MacBride 10 Dec.; MacBride to RH 15 Dec.; Holt to RH 18 Dec.; RH to Holt 21 Dec. RH discovered that his name had been given to the MoI by a Captain Ricci, whom he thanked on 14 Jan. 1940.
31. Date uncertain. Some accounts talk of his returning only just before Christmas; but it is quite probable (in view of the two missed court appearances) that he was back in Laugharne by mid Dec.
32. IND RH to R.H. Tyler 24 Jan. 1940.
33. IND This had been especially evident in Aug., when RH had joined Dylan and Caitlin at a masque in Swansea. Vernon Watkins to RH 2 July 1939, inviting him to the masque on 6 July. The other details are from Caitlin's sister Nicolette, in conv. with the present author in Judith Eagle's London flat some years ago.
34. MINNEY p.128.
35. IND – a programme for the evening.
36. MINNEY p.128.
37. Ibid. pp.18–19; see also Clough Williams-Ellis in SCRIPT pp.28–9.
38. Churchill, *The Gathering Storm* p.406.
39. Ibid. p.408.
40. Ibid. p.417.
41. IND RH to Major-General A.A. Goschen 31 Dec. 1939: 'Thomas has just rung me up about "a war job in the Persian Gulf" for which he thought me a likely candidate. I should very much like to hear a little more about it, if I may.'
42. IND *Diaries* RH: 4 Jan. 1940 Travel Liverpool; 8 Jan. 1940 Leave L.
43. IND A friend of RH (name illegible) to Rear-Admiral J.H. Godfrey 10 Jan. 1940, telling him that Hughes has abandoned his attempt to get a job in Godfrey's department; but would like to write a book on the *Graf Spee*.
44. IND RH to the Provost of Oriel 10 Feb. 1940.
45. IND RH to Edward Marsh 10 Feb. 1940; Edward Marsh to 'Dear Diccon' 13 Feb. 1940; Leigh Ashton of the Ministry of Information to RH 14 Feb 1940; and RH to Leigh Ashton 17 Feb. 1940.
46. IND Ministry of Information (to various recipients) 25 Feb. 1940.
47. Churchill, *The Gathering Storm* p.445.
48. IND RH to Chambrun 16 Mar. 1940; see also IND *Diaries* 1940, showing that in March he went (among other places) from London, to Plymouth, to London, to Bristol, to London, to Laugharne, to Bath, to London, to Liverpool, to London; and that on 10–12 Apr. he spent some two and a half days at the Admiralty.
49. MINNEY p.34.
50. IND RH to Jack [?James of the Admiralty] 2 May 1940.
51. IND *Diaries* 1940: 27 Apr. 'Began Chapter 1'; Thursday 2 May 'Began Chapter 2'; Wednesday 8 May 'Began Chapter 3'.
52. IND have a fair draft of chs. 1–3, and nine pages of ch. 4 of *The Navy is Here*.

53. IND Barclays of Carmarthen to RH 8 Jan. 1940.
54. IND Barclays of Carmarthen to RH 31 Mar. 1940.
55. IND Mr Lloyd of the Central Register advised RH of this 4 June 1940.
56. RH may have been contemplating rather than actively investigating it; but IND *Diaries* 1940 show that on 5 June (on receipt of the letter about Tunis) he went to London for six days.
57. IND Barclays, Carmarthen to RH 6 June 1940.
58. *ADMIN* p.84.
59. IND The Admiralty, Bath to RH 6 June 1940.
60. IND Mrs C. Johnson to FH 15 Aug. 1940 reassuring her about RH's decision to take up the Admiralty appointment.

Chapter 25: My Cupboard is Bare

1. IND RH to the Portreeve R.H. Tyler 24 Jan. 1940; and RHT to RH 10 Mar. 1940. There was nothing to be settled in the wider community. In late Jan. RH asked for 'the whole question of my foremanship . . . to be reconsidered'; and once he had permission for *The Navy is Here*, RHT reluctantly let him go.
2. IND RH to Jack James 16 June 1940.
3. IND Mrs C. Johnson to RH 25 Aug. 1941.
4. IND RH to Mrs Crick (who wanted to rent Parc) 12 June 1940.
5. IND RH to Jack James 16 June 1940.
6. IND Mrs Johnson to FH 15 Aug. 1940 reassuring her about RH's decision that she and the children must go abroad. Lleky Papastavrou writes: 'Frances typically often showed strong social principles. In my late teens she would not allow me to go to University on a County Grant saying these were for the poor and there were few of them because Merioneth was not a rich county.'
7. IND FH to RH telegram 26 June 1940 'APPLYING PASSPORTS CHILDREN'.
8. IND Western Union Cablegram from New York to RH 27 June 1940.
9. IND Edith Burbury to FH 31 July 1940.
10. IND Francis Cadogan to FH 21 Aug. 1940.
11. IND Mrs C. Johnson to FH 15 Aug. 1940.
12. MINNEY p.37.
13. ADMIN pp.165–6.
14. IND RH to Harold 16 Aug. 1940.
15. MINNEY p.77.
16. IND 6 July 1940 J.H. James (Ass. Sec.) TO ALL WHOM IT MAY CONCERN.
17. MINNEY p.45.
18. As n.14 above.
19. MINNEY p.37.
20. Ibid. p.38.
21. Ibid.
22. SIEVEKING pp.175–6.
23. As n.14 above.
24. IND RH to Bank 14 July 1940: impossible to reduce his overdraft 'materially' out of his salary; but funds would become available when he had finished his book.
25. IND RH to Mrs C. Johnson 31 July 1940.
26. IND Mrs C. Johnson to RH 12 Aug. 1940.
27. As n.14 above.
28. IND BBC to RH 31 Oct. 1940; the pass was for a rehearsal on 3 Nov. and broadcast the next day.
29. SIEVEKING pp.176–7.
30. IND RH to FH 13 Sept. 1940.
31. As n.25 above.
32. MINNEY p.39.
33. SIEVEKING pp.176–7 has the invitation from RH of 24 Sept. 1940.
34. SIEVEKING pp.163–4.
35. Winston S. Churchill, *The Second World War: Volume Two – Their Finest Hour* (Cassell 1949) p.290.
36. IND RH to FH 13 Sept. 1940.
37. Churchill, *Their Finest Hour* p.293.
38. Ibid. p.556.
39. IND RH to FH 4 Oct. 1940.
40. IND RH to Lee Ashton Esq. at the MoI 27 Mar. 1941. Radić had been mortally wounded on 20 June 1928 in the parliament of the kingdom of Serbs, Croats and Slovenes. Seven months later, on 6 Jan. 1929, King Alexander I (seeing no other way of uniting Croats and Serbs) proclaimed a royal dictatorship, and re-christened his kingdom Yugoslavia.
41. ADMIN p.172.
42. IND John James, Admiralty, Bath 8 May 1941.

43. MINNEY pp.47–9. Seven-and-a-half-year-old Robert had recently been sent to boarding school near Oswestry, and Kate and Lleky were too small.
44. As n.39 above.
45. Robert Hughes in a telephone conv. with the present author 6 Nov. 1992.
46. MINNEY p.55; and information in square brackets from Lleky Papastavrou to the present author in Apr. 1993. She adds that it was 'MUCH harder getting MacTaffy down the stairs again than up'.
47. Caitlin Thomas with George Tremlett, *Caitlin: Life with Dylan Thomas* (Secker and Warburg 1986) p.199.
48. IND Caitlin Thomas to FH 5 Aug. 1941.
49. MINNEY p.51.
50. IND RH to FH 14 Mar. n.d. [1942].
51. IND Margaret Storm Jameson to RH 19 Feb. 1942.
52. IND RH to Margaret Storm Jameson 31 Mar. 1942.
53. IND FH to LH Friday [31 Apr. 1942].
54. Frank Barrett, 'Bath: beauty and the bombs' the *Independent* 4 Jan. 1992 p.23.
55. MINNEY pp.51–2 with some variations from IND original.
56. IND A fragment (not in MINNEY) of RH to FH 25/26/27 Apr. 1942.
57. IND RH to LH 16 Apr. 1942.
58. Ibid.; and for Diccon's distress see also IND RH to 'Aunt Lily' at Caterham. (Lily, no longer able to run her home, was about to move; and died later in the year.)
59. IND RH to FH 6 May 1942 (a typed extract).
60. Lleky Papastavrou writes: 'The Russian family were Peter Ustinov's parents, Klop and Nadia, whom we dearly loved, friends of Thomas.'

Chapter 26: A Sweet Flavour

1. MINNEY p.55.
2. ADMIN p.166.
3. IND RH to Markham 17 Dec. 1946.
4. Ibid.
5. IND RH to FH 20 June 1942.
6. SIEVEKING pp.163–4.
7. Jocelyn Herbert in conv. with the present author 19 Oct. 1992.
8. MINNEY p.55.
9. Ibid. p.58.
10. IND RH to FH 14 Mar. n.d. [1942].
11. IND Susan Williams-Ellis to RH 14 Mar. 1942.
12. Peter Quennell in conv. with the present author.
13. IND Nancy Fielden née Stallibrass from Grimston Park, Tadcaster, Yorkshire, to RH 23rd n.d.
14. ADMIN p.174.
15. Ibid. p.175.
16. IND note n.d. by Lucy McEntee: RH used to say that 'there might have been the most appalling row over my first report for the Cabinet!' Having estimated the Navy's need for new warships to the end of 1943, he recalled an article in *Harper's Magazine* about splitting the atom, and casually remarked that atomic progress might alter these requirements; which must have made several Cabinet members wonder if there had been a leak of the 'Manhattan Project' by which attempts were being made in the USA to develop an atomic bomb.
17. MINNEY p.78.
18. IND RH to FH 3 Feb. 1943.
19. IND Ursula Otte to FH 10 Mar. 1943.
20. MINNEY pp.60–1.
21. Obituary of Vice-Admiral Sir Peter Gretton in the *Independent* 12 Nov. 1992.
22. Those months were July and Sept. 1943, and Mar. 1944 (*Ency. Brit.* 15th edn).
23. Arthur Bryant, *The Turn of the Tide* (Collins, 1957) pp.667, 658.
24. Lleky Papastavrou writes: 'Frances delivered her own baby because when she came into the delivery room at the nursing home, the midwife was drunk. That nursing home was closed down a few months later.'
25. ADMIN p.176.
26. IND RH, an enc. dated 30 Sept. 1948.
27. IND An account by RH dated 9 Nov. 1946 of his life up to that date.
28. Colin Wells in a telephone conv. with the present author Nov. 1992.
29. *Ency. Brit.* vol.8 p.768.
30. IND RH to FH 11 June 1944.
31. Dawn Macleod 'Betjeman at war' in the *Spectator* 3 Nov. 1984 p.15.
32. IND Teddy Wolfe (now working for the BBC in Bristol) to RH 11 Sept. 1944.

33. IND RH to Davies 20 Oct. 1945.
34. IND The Admiralty to RH 31 Oct. 1945.
35. MINNEY pp.78–9.
36. SIEVEKING p.164.
37. MINNEY p.76.
38. IND Mrs Johnson to FH 21 June 1945.

Chapter 27: Trying to Adjust

1. IND RH to Iris Barry 7 Nov. 1945. She had written on 27 Sept. 1945 with news of Alan Porter's death in 1943.
2. IND RH to A W-E 1 Jan. 1946.
3. MINNEY p.79.
4. IND Norman Kipping, Board of Trade, to RH 28 Dec. 1945.
5. As n.2 above.
6. MINNEY p.80.
7. IND Mrs Johnson to FH 21 June 1945.
8. As n.2 above.
9. MINNEY p.80.
10. As n.7 above.
11. Ibid.
12. As n.2 above.
13. Ibid.
14. IND RH to Sir Norman Kipping 17 Jan. 1946.
15. As n.2 above.
16. IND The WEA first wrote in July 1945; RH replied in Sept.; they wrote on 6 Oct.; and on 11 Jan. 1946 he was sent this programme:

    February 2 3p.m. Swansea
    2 7p.m. Gorseinion
    5 7p.m. Pontardulais
    6 7p.m. Ystalyfera
    7 7p.m. Port Talbot
    8 7p.m. Llanelly
    9 7p.m. Neath

    On 24 Jan. it was agreed he should be paid £2 per lecture, and treated to board and lodging throughout the tour.
17. IND *Diary* 29, 30 and 31 Jan. 1946.
18. IND RH to FH 9 Feb. 1946.
19. IND *Property* By Jan. 1946, when Mrs Starke asked about the lease, the Hugheses had sublet to Mr Kent, who stayed to Apr. 1948.
20. IND Harry V. Markham to RH 28 Mar. 1946.
21. IND RH to Harry Markham 6 Apr. 1946.
22. IND RH to Charles Prentice 12 Apr. 1940.
23. IND Charles Johnson to RH 20 June 1945.
24. IND LH to RH n.d. (but from internal refs. (a) to Victoria Sieveking suffering from phlebitis and (b) to RH's birthday, it may safely be dated Apr. 1946. IND misplace it among the 1937 letters).
25. MINNEY p.96.
26. Ibid. p.68.
27. IND RH to Uffa Fox 8 July 1946.
28. MINNEY p.96.
29. AUTHOR Amy Graves to John Graves 13 June 1946.
30. IND Arthur Koestler to RH 29 Aug. 1946.
31. MINNEY p.72.
32. As n.30 above, 24 Sept. 1946.
33. IND Report by Hilton Wright ARIBA of 11 Campden Hill Road, Kensington dated 22 Feb. 1947, when he visited Mor Edrin.
34. IND doc. dated 9 Nov. 1946.
35. IND Pamela Bianco to RH 6 Nov. 1946.
36. IND RH to Markham 17 Dec. 1946.
37. IND RH to Barclays 7 Oct. 1946.
38. IND Faber & Faber to RH 13 Sept. 1946 has: 'Mr Eliot has now seen your report, with which he very much agrees'. (IND 10 Sept. RH had said it needed pruning of much speculation.)
39. *Radio Times* for 10 May 1946 announces: '*A Comedy of Good and Evil* from the play by Richard Hughes.'

40. IND Hamish Hamilton to RH 25 June 1946, about arrangements between Harpers and Penguin for this reprint. (RH guaranteed $1500.)
41. IND RH to AW-E 14 Feb. 1947.
42. MINNEY p.80.
43. IND RH to Ed. *Daily Telegraph* n.d. April 1947.
44. RH, 'Make Parenthood Possible' pp.5–7 of the *English Digest* vol.XXXIII no.1, Mar. 1950 (condensed from *World Review*).
45. IND RH to the Sec. of the NCCL 31 Mar. 1947.

Chapter 28: Môr Edrin

1. IND RH to Maxwell Fry 14 May 1947.
2. IND FH to J.S. Morris of Portmadoc [pre-Tuesday 10 June].
3. IND RH to Thomas Cook & Son 9 May 1947.
4. IND RH to FH p.c. 16 June 1947.
5. As n.2 above.
6. IND RH to Joseph Brewer 30 June 1947.
7. See e.g. IND RH to James Hamilton of Hamish Hamilton 18 Feb. 1947; and IND RH to Cyril Connolly (who wanted something for *Horizon*) 8 Sept. 1947.
8. MINNEY p.80.
9. Ed. Sile Flower, Jean MacFarlane, Ruth Plant, *Jane B. Drew architect: A tribute from colleagues and friends for her 75th birthday 24th March 1986* (Bristol Centre for the Advancement of Architecture 1986) pp.46–67 and p.114.
10. RH, 'Make Parenthood Possible' *English Digest* vol.XXXIII no.1, Mar. 1950.
11. MINNEY p.86.
12. Ibid. pp.87–8.
13. Ibid. pp.89–90.
14. IND FH to LH 23 Oct. 1947.
15. IND RH to Maxwell Fry 11 Sept. 1947.
16. MINNEY p.85; and IND FH to 'Dear Echo' 23 Oct. 1947 (dictated).
17. IND FH to LH 23 Oct. 1947.
18. MINNEY p.88.
19. IND FH to 'Nadia' [Peter Ustinov's mother] 30 Oct. 1947.
20. IND Barclays Bank to FH 19. Jan. 1948.
21. IND FH to 'Henry' Apr. 1948.
22. IND FH to Nancy Nicholson 23 Jan. 1948.
23. It was the Mrs J.M.A. Bateman trust, which appears to have been set up by Frances's Bazley grandfather, probably in his will.
24. IND RH to Barclays 6 Mar. 1948.
25. IND. esp. RH's to Hooper & Wollen of Torquay 14 Oct. 1948 ack. FH's receipt of £2363 10s. 0d.
26. IND RH to Mr William Elias of Carmarthen 10 and 12 Mar. 1948. The coracle cost 6 guineas, and arrived in the third week of May.
27. IND RH's Admiralty warrant was dated 22 Apr. 1948.
28. IND *Travel* various.
29. IND has some n.d. letters from Evelyn Waugh which clearly refer to their meetings at this conference.
30. IND RH to LH p.c. [June 1948].
31. This comment appeared in the *Morning Advertiser*.
32. IND various corres. Jan.–Mar. 1948 between Margery Vosper Ltd and RH; also Alec Clunes (Director at the Arts Theatre) to RH 25 Mar. 1948: there had been poor houses, but 'putting on any play of distinction is always a lottery'.
33. IND Agreement dated 17 Apr. 1948.
34. IND Agreement with John Gassner signed 5 May 1948; letter telling RH of JG's intentions dated 21 May 1948.
35. IND RH to John Gassner 21 July 1948.
36. IND RH to JG 3 Aug. 1948; and JG to RH 7 Aug. 1948, telling him 'all the changes and additions are for the better'.
37. IND Michael Balcon to RH 10 Aug. 1948.
38. Address at Westminster College, Fulton, USA, 5 Mar. 1946.
39. IND A. Slonimski (describes himself as the rep. in England of the French/Polish organising committee) from 81 Portland Place, London W1, to RH 14 July 1948.
40. IND RH to Anthony Bevir at 10 Downing Street.
41. MINNEY p.100.
42. RH in the *Sunday Times* 1 Aug. 1948 (quoted in MINNEY p.101).
43. IND R.D. McAlpine of the FO to Bevir 28 July 1948 (sent on to RH on 3 Aug.).
44. RH seems to have had two briefing sessions: IND McAlpine to RH 18 Aug. 1948 declares

Hancock could see him for a further briefing on 23 Aug.

45.   IND RH to FH Monday evening n.d. [23 Aug. 1948].
46.   IND RH to FH Tuesday n.d. [31 Aug. 1948].
47.   IND Edward Crankshaw to RH 15 Sept. 1948.
48.   As n.46 above.
49.   RH, 'Polish Impressions' in the *Spectator* 17 Sept. 1948.
50.   IND 4 Sept. 1948 a ticket from Warsaw to Northolt via Berlin RAF form 2863 (paid for by the Polish government).
51.   MINNEY p.103.
52.   IND RH to J.M. Booth of London 14 Oct. 1948; present author's italics.
53.   IND John Gassner to RH 27 Sept. 1948.
54.   Ibid. 24 Oct. 1948.
55.   IND Ann Watkins to Margery Vosper 8 Oct. 1948.
56.   IND RH to Margery Vosper 10 Dec. 1948.
57.   IND RH to Charles Frend 11 Nov. 1948 refers to 'the Laugharne script'; and IND FH to Mrs Stark 16 Sept. 1948, and to Mr Watts of Laugharne 16 Sept. 1948: 'Mr Hughes has a very important bit of writing to do which he could do best at Laugharne.'
58.   IND various, esp. FH to Mrs Starke 16 Sept. 1948.
59.   Caitlin Thomas with George Tremlett, *Caitlin: Life with Dylan Thomas* (Secker and Warberg, 1986) p.96.
60.   Ibid. p.110.
61.   IND Dylan Thomas to RH 27 Sept. 1948. DT explained that he could afford the lease, because he had a long-term film contract with Rank.
62.   IND Margaret Taylor to RH 4 Oct. 1948.
63.   IND FH to MT 7 Oct. 1948. That she wrote to DT in similar terms can be seen from the content of MINNEY MSS DT to FH 10 Oct. 1948.
64.   See MINNEY p.104, Thomas with Tremlett, *Caitlin* p.110; original is in MINNEY MSS.
65.   Thomas with Tremlett, *Caitlin* pp.111–15.
66.   IND various. Completion took 15 months. In Dec. 1948 they believed the lease was sold for £650 to Mr and Mrs Bowen. They vacated the house by 1 Feb. 1949. A week later, they learned Mrs Starke intended to hold up the lease until an assessment could be made for damage to the property. In Aug. (after minor repairs) Mrs S. signed the licence to assign. Completion in Feb. 1950 brought £555 10s. 2d. after expenses.
67.   MINNEY pp.104–5.
68.   IND RH to Anthony Lousarda of Stephenson Hanwood and Tatham of Saddlers Hall, Gutter Lane, London EC2, 1 July 1961.
69.   IND RH to Charles Frend 11 Nov. 1948.
70.   MINNEY p.106.
71.   IND The festival ran from 14–19 March; the plays included *Heloise, Gaslight, Duet for two Hands*, J.B. Priestley's *The Linden Tree* and George Bernard Shaw's *Getting Married*.
72.   IND RH to Glyn Jones 19 Nov. 1949.
73.   The *News Chronicle* 23 Nov. 1949.
74.   IND LH to RH and FH 21 Feb. 1949.
75.   MINNEY p.108.
76.   IND RH to Joseph Brewer 7 May 1950.
77.   IND *Diaries* 1950, 1 and 2 Jan.
78.   IND Stella Watson to RH 9 Jan. 1950; and RH to Gwenol 16 Mar. 1950.
79.   IND Valerie to FH.
80.   IND Brenda Osborne to RH.
81.   IND *Diaries* 1950, 30 Jan.
82.   IND RH to John Cadogan 19 Feb. 1950.
83.   IND RH to Joseph Brewer 7 May 1950.
84.   IND RH to Sheila [Rowlands?] 16 Mar. 1950.
85.   IND *Diaries* 1950, 5 Feb.
86.   As n.82 above.
87.   IND RH to Miss Harris 5 Sept. 1949.
88.   This is speculative; but IND *Lico* Jack James to RH 3 Jan. 1950 has: 'The Secretary has had copious correspondence and interviews about the Admiralty Administrative story on production, as the result of which he is anxious to see you with me some time with a view to your doing it'; and *Diaries* 1950 6–10 Jan. show that RH remained in London for a few days after LH's cremation, so it seems natural that this should have been when the meeting took place.

Chapter 29: Limbering Up
1.   IND *Diaries* 1950, 5 Feb.
2.   The *Times* Monday 29 May 1950 p.8.

3.	MINNEY p.112.
4.	POOLE p.70.
5.	IND Draft of RH, *The Herring-Farm* p.107.
6.	E.g. IND Ministry of Supply Official Historians, 35–37 Old Queen Street, London SW1, to RH 22 Mar. 1950.
7.	IND J.D. Scott Cabinet Office, 35 Old Street, to RH 13 May 1950.
8.	IND various. esp. Barclays to Mrs RH 8 June and 19 July 1950. Without the invitation from JN and her husband Alexander Clifford, Director of the *Continental Daily Mail*, RH and FH could hardly have afforded such a holiday: RH expected £1700 as soon as his mother's estate was wound up, but had an overdraft of £500–£600; while FH (continually exceeding her spending limits) would return to hear that her overdraft stood at £1842, and it would soon be difficult to honour her cheques.
9.	IND RH to Jack James 31 May 1950.
10.	IND Sir John Lang, Sec. to the Admiralty to RH 26 June 1950.
11.	IND JDS to RH 10 Aug. 1950.
12.	MINNEY pp.109–13; and various members of the Hughes family (esp. Penny, Lleky and Kate) in conv. and/or corres. with the present author.
13.	MINNEY p.120.
14.	Ibid. p.109.
15.	IND RH to Tom Richards 28 Sept. 1950.
16.	IND RH to AW-E 26 Oct. 1950.
17.	Ibid. 31 Oct. 1950.
18.	IND. RH to Rupert Hart-Davis 3 Oct. 1950; the broadcast was at 9.15 on 13 November; see also *Ibid*. RH to Janet Adam Smith 1 Dec. 1950 complaining that he was unhappy about the broadcast. For extracts from the lecture, see *FICTION AS TRUTH* pp.140 and 143.
19.	IND RH to JDS post-26 Oct. 1950; pre-13 Nov. 1950.
20.	IND JDS to RH 28 Nov. 1950.
21.	IND LS to RH 25 Jan. 1951 singling out 'particularly the first instalment where there is much too much author and much too much prose description which, if the information is essential, must I think somehow or other be done by the children'.
22.	IND JDS to RH 21 Jan. 1951.
23.	IND RH to JDS 23 Jan. 1951.
24.	JDS in SCRIPT p.37.
25.	IND Margery Vosper to RH 9 Apr. 1951.
26.	Ibid. 13 Apr. 1951.
27.	IND RH to MV 15 Apr. 1951.
28.	IND Charles Frend to RH 20 Apr. 1951.
29.	Monja Danischewsky in *SCRIPT* p.41.
30.	IND MV to RH 29 May 1951 (MV commented that the contract was 'more in the author's favour than Ealing contracts usually are').
31.	IND RH to Charles Frend 14 May 1951.
32.	IND MV to RH 13 June 1951.
33.	As n.29 above.
34.	IND RH to Herbert Davies 11 Sept. 1951.
35.	IND 'Danny' to RH 25 July 1951.
36.	IND Memo Sandy Mackendrick 31 July 1951.
37.	IND 'Danny' to RH 17 Sept. 1951.
38.	IND Charles Frend to RH 24 Sept. 1952.
39.	IND RH to 'Danny' 15 Oct. 1951.
40.	IND RH to JDS 28 Sept. 1951; and JDS to RH 29 Jun. and 26 Sept. 1951.
41.	IND MV to RH 9 Nov. 1951.
42.	IND pp M Danischewsky to RH 23 Jan. 1952 (dict. 22 Jan).
43.	IND RH to Danny 14 Feb. 1952.
44.	IND 'Danny' to RH 15 Feb. 1952.
45.	IND enc. 28 Feb 1952 – lecture schedule from the British Council, Stockholm, showing RH's arrival 6 Mar. at Gothenburg on the SS *Suecia* and an intensive series of lectures until 25 Mar. (Dinner with the British Ambassador on 13 Mar.)
46.	IND RH to his children 17–18 Mar. 1952 (third instalment).
47.	IND Pamela Bianco to RH 4 Apr. 1952; and PB (in Bad Godesburg) to RH 5 May 1952, telling him how much she had enjoyed her weekend visit, one that she was certain she would remember for the rest of her life.
48.	IND MV in corres. with RH Apr./May *re* the Carol Reed film; 16 July 1952 about Boulting, who was also interested in *A High Wind in Jamaica*.
49.	IND RH to 'Danny' 2 June 1952; MV to Ealing 8 Aug. 1952; and RH to MV 20 Aug. 1952.
50.	*The Times* 2 Apr. 1952 p.7.
51.	*The Times* 20 May 1952.

52. IND 'Danny' to RH 29 May 1952.
53. IND RH to 'Danny' 2 June 1952.
54. MINNEY pp.90–1.
55. IND Memo from RH to the Sec. to the Admiralty 29 July 1952.
56. IND Cabinet Office to RH 17 Apr. 1953.
57. IND JDS to RH 8 Jan. 1954.
58. IND The Admiralty to RH 19 Mar. 1954.
59. IND Lang of Admiralty to RH 6 July 1954, asking whether he can finish the last paragraphs in the next few days.
60. MINNEY pp.119–20.
61. Ibid. p.120.
62. IND Joseph Brewer to RH 16 Aug. 1949 tells of his marriage to Jacqui (aged thirty-four) in Sept; and RH to JB in reply 7 May 1950 explains his long silence: 'I feel when I do write the letter ought to be a worthy one; and since I never can write as grand a letter as I want to write, it just means that I don't write at all!'
63. IND Joseph Brewer from The Mead, Wantage, Berks., 21 Nov. 1953.
64. IND RH to Joseph Brewer 24 Apr. 1954.
65. Diccon's letter suggests that the meat was roasted before being sent to Oxford; MINNEY p.124 gives details of the roasting on Port Meadow, but now believes it had indeed been pre-cooked.
66. IND Sir Emrys Evans to RH 12 May 1953; RH's talk on *A Welsh Journey* had been prepared at short notice after a long bout of work on *ADMIN*. RH, exhausted and despondent after the broadcast, was pleased to receive letters of praise: notably from Sir E.E. Principal of the University College of North Wales at Bangor, who wrote: 'It was really magnificent in conception and execution – an unequalled presentation of what Wales was and is. How much we all owe to you!'
67. RH, 'The Children and the Pirates' in *Radio Times* 14 Aug. 1953.
68. IND RH to Miss Helen Lehmann of the Society of Authors 16 Oct. 1953: RH protested that Equity had prevented him from taking a part himself (which would have meant 'travelling expenses, a subsistence allowance, and even a small fee'). So accepting the producer's invitation to attend rehearsals left him 'well over £60 out of pocket' after he had paid for six weekly journeys, each involving three nights in London.
69. Monja Danischewsky in SCRIPT p.42.
70. IND RH to Monja Danischewsky 19 Nov. 1953.
71. IND Danny to RH 20 Oct., 2 and 10 Nov., and 29 Dec. 1953; and RH to Danny 19 Nov. 1953.
72. IND RH to MV 10 Jan. 1954.
73. Ibid.
74. IND (draft) RH to Sir Michael Balcon 12 Apr. 1954.
75. IND (draft) RH to Sir Michael Balcon 12 Apr. 1954. RH had agreed to £400 (£100 per week for three weeks of continuous work in Jan., plus odd days in Feb.); but it took so long that his payment was only £40 per week; 'the only snag is', he wrote, 'that I can't with my family commitments afford nowadays to work for enjoyment only'.
76. IND RH to MV 17 Apr. 1954.
77. IND RH to Mrs Pollard 9 Aug. 1954.
78. IND RH to Charles Crichton 5 Jan. 1955.
79. MINNEY p.135.
80. IND *Diaries* RH 1954: 1–4 Nov. Gresham lectures.
81. POOLE p.72.
82. IND The Cabinet Office to RH 7 Dec. 1954 with galley proofs of *ADMIN*.
83. IND RH to Jessamine [Weeks] [n.d.].
84. MCENTEE RH, 'An Autobiographical Sketch' for a confidential brochure entitled *Richard Hughes* circulated in-house by Harpers in advance of their publication of *The Fox in the Attic* in 1962.

Chapter 30: *The Fox in the Attic*

1. IND *Travel* shows RH and FH flew from London to Gibraltar on 14 Jan. 1955, and went straight to Marbella. IND *Diaries* gives the date when RH began his novel.
2. *FICTION AS TRUTH* pp.51–2 (RH, 'On *The Human Predicament*' in the *Listener* 1961).
3. Rupert Shephard and his wife Nicolette (née Macnamara) and Brigid Macnamara in conv. with the present author one evening in April 1985 in Judith Eagle's flat in London. One of them had heard RH tell of the man carrying a lamb upon his back at a meeting of PEN.
4. As n.2 above.
5. MINNEY p.132.
6. As n.2 above.
7. *FOX* p.111.
8. See MINNEY pp.132–4.

9. MINNEY p.137.
10. MINNEY pp.156–7 for this and what follows.
11. MINNEY p.157.
12. IND *Diaries* RH 1955 e.g. 'Wednesday 26 January Drove with Hopes to Gibraltar; Sunday 30 Hopes dinner; Wednesday 2 February 1955 Dine Hopes'.
13. MINNEY pp.156 and 137.
14. IND RH to the Manager, Drummonds Branch, Royal Bank of Scotland, 49 Charing Cross, SW1, 19 Sept. 1955. RH says he heard of these things 'a year or two ago'; RH to Sr. Palma de Navas of Tangier 7 Apr. 1952 shows that Wyllie's report reached him in the early spring of 1952.
15. Ibid.
16. MINNEY MSS FH (taped conv.).
17. MINNEY p.134.
18. IND TS. copy of article by the rector in the *Church Times* for 11 Sept. 1963, with emendations in RH's hand.
19. MINNEY pp.134–5.
20. IND Jessamine Weeks to RH 8 Oct. 1955.
21. MINNEY p.140.
22. IND RH to Gerard Wathen [?Apr.] 1956.
23. *FOX* p.73.
24. Ibid. p.68.
25. IND *Diaries* RH 1955 23–26 Dec. Gloucestershire.
26. MINNEY p.160.
27. IND RH to Wayfarers 14 Jan. 1956; a telegram n.d. from Pia Gunzbourg telling them: 'take train leaving Munich 16.16, meet Augsburg 16.57 Wed'; and *Diaries* RH 1956 Wed. 25 Jan.
28. MINNEY p.160.
29. IND *Diaries* RH 1956: 28 Jan. Wedding at Augsburg cathedral.
30. IND *Diaries* RH 1956 3 Feb. (temperature) 8 and 12 Feb. (to Munich).
31. MINNEY p.161.
32. IND *Diaries* RH 1956 (Feb.) 15 Heidenburg; 18 to Munich; 19 to London.
33. MINNEY p.160.
34. Since MINNEY p.160 declares that 'the children, and the sledge pulled by horses, were provided by Heidenburg', the quotation describing the ride is taken from *FOX* pp.182–9.
35. POOLE p.181–2. Genji's theory as to why novels come into being was in line with RH's beliefs. Genji declared that the novelist's experience had moved him 'to an emotion so passionate that he can no longer keep it shut up in his heart. Again and again something in his own life or in that around him will seem to the writer so important that he cannot bear to let it pass into oblivion. There must never come a time, he feels, when men do not know about it'.
36. SIEVEKING pp.182–4.
37. IND RH to Professor Tillotson 13 Oct. 1955.
38. IND RH to Gerard Wathen [?Apr.] 1956; there was one more set of lectures on 11–14 June 1956 before his resignation took effect.
39. See e.g. his letter quoted in SIEVEKING p.186.
40. MINNEY p.159.
41. IND *Diaries* RH 1956: 1 July to Malta.
42. MINNEY pp.151–2.
43. IND *Diaries* RH 1956: 14 July to London.
44. IND document.
45. IND Sir John Lang to RH 27 Feb. 1956.
46. IND RH to Sir John Lang KCB 31 Mar. 1956.
47. IND Sir John Lang to RH 31 Dec. 1956; RH to SJL 26 Jan. 1957; and SJL to RH 8 Mar. 1957.
48. IND RH to J.C. Cadogan ['Uncle Johnnie' – one of the trustees of FH's trust funds] 16 Jan. 1957.
49. IND RH to Joseph Brewer 24 Jan. 1957.
50. IND FH from Pension Iberia San Rogue to Kate Hughes.
51. IND RH to Joseph Brewer 12 Apr. 1957.
52. Ian Parsons in SCRIPT p.48.
53. *FOX* p.119.
54. Ibid. pp.116–18.
55. Ibid. p.120.
56. IND RH to Joseph Brewer 27 Jan. 1958.
57. Penelope Minney to the present author 8 May 1993.
58. IND RH to Joseph Brewer 23 Mar. 1958.
59. IND RH to FH 6 and 7 June 1958; partly quoted in MINNEY p.168.
60. MINNEY p.173.
61. Ibid. p.172.

62. MINNEY p.173 explains that in the May 1958 TS (of ch.19) 'Polly's nightmare, and terrifying scream, are followed by a drawing-room discussion of how the generation brought up by Freud need have nightmares no more. He wanted to alter the sequence of events so that the discussion ... was abruptly *ended* by that despairing yell from the dark depths of the house'.
63. MINNEY p.173.
64. IND RH to FH 11 June 1958, approaching Trikeri.
65. Ibid.
66. MINNEY p.174.
67. Quoted in MINNEY p.176.
68. IND RH to FH 16 June [1958] Island of Pelagos (Northern Sporades).
69. Ibid.
70. Penelope Minney to the present author 22 Mar. 1993.
71. MINNEY pp.178–9.
72. MINNEY pp.181–2; but description of Lemnos as n.73 below.
73. IND RH to FH Dardanelles 23 June 1958.
74. MINNEY p.183, and pp.183–6 for the remainder of the journey.
75. IND MV to RH 11 June 1958.
76. IND RH to Norman Spencer 14 Aug. 1958.
77. IND n.d. draft of the (very much altered) n.78 below.
78. IND RH to Norman Spencer 14 Aug. 1958.
79. IND RH to MV 21 Jan. 1959.
80. IND RH to Norman Spencer 29 Oct. 1958.
81. As n.79 above.
82. IND Spencer to RH 11 Sept. 1958 encloses R.M. Ballantyne's *The Coral Island* (with its obvious relevance to Golding's story) and announces that he has also sent a copy to one Peter Brook.
83. IND Penelope Hughes to RH 12 Nov. 1958.
84. IND Barclays Bank Trustee of 1 Sloane Street SW1 to RH 8 May 1959 allows the cost of connecting Môr Edrin and Clogwyn Melyn to electricity, £16 from capital.
85. *FOX* p.192.
86. IND RH to Mr Gregson 25 Sept. 1959.
87. MINNEY pp.187–8.
88. IND RH to Joseph Brewer 6 Jan. 1960.
89. Rose Basketts in conv. with the present author 14 Mar. 1984.
90. IND RH to Mr Hanfstaengl 8 Feb. 1960, planning to meet him in Munich on the weekend of 6 March.
91. IND RH to Mr Madams of Percy A. Popkin of Brentwood, Essex, 1 Dec. 1960.
92. IND RH to Mr Gregson 25 Sept. 1959.
93. *FOX* pp.265–7 for this and subsequent quotations.
94. Penelope Minney to the present author 8 May 1993.
95. IND RH to Joseph Brewer 10 Feb. 1962.
96. IND A note by RH of 1 Dec. 1960 points out that his gross earnings had dwindled to nil, and that he has only financed his work by selling pictures and running into debt. (In 1960 Frances's investment income was £810; Diccon's £19 after tax.)
97. IND RH to the Baroness Pia von Aretin 15 Nov. 1960.
98. Ibid. 27 Apr. 1961.
99. Rose Basketts in conv. with the present author 14 Mar. 1984.
100. Ibid.
101. IND *Diaries* show that the journey to Paris came after much travel: RH Saturday 11 Feb. 1961 to Shrewsbury; dine at the Mytton and Mermaid; sleep at the Pengwern Hotel; 12 Feb. 8 a.m. Holy Communion in the Abbey; 13 Gloucestershire; 14 Glos–London–Glos; 15 Glos. dine Rachel; 16 Glos. to Hants; 17 Hants–Dorset–Hants; 20 to London. 3–13 Mar. to Paris; then London to 23 Mar. (Sunday 19 Mar. Robert preaches at Woolwich).
102. As n.99 above.
103. Ibid.
104. Ibid; but with some of the detail of her Coventry experiences taken from RH's account of them in *SHEPHERDESS* pp.221–2.
105. IND 9 June 1960 Selection Committee Hawthornden (Arts Council).
106. IND David Jones of Swansea to RH 28 June 1960.
107. IND The Minister for Welsh Affairs to RH 30 June 1960: invitation to a garden party at Dyffryn St Nicholas near Cardiff on 5 Aug.
108. IND the Lord Chamberlain to Mr and Mrs RH.
109. IND RH to T.E.B. Clarke 19 Aug. 1961.
110. IND T.E.B. Clarke to RH 13 Dec. 1961.
111. As n.109 above.
112. IND Anthony Curtis of the *Sunday Telegraph* to RH 18 Sept. 1961.

113. IND The interview was at 2.30 on 26 Sept. and RH was paid a £10 appearance fee, his first-class return rail fare, a night's subsistence and a room in an hotel.
114. IND Alan Bullock to RH 25 Sept. and 27 Oct. 1961.
115. IND David Garnett to RH 25 Oct. 1961.
116. IND Mrs Jane Cassidy Holran to RH 14 Nov. 1961.
117. IND RH to Jane Cassidy Holran 28 Nov. 1961.

Chapter 31: *The Wooden Shepherdess*

1. IND RH to Stavros Papastavrou, 12 Apr. 1962.
2. Ibid.
3. IND RH to [?] [1962, pre-18 Jan.].
4. IND RH to Cass Canfield 19 Jan. 1962; and cables from CC dated 19 and 23 Jan. 1962.
5. IND RH to Mr Gregson 26 Jan. 1962.
6. IND Pamela Bianco to RH 26 Feb. 1962.
7. IND Gloria Vanderbilt to RH 28 Feb. 1962.
8. IND Annie Churchill to RH 1962.
9. IND The Welsh Committee of the Arts Council to RH 5 Feb. 1962; on 7 June they suggested that the award of £100 should be presented at Cardiff on 21 June.
10. IND Royal Society of Literature to RH 5 Apr. 1962; and RH to the RSL 21 Apr. 1962.
11. IND RH to Mr Brown 21 Apr. 1962.
12. IND RH to Robert Hughes 7 May 1962.
13. IND Laurie Lee to RH 17 Jan. 1962.
14. IND RH to Joseph Brewer 7 Feb. 1962.
15. IND RH to Jim Wyllie 1 July 1962, and to Stavros 18 July 1962.
16. IND RH to Childs 15 Jan. 1961.
17. IND The Bishop of Bangor to RH 17 July and 7 Aug. 1962. The talk was fixed for 19 Sept.
18. RH, *Liturgical Language Today* (reprinted by Church in Wales Publications from *Province* vol.XIII no.4).
19. IND TS. copy of an article by the rector of Lanfihangel-y-Traethau from the *Church Times* of 11 Sept. 1963; with pencil alterations by RH.
20. IND RH to Gregson 28 Aug. 1962.
21. IND John Betjeman to RH 26 July 1962.
22. Stated as early as 1948: cf RH, 'The Writer's Duty' in the *Listener* 22 July 1948: 'not an answer, but a question'.
23. Magnus Magnusson in the *Scotsman* 23 Aug. 1962.
24. IND T.E.B. Clarke to RH 14 Oct. 1962.
25. MINNEY p.188.
26. IND RH to Cass Canfield 9 Jan. 1963.
27. IND RH to Pamela Bianco 23 Jan. 1963.
28. IND *Diaries* RH 1963: 21 Mar. plane to Milan.
29. IND RH to Joseph Brewer 10 June 1963.
30. IND RH to Dr Arnold 22 Aug. 1963.
31. IND *Diaries* RH 29 Mar. plane London.
32. As n.30 above.
33. IND *Diaries* RH 1963 2 Apr. Norah Smallwood 11.40.
34. IND *Diaries* RH 1963: 6 May to Cambridge; and IND Invit. to a dinner on 7 May 1963.
35. IND RH to Joseph Brewer 10 June 1963.
36. Ibid.
37. IND RH to Stavros 24 Nov. 1966.
38. IND Edward Garnett to RH 25 Oct. 1961.
39. As Richard Poole writes [Anglo-Welsh Review Vol.26 no.57 p.68] '[Augustine's] ignorance constitutes at once an ironic vehicle by means of which the gulf separating English and German sensibilities is revealed and explored, and Richard Hughes's trump card in persuading the reader to appreciate what Augustine can't . . . To identify himself with this young Englishman . . . is to leave himself unprotected before the continual jet of irony directed by the novelist at his hero. To escape this irony, he needs merely to open his [own] awareness to the Bavarian situation . . .'
40. *SHEPHERDESS* pp.25–9.
41. POOLE p.82.
42. Quoted in *Cambrian News* 2 Aug. 1963.
43. IND draft of speech.
44. IND T.E.B. Clarke to RH 1 Oct. 1963.
45. IND RH to Elmo Williams 2 Oct. 1963.
46. IND Elmo Williams to RH 12 Oct. 1963.
47. IND A document dated 21 Nov. 1963. The sum was made up of £3567 4s. 9d. from England, £11,163 16s. 9d. from the USA, and £4324 3s. 4d. from other foreign rights. The total would

be worth in the region of £200,000 in 1994 terms; and RH had established himself as a limited company in order to reduce his tax liabilities.

48. IND RH to Polly Hope 3 Mar. 1964.
49. IND Robert Graves to RH n.d. [clearly 1961].
50. IND RH to Miss Ruth Connell 23 Oct. 1963.
51. IND RH to the Revd Mother of the Carmelite convent, Dolgellau 24 and 27 Nov. 1963; the visit was on 28 Nov.
52. IND a doc. of 15 Dec. 1963.
53. IND Robert Graves to RH 20 Dec. 1963; Sheila Sharp had been asking for details of air flights to Majorca ten days previously, so I suspect some earlier correspondence.
54. Cf. RPG *Robert Graves: The Years with Laura 1926–1940* (Weidenfeld & Nicolson 1990) pp.127–8.
55. IND RH to Polly Hope 3 Mar. 1964.
56. IND Alan Sillitoe to RH 15 Apr. 1964.
57. IND RH to Sheila Sharp 29 Apr. and 14 May 1963.
58. IND Sheila Sharp to RH 22 Feb. 1964.
59. Ibid. 22 Apr. 1964.
60. IND RH to Sheila Sharp 22 Apr. 1964.
61. IND *Diaries* RH 1964: 14 [?4] June dine Oriel; 30 June diocesan conference Dolgellau. IND The Lord Chamberlain inviting Mr and Mrs RH to a garden party at Buckingham Palace on 16 July 1964.
62. *SHEPHERDESS* p.34.
63. Ibid. p.113.
64. Ibid.
65. IND T.E.B. Clarke to RH 2 May 1964.
66. IND RH to T.E.B. Clarke 5 May 1964.
67. IND RH to Cass Canfield 17 Oct. 1964.
68. Ibid.
69. IND Gregson to RH 27 Apr. 1966: the picture was still $5.5 million away from profit, which it would never reach.
70. IND RH to Buckley Sharp 19 Oct. 1964.
71. IND RH to 'David' 12 Nov. 1964.
72. Ibid. 5 Nov. 1964.
73. IND RH to Revd Father Peter Levi 25 Feb. 1965; and Peter Levi in conv. with the present author March 1984.
74. These were a Monsignor Vance and a Sister Mary. See IND RH to Dear Sister Mary of St Philip 25 May 1965.
75. IND *Travel*.
76. IND RH to Joseph Brewer 24 Nov. 1966.
77. Caroline Glyn in SCRIPT p.60; and IND CG to RH 24 July 1965.
78. Ibid.
79. Jane Rainey in conv. with the present author 20 June 1993.
80. Monja Danischewsky in SCRIPT p.54.
81. Caroline Glyn in SCRIPT p.61.
82. MINNEY MSS: most of these details come from a copy of the original tape-recorded interview with Caroline Glyn from which extracts were used for SCRIPT.
83. IND *Diaries* RH 1966: *March*: 8 M. 1966 to London (7.15 evening PEN); 13 to Paris; 21 Paris to London; 25 London to Birmingham; 27 arrive Môr Edrin 6.30; *April*: 2 A. speak at Sussex University.
84. IND *Diaries* RH 1966, 7–10 June diocesan conference.
85. IND RH to Penelope Minney 16 June 1966.
86. IND RH to Montagu Motor Museum 11 Aug. 1966.
87. Lucy McEntee in SCRIPT pp.51–2.
88. IND RH to Joseph Brewer 24 Nov. 1966.
89. *SHEPHERDESS* p.144.
90. Ibid. p.155.
91. Ibid. p.163.
92. Lucy McEntee in SCRIPT p.64.
93. IND RH to Robert Hughes 15 Sept. 1964.
94. IND *Travel*.
95. RH to Caroline Glyn n.d. [late 1966/early 1967].
96. IND Caroline Glyn to RH 1 Nov. 1966.
97. IND FH to Lucy McEntee telegram 19 Dec. 1966.
98. IND RH to Teddy Wolfe 11 Feb. 1967; the words in square brackets come from the earlier draft of a letter to Caroline Glyn.
99. As n.94 above.

100. IND Robin Duke of the British Council to RH 5 Oct. 1966.
101. MINNEY p.189.
102. Ibid.
103. IND RH to Mr H.T. Lawrence (British Council rep. in Kenya) 6 Feb. 1967.
104. IND n.d. circular from Mr Hilary Ng'weno with details of the Kenya national book week 1967.
105. IND RH to Lucy McEntee 18 Feb. [1967].
106. IND RH to Joseph Brewer 24 Feb. 1967.
107. Ibid.
108. IND RH to Thomas Meadows (Insurance) Ltd of London 30 Mar. 1967.
109. As no.106 above.
110. IND RH to Robin Duke of the British Council 4 May 1967.
111. IND A programme for the Kampala book week has screenings of *A High Wind in Jamaica* arranged for 13 (intro. by RH), 14 and 15 Mar. 1967.
112. Ibid. shows Blishen lecturing and taking part in discussions; and IND EB to FH 19 July 1967: he apologises for being unable to come and stay at Môr Edrin, and tells FH how excited he had been to meet her distinguished husband.
113. As n.108 above.
114. IND Sir Paul Sinker of the British Council to RH 27 Apr. 1967.
115. IND RH to the Librarian, The Foreign Office, 13 July 1967.
116. *Daily Express* 1 July 1967.
117. IND *Clubs and Societies*: North Wales Assoc. of Sheep Dog Trials Societies met on 2 Aug. Talsarnau; 3, 4, 5 Aug. trials at Machynlleth; 23–5 Aug. North Wales trials at Great Orme, Llandudno; 29 Aug. North v. South Wales trials.
118. IND RH to the Cruising Assoc. 18 Feb. 1947; and CA to RH 22 Feb. 1947.
119. IND Graham Greene to RH 22 Aug. [1967].
120. IND RH to Graham Greene 4 Sept. 1967.
121. IND RH to Jim Wyllie 25 Mar. 1968.
122. Lucy McEntee to the present author 24 Mar. 1993.
123. As n.121 above.
124. Ibid.
125. Ibid.
126. IND Caroline Glyn to RH and FH 14 July 1968.
127. IND RH to Caroline Glyn draft 25 July 1968.
128. As n.126 above 28 Dec. 1968.
129. Ibid. 2 Aug. 1968.
130. MINNEY MSS Caroline Glyn in a tape-recorded copy of the interview made when SCRIPT was being prepared.
131. Caroline Glyn in SCRIPT p.62.
132. IND Telegram to RH dated 7 Mar. 1969.
133. IND Cable 9 Mar.
134. See e.g. IND RH to Mr Paul 4 May 1969, telling him 'I have been up to my eyes in preparing a paper I have to read in New York this month'; that he had 'cribbed shamelessly' from Mr Paul's chapter on Existentialism in *Alternatives*; and that he will soon be sending Penny a copy for her comments – which she will forward to Mr Paul for his.
135. Inc. Andre Michalopoulo (Michal) and Lewis Galantiere.
136. IND RH to Robert Graves 4 May 1969.
137. IND 'Richard Hughes schedule' for this visit to New York.
138. RH, 'Fiction as Truth' in *FICTION AS TRUTH* p.71–4. (This address also appeared in the *Times Saturday Review* on 21 Mar. 1970.)
139. As n.137 above.
140. *New Yorker* 28 June 1969, quoted in POOLE p.82.
141. IND A schedule shows that they were to leave for Canada on 26 May 1969.
142. POOLE p.82.
143. IND RH to Caroline Glyn 18 Jan. 1970.
144. IND Lord Chamberlain inviting Mr and Mrs RH to garden party at Buckingham Palace on 17 July 1969; North Wales Assoc. of Sheep Dog Trials Societies to RH 21 July 1969: he is to attend the Talsarnau meeting on 13 Aug. and open trials at Phoneigr on 22 Aug. 1969.
145. Rose Basketts in conv. with the present author 14 Mar. 1984.
146. As n.143 above; and IND CG to RH Jan. 1970.
147. IND *Travel* 29 Jan. 1970 air Birmingham to Rhodes.
148. As n.143 above.
149. IND FH from Lindos, Rhodes, to Lucy McEntee 11 Feb. 1970.
150. IND Caroline Glyn to RH 1 Mar. 1970.
151. IND FH from Lindos to Lucy McEntee 21 Feb. 1970.
152. IND Robert Graves to FH 3 Sept. 1970.
153. IND 23 Feb. 1970 Merioneth Rural Community Council asks RH to be patron of the County

Drama Festival at Dolgellau; and 30 Nov. 1970 RH to Buckley of the North Wales Assoc. of Sheep Dog Trials Societies asks whether he should stand down, after being president since 1968. In the event, he carried on.

154. Lucy McEntee in a telephone conv. with the present author June 1993. On their first meeting, MJ and MF had been staying with JR at Glyn; and she had brought them over to Môr Edrin for tea. JR in telephone conv. 20 June 1993 also recalls this.
155. Lucy McEntee to the present author 24 Mar. 1993.
156. Frances and Jenny West (née Lousarda, daughter of Jocelyn Lousarda née Herbert) in conv. with the present author 20 Oct. 1992.
157. POOLE p.82.
158. SHEPHERDESS p.320.
159. Ibid. p.339.
160. Ibid. p.336.
161. Ibid. p.338.
162. Ibid. p.368.
163. Ibid. p.363.
164. Ibid. p.372.
165. Ibid. p.384.
166. Ibid. p.387.
167. IND 38th International PEN Congress Dublin 12–18 Sept. 1971. RH met 'Sean O'Faolain and others' on the 12th.
168. IND Travel 4 Feb. 1972 landing conditions Gibraltar bad, so on 5th flew direct to Tangier; then on to Spain (cf. Lucy McEntee 10 Apr. 1972 to Wayfarer's Travel Agency of London).
169. MCENTEE A detailed account by LM of the stages through which The Wooden Shepherdess progressed during these years.
170. IND A letter of July 1966.
171. IND Finance: Financial difficulties (for 1972–1973, RH's expenses of £5535 exceeded his income by £152) had recently been eased by the sale of MSS to the Lilly Library, Indiana, for approx. £10,000.
172. MINNEY pp.189–90.
173. Edward Blishen in SCRIPT p.68.
174. POOLE pp.82–3 gives an extensive account of the reviews.
175. POOLE p.8.
176. IND Caroline Glyn to RH 3 June 1973.
177. David Divine in a published tribute written in May 1976.
178. MINNEY p.190.
179. IND has the dates: the w/e was from Sat. 1 Sept. to Mon. 3 Sept.; RH's talk was on Sat. at 5 p.m.; RP's lecture on Sun. at 10 a.m. POOLE p.7 has details.
180. IND Richard Poole from Coleg Harlech to RH 25 Oct. 1993.
181. Penelope Minney to the present author, 25 Mar. 1993.
182. IND 21 July 1973.
183. IND Lucy McEntee to Richard Poole 29 Oct. 1973.
184. IND (Among sheep-dog-trials material) RH to C.R. Buckley 2 Jan. 1974.
185. IND Caroline Glyn to RH 3 Feb. 1974.

Chapter 32: Unfinished Business

1. MCENTEE Quotations are taken from Last Twelve Chapters, the TS of the final 12 chs. of The Human Predicament.
2. MCENTEE Detailed notes by LM on the events of RH's life during his writing of the last 12 chs. of The Human Predicament.
3. POOLE p.83.
4. Last Twelve Chapters p.26.
5. Ibid. p.46.
6. Ibid. p.50.
7. As n.2 above.
8. IND Owain Hughes to RH and FH [?18] Aug. 1975.
9. IND a note by FH of Jan. 1978 to accompany a tea-cloth map of Long Island commemorating 'Dicken's [sic] best day in the last six months of his time'.
10. IND RH to Mr Gregson 25 Sept. 1959.
11. POOLE pp.233–4.
12. From IND RH to Mr Gregson 25 Sept. 1959; quoted in POOLE p.234.
13. MINNEY p.190.
14. Ibid. p.190.
15. POOLE p.84.
16. FH in SCRIPT p.68.

17. IND RH to Richard Poole 23 Jan. 1976.
18. MINNEY pp.190–1.
19. IND Circular letter from Robert Hughes to Penny, Lleky, Kate and Owain 2 Apr. 1976.
20. MINNEY pp.191–2.
21. Ibid. p.192.
22. Ibid. pp.191–2.
23. Ibid. p.192.
24. Ibid. p.193.
25. IND Lucy McEntee to Professor B.P. Reardon 12 Apr. 1976.
26. MINNEY p.193–4.
27. Ibid.
28. IND Copy of a teleg. from FH: DICCON VERY PEACEFULLY & SUDDENLY DIED EARLY THIS EVENING LOVE AND MUCH LOVE FRANCES.
29. Lucy McEntee to the present author 27 May 1993. LM 'organized the police who gave us parking help and guarded the house while all were out against the press raiding the attics for unpublished MSS'.
30. Thursday 10 June 1976.

Select Bibliography

A.E. Coppard, *It's Me, O Lord!* (Methuen 1957) contains some fine vignettes of RH's time at Oxford.

Charles Graves, *The Bad Old Days* (Faber & Faber 1951) contains some useful details about RH, especially during his time at Charterhouse.

Richard Perceval Graves, *Robert Graves: The Assault Heroic 1895–1926* (Weidenfeld & Nicolson 1986) and *Robert Graves: The Years with Laura 1926–1940* (Weidenfeld & Nicolson 1990). These two books provide the most reliable account of RG's life to date.

Gwenol Heneker, *The Waters and the Wild* (Macdonald 1972). RH's friend Gwenol Satow later became Mrs David Heneker; and in 1972 she published this autobiographical novel in which RH appears as 'Emlyn'.

Penelope Hughes, *Richard Hughes: Author, Father* (Alan Sutton 1984). This fascinating memoir contains much original information.

Paul Morgan, *The Art of Richard Hughes: a Study of the Novels* (University of Wales Press 1993). Apart from being a fascinating study in its own right, also contains many interesting details of Hughes's relationship with his publishers, and the fullest and most up-to-date bibliography.

Richard Poole, *Richard Hughes: Novelist* (Poetry Wales Press 1987). The best critical account of Hughes's literary work.

Peter Quennell, *The Marble Foot: An autobiography 1905–1938* (Collins 1976). Not a great deal is said about RH; but the book is rivetting on the subject of Nancy Stallibrass (discreetly referred to as S).

Lance Sieveking, *The Eye of the Beholder* (Hulton Press 1957) contains a chapter which is one of the wittiest and most revealing portraits of RH, by one of his oldest friends.

Caitlin Thomas with George Tremlett, *Caitlin: Life with Dylan Thomas* (Secker and Warburg 1986). A rare unfriendly view of RH.

Amabel Williams-Ellis, *All Stracheys are Cousins* (Weidenfeld & Nicolson 1983) contains several anecdotes about RH; but is more interesting as a self-portrait by one of Diccon's closest confidantes.

Principal publications by Richard Hughes

Gipsy-Night and Other Poems (Golden Cockerel Press 1922) poems.

The Sisters' Tragedy (Basil Blackwell 1922) play.

The Sisters' Tragedy and three other plays (Heinemann 1924) plays.

A Rabbit and a Leg (A.A. Knopf 1924) plays.

ed. John Skelton, *Poems* (Heinemann 1924) critical.

[ghost] Nigel Playfair, *The Story of the Lyric Theatre Hammersmith* (Chatto & Windus 1925) history.

Confessio Juvenis (Chatto & Windus 1926) poems.

A Moment of Time (Chatto & Windus 1926) stories.

The Innocent Voyage (New York, Harper and Brothers); and as *A High Wind in Jamaica* (London, Chatto & Windus 1929) novel.

An Omnibus (Harper and Brothers 1931) miscellany.

The Spider's Palace and other stories (Chatto & Windus 1931) children's stories.

In Hazard (Chatto & Windus and Harper and Brothers 1938) novel.

Don't Blame Me! (Chatto & Windus 1940) children's stories.

J.D. Scott and Richard Hughes, *Administration of War Production* (Her Majesty's Stationery Office and Longmans, Green & Co. 1955) history.

The Fox in the Attic (Chatto & Windus 1961, Harper and Brothers 1962) novel.

Gertrude's Child (Harlin Quist 1966) children's stories.

The Wooden Shepherdess (Chatto & Windus and Harper and Brothers 1973) novel.

The Wonder Dog (Chatto & Windus 1977) collected children's stories.

ed. R. Poole *In the Lap of Atlas* (Chatto & Windus 1979) stories.

ed. R. Poole *Fiction as Truth: Selected Writings by Richard Hughes* (Poetry Wales Press 1983) critical, literary, philosophical etc.

Index